SOCIETY OF BIBLICAL LITERATURE
1976 SEMINAR PAPERS

SOCIETY OF BIBLICAL LITERATURE SEMINAR PAPERS SERIES

edited by

George MacRae

Number 10

Society of Biblical Literature

1976 Seminar Papers

edited by

George MacRae

SCHOLARS PRESS

Missoula, Montana

SOCIETY OF BIBLICAL LITERATURE
1976 SEMINAR PAPERS

edited by
George MacRae

One Hundred Twelfth Annual Meeting
28-31 October 1976
Stouffer's Riverfront Towers, St. Louis, Missouri

Published by
SCHOLARS PRESS
for
The Society of Biblical Literature

Distributed by

SCHOLARS PRESS
University of Montana
Missoula, Montana 59801

SOCIETY OF BIBLICAL LITERATURE
1976 SEMINAR PAPERS

edited by

George MacRae

ISBN: 0-89130-097-X

Printed in the United States of America

Printing Department
University of Montana
Missoula, Montana 59801

TABLE OF CONTENTS

Introductory Note . . . . *viii*

S 21 *Dynastic Oracle in Dtr: A Workshop in Recent Trends*
Richard D. Nelson 1

S 23 *Jonathan: A Structural Study in 1 Samuel*
David Jobling 15

S 54 *Jews and Christians in Antioch in the First Four*
A 75 *Centuries*
Wayne A. Meeks 33

S 55 *The Jews of Antioch*
A 76 Robert L. Wilken 67

S 75 *Catalogue of Hebrew Letters Seventh Century B.C. to Second Century A.D.*
Dennis Pardee 75

S 81 *Categories of Greek Papyrus Letters*
-83 John L. White and Keith A. Kensinger 79

S 90 *The Oracular Style of the Cultic Proclamations of Antiochus I of Commagene*
Robert W. Allison 93

S 91 *Music and Ritual in Primitive Eleusis*
Apostolos N. Athanassakis 99

S 92 *A Problem of Power: How Miracle Doers Counter Charges of Magic in the Hellenistic World*
Anitra Bingham Kolenkow 105

S 93 *A Critique of Kelber's "The Hour of the Son of Man and the Temptation of the Disciples: Mark 14: 32-42:*
Gene Szarek 111

S 101 *Christian Prophecy and the Q Tradition*
Richard A. Edwards 119

S 103 *Christian Prophecy and Matthew 10:23: A Test Exegesis*
M. Eugene Boring 127

S 121 *Migration Theories vs. Culture Change as an*
A 184 *Explanation for Early Israel*
George E. Mendenhall 135

S 122 *Early Israel and "The Asiatic Mode of Production"*
A 185 *in Canaan*
Norman K. Gottwald 145

S 123 *The Role of the Peasant in the Amarna Period*
A 186 John M. Halligan 155

S 137 *Joseph and Asenath and the Greek Novel*
Richard I. Pervo 171

S 139 *The Socio-Religious Setting and Aims of Joseph and Asenath*
Howard C. Kee 183

S 140 *Illustrated Manuscripts of the Romance of Joseph and Aseneth*
Gary Vikan 193

S 155 *The Lukan Birth Narratives in Tradition and Redaction*
Lloyd Gaston 209

S 156 *The Lukan Sitz im Leben: Methodology and Prospects*
Robert J. Karris 219

S 179 *The Discourse Structure of the Flood Narrative*
Robert E. Longacre 235

S 186 *John Dominic Crossan, "Empty Tomb and Absent Lord" - A Response*
John E. Alsup 263

S 187 *Empty Tomb and Absent Lord: Mark's Interpretation of Tradition*
Thomas R. W. Longstaff 269

S 188 *The Sources of Luke: A Proposal for the Consultation on the Relationships of the Gospels*
Joseph B. Tyson 279

S 189 *Joseph B. Tyson's Proposal for the Consultation on the Relationships of the Gospels: A Response*
William O. Walker, Jr. 287

S 190 *Joseph B. Tyson's Proposal: A Response and Counter-Proposal*
Charles Thomas Davis, III 291

S 194 *Christian Prophecy in Lukan Thought: Luke 4:16-30 as a Point of Departure*
Waldemar Schmeichel 293

S 196 *Christian Prophecy and Matthew 23:8-12: A Test Exegesis*
J. Ramsey Michaels 305

S 213 *Revolutions in Northern Israel*
A 362 Simon B. Parker 311

Panel Discussion on Divination Techniques

S 228 *Techniques in Early Dream Interpretation*
Robert J. White 323

S 229 *Fate and Freedom: Astrology vs. Mystery Religions*
Jean Rhys Bram 326

S 230 *The Two-Bean Method at Delphi*
J. O. and C. Grandjouan 330

S 231 *Omens and Oracles in the Classical Historians*
Tamara M. Green 333

S 238 *The Study of Rabbinic Parables: Some Preliminary Observations*
Robert M. Johnston 337

S 239 *Hidden Treasure Parables in Late Antiquity*
John Dominic Crossan 359

S 240 *By Land and by Sea: A Study in Acts 13-28*
Vernon J. Robbins 381

S 241 *The Portrait of Paul in Acts and the Pastorals*
Stephen G. Wilson 397

S 246 *Metaphor and Reality in Hosea 11*
A 409 J. Gerald Janzen 413

S 259 *The Portrait of Moses in Ezekiel the Tragedian*
Carl R. Holladay 447

S 260 *The Rule of Tyche and Hellenistic Religion*
Luther H. Martin 453

S 268 *Approaching the Synoptic Problem from the Second Century: A Prolegomenon*
Arthur J. Bellinzoni, Jr. 461

S 274 *Beyond Bruxism*
A 458 Kent Harold Richards 467

INTRODUCTORY NOTE

This volume contains papers to be discussed but not read at the One Hundred Twelfth Annual Meeting of the Society of Biblical Literature, St. Louis, Missouri, 28-31 October 1976. They have been photographically reproduced from typescripts supplied by the authors in most cases. The Editor is responsible for assembling the volume and preparing it for the printer; he has also done minor copy editing. The book includes those papers received by the Editor before 23 July 1976.

It should be remembered that these papers represent only working documents submitted for discussion at Seminar and Group sessions of the Annual Meeting. They are not intended to be finished products of the scholarly discussion.

The papers are printed in the order of their appearance on the program of the Annual Meeting. The identifying numbers prefixed to each title refer to the program, the letter *S* indicating presentations of the Society of Biblical Literature and the letter *A*, joint presentations with the American Academy of Religion.

The Editor wishes to thank the authors and the various Seminar and Group Chairmen for their cooperation in the preparation of this volume.

S 21

DYNASTIC ORACLE IN DTR
A WORKSHOP IN RECENT TRENDS

Richard D. Nelson
Pittsburgh, Pennsylvania

1. Recent Trends

For a general overview of the trend of scholarship on the issue of the Deuteronomistic history (Dtr), the reader is directed to the bibliographic studies of Jenni and Radjawane.[1]

The present writer believes that recent study of Dtr may be summarized into four general trends: 1) The search for unifying theological principles. 2) The discovery of subtle editorial devices and activity. 3) The devaluation of the importance of literary criticism in working with Dtr. 4) The growing popularity of the opinion that Dtr is the product of a two-stage redaction process.

We shall examine each of these trends briefly, then move on to consider how each is illustrated by a fresh examination of the various dynastic promises in Dtr.

A. Unifying theological principles. Section 13 of Martin Noth's Überlieferungsgeschichtliche Studien[2] outlined his insight into Dtr's theological purpose: to explain why disaster came upon Judah. Dtr had no hope for the future; this end was decisive. Since Noth's original study, however, our understanding of the unifying theological themes of Dtr has been considerably refined.

Enno Jansen found a certain amount of hope for the future in Dtr. Obedience to the law can give the people confidence, even though the future remains unknown, for God's promise still stands.[3] The discussion over whether Dtr's view of the future is positive or negative has centered on the final paragraph of the work in its present form, the release of Johoiachin.[4] H. W. Wolff discovered the importance of "turning" (šûb) as a unifying theme in Dtr. In the days of the judges the rebellious were rescued when they "turned" to Yahweḥ. The historian was urging his contemporaries to do the same.[5] Much the same positive note was struck by Walter Brueggemann, who raised a countertheme to Wolff's return motif in the concept of the "good" (ṭôb) as the motivation for repentence. This "good" is found in the prophetic word, the gift of the land, and the Davidic house.[6] A third unifying theme was developed by von Rad, the "word." Yahweh's word unites the history through an overarching prophecy and fulfillment schema. "Jahweh's word, once uttered, reaches its goal under all circumstances."[7] The Davidic kingship provides yet another unifying theme according to von Rad. David provides a prototype for the perfect king and a focus for God's grace to Judah.[8]

It is in this area of the Davidic kingship that recent scholarship has continued to look for unifying theological themes. Hans Boecker has made it clear that Dtr's evaluation of kingship is not negative at all. Rather, the institution of kingship is the result of Yahweh's gracious accommodation to the wishes of the people.[9] R. E. Clements has sharpened his insight to differentiate between kingship in general and those kings chosen by Yahweh.[10] It is appropriate, then, that this paper should look to the conditional and unconditional dynastic promises for further clarification of Dtr's unifying themes.

B. Editorial devices. Dtr is held together by various editorial techniques like a dual overlapping chronology,[11] recurrent speeches and summaries at critical junctures that interpret the course of events,[12] and the prophecy-fulfillment schema.[13] The trend in the study of Dtr has been to trace some more subtle editorial techniqes as well. Jansen has demonstrated that the "end of era" speeches exhibit a common structure.[14] McCarthy has shown that these transitional speeches always point forward to double events in the future.[15] Herbert Timm has explained how Dtr used the Ark Story to provide a transition between the judges and the kings.[16] Norbert Lohfink has used the "new stylistics" to postulate subtle editorial work by Dtr in Deuteronomy.[17] This paper will explain how Dtr uses the dynastic promises in a subtle way to create editorial unity.

C. Literary criticism. It is fair to say that literary criticism has fallen out of of favor with the avant-guard of OT scholarship. It is often said to be old-fashioned and overly subjective, unproductive and sterile. This attitude has led to a certain loss of rigor in literary critical matters in a distressingly large number of recent studies in Dtr, at least by Americans. This problem is most obvious in the consideration of Dtr's limits, his sources, and the problem of later insertions.

It is a little appalling to discover that studies of Dtr's view of history can appear in print which blithely accept Judges 17-21 as part of Dtr without any attempt to justify this surprizing thesis[18] or with only the sketchiest arguments to counter the solid literary-critical work of Noth and his predecessors.[19] The objection is not that some commentators and authors are making unorthodox literary-critical decisions, but that their decisions are so often made on such casual grounds without any consideration of the larger literary-critical situation.

Strict and objective literary criticism in Dtr is vital and is just the opposite of sterile. A glance into the recent work of Richter, de Tillesse, Cazelles, Beyerlin, and others should make this clear. Certainly a good deal of divergence of opinion in literary-critical matters is to be expected, but a refusal to do one's literary criticism is inexcusable. In this workshop on dynastic promise, the present writer hopes to rehabilitate the reputation of strict literary criticism in the eyes of some skeptics.

D. A pre-exilic historian. The concept that the book of Kings, and by extension Dtr, was produced in pre-exilic times and later revised during the exile goes back at least to Abraham Kuenen. Enthusiastically approved by Wellhausen, the theory was generally accepted by scholars until Noth's discovery of Dtr.[20] Noth insisted on a single, exilic historian.

Recently, Noth's single exilic historian has come under fire. Rudolph Smend attempted to trace the hand of a second redactor in Joshua and Judges (DtrN revising DtrG).[21] His student Walter Dietrich has attempted a similar task in Kings, tracing another redactor (DtrP).[22]

The present writer believes that the trend of the future lies with the approach taken by Frank Cross, who supports Albright's earlier position that Dtr was issued in the time of Josiah as propaganda for that king's policies and that this was later brought up to date around 560 BC by means of several additions which modified the theological thrust of the original.[23]

This new look at the dynastic promises will provide further evidence that this is correct.

2. Conditional Promise as a Unifying Theological Principle

In the business of tracing the broad unifying theological themes of Dtr, most people assume that the conditional promises of 1 Kgs. 2:4; 8:25; and 9:4-5 represent his central theological opinion concerning the Davidic dynasty. Yahweh had promised that dynasty a secure rule, but only so long as its members toed the line in regard to obedience to him. Dtr is supposedly tracing the history of the fall of Judah through the operation of this conditionalized dynastic promise.[24]

However, a closer look at these three passages shows that the historian actually did not intend that this condition of obedience be applied to the subsequent continuity of the Judean dynasty at all.

In 1 Kgs 2:4, the conditional oracle has been inserted with vss. 2 and 3 into David's admonition to Solomon at the start of his reign. Since the historian had to break into a continuous source, the Succession History, in order to place this oracle in precisely this spot, this location at the very start of Solomon's reign must have been of great importance to him. Dtr's reluctance to interfere with his sources is one of the characteristics of his techniques.[25] He could have easily waited until his source ended at 1 Kgs. 2:46 if he had not wanted this promise at exactly this location. Only this location would do.

This is further supported in that the oracle was put into the mouth of David as one communicated to him by Yahweh and here only repeated to Solomon. Yet the delivery of such an oracle to David is never recorded in the presentation of David's history. If Dtr had wanted to report this promise in David's own time, he could easily have done so while inserting 2 Sam. 7:13a or in the prayer of 2 Sam. 7:18-29. David's advice to Solomon simply serves as a handy vehicle for this conditional dynastic promise which Dtr insisted on placing at the very start of Solomon's reign.

It is sometimes assumed that the historian is referring to the Nathan Oracle (2 Sam. 7:13b-16) here in 1 Kgs. 2:4.[26] This is quite wrong. None of the words of the Nathan Oracle are quoted, none of its circumstance recalled. The Nathan Oracle is definitely unconditional; this promise is just as clearly conditional. Only this location would do. Why, one immediately wonders, were these conditional oracles all deliberately concentrated in the reign of a single king if they were intended to apply to all? Why did it have to be mentioned right at the beginning of Solomon's reign if it applied to David's house as a whole?

In 1 Kgs. 8:25, Solomon quotes the oracle given to his father in his dedicatory prayer and calls upon God to keep his promise. Again the reference to this conditional promise occurs in a rather strange place, in the midst of a prayer about the Temple (cf. vss. 24, 28-29). It seems that Dtr is purposefully reminding his readers of this conditional oracle precisely at the very apex of Solomon's obedience to its conditions, just as he was careful to mention it right at the beginning of Solomon's rule.

This oracle is repeated for the third time in 1 Kgs. 9:4-5. This time Yahweh himself speaks with specific reference to the dedicatory prayer. The obedience that had been required in a general way of David's "sons" in 1 Kgs. 2:4 and 8:25 is specifically narrowed to Solomon and Solomon alone. This issue is, as before, the eternal security of the "royal throne over Israel."

Although vss. 6-9 go on to expand the subject to include the obedience of Solomon's descendants, there is an abundance of literary-critical evidence that these verses are later than Dtr. They are literarily dependent upon Deut. 29:23-25, a section added to Deuteronomy later than the time of Dtr.[27]

1 Kgs. 9:4-5 makes it clear that it is specifically Solomon's obedience that was vital to this conditional promise, not that of David's descendants in general. The potentially misleading application of the oracle to David's "sons" in 2:4 and 8:25 was forced upon the historian by the flow of events in his source, the Succession History. Dtr was well aware that it would be ludicrous for him to insert a promise supposedly given sometime in the reign of David which would have specifically anticipated Solomon's successful bid for the throne. The outcome of the dynastic struggle was unclear up to the last moment.

What is actually happening is that the historian is offering in a subtle way his own reflection upon the theological meaning of the events of the succession. David's other sons refused to behave according to Yahweh's will and thus did not come to the throne. Both 2:4 and 8:25 referred to the original communication of this promise and had to use the term "sons" appropriate to the days of David's own reign. In contrast, in 1 Kgs. 9:4-5, Yahweh communicates the promise to Solomon himself. Now the historian was able to apply it exclusively to Solomon. We need not doubt that the historian was willing to pin dynastic continuance on the actions of a single kind, for much the same promise was made to Jeroboam (1 Kgs. 11:38).

These observations suggest three conclusions. First, the conditional oracles were carefully restricted by Dtr to the reign of Solomon because they were intended to apply only to him. Second, the three-fold repetition indicates that Dtr was trying to make an important theological point. He is also tying together the history of Solomon, just as he used the formulaic oracles of doom for the three Northern kings, Jeroboam, Baasha, and Ahab (1 Kgs. 14:10-11; 16:4, 11; 21:21, 24), to unite the history of Israel up to Jehu's time. Third, the clarification of 1 Kgs. 9:4-5 that it is exclusively Solomon's obedience that is under consideration (and not the piety of his successors) indicates that the crisis of the fulfilment or non-fulfilment of this promise must have been worked out within the confines of the reign of Solomon.

Yet what exactly is the content of this promise? A Davidide would always sit on the "throne of Israel." In 9:4-5 this is interpreted further: Yahweh will establish "your royal throne over Israel forever."

It has generally been assumed that these promises refer to the Davidic rule over Judah. If this were really the case, Dtr could easily have found a less misleading expression to make his point (as in 2 Sam. 7:13; 1 Kgs. 11:36; 13:2; 15:4; 2 Kgs. 8:19; 17:21). As a matter of fact, the phrase "throne of Israel" is used four other times in Dtr. Twice it clearly refers to the rule of the kingdom of Israel, that is dominion over the Northern tribes (2 Kgs. 10:30; 15:12). The other two undoubtedly refer to the throne of the United Kingdom (1 Kgs. 8:20; 10:9). Certainly this phrase never refers to rule over Judah.

Let us simply take these conditional promises at face value. They refer to the throne of Israel, a united throne including rule over all the tribes. They refer specifically to Solomon. It is clear that Dtr is making a theological comment on the loss of the throne of Israel to the Davidic dynasty because of the disobedience of Solomon. They provide a unifying theological theme that helps unite the succession to David's throne, the reign of Solomon, and the division of the nation. What they do not do is provide us with Dtr's theological attitude about Yahweh's promise of a rule over Judah to David's family, as is so often assumed. They have nothing to do with Judah; they have nothing to do with the behavior of Solomon's descendants. For this we must turn to the unconditional dynastic oracles (2 Sam. 7:13b-16; 1 Kgs. 11:36; 15:4; 2 Kgs. 8:19).

3. The Nathan Oracle as a Subtle Editorial Device

The Nathan Oracle has been one of the most studied chapters in the OT, so that anything but the most superficial reference to the problems involved is impossible. The present writer is convinced that the oracle has an overarching unity, connecting the monarchy and the older amphictyonic traditions through the subject of the ark. 2 Sam. 7 was at one time propaganda for the transfer of the ark and election of the dynasty, along the lines of an Egyptian Königsnovelle.[28] Of course, we are more concerned here with the use made of this material by Dtr.

A recent study by Dennis McCarthy has pointed out that 2 Sam. 7:1-17 actually performs the same function as the transitional speeches in Dtr. In its present position it is closely integrated with its context and and has been made the central element of the transition from Saul to David. 1 Sam. 12 concludes the era of the judges, but the era of the monarchy as a positive instituion does not really begin until 2 Sam. 7. McCarthy's most valuable insight is that these transitional elements in Dtr always point forward to double events in the future. The speech of Moses commands both conquest and distribution. Josh. 23 points to both the breaking of the covenant in Judg. 2 and the rejections of Yahweh's kingship in 1 Sam. 8. In the same way the Nathan Oracle foreshadows two events: the erection of the Temple and, in McCarthy's opinion, the ultimate failure of the kingship.[29]

McCarthy is wrong about this second foreshadowed event. The oracle clearly refers, not to the ultimate fall of the monarchy, but to the punishment that was to come upon Solomon (2 Kgs. 11:9-13; 31-39). 2 Sam. 7:14-15 could not be clearer:

> When he [David's seed] commits iniquities, I will punish him with the rod of men and with the stripes of the children of men; but my covenant love will not depart from him as I made it depart from Saul, whom I made to depart from before you.

These words can hardly be taken to apply to the fall of the Davidic monarchy. Their most natural application is to Solomon and the limited punishment which he incurred.

These words are not from Dtr's own hand, of course.[30] It is precisely McCarthy's realization that a section of the history not directly created by the historian may still have been used by him as a deliberate editorial signpost that is a significat advance over Noth's more limited approach. In this case, Dtr laid so much weight on the Nathan Oracle as a structural element that he went on to refer to it a couple of times in regard to Solomon's Temple building activities (1 Kgs. 5:9; 8:19). In fact, Dtr actually went so far as to add words to his traditional source here in regard to Temple construction. He was usually extremely reluctant to do this.[31] The clearest example of his interference is the addition of vs. 13a.[32]

All this should make us look at the unconditional promise of grace to David in the Nathan Oracle a liitle more closely. Dtr permitted this strongly unconditional dynastic promise (11b-16) to remain, making no attempt to conditionalize it.

When Dtr did not agree with his traditional sources, he was quite willing to speak for himself. The introduction of the monarchy in 1 Sam. 7-10 is a transitional section like 2 Sam. 7. Out of his usual respect for his sources, Dtr reproduced 1 Sam. 9:1-10:16, 11:1-15; and 13:1ff, materials already linked together for him.[33] However, he disagreed with the exessively positive attitudes toward the monarchy in this source. So he did not hesitate to insert his own opinions in 1 Sam. 8, 10:17-27, and 12.[34] Dtr relieved the tension created by his inherited pro-monarchy material and his own less enthusiastic opinion by making the institution of the monarchy a command of Yahweh (1 Sam. 8:22) and laying down the program for the new order of things.[35]

We would expect a similar state of affairs in 2 Sam. 7, a passage just as important to the structure of the history as 1 Sam. 7-10, if the historian disagreed with the concept of an eternally valid promise to the Davidic house. He does not speak for himself on this issue, however, and we must assume that he is in basic agreement with what he found in the Nathan Oracle. This is borne out by Dtr's inclusion of promises dealing with an eternal n̂r for David.

The Nathan Oracle, then, functions as a subtle editorial device, pointing forward to the construction of the Temple and the limited punishment for Solomon. Its inclusion without any limiting or contradictory statement shows that Dtr accepted the eternally valid, unconditional promise to David.

4. A *nîr* for David: A Workshop in Literary Criticism

With 1 Kgs 11:36; 15:4 and 2 Kgs. 8:19, Dtr goes beyond the point of merely allowing a traditional unconditional promise to stand in his work. He inserts some himself. In contrast to those conditional promises concerning Solomon alone and referring to the future of the throne of Israel alone (1 Kgs. 2:4; 8:25; 9:4-5), these unconditional ones are not confined to any one reign and speak unambiguously of a projected eternal reign over Judah and Jerusalem, promising David an eternal *nîr* or dominion.[36]

Of these three, 1 Kgs. 11:36 is most instructive from a literary-critical point of view. 1 Kgs. 11:1-13 is entirely Deuteronomistic, while 11:14-28, 40 is in a different, more annalistic style and seems to be from a source dealing with the enemies of Solomon throughout his reign. Vs. 29 clearly marks a new beginning. Vss. 29-39 interrupt the clear previous connection of vss. 26-28 and 40 and have the same style, character, and subject matter as vss. 1-13.

To discover just what function the *nîr* promise of vs. 36 plays within Dtr, we must answer three questions. Did Dtr use a prophetic source to create vss. 29-39? Did that source supply the *nîr* promise or did Dtr add it? Should the hint of a return of a full hegemony to David's house in vs. 39 be eliminated as a gloss?

A. *The prophetic source*. Martin Noth, in his recent commentary on Kings, attempted to demonstrate that these verses, except for a few later glosses, are entirely the work of Dtr. Noth saw a basic unity of purpose and outlook and believed that Dtr picked up the figure of Ahijah from 1 Kgs. 14:1-8 and the motif of the tearing of the kingdom from 1 Sam. 27b-28.[37]

Nevertheless, it is almost certain that Dtr did use an earlier source. The number twelve is not consistently carried out.[38] The parenthetic circumstantial notice of Jeroboam's departure from Jerusalem in vs. 29 is a rather awkward insertion into a sentence with an already established consecution, designed apparently to provide a link to information provided by Dtr's source in vs. 27.

The concern of the narrative to place the interview in the open country away from prying eyes or ears is not characteristic of Dtr himself. His own insertions of oracles where none had been provided by one of his sources contain an absolute minimum of circumstatial detail. Sometime Yahweh speaks without any intermediary or any background (1 Kgs. 6:11-13; 11:11-13; 2 Kgs. 10:30-31). Sometimes Dtr offers the prophets' name, but nothing more (1 Kgs. 12:21-24; 16:1-4). In contrast, here we have the prophet's name, the location of the announcement, and even the accompanying symbolic action. An interest in the technical side of prophecy, the newness of the cloak,[39] is also not characteristic of Dtr.

The narrative seems to reflect a Northern viewpoint. The absolute use of "the kingdom" (*hammamᵉlākāh*) to refer to the ten tribes is one example. Up to vs. 32 it is rather sympathetic to Jeroboam, towards whom Dtr was violently antipathetic. The term "the ten tribes" must be thought to include Levi, no matter which of the several solutions to the mathematical puzzle of ten plus one equals twelve one accepts.[40] It is difficult to believe that Dtr thought that Yahweh had assigned Levi to the apostate North.

There are several indications of an older source in vs. 34a. Dtr clearly wanted to contrast vss. 34 and 35 (Yahweh will not take the kingdom from Solomon's hand, but from the hand of his son), but the presence of "all" in vs. 34a disturbs this intended contrast.[41] Vs. 34a, taken by itself, indicates that Yahweh will not tear the entire kingdom from Solomon because Yahweh intends to demote him from king to <u>nāsi'</u>. Dtr converts this demotion into an element of Yahweh's <u>election</u> of David in vs. 34b and distorts the point of 34a (the partial nature of the punishment) into a delay of the punishment by adding vs. 35. This vs. 35 shifts the "kingdom" (<u>mam^{e}lākāh</u>) of vs. 31 and 34a into "kingship" (<u>m^{e}lûkāh</u>).

There can be little doubt that Dtr has used a prophetic source here. It has much in common with the anointing of Jehu (2 Kgs. 9:1-6, 10). In both narratives the situation and location of the event, the action of the prophet, and the accompanying word of Yahweh play a prominent part. Such narratives would have been preserved among the prophetic brotherhood with the intent of demonstrating how even the legitimacy of a king is subservient to Yahweh's use of the prophet's office.

B. <u>Dtr's own contribution</u>. The historian's own purposes and interests are clearly set forth for us in 1 Kgs. 11:1-13. The division of the kingdom as punishment for Solomon's sins will take place after his death (vs. 12) and the loss will be limited in extent (vs. 13). Vss. 33 (foreign worship) and 35 (postponement) are Dtr's. Deuteronomistic phrases in 32a<u>b</u>b, 34b, 36b<u>b</u>, and 38a deny them to the prophetic source and require us to assign them to Dtr (or, of course, to some later Deuteronomistic writer). We have already found traces of the prophetic source in vss. 29-31 and 34a.

The plural of vs. 33 fits poorly with the grammatical antecedent of its subject, Solomon, in 32a<u>a</u>. In vs. 34a, however, the source continues this singular from 32a<u>a</u>. Whether these verses now separated by 32a<u>b</u>-33 were once directly connected or whether something has dropped out cannot be determined, but they do make sense together: "But one tribe shall be his and I shall not take the whole kingdom from his hand, for I shall make him a <u>nāsî'</u> as long as he lives." Dtr in vs. 33 used the plural in order to extend the sin to the whole people, carelessly assimilating the grammatical number of the subject of vs. 33 to the last word of vs. 32 and overlooking or ignoring the singular of his source. Dtr then returned to the singular with his familiar "David his father" at the end of vs. 33.

Dtr created vss. 31-36 in an oddly repetitive way. The idea of a limitation on Solomon's punishment by restricting the loss to ten tribes was already present in his source (vss. 32, 34a). To this Dtr added his own concept of the delay of the punishment for a generation. His procedure is quite interesting and may be outlined in columns. Capitalized words in the first column are from the prophetic source. Underlined words in the second are Dtr's use of what he had already written about the limitation of punishment to produce what he wrote about its delay.

limitation of punishment
vss. 31-34

BEHOLD, I AM ABOUT TO TEAR THE KINGDOM FROM THE HAND OF SOLOMON AND WILL GIVE YOU TEN TRIBES, BUT HE SHALL HAVE ONE TRIBE for the sake of ($l^{e}ma$ʿan) my servant David and for the sake of Jerusalem, the city which (ʾăšer) I have chosen out of all the tribes of Israel, because they have forsaken me . . . as David his father did. NEVERTHELESS I WILL NOT TAKE THE WHOLE KINGDOM OUT OF HIS HAND, FOR I WILL MAKE HIM PRINCE ALL THE DAYS OF HIS LIFE for the sake of David my servant whom I chose, who kept my commandments and my statutes.

delay of punishment
vss. 35-36

But I will take the kingship from the hand of his son and will give it to you, ten tribes, but to his son I will give one tribe, that ($l^{e}ma$ʿan) there may be a nîr for David my servant forever before me in Jerusalem, the city where (ʾăšer) I have chosen to put my name.

It is easy to see how the words of his source in 32aa gave Dtr an opportunity to expound upon his theme of the limitation of the punishment with 32abb. In vs. 33 he went into greater detail about the nature of the people's sin. He then continued with 34a to lead into his second theme, the delay of the punishment. For this part of his exposition, Dtr used vss. 31-32 from what he had already written as a model to construct vss. 35-36. In so doing, he replaced the key verb of his source ("tear," vss. 30, 31) with the less colorful "take" and the "kingdom" of his source with the less objectionable parallel "kingship."

Further evidence that this analysis is correct is provided by the maverick "ten tribes" of vs. 35. This expression is completely superfluous in that verse and does not fit with the feminine singular object suffix of the preceding verb. A second bit of evidence is the return in vs. 36 to the theme of the limitation of punishment, a subject already completely covered in vss. 31-32. Both these anomalies can best be explained by our hypothesis that Dtr used vss. 31-32 to create vss. 35-36.

The upshot of all this rather unexciting literary-critical drudgery is that the nîr promise of vs. 36 must be from the historian's own hand and thus is part of his own theology. Just as vs. 32 provides the motivation for the limitation of the punishment (for the sake of David and Jerusalem), vs. 36 supplies the motivation for the restraint shown to Rehoboam: for the sake of David's nîr. Indeed, the nîr promise would hardly have been present in a Northern prophetic narrative, the object of which was to demonstrate the ascendancy of prophetic revelation over royal succession!

C. Is vs. 39 a later gloss? Vss. 37 and 38 extend a conditional dynastic promise couched in Deuteronomistic terms to Jeroboam. If Jeroboam is as pious as David was, then Yahweh will give him a "sure house." In other words, if Jeroboam meets the same conditions that David has already met, he too will receive the promise of an enduring dynasty.[36] Of course Jeroboam immediately flunked the test.

Vs. 39 is a crucial verse for the proper understanding of Dtr. The loss of the Northern tribes to the seed of David would not last forever. This verse is a clear indication of a date for Dtr during the reign of Josiah, for at no other time in Judean history did it look so much as though this promise was likely to be fulfilled. Yet scholars have been almost unanimous in declaring 38bb-39 a secondary gloss.[37]

They have pointed to the change in subject matter from David, his son, and grandson, to the more extended expression "seed." This, however, is not so much a change of subject as it is a natural broadening of the author's horizon towards the future.

They have also asserted that the sentiments expressed in vss. 38bb-39 must be those of post-exilic messianism. Actually, however, the nationalistic hope of a new ascendancy for the Davidic dynasty over the North was a recurring feature of pre-exilic Judean political life. We need only think of the wars of Rehoboam and Asa (1 Kgs. 14:3; 15:16-22), Amaziah's trial of strength (2 Kgs. 14:8-14), Hezekiah's reform[38] and revolt, Josiah's expansionistic policy, or even that last flicker of hope centered upon Jehoiachin (Jer. 28:1-4).

They have suggested that the imperfect with the weak waw for the future at the beginning of vs. 39[39] must be the work of a later hand. As it stands, however, vs. 39 is surely a final clause dependent on the main sentence 38bb. Even though it must be admitted that precisely this consecution does not seem to occur elsewhere in such a construction,[40] there are plenty of examples of a final clause introduced by a weak waw and the imperfect following the imperative.[41] There is no real grammatical difficulty here, and in any case, the "problem" occurs within the supposed gloss, not at its start. Left with its Masoretic poining the sentence makes perfect sense and is in perfect harmony with what the historian was trying to say: "I am going to give you Israel, that I might humble the seed of David."

Finally, scholars have suggested that vs. 38bb is tautological and superfluous.[42] This is not true. It does repeat the substance of vs. 37, but Dtr simply had to do so after his excursus concerning the possibility of a lasting dynasty for Jeroboam in 38aba in order to prepare for his explanation of the purpose of the transfer of power in vs. 39.

We must conclude, therefore, that vss. 38bb-39 are from Dtr. To summarize, in constructing 1 Kgs. 11:29-39, Dtr took over an old prophetic source, fragments of which remain as vss. 29-32a, 34a. Part of his own contribution to this was the promise of an eternal dominion to the Davidic house and the hint that the loss of the North was only a temporary punishment. Dtr went on to use the nîr promise two more times.

D. 1 Kgs. 15:4 and 2 Kgs. 8:19. 1 Kgs. 15:4 applies this promise to Abijam to explain Yahweh's tolerance of his sins. Several scholars have considered this to be an insertion.

Martin Noth first argued that vs. 4 must be an intrusion simply because vss. 3 and 5a (without David) fit together.[44] Yet certainly the circumstance that these verses could fit together does not automatically prove that they ever did. Noth abandoned this line of reasoning in his recent commentary, pointing instead to the odd use of *kî* at the beginning of vs. 4. Noth insisted that this *kî* be taken as causal, indicating that vs. 4 was later added to substantiate the idea, taken from 3b*b*, that Abijam ought to have followed David's example because of Yahweh's gracious favor towards David: "as the heart of David his father, because for David's sake . . . ." Noth concluded, quite rightly, that to take this *kî* as causal creates a grammatical mess so complex as to be explainable only by taking vs. 4 as a later insertion.[45]

However, we are not forced to understand this *kî* as causal, for the range of the function of this conjunction encompasses an adversative use when it follows a negative.[46] We should translate this as "however" or "nevertheless" as do most versions, which gives us a perfectly clear sentence.

Dtr, therefore, use the *nîr* promise a second time to explain why Yahweh did not punish Abijam for his apostasy. The singular ("his son") should not disturb us, for the promise is still seen from David's own standpoint.

This promise occurs for the third time, 2 Kgs. 8:19, in Dtr's presentation of Jehoram of Judah. Here again he uses it to explain why Yahweh did not destroy Judah. This time Dtr extends the promise explicitly into the indefinite future. No serious effort has ever been made to deny this verse to Dtr.

Why is explicit mention of the unconditional dynastic promise made only for Abijam and Jehoram? There does not seem to be anything special about these two kings or their reigns. However, they are the first two kings after Rehoboam whom the historian judges negatively. Perhaps he considered that his point had been made by the time he got to his negative verdicts on Ahaziah, Ahaz, and Manasseh.

But what point was he making? Surely Noth does not go nearly far enough when he explained the reason Dtr cited this promise for Jehoram: "Die Reflexion von Dtr in V. 19 geht von der geschichtlichen Tatsache des Weiterbestehens des Staats Juda aus."[47] If this were all Dtr had in mind, he was using a theological cannon to kill a fly. Why should he call into play the concept of an eternal Davidic dynasty, a concept with which Noth's postulated exilic and pessimistic historian would have been in violent disagreement, merely to explain the continuance of Judah for another two and a half centuries? He already had at hand other, less radical, theological tools with which to explain the continued existence of the nation in the face of deserved punishment (2 Kgs. 13:4-5; 14:26-27). Dtr must have had more in mind.

Perhaps this study has helped to rehabilitate the reputation of literary criticism as a valuable tool and may encourage its more careful use in the study of Dtr.

5. A Pre-exilic Historian

The triple invocation of the eternal and unconditional covenant with David cannot be construed to mean anything less than that Dtr was fully in sympathy with that promise and considered it still in force. Dtr used this dynastic promise once to explain the retention of one tribe by David's house (1 Kgs. 11:36) and twice to clarify why Yahweh failed to wipe out Judah (1 Kgs. 15:4; 2 Kgs. 8:19). Dtr also left the explicitly eternal and unconditional promise of Nathan (2 Sam. 7:11b-16) unrevised, even though he did interrupt it to insert permission for Solomon's Temple construction and even though this oracle was of great structural importance to his work.

On the other hand, the three conditional promises to Solomon (1 Kgs. 2:4; 8:25; 9:4-5) cannot be used as a correction to or a conditionalization of the eternal dynastic promise, for they are clearly limited to Solomon alone and refer explicitly to the retention of the throne of Israel, not Judah.

Such unquestioning acceptance of the unconditional and eternal nature of the place of David's house in Yahweh's scheme of history points clearly to a pre-exilic historian. The hint of a return of Davidic hegemony over the North in 1 Kgs. 11:39 pinpoints this pre-exilic historian to the time of Josaih and his expansionistic policies.

This study has attempted to look at four major trends in the study of Dtr and to see how a fresh examination of the dynastic promises in that work can advance our understanding in each area.

NOTES

[1]Ernst Jenni, "Zwei Jahrzehnte Forschung an der Büchern Josua bis Könige," ThRu 27 (1961) 1-32, 97-146. Arnold N. Radjawane, "Das deuteronomistische Geschichtswerk: ein Forschungsbericht," ThRu 38 (1974) 177-216.

[2]Martin Noth, Überlieferungsgeschichtliche Studien: Die sammelnden und bearbeitenden Geschichtswerke im Alten Testament (3. unveranderte Aufl.; Tübingen: Max Niemeyer Verlag, 1967) 100-110.

[3]Enno Janssen, Juda in der Exilszeit (FRLANT 69; Göttingen: Vandenhoeck & Ruprecht, 1956) 74-75.

[4]Martin Noth, "Zur Geschichtsauffassung des Deuteronomisten," Proceedings of the Twenty-Second Congress of Orientalists (ed. Zeki Velidi Togan; Leiden: E. J. Brill, 1957) 2. 558-565. Erich Zenger, "Die deuteronomistische Interpretation der Rehabilitierung Jojachins," BZ 12 (1968) 16-30.

[5]H. W. Wolff, "Das Kerygma des deuteronomistische Geschichtswerkes," ZAW 73 (1961), 174-179, 183-185.

[6]W. Brueggemann, "The Kerygma of the Deuteronomistic Historian," Int 22 (1968) 387-402.

[7]G. von Rad, Studies in Deuteronomy (SBT 9; London: SCM, 1953) 78.

[8]Ibid., 84-90.

[9]H. J. Boecker, Die Beurteilung der Anfänge des Königtums in den deuteronomischen Abschnitten des 1. Samuelbuches (WMANT 31; Neukirchen-Vluyn: Neukirchener Verlag, 1969) 89.

[10]R. E. Clements, "Deuteronomistic Interpretation of the Founding of the Monarchy in 1 Sam. VIII," VT 24 (1974) 398-410.

[11]Noth, UgS, 18-26.

[12]Ibid., 5-6.

[13]von Rad, 79-82.

[14]Janssen, 107.

[15]D. J. McCarthy, "II Samuel 7 and the Structure of the Deuteronomic Historian," JBL 84 (1965) 131-138.

[16]H. Timm, "Die Ladeerzählung und das Kerygma des deuteronomistischen Geschichtswerks," EvT 26 (1966) 509-526.

[17]N. Lohfink, "Darstellungskunst und Theologie in Dt. 1, 6--3, 29," Bib 42 (1960) 105-134; "Der Bundesschluss im Land Moab, BZ 6 (1962) 32-56.

[18]W. Harrington, "A Biblical View of History," IThQ 29 (1962) 207-216.

[19]G. Wenham, "The Deuteronomic Theology of the Book of Joshua," JBL 90 (1971) 140-156.

[20]For a detailed history of opinion, see Richard D. Nelson, The Redactional Duality of the Deuteronomistic History (unpublished dissertation, Union Theological Seminary in Virginia, 1973) 5-23.

[21]R. Smend, "Das Gesetz und die Völker: Ein Beitrag zur deuteronomistischen Redaktionsgeschichte," Probleme Biblischer Theologie: Gerhard von Rad zum 70. Geburtstag (ed. H. W. Wolff; Munich: Chr. Kaiser Verlag, 1971) 494-509.

[22]W. Dietrich, Prophetie und Geschichte (FRLANT 108; Göttingen: Vandenhoeck & Ruprecht, 1972).

[23]F. M. Cross, Jr., "The Structure of the Deuteronomic History," Perspectives in Jewish Learning (Chicago: Spertus College of Judaica Press, 1967) 3. 9-24.

[24]Noth, UgS, 66, 93-94, 100. Idem., Könige (BKAT 9/1; Neukirchen-Vluyn: Neukirchener Verlag, 1968) 30. L. Rost, Die Überlieferung von der Thronnachfolge Davids (BWANT 3/6; Stuttgart: W. Kohlhammer, 1926) 89-90. Wolff, 174. Janssen, 13-14.

[25]Noth, UgS, 95.

[26]Ibid., 66.

[27]Nelson, 143-149.

[28]Noth, "David and Israel in II Samuel VII," The Laws in the Pentateuch and Other Essays (Edinburgh: Oliver & Boyd, 1966) 250-259.

[29]McCarthy, 131-138.

[30]Rost, 61.

[31]For example, Dtr reproduced the Rise of David (I Sam. 16:4--2 Sam. 5:12) with the most minimal interference: 2 Sam. 2:10, 11; 5:4-5.

[32]Rost, 56. Noth, "David and Israel," 251.

[33]The command in I Sam. 10:8 to go to Gilgal points forward to the events of I Sam. 13. The tension created by 10:16 is not resolved until Saul's kingship is revealed in chapter 11.

[34]Noth, UgS, 54-59.

[35]Boecker, 89-90.

[36]Cf. I Sam. 2:35, where a "sure house" clearly means an external continuance.

[37]Noth, UgS, 72 n. 1; idem., Könige, 262; and many others.

[38]John Bright, A History of Israel (2nd. ed.; Philadelphia: Westminster, 1972) 280-282.

[39]Gesenius, Kautzsch, and Cowley, Hebrew Grammar, art. 23d. To repoint this as a waw-consecutive imperfect makes nonsense out of the sentence.

[40]Ibid., art. 165a.

[41]R. Meyer, Hebräische Grammatik (3. Aufl.; Berlin: Walter Gruyter, 1972) vol. 1, art. 117, 1.

[42]Noth, Könige, 262; John Gray, I & II Kings (2nd ed.; Philadelphia: Westminster, 1970) 292, n. a.

[43]The absence of this sentence from the Old Greek has often been cited against its originality. However, the translator of this portion of Kings often let his theology control his accuracy and took great pains to safeguard God's majesty. Since David's house never did regain Israel, the sentence would have been considered destructive to God's reputation. H. St. J. Thackery, "The Greek Translators of the Four Books of Kings," JTS 7 (1907) 262-278.

[44]Noth, UgS, 82, n. 1.

[45]Noth, Könige, 334.

[46]Gesenius, Kautzsch, and Cowley, art. 163a.

[47]Noth, UgS, 84, n. 1.

S 23 JONATHAN: A STRUCTURAL STUDY IN 1 SAMUEL

David Jobling

ABSTRACT

The theological problem, why Israel has a human monarchy when YHWH is her king, having been treated in 1 Sam 8-12, the remainder of the book has the function of treating another: Since monarchy is dynastic, how is it that Israel's monarchy is not traced from her first king? The hypothesis is presented that the character Jonathan has a key role in the solution. After exegetical treatment of the chapters in which he appears, various approaches to his significance are laid out, based on structuralist and literary methods. These methods have in common the assumption that Jonathan's significance is to be discovered primarily from his function in the narrative, and only secondarily from assessment of the historicity of the traditions about him. It is concluded that the use of the character Jonathan provides the only plausible affirmation of the legitimacy of David's kingship.

*

> Only after the function and structure of the work itself have been studied should the more traditional tasks of relating it to history or psychology or of establishing its connections with other disciplines or with the world be undertaken (De George: xxii).

> Some psychologist has proved that Benjy is not a true psychotic but a literary construct. This being so, it is fortunate that Benjy is in a book, where he belongs (Scholes and Kellogg: 199).

0.1 That the narrative parts of the Old Testament, including the Deuteronomic History, were compiled for primarily theological reasons, will hardly be disputed. But since the rise of historical criticism, it has been assumed that theological insight is to be had first of all through understanding of the processes by which the texts reached their canonical form, and through an assessment of the historical veracity of the traditions they present. Recently, it has been questioned whether this assumption is appropriate to the task, and whether, rather, the canonical texts should not be approached as integral pieces of theological literature, whose meaning is to be sought primarily from their inner structure. In particular, there have appeared many confessed "structural analyses" of canonical texts (e.g. Int 28/2 (April, 1974); Semeia 1, 2, 3:99-127; Barthes: 1974; Leach: 1962, 1966; for bibliography, Etudes théologiques et religieuses 48 (1973) 113-119).

0.2 In this paper, we apply to a part of the Old Testament which has usually been approached by historicizing methods, other methods drawn from structuralism and literary criticism. We do so not in a doctrinaire way, for, with Culley (169), we take structuralism as a suggestive set of methods, rather than as a "philosophical option". We draw on fields in which we have no expertise, as they have proved stimulating. These methods have suggested, where others have not, the key significance of Jonathan in the theology of 1 Sam.

Our conclusions provide new perspective on the results of historical study, and, if space were available, we should enter into a discussion of this /1/. We have made no attempt to do this, though we allude to the results of historical criticism from time to time.

0.3 The first section justifies the scope of the investigation (1 Sam 13-31) and the concentration on the character Jonathan. The second is a close examination of this section, and particularly of the contribution Jonathan makes to it. The third applies a variety of methods to the illumination of the character Jonathan, and hence to the confirming of the significance of these chapters.

1. The theological problematic of 1 Sam 13-31

1.1 Most commentators find a major division in 1 Sam at the end of ch. 15, seeing either chs. 7-15 or chs. 8-15 as a major section (recently, e.g. Ackroyd, Hertzberg, Stoebe: 1973). An essay by McCarthy (1973) suggests, however, that the major division is after ch. 12. He deals with chs. 8-12, the section on the beginning of kingship in Israel, and, going beyond the numerous theories of different sources in these chapters, sees the whole section as a closely-edited treatment of a severe theological problem: How can a people of whom YHWH is sole king become a human monarchy under YHWH? The problem _is_ severe, for the theological legitimacy of the system under which Israel lives is in question. The answer goes roughly like this: YHWH is Israel's king; for Israel to desire a human king is sinful; YHWH meets Israel halfway--after due expiation of the sin, YHWH looks with favor on the sinful wish, and approves Israel's human king. The firm formal structure of these chapters--three assemblies of all Israel alternating with two traditional stories about Saul--proves a very effective vehicle for the _theology_, but presents a sequence which is the _historian's_ despair, or should be!

1.2 The present paper took its start from reading McCarthy's, being satisfied with it, and asking, what next? If one problem has been laid to rest, what new one do the following chapters take up? The answer is immediately clear. Monarchy is, from the deuteronomic point of view, dynastic /2/. If YHWH approved Israel's monarchy, why then do her later kings not trace their descent from her first king? Why Davidides, not Saulides? YHWH swore with David an eternal covenant (2 Sam 7) that one of his descendants would always sit on his throne, a covenant which even sin could not annul. Did YHWH swear such a covenant with Saul? If so, how could it be annulled? If not, was Saul's kingship real, was YHWH "for real" in approving it? Again, the theological stakes are high, nothing less than the legitimacy of David's line, under which Israel lives. This problem, we suggest, dominates the whole rest of the book /3/.

1.21 The section 1 Sam 13-31 is noted for the profusion of doublets, _non sequiturs_, and narrative implausibilities which it contains; this is usually explained as the result of editorial activity (e.g. Weiser, 1961: 159-160). But why is the editorial work so "poor"? Admittedly we are dealing with canons of narrative construction of which we have limited understanding, but it seems worth hazarding a different suggestion, that the narrative problems are a marker of the severity of the theological problem to be solved.

1.3 The thesis of this paper is that 1 Sam 13-31 is Israel's theological solution to the theological problem outlined; and further, that the character Jonathan is much the most important of the means of solving (of "mediating", in a sense to be defined) this problem. The transition from Saul to David, otherwise theologically implausible, is by Jonathan made theologically plausible. And we suggest that the testing of this thesis should assume precedence over attempts to assess the historicity of the Jonathan traditions, in other words that he is better approached as a literary character than as a historical figure.

2. The structure of 1 Sam 13-31

2.0 The following description of the shape of the section, based on the appearances of Jonathan, is a working tool, whose value is to be judged by the insight it provides. The movement towards David's kingship begins before he even appears, in the account of Saul's rejection. Chs. 13-15 we therefore call preamble. 16:1-13, the secret anointing of David, is a focal scene. Thereafter, sections describing the relation of David to Saul, and lacking Jonathan, alternate with sections where Jonathan appears. The Saul-David sections are usually much longer than the Jonathan ones (20:1-21:1 is the exception). By the fourth Saul-David section (21:2-23:15a) other material enters in, but their relationship is still the major theme. After 23:18, it becomes one theme among several, though still important. It is not merely in a formal sense that the Saul-David sections lack Jonathan. With the single exception of 22:8, there seems to be nothing in them that would be different if Jonathan did not exist /4/.

2.01 Schematically, the structure is as follows:

Preamble: The rejection of Saul	chs. 13-15
Focal scene: The anointing of David	16:1-13
1st Saul-David section	16:14-17:58
1st Jonathan section	18:1-5
2nd Saul-David section	18:6-30
2nd Jonathan section	19:1-7
3rd Saul-David section	19:8-24
3rd Jonathan section	20:1-21:1 (MT)
4th Saul-David section (with other material)	21:2-23:15a
4th Jonathan section	23:15b-18
5th Saul-David section (with much other material)	23:19 onward

2.1 The preamble

2.11 The formal rejection of Saul is a prerequisite for the movement towards David's becoming king. Elsewhere we have tried to show that chs. 13-15 have the purpose of stating this formal rejection, and that in particular 14:1-46 depicts Saul as the rejected king:

> Saul in this story is not so much wicked as foolish and frustrated. His intentions are good, indeed thoroughly pious, but he pursues them in self-defeating ways, and events thwart them . . . . The passage presents a skillful portrait of a rejected king, wholly coherent with the rejection oracles of chs. 13 and 15. His character and fate bear out his rejectedness (Jobling, 1976).

To achieve this portrait, we further suggested, the traditional view of Saul, mostly positive, has been much altered. But if 14:1-46 shows a tendency in relation to Saul, so it does also in relation to Jonathan. He receives such marks of divine approval, and such acclaim of the people, as befits a king, and does so in the very context of his father's rejection. Our study concluded as follows:

> We have shown how the redaction of 1 Sam 14:1-46 tends to diminish Saul and exalt Jonathan. We have discussed in detail how this meant the alteration and even reversal of traditions. We have suggested that the reader, coming to the section aware of Saul's rejection, must ask at the end whether Jonathan is not the successor appointed by YHWH.
>
> But, for the attentive reader, this contradicts the apparent implication of 13:13-14, that the rejection of Saul was the rejection of his dynasty too. What, then, can the exaltation of Jonathan mean? This question receives no answer in 14:1-46. The answer is undoubtedly to be sought in the mediary role which Jonathan is later to play in the transition from Saul's kingship to David's (Jobling, 1976).

2.12 To this we add a footnote at a more formal level. The relationship between Saul and Jonathan shows <u>both</u> role-identification between the two (13:2, 22; 14:21) <u>and</u> replacement of Saul by Jonathan, in the fighting of Saul's battles (13:3; 14:1-15, cf. 9:16), and in the affection of the people (14:45). This pattern of identification and replacement /5/ will be extremely important for our further discussion.

2.2 The focal scene, the secret anointing of David, is reminiscent of the witches' scenes in <u>Macbeth</u>; brief and formal in structure, mysterious in content, and secret, but providing the motive and explanation for the surrounding narrative. David, apparently, knows his destiny from the start, though others do not.

2.3 The Saul-David sections

2.30 The programme of these sections is stated at the outset. YHWH has departed from Saul (16:14), but is with David (16:18; cf. 16:13; 18:14). Saul is rejected, David elected, and everything in these sections drives this home. Saul is shown negatively in almost every incident, but even more he is shown as frustrated--his plans to harm David are always turning out to David's advantage, his descent to the depths is the very cause of David's rise. David is shown positively /6/, and as successful in what he intends. This is a first level in the contrast between the rejected and the elected; in character, bad <u>versus</u> good, in intentions, frustration <u>versus</u> success (cf. Conrad: 68-71; Grønbaek: 110). A second level is the effect each character has on the relationship between them. Saul, as rejected, is disloyal to David, and tends to drive him away. David, as elected, is loyal to Saul, and tends to seek his presence. This sets up a great tension--the relationship finds no stability whether they are together or apart.

2.31 In the first section, 16:14-17:58, Saul accepts David, and the two become intimate. Within the intimacy, however, David soon asserts his independence of, and superiority over, Saul, in the Goliath affair. Not even by the offer of his armor can Saul gain a share of the credit, for David must reject it (17:38-39).

2.321 The next section, 18:6-30, excellently exemplifies the structure of the relationship--Saul ever trying to do David undeserved harm, but succeeding only in helping him. The son-in-law motif (18:17-29) deserves particular attention. Saul offers to David, in turn, two of his daughters as wife, and David actually marries the second, Michal. It is plausible to see in this a point in favor of the legitimacy of David's kingship, the theological problem of our section. Under certain circumstances, to be a king's son-in-law is to be his legitimate heir; one need think only of the common fairy-tale ending, "my daughter and half my kingdom" as the hero's reward on the accomplishment of his task (Propp: 63-64). Perhaps, historically, David's status as Saul's son-in-law did have something to do with his succession /7/. Morgenstern (1959) finds evidence for such a system of succession in Edom not long before Saul's time, and builds up from certain hints in the text (for example, David's demand in 2 Sam 3:14 for Michal's return) the case that it was precisely under this system that David came to the throne.

2.322 This, however, cannot possibly be the function of the son-in-law motif in the present narrative, whose point of view is that kingship passes through the male line. No one is ever represented as assuming otherwise! Morgenstern's work is an example of finding the meaning of narrative rather from imported historical data than from implicit literary considerations (cf. Barthes, 1972: 249-254). The motif performs here, in fact, under the constraint of the overriding theological agenda, a function not natural to it. According to the account, Saul's motive in offering his daughters was deceitful from the start. In the fairy-tale motif, the king's offer, though fraught with peril, is sincere, so that Saul's deceitfulness represents an ironic use of the motif /8/. The account serves the character-portrayal of Saul (and also of David, who has occasion to show becoming modesty!) as well as fitting the pattern of frustration and success.

2.33 The same theme continues in the next section, 19:8-24, for Michal becomes David's ally against Saul. The scene in vss. 18-24 merits comment. Saul's intention to do David harm is again frustrated, for his pursuit ends in his deep humiliation (as Saul's pursuits always do--cf. not only chs. 24 and 26, but also his pursuit of the Philistines in 14:1-46!) The similarities with 9:1-10:16 are so striking, above all in the repetition of the proverb "Is Saul also among the prophets?", that we should regard it as a satirical recapitulation of the earlier passage. Saul's previous visit to Samuel, and his first experience of prophesying, showed him as the elected one on his way to the height of fortune; the recapitulation shows the rejected one far gone in degradation. Stoebe comments appositely:

> Der vom Geist ergriffene Saul wird nicht zu Taten ermächtigt (10,7), sondern völlig entmächtigt. Das ist der eigentliche Skopus, dem der Gedanke der Rettung Davids völlig untergeordnet ist . . . . Die Kleider, die hier abgerissen werden, sind die Kleider eines Königs, der nun nicht nur in schimpflicher Nacktheit, sondern zugleich entblösst von Macht, unfähig zur Tat am Boden liegt (1973: 368). /9/

2.34 On 21:2-23:15a little need be said. Material on Saul's relationship to David is now broken up by other material. David is glorified as a kind of Robin Hood. He befriends a priest, while Saul is a slaughterer of priests /10/. And Saul's intentions against David are, as ever, frustrated; as the section ends, he has lost control of the oracular ephod by his actions, and David, having possession of it, uses it to frustrate Saul! (on this, excellently, Weiss: 187-188). It is also significant that, in his action against the priests, Saul can find only a foreigner to support him (22:17-19).

2.35 Similar themes continue after 23:18; but now something new occurs, Saul's acknowledgement of David's coming kingship (24:20; the doublet 26:25 has only a general blessing). We shall consider this below (4.2).

2.4 The Jonathan sections

2.40 According to Leach, "From (1 Sam 18) through to 23 <u>every</u> reference to Jonathan serves to emphasize his role identification with David. This equation implies that David ultimately replaces Jonathan as Saul's 'rightful' successor" (1966: 67). This correct insight is only a partial one. The character Jonathan stands in a twofold relationship, to Saul and to David, and the two parts have parallel structures. In relation to Saul, he moves between close identification and an independence which frequently suggests his replacing Saul. In relation to David, he moves between close identification and a self-emptying into David, a readiness to <u>be replaced</u> by him. We must demonstrate this twofold pattern of identification and replacement in detail.

2.41 We have already mentioned (2.12) this pattern between Saul and Jonathan in chs. 13-14. No identification with David was possible there, of course; but before going on to the later Jonathan sections we may note, even in ch. 14, two Jonathan themes which will find recapitulation in David. First, Jonathan's single combat (independent of Saul) against the Philistines is echoed in David's combat with Goliath. Second, Jonathan's infraction of a food tabu, interpreted by the narrative to his credit, finds a close echo in the account of David and the priest at Nob (21:2-7) /11/.

2.421 Jonathan's first appearance after ch. 14, in 18:1-5, is sudden and brief, but in a sense this remarkable passage (understood along with ch. 14) tells everything that is to be told about him /12/. It follows David's defeat of Goliath and reintroduction to Saul, and expounds his relationship to Jonathan in a beautifully structured way:

Ia (vs. 1) Jonathan establishes identification with David: "Jonathan loved him as his own self".

IIa (vs. 2) Saul confirms the identification of Jonathan with David by adopting David: he "would not let him return to his father's house" /13/.

Ib (vss. 3-4) Jonathan makes David his replacement, by handing over to him his clothes and weapons.

IIb (vs. 5) Saul confirms the replacement of Jonathan by David, sending David out to fight his battles, which Jonathan previously did.

The identification-replacement pattern between Jonathan could not be more effectively exhibited.

2.422 But there is more to say. When we last took leave of Jonathan, in ch. 14, he was at the high point of his fortunes, to the extent that the reader might see in him the legitimate heir, with all the signs of Saul's lost kingship (above, 2.11). At this level, 18:4 can be read only as an abdication--it is the <u>royal</u> garments and the <u>royal</u> weapons that he hands over (Morgenstern: 322, cf. Thompson: 335; dissenting from this, Stoebe, 1973: 348). David is now king not only in the secret counsels of YHWH, but by the abdication in his favor of the "acting" king! Taken together, 14:1-46 and 18:1-5 have an inner significance which runs ahead of the external appearances--the kingship has passed from Saul to David by the mediation of Jonathan. The remaining Jonathan sections do little more than reinforce this.

2.431 In 19:1-7, Jonathan's double role-identification is very clear. Saul tries to enlist him against David (vs. 1a). But his identification with David is at once reaffirmed (vs. 1b), and he warns David of Saul's intentions (vss. 2-3). For the time being, however, this is not at the cost of Jonathan's unity with his father: "Saul listened to the voice of Jonathan" (vs. 6). The two act as one in restoring David to his place as Saul's adopted (cf. 18:2), and Jonathan at once disappears (vs. 7).

2.432 The heavy theological freight of this passage is the cause, perhaps, of two infelicities of style. First, the redundant use of "father" and "son" in vss. 1-4 suggests the importance of their identification at the point where it is endangered (for another significant use of "father" and "son", see below, 4.2). Second, the repetition of the name "Jonathan" at the end, four times in vss. 6-7 (cf. Stoebe, 1973: 357), makes clear the importance of Jonathan's mediating role. We note one further point. There are close parallels, down to vocabulary and phraseology, between this passage and the final scene of 14:1-46. In one case, Jonathan is under Saul's death sentence, in the other, David. Each is saved by an external mediation, in which Saul acquiesces. Here, once more, David's experience recapitulates Jonathan's!

2.441 Ch. 20, even more than ch. 14, is Jonathan's big chapter. He appears throughout, sometimes in David's, sometimes in Saul's, company. In vss. 1-23 he is with David. During Saul's temporary indisposition (he is naked at Ramah), Jonathan is presented unmistakably as a king. David enters his presence (p̄anim), and we are made to think of the royal "presence" of Saul which David enters and leaves (16:21, 22; 17:57; 19:7). Jonathan speaks as a king: "Far from it, you shall not die" (cf. 19:6!) The role identification Saul-Jonathan is tremendously strong in the first verses: "Behold, my father does nothing either great or small without disclosing it to me" (vs. 2) /14/. The following verses (4-11), display great subtlety. Even while acting as king, Jonathan strongly affirms his identification with David (vs. 4), and allows himself to be enlisted as mediator. David at first seems to accept the identification of Jonathan with Saul, regarding the son as the father's plenipotentiary (vs. 8b), and adopting the attitude of a suppliant (vs. 8a, cf. Hertzberg: 172). But David's hints that Jonathan might act against him elicit a forceful denial: "Far be it from you!" (vs. 9). The remainder of the passage, vss. 12-23, moves entirely in the identification-replacement pattern of Jonathan and David. Jonathan's abdication is clear: "May YHWH be with you, as he has been with my father" (vs. 13), and he appeals to be identified with David the coming king.

2.442 In 20:1-23 we witness a great collision between the Saul-Jonathan pattern of identification and replacement and the Jonathan-David pattern of identification and replacement. Perhaps even more plainly than in 14:1-46 and 18:1-5, kingship passes from Saul to David by means of Jonathan; it is when Jonathan has most clearly "become king" that he most clearly "abdicates"!

2.443 20:24-34 finds Jonathan with Saul. Implying the Jonathan-David identification, Saul questions Jonathan about David (vs. 27). Implying the Saul-Jonathan identification, Jonathan replies (vs. 28) that David requested something of him as of a king (Saul's deputy!) But Saul is not bluffed. "You have chosen the son of Jesse" (always a pejorative appellation, Stoebe, 1973: 388) " . . . to the shame of your mother's nakedness", and while David lives "neither you nor your kingdom shall be established"(vss. 30-31). In this, the only use of a <u>mlk</u> word in connection with Jonathan, Saul simultaneously affirms the point of view of the narrative, that kingship is dynastic, and "forgets" the terms of the oracle of rejection in 13:13-14, which applied to his whole house /15/. Jonathan falls into his accustomed role of mediation (vs. 32), which Saul rejects not by word, but by deed. In one of the most revealing verses (33) of the whole narrative, and without narrative logic, Saul tries to impale Jonathan (Jonathan's experience now recapitulating David's in 18:11 and 19:10!) and from this Jonathan deduces that his father seeks <u>David's</u> life. The identification of Jonathan and David is total--an act directed at one is an act directed at the other /16/.

2.444 20:35-21:1 sees Jonathan back with David, and partly recapitulates vss. 1-23. David accepts Jonathan as king, doing obeisance (vs. 41), and they reaffirm their covenant identification.

2.45 The last brief passage, 23:15b-18, provides a neat counterpoint to the last; Jonathan goes out to David as to a king, reversing 20:1. The identifications are present: Jonathan's acknowledgement of David is also Saul's ("my father also knows this"); and Jonathan again appeals to his past relation with David ("I shall be next to you"). But they are swallowed up in the completeness of the replacement, which is unambiguous: "You shall be king over Israel".

3. Approaches to the character Jonathan

3.0 It is out of readings in structuralism and literary criticism that the stimulus for this paper has come. Since these are still relatively foreign fields, some of the following may be methodologically problematic; but the final test of method is its power to illuminate.

3.1 An "actantial" model for 1 Sam 13-31

3.11 Greimas (172-191) has suggested a <u>schema actantiel</u>, by means of which narrative can be analyzed according to its participants, or "actants" (anglicizing the identical French), who need not be people, and their relationship to the movement of the narrative, as follows:

```
Destinator ------ Object ------- Destinary
                    |
 Adversary ------ Subject ------ Helper      /17/
```

The <u>destinator</u> brings the action about, with the aim of getting the <u>object</u> to the <u>destinary</u>. The <u>subject</u> is the protagonist of the action, which is aided and opposed by various <u>helpers</u> and <u>adversaries</u>.

3.12 The actantial scheme which we propose for 1 Sam 13-31 is

```
                 (Saul's)
    YHWH ----- kingship ------ David
                   |
    Saul ------ David -------- Philistines
JONATHAN                       JONATHAN
(others)                       (others)
```

It is the categories "helper" and "adversary" which claim special attention.

3.13 To digress briefly, the placing of the Philistines is most interesting. Historically, it is likely that although they were responsible for Saul's downfall their threat was also the major cause of his rise; and that he enjoyed considerable successes against them. In our chapters, none of this ambiguity is preserved. The Philistines in their every appearance assist the narrative's movement towards David's takeover--even the accounts of the victories over them in chs. 13-14, for these are Jonathan's, not Saul's! David's successes against the Philistines advance him at Saul's expense. Saul's attempt to use the Philistines to destroy David misfires (18:20-29). The Philistines even recognize David's kingship early in the story (21:11). And they prevent his participation in the disastrous final battle (ch. 29), from which, whatever the outcome, he could have gained no credit in Israel. Greimas's model shows this consistent function of the Philistines <u>in relation to the aim of the narrative</u>, even where their activities seem to make poor historical sense.

3.14 Jonathan, by his mere existence, is the opponent of the action. He is heir to the throne, so that David must replace not only a legitimate monarch, but also a legitimate heir. But in all his appearances after ch. 14 he is, in action and word, the helper of the action--he saves David's life, tries to maintain his high position in Saul's court, and as it were hands over the future to David. And when his function is performed, he disappears (not only for good, after 23:18 (the notice in ch. 31 is but a passing one), but also after his earlier appearances) quite abruptly. Greimas's scheme alerts us to this extraordinary ambiguity of the character Jonathan in relation to the theological problematic.

3.2 Jonathan as mediator

3.20 We here consider the work of Lévi-Strauss on myth, especially as it has been applied to the Old Testament by Leach (for the following, Lévi-Strauss: 206-231; Leach, 1962, 1966, especially 1962: 7-11; Lane: 13-19; Jacobson: 149-157).

3.21 The function of myth is as follows. Any belief system contains contradictions that are essentially irresoluble; for instance, how could the human race have descended from the first parents without violation of the absolute incest tabu? Myths soften, or "mediate", such contradictions, by making it appear that they are resolved, though they never are. For it is vital to a society that its belief not <u>appear</u> to be based on contradictions. In the enormous variety of myths within societies and across societies, it is the same essential problems which are at issue.

3.22 Belief systems, in other words, abound in <u>binary oppositions</u> (Leach, 1962: 9-10; Lane: 16), life and death, endogamy and exogamy, etc., which are not capable of final resolution. A characteristic of the myths which mediate them is <u>redundancy</u>, the saying of the same thing in many different mythical ways:

> Any particular myth in isolation is like a coded message badly snarled up with noisy interference. Even the most confident devotee might feel a little uncertain as to what precisely is being said. But, as a result of redundancy, the believer can feel that, even when the details vary, each alternative version of a myth confirms his understanding and reinforces the essential meaning of all the others (Leach, 1962: 9).

The underlying agenda of a myth is its <u>deep structure</u> (Lane: 14-16), as opposed to the surface structure, that is, its narrated form(s). In their surface structure, myths are <u>diachronic</u>--they tell stories in which the passage of time is an element. But their deep structure is <u>synchronic</u>--they express relationships within a belief system which need not take any particular view of the time element. The priority of synchrony over diachrony is characteristic of structuralism: "History is seen as the specific mode of development of a particular system, whose present, or synchronic nature must be fully known before any account can be given of its evolution, or diachronic nature" (Lane: 17).

3.23 Leach (1966: 25-31) has challenged Levi-Strauss's insistence that his methods are not appropriate for the Old Testament. Boldly applying the term "myth" to his material, Leach presents the accounts of the struggles over the succession to David as a mediation between principles of endogamy and exogamy in Israel (1966). In what follows, we certainly go beyond Leach's intentions, for he is still working with themes of direct concern rather to the anthropologist than to the theologian. Without implying acceptance of his view of the nature of the deuteronomic narrative, we make use of a method which has been suggested by his.

3.24 The theological problematic discovered in 1 Sam 8-12 by McCarthy (above, 1.1) may be readily expressed in binary form:

1. Human monarchy is alien to Yahwism, but
2. Israel is a human monarchy under YHWH.

So, likewise, may the problematic of the succeeding chapters:

1. Monarchy is inherently dynastic, but
2. Israel's monarchy is not traced from her first king.

This opposition Jonathan mediates. In a dynastic system, the only way in which an outsider may legitimately succeed is as a result of an abdication. For reasons to be considered (cf. 4.1), Saul <u>cannot</u> abdicate in David's favor, and this means an <u>impasse</u>. But what he cannot himself do, perhaps he can do in the person of his legitimate heir. At least, this is the best way out of the <u>impasse</u> available. Jonathan's identification with, his heirdom to, Saul, provide him with the royal authority to abdicate; his identification with David enables the emptying of his own heirdom into David.

3.25 Other structuralist categories provide insight into the narrative. The use of Jonathan certainly exhibits <u>redundancy</u>. All that is essential is in 14:1-46 and 18:1-5 (cf. 2.421-422), but there follow three more Jonathan sections; that is, sections where the theological problem can only be broached alternate with ones in which it is "resolved". To speak of redundancy is to stress the <u>synchronic</u>. Although the Jonathan sections do exhibit <u>diachrony</u> (e.g. Jonathan's declarations of David's coming kingship grow in clarity, 18:4; 20:13-16; 23:17), synchrony is at least equally clear; a good example is David's obeisance to Jonathan in 20:41, recalling vss. 1-11 and making little sense "after" Jonathan's declaration in vss. 13-16.

3.26 As to <u>deep structure</u>, we have already pursued the implications of the Jonathan sections below the narrative level. But may we not go deeper, and suggest that we see here a manifestation of one of the most basic of biblical oppositions, that between divine demand and divine grace, or between the conditional and the unconditional covenant? Between these there is in the Old Testament not a static choice but an ultimately irresoluble conflict; YHWH's grace is utterly free,

YHWH's demand is utterly binding. Saul sins, and must be rejected. But YHWH made him a promise, which must be kept. Therefore, the passing of Saul's kingship must express the radical discontinuity caused by sin (the kingship is torn from him), but also the radical continuity guaranteed by grace--the kingship passes by legitimate means to one who has become his heir.

3.3 Character and plot

3.31 Scholes and Kellogg make these statements about ancient narrative: "As in the epic, character in the saga is conceived in terms of plot. In this perfectly self-contained narrative world, the characters are not endowed with any attributes extraneous to the action being presented" (173), and "Characters in primitive stories are invariably 'flat,' 'static,' and quite 'opaque'" (164). Apparently, however, they do not intend to include the Old Testament in such judgments, for elsewhere they contrast it with Greek literature:

> The heroes of the Old Testament were in a process of becoming, whereas the heroes of Greek narrative were in a state of being. Process in Greek narrative was confined to the action of a plot. And even so, the action exemplified unchanging, universal laws; while the agents of the action, the characters, became as the plot unfolded only more and more consistent ethical types. Abraham, Jacob, David, and Samson, on the other hand, are men whose personal development is the focus of interest (123).

We suggest, however, that in our section character _is_ very much subordinate to plot; not, perhaps, because character is unimportant, but because _here_ plot, the theological agenda, is overwhelmingly important.

3.321 Before discussing Jonathan, it is instructive to consider the two major protagonists, Saul and David. They show character traits, and appear to act from discernible motives. Saul acts to keep the kingship for himself and his house. But here two difficulties arise. First, why should he do so, having been plainly told that kingship will depart from him and his house (13:13-14)? Second, why does he do so so badly, in such consistently self-defeating ways? David, on the other hand, in the usual (historicizing) view, early set his sights on the kingship, and pursued it with patience and opportunism. But why should he do so, having been already anointed king?

3.322 It seems accurate to say that even in Saul and David character is almost entirely (making allowances for the strength of tradition and the exigencies of story-telling) in the service of plot. Saul is rejected, David elected, and the character and experience of each bears out that rejection and election; must bear them out, for the success of the narrative. The rejected is bad, the elected is good, and to ask after cause and effect is pointless. The rejected is frustrated by events (so that his bad acts turn out for good!), while the elected is advanced by events.

3.33 Jonathan is the extreme case of character emptied into plot; at least after ch. 14 /18/ he is flat, static, and certainly opaque (3.31), his attitudes and actions lacking any normal motivation. He is the heir, and the heir does not normally champion the cause of an upstart against his own. Morgenstern's view, that Jonathan accepted the custom of son-in-law succession, we have already rejected (2.322; one may reasonably doubt whether there is any traditio-historical link, in any case, between Michal and Jonathan). Psychologizing solutions are suggested particularly by Hertzberg: "On Jonathan's side (the friendship with David) is completely disinterested" (154), and "In the figure of Jonathan, the Old Testament has a real nobleman of high sensibility" (172). It is one thing, however, to show even an extreme case of a human virtue, but quite another to act without reason against oneself! Jonathan after ch. 14 is so lacking in features that might grow out of traditions about him that one is forced to wonder whether there were any such traditions, whether he is not a purely literary construction.

3.341 Conrad (67) finds a motivation for Jonathan from another direction; he takes the initiative on David's side "nicht nur aus menschlicher Liebe und Zuneigung, sondern vor allem deshalb, weil ihm . . . bewusst wird, dass dieser der Erwählte Jahwes ist, und er das anerkannt (20,13ff.; 23,16f.)" This hardly means that Jonathan "saw which way the wind was blowing" and acted opportunistically, for on more than one occasion he could have allowed David to be killed simply by doing nothing. Rather, he came to know the divine plan, and acted in accordance with it. The theme of <u>knowledge</u>, of who knows what is going on in the narrative, is a very important and also a very problematic one, requiring a separate study /19/, but we must sketch the problem. As a pointer, we may quote Hertzberg (156), speaking of Saul's first mistrust of David: "Anyone who knows how events are to turn out, of course, knows the deeper justification of his mistrust: David is really destined to be Saul's successor". On the face of it, this statement is meaningless, for what has the narrator's knowledge of the outcome to do with Saul's mistrust? But such knowledge is pivotal for the narrative.

3.342 David is made privy to the theological agenda at his anointing, and his knowledge of what YHWH is doing never becomes a major issue /20/. Saul does not learn who his successor is, but he does learn of the rejection of his house, so that ignorance of this on his part is <u>refusal to know</u>. Leach (1966: 67) notes that the narrative makes Saul, rather than David, the rebel; and wherein can Saul's rebellion against YHWH lie but in this refusal to know? It is tempting to find a marker of this "epistemological" rebellion in Samuel's words to Saul: "Rebellion is as the sin of divination" (15:23). The one who refuses to know by direct prophetic oracle (13:13-14) seeks to know by witches (ch. 28)!

3.343 Jonathan receives no revelations, and yet he knows. Mysteriously, the divine plan is open to him. His discernment is clear enough in 20:13-16, but in 23:17 he speaks to David as a prophet speaks: "The hand of my father shall not find you; you shall be king over Israel, and I shall be next to you."

3.35 In his reckless courage, his mysterious insight into events, his utterly selfless surrender of himself to this insight, who are Jonathan's literary counterparts? In different ways, we may perhaps look to Perceval, to Dostoevsky's

Idiot, even to Don Quixote. Like Myshkin, "He was an ideal character, a God's fool" (Gibson:105, and cf. Welsford: 88-112, on the clairvoyant fools of Ireland). His motivation is YHWH's motivation, ultimately unknown. His initiative on David's behalf (Conrad: 67) is YHWH's initiative. He has, as Hertzberg (193) instinctively discerns, one notable biblical counterpart in John the Baptist, in whom the old age recognizes and yields to the new.

4. Conclusions

4.0 From this investigation we attempt a summary statement of the role of Jonathan in 1 Sam 13-31. These chapters must make theologically acceptable the transition from Saul's kingship to David's. We are concerned not with how this took place historically, and what reasons, if any, were then given, but rather with the answers given in the text, and coherent with its implicit point of view. Saul's incapacity to rule does not legitimize David (cf. Grønbaek: 119). Nor does any amount of support from various individuals and factions (Grønbaek: 273). Nor does being Saul's son-in-law, though in another frame of reference it would (2.322).

4.1 The Saul-David sections through 23:15a work well in their own terms. They depict the rejected one as bad and appropriately rejected, the elected one as good and appropriately elected. They create superb narrative tension in the interplay between Saul's disloyalty to David and David's loyalty to Saul. But these sections cannot show David's legitimacy, and do not try. David can be king only if Saul gives place to him. But Saul cannot give place to David and still "be himself"--this would call for knowledge of YHWH's plan and obedience to it. These the rejected one cannot have; his lack of them goes along with his rejection!

4.2 The impossibility of solving the theological problem by means of Saul and David alone is shown after 23:19; for here the attempt is apparently made to do so (perhaps a relic of a stage of the tradition which lacked the Jonathan sections) /21/. The attempt is made, that is, to show Saul both as the rejected one and as willingly abdicating to David. In ch. 24, he begins by seeking David's life, and ends by confessing David's future kingship (vs. 20). Their next encounter, in ch. 26, is a "redundant" repetition of this cycle, though without the specific confession. Noteworthy in these chapters is the frequent use of "father" and "son" (24:11, 16; 26:17, 21, 25; cf. above, 2.432). But in the very next verse (27:1) David complains of the continuing danger to his life from Saul. The attempt fails; the theological aim is here pursued at the cost of narrative coherence, and even of psychological conviction; at no level does the account make sufficient sense.

4.3 The introduction of Jonathan appears at first to add to the problems; David must now supplant not only a king, but a legitimate heir. But this is illusory; Jonathan will die with Saul, since Saul's house is rejected. Meanwhile, Jonathan provides what is needed. As Saul's heir, he has the kingly power to abdicate; as separate from Saul, he can do so without disrupting Saul's character-portrayal. David can receive Jonathan's armor (18:4) where he cannot receive Saul's (17:38-39)! The theological aim is pursued first by a beautiful technique of interlacing the Jonathan sections with the Saul-David sections; again and again we are put in touch with the resolution of the problem which the Saul-David sections necessarily leave unresolved. Second, Jonathan's mediation of the theological problem is shadowed by his mediation between Saul and David at the narrative level. Third, at the deeper level, and coming to the surface in a variety of ways, are the structural patterns which bear the burden of the theology, the double pattern of identification and replacement between Saul and Jonathan and between Jonathan and David.

4.4 The narrators worked with a theological paradox, admitting no "solution". We may admire their skill, though we cannot know the extent to which the phenomena we have studied were consciously intended. But a judgment on their "success" is meaningless. That their work was a <u>sufficient</u> treatment of the paradox is demonstrated simply by its survival as sacred scripture /22/.

NOTES

/1/ On a more limited scale, we attempted this in Jobling, 1976.

/2/ The problematic question, whether the historical Saul expected to found a dynasty, is irrelevant here. On 13: 13-14, cf. Grønbaek: 125.

/3/ Weiser (1966: 354) sees the account of David's rise as a "Tendenzschrift . . . die zwar verschiedenartige Einzelüberlieferungen von ungleichem historischem Wert in zeitlicher Abfolge zusammenordnet, ihr Ziel aber in der göttlichen Legitimation des Königs David und seiner Dynastie über Israel . . . sieht" (the article contains numerous details of how this goal was pursued).

/4/ On the possibility that the Jonathan traditions were originally separate, cf. below, 4.2.

/5/ Of the interplay between the identification and the separation of Saul and Jonathan, the two lots in 14:40-42 provide a neat parable--first the two together over against the people, then the two over against each other!

/6/ A negative view of David is perhaps implied in 21: 2-7 (his misrepresentation of the facts to Ahimelech), or in ch. 25 (his intended violence against Nabal's house, not carried out). But even these are readily to be understood under the rubric that everything turns out for the best for him. By no means is there anything negative about David in ch. 22--Saul's words (vss. 7-8) simply confirm the king's vindictiveness, and David's own (vs. 22) show him truly penitent over consequences of his action which were scarcely his fault. Any negative hints in the account of David's rise are put in perspective when contrasted with the "realistic" and damning account of his actions towards Uriah (2 Sam 11).

/7/ On the extraordinary complexity of the traditions involved, cf. Stoebe, 1961; Grønbaek: 104-109.

/8/ Grønbaek (104-105) suggests that, in the tradition, Saul may have had positive intentions in offering Michal.

/9/ Grønbaek (119-120) sees the incident as fictional, composed precisely as an expression of Saul's rejectedness, and further to confirm David's legitimacy (but cf. below, 4:0). On the *crux* between 15:35 and 19:18-24 (Samuel *does* see Saul again) it is best to conclude that this is one of the narrative tensions occasioned by the theological urgency of showing Saul rejected.

/10/ On Saul's relationship with the house of Eli, cf. Jobling, 1976: In ch. 14, he is only hindered by the Elide priest, and his very association with a rejected house (cf. 2:27-36) is a further indication that his own house is rejected. The scene in 22:11-19 thus lies on two axes of divine rejection.

/11/ We owe this suggestion to D. J. McCarthy.

/12/ The absence of this section, and of large parts of ch. 17, from the LXX, we here ignore, despite its importance for historical investigation. Our present purpose is literary investigation of the MT.

/13/ Some scholars see vs. 2 as inserted into the immediate context, being the original conclusion to 17:55-58 (Grønbaek: 92; de Vries: 27-28; dissenting, Stoebe, 1973: 347-348). If this is correct, it makes the structuring of vss. 1-5 only the more striking.

/14/ Hertzberg speaks of "Jonathan, who imagines himself to be in full possession of his father's confidence" (172). This psychological interpretation is too shallow to account for Jonathan's formal declaration.

/15/ For reasons which are not clear, Stoebe (1973: 389) regards it as impossible (in 20:31 and 23:17) to see Jonathan as regarding himself as heir apparent, but as giving up his claim and taking second place. Perhaps he has in mind simply the historical implausibility (cf. 3.33).

/16/ The spear is cast "im Grunde gegen David" (Stoebe, 1973: 388).

/17/ There are no standard English equivalents for Greimas's terms. We use Jacobson's (160) with one small change.

/18/ It is not clear whether there is significance in the orthographic change in Jonathan's name (*yō-* in chs. 13-14, except 14:6, 8; *yᵉhō-* in 14:6, 8 and after ch. 17).

/19/ Such a study would need to take account of the prevalence of the theme of ignorance even at the narrative level: e.g. Saul's ignorance of what is going on in ch. 14; his having to ask who David is after the fight with Goliath (17: 55-58; for a summary of attempts to deal with this famous *crux*, and a new suggestion, Willis: 295-302); his "no one tells me anything" (22:8).

/20/ Historically correct, no doubt, but nonetheless quite

facile, is Hertzberg's remark: "For the further course of this history the anointing remains, of course, without importance" (139).

/21/ Conrad (66-67) seems to suggest this.

/22/ For clarity of focus, we have left unconsidered any other theological significance of Jonathan than in relation to the major theological problem of the section. The reincorporation of the tribe of Benjamin into a Davidic monarchy, which becomes a problem in 2 Sam, is already prepared for here (cf. 20:15 and 23:17 in particular). The problem is eased if it is accepted that Saul's troubles came from YHWH, that his family assisted David, and above all that Jonathan's non-succession was volitional.

*

WORKS CONSULTED

Ackroyd, P. R. 1971 — The First Book of Samuel. The Cambridge Bible Commentary. Cambridge: University Press.

Barthes, R. 1972 — Critical Essays. Trans. by R. Howard. Evanston: Northwestern University Press.

1974 — Et al., Structural Analysis and Biblical Exegesis. Trans. by A. M. Johnson, Jr. Pittsburgh: Pickwick Press.

Conrad, J. 1970 — Die junge Generation im alten Testament. Stuttgart: Calwer Verlag.

Culley, R. C. 1974 — "Structural Analysis: Is it Done with Mirrors" Int 28:165-181.

De George, R. T. and F. M., eds. 1972 — The Structuralists from Marx to Levi-Strauss. Anchor Books. Garden City, New York: Doubleday & Company.

De Vries, S. J. 1973 — "David's Victory over the Philistine as Saga and as Legend" JBL 92:23-36.

Gibson, A. B. 1973 — The Religion of Dostoevsky. Philadelphia: The Westminster Press.

Greimas, A.-J. 1966 — Sémantique structurale: Recherche de methode. Paris: Larousse.

Grønbaek, J. H. 1971 — Die Geschichte vom Aufstieg Davids (1 Sam. 15-2 Sam. 5): Tradition und Komposition. Copenhagen: Munksgaard.

Hertzberg, H. W. 1964 — I and II Samuel: A Commentary. Trans. by J. S. Bowden. Phildelphia: The Westminster Press.

Jacobson, R. 1974 — "The Structuralists and the Bible" Int 28: 146-164.

Jobling, D. 1976 — "Saul's Fall and Jonathan's Rise: Tradition and Redaction in 1 Samuel 14:1-46" JBL 95/3: pagination not available.

Lane, M., ed. 1970 — Introduction to Structuralism. New York: Basic Books.

Leach, E. 1962 — "Genesis as Myth" Discovery 23. Cited from Genesis as Myth and Other Essays. London: Jonathan Cape, 1969: 7-23.

1966 — "The Legitimacy of Solomon" European Journal of Sociology 7:58-101. Cited from Genesis as Myth and Other Essays: 25-83.

Lévi-Strauss, C. 1963 — Structural Anthropology. Trans. by C. Jacobson and B. G. Schoepf. New York: Basic Books.

McCarthy, D. J. 1973 — "The Inauguration of Monarchy in Israel: A Form-Critical Study of I Samuel 8-12" Int 27: 401-412.

Morgenstern, J. 1959 — "David und Jonathan" JBL 78:322-325.

Propp, V. 1968 — Morphology of the Folktale. Trans. by L. Scott. Second edition revised and edited by L. A. Wagner. Austin: University of Texas Press.

Scholes, R. and Kellogg, R. 1968 — The Nature of Narrative. New York, etc: Oxford University Press (1966, paperback 1968).

Stoebe, H.-J. 1961 — "David und Mikal" in Von Ugarit nach Qumran, BZAW 77, edited by J. Hempel and L. Rost. Berlin: Verlag Alfred Töpelmann: 224-243.

1973 — Das erste Buch Samuelis. Kommentar zum alten Testament, 8/1. Gütersloh: Gerd Mohn.

Thompson, J. A. 1974 — "The Significance of the Verb Love in the David-Jonathan Narratives in I Samuel" VT 24:334-338.

Weiser, A. 1961 — The Old Testament: Its Formation and Development. Trans. by D. M. Barton. New York: Association Press.

1966 — "Die Legitimation des Königs David: Zur Eigenart und Entstehung der sogenannten Geschichte von Davids Aufstieg" VT 16: 325-354.

Weiss, M. 1965 — "Weiteres uber die Bauformen des Erzählens in der Bibel" Bibl 46:181-206.

Welsford, E. 1935 — The Fool: His Social and Literary History. New York: Farrar & Rinehart.

Willis, J. T. 1973 — "The Function of Comprehensive Anticipatory Redactional Joints in 1 Sam 16-18" ZAW 85: 294-314.

S 54, A 75

JEWS AND CHRISTIANS IN ANTIOCH IN THE FIRST FOUR CENTURIES

Wayne A. Meeks, Yale University

If the identity of a group, like that of an individual, is shaped in large measure by the "significant others" within its horizons, then we stand to learn a great deal about the early Christians in Antioch if we can discover something about the relationship between them and the Jewish groups of that city and its villages. In the beginning, of course, they *were* one of the Jewish groups. However, it was precisely in Antioch, according to our earliest sources, that they first were perceived as a distinct movement and there that they first crossed the boundaries of Judaism and sought gentile proselytes. At that moment began the powerful ambivalence which has marked the relationship between the parent community and its somewhat unnatural offspring throughout the history of their encounters. The Pauline school, which originated in Antioch although its center soon shifted elsewhere, fought most vigorously for the freedom of gentiles to become Christians without becoming Jews, yet it also made the unity of Jew and gentile in the new community a primary theological paradigm. Emerging from Judaism, the new movement would inevitably inherit some of the gains and losses which had accrued to the Jewish diaspora in its long struggle to live well and truly in the midst of a pagan society. But equally inevitably, the Christians would complicate life for the Jews and even threaten the delicate balance of their social and political position. Indeed, they would become active competitors with the Jews for the social as well as religious favors of the larger society, and finally the synagogue's most dangerous enemy. The ambivalence is amply exhibited in Christian literature from Antioch. From Ignatius to John Chrysostom, Isaac, and Symeon Stylites, attacks on Judaism and on "Judaizing" Christians grow in both ferocity and specificity. Yet those very attacks were occasioned by the attraction which Judaism continued to exert on Christians, in one way on ordinary church folk, in another way on their theologians, even those who attacked "Judaizing" most vehemently. The ambivalent relationship did not, of course, develop in a vacuum, but was intertwined with the complex attachments and reactions of each group to the Greco-Roman culture and government. Consequently an investigation of Jewish-Christian relations will shed some light on the broader question of each group's place in the larger society.

The Jewish Community in Antioch[1]

Josephus says that the Jews were particularly numerous in Syria, because of the proximity of the homeland, and especially in Antioch, "partly owing to the greatness of the city, but mainly because the successors of King Antiochus had enabled them to live there in security" (*JW* 7.43).[2] Kraeling estimates a Jewish population in the city of 45,000, twelve to thirteen per cent of the total, in the time of Augustus, and 65,000 in the fourth century, but these figures are perhaps a little high.[3]

Not very much is known about the organization of the Jewish groups or about their internal divisions. There was one principal official who could be called "the ἄρχων of the Antiochene Jews" in AD 69/70 (*JW* 7.47). Three centuries later a letter from Libanius calls this office the "chief of their rulers" (τὸν τῶν ἀρχόντων τῶν παρ' αὐτοῖς ἄρχοντα). Both are evidently referring to the head of the council of elders, the γερουσίαρχος. The family tomb of one Gerousiarch of Antioch, Aidesius, was found in the cemetery of Beth She'arim.[4] Libanius' letter appealed to an advisor of the prefect to permit the chief to remove from office "a certain wicked old man."[5] What office (ἀρχή) the old man held is not clear; presumably something more than simply one of the elders, for the whole Jewish community had experienced trouble (θόρυβος) since he took office. Perhaps he was the ἀρχισυνάγωγος of one of the synagogues. The latter office is attested from two inscriptions in Apamea, for in the year 391 Ilasios, "Archisynagogos of the Antiochenes," made a substantial contribution for the mosaic floor of the synagogue there, where he had close family connections.[6]

We cannot be certain how many synagogues existed in Antioch, for the literary evidence is spotty and the archaeological data nil.[7] From Seleucid times there was one in the city itself.[8] In the Roman period the main synagogue was located in the southern quarter of the city, the Kerateion.[9] It was probably the one supposed to have been built over the tomb of the Maccabee martyrs and thus called, at least in one medieval source, *kenneset ḥašmûnit*,[10] i.e., Synagogue of the Hasmoneans. The same source, however, says that this was the first synagogue built after (the destruction of) the Second Temple.[11] It was surely not the only synagogue within the city. One of the synagogues burned in the disorders of the late fifth century was named for Asabinus, perhaps the same as the Jewish *curialis* of that name whose property, according to Malalas, had been purchased to build a new Plethrion in AD 193.[12] This was obviously different from the Hasmonean synagogue and, assuming its foundation to have been near the time of the Asabinus known to us, it must have existed simultaneously with the Hasmonean rather than having been built to replace the latter when it was seized by the Christians in the fourth century.[13] In addition, there was a synagogue in Daphne; Kraeling even suggests that Onias' taking refuge in a pagan shrine at Daphne (2 Macc 4:33 f.) may indicate the presence of a Jewish settlement there as early as 171 BC.[14] Whether there was also an organized Jewish community to the north of the city, on the plain of Antioch, as Kraeling argues, is more uncertain.[15]

There certainly were rural Jews in the vicinity of Antioch; the question is what their status was. As Kraeling pointed out, the Tosefta speaks of rice grown in the *Ḥulat* of Antioch, so there must have been Jewish farmers. Moreover, his argument that the *ḥulta' šel 'Anṭiokia'* is the same as the οὐαλαθά mentioned by Josephus, *Ant* 17.24, and τὸ τῶν 'Αντιοχέων πέδιον in Strabo, *Geog.* 16.2.8, is both ingenious and convincing.[17] But it will not do to regard that area as a "Jewish suburb."[18] From Libanius' Oration 47.13-16, "On Patronages," we learn of Jewish peasants who had worked Libanius' family land for four generations. Although some earlier scholars argued that the estate must have been in Palestine, L. Harmand has shown that it must have lain near Antioch, in the Orontes valley--i.e., probably in the *Ḥulat* of Antioch by Kraeling's reckoning.[19]

These tenants of Libanius were not like the small free proprietors who lived in the large villages (κῶμαι μεγάλαι) and owned tiny portions of the communal fields, though since Libanius also describes the troubles of the latter, they were evidently to be found in the same area, and there may well have been Jews among them, too.[20] Nor were they hired free workers (ἐργάται = *operarii* or μισθωταί = *mercenarii*). Rather, they were tenants of the most restricted sort (γεωργοί = *coloni*). Even though the colonate in the strict legal sense (which made the *colonus* virtually a serf) probably did not yet exist in Syria in Libanius' time, Harmand argues that workers like these had lost their original liberty by *consuetudo*.[21] The terms of their work and their share of the crop were determined entirely by the landowner. In a desperate attempt to "shake off the old yoke and henceforth to dictate the terms" of their employment, they went on strike.[22]

Unfortunately we do not learn what kind of connections there may have been between these Jewish peasants and their more affluent coreligionists in the city. It may be significant, however, that their confrontation with Libanius does not seem to have affected the congenial relationship which he had both with the patriarch Gamaliel V in Tiberias and with leaders of the Jewish community in Antioch,[23] and that the peasants did not, so far as Libanius informs us, try to get either of these to intercede with him on their behalf. Whether they were separated from the urban Jews by language (the latter used Greek), by religious practice,[24] or only by economic class, one can only guess.[25]

In one respect, however, the peasants of Libanius and the urban Jews of Antioch were alike. When in difficulties, both sought help from a strong patron, who was likely to be connected with the imperial government. In the case of the peasants, this was a military commander, perhaps the *magister militum per orientem*.[26] Such military patrons are the chief object of Libanius' complaints to the emperor, for they have usurped a role which used to belong to the local aristocracy.[27] The power of this new form of patronage is well illustrated in the fact that Libanius lost his case. The fact that he had to file suit against his workers already shows that disadvantaged groups like the Jews could count on some protection from Roman law. Nevertheless, Libanius' case, at least on grounds of breach of contract, would appear to have been very strong[28]--certainly he thought it was--had it not been for the superior power of the patron. Those peasants who lacked such a patron--a person of influence standing outside the old structures of the aristocracy that oppressed them--were little better off than slaves.[29]

For the patron, on the other hand, intervention in such cases provided opportunity to increase his power as the number of clients dependent upon him grew. That is likely to have been a more important factor in his self-interest than the amount of money he could squeeze out of them, which Libanius dwells on. The whole episode, as Libanius himself emphasizes, was part of a very general shift in the forms of social and economic power, and during the transition there were enormous opportunities for entrepreneurs of all sorts, via the military, the rapidly growing imperial civil service, the law, and--already--the church.[30]

Not all the Jews had thrown in their lot with the new power brokers. Ironically Libanius himself acted as a patron for the whole Jewish community of Antioch on one occasion, in the letter to Callistio already quoted,[31] and he often intervened informally as a patron for individuals in the correspondence he conducted with Gamaliel V between the years 388 and 393. Eight of his letters "To the Patriarch" are extant.[32] They provide an interesting and, to those accustomed to handbook generalizations about rabbinic Judaism's anti-hellenism after Bar Kochba, astonishing picture of the relationship between cultured Jews and pagans at the end of the fourth century. One letter is a response to a complaint from the Patriarch about anti-Semitic (or perhaps just anti-Gamaliel) tracts or letters which have been circulating, which Gamaliel thinks originate in or near Antioch (*Ep*. 914). The others all are written on behalf of individuals, as introductions (973) or appeals for help against opponents (917), for financial help (974), or unspecified favors (1084, 1097). One (1105) asks the Patriarch to assist in the defense of Libanius' former pupil who, as proconsul of Palestine AD 392/93, has committed some misdeed resulting in criminal charges. And one is a charming letter on behalf of Gamaliel's son, who has dropped out of school after studying briefly with Libanius. Libanius asks the old man to be neither harsh nor perplexed, for at this stage of life "it is as profitable for him to see many cities as it was for Odysseus." It is apparent that Gamaliel himself has continued the Hillelite interest in Greek culture, for Libanius flatters him for his love of books and the excellence of his letters (1084; cf. 1004).[33] It is also clear that for some Jews in Antioch it was perfectly natural to work through the network of relationships involving the curial class and the old rhetorical schools.

The urban Jews of Antioch were of all classes. The *curialis* Asabinus has already been mentioned.[34] The donors of the fourth-century mosaics in the Apamea synagogue, including the Antiochene *archisynagōgos*, were both wealthy and Greek-speaking and bore hellenic names. But there were also Jewish shopkeepers and artisans, still in the time of Chrysostom and doubtless from the beginning.[35] A few members of these groups were able to gain wealth, but for the most part they were poor, burdened directly or indirectly by the heavy traders' tax (*collatio lustralis*) and subject to abuse by soldiers and officials.[36] There were certainly Jewish slaves as well. In between, upward mobility will have been obtained by Jews as by others in several ways: as veterans of the Roman army, as lawyers,[37] as notaries.[38]

I have said nothing so far about the formal legal and political status of the Antiochene Jews. There is little which can be said with certainty, for it would be hazardous to assume with Kraeling that the better-known arrangements in Alexandria were "normative" elsewhere.[39] We do have a series of glimpses of the interaction between the Jewish community and the imperial government. Josephus reports that "the Jews residing in Antioch are called Antiochenes, for the founder Seleucus granted them citizenship (τὴν πολιτείαν αὐτοῖς ἔδωκεν)" (*CAp* 2.39; cf. *Ant* 12.119). This statement is contradicted by *JW* 7.44, which says that it was the successors of Antiochus Epiphanes who gave them rights "equal to the Greeks."[40] In practice, their rights do seem to have been on a par with those of others, class by class, in the city, but it is unlikely that they enjoyed, as a group, actual citizenship in the polis, any more than Alexandrian Jews, who sought it in vain until Claudius rejected their petition once and for all.[41] Their rights were preserved repeatedly by Roman emperors and their representatives, often against local opposition.

A series of crises faced by the Jews of Antioch illustrates the protection afforded them by Roman law until it was eventually traduced by Christians. Malalas reports an attack on Jews in the third year of Caligula's reign (AD 40), resulting in many deaths and the burning of synagogues. Although the story related by Malalas is fantastic, including a retaliatory expedition of 30,000 men led by Phineas, high priest in Jerusalem, both Kraeling and Downey point out that a disturbance involving Jews is quite believable at that time--two years after a pogrom in Alexandria and the very year of Caligula's attempt to install a statue of himself in the Jerusalem temple. That the emperor then settled the strife (this must, however, have been Claudius, who did the same in Alexandria) is also credible.[42]

The next crisis came at the time of the revolt of AD 66-70. At first, although there were massacres of Jews throughout Syria (Josephus *JW* 2.457-79), Jews in Antioch, Sidon, and Apamea were not affected (*JW* 2.479). However, shortly after Vespasian arrived in Syria, an apostate named Antiochus, son of the *archōn* of the Antiochene Jews, encited the pagans with a story of a Jewish plot to burn the city (*JW* 7.47). The pogrom which followed brought terror to the Jews, and four years later they were threatened with a recurrence of the same violence when fire actually broke out and destroyed several public buildings, appearing to confirm Antiochus' charges.[43] This time the Jews were saved from mob action by Gnaeus Collega, the deputy governor, who carefully investigated the affair and cleared the Jews of any complicity (*JW* 7.58-61). However, Josephus suggests that the Jews were still in danger until the coming of Titus Caesar, for when he arrived at Antioch the population greeted him with cries urging the expulsion of the Jews (*JW* 7.100-103).[44] The petition was repeated at Zeugma on the Euphrates, where Titus refused it on grounds that, Judea being destroyed, the Jews had nowhere to go if they were banished (7.109). Thereupon the Antiochenes demanded that the privileges of the Jews inscribed on bronze tablets be removed. That also was refused by Titus, "leaving the status of the Jews of Antioch exactly as it was before" (7.110-11).[45]

If the revolts in Bithynia in the early second century or the Bar Kochba revolt under Hadrian were reflected in special difficulties for the Jews in Antioch, we have no record of it. It was not until Constantine granted special privileges to the church that Jews found themselves in serious and growing trouble. Since this involved direct interactions between the Jews and the Christians, it is better discussed below in the context of the history of those interactions. One fact needs to be noted here: even though anti-Jewish language began to creep into the codes from Constantine on,[46] the imperial power generally sought to protect the basic rights of the Jews until quite late.[47]

Beginnings of Christianity in Antioch

For the story of Christianity's beginnings in Antioch, and consequently of the first interactions between Jews and Christians there, we have to depend upon the account in the book of Acts, together with the clues in a few verses of Galatians. If there is one thing that has been made clear by scholarship from F. C. Baur until the most recent "redaction critics," it is that historians have to read the Acts' account with a sharp eye open for its functions within the literary and theological plan of the whole two-volume work. When that is done, however, it becomes a very useful document for our purposes.

In Acts Antioch is singled out as the scene of the first deliberate mission to gentiles (11:19-26) and as the locus of the decisive controversy over terms of their admission to the church (chap. 15). There is no reason to doubt the accuracy of the former, and comparison with Gal 2:11 f. suggests that the second as well has some factual basis. The account begins with a sentence (Acts 11:19) which is probably entirely a Lucan construction. It links the Antioch report with the preceding story of Stephen, the subsequent persecution, and the "scattering" of the Jerusalem disciples--actually of the Jewish-Christian "Hellenists" in the consensus of most modern scholarship. In between, the author has inserted the story of Paul's conversion and the story of Peter's instruction and baptism of Cornelius--both important for the significance which our author wants to give to the gentile mission that begins in Antioch. Since the notion that the persecution produced a wider spread of the Word is an important Lucan motif, the final phrase of 11:19, "speaking the Word to no one except to Jews alone," is Lucan. It looks as if he wants especially to avoid the impression that the "Hellenists" were directly responsible for the beginning of the gentile mission. Rather (vs.20) it was certain anonymous individuals of Cyprus and Cyrenaea. If so, his purpose is partly defeated by vs.20, for the Cypriot and Cyrenaean preachers were also among the scattered "Hellenists" (τινες ἐξ αὐτῶν ἄνδρες). Perhaps the author has merely chosen an awkward way of saying that in general the Hellenists spoke only to Jews, but some few of them, who happened to be Cypriots and Cyrenaeans (thus distinct from those who had previously been living in Jerusalem, chap.6?), by exception began preaching to gentiles. Nevertheless, it is worth asking why so competent an author was led into such awkwardness. One plausible answer is this: he had a tradition or source that connected the origin of the gentile mission with Antioch, beginning in the mission of certain Greek-speaking Jews associated with the "hellenistic" wing of the Jerusalem Christians. (It may be significant that one of the seven hellenist Diakonoi elected in Jerusalem was an Antiochene proselyte, Nicolaus [Acts 6:5]). The disclaimer of vs.19 is Luke's own, for he wants to tie this beginning in Antioch firmly to the authoritative figures in Jerusalem and also properly to introduce Paul, who is for him the paradigmatic missionary to the gentiles.[48] Hence he sets before this report the vision of Peter and the conversion of Cornelius, so that a *nihil obstat* for the conversion of gentiles has already been provided among the Jerusalem apostles, under the authoritative person of Peter. And he inserts the story of Paul's conversion, tying it artificially to the martyrdom of Stephen, to prepare Paul for the role given him in 11:25. Then appears Barnabas, himself a Cypriot (4:36),[49] who has been introduced before as one with impeccable Jewish credentials (a Levite 4:36) and a particularly devoted disciple directly and obediently related to the apostles in Jerusalem (4:36-37).[50] Finally Paul is introduced to the Antioch situation at second-hand, by Barnabas, who has been made the official Jerusalem delegate at Antioch (11:25).

From this brief report, which is a keystone in the structure of Luke's second volume, what trustworthy information can be gleaned then? That Antioch was the starting point for self-conscious mission to gentiles who had not previously become Jewish proselytes; that this mission was initiated by Greek-speaking Jewish Christians, "Cypriotes and Cyrenaeans," among whom Barnabas was probably the leading figure.

This tiny glimpse of the early leadership at Antioch is augmented very slightly at the beginning of Luke's next major section, 13:1, by another bit of information: a list of "prophets and teachers" in Antioch.[51] The list is traditional; Symeon called the Black, Lucius the Cyrenaean, and Menaen (= Menaḥem) the σύντροφος of Herod the Tetrarch (Antipas). One might be tempted to doubt whether the names which Luke puts in the prominent positions at the head and tail of this list, Barnabas and Paul, belonged to the traditional list, since this author often manipulates the comings and goings of his chief characters. In this case, however, we have confirmation from Galatians that both Paul and Barnabas were closely connected with Antioch in the earliest days of their mission. The presence in the Antiochene church of a *syntrophos* of Herod Antipas is interesting, for while we have no record of any significant connection between the Tetrarch and Antioch, his father had been a major benefactor of the city.[52] The honorific ("childhood companion," "foster brother"; Haenchen: "Milchbruder") obviously implies high social status. If Menaen was a native of Antioch, of which we cannot be sure, the Herodian connection may have been advantageous. Of the five names, all but Lucius are Semitic, but only because Luke up to this point calls Paul "Saul."

In 11:26 Luke adds another "first" for Antioch: "And in Antioch they first called the disciples 'Christians.'" This detail is not likely to have been invented by the author of Acts. Considerable ingenuity has been expended on attempts to explain its significance,[53] but the most satisfactory remains the simplest: that the disciples were called "Christians," i.e. "Christus-people," by pagans, because it was in Antioch that they first stood out from Judaism as a distinct sect.[54] It is interesting that among Christian writers Ignatius of Antioch is the first to use the term "Christianity" (Χριστιανισμός).[55] And later Theophilus writes to Autolycus, "You call me a Christian as if I were bearing an evil name . . . ."[56] Whatever the reason for the original designation, the author of Acts thought it significant that it took place precisely in Antioch. Even if it is only the accidents of transmission that make Ignatius' usage appear unique, it also calls attention to the fact that the "Christ-movement" attained a degree and kind of self-identity at Antioch which made it visible to outsiders as a distinct movement very early in its history. Antioch was the birthplace of "gentile Christianity."

It was also the place where controversy between Jews and gentiles first erupted within the church.[57] I cannot touch on all the issues which have been raised in the long debate over the "Jerusalem Council" and the conflicting descriptions of it in Acts 15 and Galatians 2. Olof Linton's suggestion, made a number of years ago, is likely correct: the version of the events which Luke had was just the kind of interpretation Paul was trying to refute in Galatians.[58] But both versions agree on a few points that are clear and significant. (1) The question of the terms of admission of gentiles to the Christian community, with circumcision as the focal issue, arises at Antioch and is sent up to Jerusalem for ajudication. (2) The principal delegates from Antioch are Paul and Barnabas. Paul adds the name of Titus, not as a delegate but as a test case, unmentioned by Acts, though Acts does mention "certain others" (15:2). Paul implies that the decision for the trip was primarily his own, "by revelation," while Acts records a formal action (ἔταξαν) by the Antioch congregation to send them. But if the decision was made by prophetic leadership, like that described in Acts 13:2 f., both could be talking about the same procedure.[59] (3) The issue is raised by a particular group among the Judean Christians, not identified with the leadership. In the Acts version, these were already active at Antioch, precipitating the whole issue; Paul has them first intervene in the discussions at Jerusalem.[60] Acts calls them former Pharisees; Paul does not identify them but calls them "false brothers." (4) The upshot of the debate is agreement between the Antioch delegates and the Jerusalem leadership that the former are to pursue the gentile mission as before, and that circumcision is not to be required of gentile converts. The Acts version, however, goes on to record a "decree" requiring a modified form of kashrut as well as forbidding idolatry and sexual immorality.[61] The only requirement Paul acknowledges is "remember the poor," and it is commonly understood that his concern for the "collection" for Jerusalem was his way of carrying out that part of the agreement.

Acts and Galatians further agree that Paul and Barnabas had a major disagreement soon after these decisions were made (Acts 15:39 calls it a παροξυσμός; Gal 2:13 accuses Barnabas of "hypocrisy"). The reasons given for this break, however, are quite different. Acts knows nothing of a visit of Peter to Antioch or of the confrontation there between him and Paul, nor of a delegation from James that wrecked the previous agreement and provoked such a confrontation.[62]

There is one further area of agreement, of a negative sort. Neither in Acts nor in Paul's letters does Paul have any further important connection with Antioch. After the "first missionary journey," which has Antioch as its base,[63] Acts has Paul pay only one further, obscure visit (18:22); in his letters Paul never mentions Antioch outside Galatians.[64] Now John Schütz has made the shrewd deduction that Barnabas' turnabout and support for Peter (Gal 2:11-21) and Paul's subsequent separation from him do not represent merely a personal disagreement, as Acts would have us believe, but a fundamental crisis of authority affecting the relationship between Paul and Antioch.[65] What Paul was resisting, in his confrontation with Peter, was the attempt of Jerusalem to extend its authority to Antioch. When not only Peter but even Barnabas, whose connection with Antioch was older and more intimate than Paul's, accepted compromise with the James group, Paul made himself independent of Antioch as well as of Jerusalem.[66]

Antioch at this earliest point in the church's history looks then like a place of compromise, a bridge between Jewish and gentile Christianity. Neither in Acts nor in Paul do we learn of any locally bred division between Jewish and gentile Christians; division occurs only at the instigation of certain people from Jerusalem.[67] The form of the compromise after the crisis and Paul's withdrawal is not altogether clear, although it looks from Gal 2:12 f. as if former Jews and former gentiles formed henceforth separate fellowships, presumably meeting in different houses. There is also no mention of hostility from synagogue authorities in Antioch,[68] although an argument from this silence would be precarious. Had the emergence of the *Christianoi* as a distinct religious movement not yet occurred?

William Farmer has argued that the decisive break came in fact, and precisely at Antioch, a generation later: in the aftermath of the Jewish revolt of AD 66-70.[69] The war must have had a strong effect on Antioch, he argues, because troops would have been recruited there to take part in putting down the rebellion, resulting in an increase of the "perennial anti-Jewish feelings."[70] Farmer thinks the Christians would consequently have had very good reasons for distinguishing themselves from the Jews. It is an attractive hypothesis, even though there is hardly any evidence to support it.[71] Josephus' reports of the pogrom in 66/67 and the uproar following the Antioch fire of 70 certainly show the intensity of anti-Jewish feeling.[72] The desire of some Christians to separate from them is a plausible conjecture. However, this would have amounted to a reinforcement of the division along lines of religious practice which had been effected by the Peter-Barnabas concessions, rather than an abrupt breakdown of the successful Jerusalem compromise, as Farmer sees it.[73] Moreover, if such a separation did take place around 70, it certainly did not mean the once-for-all isolation of the Judaeo-Christians from gentile Christians nor of Jews from Christians. We shall see that the active influence of Judaism upon Christianity in Antioch was perennial until Christian leaders succeeded at last in driving the Jews from the city in the seventh century.

Christians and Jews in the Second and Third Centuries

Sources of information about Christian-Jewish relations in the second and third centuries are fragmentary, mostly indirect, and almost entirely from the Christian side. During this period it is also difficult or impossible to distinguish between continuing direct Jewish influence on Christianity and the independent internal development of Christian exegesis of the common scriptures. Consequently the "Jewishness" posited of certain schools of Antiochene theology by ancient as well as modern writers may sometimes be so vague as to be of little help.

Ignatius, although his letters address directly the problems of the Asian churches to which he is writing and speak only allusively of the situation in Antioch, nevertheless allows some inferences to be drawn for our topic. Certain passages in the letters to the Smyrnaeans, the Magnesians, and the Philadelphians are particularly important. The letter to Smyrna opens with an epistolary thanksgiving (1:1 f., not usual in Ignatius' letters) which probably echoes the liturgy of baptism at Antioch.[74] It is therefore particularly interesting that it contains a version of the "baptismal reunification formula" which in the New Testament is found in writings of the Pauline school:[75] ". . . that 'he might set up an ensign' [Isa 5:26] for all ages through his Resurrection, for his saints and believers, whether among the Jews, or among the heathen, in one body of his church."[76] Furthermore, just as in the Pauline school, it is the unification of Jew and gentile in the one body of Christ that is the paradigm instance of God's will to make all one.[77] Ignatius himself, however, is far from positive toward continuing Jewish elements in Christianity. He can equate Jewish teachings (though of what sort is not said) with heterodoxy and "fables (μυθεύματα) which were unprofitable to those of old" (Magn 8:1).[78] To live "according to Judaism"[79] would mean to confess "that we have not received grace" (Magn 8:2). He warns that "It is monstrous (ἄτοπον) to talk of Jesus Christ and to practise Judaism. For Christianity did not base its faith on Judaism (εἰς 'Ιουδαϊσμὸν ἐπίστευσεν), but Judaism on Christianity, and every tongue believing on God was brought together in it" (10:3, Lake). Similarly Ignatius warns the Philadelphians against Judaeo-Christianity:

> But if anyone interpret Judaism to you do not listen to him; for it is better to hear Christianity from the circumcised than Judaism from the uncircumcised. But both of them, unless they speak of Jesus Christ, are to me tombstones and sepulchres of the dead . . .
> (Philad 6:1)

These polemical passages may be occasioned by controversies in Magnesia and Philadelphia, but almost certainly they reflect also Ignatius' experience of Judaeo-Christians in Antioch.[80] Note that it is the *Judaeo*-Christians, Christians adopting Jewish practices, not *Jewish*-Christians, i.e. those of Jewish origins, who attract Ignatius' ire. If his language in Philad 6:1 is careful, not just a rhetorical flourish, then both sorts of Christians are known to him. The other group whom Ignatius takes pains to refute in his letters are the docetists, and it has become customary to think of these as the opposites of the Judaeo-Christians. That may be misleading, however, for there are prominent elements drawn from Jewish or Judaeo-Christian tradition in most of the gnostic movements associated with Syria.[81] This seems to have been true, for example, of Menander, the first of the gnostic teachers known by name in Antioch,[82] whose christology was undoubtedly docetic. To be sure, Ignatius does say of his docetists, "These are they whom neither the prophecies nor the law of Moses persuaded, nor the gospel even until now, nor our own individual sufferings" (Smyr 5:1, Lake), but that does not necessarily mean that they opposed the Jewish scriptures--only that they interpreted them differently than Ignatius. His own hermeneutic principle is stated in Philad 8:2:

> For I heard some saying, 'If I do not find it in the archives (ἀρχεἰοις), I do not believe in the gospel.' And when I said to them, 'It is written,' they replied, 'That is just the issue.' But for me 'the archives' are Jesus Christ; the inviolable archives are his cross and death and his resurrection and the faith which comes through him . . .

In practice, however, at least in the extant letters, Ignatius does not offer any extended exegetical arguments. Laeuchli even goes so far as to deny that he knew much of the Old Testament: "Ignatius, therefore, cannot have grown up in a Septuagint-diaspora community, nor can he have lived very long in a Christian congregation that was familiar with Old Testament models."[83]

If traditions of Septuagint-exegesis are lacking in Ignatius, the lack is amply made up by his successors, for exegesis depending ultimately on Jewish models becomes a hallmark of the Antioch school. This is quite clear in Theophilus, who wrote his apology to Autolycus around 180, for "almost everything in his exegesis can be paralleled in Jewish haggadic literature."[84] It is not only with Palestinian aggadah that Theophilus' exegesis has parallels, however, for Grant has shown that many of the apologist's basic theological phrases and ideas are drawn from the synthesis of biblical and Stoic language which had been worked out in hellenistic Judaism and best known to us through Philo.[85] Theophilus' expositions, however, never attain the profundity of Philo's, nor his allegorical complexity; it is doubtful that he knew Philo's works at first hand.[86] Theophilus' attitude toward the Law also sounds superficially like that of Alexandrian Jews: "Of this divine law the minister (διάκονος) was Moses, the servant of God, not only to all the world but especially the Hebrews (also called Jews) . . ."[87] The positive emphasis upon the Law probably carries a specifically anti-Marcionist thrust,[88] thus providing evidence for a Marcionite--and consequently counter-Jewish--influence in Antioch at this early date. He can call Moses "our prophet and the minister of God" (3.18), the Hebrews "our forefathers" (3.20), and David "our ancestor" (3.25). Yet it is also clear that "this great and marvellous law" is understood by Theophilus as the moral law epitomized in the "ten chapters" (κεφάλαια) (3.9), distinct from the ritual commandments which Christian commentators were by now regularly interpreting as a secondary addition pertinent only to Jews.[89] Furthermore, this strong emphasis on the continuity of the revelation to "the Hebrews" with that to the Christians does not carry any necessary implication of continued positive relationship with living Jews. On the contrary, Theophilus commonly speaks of "our scriptures" (τὰ ἡμετέρα γράμματα) with casual disregard for the continued existence of Judaism. When he argues, for example, that the true picture of the world's origin and the early spread of its peoples is found only in the scriptures (and the Sibyllene oracles that depend on them) rather than in pagan writings, he concludes that "it is plain that all the rest were in error and that *only the Christians* have held the truth . . ." (2.33).[90]

During the whole of the second and third centuries we have evidence for the continued influence of Jewish scriptures and thought on Antiochene Christianity, but virtually none from which we can get a picture of relationships between Jewish and Christian communities. The presence of Jewish elements in the local liturgy, which Grant has demonstrated,[91] does not prove continued contact with the synagogue, for they may have been included earlier. They are not like the entire book of prayers incorporated into the eucharistic prayer in the seventh book of the Apostolic Constitutions, which Simon thinks must have resulted from a mass conversion of a whole Jewish community, probably in Alexandria.[92] Even the intensive textual and exegetical work accomplished by Lucian and his school, though it indicates a certain continuity of tradition from the rather naive expositions by Theophilus to the mature work at the turn of the third to fourth centuries, does not prove that Lucian and his associates were in close contact with the synagogue. It is true that Eusebius describes a certain Dorotheus, a contemporary of Lucian, who "made so careful a study of the Hebrew tongue that he read with understanding the original Hebrew scriptures."[93] One may speculate that he, like Jerome, learned his Hebrew from the rabbis, but that is by no means a necessary conclusion.

Yet at one point, around AD 200, we hear of a conversion from Christianity to Judaism, proving that the kind of contact and attraction which would become chronic in the fourth century was not unknown earlier. The case was important enough for the apostate, a certain Domnus, to receive a letter from his bishop, Serapion, which Eusebius mentions but unfortunately does not quote.[94]

More problematic for our topic is the significance of Paul of Samosata, who was bishop of Antioch, as well as its chief financial officer, during the period of Palmyrene rule, AD 260/61 to 272. John Chrysostom calls him "a Jew wearing a Christian mask,"[95] and the nickname may well have been coined earlier by Paul's opponents, for reports circulated which connected his teaching with Judaism, and Athanasius even asserted that he was pro-Jewish in order to please his protector, the Palmyrene queen Zenobia, herself a Jewess![96] Both Loofs and Bardy, however, after independently examining the sparse evidence, conclude that there is no historical substance in the reports that Zenobia had a special relationship to Judaism.[97] Loofs thinks all the reports originated in Antiochene gossip, perhaps fueled by the fact that Zenobia had a Semitic (probably good Palmyrene) name, Bat Zvi. Athanasius' statement that Zenobia was Paul's "patroness"--if indeed προέστη has here that narrow sense and does not mean simply that she was his sovereign--probably referred to her helping him avoid the execution of the sentence of excommunication decreed by the Council of Antioch.[98]

That Paul belonged in some sense to the "Palmyrene party" in Antioch, as Harnack conjectured,[99] is now generally accepted.[100] But that does not clarify his relationship, if any, to Judaism. Bardy supposes that Paul had to gather around him all those who were pro-Palmyrene, be they Christians, Jews, or pagans.[101] Downey thinks it likely that support would have come especially from "people of Semitic stock in and around Antioch who hated the Romans and looked to the East for sympathy and possible rescue."[102] There may have been Aramaic-speaking Jews around Antioch who would have welcomed a Semitic government between themselves and the Romans. But the only Jews in Antioch about whom we have any information were Greek-speaking and depended upon the central government and its representatives for their safeguards. As Bardy says, "Au pouvoir de Palmyre qui était près, ils préféraient encore, du moins beaucoup d'entre eux, l'autorité de Rome qui était loin."[103] And it is certainly significant, as Bardy points out, that the letter of the Council of Antioch that condemned Paul contains not a word about his "Judaism," which would later become the standard accusation.[104] What, then, was the origin of these assertions? John Chrysostom's statements about the Samosatan are typical and instructive. The reason he calls Paul a Jew is simply because of the latter's "low" christology; he does not hint of any actual Jewish connection.[105] Epiphanius observes that the Samosatans did not practice circumcision or observe the Sabbath;[106] the reason they deserved the name "Jews" is purely the fact that their theology sounded "Jewish" in orthodox ears. Possibly Paul's connections with the Semitic rulers of Palmyra helped the slander along. Probably, too, there were Jews in Antioch who prudently sought good relations with the new regime. But in all of these possibilities and probabilities there is nothing which could count as evidence for specific influence of Judaism on Paul's thought or practice, nor for positive relations between his Christian supporters and the local synagogues.[107]

From the time of Ignatius to the flourishing of Lucian's school, then, we may surmise that active contact between Christians and Jews continued. But only at one point, Domnus' conversion around AD 200, is there any firm evidence. We have to remember, as both Downey and Corwin stress,[108] that there were without doubt numerous "house churches" in the early decades of Christianity in Antioch, and that this division into small, natural groupings, each of which would evolve its own leadership, would facilitate growth and persistence of diversity in doctrine and practice.[109] Most likely some previously existing groupings, related to networks of *clientela*, kinship, and of course ethnic and language groups, affected the formation of these early Christian congregations. Some of these groups were closer to Jewish traditions, thought, and exegesis than others. But none of them emerges into clear light in the extant sources, nor can any straight lines be drawn from early ones to later; for example, from the Judaeo-Christians opposed by Ignatius to the Paulists or the Arians. Fortunately, from the fourth century much more evidence is at hand.

The Fourth Century

Constantine's pro-Christian policy obviously marked a shift in the political situation which worked increasingly through the fourth and fifth centuries to the advantage of the Christians and the detriment of the Jews. In 315 conversions to Judaism were forbidden anew, and subsequent legislation proscribed the kinds of situation which would facilitate proselytism, such as intermarriage and Jewish ownership of gentile slaves.[110] During the fourth century, however, the new legislation did not yet attack the fundamental rights of the Jewish community, which continued to be protected by most of the emperors and the imperial officers in the province. Its aim seems rather to have been the isolation of the Jews, and even that aim does not seem to have been achieved until the turn of the century brought much harsher measures against them.[111]

During the same period a more subtle and pervasive shift in the foci of power was taking place. The letters and orations of Libanius give an unusually full picture of the changes, as seen by a deeply interested participant, and Liebeschuetz has described them brilliantly in his monograph.[112] The social and economic distance was growing between the higher and lower classes of the old urban order, and both ends of the scale were subject to increased pressures. The artisans and shopkeepers in the city had to cope with heavy taxes and, at intervals, rapid inflation; peasants in the plain, unless they were able to secure the help of a more or less honest patron, were reduced to serfdom. At the other end, the curial class was being squeezed; the council was reduced to a fraction of its earlier size as many landowners escaped from its heavy financial duties either by selling their land or by obtaining an imperial appointment immune to conciliar duties. A small number of *principales* connived in this in order to concentrate land and power in their own hands. However, a new aristocracy was developing at the same time, composed of former imperial officials (*honorati*), both civilian and military.

These shifts brought with them new opportunities for both upward and horizontal mobility. As the century passed, Christians seem to have been in a position to take more and more advantage of them. There were, for example, a number of Christians among Libanius' students, all of them of families that were well off.[113] The rhetorical training they were receiving was still a sure means of advancement, envied by those who could not afford it. Incidentally, only one Jew is identifiable in Libanius' school, the son of Gamaliel V already mentioned. Yet Libanius did have acquaintances and clients in the Antiochene Jewish community; is it only accidental that we do not hear of their sons taking this traditional road to success?

Libanius, however, complains that pupils are deserting him for the newer and surer ladders to the top: the study of law, Latin, and even shorthand.[114] He might also have mentioned the church, for those who lacked the means for rhetorical schooling were able to use the bishops' schools and, in place of the old-boy system of the rhetors, the new connections between the church itself and the imperial court.[115] The new form of patronage, both ecclesiastical and military, could occasionally work to the benefit of oppressed groups, like the Jewish peasants of Libanius.[116] That these happened to be Jews is quite incidental to Libanius' discussion of the case; countless others, by his own report, were using the military patrons in similar ways. There were doubtless Jews, Christians, and pagans among them. Further, a new figure was emerging whose power, first in the rural areas, later even in the city, could rival even that of the generals: the monk.[117] The Jews had nothing quite like this, although in Babylonia the rabbis in this period and even earlier sometimes functioned very much like *magi*, and in Antioch, as we shall see, Jews commanded attention as adepts in both religion and magic.

These shifts in the relations of power have to be seen also within a more general picture of unsettled social and economic conditions. During the fourth century as a whole, Antioch appears to have been very prosperous. But that general affluence not only was very unequally and changeably distributed, it was also punctuated by occasional severe shortages and violent swings in the economy--like the sharp inflation in the time of Julian. As Peter Brown has discerned, it was a time when new institutions were being formed, and in the meanwhile inarticulate forms of power had their opportunity, though they must clash with the articulate forms of the old order. In such a time, also, resort to occult means of explanation and influence was attractive: the urbane, rational Libanius was accused four times of sorcery and believed himself on one occasion a victim of black magic.[119] Moreover, the emerging forms of articulate power, tied as they were to the imperial service, tended to be in conflict with the local, urban loyalties of the conservative aristocracy.[120] That is the reason why upward mobility was linked with horizontal mobility: success in the civil service or the military required loyalty to the central authorities and a sharp eye for the next plum appointment, wherever it might be. The Christians, who from the beginning had developed effective practical forms of cosmopolitanism and, by the fourth century, an elaborate international organization, were in a way ideally suited to take advantage of this situation. For this reason the hostility toward them on the part of the old urban aristocracy was quite understandable.

But the trans-nationalism of the Christians was in large measure directly inherited from Judaism, and in earlier years, as we have seen, the urban Jews were skillful in trading on Roman law and Roman power to protect their local rights and opportunities. Why were they unable to retain these advantages in the latter part of the fourth century? What forces had dealt them weaker hands than the Christians in the game of power? There is no simple answer to these questions; it is no adequate explanation merely to name Constantine or to point to the anti-Jewish legislation of later Christian emperors, for these were themselves in part responses to the facts of Christian power. This much can be said: in the late fourth century Christians and Jews were competitors for power and influence in the new society of the eastern Empire, and the advantage of the Christians brought the direct decline of the Jews.

At one revealing point they are pitted directly against one another by imperial power: in the religious reform of Julian. It seems curious that Julian would have thought the Jews a natural ally for his program to restore pagan worship to the Empire, but so it was. Downey even suggests that one of the reasons why Julian decided to make his residence in Antioch at the beginning of his reign was in order to win support from the large Jewish community there.[121] It was during his stay in Antioch, at any rate, that he decided to rebuild the Jerusalem temple. According to Ammianus Marcellinus (23.1.2) he put an Antiochene, Alypios, in charge, with ample funds at his disposal. The attempt was unsuccessful, because some disaster, perhaps an earthquake, interrupted work as soon as the old foundations had been uncovered--naturally the Christians interpreted this as divine intervention, and later accounts expand the miraculous features.[122] Julian himself, speaking in retrospect of the failure, shows some bitterness and makes it clear that the attempt would not be renewed.[123] Why, then, did he undertake it, especially since he frequently makes remarks showing that he regarded Judaism as far inferior to paganism?[124]

Vogt has shown that in the Neoplatonic tradition in which Julian was schooled, the alliance of paganism with Judaism against Christianity was not unprecedented. It first appears vividly in Celsus, who in his dialogue of a Jew refuting Jesus makes most of the points raised by Julian.[125] In the third century, with Porphyry's attack on Christianity, the common front became still clearer.[126] This tradition explains the source of intellectual legitimation of Julian's alliance, but not its purpose. Chrysostomus Baur's suggestion, that Julian depended on Jewish financing,[127] is advanced without any evidence to support it, and looks like a reading of medieval practices back into the fourth century. We might speculate that Libanius' connections with the local Jewish leaders and his friendship with Gamaliel may have influenced the Emperor, who was a friend and onetime pupil of the rhetorician. Unfortunately, Libanius' letters from the time when Julian was in Antioch have not been preserved--one of the few gaps in his voluminous correspondence--and there is no mention of Julian's relationship with the Jews in those that survive. Chrysostom says that the attempted reconstruction followed Julian's admonition to the Jews to resume their ancestral sacrifices, for they told him they were not permitted by their law to do so outside Jerusalem.[128] That tallies well with what Julian himself says in two places. In his letter appointing the pagan priest Theodorus to oversee and reform all temples in Asia, he holds up the Jews as models of religious fervor who ought to be emulated by the pagans, while contrasting the "disease of the Galileans."[129] And in his tract "Against the Galileans," he says:

> . . . the Jews agree with the Gentiles, except that they believe in only one God. That is indeed peculiar to them and strange to us; since all the rest we have in a manner in common with them--temples, sanctuaries, altars, purifications, and certain precepts. For as to these we differ from one another either not at all or in trivial matters. . . .[130]

Julian wanted to link the Jews and pagans together as defenders of ancient traditions and cultivators of the rites and ceremonies which, for the Roman, constituted and manifested *religio*. They had to form common ranks against the Christians, whose great fault in Julian's eyes was their destruction of the links with the past--even their own Jewish past. While the evidence does not permit us to be very precise, it is worth asking what this alliance would have meant in the context of fourth-century Antiochene society. The insults which Julian received upon his arrival in Antioch made it plain that he could expect little support from those who were presently in power in the city.[131] Indeed, his rather eccentric crusade led to something like an inversion of the ordinary connections. The old pagan aristocracy, whose primary loyalty had always been to the city first and the Empire only when need be, now had to be his first resort;[132] Libanius is the perfect example. The newly wealthy and powerful classes which had been created by the central government, beginning especially with Diocletian's reforms that multiplied the bureaucracy, were now largely in the hands of Christians. Correspondingly, the Jews were also in a peculiar position. Their traditional alliance had been with the central government rather than with the local, but since Constantine that relationship, while not entirely destroyed, was more and more precarious. Meanwhile, the wealthier members of the Jewish community found more in common with the old Greek aristocracy than with the *honorati*. Among the leadership classes of the city, pagan and Jew found themselves similarly excluded from the revised channels of power, while the pagan emperor found those same channels of power recalcitrant to his will. Thus the seemingly improbable religious alliance joins people who had been forced by a social and political shift to become bedfellows. This is not to say that the religious factors are mere disguises of the social facts, for it was precisely Julian's deeply held beliefs and his puritanical reform measures that brought about the alliance. The point is rather that the religious and social factors are inextricably knitted together.

On the ideological side, there was one further reason why support for the Jews, and particularly the rebuilding of the Jerusalem temple, were attractive to Julian. From his Christian training he was doubtless familiar with the apologetic *topos* which made the destruction of the temple and the apparently permanent interruption of the sacrificial cultus a sign that God willed for his promises to pass at that moment from the Jews to the Christians. What better way to refute the Christians than to rebuild the temple and reestablish the cultus? Unfortunately the failure of the attempt appeared so dramatically to confirm the Christian claim that it became itself a regular part of subsequent Christian arguments against the Jews.

Shortly after the end of Julian's reign, Antiochene Christians begin to manifest increasing hostility toward the Jews, which could be construed as a backlash against Julian's use of the Jews against the Christians.[133] It was at this time that the Synagogue of the Hasmonean Martyrs was seized by the Christians and made into a church,[134] the first of many such incidents.[135] And twenty-three years after Julian's death, John Chrysostom, newly ordained to the priesthood, began a series of eight sermons against the Jews in his native Antioch.[136] The highly rhetorical invective of these sermons, combining elements of popular pagan anti-semitism with anti-Jewish exegetical traditions from the Christian apologists, established Chrysostom as "le maître de l'imprécation anti-juive...sans conteste...."[137] Two of the homilies (actually one very long sermon interrupted by hoarseness) make particular reference to Julian's restoration project.[138] Chrysostom compares the outburst of flame that stopped the rebuilding of the foundations with what happened to Aaron's sons, who were burned up when they sought to offer sacrifice illegitimately. The miracle, like the Jews' defeats under Vespasian and Titus, under Hadrian, and again under Constantine, proved that the temple had been destroyed in accordance with God's will, making it clear to all "that the wreath belongs indubitably to the church."[139] Chrysostom thus draws the conclusion which is implicit in the anti-Jewish polemic of the Christian apologists from Pseudo-Barnabas and Justin--if not actually from the Acts of the Apostles--on: the Jews' rejection of Jesus as Messiah meant the end of their role in the history of salvation, and the destruction of their city and temple was God's public pronouncement of their rejection. Consequently there seems hardly any limit to his invective. Jewish souls, like Jewish buildings, are haunts of demons (*PG* 48.847; 852B; 861A; 940B); no Jew worships God (*PG* 48.847B); Jewish festivals are no better than theatre spectacles, occasions of "gluttony and drunkenness, sexual license, and "dancing barefoot in the *agora*" (1.2, 846B, 1.3, 848B; 6.6, 912B-913A; 7.1, 916; 8.1, 927). To be sure, much of this belongs to stereotyped insults of the rhetorical tradition,[140] but there are ominous new elements. In the first of these homilies Chrysostom urges his congregation to use every means possible, including force if necessary (κἂν βίαν ποιῆσαι, κἂν ὑβρίσαι) to save a brother from "the trap of the devil, and to separate him from the fellowship of the Christ-killers" (*PG* 48.849A). He may not have been the first to use this last dreadful term,[141] but he uses it with deadly seriousness.[142] He can even compare the Jews with "dumb beasts" which "when they are not useful for work, become useful for slaughter," reinforcing this with the words of Luke 19:27, "Those enemies of mine, who did not want me to reign over them--bring them here and slaughter them" (1.2, *PG* 846B).

Nevertheless, Chrysostom's aim in these homilies is not an attack on the Jews as such, but the deterrance of Christians from participating in Jewish rites. Far from representing a popular hostility toward Judaism among Christians in Antioch, Chrysostom's imprecations reveal the exact opposite: a widespread Christian infatuation with Judaism. Seven of the eight homilies are timed to precede the High Holy Days of autumn; the remaining one (No. 3) concerns Passover. The reason, as Chrysostom explains, is that large numbers of Christians are drawn to observe the "spectacle" of these festivals and fasts and even to participate in them (1.1, 844). Not only at festival time, however, but throughout the year the synagogues appear to some Christians as awesome, numinous places. Chrysostom relates the case of a Christian matron required by a man, also claiming to be a Christian, to go to the synagogue to take an oath for some business transaction, since "many had told him that oaths taken there were more awesome" (1.3, 847B-848A). Chrysostom has also heard that many believers go to the synagogue in Daphne for incubation when they are ill (1.6, 852A). The sanctity of the synagogue seems in the mind of these Christians to stem particularly from the presence of the scrolls of the Torah in the ark, for Chrysostom takes pains to refute this notion, and ridicules these arks, which are such feeble substitutes for the implements of the former Temple (6.7, 914A-915A; 1.5f., 850B-852A).[143] So strong is the attraction of the Jewish rites that some Christians in Antioch--or at least one known to Chrysostom--have been circumcised (2.2, 848B-860A; cf. 1.8, 855B). What is most interesting here is that it is not simply a case of conversion to Judaism, for the man regards himself as still a Christian. It is Chrysostom who, appealing to Galatians 5:3, insists that the man has in fact become apostate, but even he still calls him a "brother," hidden in Judaism "like an animal in the bushes" (857B).

Marcel Simon, who has made a very careful study of Chrysostom's anti-Jewish polemic,[144] concluded that Chrysostom was responding to an active proselytizing effort mounted by the Jews.[145] That is doubtful. True, Chrysostom can say things like, "The Jews, worse than any wolves, prepare at the approach of their festivals to attack the flock" (4.1, 871B), but that is exceptional. Chrysostom sometimes is carried away by his own metaphors; in one of the last of the anti-Jewish homilies he admits to his congregation that, like a gentle animal that has acquired the taste for human blood, he has come to lust for combat against the Jews (6.1, 903B). The dominant note in the homilies is not that the Jews are agressors, but that they are ungodly and that Christians should restrain their own and their brothers' strange attraction to them. The recurrent themes in Chrysostom's sermons show that there are three principal factors which lead Christians to become "infected" with the "disease of Judaism"[146]: (1) the great festivals and fasts of the Jewish year exerted great power; (2) the Jews and their places of worship were endowed with a numinous aura, expressing itself, for example, in miraculous healing;[147] (3) they were after all the people of the Old Testament, still observing the impressive rites and celebrations found in the Law, and prominently displaying the sacred scrolls in their synagogues. So many Christians are caught up in the attraction of Judaism that Chrysostom warns in September 387 not to say how many, lest the public reputation of the church suffer (8.4, 933). The remedies which Chrysostom prescribes also support the impression that he feared Christian fascination with Judaism more than active Jewish recruitment of Christians. He does not yet urge attacks on the Jews as such, even though there are ominous notes in his polemic which would reappear in his successors in justifying Christian pogroms. Rather, he undertakes to isolate the Jews from the church. On the one hand, he undertakes to convert the numinous halo of the synagogues into a taboo. He does not deny that healings take place in the synagogues, but asserts that they are accomplished through evil powers (1.6f., 851B-855B; 8.5-7, 935-41). He insists over and over again that the synagogues are "dens of thieves" and "lairs of demons"; they are no different from pagan temples (1.6, 851B); the festivals no different from the theatre, which is forbidden to Christians (4.7, 881B). He warns husbands not to permit their wives to go there; "Are you not afraid they will return from there possessed of demons?" (2.3, 861A). Even the Christ-killer theme serves the same purpose: Christians found in the company of Jews run the risk of guilt by association, just as after the Riots of the Statues many innocent bystanders were dragged into court and punished, simply because they were present where the mischief took place (6.6, 913 middle). On the other hand, he urges each Christian to become the policeman of his brother's conscience, "to track down and win back" those Christians infected with Judaism (2.1, 857A). The sermons are intended to equip them all with arguments, which they can use "like a bridle" to seize anyone they see running to the synagogue and "lead him into the church" (6.7, 915A; cf. *Or* 8 passim). Not to do so would be as irresponsible as for a soldier finding a Persian sympathizer in his camp to fail to report it to his commander (1.4, 850A).

From the end of Julian's reign until the expulsion of Jews from Antioch in the seventh century, there was a rising campaign to contain and isolate the Jewish community. Inside the church this was carried out by invective like Chrysostom's and, not long after, incitement to violence against the Jews. Outside, pressure on the Christian emperors brought changes in the imperial legislation to the same effect. These attempts to insulate Christians from Jewish influence cannot be regarded as simply a reaction against Julian's short-lived Jewish-pagan front. On the contrary, the direct impetus comes from the discovery by ecclesiastical leaders of a very strong "Judaizing" movement within the church.[148] The picture which emerges from Chrysostom's sermons is of a naive infatuation with Jewish rites benignly tolerated or ignored by those who do not participate. It is only he, the zealous young ascetic priest, who sees mortal danger. Can the Jewish sympathizers be identified? Sometimes it is supposed that they were found chiefly among the Arians or Neo-Arians. Chrysostom and subsequent church writers do use the term "Jew" as a pejorative for these and other heretics, but that does not prove that they saw themselves in the light. The fact that Jews are reported to have taken sides occasionally in the Arian-Athanasian conflict in Alexandria[149] may also be only orthodox slander or, if true, local opportunism. Chrysostom interrupted a series of sermons against the Anomoeans to begin his attacks on Judaizing Christians and, while he excuses this shift by saying that the Anomoeans are after all "akin to the Jews" (*Or. adv. Jud.* 1.1, *PG* 48.845), he does not suggest anywhere that they are the ones "infected with Judaism." On the contrary, he talks about members who are in communion with his own church; otherwise the recurrent appeal for mutual vigilance and correction would be meaningless. Simon, following Chrysostom, says that the Christian Judaizers were principally to be found among women and the relatively uneducated.[150] That may be, but such assertions are common coin in ancient attacks on religious deviance, so they should not be taken too literally. Thus we do not obtain any clear idea just who the Christians were who were flocking to synagogues in Chrysostom's day.

Perhaps, indeed, it is more profitable to ask what was the source of the *anti*-Jewish sentiment. Perhaps it is Chrysostom himself and other leaders of the church who are exceptional. Chrysostom is a strikingly complex figure, for he combines in his person two utterly divergent cultures: the aristocratic world of Greek rhetoric[151] and the ascetic Christianity of the monks in the hills.[152] Yet in this period the two had one thing in common: advancement, whether construed in spiritual terms or in terms of a career, was achieved by means of talent, discipline, and personal exertion, within the context of connections which were more personal than institutional. Now consider the observations by Peter Brown that, where articulate and inarticulate forms of power meet, in the realm where it is charismatic authority that counts, accusations of witchcraft arise.[153] Rhetoricians who lose their following and chariot drivers who are upset accuse one another of sorcery; the monks combat a world with devils filled; and Chrysostom portrays the synagogue and the individual Jew as "full of demons."

The church had won its political struggle. After Julian's failure, paganism was no longer a significant enemy. The human embodiment of the demonic opposition to Christianity, which throughout the period of the apologists had become so prominent a motif in the Christian portrayal of their place in the world, had to be sought elsewhere, in heretics within and Jews without. The Jews were a most convenient enemy for those who had need of an enemy in order to map out a meaningful world. A quite visible minority, they were for the ordinary Christian now both somewhat exotic and in some sense sanctified by the Christian's own traditions. But for the church leader of the dynamic new sort represented by Chrysostom, this benign acceptance of the Jew was a direct challenge to the theologically ordered world in which his own powers were plausible and effective. Infatuation with Judaism was a symptom of a fatal laxness and softness in Christianity, which the ascetic wants to root out, and about which the rhetor can be wonderfully eloquent. It is not surprising that the Fourth Gospel provided some of the most vivid texts for Chrysostom's attack, and the Pauline texts (with Hebrews) and the judgment oracles of the Old Testament prophets take on quite a different character when set into the framework of Johannine dualism. For many an ordinary Christian, the Jew brought an element of mystery and awe into a world that had become rather humdrum; for the future bishop of Constantinople the mystery was that of the Devil.

Lacking both space and competence to pursue this investigation down to the end of the Jewish community in Antioch in the early seventh century, I conclude with two observations about the later developments, which may reinforce the somewhat speculative interpretation advanced above. First, the measures taken to isolate the Jews did not succeed immediately. A Syriac homily "On Magicians, Enchanters, and Diviners," thought to be by Isaac of Antioch, some half-century or more after Chrysostom's anti-Jewish sermons, reveals that many Christians, including even clergy, resort to the Jews for protective amulets and healing spells. Isaac insists that the names of the angels which are prominent in these spells are really names of demons, "the ministers of the devil." The language of his anathema is significant:

> Whoever eats with the magicians,
> Does not eat the body of our Lord.
> And whoever drinks with the charmers,
> Does not drink the blood of the Messiah.
> These three, bloated with blood, will be (assigned) to
>   the fire.
> And whoever mingles with them,
> The Jews and the magicians
> Together with Satan, their leader.[154]

Clearly there were Christians still associating intimately with Jews, and precisely because Judaism still seemed charged with mysterious power.[155]

It is to be observed, too, that Isaac was a monk and preached in Syriac. That is the second point: it was the monks who exercised their power on the borderline between rural and urban, Syriac and Greek cultures, who were prime movers in the fifth and sixth century assaults on Judaism in Antioch. To be sure, other factors were involved as well, especially the class conflict which manifested itself in the recurrent riots between the hippodrome factions. In these the Jews tended to get caught up on the side of the Blues, who generally were identified with Christian orthodoxy and the imperial establishment, against the Greens, who included Monophysites and local Syrian elements.[156] But the instigators of attacks on the Jews and their synagogues were the monks, preeminently that most exotic of holy men, Symeon Stylites, and others who emulated his ostentatious asceticism.[157] The holy men could not endure competition from another center of charismatic power. The magic of the Jews had proved too potent and too persistent; it had finally to be rooted out of the city. Soon the importance of the city itself and of the Christian patriarchate there would decline rapidly, after devastating earthquakes followed by Arab invasion. The history of Antiochene Christianity is thus marked for almost its entire span by an ineluctable but finally terribly destructive ambivalence toward the people that gave it birth.[158]

Notes

[1]Since C. H. Kraeling published a comprehensive survey of "the significant data concerning the history and life of the Antiochian Jews" ("The Jewish Community in Antioch," *JBL* 51 [1932] 130-60), only a brief summary is needed here. There are but a few particulars in which Kraeling's study has to be corrected or supplemented, principally from Libanius, whom he seems not to have used. The archaeological expeditions of 1932-39 uncovered surprisingly little that is pertinent to the Jews of Antioch. Further, the whole published corpus of Jewish inscriptions provides almost no information about the region of Antioch, apart from the dedicatory inscriptions in the Apamea synagogue floor (below, n.6) and the tomb of the Antiochene Gerousiarch at Beth She^carim (below, n.4). From the Antioch excavations, only one Jewish inscription was reported, a marble funerary slab roughly inscribed with a menorah and the Greek letters ΓΟΛΒ (*Antioch-on-the-Orontes* [Publications of the Committee for the Excavation of Antioch and its Vicinity] 2, ed. R. Stillwell [Princeton, 1938] 150 f., No. 24). (At the time Downey thought it might have been Christian, but E. R. Goodenough's collection of examples of the Menorah as a primary Jewish symbol in the Greco-Roman period enables us to be confident that it was Jewish. See *Jewish Symbols in the Greco-Roman World* [Bollingen Series 37; New York: Pantheon, 1953-65] Index, vol. 13, s.v. "menorah.") Downey offers several possible explanations of the word, which seems most likely Aramaic. He also suggested that No. 111 was from a Jewish inn, because of its semitic phrases, but since H. Immerwahr pointed out that those phrases were a modified quotation from 1 Kdms 16:4, it could as easily be Christian as Jewish (Jalabert and Mouterde, *IGLS* 3/1.442). D. Levi doubts Downey's identification of the triclinium as part of an inn, since σταθμοῦχος does not necessarily mean "inn-keeper" (*Antioch Mosaic Pavements* [Princeton: University Press, 1947] 1.320). The mosaic is perhaps sixth century (Downey in *Antioch-on-the-Orontes* 3.84). For the general history of the Jews in Antioch, besides Kraeling, who cites the important earlier literature, see the excellent discussions in G. Downey, *A History of Antioch in Syria* (Princeton: University Press, 1961) Index, s.v. "Jews," "synagogues." For references to Antioch in rabbinic literature, see the arts. "'Anṭiokia'" and "Dap̄nē šel 'Anṭiokia'" in *'Ensyklopedia' l^eGe'ograp̄ia' Talmudit*, ed. Phinḥas Na'aman (Tel Aviv: Joshua Chachik, 1972) vol. 1, cols. 87-102.

[2]Trans. Thackeray in the Loeb ed. Thackeray (p.517, n.c.) supposed that the Antiochus named here is Antiochus I Soter, but the context requires Antiochus IV Epiphanes, even though *CAp* 2.39 is thereby contradicted.

[3]He assumes the same percentage as in Egypt and accepts Beloch's estimates for the whole of Syria and Antioch in Augustan times and Chrysostom's figure of 200,000 plus children, slaves, and suburbans for the later period. For a more conservative estimate, see W. Liebeschuetz, *Antioch: City and Imperial Administration in the Later Roman Empire* (Oxford: University Press, 1972) 92-97. F. M. Heichelheim in T. Frank, *Economic Survey of the Roman Empire* 4.158, supposes on the contrary that "the population must have been much larger in the first and second century A.D., perhaps twice or three times its later size." Hardly correct.

[4]M. Schwabe, "Greek Inscriptions found at Beth She^carim in the Fifth Excavation Season, 1953," *IEJ* 4 (1954) 252-56. John Chrysostom in one place mentions ἄρχοντες and προστάται

(*PG* 48.887), and Kraeling supposes that the προστάτης was "as usual" the presiding officer of the council of elders, while the ἄρχων was a member of the council "with special executive obligations" (*JBL* 51.137), but it is not at all apparent that these are technical terms, or that Chrysostom knew very much about the Jews' internal organization.

[5]Ep.1251, ed. Foerster. Because the letter is also important in illustrating the relations between the Jews of the city and prominent pagans as well as the connections between internal self-government and the imperial bureaucracy, it is perhaps worth translating here in its entirety: "Trouble has come to the Jews among us [i.e. in Antioch] since a certain wicked old man came into office, whom they had expelled when he held it previously because he had turned his office into a tyranny. They are of the opinion that the chief of their governors will put this in order if you are willing, for (they think) that you accepted the petition of the old man without knowing his character, which not even age has been able to improve. Those who are agitated believe this to be the case, and although they could not convince me, they did succeed in compelling me to write. But please forgive both me and them--me for yielding to so many, them because of their great suffering--for it is the nature of crowds to be easily deceived." The addressee of the letter is not clear; it is headed τῷ αὐτῷ in the mss, and the preceding letter is to Priscian, but Priscian seems never to have held an office which would have permitted such a request. O. Seeck (*Die Briefe des Libanius* [Leipzig, 1906; rp. Hildesheim: Olm, 1966] 103) argues persuasively that it was addressed to Callistio, who according to Ep. 1233 was assessor of the prefect Salutius in A.D.364. (Consequently J. Vogt, *Kaiser Julian und das Judentum* [Morgenland, Heft 30; Leipzig, 1939] 51, is to be corrected.)

[6]Frey, *CIJ* 2, Nos. 803, 804.

[7]Apparently no remains of synagogues were found in the Princeton-French Academy excavations, even though the site of the Daphne synagogue, which Malalas says was pulled down to make way for a theatre (Downey, *History* 206 f.), was excavated, producing fragments of the theatre (*Antioch-on-the-Orontes* 2.57-94). The notebooks of the expedition, in the archives at Princeton, should be checked to see if there were clues not published.

[8]Josephus, *JW* 7.44, says that the successors of Antiochus Epiphanes restored to the Jews in Antioch the brass votive plaques which had been seized from the Jerusalem temple, "to be installed in their synagogue." Downey, *History* 109, doubts the trustworthiness of the report, but the existence of an Antioch synagogue in that period is not thereby called into question.

[9]Downey, *History* 544, n.179; cf. p.109 and the map, plate 11.

[10]Kraeling makes the identification, p. 140, and Downey seems to concur, as does M. Simon, "La Polémique anti-juive de S. Jean Chrysostome et le mouvement judaisant d'Antioche," in *Annuaire de l'Institut de Philologie et d'Histoire Orientales et Slaves* 4 (=*Mélanges F. Cumont*) (1936) 414. See also the pioneering work of Card. Rampolla [y Tindaro], "Martyre et sepulture des Machabées," *Rev. de l'Art Chrétien* 4e sér., 10 (1899) 302, 383-87.

[11]J. Obermann, "The Sepulchre of the Maccabean Martyrs," *JBL* 50 (1931) 255 f. The source is a Judeo-Arabic Farag-book (*The Arabic Original of Ibn Shahin's Book of Comfort*, ed. J. Obermann [Yale Oriental Series, 17; New Haven: Yale, 1933] 25-28). For further literature on the question see Downey, *History* 109-11 and nn. 116, 118, 121. See also the comments in W. F. Stinespring,

The Description of Antioch in Codex Vaticanus Arabicus 286 (Unpublished Yale Dissertation 1932) 48-50 (on 18.16-10.10 of the translation).

[12]Downey, *History* 499 and 237.

[13]Chrysostom preached four sermons there and Augustine spoke of its (recent) acquisition (Simon, "Polémique" 414; Rampolla, 387-92, 457-58).

[14]Kraeling 141. When the Talmud makes Nebuchadnezzar meet the men of the Great Assembly at Daphne (pShekalim 6, 50a bottom; bShekalim 6b), however, it probably reflects the story of the 100 delegates from Jerusalem who met Marc Antony there in 42/41 B.C. to oppose the accession of Herod and Phasael (Josephus, *JW* 1.243). It does not imply anything about the Jewish community in Antioch or Daphne. Kraeling is mistaken, by the way, when he locates in Antioch the meeting of Jerusalem delegates with Petronius in A.D. 40 (p. 149). Josephus says the meeting was "in the plain of Ptolemais" after Petronius had left Antioch (*JW* 2.187).

[15]Ibid. 141-43. Kraeling, following ancient convention but not the compass, places the plain to the East of Antioch; it should rather be North or Northeast: see Downey, *History*, Excursus 9; although J. Lassus, *Antioch-on-the-Orontes* 5.140, insists that the ancient practice, in which the main street was designated West-to-East, was not an "error," but only a convention. H. H. Tanzer, *The Villas of Pliny the Younger* (N.Y.: Columbia, 1924) points out that the cardinal compass points were generally avoided in the siting of ancient cities, though the deviation of 22° West of true North she cites is not enough to explain the Antioch streets' deviation.

[16]"R. Leazar ben R. Jose says: 'Rice of the Ḥulat of Antioch is permitted as far as BORO'" (Some mss read 'as får as Beirut') TDemai 2:1 (ed. Liebermann, p.68); cf. pDemai 2:1, 22d.

[17]Kraeling 141-43. Josephus tells of a Babylonian Jew named Zamaris who with a retinue of 500 mounted archers and a hundred kinsmen (Kraeling calls him an "emir") had settled in "a place called Οὐαλαθά" when Saturninus was governor of Syria. Later Herod the Great moved him to a village he was founding in Batanaea (*Ant.* 17.23-29).

[18]Much less to fancy that the road, 20 stadia long, paved by Herod (Josephus, *JW* 1.425) was built to connect this "suburb" with the city (Kraeling 144 f.). Josephus clearly is describing the main street of Antioch itself, "once shunned on account of the mud" but paved by Herod "with polished marble, and, as a protection from the rain, adorned . . . with a colonnade of equal length." Cf. Downey, *History* 173 f. and, on excavations in this street, J. Lassus in *Antioch-on-the-Orontes* 5.

[19]L. Harmand, *Libanius: Discours Sur les Patronages* (Paris: Presses Universitaires de France, 1955) 73-87. His argument is accepted by Liebeschuetz 44, who points out, however, that the estate would therefore not have been fortified like the farm near the wilderness at Et-Touba, the plan of which Harmand uses as an illustration, p.142.

[20]*Or.* 47.4-6.

[21]Harmand 138 f.

[22]Libanius, *Or.* 47.13. Liebeschuetz, 45, thinks their situation may have been like that of Jewish peasants in Babylonia, where the landlord controlled the crops the tenant could grow and even the time of the harvest.

[23]See below.

[24]I do not find anything in Libanius' account to justify Downey's description of them as "very orthodox" (*History* 447).

[25]On the sharp separation in general between city and country dwellers, see R. MacMullen, *Roman Social Relations* (New Haven & London: Yale, 1974) chap. 2, and Liebeschuetz 61-73.

[26]Liebeschuetz 44.

[27]*Or.* 47 *passim*; note especially §§19-21, where he insists that the only proper patron and judge of peasants, *as of slaves*, is the owner. That is, he takes for granted their reduction to serfdom, and grandly asserts that the owner's *noblesse oblige* is the only protection they need.

[28]Harmand, chap. 6, discusses in some detail the probable form of Libanius' complaint and its legal basis.

[29]Cf. Liebeschuetz 66 and above, n.27. Liebeschuetz, 71-73, points out that in the period Libanius describes in *Or.* 47 the situation was aggravated by a depression following the battle of Adrianople.

[30]Liebeschuetz has described the transition very effectively. For the place of the church, in both its formal and "charismatic" opportunities, see P. Brown, "The Rise and Function of the Holy Man," *JRomSt* 61 (1971) 80-101, and T. Kopeček, "Social Aspects of the Neo-Arian Movement," a paper distributed to the working group on "The Social World of Early Christianity" 1975.

[31]*Ep.* 1251 (Foerster); n.5 above.

[32]In Foerster's edition, Nos. 914, 917, 973, 974, 1084, 1097, 1098, and 1105. *Ep.* 1097 is problematic because it is addressed τοῖς πατριαρχαῖς (the Sinaiticus ms reads τοῖς ἀρχιερεῦσιν ἀντιοχείας--an impossible office). Foerster thinks this could be shorthand for τῷ πατριάρχῃ καὶ τῷ συνεδρίῳ.

[33]On the philohellenism of the patriarchal family, beginning with Judah ha-Nasi, see M. Simon, *Verus Israel* (Paris: Boccard, 1948) chap. 10.

[34]Above, n.12.

[35]Kraeling 134. But I do not know how Kraeling can be certain that the ἀναθήματα sent by Antiochene Jews to the Jerusalem temple (Josephus *JW* 7.45) were gold, or that they were necessarily made by Jewish metalsmiths.

[36]Liebeschuetz 52-61.

[37]Libanius' *Ep.* 974 is on behalf of the lawyer Euthymos, presumably a Jew, since Libanius appeals to the Patriarch and the Archon together to stake the beginning of his professional career.

[38]Libanius complains bitterly about people leaving his school to study law or Latin and shorthand instead of rhetoric; cf. Liebeschuetz 41-51.

[39]Kraeling 139.

[40]See Kraeling 139, who remarks that the Jews doubtless did call themselves Antiochenes, but without the legal right to do so.

[41]See H. I. Bell, *Jews and Christians in Egypt* (Greek Papyri in the British Museum, 6; London: Brit. Mus., 1924) 10-19. Kraeling thought 2 Macc 4:9, where Jason offers money for Antiochene citizenship for Jerusalem Jews, presupposes similar

rights already for Jews living in Antioch, but that does not follow. On the question of "Antioch-in-Jerusalem," see E. Bickermann, *Der Gott der Makkabäer* (Berlin: Schocken, 1937) 59-65, and V. Tcherikover, *Hellenistic Civilization and the Jews* (Philadelphia: Jewish Publication Society, 1959) 161-69.

[42]Malalas, *Chronographia* (ed. Dindorf) 50.10 (pp.254.15-246.2); Kraeling 148; Downey, *History* 192-95.

[43]Kraeling thinks the two accounts are doublets of one event (150 f.), but Downey, *History*, Excursus 4, 586 f., effectively defends Josephus' version.

[44]For the practice in Antioch of presenting such petitions to an official upon his arrival, see Liebeschuetz 208-19 and his appendix on the claque, 278-80.

[45]Downey, *History* 206, calls attention to Malalas' report (260.11-261.12 in Dindorf's ed.) that Titus in compensation did give to Antioch some of the spoils of Judea and set up the "Cherubim Gate" facing Jerusalem as a memorial of the Jews' humiliation.

[46]As Simon observes, successive editions of Theodotian's code took on more and more of the language of anti-Jewish pamphlets (*Verus Israel* 267 f.).

[47]See Simon, *Verus Israel*, chap. 8; Kraeling 159 f.; Downey, *History* 460 f., 499, 505 f., 571.

[48]Cf. E. Haenchen, *Die Apostelgeschichte* (KEK, 12. ed., 1959) 314.

[49]Was Barnabas therefore one of the ἄνδρες Κύπριοι 11:20? So E. Schwartz conjectured. Was he in fact the founder or leader of the group that founded the Antiochene church? Cf. Haenchen 314.

[50]On the significance of Barnabas' laying his money "at the feet of the apostles" as a symbol for Luke of the continuity of authority through the spirit-filled leaders representing the Prophet Jesus, see now L. Johnson, *The Literary Function of Possessions in Luke-Acts* (Yale Dissertation, 1976).

[51]"Prophets" are not to be distinguished from "teachers" as distinct "offices"; see Haenchen 337 f. and E. E. Ellis, "The Role of the Christian Prophet in Acts," in *Apostolic History and the Gospel* (F. F. Bruce Festschrift), ed. W. W. Gasque and R. P. Martin (Exeter: Paternoster, 1970) 64.

[52]Josephus, *JW* 1.425; see n.18 above.

[53]See the arts. by E. Peterson, E. Bickermann, J. Moreau, and others cited by Haenchen 312; further bibliography in H. Conzelmann, *Die Apostelgeschichte* (HNT 7, 4th ed.; Tübingen: Mohr, 1963) 68, and Downey, *History* 275 f., n.19.

[54]Cf. Haenchen 312.

[55]Mag 10:1, 3 (bis); Rom 3:3 (with Χριστιανός as var.lect.); Philad 6:1. Elsewhere in the Apostolic Fathers only in Mart Polyc 10:1, τὸν τοῦ Χριστιανισμοῦ . . . λόγον; cf. V. Corwin, *St. Ignatius and Christianity in Antioch* (Yale Studies in Religion, 1; New Haven & London: Yale, 1960) 189. In general Ignatius likes compounds in Χριστ-. According to Kraft's index he is also the only "Apostolic Father" to use the noun Χριστιανός (7x), also used fairly often by second-century apologists Justin, Aristides, and Athenagoras. Also Χριστιανικός Trall 6:1; Χριστομαθία Philad 8:2; Χριστόνομος or Χριστόνυμος Rom inscr.; Χριστόφορος Eph 9:2.

[56]*Ad Autol.* 1.1, trans. R. M. Grant (Oxford: Clarendon, 1970). He goes on, "I bear this name beloved of God in the hope of being useful (εὔχρηστος) to God. It is not the case, as you suppose, that the name of God [sic] is offensive." The statement is the more remarkable since Theophilus does not elsewhere mention "Christ" or "Jesus" in his apology. He takes up the question again in 1.12, this time combining his play on Χρηστός with examples of "anointing" that makes objects "useful." "Do you not want to be anointed with the oil of God? We are actually called Christians just because we are anointed with the oil of God."

[57]I pass over the account in Acts 11:27-30 of the Antioch congregation's famine-relief for Jerusalem. If the report could be taken at face value, it would afford evidence for the early importance of the Antioch church and of its strong ties with Jerusalem. However, the internal difficulties with the passage and the problems involved in attempts to harmonize it with Paul's reports of trips to Jerusalem in Gal 1-2 make its historical value precarious.

[58]"The Third Aspect: A Neglected Point of View. A Study in Gal.i-ii and Acts ix and xv," *ST* 3 (1949) 79-95; cf. J. Hawkins, *The Opponents of Paul in Galatia* (Yale Dissertation 1971) 317-40, 348.

[59]Codex D has the intervening group from Jerusalem "command" Paul and his associates to come.

[60]At least that is the most natural reading of Gal 2:4.

[61]The "Western" text is undoubtedly secondary.

[62]Acts 21:25 does have James refer to a letter which he and the Jerusalem elders have sent, containing the "Jerusalem decree." Some commentators have identified this letter with the action by the James party mentioned in Gal 2:11 and have surmised that the author of Acts has mistakenly or deliberately presented it as an action of the Jerusalem Council for the sake of a more harmonious picture. See the standard commentaries.

[63]Note the *inclusio* formed by the commissioning, 13:2 f., and the report, 14:26-28.

[64]Antioch is also absent from the deuteroPauline literature, for 2 Tim 3:11 probably depends on Acts 13:50 and therefore refers to Pisidian Antioch.

[65]J. Schütz, *Paul and the Anatomy of Apostolic Authority* (SNTSMS; Cambridge: University Press, 1975) 138-40.

[66]Schütz 151 f.

[67]Downey, *History* 278, thinks the separate groups existed before Peter's arrival, but I do not think that can be read out of μετὰ τῶν ἐθνῶν συνήσθιεν. Paul, at least, wants the reader to believe that division is an innovation.

[68]οἱ ἐκ περιτομῆς who were "feared" by Peter (Gal 2:12) are evidently Jewish *Christians*.

[69]"Jesus and the Gospels," *Perkins Journal* 28/2 (1975) 31-36; expanded somewhat in his paper read at the SBL Annual Meeting 1975.

[70]Ibid. 34. Recruitment was more often from rural areas, so the villages may have been affected more than the city. Josephus in fact tells us that Antioch, Sidon, and Apamea were exceptions at first to the general wave of anti-Jewish feelings and action at this time (*JW* 2.479).

[71]As L. E. Keck pointed out in his response at SBL 1975.

[72]See above.

[73]One may also ask whether the Jewish-Christian group may have been strengthened by refugees from Jerusalem; cf. Downey, *History* 286 f.

[74]Its form is "baptismal Anamnesis"; cf. N. A. Dahl, "Anamnesis," *ST* 1 (1947 [1948]) 69-95.

[75]W. A. Meeks, "The Image of the Androgyne," *HR* 13 (1974) 165-208.

[76]1:2, trans. K. Lake (Loeb).

[77]See W. A. Meeks, "In One Body: The Unity of Humankind in Colossians and Ephesians," forthcoming in *God's Christ and His People: Essays in Honor of Nils Alstrup Dahl*, ed. J. Jervell and W. A. Meeks (Oslo: Norwegian Universities Press, 1976). For the importance of the symbols of unification in Ignatius' theology, see Corwin 85f., 165, and chap. 7 *passim*.

[78]Lake takes παλαιοῖς to modify μυθεύμασιν, but the syntax seems a little clearer by treating τοῖς παλαιοῖς as a substantive, as I have translated.

[79]κατὰ Ἰουδαϊσμόν; var. lect. νόμον Ἰουδαϊκον, νόμον Ἰουδαϊσμόν.

[80]Corwin 61-64; R. M. Grant, "Jewish-Christianity in Antioch in the Second Century," *Rech.Sci.Rel.* 60 (Danielou Festschrift, 1972) 101. Corwin thinks the Antiochene Judaizers resembled the Qumran sect and must have been of Essene background; Grant agrees that "the more extreme Judaizers had affinities with Qumran." The evidence adduced seems too slim, however, to be confident about this identification.

[81]Particularly emphasized by Grant, "Jewish Christianity in Antioch." Grant also argues, however, that gnostics like Saturninus (in Antioch in Hadrian's time) formed a front apposing the kind of Judaeo-Christianity represented later by Theophilus (p.105).

[82]According to Justin, *I Apol.* 26.4.

[83]S. Laeuchli, "The Drama of Replay," in *Searching in the Syntax of Things* (Philadelphia: Temple Univ. Press, 1974) 89.

[84]R. M. Grant, "Theophilus of Antioch to Autolycus," in *After the New Testament* (Philadelphia: Fortress, 1967) 136 (originally in *HTR*, 1947). Grant, who depends for this judgment mainly on research by L. Ginzberg, cites numerous examples here (136-41) and in the notes to his translation, *Ad Autolycum* (Oxford: Clarendon, 1970).

[85]*After the New Testament* 129.

[86]One example may illustrate the relationship and difference. Like Philo and the rabbis, Theophilus knows traditions that seek to explain the different names of God, especially θεός = אלהים and κύριος = יהוה. (On the development of these traditions, see A. Segal, *Two Powers in Heaven* [Yale Diss. 1975] and the paper by N. A. Dahl and A. Segal at the 1975 Annual Meeting of SBL.) Theophilus is closer to Philo than to the rabbis in depending entirely on the LXX, in his explanation of κύριος as referring to God's rule (κυριεύειν) of the universe, and in connecting θεός with τίθημι and equating it with God's creative power. However, he adds yet another etymology, from θέειν, and goes on to mention other "names," πατήρ, δημιουργός, ποιητής, ὕψιστος (*Ad Autol.*1.4).

One of the traditional motifs taken up by Theophilus is illustrated by an Antioch mosaic. In his exposition of the creation story, Theophilus says that the eschatological restoration of man will also bring gentleness among the animals (*Ad Autol*.2.17). This seems to be the theme of the *Philia* mosaic in which four pairs of animals, one carnivore, the other gentle, face each other on sides of a rectangle (Levi 2, Pl. LXII). The exegetical basis is presumably Isa 11:7, quoted explicitly in a similar mosaic from the "hall church" at Ma'in in Madaba, Transjordan (Levi 1.318 f.), and Levi thinks the animal pair in the synagogue at Beth Alpha probably has the same meaning.

[87]3.9, trans. Grant.

[88]Theophilus constructs "syntheses" of OT and NT passages, which may be intended to counter Marcion's "Antitheses" (Grant, *After the NT* 144). According to Eusebius, *HE* 4.24, he also wrote a tract against Marcion, now lost.

[89]On the notion of the δευτέρωσις, suggested already in Diognetus, Aristides, and Barnabas, and receiving its classic expression in the Didascalia, see M. Simon, *Verus Israel* 114-17.

[90]Trans. Grant, italics added. This claim on the Jewish scriptures is of course important for Theophilus' apologetic, for Autolycus thinks "that our scriptures are new and modern" (3.1).

[91]"The Early Antiochene Anaphora," *ATR* 30 (1948) 91-94, followed by Downey, *History* 301.

[92]*Verus Israel* 436.

[93]*HE* 7.32.2, trans. Lake. It is often supposed that he assisted Lucian in the latter's famous recension of the Greek Bible, but there is no direct evidence of this. Grant thinks both Lucian and Dorotheus "studied with Jewish teachers" ("Anaphora" 93).

[94]*HE* 6.12.1. Domnus, he says, "had fallen away from the faith of Christ, at the time of the persecution, to Jewish will-worship (ἐθελοθρησκεία)." It is not clear which persecution is meant--not likely the measures taken against Christianity by Septimius Severus while Serapion was bishop, since these forbade conversion to either Christianity *or Judaism* (Downey 305). Possibly then Domnus had defected in the time of Marcus Aurelius. The use of the rare word ἐθελοθρησκεία is doubtless dependent on Col 2:23 and shows that the Christians are still looking for scriptural models for their opposition to Judaism--but this word is likely Eusebius' rather than Serapion's.

[95]Ἰουδαῖος . . . πρόσωπον Χριστιανοῦ περιφέρων; *Exp. in Ps. 109*. 1 = *PG* 55.267. Cf. Simon, *Verus Israel* 123.

[96]*Hist. Arianorum ad monach*. 71 = *PG* 25.777B, cited by F. Loofs, *Paulus von Samosata* (TU, 3.Reihe, 14/5; Leipzig: Hinrichs, 1924) 18, who has assembled all the significant sources. See also G. Bardy, *Paul de Samosate* (Spicilegium sacrum Lovaniense, Etudes et Documents, 4; Louvain, 1923) 23 f., 32, 382-84.

[97]Loofs 20-34; Bardy 23 f., 32, 172-74, 384.

[98]As stated explicitly by Bar Hebraeus I: cui gratissimae Pauli sententiae exstiterunt; cited by Loofs 32 f.

[99]*Dogmengeschichte* 1^1.589 = 1^4.723, cited by Loofs 34.

[100]See beside Loofs and Bardy, Downey *History* 310-15. Loofs, however, thinks it "unwahrscheinlich" that Zenobia elevated Paul to the office of *ducenarius*. No credence is to be given to late

reports that she was even responsible for his installation as bishop, though Bardy accepts this (197).

101Bardy 194.

102Downey, *History* 311.

103Bardy 197.

104Bardy 384.

105*Exp. in Ps.109.1=PG* 55.265.

106*Haer.* 65.2; Bardy 32. · Epiphanius says they are called "second Jews" (δεύτεροι Ἰουδαῖοι).

107It is another question, which cannot be taken up here, just which groups of Christians in Antioch and vicinity rallied to Paul's cause. Do the allegations about his social climbing, made by the Council letter (Eusebius *HE* 7.30.7) suggest a difference in social class between the Paulists and the Catholics? (Cf. T. Kopecek.) Paul's chief opponent was the presbyter Malchion, who was head of a rhetorical school and hence probably of relatively high socio-economic class (see P. Petit, *Les Etudiants de Libanius* [Paris: Nouvelles Editions Latines, 1957])--in effect thus a member of the Greco-Roman "establishment" which would naturally oppose the Palmyrene hegemony. Does Paul's show of asceticism, to the point of keeping *virgines subintroductae* (*HE* 7.30.12 f.), also point to connections with the Syriac-speaking Christians East of Antioch and, probably, also in the Antiochene villages? If so, the connection would count against positive relations with Judaism, for the Syriac Christian leaders apart from Aphrahat seem to have been outspokenly hostile toward the Jews (see R. Murray, *Symbols of Church and Kingdom* [Cambridge Univ. Press, 1975] 41, referring however principally to fourth-century sources).

108Downey, *History* 277 f.; Corwin 49, 76 f., 85 f.

109Ignatius' preoccupation with the question of unity is implicit testimony to this diversity; cf. Corwin 85 f.

110See Simon, *Verus Israel* 337-41.

111For a digest of the main laws see J. Juster, *Les Juifs dans l'empire romaine* (Paris: Geuthner, 1914) 1.160-72; cf. 226-38, 248-51. Note particularly the sequence of legislation from Constantine to Theodosius II, alternately restricting and defending the Jews, in *C.Theod.* 16.8.1-29 (ET in C. Pharr, *et al.*, *The Theodosian Code* [Princeton Univ. Press, 1952] 467-71).

112See n.3 above.

113Of 100 students whose religion is ascertainable, Petit finds 12 Christians, most of them from Cappadocia and Armenia (only two from Antioch). All Libanius' students were from the three highest provincial classes, and the Christians were all of the top two, sons of either imperial officials or *curiales*. They are thus examples more of the results than of the process of upward mobility (Petit 113-17 and Tables I and II). An example not counted by Petit (since this person's study with Libanius is not confirmed in the authentic letters of Libanius) was John Chrysostom, whose father and grandfather had served in the *officium* of the *magister militum per orientem*, but who aspired by his rhetorical training to a still higher career in the civil service (see A. H. M. Jones, "St. John Chrysostom's Parentage and Education," *HTR* 46 [1953] 171-73).

114See Liebeschuetz 50 and 247-51.

[115]For the case of the Neo-Arians, demonstrated by Kopeček (see n.30 above). Paul of Samosata, if we are to believe the accusations of his opponents, had also mastered the art of combining ecclesiastical and political power a century earlier (see above).

[116]See above.

[117]Brown, "Holy Man"; the cases of Aetius and George in Kopeček. In a different way Paul of Samosata presented an earlier example. The council's accusation that he intervened in lawsuits for money parallels the kind of accusation Libanius would make against military patrons, and suggests the kind of mediation which patrons of both the older and newer types were expected to provide. Libanius, *Or.*30(*Pro templis*).8, says the monks, who have led attacks on pagan shrines, "eat more than elephants." Harmand, 28 n.3, compares this with Libanius' words about the gluttony of military patrons.

[118]J. Neusner, *A History of the Jews in Babylonia* 2 (SPB, 11; Leiden: Brill, 1966) 147-50.

[119]C. Bonner, "Witchcraft in the Lecture Room of Libanius," *TAPA* 63 (1932) 34-44; P. Brown, "Sorcery, Demons and the Rise of Christianity . . . ," in *Religion and Society in the Age of St. Augustine* (London: Faber & Faber, 1972) 119-50 (originally in M. Douglas, ed., *Witchcraft Confessions and Accusations* [1970] 17-45).

[120]On Libanius' primary loyalty to the city, and the city as focus of conservative views of society, see Liebeschuetz 12 f.

[121]Downey, *History* 381 f.

[122]See J. Vogt, *Kaiser Julian und das Judentum* (Morgenland, Heft 30; Leipzig, 1939) chap. 6.

[123]*Ep.* 89b (Bidez-Cumont) 295C; ET in the Loeb ed. by W. C. Wright, 2.296-339. Vogt even thinks Julian's parody of judgment oracles by Jewish prophets, "Tremble, be afraid, *fire*, *flame*, death, a dagger, a broad-sword!" may allude to the "fire" which sprang from the earth to stop the restoration, but he has misread the passage. Julian is not talking about contemporary prophets in Antioch who persuaded him to undertake the futile project, as Vogt believes (50, cf. 47, 59), but the OT prophets, who make the profanation of pagan temples "a reproach against us."

[124]E.g. the first portions of "Against the Galileans" (in vol. 3 of the Loeb ed.).

[125]Origen, *C.Cels.* 1.28-71; 1.1-79; for ET see H. Chadwick, *Origen: Contra Celsum* (Cambridge Univ. Press, 1953).

[126]Vogt 9-18.

[127]*John Chrysostom and his Time* (London & Glasgow: Sands, 1959 [The 1st German ed. was 1919-30]) 1.66. Contrast Simon, *Verus Israel* 241 and n.1, who points out that there was no economic basis for anti-semitism in antiquity. The role of "money lovers" in ancient stereotypes was played rather by Egyptians and Phoenicians.

[128]*Or. adv. Jud.* 5.11 (*PG* 48.900B). This homily was delivered twenty years after the event. The "Letter to the Jewish Community" attributed to Julian (No. 204 Bidez-Cumont=No. 51 in the Loeb ed.) asks the Jews to pray for him, "in order that, when I have successfully concluded the war with Persia, I may rebuild by my own efforts the sacred city of Jerusalem, which for so many years you have longed to see inhabited, and may bring

settlers there, and, together with you, may glorify the Most High God therein" (trans. Wright, Loeb). This letter, however, is probably a forgery, despite Wright's defense of it: so Schwartz, Klimek, Geffcken, Bidez-Cumont; see esp. Vogt 64-68. If so, only a single line of his authentic letter to the Jews remains (quoted by Lydus, *De mens.* 4, p.110.4 ed. Wünsch=Ep.134 Bidez-Cumont): "I shall with all enthusiasm raise up the temple of the Most High God."

[129]*Ep.* 20 in the Loeb ed.=89 Bidez-Cumont.

[130]306B, trans. Wright (Loeb, vol. 3).

[131]See his *Misopogon* and the Julianic orations of Libanius, conveniently collected and translated in vol. 1 of the new Loeb ed. by A. F. Norman.

[132]Liebeschuetz has aptly described the significance of this alliance: "Belief in the city as the essential form of social organization, and in the value of the cults of the city are different aspects of the same attitude of cultural conservatism" (13).

[133]M. Simon, "Polémique" 414; Vogt 68-72.

[134]Rampolla 387-88; Simon, "Polémique" 414; cf. above, n.11.

[135]Baur 1.52 accepts as factual the report by Ambrose, *Ep.* 40.15 *Ad Theodosium*, that the Jews under Julian had burned several churches in Damascus, Alexandria, Gaza, Askalon, Beirut, and elsewhere. If that happened, it is surprising that we do not hear of earlier and more extreme reactions than is in fact the case. If Chrysostom had heard of such incidents, he would almost certainly have mentioned them somewhere in his vituperations against the Jews. Cf. J. Parkes, *The Conflict of the Church and the Synagogue* (London: Soncino, 1934) 188.

[136]*PG* 48.843-942. The sermons extended over three years, from 2 Sept. 386 until 2 Sept. 389, according to dates worked out by H. Usener and corrected by E. Schwartz; see Juster 1.62, n.1.

[137]Simon, "Polémique" 256.

[138]*Or. adv. Jud.* 5 and 6, *PG* 48.899B-901B, 905A-907A. The sermons were delivered on 28 and 30 Sept. 388.

[139]900A, 900B-901A.

[140]Compare Liebeschuetz's remarks about Libanius' conventions of abuse, 31-39.

[141]Lampe's *Patristic Greek Lexicon*, s.v. Χριστοκτόνος, gives examples from *Apoc. Pauli* 49; *Const.Ap.* 2.61.1; 6.25.1; Athanasius fr. (*PG* 26.1224B), and Proclus, *Constant.Or.*12.2 (*PG* 65.789A), as well as several instances from Chrysostom. Most of these, however, seem to refer to those actually involved in Jesus' death, such as Caiaphas, rather than the nation as a whole. But Chrysostom likes to quote Matt. 27:25. It is possible that this is another instance of the influence of Syriac Christianity on Chrysostom, for Ephrem regularly uses the words *ṣālôḇâ* and *zāqôp̱â*, 'crucifier,' as synonyms for 'Jew' (Murray 41).

[142]See especially 1.5 (*PG* 48.850A-851B), 2.3 (862A); and 6.2 (907A).

[143]The viewpoint he opposes provides evidence in favor of E. R. Goodenough's hypothesis, that the ark of the Torah served in synagogues of the Greco-Roman period as numinous objects functionally analogous to the statue in the inner shrine of a pagan temple (*Jewish Symbols* 4 [1954] 99-144; 12 [1965] 83-86).

[144]"Polémique" *passim*; cf. *Verus Israel* 256-64. See also Baur 1.274-76.

[145]"C'est véritablement une campagne de propagande, amplement orchestree" (*Verus Israel* 336).

[146]1.1, 844; 1.8, 855B; 3.1, 862; 5.12, 904; 7.6, 926B-927A; 8.9, 941 f. Julian had spoken of the "disease of the Galileans," *Ep.* 89 Bidez-Cumont=20 Loeb, 454B. A common pejorative term for false opinion; similar language is found already in the Pastoral Epistles.

[147]It is well known that the Jews had a reputation as magicians in antiquity; see e.g. Simon, *Verus Israel* chap. 12. "Throughout this age the Jews share with Persians and Chaldaeans a reputation as expert sorcerers second only to the Egyptian past masters" (A. A. Barb, "The Survival of Magic Arts," in *The Conflict Between Paganism and Christianity in the Fourth Century* [Oxford-Warburg Series; Oxford: Clarendon, 1963] 118). In private conversation Barb has ventured the guess that in both Antioch and Alexandria, which were apparently the chief centers for the production of magic gems, Jews were responsible for very many, if not most of these objects.

[148]Cf. Parkes 150-95. Simon, *Verus Israel* 272 f., says Parkes goes too far in claiming that anti-semitism was imposed from above by the ecclesiastical hierarchy; it was also a popular movement. But he agrees that there was also a popular philo-Judaism, and that Christian anti-semitism was above all a defensive reaction to it.

[149]See Simon, *Verus Israel* 264, who cites Athanasius, *Ep. encycl.* 3 (*PG* 25.228) and Theodoret, *HE* 4.18-19.

[150]"Polémique" 405.

[151]Sozomen reports that he studied under Libanius, and Chrysostom's rhetorical style makes that believable. See Baur 1, chap. 4, esp. pp.22 f., and Jones (n.113 above).

[152]Palladius says he lived four years with an old Syrian monk, practicing self-mortification. Baur thinks this may have been Carterius, and the time with him that period which Chrysostom, Theodore of Mopsuestia, and Maximus (later bishop of Isaurian Seleucia) spent in the *Asketerion* of Diodorus (1.109 f.). Though ascetic Christianity was especially identified with the Syriac-speaking population, it had already begun to penetrate the urban, Greek-speaking church, particularly the anti-Arians. Diodorus and Flavian, the two laymen who became leaders of the pro-Nicene faction, became closely allied with rural monasticism, although their own background was aristocratic with classical training. Under Meletius they introduced the antiphonal chanting of Psalms from the villages into the churches of Antioch. Theodoret reports that they were joined in the struggle against the Arians by a Syriac-speaking hermit from Edessa, the "Persian" Aphrahat, and later, during Meletius' second or third exile, by another Osroenean holy man, Julian (*Relig.hist.* 2 and 8 [*PG* 82.1317C-D and 1368C-76C] and *HE* 4.25-27 [GCS 44, 2nd ed. 1954]). As a youthful eyewitness, Theodoret's report cannot be ignored, yet this Aphrahat, who came to Antioch ca.360 and remained there until his death after 400 (S. Schiwietz, *Das morgenländische Mönchtum*, vol. 3 [Mödling bei Wien: St. Gabriel, 1938] 278-80; A. Festugiere, *Antioche païenne et chretienne* [Paris: Boccard, 1959] 267-76), cannot be the well-known Syrian church leader and author (A. Vööbus, "Aphrahat," *JAC* 3 [1960] 153). But none of the authors I have consulted discusses the remarkable coincidence

of origin, date, and name, or asks whether Theodoret has muddled the identity of his pro-Nicene hero.

153Brown, "Sorcery" (above, n.119).

154Trans. S. Kazan, "Isaac of Antioch's Homily against the Jews," *Oriens Christianus* 46 (1962) 94 f.; see his extended discussion of Isaac's other anti-Jewish writings within the context of other Syriac Christian literature, ibid. 45 (1961) 30-53; 46 (1962) 87-98; 47 (1963) 89-97; 49 (1965) 57-78. The homily *De magis* is preserved with the works of Ephraem (ed. Lamy, 1886, 2.393-426) but Burkitt's identification of the author as Isaac is now generally accepted. See A. Baumstark, *Geschichte der syrischen Literatur* (Bonn: Marcus u. Weber, 1922) 65, n.4; Simon, *Verus Israel* 416-18; Baur 1.274, n.20.

155The fact that an early fifth-century deacon of the "Cruciform Church" in Kaouseia had the name Akkiba may indicate continuing Jewish influence (Inscription No.66, *Antioch-on-the-Orontes* 2.42). On the other hand, the appearance of biblical names like Ephraem and Reuben proves nothing.

156Kraeling 159; more fully Downey, *History* 499.

157The story by Symeon's Syriac hagiographers that his threats persuaded the emperor Theodosius II not to force the Christians to make reparations for the synagogues they had destroyed is exaggerated at best. See Downey, *History* 460 f. and n.50. The story intrudes into the account of Symeon's death in the Syriac vita; see the German translation by Hilgenfeld in H. Lietzmann, *Das Leben des heiligen Symeon Stylites* (TU 32/4; Berlin, 1908) §§130-31, and English by F. Lent, *JAOS* 35 (1915-17) 188 f. (=Bedjan's text, pp.635-38). The story is repeated by later biographers, but the earliest hagiography of Symeon, by Theodoret in *Relig.Hist.* 26, contains only the statement that Symeon "fought against the Greek impiety and sought to destroy the audacity of the Jews" (§25).

158My research on this topic has been made possible by a Senior Fellowship from the National Endowment for the Humanities and a special leave of absence from Yale University, for both of which I am grateful.

S 55, A 76

THE JEWS OF ANTIOCH

Robert L. Wilken
University of Notre Dame

Surveys of the history of the Jewish community in Antioch during Hellenistic and Roman times can be found in S. Krauss, "Antioche," *Revue des Etudes Juives* 45 (1902) 27-49; C. H. Kraeling, "The Jewish Community at Antioch," *JBL* 51 (1932) 130-160; B. T. Lurie, *The Jews in Syria* [in Hebrew] (Jerusalem, 1957); and G. Downey, *A History of Antioch, passim*. The Kraeling article, though over forty years old, is the most comprehensive; Krauss gives more information from Talmudic and Midrashic sources; Lurie, somewhat too general and superficial, is useful because he had access to epigraphic sources unknown to Kraeling, and he discusses Antiochene Jewry in relation to Jewish communities in other Syrian cities; Downey is helpful as on specific points, but his comments are scattered throughout the book and from him it is difficult to get a total picture of the place of the Jews in the life of the city. In this report I briefly summarize what we know about the history of Jews of Antioch and then discuss the epigraphic evidence (which was not available to Kraeling and which is mentioned only briefly in Downey) and relate this information to the literary sources.

Jews were among the original settlers of Antioch when the city was founded by Seleucus Nicator in 300 B.C.E. (Josephus, *Contra Apionem* 2.39; *Antiquities* 12.119). Antioch's proximity to Palestine (the lake of Antioch was thought to be one of the seven lakes surrounding Eretz Israel), as well as its importance as an administrative and commercial center, made it attractive to Jews. Its accessibility to Asia Minor also made it a convenient stopping place for Jews traveling between Palestine and Asia Minor, either by land through Cilicia or by ship to the coastal cities. Paul, for example, sailed to Pamphylia from Antioch.

By the middle of the 2nd century at least, and perhaps earlier, the Jews were recognized as a distinct group within the city free to follow their own customs. (Josephus, *Bellum* 7.44; *Ant.* 13.119). This probably meant that they were organized as a πολίτευμα within the larger community. Josephus says they were called "Antiochenes" (*C. Apionem* 2.38), but the legal significance of this term is unclear. For most of the Hellenistic period the Jewish community was able to carry on its affairs undisturbed, except for the brief interlude under Antiochus Epiphanes (175 B.C.E.). His policy of repression of Judaism surely had consequences for the Jews of Antioch, because the capital of his kingdom was located there, but it is noteworthy that most of the events associated with his reign occurred in Jerusalem, not Antioch. Josephus does say, however, that his successors restored to the Jews of Antioch what had been taken from them by Antiochus and reaffirmed the rights they had possessed, implying that these rights were curtailed by Antiochus. Possibly captives from Jerusalem were brought to Antioch. Later Jewish tradition spoke of three "exiles," one of which was at Daphne near Antioch (Jerusalem Talmud, *Sanhedrin* 29c; *Pesikta Rabbati*, ch. 31.10, Krauss, p. 30), and John Chrysostom speaks of a "captivity" under Antiochus Epiphanes (*Hom. ad Iud.* 5). Further, the Maccabean martyrs are sometimes associated with Antioch, though it seems more likely that the martyrdoms actually took place in Jerusalem. One of the synagogues of Antioch, called Kenesseth Hasmunith [synagogue of the Hasmonaeans], was dedicated to the martyrs and for a time the bones of the martyrs were buried there (E. Bickermann, "Les Maccabées de Malalas," *Byzantion* 21 [1951] 63-82).

All this suggests that Antiochene Jewry was affected by the policies of Antiochus, but details are sparse. Josephus, our chief source, emphasizes, no doubt intentionally, that except for the rule of Antiochus Epiphanes the Jews lived in peace and tranquility under the Hellenistic kings and the community grew and prospered. Jews were, he writes, "particularly numerous in Syria, where intermingling is due to the proximity of the two countries. But it was at Antioch that they specially congregated, partly owing to the greatness of that city, but mainly because the successors of King Antiochus had enabled them to live there in security. For, although Antiochus surnamed Epiphanes sacked Jerusalem and plundered the temple, his successors on the throne restored to the Jews of Antioch all such votive offerings as were made of brass, to be laid up in their synagogue, and, moreover, granted them citizen rights on an equality with the Greeks. Continuing to receive similar treatment from later monarchs, the Jewish colony grew in numbers, and their richly designed and costly offerings formed a splendid ornament to the temple. Moreover, they were constantly attracting to their religious ceremonies multitudes of Greeks, and these they had in some measure incorporated with themselves" (*Bellum* 7.44-45, trans. Thackeray).

During the Hellenistic period Jews also settled in Daphne, the lovely suburb on a plateau south of the city. At least since Tiberius there was a synagogue in Daphne (Malalas, 261) and it is possible there had been one earlier. Rabbinic sources speak of Daphne as a Jewish center, even locating a meeting there between King Nebuchednezer and the Sanhedrin (*jer Shekalim* 6; 50a). The account is legendary, but it indicates the importance of Daphne in Jewish tradition. In John Chrysostom's day there was a synagogue in Daphne (*Hom. ad Iud.* 1.6).

A third Jewish settlement was located in the vicinity of Antioch. Its origins are unclear but its existence is well attested. This area, called חולתא, must have been outside of the walls of the city, north and east of the great plain adjacent to the Lake of Antioch. The Jews who lived there grew rice and the rabbis discuss the question whether rice grown there should be considered מותר or ח״ב, i.e. subject to the same laws which apply to produce grown in Eretz Israel. At several places in Midrash Rabbah there is a story of a visit to this area by several rabbis to collect money for Eretz Israel (*Deut. Rabbah* 4.8; *Lev. Rabbah* 4.3). The account makes clear that the rabbis came regularly to the area to collect funds. Confirmation of the existence of Jews living in the vicinity of Antioch also comes from Libanius, who had dealings with Jews who had worked his family's land for four generations (*Or.* 47.13 ff.).

The Romans captured Syria in 64-63 and made it into a Roman province. The new rulers brought changes, but their policies had little immediate effect on the status of the Jews in Antioch. If the analogy of other Jewish communities within the empire is used, the Jews of Antioch will have been allowed to exist as a distinct group within the city, to use their own laws on matters which pertained to their common life, to maintain relations with Eretz Israel and to send funds to Jerusalem, to follow their traditional mode of worship. (See, for example, the decree in Josephus concerning the Jews in Sardis, *Ant.* 14.259.)

But the rule of the Romans was not an unmixed blessing because of the growing conflict between the Jews and Romans in Palestine. Inevitably the Jews of Antioch were drawn into the conflict. For example, the Emperor Caligula ordered his statue placed in the temple in Jerusalem; the decree was transmitted via the governor of Syria. He consulted with the Jews in Antioch about the matter and said that if they did not concur his army was "ready at hand" and would "strew the land with the dead." The Jews refused, and when the governor went to Jerusalem to carry out the order Jews lined the roads to protest his action (Philo, *Ad Gaium*, 222-24; Josephus, *Ant.* 18.262-272). The initial impetus to protest probably originated in Antioch. Actions such as these did not bode well for their future relations with Roman officials in Antioch as well as with the populace of the city. Opposition to the Jews grew and some asked the governor to revoke their sabbath privileges, i.e. the right to close one's shop on the sabbath or to refuse to appear in court. The Roman official refused the request, however, and later, after the war, when Titus was asked to drive the Jews out of the city, he refused. "Now that their city is destroyed there is no place for them to live but where they do live" (*Bell.* 2.462-3, 479, 481; *Bell.* 7.100-111). Again our source is Josephus, who wished to show that, in spite of what happened in Palestine, life continued undisturbed in the diaspora. Malalas, however, reports that the emperor set up several bronze figures, presumably from the temple, outside the southern gate of the city. Since Jews were concentrated in that part of the city, the figures served as an affrontery to Jews every time they passed through the gate, reminding them of the fall of the city. Malalas (260-61) also says that a theater was built on the site of the Jewish synagogue in Daphne with the legend: "From the Jewish spoils."

In the years following the fall of Jerusalem information on Antiochene Jewry is meager. It is possible that the war and the events surrounding the war altered the status of the Jews there, but there is no evidence for it. The legacy of the war was to linger on in attitudes toward the Jews (e.g. Tacitus, *Histories* 5), the imposition of an onerous tax, the *fiscus judaicus*, and the devastation of Palestine and the loss of Jerusalem. The long-range consequences of the war affected Jewish life in Palestine more than in the diaspora; for example, the center of Palestinian Jewry shifted from Jerusalem to the cities in the north, e.g. Tiberias, Sepphoris, *et al.* The Bar Kochba revolt in 135 C.E. again brought great destruction and desolation to Palestine, but its significance for the diaspora communities was minimal. Under Antoninus Pius (138-161) relations with Rome began to improve. Hadrian's ban on circumcision was modified to allow Jews to circumcise their own sons (Justinian, *Dig.* 48.811), and in Palestine as well as in diaspora cities Jews began gradual recovery. It is in this period e.g. that a large building in Sardis was bought and made into a Jewish synagogue. (See M. Avi Yonah, *In the Days of Rome and Byzantion* [in Hebrew], 1970, pp. 44-73; S. Liebermann, *Jewish*

Quarterly Review 36 [1946], 329ff.; J. Gager, *HUCA* 44 [1973]; A.T. Kraabel, *Judaism in Western Asia Minor* [Ph.D. dissertation, Harvard, 1968].)

In the beginning of the 3rd century with the establishment and official recognition of the patriarchate, and the new law (*Constitutio Antoniana*) recognizing all inhabitants of the Empire as citizens, the Jews, in Palestine and in the diaspora, were more fully integrated into the civic life of the Empire. In the next several hundred years the Jews are a significant factor in the life of the Greek speaking cities of the East: (1) Jews served on a city council in the cities in which they lived. They performed liturgies and held positions as magistrates. They served as watchmen, clerks in the markets, police officers. In Sardis several served as members of the provincial administration. According to Malalas (290) Antioch had a Jewish magistrate ca. 190 C.E. (See Amnon Linder, "The Roman Imperial Government and the Jews under Constantine," [in Hebrew] *Tarbiz* 44 [1973] 110-114). (2) Numerous dedicatory inscriptions of synagogues built during the 3rd and 4th centuries have been found in cities scattered throughout Asia Minor, Syria (and Greece), and of course Palestine. These inscriptions, e.g. in Pergamon, Phocaea, Smyrna, Teos, Myndos, Tralles, Side, Acmonia, Apamaea, *et al.* indicate that the Jews were able to continue their way of life undisturbed and that they had the resources to build and decorate suitable structures for religious educational and social purposes (see B. Lifschitz, *Donateurs et fondateurs dans les Synogogues juives* [1967]). (3) Even after Constantine there was little change in the legal status of the Jews, and opposition to the continuation of privileges to Jewish leaders (e.g. exemption from liturgies) indicates that the cities counted on and could not dispense with the contributions of the Jewish citizens. (See especially *Codex Theodosianus* 12.1.157-158; A. Linder, *op. cit.* 95-110, Avi Yonah, *op. cit.*, 158-177.) I mention these general conditions because we can only discuss Antiochene Jewry by analogy to Jewish life in other cities in the Empire. Precise knowledge about Jewish life in Antioch is limited to scattered references (e.g. mention of visits to the city or the vicinity by Palestinian rabbis such as those in Midrash Rabbah or in the Jerusalem Talmud, e.g. *Horayyoth* 3; 48a, a visit of R. Akiba). By the 4th century the sources begin to yield a clearer picture (as they also do for Christianity and paganism), and there is no reason to think that what we learn from the later period does not stand in continuity with the earlier. And what we do learn indicates that Jews in Antioch still held an important place in the city's life as did Jews in other cities in the eastern Empire. A series of inscriptions from Apamaea in Syria and Beth She'arim and Tiberias in Palestine allow us a glimpse of Antiochene Jewry in the 4th century.

1) *Beth She'arim*, a center of Talmudic study, for a time the seat of the sanhedrin and patriarchate. Excavations there have uncovered a large number of Jewish tombs with many inscriptions, largely in Greek, but some in Hebrew. One room at Beth She'arim, comprising six tombs, was the burial place for members of a distinguished family from Antioch. An inscription from the early 4th century C.E. reads as follows: "Apse of Aidesios, head of the council of elders of Antioch." A second indicates that the six tombs in the "burial chamber" belong to Aidesios. (Text in M. Schwabe and B. Lifshitz, *Beth She'arim*

[1973-4], nos. 141 and 142.) Aidesios was head of the gerousia, the ruling body of the Jewish community in Antioch, and was well enough known that his father's name is not even mentioned on the tombstone for identification. The tomb was of course in Palestine, not in Antioch, suggesting that the head of the gerousia in Antioch was also known in Palestine, and that the Jews in Antioch had close relations to Eretz Israel. The practice of burial in Eretz Israel, which was actually a re-burial because the bones of the deceased were normally brought there only later, was also an act of piety (see E. Meyers, *Jewish Ossuaries: Reburial and Rebirth* [1971], pp. 73-91). To be buried in Israel was an act of atonement: "As soon as they are buried in the land of Israel or even a handful of soil of the land of Israel is placed upon them it will make expiation for them as it is said 'And His Land shall make expiation for His people'" (*Pesikta Rabbati* 1.6).

2) *Apamaea*. Several inscriptions from a synagogue in Apamaea, south of Antioch on the Orontes, dated in 391 C.E. mention descendants of the same Antiochene family. The inscriptions are written in Greek and in the same style as dedicatory inscriptions found in other synagogues in this period and in the Christian church dedicated at Antioch several years earlier (D. Levi, *Antioch Mosaic Pavements*, p. 426). "At the time of the most illustrious archisynagogoi Eusebius, Nemesios and Phineos, and the gerousiarch Theodoros, and the most illustrious presbyters, Isakios, Saulos, and the others, Ilasios, archisynagogos of the Antiocheians made the entrance of mosaic, 150 feet, in the year 703 (391), the 75th day of the month of Audynaios (Jan. 7). Blessings to all." Ilasios was the grandson of Aidesios who was buried in Tiberias. "Ilasios, son of Isakios, archisynagogos of the Antiocheians, for the welfare of Photios his wife, and of their children, and for welfare of Eustathia his mother-in-law, and in memory of Isakios, Aedesios, and Hesychios his ancestors, made the mosaic of the entrance. Peace and mercy on all your holy people." (Inscriptions in E. L. Sukenik, *HUCA* 23 [1951-52], 541-551, and Frey, *CIJ*, nos. 803, 804, 805). On the basis of this inscription we can establish the family tree of Ilasios on both his father's and his mother's side. And if Ilasios was a middle aged man at the time, i.e. in 391 C.E., his grandfather was active at the beginning of the century.

3) *Tiberias*. A very fragmentary inscription dated in the late 3rd or early 4th century mentions a certain Leontine who was the daughter of Samuel, the gerousiarch of Antioch and wife of Thaumasios, the archisynagogos of Antioch. The inscription, because it is so fragmentary, can be used only to show that members of another family were brought to Israel for burial and that this family also held a prominent position in the Jewish community of Antioch. (M. Schwabe, "On the History of Tiberias," [in Hebrew] in *Sepher Jochanan Levy* [Jerusalem, 1949], ed. M. Schwabe and J. Gutman, pp. 216-221.)

These inscriptions indicate that the Jewish community of Antioch was Greek speaking, that its leaders were men of wealth and standing, which meant that they owned property, that they cherished family ties and traditions, as did the wealthy pagans in the city, and that they received a similar education to that of wealthy pagans. They had close ties with Jews in the neighboring city of Apamaea as well as in Israel and they had the money as well as the social standing and confidence of their own position to contribute to the building and decoration of a neighboring synagogue. The community was organized along lines familiar from other communities in the East, i.e. the gerousia was made up of representatives of the various synagogues in the city, and it served as the governing body for all the Jews in the city.

The Jews of Antioch, who had been there for centuries, assumed that in the future they would have freedom to pursue their way of life, to conduct their own businesses (John Chrysostom mentions that Jews closed their shops early on Friday afternoon because of the Sabbath, PG 51, 176), to build and maintain their own synagogues, and for those with wealth to pass on inheritances to their children, to provide a liberal education for their sons, to seek public office or a profession, to perform liturgies, in short to live with few changes from the way they had lived for centuries. Up to the beginning of the 5th century, the rise of Christianity had little social or legal significance for the Jews in the Roman Empire, except in the matter of non-Jewish slaves. And even in this area, writes Avi Yonah, the "Jews were able to oppose, with distinct success, the edicts [concerning slaves]. And in other economic matters the state did not touch them. Freedom to carry out their commercial affairs was not restricted and most economic activities were carried on as previously. Thus the Jews were permitted to own land and to cultivate it. It was clear also that in the passing of new laws there was still sufficient opportunity for the Jews to carry out their way of life" (*In the Days of Rome and Byzantion* [in Hebrew], p. 184).

Antiochene Jews were friends with Libanius and were treated as equals. Libanius became involved in an internal matter concerning a local Jewish leader, possibly gerousiarch, who was deposed by the community there (*Ep.* 1251; see G. Alon's comments in his *Studies in Jewish History* [in Hebrew], Tel Aviv, 1970, Vol. 2, pp. 315-6). And Libanius wrote a number of letters (*Ep.* 914, 917, 973, 974, 1084, 1085, 1098, 1105) to the Jewish Patriarch in Israel touching on Jewish affairs (M. Schwabe, "Letters of Libanius to the Patriarch in Eretz Israel" [in Hebrew], *Tarbiz* 1 [1930] 85-110).

From Jewish sources we know that Antioch had a Beth Din during this period (*jer Sanhedrin* 3.2; 14a), and that a number of rabbis from Palestine had continuing contacts with the Jews of Antioch. R. Tanhuma bar Abba (4th century), who is noted for his defense of Judaism against non-Jews, had disputes in Antioch (*Gen. Rabbah* 19.4). The issue concerned the use of plural forms to refer to God in the Scriptures (see also *jer Berachoth* 9.1). R. Simlai (3rd century) was also associated with Antioch. According to *jer Kiddushin* (3.13; 35a) R. Simlai rendered a decision concerning the sons of a Mamzer in Antioch. On occasion the Patriarch traveled to Antioch because of dealings with the Roman legate of Palestine who was often in Antioch (*Siphre Num.* 4.22, ed. Friedmann). After the revolt under Gallus two rabbis visited Ursicinus in Antioch and from the account in the Jerusalem Talmud they seemed to be respected by the Roman general and on good terms with him (*jer Berachoth* 5.1; 9a). These scattered references indicate that Jews from Palestine had continuous relations with the Jews of Antioch (and the community outside of the city, *Lev. Rabbah*, 5.3; *Deut. Rabbah* 4.8) and with Roman officials in the city.

From John Chrysostom, who was ordained to the presbyterate in Antioch in 386 C.E., we learn that the Jews observed the Sabbath (PG 51, 176), that they celebrated the three major festivals in the fall, Rosh Hashanah, Yom Kippur, Sukkoth (*Hom. ad Iud.* 1), that they celebrated the Passover (*Hom. ad Iud.* 3), practiced circumcision (*Hom. ad Iud.* 2). They also venerated the Maccabaean martyrs (Malalas 324; E. Bickermann, *Byzantion* 21 [1951] 63-82). It seems that they hoped for the restoration of the temple in Jerusalem and the eventual resettlement of Jerusalem by Jews (*Hom. ad Iud.* 5). This hope was nurtured by Julian's effort to rebuild the temple in 363 C.E. The man appointed by Julian to oversee the rebuilding of the temple, Alypius, was from Antioch. From John we learn that the Jews in Antioch continued to proselytize among non-Jews (*Hom. ad Iud.* 8.4-5). The Jews of Antioch contributed money to the patriarch in Palestine (PG 48, 835). Like Jews elsewhere in the Roman Empire, some of the Jews practiced magic, especially for healing. John complains that the Jewish amulets and incantations are attracting Christians because the Jewish magical rites seem to have greater power. That is, the Jewish magicians were probably more successful than the pagan or Christian magicians (*Hom. ad Iud.* 8). It is likely that the Jews who practiced magic were devout and pious and saw no contradiction between the use of magic and Jewish religion. Magic helped them deal with fears, anxieties, sicknesses, and to soften the abuse and mistreatment lower class citizens received from the wealthy and powerful. The recently discovered book of magic from this period written in Hebrew, the *Sepher HaRazim* (ed. Margoliouth [Jerusalem, 1966], was produced by a person without power and influence, dependent on the whims and desires of those in authority. He uses magic to impress "kings," the "head of a city," a "Judge," or "military officer," or a "rich or famous woman." (*Sepher HaRazim* 1.218-20; 2.45-47; 2.133-34). What this may suggest is that the presence of magic among the Jews of Antioch provides us a glimpse of another side of Antiochene Jewry than what we learn from the Greek inscriptions or the Jerusalem Talmud or Midrashim.

Finally a word about judaizing Christians or Jewish Christianity in Antioch. Here too the most extensive evidence comes from the 4th century, specifically in the writings of John Chrysostom, and in other works from Syria, e.g. the *Apostolic Constitutions*, the Canons of Laodicaea, and the canons of the Council of Antioch in 341. But it is clear from earlier sources, e.g. Ignatius and Theophilus in the 2nd century, and Paul of Samosata, bishop in the 3rd century, that the Jewish presence had a continuing impact on Christianity in the city. John's homilies on the Jews were preached in the fall of 386 immediately prior to the festivals of Rosh Hashanah, Yom Kippur, and Sukkoth (*Hom.* 1.2). He was preaching against the Arians but he broke off that series because, he said, at this time of the year the Jewish festivals come "continuously and one after another" and Christians were joining with the Jews in large numbers. Christians also believed that the synagogue was more holy than the church because the sacred books were kept there; they kept the Pasch according to Jewish calculations; others sided with the Jews against the Catholics on the importance of rebuilding the Jewish temple and continuing to observe the Jewish law. Christians kept the Sabbath with Jews (PG 62.679). The Canons of Laodicaea responding to a similar situation prohibit any intercourse with Jews, e.g. "celebrating festivals with them," "keeping the Sabbath," "eating unleavened bread" during the Pasch, bringing gifts on festival days. Christians were urged to work on the Sabbath and to read the Gospels as well as the Jewish Scriptures on Saturday (Canons 16,29 37,38). The *Apostolic Constitutions* (2.61; 4.17; 6.27) forbid Christians to enter the synagogues of the Jews and probhibit participation in "Jewish feasts," and order them to close their ears to Jews who say "you are unclean because of nocturnal pollutions" or "menstruation."

The existence of large numbers of judaizing Christians in this period is evidence not only of the continuing attraction of Judaism to outsiders, but of the strength and vitality within the Jewish communities in Syria and in Antioch. Other than the cities already mentioned, e.g. Apamaea, Laodicaea, other cities close to Antioch with Jewish communities are Ihmestar near Chalcis (Socrates, *Historia Ecclesiastica* 3.7.16), Aleppo (*CIJ*, 819), Cyrhhus (Theodoret wrote a commentary on Daniel directed against the Jews, PG 81, 1255-1546), Emessa (see Juster, *Les Juifs dans l'Empire Romain* [1914], I, 197). That the Jews in Apamaea would build and decorate a synagogue in the last decade of the 4th century, some ten years after Theodosius' edict *Cunctos populos* making the Empire officially Christian, is testimony not only to their status within the Greek speaking cities of the later Roman Empire but also their confidence in the future. That these hopes and expectations should be disappointed by later events is no evidence that they were misplaced in the 4th century. To the historian looking back from the perspective of a Christian civilization, the events in the 4th century appear to be moving swiftly and inexorably, but neither Jew nor Christian could see this in the 4th century even as late as the last decade. Elias Bickermann writes, "The contemporaries of Chrysostom did not yet know that they were opening the Christian period. Julian was yesterday, the persecutors the day before yesterday. Ambrose knew some magistrates who could boast of having spared Christians. At Antioch the catholics had just endured the persecution of Valens where unbelievers of every sort dominated the capital of Syria. The army, composed of peasants and barbarians, could acclaim tomorrow another Julian, another Valens, even another Diocletian" (*Byzantion* 21 [1951] 82).

S 75 CATALOGUE OF HEBREW LETTERS SEVENTH CENTURY B.C. TO SECOND CENTURY A.D.

Dennis Pardee

	Provenience	Museum No.	Easy Access	*Editio Princeps* or Preliminary Publication
1	Meṣad Ḥashav-yahu (Yavneh Yam)	IDAM 60-67	*TSSI* 1, p.26 *KAI* 200	J. Naveh, *IEJ* 10 (1960) 129-39
2	Lachish II	BM 125 702	*TSSI* 1, p.37 *KAI* 192	H. Torczyner, *The Lachish Letters*, Lachish I (London: Oxford University Press, 1938), No. 2.
3	Lachish III	IDAM 38-127	*TSSI* 1, p.38 *KAI* 193	Ibid., No. 3
4	Lachish IV	IDAM 38-128	*TSSI* 1, p.41 *KAI* 194	Ibid., No. 4
5	Lachish V	BM 125 703	*TSSI* 1, p.43 *KAI* 195	Ibid., No. 5
6	Lachish VI	IDAM 38-129	*TSSI* 1, p.45 *KAI* 196	Ibid., No. 6
7	Lachish VII	BM 125 715		Ibid., No. 7
8	Lachish VIII	BM 125 704		Ibid., No. 8
9	Lachish IX	BM 125 705	*TSSI* 1, p.47 *KAI* 197	Ibid., No. 9
10	Lachish XII	BM 125 713		Ibid., No. 12
11	Lachish XIII	BM 125 714	*KAI* 198	Ibid., No. 13
12	Lachish XVI	BM 125 706		Ibid., No. 16
13	Lachish XVII	BM 125 707		Ibid., No. 17
14	Lachish XVIII	BM 125 708	*TSSI* 1, p.48	Ibid., No. 18
15	Lachish XXI	L 12:1065		D. Diringer in Olga Tufnell *et al.*, *The Iron Age* (London: Oxford University Press, 1953), p. 339 and Pl. 48 A:3.

	Provenience	Museum No.	Easy Access	*Editio Princeps* or Preliminary Publication
16	Arad I	IDAM 67-631	*Inscriptions Reveal*, 2d rev. ed., E. Carmon, ed. (Jerusalem: Israel Museum, 1973), No. 62.	Y. Aharoni, *EI* 9 (1969) 16 (Pl.3, No.2); *BASOR* 197 (1970) 27-32.
17	Arad II	IDAM 72-126	Ibid., No. 56	Unpublished
18	Arad III	IDAM 67-669	*TSSI* 1, p. 52 *Inscriptions* No. 166	Aharoni, *Yediot* 30 (1966) 36 (Pl.1); *IEJ* 16 (1966) 5-6 (Pl. I, B-C).
19	Arad IV	IDAM 67-713	*TSSI* 1, p. 51 *Inscriptions* No. 49	Aharoni, *Yediot* 30 (1966) 33 (Pl.1); *IEJ* 16 (1966) 2-3 (Pl. I, A).
20	Arad V	IDAM 67-623	Ibid., No. 52	Unpublished
21	Arad VI	IDAM 67-625	Ibid., No. 50	Unpublished
22	Arad VII	IDAM 67-627	Ibid., No. 55	Unpublished
23	Arad VIII	IDAM 72-127	Ibid., No. 53	Unpublished
24	Arad IX	IDAM 67-990	Ibid., No. 51	Unpublished
25	Arad X	IDAM 67-624	*TSSI* 1, p. 53 *Inscriptions* No. 54	Aharoni, *BA* 31 (1968) 14 (fig. 9); *BASOR* 184 (1966) 14-16.
26	Arad XI	IDAM 72-721	Ibid., No. 63	Aharoni, *EI* 9 (1969) 10 (Pl.3, No.1); *BASOR* 197 (1970) 17-20.
27	Murabbaat I (papMur 17)		*TSSI* 1, p. 31	*DJD* II, No. 17
28	Murabbaat II (papMur 42)		Y. Yadin, *Bar-Kokhba* (New York: Random House, 1971), pp. 135-36.	Ibid., No. 42
29	Murabbaat III (papMur 43)		Ibid., p. 137	Ibid., No. 43
30	Murabbaat IV (papMur 44)		*Inscriptions* No. 188	Ibid., No. 44
31	Murabbaat V (papMur 45)		Yadin, *Bar-Kokhba*, p.139 (partial)	Ibid., No. 45

	Provenience	Museum No.	Easy Access	*Editio Princeps* or Preliminary Publication
32	Murabbaat VI (papMur 46)		*Inscriptions* No. 194	Ibid., No. 46
33	Murabbaat VII (papMur 47)			Ibid., No. 47
34	Murabbaat VIII (papMur 48)			Ibid., No. 48
35	Naḥal Ḥever I		Yadin, *IEJ* 11 (1961) 43, No. 5 (partial)	Unpublished
36	Naḥal Ḥever II		Ibid., p. 44, No. 7 (partial)	Unpublished
37	Naḥal Ḥever III		Ibid., p. 45 No. 9 (partial)	Unpublished
38	Naḥal Ḥever IV		Ibid., pp. 46-47, No. 12 (partial)	Yadin, *Bar-Kokhba*, p. 133 (partial)
39	Naḥal Ṣeelim		J. T. Milik, *VTSup* 4 (1957) 21 (partial)	Unpublished

Abbreviations:

BA — *Biblical Archaeologist*

BASOR — *Bulletin of the American Schools of Oriental Research*

DJD II — P. Benoit, J. T. Milik, *et al.* *Les grottes de Murabba'ât*, Discoveries in the Judaean Desert II. Oxford: Clarendon Press, 1961.

EI — *Eretz Israel*

IEJ — *Israel Exploration Journal*

KAI — H. Donner and W. Röllig. *Kanaanäische und aramäische Inschriften*. 3 vols. Wiesbaden: Harrassowitz, 1971, 1973, 1969.

TSSI 1 — John C. L. Gibson. *Textbook of Syrian Semitic Inscriptions*. Vol. 1: *Hebrew and Moabite Inscriptions*. Oxford: Clarendon Press, 1971.

VTSup — *Supplements to Vetus Testamentum*

S 81-83 CATEGORIES OF GREEK PAPYRUS LETTERS

Part I: John L. White
Missouri School of Religion

Part II: Keith A. Kensinger
University of Wisconsin-LaCrosse

I

Third and Second Century B.C.E. Letters

Two hundred letters were analyzed from the third and second centuries B.C.E.; one hundred from the third century Zenon archive,[1] fifty from various smaller third century archives and fifty from the second century.[2] These letters seem to fall into three functional categories; orders or instructions, letters of request and letters whose primary purpose is to impart information. These three categories, as well as various subdivisions within each classification, are examined below.

Letters of Request

The writer's primary motivation for writing, in many cases, is his need of something (or various things) from the recipient. The recipient may be requested, for example, to deliver something to someone, to send something to the writer or to send (write) information. Those letters of request which cannot be defined more specifically, according to type, tend to have the following general features. The form of the opening salutation, like most letters in the period, is: "A(=writer) to B(=recipient) χαίρειν(="greeting")" and the closing formula is ἔρρωσο (="farewell"). A health wish may immediately follow the opening address or immediately precede the farewell, both in letters of request and letters of information, if the correspondents are familiar with each other, relatively equal in rank, or family members. The opening health wish usually conveys the writer's concern about the addressee's health and informs the addressee of the writer's own welfare, i.e., εἰ ἔρρωσαι, εὖ ἂν ἔχοι· ὑγίαινον δὲ καὶ ἐγώ ("If you are well, it would be excellent, I too am in good health.").[3] The closing health wish, much less frequent in this period, is simply the wish that the recipient take care of himself, e.g., τὰ ἄλλα σαυτοῦ ἐπιμελόμενος ἵν' ὑγιαίνῃς ("...and for the rest, take care of your health").[4]

More specifically, the occasion of the request is usually given and, since it tends to precede the request, we may refer to it as the "background" element.[5] The request itself is very often expressed as a polite circumlocution for the imperative, i.e., καλῶς οὖν ποιήσεις ("Therefore you would do well to.." or "Please..") and the subject of the request is expressed by means of the aorist participle, e.g., καλῶς οὖν ποιήσεις <u>ἀγοράσας</u>..("Please <u>buy</u>..").[6] Letters of request are sent regularly from inferiors to superiors and between equals, much less often from superiors to inferiors. The request is sometimes strengthened, either by the writer's promise to repay the favor or by referring to the negative consequence(s) (sometimes expressed as a threat) that may result from failure to fulfil the request.[7]

We may now identify the discrete types of letters of request: letters of recommendation (ἡ ἐπιστολὴ συστατική), petitions (ἡ ἔντευξις) and memoranda (τὸ ὑπόμνημα). Letters of recommendation were identified by ancient letter theorists and they have been analyzed formally by modern authors.[8] The following elements are characteristic: the salutation is "A to B χαίρειν" and ἔρρωσο is the farewell, often followed immediately by the date. A health wish is sometimes expressed, after the salutation, in the opening. The opening phrase in the body concerns the credentials of the letter bearer (the one being recommended) and/or his relation to the writer, e.g., in P.Mich.I, 33, 2-8, Νικάνωρ ὁ τὴν ἐπιστολήν σοι ἀποδιδούς ἐστιν ἡμῶν ἐν φιλίαι, ἀποδεδήμηκεν δὲ πρὸς ὑμᾶς διὰ τὸ τὸν υἱὸν αὐτοῦ εἶναι τῶν ἐπιγόνων τῶν καταμεμετρημένων ἐν τῶι Ἀρσινοείτηι ("Nikanor who is handing you this letter is a friend of ours, and he has gone on a journey to your district on account of his son being one of the epigonoi who have received allotments in the Arsinoïte province"). This formula is followed, in turn, by a request on the letter bearer's behalf, e.g., in the lines immediately following the preceding quotation, καλῶς ἂν οὖν ποιήσαις ἐπιμέλειαν ποιούμενος αὐτοῦ περὶ ὧν ἄν σοι ἐντυγχάνηι· ("Be kind enough then to show him consideration in any matter about which he may speak to you;.."). Then, the writer states that the recipient will favor him by aiding the letter bearer and/or he promises to repay the favor, e.g., once again in P.Mich.I,33 (11-13), ..χαριεῖ γάρ μοι. γράφε δὲ καὶ σὺ ἡμῖν περὶ ὧν ἂν βούληι ("..; for you will be doing a favor to me. And write to us yourself about anything that you may desire at any time").[9]

All but one of the letters of recommendation in this study (P.Teb.I,20, which is a questionable example) are from the Zenon archive. Given the social relations of correspondents in these letters, we may deduce that letters of recommendation tend to involve equals of relatively high social rank, that they are personal, friendly and private (not official) letters.[10]

Petitions are letters submitted by inferiors (almost always) to officials for redress of some injustice or grievance[11] or, in the case of private letters of petition, they are sent, generally, as a plea for help. The following elements are common: the salutation is either "To B χαίρειν A" or "To B παρὰ A" and the word of farewell is εὐτύχει. Note that the recipient's name is written prior to the writer's, signalling the recipient's superiority in the epistolary situation. The health wish is not used in petitions. The first item in the body is the plaintiff's recital of the facts which necessitate the request (the "background" portion of the petition), followed by a formulaic request for redress (the customary verbs of entreaty are ἀξίω, δέομαι and ἱκετεύω) and, near the close of the petition, it is customary for the petitioner either to appeal pathetically for help and/or to state the anticipated benefit that the recipient will render.

Several letters in this study are petitions in the official sense,[12] but a number are private in nature and all of these are addressed to the influential Zenon. Two were sent to Zenon by correspondents of comparable social rank (P.Col.Zen.I,6 and 9) and their equality is reflected by the order of names in the salutation (the writers' names are in first position) and by the correspondents' promise to return the favor. Nevertheless, the letters are clearly petitions (see the letter contents, the stereotyped language, and the word of farewell, εὐτύχει). We may explain the recourse to petition, in these two cases, either by means of the lack of familiarity between correspondents and/or the exigencies of the situation(s) which necessitated the special entreaty. The seven remaining private petitions[13] may be accounted for by observing that all were written by Zenon's inferiors. In these cases, lack of rank may have been the most important factor in the use of the petition format.[14]

The memorandum may also function as a type of letter of request. Four of the six memoranda in this sampling are from inferiors (P.Hib.II,240; P.Col.Zen.I,44;II,86; P.Mich.I,100), one is between equals (PSI IV,413) and one is from a superior (P.Col.Zen.II,107). Consequently, this epistolary type functioned in various ways, i.e., as a means of conveying instructions (superior to inferior), as a means of making a request (inferior to superior) or as a reminder (between equals). The five memoranda from inferiors, or between equals, may all be considered a type of letter of request, formally akin to letters of petition. For example, four of the five have ὑπόμνημα to B παρά A ("Memorandum to the recipient from the writer") in the salutation and three of the four take εὐτύχει as the word of farewell. Again, the body of the letter commences with a recital of the circumstances which occasion a subsequent request.[15]

Letters of Information

The primary motivation for many letters is the need to impart information and this information is often stated explicitly as a disclosure, e.g., a word of disclosure may introduce the body of the letter (usually in the imperative mood in this period, γίνωσκε ("Know..") or γνώριζε ("Recognize..") or, occasionally, a formulaic phrase of disclosure closes the body (γέγραφα οὖν σοι ἵνα εἰδῇς="Therefore I wrote to you that you may know").[16] The information is sometimes sent in response to previous correspondence, as actual references to such correspondence (e.g., the formula, ἐκομισάμην τὴν ἐπιστολὴν ἣ ἔγραψας καί..="I received the letter which you wrote and.." or ἔγραψας μοι ὅτι..="You wrote me that.."),[17] or more oblique references to writing (either περὶ δὲ τοῦ.. or ὑπὲρ δὲ τοῦ..="concerning the.."), attest.

A few specific types of letter of information may be identified. For example, the writer occasionally states that he has acted in accordance with the recipient's instructions. The following examples illustrate this kind of letter.

C.P.Jud.I,5,1ff., καθάπερ μοι ἔγραψας ἀποστεῖλαι τῶι βασιλεῖ.., "Just as you wrote I sent to the king.."

P.Mich.I,12,2ff., ἐκομισάμεν τὴν ἐπιστολὴν ἣν ἔγραψας..καὶ ἀπέστειλα..καθὰ ἔγραψας. "I received the letter that you wrote..and..I sent..as you wrote."

P.Col.Zen.I,15,1ff., ἔγραψας μοι δοῦναι..ἔσται οὖν ὥσπερ ἐφεσταλκας. "You wrote me to give.. It will be carried out, therefore, as you ordered."

P.Cair.Zen.III,59426,3f., καὶ καθότι μοι ἔγραψας..ποιοῦμαι.. "..and in accordance with what you wrote to me.., I am taking.."[18]

I designate these letters, for want of a more precise name, "Letters of compliance," i.e., the writer sends information in accordance with the recipient's instructions. Though the addressor's name is in first position in the opening address (this could suggest the equality of the correspondents), and the word of farewell is ἔρρωσο, most of these letters appear to be reports from inferiors. The only recognizable convention in the body of the letter is the statement of compliance, indicated by the words καθάπερ (or καθότι, καθά, ὥσπερ) μοι ἔγραψας ("Just as you wrote"), underlined in the above examples.

Another kind of letter of information is the epistolary receipt. It may be set out explicitly as an acknowledgment of the receipt of payment for something, e.g., ὁμολογῶι ἔχειν παρ' ὑμῶν.., "I acknowledge that I have received from you.." (P.Amh. II,55,4. See also P.Teb.I,11) or, more often in the letters of this survey, as a simple notice of the addressee's payment of something, e.g., ἔχω παρα Πτολεμαίου.., "I have received from Ptolemaios.." (P.Yale 47,3f. See also P.Col.Zen.II,84; P.Amh. II,56 and 57). Neither the opening address or the closing is unusual in these epistolary receipts except, like many other legal documents, various credentials of the correspondents (e.g., vocation, patronymic, residence) are cited in connection with their names in the salutation. And, like many legal documents, the date of the receipt is stated within the body of the letter and/or after the word of farewell.[19]

Orders and Instructions

The final epistolary category in this sampling concerns the orders which a superior sends to his underlings, whether they be subordinate government officials or employees. Though the use of the imperative mood of the verb is not restricted to epistolary orders, and though orders are not always conveyed by the imperative, it is used considerably more often in orders than in other kinds of letters. Commands are often sent without any explanation. Other times, like letters of request, an explanation is given (=the "background") for the instructions.

It was suggested previously that the writer may strengthen his request by promising to repay the favor or, negatively, by threatening the recipient. The negative dimension abounds in epistolary orders, as the numerous conventions spawned by the process attest. The superiority of the writer and/or the assumed incompetence of the recipient is reflected, broadly, in three ways: (i) by reference to the unnecessary delay and/or negligence of the recipient; (ii) by the demand for immediate and/or responsible action; (iii) by the writer's threat(s). Reference to the addressee's negligence or delay is sometimes the introductory statement in the body of the letter and it may be set out in stereotyped phrases, e.g., by referring to former correspondence on the same matter, by charging the addressee directly with negligence or senselessness or by expressing astonishment at the addressee's behavior.[20] The demand for urgency or responsibility, another type of coercive measure, appears at various points in the body. And, the command to do something immediately upon receipt of a letter, the general emphasis upon haste, the command to come or go quickly, the command to act in accord with some instruction(s) or for the recipient to make something a matter of concern, are all conventional means of expressing this kind of emphasis.[21] The third type of coercion, which the writer may use, is the threat. It is usually stated after the instructions and immediately preceding the farewell or date (many epistolary orders do not have a word of farewell). The threat is often expressed with the phrase, μὴ οὖν ἄλλως ποιήσηις ("Therefore, do not act otherwise") or a near equivalent, εἰ δ' ἄλλως ἔσται ("If you should act otherwise..").[22] Less frequently, there is the phrase, ὡς πρὸς σὲ τοῦ λόγου ἐσομένου ("knowing that you will be held accountable").[23] Also, various uses of the conditional clause and the imperative are employed to make threats.

Though the aforementioned stereotyped phrases and/or other concatenation of items may prove, eventually, a means of positing identifiable types of epistolary orders, I am not presently able to make such distinctions. When orders upon a bank[24] or notifications of payments due to the bank[25] are in epistolary form, however, they are readily identifiable. Another possible type of epistolary instruction is the memorandum from a superior. But, though such memoranda are referred to occasionally in the present sampling, only one memorandum actually occurs[26] and it will be necessary to expand the sampling before drawing any conclusions.

Observations, Problems, Epistolary Aspects Needing Analysis

One major functional epistolary category which did not appear in this third and second century B.C.E. sampling was family letters. There are letters between family members but the kind of letter so common in the Roman period, whose primary or sole intent is the maintenance of personal contact, does not appear. All the letters in this study have a more specific occasion for being written.

Regarding the preceding classification of letters according to function--letters of request, letters of information and orders--the majority of these letters will probably resist more specific identification according to type. Moreover, many letters serve more than one function, e.g., a writer may request something, as well as convey information and, if the correspondents are friends or family members, the letter may serve the additional purpose of maintaining contact.

Nevertheless, I am not suggesting either that letters are formless or that classification is impossible. I am suggesting that we must often recognize the variegated function of letters and that we should have the total contours in mind when classification is made. Having recognized these difficulties, it can be stated, positively, that letters serve more or less customary purposes and there are, generally speaking, a limited number of conventions at hand to express these functions. Moreover, the limited range of many conventions often facilitate broad classification, quickly and accurately. For example, the use of either the formulaic promise to repay a favor or the health wish assumes the relative equality of the correspondents, as well as a degree of familiarity. Hence, it is unlikely that letters with these conventions are epistolary orders. Or, by contrast, if the petition-type address or closing is employed (the kind of letter written by inferiors), one should not expect to see the health wish, the promise to repay a favor or similar conventions which assume a degree of cordiality and social equality. Exceptions to these rules exist, to be sure, but, in these instances, we should seek the social exigencies which have produced the unexpected.

Regarding the problematic areas of this research, much of the usual opinion regarding the order of names in the salutation and the nature of epistolary clichés is unsatisfactory. It has been suggested, for example, that the order of names in the salutation is a guide for determining the relative rank of the correspondents, i.e., if the writer's name is first, he is either the superior or an equal and, if the writer's name is in second position, he is the inferior. On the basis of my examples, the order of names in the salutation is not a sure guide for determining rank. Regarding the use of clichés, since many appear to recur in specific epistolary categories (e.g., the cliché, εἰ ὑμῖν δοκεῖ, "if it seems good to you," is found in letters making a request, especially petitions), the notion that clichés are an accidental type of statement also seems unsatisfactory. Both of these areas need to be reconsidered.

Regarding the epistolary aspects that were not treated in this analysis, but which should be kept in mind as the Epistolography Group continues, the following seem noteworthy. The function of the attributes, credentials or other qualifying words, which are used in connection with the correspondents' names in the salutation, should be examined in connection with the various epistolary types. Another matter warranting consideration is the manner in which first ("rough") drafts of letters and letters quoted in another letter (=appended letters) seem to be abbreviated versions of the good clean copy and the original, respectively. That is to say, was it customary to abbreviate first drafts and appended letters according to an established manner? Thirdly, it would probably be worthwhile to examine the manner in which letters were docketed when received. And, finally, do letters that bear a date--or, more specifically, letters which state the date in a specified manner or at a certain point--belong to specific epistolary categories?

II
Second and Third Century C.E. Letters

Two hundred letters, from the second and third centuries C.E., were examined; forty-one from the University of Michigan collection (P.Mich.), ninety-eight from the Oxyrhynchus collection (P.Oxy.), and sixty-one from other smaller collections.[1] It is possible to classify these letters according to the categories delineated in section one of this paper, namely, letters to inform, letters of request, and orders or instructions.[2] The dominant feature of these letters is that they reflect familial relationships. In one hundred twenty-five the address suggests family connections, e.g., they are addressed to πάτηρ, μήτηρ, ἄδελφος, ἀδέλφη, τέκνον, υἱός, υἷα and σύμβιος.[3] The structural features of the "family" letters, however, appear to be the same as, or similar to, the aforementioned categories.

Letters of Information

The desire to keep others informed motivated many letter writers in this study. And, the information is frequently expressed as a form of disclosure. Forty-one letters employed the disclosure formula, γινώσκειν σε θελῶ ("I wish you to know.."), six used the imperative, γίνωσκε ("Know.."), while seven conclude the background period of the body with the phrase, "..ἵνα εἰδῇς.." ("..in order that you may know.."). Eight other letters employ less common expressions of disclosure.

The disclosure formula usually introduces or concludes the "background" period of the letter, the portion of the letter that precedes a request. Only four letters (BGU,I,261;P.Mich. VIII,475;480;493) may be classified, formally, as letters of information. The epistolary structure of such letters is, usually, the salutation, "A(=writer) to B(=recipient) χαίρειν," the body, introduced by the disclosure formula,and the closing, with its greeting and health wish (ἐρρῶσθαί σε εὔχομαι).[4]

Information may be introduced also by referring to previous correspondence, e.g., the phrases, ἔγραψας μοι..("You wrote to me..") and ἔγραψα σοι.. ("I wrote to you.."), introduce reports of compliance, recommendations or personal circumstances. This information, like that which follows disclosure formulae, is often part of letters which serve additional purposes.

Letters of Request

Letters of request seem to differ from orders and instructions in respect to their use of formulae, not because of difference of content. The letter of request usually has the following letter elements: the opening salutation, the body, which includes a request formula, and the closing. The salutation is, ordinarily, "A to B χαίρειν" and the relation of writer and recipient is often conveyed by means of qualifying words in the salutation (including familial, vocational, honorific, or personal emotional titles). The word greeting in the salutation, χαίρειν, may be modified by such words as πλεῖστα and πόλλα. The letter opening may also include expressions described by H. Koskenniemi as parousia (="presence") phrases. These include the health wish and the greeting.[5]

It is not always clear where the letter-opening concludes and the body begins. For example, is the formulaic phrase in P.Amh.,II,133, πρὸ τῶν ὅλων ἀσπάζομαι καὶ εὐχαριστῶ σαι ὅτι ἐδηλοσάς μοι τὴν ὑγείαν σου ("Above all I greet you and thank you for telling me of your health."), a letter-opening formula or the introductory phrase in the body?[6]

The body of the letter of request divides into two parts, the background and the request. The background consists either of general information or of conventional phrases.[7] In some cases, the background material follows the request.[8] The request itself employs two distinct formulae: the "petition" formula and the "favor" formula. These two formulae distinguish letters of request from orders and letters of instruction.[9]

The letter of request, like most letters, has a closing section. It may consist of as many as six items, five of which appear to be formulaic. They are: (1) the closing greeting (ἀσπάζομαι or προαγορεύω), (2) the health wish (generally ἐρρῶσθαί σε εὔχομαι), (3) the ἐπιμελέσθαι period, (4) the farewell formula (generally ἔρρωσο), (5) the date, and (6) miscellaneous matters. Letters of the ii and iii C.E. usually employ one or more of these elements (most often the greeting, the health wish and the date).

Some of the letters of this study were "simple" letters of request, i.e., they consisted of the opening salutation, the body, composed of the background and request, and the closing. A number of letters, however, were more complex; consisting of multiple requests or a combination of request and orders or instructions. The latter require their own analysis.

Letters of Order and Instruction

One hundred twenty-seven of the two hundred ii and iii C.E. letters examined contain orders and/or instructions (or requests not framed in formulaic language). The order or letter of instruction may be directed by a superior to his underlings or employees or they may be sent between family members. The body consists of the background and the instruction or order. The instruction or order may include the following items: (1) the verb, usually in the aorist imperative mood, though occasionally in the future indicative or subjunctive mood, (2) the attenuating or circumstantial phrase, (3) the predicate complements, and (4) the causal or resultative clauses. The order or instruction period may also include an inferential conjunction (οὖν or δέ).

The writer may reinforce his request in various ways, it was suggested in section one, by promise of special favor or by threatening the addressee. Family letters are especially replete with conventions conveying the writer's attitude toward the recipient. These matters frequently form the background segment of the letter, though they may close the request period. The threat is most often the concluding sentence in the body. It is not known, presently, whether the clichés, designated by Steen as "expressions of intensity or severity" belong to a particular type of letter.

General Letters, Observations, and Issues for Further Study

Several letters of this ii and iii C.E. study do not fall into the three epistolary classifications suggested above. Many may be considered "family" letters or letters of friendship.[10] Condolence is expressed,in P.Oxy.,I,116, to the bereaved of Eumoerus, following his death.[11] And, P.Flor.,II, 176 is a letter of criticism; containing no explicit orders, requests or instruction. It lacks the usual social amenities in the salutation and the closing.

It is not clear at this stage in the study of ii and iii C.E. letters what may be considered the distinguishing features of the "family" letter. If the family letter has as its primary intent the maintenance of personal contact, further analysis is necessary to determine those structural and formulary items which distinguish them from other letter types.

The function of credentials, attributes, and other identifying designations of the correspondents, both in the salutation and elsewhere in the letter (in the vocative case), requires further study. It is not clear, at this stage of the study, when the title ἀδελφος ("brother"),or its female equivalent, refers to a familial relationship and when it refers to a collegial relation. Nor is it clear when this and similar terms indicate the relative rank of correspondents.

Notes to Part One

[1]The Zenon archive, found in the Fayum area of Egypt near ancient Philadelphia, spans a period of about a quarter of a century. Zenon spent most of this period in uninterrupted relation with his chief, Apollonios, the dioiketes of Ptolemy II ("Philadelphus"). For a good treatment of the archive, cf. M. Rostovtzeff, A Large Estate (Madison, Wisc., 1922) and C. C. Edgar, "Introduction," Zenon Papyri in the University of Michigan Collection (Ann Arbor, 1931), 1-60.

Abbreviations for editions of papyri, in this study, conform to those proposed by J. Oates, R. Bagnall and W. Willis in their "Checklist of Editions of Greek Papyri and Ostraca," BASP 11, No.1(1974). P.Col.Zen.I,7,1f.,for example, refers to the Columbia Papyri, volume one of the Zenon Papyri, document number seven, line one and following. Dates are indicated thus: i, ii and iii refer to the first, second and third century, with the qualification B.C.E. or C.E. immediately following.

[2]The small number of second century B.C.E. letters is due, in part, to the smaller number of extant letters from the period and, partly, to the author's greater unfamiliarity with letters of this period.

[3]Exx. of the health wish in the iii B.C.E. Zenon correspondence: P.Col.Zen.I,7,1f.;9,1f.;10,1ff.;P.Mich.I,10,1 and 6f.; 13,1f.;23,1f.;55,1ff.;58,2ff.;C.P.Jud.I,4,1ff.;PSI V,500,1f.; 502,1f. Due to the administrative nature of the correspondence (written by superiors to inferiors), only one letter in the iii B.C.E. correspondence other than Zenon contains a health wish (P.Yale 42,2ff.). The health wish is relatively frequent, however, in private letters and between epistolary equals in the period, e.g., cf. the elaborate health formula in P.Hib.I, 79,2ff. (*ca*.260 B.C.E.). Exx. in the ii B.C.E.: P.Par.43,1f.; P.Teb.III,755,2ff. Note that in the ii B.C.E. the health wish begins to be combined syntactically with the opening greeting, i.e., A to B χαίρειν *και ἐρρῶσθαι* ("A to B greeting *and good-health*." Exx.: P.Par.49,1f.;P.Teb.I,12,1f.;20,1;55,2;754,1f.).

[4]The closing health wish appears to be more frequent in the ii than in the iii B.C.E. Exx.: P.Teb.I,12,12f. and 26 (letter draft);19,14f.;20,10;55,9f.;P.Par.49,36.

[5]When the request itself is the first item in the body, the information that would have been given as the occasion ("background") for the request is stated subsequently by ἐπει (ἐπειδή), ἵνα, ὅπως or γάρ clauses.

[6]Exx. of the καλῶς οὖν ποιήσεις formula in Zenon: P.Ryl.IV, 557 and 558;P.Col.Zen.I,16;P.Mich.I,21;22;28;32;34;43;48;55;69; 72;PSI V,502. Exx. in other iii B.C.E. letters: P.Yale 29;40; 42;P.Hib.I,63;65-66;II,206;P.Teb.III,745. Exx. in ii B.C.E. letters: P.Teb.I,23;III,755;764;767;P.Amh.II,41;P.Par.43.

[7]Exx. of the promise to repay a favor in Zenon: P.Col.Zen. I,3;7,4f.;9-10;16;P.Mich.I,6,5-7;10;23;33,11f.;42,5f.;69,7f. (favor only,no promise);85,5-7;PSI IV,333,16f.;P.Cair.Zen.V, 59804,11f.;59805,3f.;59823,8f. Ex. in other iii B.C.E.: P.Hib. I,66,4f. Exx. in ii B.C.E.: P.Teb.I,12,25f.;55,6ff. (only statement of favor the recipient will render).

Exx. of negative consequences following from failure to fulfil the request in Zenon: P.Mich.I,21,7f.;22,6-8;55,6ff.; 72,17ff.

[8]Cf. Clinton W. Keyes, "The Greek Letter of Introduction," *American Journal of Philology* 56(1935), 28-44 and Chan-Hie Kim, *Form and Structure of the Familiar Greek Letter of Recommendation*, SBL Dissertation Series, no.4 (SBL,1972).

[9]The writer's statement regarding the recipient's favor in aiding the recommended is combined syntactically, on occasion, with the request for recommendation, e.g., in P.Cair.Zen.V, 59805,3-5, χαριεῖ δή μοι σπουδάσας τε ὅπως ὅ τι τάχος λάβηι καὶ ἐὰν καταπλῆι πλοῖον ἐπιβιβάσας αὐτόν· ἔστι γὰρ ἄπερος· εἰ δὲ μή, τό γε κερμάτιον λαβὼν παρ' αὐτοῦ ἐσφραγισμένον καὶ ἀποστείλας πρὸς ἡμᾶς, ἵν' ἀποδῶμεν ἡμεῖς αὐτοῖς. ἔρρωσο. ("You will do me a favor, then, if you help him to obtain it as soon as possible and put him on a boat if any is sailing down, for he is inexperienced, or else take the money from him under seal and send it to us to pay them. Farewell.").

[10]We could draw similar conclusions on linguistic grounds, e.g., both the promise to repay the favor and the general

function of letters of recommendation suggest the social equality of correspondents. Letters of recommendation: P.Col. Zen.I,7 and 41;P.Mich.I,6 and 33;P.Cair.Zen.II,59192;V,59805 and 59853. P.Col.Zen.I,48 and II,111, though fragmentary, are probably letters of recommendation. P.Col.Zen.I,11;II,112 and P.Teb.I,20, though not using the conventional phrases, appear to function like, and/or have affinities with, letters of recommendation. Epistolography Group members may refer to letters 5, 47 and 72 of the Kim and White, <u>Letters From the Papyri</u>.

[11]Regarding the petitioning process, as well as bibliographical information, see the introductory comments to letters 95-98 of Kim and White, <u>Letters From the Papyri</u>. See Gueraud, Ἐντευξις, pp.xxii-xxvii and John L. White, <u>Form and Structure of the Official Petition</u> (SBL,1972), concerning letter elements and the conventional phrases.

[12]See P.Col.Zen.II,83;P.Teb.I,40-41;43;45;III,771;P.Amh.II, 33;P.Ryl.IV,557 and, though fragmentary, P.Col.Zen.II,72. See letters 95-97 in the Kim and White handbook.

[13]P.Mich.I,29;46;87;C.P.Jud,I,12;P.Cair.Zen.V,59838; 59852;P.Col.Zen.II,66.

[14]Had these writers been higher up the social ladder, we can imagine them writing a different type of letter. This is intimated in three of the letters which use the polite circumlocution, καλῶς ἂν οὖν ποιήσαις, instead of the usual petitionary words (i.e., καλῶς ἂν ποιήσαις is used in ordinary private letters of request) and in one of the letters, though the ordinary petition-type conventions are used in the body, the writer's name is in first position in the salutation and the word ἔρρωσο is used in the closing (i.e.,the ordinary salutation and farewell in common Greek letters, suggesting the writer's sense of inferiority led him to couch his request in the form of a petition).

[15]Epistolography Group members may refer to letters 51 and 52 in the Kim and White handbook for examples of this letter type.

[16]Opening disclosure formulae in Zenon: P.Mich.I,6,1f.; 28,f;32,1;P.Cair.Zen.V,59812,1;P.Col.Zen.II,70,2;103,2. No iii B.C.E. letters,other than Zenon in this study, had opening disclosure formulae. Exx. from ii B.C.E.: P.Teb.III,764,2; 12,2ff.

Closing disclosure formulae in Zenon: P.Cair.Zen.V,59804, 10f.;59812,3;P.Col.Zen.I,3,10f.;51,22;II,102,5;C.P.Jud.I,5,7; 4,5;6,8;P.Ryl.IV,557,6. Ex. from iii B.C.E. other than Zenon: P.Teb.III,747,16ff. Exx. from ii B.C.E.: P.Par.43,4;P.Teb.I, 15,10f.;16,21f.;26,21-23.

[17]Exx. in Zenon: P.Mich.I,12;28,1ff.;PSI V,502,11ff.; P.Cair.Zen.V,59815,1f. Exx. from other iii B.C.E. letters: P.Yale 30,3f.;29,2ff.;P.Teb.748,2f. Exx. from ii B.C.E.: P.Teb.I,12,2ff. and 15f.;19,2ff.;21,2ff.;III,764,28.

[18]Exx. in Zenon: P.Mich.I,43,4;PSI IV,333,5 and 12. Other iii B.C.E. letters: P.Hib.I,41,8f.;51,2f.;P.Yale 33,3;32,6f.; 36,2-4;39,9f.;P.Teb.III,746,31f. Exx. from ii B.C.E.: P.Teb.I, 27,9,14f.,23,89,92;26,4-6 and 9.

[19]See letters 107 and 108 in the Kim and White handbook.

[20]Reference to former correspondence: P.Hib.I,44,1. Reference to negligence: P.Hib.I,44,4;46,10ff. Reference to the recipient's senselessness: P.Yale 39,3ff.;P.Col.Zen.II,121,1ff.; P.Teb.III,758,4ff. Expression of astonishment: P.Teb.I,27,34 (cf.P.Cair.Zen.I,59060,10).

[21]Exx. of the command to act immediately upon receipt of a letter: C.P.Jud.I,9,1f.;P.Mich.I,43,6f.;P.Hib.I,44,5;45,3f.; 57,1f.;58,2ff.;59,2ff.;61,2f.;P.Teb.III,748,8ff.;749,1f.;I,26, 2f.;27,83f.;P.Col.Zen.II,121,4ff.;122,2ff. Emphasis upon haste: P.Cair.Zen.V,59815,4;P.Col.Zen.I,42,1;44,6f.;46,3f.;62,10f. The command to go or come quickly: P.Yale 34,2; 32,2f. The command to responsibility: "Take care that.."(φρόντισον ὅπως) and "Make it a concern that.." (ἐπιμέλειαν δὲ ποίησαι ὅπως): P.Teb. I,27,21,27,60,92,95;10,6f.;33,2;P.Hib.I,41,20f.;43,5ff.

[22]P.Mich.I,72,20;P.Col.Zen.II,122,5f.;103,12;P.Cair.Zen.V, 59824,3f.;P.Hib.I,58,11f.;60,8f.;62,16;69,8f.

[23]P.Hib.I,53,3f.;P.Teb.I,27,5f.

[24]P.Col.Zen.I,45;P.Hib.I,67 and 68.

[25]P.Hib.I,163;70(a);70(b).

[26]The memorandum is written as a postscript in P.Col.Zen. I,107. See the reference to a memorandum from a superior in PSI V,500,2.

Notes to Part Two

[1]Seven letters are from the Amherst Papyri (P.Amh.), eighteen from Aegyptische Urkunden aus den Staatlichen Museen zu Berlin, Griechische Urkunden (BGU), four from the Papiri greco-egizii, Papiri Fiorentini (P.Flor.), eight from the Griechische Papyri im Museum des oberhessischen Geschichtsvereins zu Giessen (P.Giss.), four from A Descriptive Catalogue of the Greek Papyri in the Collection of Wilfrid Merton(P.Mert.), and twenty from fourteen miscellaneous sources.

[2]Judgment must be reserved on the adequacy of these categories until the broad spectrum of data is examined. They will serve as temporary frames of reference.

[3]Twenty-one of the letters identify the relationship of the writer to the recipient as πάτηρ, seventeen as μήτηρ, fifty-four as ἄδελφος (or its plural), nineteen as ἄδέλφη, six as τέκνον, eleven as υἱός or υἷα and five as σύμβιος. Some of the occurences of ἄδελφος clearly refer to a husband-wife relationship rather than to that of brother and sister. In P.Grenf.II,73 ἄδελφος is employed in a Christian context as "a brother in the Lord," that is, as a fellow member of the Christian community.

[4]Ten letters follow this general structure but lack a specific disclosure formula; six were written exclusively to impart information.

[5]The customary health wish in the ii and iii C.E. is the ὑγιαίνειν-wish. Like the ἐρρῶσθαι-wish, in earlier periods, the health wish has two parts. The ὑγιαίνειν wish differs from its earlier counterpart in the following way. In the ἐρρῶσθαι wish the sentence was conditional (εἰ...ἄν, "If...,then.."); the protasis expressing the writer's concern for the reader and the apodosis expressing the writer's own situation. In the ὑγιαίνειν wish, the entire wish expresses concern for the recipient. The first part expresses hope that the reader is well (usually

πρὸ (μὲν) πάντων εὔχομαι σε ὑγιαίνειν(ὁλοκλήρειν), "Above all, I pray for your health.") and the second part intensifies the first part through the use of the proscynesis(prayer) phrase (usually τὸ προσκύνημα σου ποιῶ τῷ κυρίῳ Σαράπιδι, "I make prayer for you to the Lord Sarapis.."). This concern for the addressee's welfare is frequently repeated in the letter closing.

The greeting wish (ἀσπάζομαι) is less frequent in the letter opening than the health wish. It is more common in the closing.

[6]In BGU I,332 and IV,1081, the entire letter concerns matters of health.

[7]For example, the following conventional phrases are used: the disclosure formulae, the wonder element (introduced by θαυμάζω, "I am amazed..," or a similar expression. Cf.P.Mich.III, 209; VIII,479;500), a reference to previous correspondence, or an expression of thanksgiving (introduced by εὐχαριστῶ, χάρις or ἐχάρην. Cf.BGU I,332;II,423;IV,1081;P.Mich.VIII,465;473; 474;498).

[8]P.Mich.VIII,507 and P.Teb.II,412 are examples of letters in which the background follows the request.

[9]The "petition" formula reflects the style of the formal petition. Its structure may consist of (1) the petition verb (παρακαλέω, ἐρωτάω, ἀξίω and δέομαι), (2)the address (σέ, sometimes the vocative is added), (3) the desired action expressed by the imperative, the infinitive, or the participle, (4) the causal or resultative clause, (5) the attentuating phrase, and (6) the inferential conjunctive (A common feature in the letter is the use of μέν...οὖν or μέν...δέ. The μέν generally occurs in the letter opening, i.e., πρὸ μὲν πάντων. The conjunction οὖν occurs in the initial phrase of the request period, i.e., καλῶς οὖν ποιῶ. Cf. BGU I,332;II,423;P.Bour.23. The conjunction is also used in the request period when μέν is employed. Further study of this feature is warranted).

The "favor" formula is the most frequent stylistic device of the ii or iii C.E. request. The structure of the formula is commonly (1) καλῶς ποιήσεις ("You do well.." or "Please.."), (2) the desired action, expressed by a participial phrase, an infinitive clause, an imperative, or a verb in the second person indicative or subjunctive, (3) the vocative, (4) the causal or resultative clause, (5) the attenuating circumstance phrase, and (6) the inferential conjunction (cf. P.Giss.III,97 and P.Oxy.VIII,1158).

The attentuating circumstance clause appears to be optional in both of the above formulae. Such clauses are variously described as "courtesy" phrases, modifying expressions, and conditional phrases (Note the formulae identified in Steen's Tables Chronologiques, in A.H.Steen, "Les Clichés epistolaires dans Lettres sur papyrus grecques," Classica et Mediaevalia, I(1938), pp.168-172). These phrases suggest the customary hindrances which could interfere with the recipient's execution of the desired action. The attentuating circumstance clause seems to be more common in orders (or letters of instruction), but the number in letters of request warrants inclusion in the structure of letters of request.

Chan-Hie Kim identified an additional structural unit in the request period, earlier in the Epistolography Group's research, the concluding sentence. Three types of concluding sentence may be identified, on the basis of this sampling:

(1) the repeated request, (2) the appreciation sentence, and (3) the warning sentence (repeated requests: P.Mich.III,202; VIII,508b;P.Oxy.VII,1068;BGU I,164;P.Amh.II,133;RevEg 1919, p.201; Appreciation sentences: P.Oxy.XIV,1672;P.Mich.VIII, 485. The Warning sentence: BGU III,816;P.Mich.VIII,507.).

[10]Three "family" letters desire information about the well-being of a family member (P.Mich.VIII,494;P.Oxy.I,117; 118). Several letters merely share information about a personal situation (P.Oxy.IX,1217;X,1296) or express the desire to see family members in the near future (P.Oxy.XIV, 1761).

[11]The letter was sent by a certain Irene, who was acting in concert with other concerned people. The salutation does not contain the usual word of greeting, χαίρειν, but the word, εὐψύχειν. The letter closes with the infrequent expression, εὖ πράττετε.

S 90 THE ORACULAR STYLE OF THE CULTIC PROCLAMATIONS OF ANTIOCHUS I OF COMMAGENE

Robert W. Allison
University of Chicago

The famous inscription from the syncretic Greco-Persian cult at Nemrud Dağ, the highest peak in ancient Commagene, was one of a series of similar texts set up by Antiochus I of Commagene (who ruled from before 69 to *ca.* 35 B.C.) in his reform of the state cult. At each cult site throughout Commagene where the state cult was to be held the text was inscribed on stone, with variations related to the history and character of the particular site.[1] Thus, Nemrud Dağ, central sanctuary of the state cult under Antiochus, was also to be his hierothesion, *i.e.*, his tomb and site of its attendant services. Arsameia-on-the-Euphrates was the ancestral burial ground of his dynasty down to his father, Mithradates I Callinicus. Arsameia-on-the-Nymphaeus was the site chosen by Mithradates for his own hierothesion.

These texts are cultic foundation documents (*Stiftungsurkunden*). They conform to the broad outline commonly in use throughout the ancient Near East for sacral and civil codes of law: superscription, proem, law, epilogue, and a series of curses and blessings. The law, central to the conception of the text, is set off in every inscription with the title, *Nomos*. It promulgates a series of prior enactments which included selection and development of a site, establishment of the monthly and yearly festivals of the state cult, and endowment of the festivals and the individual sanctuaries.

Perhaps the best indication of Antiochus' own conception of the text--and the basis for our use of the term cultic proclamation throughout this paper--occurs in the superscription to the text at Arsameia-on-the-Nymphaeus (A), where the text is characterized as an ἀθάνατον κήρυγμα. The two central portions (proem and law) are referred to in the phrase μνήμην τε αἰώνιον καὶ νόμον ἀκίνητον ἀσύλῳ στήλῃ παραθέμενος.

All of these closely related texts exhibit the same style, which Eduard Norden[2] characterized as representative of the luxuriant and bombastic style of Asianism. He labeled the Nemrud Dağ text a dithyramb in prose, characterized by grandiosity of expression, passionately exalted style, highly poetic vocabulary, avoidance of hiatus, and rhythmical clausulae and internal rhythms for the sake of which the word order is often strangely contorted. The purpose of the style in this setting was, in his view, the glorification of the Commagenian king.

Recently Heinrich Dörrie[3] advanced Norden's thesis, delving more deeply into the function of the court rhetor's style relative to the purpose of the inscription in the cult. Rejecting the theory which had become popular in the interim that the rhetor's native language was Aramaic--suggested by the unusual omission of the article in these texts--Dörrie demonstrated the language to be excellent Hellenistic formal speech, and the proclamations, masterpieces of the γένος ὑψηλόν. The article was avoided, he argued, in imitation of Homeric poetry to exalt the tone of the texts in keeping with the divinity of the Commagenian god-king.[4] The effect was augmented by a systematic preference for the aorist and corresponding absence of the imperfect as well as by avoidance of the helping verbs ειμι and γίγνομαι. The absence of iterative or durative verbs, which remind the reader of historical process, give to the royal acta a supra-human quality of the absolute. Another stylistic feature contributing to this effect is the elimination of virtually all hypotaxis--causal, consecutive, conditional, temporal and final clauses.

Norden's thesis, which Dörrie develops, that the style of the Commagenian inscriptions is directly attributable to the artist's attempt to exalt the king's glory (Dörrie: the king's divine glory), however, introduces a degree of distortion into the picture. One searches the collections of Greek Stiftungen in vain for a text composed for that reason in a style and tone even remotely similar to the Commagenian texts. Although numerous inscriptional parallels survive in which a tone worthy of royal majesty is sought,[5] there is no evidence for such an extreme poetic device as avoidance of the article. The simple fact that omission of the article, as a poetic device, can be analyzed after the fact as contributing to a tone of exaltation cannot outweigh the objection that it was not otherwise among the features of poetry taken over into literary prose. Its strangeness would have excluded it from the rhetor's consideration had he been seeking merely to evoke a sense of royal exaltation. Nor can it be interpreted simply as an attempt to express the king's divinity. Helmut Waldmann argues convincingly that Antiochus was well aware of the distance between his own mortal state and that of the great gods. Nor does the literature of the time preserve any examples of divine utterance expressed in this style. The style of the Commagenian inscriptions, therefore, cannot satisfactorily be explained simply as an expression of the majesty or the alleged divinity of the Commagenian dynast.

It may have become evident in the preceding paragraphs that the crux interpretum in this case is the peculiar omission of the article, and it is consideration of this phenomenon which leads to the solution of the problem. The omission of the article was known from other contexts than Homer and Homeric poetry. Aside from the fact that it might have been considered as a characteristic of archaic language in general--inapplicable here, since Dörrie's excellent analysis of their language shows us that the Commagenian texts are not otherwise archaizing in character--the most obvious context in which omission of the article was known was the oracle.

The thesis that the style of the Commagenian inscriptions is an artificial prose adaptation of oracular style has considerable evidence, both internal and external, to commend it. It is clear that an oracular response stood behind the cult reform by which Antiochus I and his father Mithradates I Callinicus introduced a Greco-Persian syncretism as the state religion of Commagene. The references to the validation of the gods in the cultic decree of Antiochus I can imply nothing else. The proclamation inscription of Arsameia-on-the-Nymphaeus injects this element at the very beginning of the proem:

> περὶ πατρῴων δαιμόνων ἰδίας τε τιμῆς, ἣν θεῶν κρίσις ἐκύρωσε. . . (A 8-10; cf. N 206).

As Dörrie points out, τιμή for the heroic ancestors and for Antiochus I himself stands at the very center of the state cult under the latter's administration. The θεῶν κρίσις was clearly the oracular validation for the foundation of the state cult. This oracular mandate is mentioned frequently throughout all of the Commagenian inscriptions of Antiochus I. It occurs again at A 82 par.:

> Διαμονῆς δὲ τούτων ἕνεκεν, ἣν ἐν φρονίμοις ἄνδρασιν
> εὐσεβὲς ἀεὶ τηρεῖν, οὐ μόνον εἰς τιμὴν ἡμετέραν
> ἀλλὰ καὶ μακαριστὰς ἐλπίδας ἑκάστου τύχης, ἐγὼ
> καθοσιώσας ἐν στήλαις ἀσύλοις ἐχάραξα γνώμῃ θεῶν
> ἱερὸν νόμον. . . .

That the Delphic oracle itself may have provided Antiochus with his mandate may be assumed from the allusions to "images of Delphic power" and to the punishment of the Galatians who had attacked Delphi, which occur in the curses in the Nemrud Dağ processional way inscription (Np 37-39):

> ...οὗτος (κακοῦργος) ἰκόνας ὁράτω Δελφικῆς δυνάμεως ἔνθα
> Παρνασίοις πέτραις ὁμογενεῖ φύσει Γαλατικὰς τείσειεν δίκας.

More suggestive for the question of style, however, are those passages in the inscription in which the stele is personified as the προφῆτις of the divinity. The curses and blessings with which the texts conclude are preceded in all texts by such a passage, in which explicit reference is also made to the oracular validation (A 189ff., par.):

> Δαιμονίῳ δὲ γνώμῃ ταύτην ἀναγραφὴν εὐσεβείας
> προφῆτιν ἐποιησάμην, ἐφ' ἧς ἱερὰ γράμματα δι' ὅλης
> φωνῆς θεσπίζει μέγαν θεῶν νοῦν πολίταις καὶ ξένοις,
> ὁμοίως βασιλεῦσιν, δυνάσταις, ἐλευθέροις, δούλοις
> πᾶσιν ὅσοι φύσεως κοινωνοῦντες ἀνθρωπίνης ὀνόμασι
> γένους ἢ τύχης διαφέρουσιν. . . .

Here the oracular validation is expressed in the words δαιμονίῳ γνώμῃ. The personification of the ἀναγραφή (Np: στήλη) as the προφῆτις is developed through the image of the ἱερὰ γράμματα uttering the great will of the gods in a low voice, a fine example of antithetical "point" as well. The main verb also carries out explicitly the idea of oracular utterance, being commonly used of the προφῆτις who expounds the will of the gods (cf. χρήζω, A 198 par.). Finally, the reference to human nature reinforces the conception of the divine source of the text, which, through the person of the προφῆτις, speaks from the perspective of deity.

While this prosopopoeia does not go so far as to entail composition in the first person representing the direct utterance of the deity, as a genuine oracle would have, neither does the king use the first person of himself after this point in the text (a detail which Dörrie noticed[6]). This fact is not to be attributed to the notion that the king is now a god, and that, in Dörrie's words, "sein Wort den Willen der Götter ausdruckt."[7] Rather the style is adjusted to support the figure of the stone as the προφῆτις of the gods. The emphasis on the validation of the gods throughout these texts demonstrates clearly that Antiochus did not speak with the authority of his own divinity,[8] but on the authority of an oracle. The image of the stone as προφῆτις is repeated in its entirety, with characteristic variatio,[9] in the sentence immediately following (A 196-98 par.), in order to introduce precisely those deities whose authority does validate the cultic reform and its νόμος:

> Τούτοις Διὸς Ὠρομάσδου φροντίσιν ἄλλων τε γνώμαις
> θεῶν λίθος οὗτος ἡσύχῳ φωνῇ ταῦτα χρήζει.

If the argument from internal evidence of the Commagenian cultic texts is accorded a high degree of cogency in its own right, external evidence surviving in the form of a text composed in a closely similar style for similar purposes should dispel any remaining doubt. An impressive parallel does survive--enough to prove that the late Hellenistic rhetor who composed the model on which these various Commagenian cultic proclamations were based did not evolve its style in isolation.

The parallel occurs in the Republic of Plato, who was esteemed throughout the Hellenistic period and beyond as an accomplished stylist in Greek prose composition. In the following passage from Plato's description of Ananke in the myth of Er, son of Armenius, persons approaching her throne to draw lots preparatory to selecting the life they would lead in their next cycle of incarnation are addressed by "a certain prophet" (προφήτην τινά) prior to their appearance before "Lachesis, maiden daughter of Necessity":

> Σφᾶς οὖν, ἐπειδὴ ἀφικέσθαι, εὐθὺς δεῖν ἰέναι πρὸς τὴν Λάχεσιν. προφήτην οὖν τινὰ σφᾶς πρῶτον μὲν ἐν τάξει διαστῆσαι, ἔπειτα λαβόντα ἐκ τῶν τῆς Λαχέσεως γονάτων κλήρους τε καὶ βίων παραδείγματα, ἀναβάντα ἐπί τι βῆμα ὑψηλὸν εἰπεῖν· Ἀνάγκης θυγατρὸς κόρης Λαχέσεως λόγος. ψυχαὶ ἐφήμεροι, ἀρχὴ ἄλλης περιόδου θνητοῦ γένους θανατηφόρου. οὐχ ὑμᾶς δαίμων λήξεται, ἀλλ' ὑμεῖς δαίμονα αἱρήσεσθε. πρῶτος δ' ὁ λαχὼν πρῶτος αἱρείσθω βίον ᾧ συνέσται ἐξ ἀνάγκης. ἀρετὴ δὲ ἀδέσποτον, ἣν τιμῶν καὶ ἀτιμάζων πλέον καὶ ἔλαττον αὐτῆς ἕκαστος ἕξει. αἰτία ἑλομένου· θεὸς ἀναίτιος. ταῦτα εἰπόντα ῥῖψαι ἐπὶ πάντας τοὺς κλήρους, τὸν δὲ παρ' αὑτὸν πεσόντα ἕκαστον ἀναιρεῖσθαι, πλὴν οὗ· ἓ δὲ οὐκ ἐᾶν· τῷ δὲ ἀνελομένῳ δῆλον εἶναι, ὁπόστος εἰλήχει.[10]

The prophet speaks once again, to reassure the last to come before Lachesis that even they will be able to exercise wisdom and select a good and acceptable life. In spite of the brevity of the second utterance, the same style is apparent in the prophet's speech:

> Καὶ δὴ οὖν καὶ τότε ὁ ἐκεῖθεν ἄγγελος ἤγγελλε τὸν μὲν προφήτην οὕτως εἰπεῖν· καὶ τελευταίῳ ἐπιόντι, ξὺν νῷ ἑλομένῳ, συντόνως ζῶντι κεῖται βίος ἀγαπητός, οὐ κακός. μήτε ὁ ἄρχων αἱρέσεως ἀμελείτω μήτε ὁ τελευτῶν ἀθυμείτω.[11]

Plato does not follow the Isocratean rules of hiatus avoidance, or favor the cretic-spondee clausula; both of these features of style are general characteristics of the γένος ὑψηλόν in the first century B.C. Plato does most strikingly omit the article[12] in the utterances of the prophet, however, by which device he gives oracular quality to the phophet's words. It is unlikely that this device would have been overlooked by the Hellenistic teachers of rhetoric, and it is not surprising that omission of the article--even if for lack of other Hellenistic evidence we cannot go so far as to identify it as an artistic convention--should again have been employed to affect an oracular or prophetic style. The sense of the absolute described by Dörrie with respect to the Commagenian texts is evoked likewise by Plato in this passage through use of the aoristic future tense, but also through omission of the copular verb to be.

On the basis of both internal and external evidence, therefore, we conclude that Antiochus' cultic foundation proclamations are composed in an artificial prose adaptation of oracular style, the most striking feature of which is the omission of the article. Indeed, the example of prophetic language is precisely the model chosen by Longinus in his approximately contemporary treatise peri hypsos, where the author compares to "noble passion," as that which can produce the most sublime style, the divine inspiration of the prophet:

> . . . for I would confidently lay it down that nothing is so grand as noble passion--when in place--which, as in the stress of madness and inspiration, breathes forth its language as one possessed by a god, and, as it were, utters it with all the divine afflatus of a prophet.[13]

Bernhard Laum, who includes N in his collection of Stiftungen, noted that Stiftungsurkenden were never legal documents in the narrow sense that modern legal documents are.[14] They did not exist solely um ins Leben zu rufen. It seems quite clear, in fact, that these texts are more political than legal in nature. They are a form of propaganda, not unlike slogans on coins in their purpose to articulate and promulgate the official ideals of the age of Antiochus in Commagene--in a word, εὐσέβεια--and at the same time to realize that ideal to the greater prestige of the regime. All of the works of art commissioned by Antiochus for the cult sites throughout the realm and all of the pomp of his proclamations are intended to the latter end; they are offered as models of εὐσέβεια to be emulated by Antiochus' successors[15] and to be admired and respected by the populace. Finally, central to cultic reform under Antiochus, and to his proclamations, is the promulgation in Commagene of the cult of the ruler. Commagene, on the model of the Seleucid Empire, was to be devoted to the worship of Antiochus' dynasty along with its Greco-Persian deities, and preeminently to Antiochus himself, as the greatest in his line. By bringing to grandiose expression the official Greco-Persian heritage of the Commagenian dynasty, and by providing for willing participation in those traditions by the indigenous people of Commagene, which was neither Greek nor Persian, Antiochus sought to place the stamp of his dynasty upon his realm.[16]

It is precisely at this point that the purposes of the king and the aspirations of Greek rhetors of the time found themselves in closest harmony. The prestige of the king might be expressed in Persian or even indigenous style in sculptures, ritual garb, and cultic endowments. In language and rhetoric, however, Greek reigned supreme; only the art of a Greek orator could satisfactorily manifest the prestige of a royal house. For his part, the Greek rhetor was committed through an extensive training in the theory and practise of Greek epideictic oratory to carry on the epideictic tradition in his own teaching and practise. A Greek rhetor in the court of Commagene, compelled to deal with essentially oriental phenomena, succeeded in imposing his own Greek heritage on his subject by articulating it in the terms of his own art. He created a masterpiece of the γένος ὑψηλόν in which, by utilizing an artificial oracular style in prose, he added a new dimension to the rhetoric of Antiochus' propaganda, reinforcing the king's allusions to divine sanction and appealing to popular acceptance of the oracular authority of Delphi.

NOTES

1. For descriptions and editions of all pertinent texts discovered to date, see Helmut Waldmann, Die kommagenischen Kultreformen unter König Mithradates I Kallinikos und seinem Sohne Antiochos I. Études Préliminaires aux Religions Orientales dans l'Empire Romain, vol. 34. Leiden: Brill, 1973.

2. Die antike Kunstprosa. 2 vols. Darmstadt: Wissenschaftliche Büchgesellschaft, 1958, vol. 1, pp. 140-46.

3. Der Königskult des Antiochos von Kommagene im Lichte neuer Inschriften-Funde. Abhandlungen der Akademie der Wissenschaften in Göttingen philologisch-historische Klasse, ser. 3, no. 60. Göttingen: Vandenhoeck & Ruprecht, 1964.

4. According to Dörrie's interpretation of the royal theology, Antiochus had become a ϑεὸς δίκαιος ἐπιφανής through his καταστερισμός which had occurred on 7 July, 62 B.C. This date and the heavenly event are represented on the famous lion horoscope on Nemrud Dağ which portrays the conjunction of Jupiter, Mercury and Mars together with the Moon in Leo. Hence, according to Dörrie, Antiochus describes himself as being σύνϑρονος with the great gods.

5. Cf. the texts cited as parallels to N by Norden, pp. 146ff.

6. Der Königskult, p. 98. 7. <u>Ibid.</u>

8. Cf. the argument against the thesis of the apotheosis of Antiochus in Waldmann, pp. 199f.

9. See the excellent discussion of <u>variatio</u> in the Commagenian cultic inscriptions by Dörrie, pp. 145-55.

10. Plato Republic 10.617 d-e. 11. <u>Ibid.</u>, 10.619 b.

12. The article is used by both Plato's prophet and Antiochus in his proclamations, however, with participial substantives.

13. Longinus 8, trans. Benedict Einarson in Longinus on the Sublime and Sir Joshua Reynolds: Discourses on Art, eds. Benedict Einarson and Elder Olson. Chicago: Packard & Co., 1945, p. 15.

14. Stiftungen in der griechischen und römischen Antike, 2 vols. Leipzig: B. G. Teubner, 1914, vol. 1, p. 1.

15. A 174-89.

16. The identification of the kingdom which Antiochus inherited as βασιλείαν ἐμοῖς ὑπήκοον ϑρόνοις is significant with respect to the tension between the Greco-Persian dynasty and the indigenous Anatolian races inhabiting the area. See Waldmann, pp. 145 f.

MUSIC AND RITUAL IN PRIMITIVE ELEUSIS

Apostolos N. Athanassakis
University of California at Santa Barbara

The story of Persephone's rape and of Demeter's arrival in Eleusis is told primarily in the Homeric Hymn to Demeter. Interestingly enough, once Demeter finds herself inside the palace of Keleos, it is not Metaneira, the queen, but wise old Iambe who knows how to entertain her (184-211). Demeter turns down the queen's throne for a humbler seat covered by a sheepskin offered by Iambe. It is Iambe's jests which restore smiles and laughter to the grief-stricken guest. Demeter also turns down the customary wine offered by the queen and bids her make a κυκεών, a mixed drink consisting of barley groats (ἄλφι), water (ὕδωρ), and penny-royal (γλήχων). The version given in the Orphicorum Fragmenta (Kern 46-53) is rather different. The most articulate version is the one given by Clement of Alexandria in Protr. 20, 1-21, 2 (Kern 52). According to this account when Demeter reached Eleusis the most important local ruler was Dysaules, and his wife's name was Baubo. The lesser kings or barons were Triptolemos, the cowherd, Eumolpos, the shepherd, and Euboulos, the swineherd. Baubo offered Demeter the kykeon but the goddess demurred because she was in mourning. Then Baubo resorted to an unusual means of persuasion:

> ὥς εἰποῦσα πέπλους ἀνεσύρετο δεῖξε δὲ πάντα
> σώματος οὐδὲ πρέποντα τύπον. παῖς δ'ἦεν Ἴακχος
> χειρί τέ μιν ῥίπτασκε γελῶν Βαυβοῦς ὑπο κόλποις
> ἡ δ'ἐπεὶ οὖν μείδησε θεά, μείδησ' ἐνὶ θυμῷ
> δέξατο δ'αἰόλον ἄγγος, ἐν ῷ κυκεὼν ἐνέκειτο.

Thus Baubo induced the goddess to smile and to accept the kykeon by showing the unseemly 'impression' of her body, that is, her pudenda. The two versions differ in several respects, but the important point to be stressed is that Keleos and Dysaules, Iambe and Baubo are the true counterparts in the Homeric and Orphic traditions. Metaneira is an awkward and obscure figure. She does not act with insight in the Homeric Hymn and she is replaced with Baubo, Iambe's counterpart, in the Orphic fragment.

Limitations of space and time permit me only to mention that the poet of the Homeric Hymn to Demeter is intentionally vague on the nature of Iambe's jests for which scholars find a parallel in the gephyrismoi, the insults hurled by people standing on the bridge of the Eleusinian Kephisos at participants in the processions to and from Eleusis. Baubo's more drastic gesture of exposing her genitals is the well-known ἀνασυρμός, which some scholars on account of a passage in Herodotus (II.60) trace to Egypt. But statuettes of the θεὰ ἀνασυρομένη have been found all the way from the Italian peninsula and Anatolia to the Nile Delta, and the same gesture - pregnant with ritualistic significance - is found in the Japanese Ko-Ji-Ki.

To stress that the cult of Demeter-Kore was primarily and at any rate originally a fertility cult would be to belabor the obvious. The kykeon itself was doubtless of a nature calculated to increase fertility and sexual potency. The verbs κυκάω (stir) and μίγνυμι (to mingle sexually) present us with interesting semantic possibilities. The ingredients of the kykeon may not have been symbolically insignificant either. It is natural that the drink of the goddess who has power over growth and fertility should contain water. The idea that the sky god impregnates the earth goddess through rain is expressed in the well-known Aeschylean line ὄμβρος ἔκυσε γαῖαν (fr.44) as well as in the ritualistic formula ὕε - κύε (rain-conceive). The second ingredient, cracked or ground barley seed (ἄλφι), is symbolic of all seeds, including the human seed, which must be kept inside the moist earth - or the moist womb - before they sprout and come to life. In Homer ἄλφιτον, of which ἄλφι is a shortened form, always occurs in the phrase ἀλφίτου ἀκτή which in Iliad 11, 631 is qualified by the significant adjective ἱερός. Thus ἄλφι-(τον) was usually cracked grain (ἀκτή < ἄγνυμι) and sometimes, if the occasion was ritualistic, it must have been cracked in some religiously meaningful way. The third ingredient of the kykeon, the pennyroyal (in Ionic γλήχων / γληχώ but βλήχων / βληχώ in Attic), may have been chosen for a very special reason, too. Kerenyi's opinion that it was a mild narcotic finds no support in ancient literature. Proof from the Greek medical writers shows abundantly that its main use was gynecological and that it was primarily associated with fertility and with vaginal and uterine hygiene. In Aristophanes Lysistrata 89 the depilated βληχώ is surely to be equated with the pudenda (cf. also Pax 709-12 and Acharnians 874). Hesychios also confirms this association. Indeed it is not unlikely that the third ingredient of the kykeon symbolized the female reproductive organs.

After this brief consideration of the Iambe-Baubo episodes and of the possible symbolism attached to the kykeon, I propose to turn my attention to the risky game of offering a purely Greek etymological explanation for the names Dysaules-Baubo and Keleos-Iambe and of reconstructing the primitive substratum of the Eleusinian mysteries on a basis which combines the etymology of these names with music produced in grain-pounding rituals.

For Δυσαύλης I propose the perfectly possible derivation from δυσ-, 'ill, hard,' and αὐλός, 'flute' as opposed to δυσ- + αὐλή, 'court,' and I suggest that Δυσαύλης is descended from a personified phallus called in jest something like "Old Flute" simply because of the fact that of all musical instruments the single flute bears the greatest resemblance to the penis. This is not as astonishing as it sounds since scholars have already suggested the Βαυβώ is a personified vulva coupled with a personified Βαυβών (=ὄλισβος). In Greek αὐλίσκος in some cases means the male member and in English the "living flute," the "silent flute" and the "one-eyed flute" are bywords for the penis. The name Βαυβώ is quite strange. Like Δυσαύλης it does not occur as a personal name and this in itself may indicate that originally it was not a person's name or that, whatever it was, its semasiological associations and sound were not sufficiently desirable. Inscriptional evidence suggests uncertainty as to whether the name was Βαυβώ rather than Βαβώ. Both forms suggest an onomatopoetic βαυ/βα (cf. βαΰζω, βαυβάω, βαμβαλιαστύς, Homeric βάζω, etc.) which might have come about as an imitation of the sound of a percussion instrument such as the drum (cf. such names for drums as tam-tam, tom-tom, the Vedic dundubhih, the Tamil Tambaṭṭam, the Russian baraban, etc.). I have proposed αὐλός as the basic etymon of Dysaules and I now proceed to suggest that Βαυβώ/Βαβώ originally was some sort of τύπανον whose name was later identified with the name of the priestess who was attached to its care and worship. The drum I have in mind would not be the little drum carried by one hand and struck by the other which we see so frequently in the art of the Aegean basin and the Near East but a bigger kettle drum or cauldron drum requiring a drumstick or a pestle used as a drumstick. The primitive version may have been some sort of wooden or earthenware pot used not only to make music, or to beat time, but also to pound grain necessary for the fertility ritual. Now the identification of such a vessel drum with the female pudenda is not only logical but also very widespread among primitive peoples. The same tribes which identify the drum with the vulva also identify the drumstick with the penis. This is the place to point out that in Empedocles (Diels PPF 135) Βαυβώ means κοιλία ('belly') - an inflated stomach is like a drum - and that in Hesychios we find the gloss βαυβάλιον· γυναικὸς μόριον. It should also be said that some significance could be attached to the fact that Baubo's pudenda are also called τύπος, 'impression,' a word which, much like τύ(μ)πανον, 'drum,' goes back to τύπτω, 'strike.' The existence of ἴαμβος makes the connection of Ἰάμβη with music a very probable one. It has been noticed by scholars that there is a musical instrument, ἰαμβύκη, which bears morphological resemblance to the better known σαμβύκη. It is possible that ἰαμβύκη was fashioned from Ἰάμβη on the analogy of σαμβύκη. The details for previous etymologies of ἴαμβος and for the precise natures of σαμβύκη and ἰαμβύκη are complex. For Ἰάμβη I propose the etymology ἴαν+βα, that is, the singular accusative of the numeral ἴα ('one') and the onomatopoetic βα, a byform of which I have already used to explain the origin of Βαυβώ, Iambe's Orphic counterpart. Iambe then originally was the cry accompanying the pounding of grain in a drum which eventually came to take on that name and which was later personified. In my scheme Iambe's male counterpart would be Keleos, the king of Eleusis. The word κελεός in Greek is the name for the green woodpecker. The root κελ- is not confined only to this word but is found in its ablaut variation κολ- and zero grade κλ- in several well-known words, all of which have to do primarily with 'striking' (thus κελεΐς, δίκελλα, κέλετρον, κολάπτω, κόλαφος, κλάω, etc.). The root does mean 'to strike, to smite, to beat,' and the green woodpecker was named κελεός because he strikes or pecks at tree trunks and branches with his beak. The original meaning of the name Κελεός must have been 'pecker, beater, striker,' and the like. Therefore it is quite possible that originally κελεός was some sort of pestle used to pound corn inside a naviform slit-drum or kettle-drum called Ἰάμβη. And just like their Orphic counterparts Βαυβώ/Δυσαύλης, Ἰάμβη/Κελεός could easily become personifications of the male and female genitals. The personification of the cry of the mystics - I am referring to Ἴακχος of course - shows that such a process might be possible.

Clement of Alexandria has preserved for us a _synthema_, a password uttered by the initiates at Eleusis, which has given birth to diverging and even contradictory theories: ἐνήστευσα, ἔπιον τὸν κυκεῶνα, ἔλαβον ἐκ κίστης, ἐργασάμενος ἀπεθέμην εἰς κάλαθον καὶ ἐκ καλάθου εἰς κίστην: "I fasted; I drank the kykeon; I took from the kiste; having done my task, I placed in the basket, and from the basket into the kiste" (_Protr._ 21). With Lobeck and Mylonas as notable exceptions, most scholars have thought that this passage refers to the manipulation of representations of human genitalia. Perhaps, we shall never know what the objects themselves exactly were, but we may venture to conjecture that the kiste, at least, as a receptacle and repository, could represent the _pudenda muliebria_ (cf. the controversy on the _kteis_) and that it and the male counterpart handled by the initiate were the symbolic substitutes for the drum-mortar and drumstick-pestle of an earlier, more primitive Eleusis.

By now one may wonder whether my suggestions are products of a prurient imagination with no basis in human reality. What does music have to do with the pounding of grain, and what does all this have to do with sex? But Malayans and Siamese make music while they pound rice in slit-drums. This primitive musical instrument, found in parts of Asia, Africa, and the Pacific Islands, frequently takes on a sexual significance of such symbolic importance in the lives of certain peoples that priestesses may be attached to its worship and care. Ξανθὴ and ἀγλαόκαρπος Demeter is the grain goddess. An ear of corn may have been part of the sacred objects exhibited to the mystai at a high point of their initiation, the epopteia (see Hippolytos, Philosophoumena V, 38-41 and cf. Himerios Orat. Z,2, p. 512). A modern Greek analogue not for producing music while pounding grain but for accompanying the pounding of grain with music is found in the custom of the raisin, the Cypriot wedding meal. The word itself is interesting in that it may go back to Homeric ῥαίω, 'to break, to dash to pieces.' Its main feature is the pounding of the wheat used for the wedding meal by means of a pestle called faouta, and it may indeed be descended from some ancient agricultural festival in which the ritual of an ἱερὸς γάμος was performed. By the way, a modern version of a festival which centered round a ritualistic wedding still survived in the beginning of the twentieth century in Thracian Viza (ancient Βιζύη). Some evidence that in certain mystic cults corn was offered to a goddess not much unlike Demeter is seen in the lines

τίς οὐκ ἀπαρχὰς ὀσπρίων τε καί σίτων
ἁγνῷ φέρων δίδωσι τυμπάνῳ 'Ρείης;
(Babrius 141, 9).

And we should not forget that the Mother of the Gods is pleased by the sound of κρόταλα, τύπανα, and αὐλοί. But the specific mention of any connection between drums (and cymbals) and Demeter is found in a mystic symbolon preserved by Clement of Alexandria: "I ate from a drum; I drank from a cymbal; I carried the sacred kernos; I stole into the bridal chamber" (Protreptikos, Loeb edition, transl. G.W. Butterworth, p. 13 ff.). Mylonas points out that the phrase ἐκ τυμπάνου βέβρωκα, ἐκ κυμβάλου πέπωκα, γέγονα μύστης Ἄττεως in Firmicus Maternus shows that Clement's "Mysteries of Deo" were the mysteries held by the Phrygians in honor of Rhea-Kybele-Attis. But Clement specifically mentions Deo, and his formula does not contain the phrase γέγονα μύστης Ἄττεως. However, the phrase ἐκ τυμπάνου βέβρωκα ἐκ κυμβάλου πέπωκα may have been part of a ritualistic formula both at Eleusis and in Phrygia.

Clement and Firmicus Maternus are not our only sources for the connection between drums and cymbals and the worship of Demeter. In the Helena Euripides has dedicated a beautiful ode to the sorrow of Demeter over the rape of her daughter and to the way in which Zeus chooses to humor the anger of the goddess. The most pertinent lines from the ode are 1341-1352. This passage seems to preserve an Orphic tradition according to which Zeus through music made Demeter relent her anger. The Graces and the Muses danced and sang, but Aphrodite, obviously part of Zeus' embassy to Demeter, went along equipped with an instrument made of copper or brass and a drum. Although in I Corinthians ch.13 the expression is χαλκὸς ἠχῶν ἢ κύμβαλον ἀλαλάζον, it is possible that χαλκοῦ αὐδὰν χθονίαν (1346) stands for the sound of a copper cymbal (cf. χαλκοτύπων βόμβοις κυμβάλων in Diog. Ath. TGF, p. 776) and that we have here a much more ancient testimony for the cymbal and the drum mentioned in the formulae preserved by Clement of Alexandria and Firmicus Maternus. Even more important for my argument is the role of the βαρύβρομος αὐλός. It is interesting that Demeter, who in the Homeric Hymn smiles and laughs because of Iambe's jests and in the Orphic fragment smiles because of Baubo's exposed pudenda, here laughs when she takes the "heavy-sounding flute" into her hands. In the two other instances Demeter is induced to laugh or smile as a result of some overtly or covertly sexual act. Is it not possible that in this third instance she laughs because in the flute she sees a symbol of the male sexual organ? And is it not possible that the Δυσαύλης of another Orphic tradition is not very different from the all-important αὐλός of the Euripidean version?

Summary and Conclusion

The important role of music and musical instruments both in the rude beginnings of the Eleusinian cult and in its later more sophisticated form is strongly and quite overtly suggested by several of the names associated with the cult. Eumolpos, "the Good Singer," was the ancestor of the powerful clan of the Eumolpidai from which the highest Eleusinian priest, the hierophant, was chosen by hereditary right. Eumolpos may have been an aoidos who sang songs about Demeter's story. The name of Dysaules hardly needs an etymological probing to be connected with αὐλός, the flute. "Hard-Flute" originally may have been a flute with phallic significance and later also the priest-musician attached to it. The process of taking a sound or cry and personifying it is well-illustrated by the derivation of the name of Baubo's child, Iakkhos, from the cry of the initiates. If the child's name can be onomatopoetic, so can the mother's: Βαυβώ comes from a reduplicated Βαύ/βα, and her counterpart, Ἰάμβη, from the same βα preceded by the accusative of ἴα: ἴαν+βα > *'Ιάμβα > 'Ιάμβη. (Cf. ἄβα, Ἄβας, and perhaps βαμβαλιαστύς for βα as an onomatopoetic component.) Finally, Κελεός, the "Beater" or "Striker" may well be derived from the well-known root κελ- = to strike, to beat (cf. κελεός, δίκελλα, κέλλω κέλετρον etc.).

A look into primitive agricultural ritual shows that the pounding of grain is sometimes done with instruments associated with the male and female genitals. The existence of such customs as that of the Cypriot raisin and that of the Thracian festival at Viza on Cheese-Monday suggests the possibility for the pounding of grain to the sound of music at a wedding and for the practice of mock-weddings and of ritualistic ploughing. Given the suggested etymologies of Δυσαύλης - Βαυβώ, Κελεός - 'Ιάμβη, the pertinent material from the practices of people still close to the soil, and the fact that ἄλφι (τον), cracked barley, was the primary ingredient of the kykeon, we may be justified in imagining that Baubo and Iambe were once drums in which sacred grain was pounded - perhaps to the sound of a flute - and that Keleos was a phallic drumstick. (Here the Hindu veneration of the Lingam - Yoni combination may offer helpful parallels). In time the functionaries attached to these instruments were identified with them in name and in the mythological aition of a more advanced culture they became kings, queens and royal handmaids. The fact that Keleos and Dysaules hardly play a role in Demeter's visit to Eleusis is in keeping with the principally matriarchial and feminine nature of the cult. It is also indicative of the vigor and survival of patently pre-Indo-European religious beliefs and rituals. Keleos and Dysaules are as inconspicuous and secondary as the consorts of the various personae of the Anatolian and Mediterranean mother goddess. That the names of the principal actors of the Homeric and Orphic versions of the Eleusinian drama might be explained in Indo-European terms should not come as a surprise. It was a process of superficial Hellenization conforming to the realities imposed by the dominant group, and a gesture not much unlike the Americanization of the personal names and institutions of many immigrant groups in the United States.

The interpretation set forth in this inquiry is not only consonant with the proposed etymologies but also gives meaning to an important mystic "symbolon," which may have eventually lost the significance it had in the humbler and more primitive Eleusinian cult. Indeed, when the initiate cried out ἐκ τυμπάνου βέβρωκα, he, much like Clement of Alexandria, may not have known that, when his forefathers "ate from the drum," they did so from an actual sacred drum named Ἰάμβη in one tradition and Βαυβώ in another.

A PROBLEM OF POWER: HOW MIRACLE DOERS COUNTER CHARGES OF MAGIC IN THE HELLENISTIC WORLD

Anitra Bingham Kolenkow

Why and how do miracle doers defend themselves in Hellenistic literature? R. Bultmann cited no real Hellenistic/Jewish parallels to the Christian gospel miracle controversy stories. However, as Vermes has emphasized, stories tell of miracle doers attacked in a Jewish milieu.[1*] In these stories, the attempts to entrap miracle doers are similar to the situation outlined in the Christian gospel miracle controversy stories -- a situation (of the activity of the miracle worker) giving rise to questioning with an answer (maintaining the validity of power or act) given by the miracle worker. Once one recognizes the adversative structure or situation, one may recognize accounts of similar structures or situations in the Hellenistic world as a whole. Miracles were a problem in a world where miraculous power was respected or feared (as well as mocked or considered nonsense). The adversative situation became a method both for control and yet affirmation of the miraculous. This paper will discuss the materials available to study such structures and situations. These materials show the accusations placed against miracle doers and yet the intertwining of miracle power with two forces which tried to combat it, the state and philosophy. The materials show how miracle doers (including both philosophers and politicians) avoid charges of goeteia in the Hellenistic world and yet affirm their own powers.

I. The Materials Available for the Study

There are three major types of material available for such studies. First, there are legal and related statements (cf. Deut 13:1-5 and other Jewish materials; Plato <u>Rep</u> 2:364-5, <u>Laws</u> 11:933a-e, Roman law codes[2]) about those who use miracle power as part of a basis for actions inimical to the society. In general such texts show the views of organized society which sees magic or prophecy as a possible subversive activity which must be strictly controlled. In this category one should also include references in works like Philostratus' <u>Lives of the Sophists</u> which say both that sophist rhetors are accused of magic (590) and that a well educated man would never be led astray to the practice of magic arts (523, 590, cf. Tacitus <u>Ann</u> 2:27 where Libo is "thoughtless").

Secondly, there are stories of miracle doers (such as Eunus: Diodorus Sic. 34; Vespasian: Tacitus <u>Hist</u> 4:81; Hanina ben Dosa and others: Ta'an 23b-25a; Eliezer ben Hyrcanus: BM 59b; and the longer lives of Apollonius and Pythagoras) which show the various roles of miracle workers. Here one may also extract pieces of arguments made for and against miracle workers.

Thirdly, one has formal defenses of miracle doers -- apologies or stories arguing that the figure is either not a magus or (if he is) is not doing evil in the society. Here one sees both typical accusations against miracle workers and how the accused answers such accusations. In this category are the extended defenses of Apollonius of Tyana (in Philostratus' <u>Life</u>) and Apuleius (<u>Apology</u>) -- as well as Eusebius' defense of Jesus (<u>Dem</u> 3:103-134). There are also short accounts of (attempted) accusation and reply in the "story" category.

*Notes to this article are available separately from the author.

II. The Role of the Miracle Worker-Prophet

In studying such materials, one gains a perspective on how miracle doing related to the life of the society. Miracles and related activities served to strengthen the hand of philosophers and, at the same time, the activities of philosophers are used to defend the deeds of the magi-vates.

Although magicians and prophets-astrologers are differentiable (and both Cramer and MacMullen separate the categories), in the general syndrome where miracle gives power to a word, the two may be joined into what will be called magi-vates. Apollonius says that wizards make forecasts (5:12). Eunus is both a prophet and magician (vs. Cramer, 59, who emphasizes prophecy). Deut 13 speaks of prophets who do signs. Hanina is asked if he is a prophet when he does a miracle (Ber 34b, BK 50a). Jose ben Kisma is asked for a miracle when he gives a prophecy (cf. Mark 13:22, John 2:18).[3]

Philostratus (Sophists 481) says that the "Method of the philosophers resembles the prophetic art which is controlled by man and was organized by the Egyptians and Chaldeans and, before them, by the Indians, who used to conjecture the truth by the aid of countless stars: the sophistic method resembles the prophetic art of soothsayers and oracles." The same author has Apollonius taught by eastern sages (shown doing healings: Life 3:39) and then tells of Apollonius exorcizing a young man and thus converting him to philosophy (4:20). Philostratus also has Apollonius cite the life style or actions of philosophers as the same as, and thus justifying, his own which are attacked as part of the accusation of magic (8:7:4, 5; cf. Apuleius Apol 4-22). Apollonius particularly defends foreknowledge as the province of the wise which sets them between gods and men (8:7:9). However, this knowledge means that he knows "the genius of the pestilence ... took the form of a poor old man" whom he seems to exorcize.[4]

Men also recognize those who do wonder works as worthy of power. Eunus who had served as court jester (note Apollonius' negative comments on similar people: Life 8:7:3) and magician becomes the leader of a slave revolution. Such powers may certainly be the certifiers of power for those not in power. Those in power accuse of subversion those out of power who do miracles; in contrast the miracle worker may naturally become the recognized leader of a group which is not in power. Not only Moses, Eunus, the Jewish leaders described by Josephus (cf. Ant 20:97 for example) and the group represented by Eliezer ben Hyrcanus,[5] but also Vespasian seems to have been an example of this truth. The advisors of Vespasian are right when they tell him that if he tries to heal and does not (as he feels he could not) the attempt will not redound to his disfavor. However, he may be successful. This story may also contain an apologetic motif; Vespasian did not seek to do the miracle -- he is not seeking his own power in healing. Those in power also have or seek the help of those who have such special abilities -- cf. the career of Thrasyllus as advisor to emperors as well as the career of Hadrian. Judah the Patriarch has the miraculous power of foresight as well as other powers.[6] Thus those who have or would have power in the society often use or claim mantic powers.

III. Accusations against Miracle Doers -- What Threatens Society

Using the materials discussed in the preceding sections, one can look at the several accusations made against miracle workers. If one excludes manner of dress and use of magicians' tools,[7] one may note three major types of accusations against or assumptions about miracle workers.

The first accusation is that of subversion. The legal code of Deut 13:1-5 serves as an example: "if a prophet arise among you....and gives you a sign or wonder .... and if he says go after other gods... that prophet shall be put to death because he has taught rebellion." As Tacitus and others describe the the upper echelons of Rome, the emperors fear forecasts of the future -- even though they have their own horoscopes drawn. In these stories, both magic and astrology are feared and condemned in that they tell of and/or can bring about the demise of an emperor.[8] Libo is accused of revolution and resorted to "astrologers' promises, magical rites and interpreters of dreams." (Tacitus Ann 2:27) The use of magical rites both for prophecy of and bringing about a death seems common -- enough that Apollonius defends himself against a charge of participating in a rite with Nerva (Life 7:36, 8:7:10). Inquiry into an emperor's time of death was a crime (done by any means) according to the Augustan edict of 11.

The second of the accusations is related to the first. Magicians are charged with use of their power for evil purposes (maleficia). Plato's Laws speak of those who harm people and are also magicians. The charges seem natural since many magical incantations or papyri seem to concern curses where they do not contain love charms. Both Apollonius (Life 8:7:12) and Apuleius (Apol 2, 42) are accused of harming young boys. The charge of bringing a plague on Ephesus is also made against Apollonius (8:7:10). It is assumed a magician could harm his enemies (Apuleius Apology 26). Apuleius curses by Mercury (64). Eliezer ben Hyrcanus brought about natural disaster (BM 59b). Aelius Aristides believed he could cause earthquakes (Sacred Discourses 39-42).[9]

The third type of accusation is that of the use of miracle to gain riches or other power. Even if a person is not doing evil, he may be gaining power too quickly. Philostratus tells of rhetors who are accused of magic because they advance so fast (590 -- and also perhaps because rhetors are felt to defeat just argument by unjust for money: 483). Apuleius is accused of using magic to marry a widow and thus gain wealth (Apol 67, 102). Servilea is said to have spent her dowry to learn the future from a magus (Tacitus Ann 16:30ff.). Aesop (Fables 65) tells of a witch who has great gain from her work. A Roman edict of 139 BCE emphasizes the financial exploitation of the gullible.[10] The Jews tell the story of Hanina ben Dosa who uses his powers both to get and to get rid of a gold table leg. When he gets the leg he sees a vision of heaven where the pious are sitting at three legged tables but he himself is sitting at a two legged table. He therefore rids himself of the table leg (Ta'an 25a). The story gracefully combines an emphasis on Hanina's own purity, the possibility of wealth from magic and the lack of reward in heaven if one has reward on earth.

IV. In Defense of Miracle Workers -- Apology and Claim of Power

The ambiguities of the value of miracle power and society's opposition to magic are illuminated by the defenses made both in apologies and stories. Because Philostratus' Life (with apology) of Apollonius of Tyana is separated by a hundred years of formalization and idealization from the actual life of Apollonius, the work enables one to see common defenses against charges of goeteia.

Apollonius arguing against charges of subversion (type 1) defends himself as one who does not seek money or power (type 3), unlike those wizards who seek gain from their skills (8:7:3). Vespasian, indeed, is said to have sung the praises of Apollonius' poverty (8:7:3). Apollonius jokes about the accusation of crimes; who would commit crimes for no money at all. Again Apollonius says that he does not seek his own power. He contrasts himself with wizards that he does not call on Zeus for testimony (cf. John 5:37, Eliezer ben Hyrcanus) and that he acts in public. He also says he does not ask people to pray to him (although they do and are made better: 8:7:2).[11] He also says that he exorcizes people by prayer to Hercules and asks would he do this if he wanted to affirm his own power.

> Cf. the account in Philostratus' Lives of the Sophists which says that the Magi involve gods in their secret rites, but that they avoid any public profession of belief in a deity because they do not wish it thought that their own powers are derived from that source (494).[12]

In arguing both against the idea of harming the state or the emperor and his own enemies, Apollonius says that he has not avenged himself on cities which persecuted him. He did not bring a plague upon them, but rather stopped the plague by his special knowledge. The apology here becomes self-affirmation.[13] He tells how wise men have actually saved cities and how wise men would defend themselves against an attempt to destroy a city (8:7:8; cf. the story of Onias who dies rather than hurt fellow Jews who are enemies: Josephus Ant 14:25-28).[14]

In the Apology of Apuleius (defending himself against use of magic for the quick gain of money, type 3), Apuleius defends himself on the bases of philosophers' poverty plus saving the widow money. Did not the philosophers proclaim poverty? Was not the widow's best interest served by avoiding spending on wedding festivities (commonly exacted by "benefactor" codes).

Apuleius further defends himself against magic charges by saying that he helps people-- and asking whether a magician would heal disease (51, cf. 80; thus using type 2). Apuleius uses the image of a physician (acting for healing and not for profit) but raises himself one step above physicians. Physicians are unable to heal the lady and bring the lady to him (thus he had more power than they, 51).

As the reader becomes aware that Apuleius, like Apollonius, might indeed be proclaiming himself a figure with special knowledge, the reader remembers other notes. Apuleius believes in magic (cf. Deo Soc 6, where the daimon is a vehicle both of prophecy and the magic of magicians). Apuleius affirms what Persian magi do in their service of the gods -- which Plato proclaimed (25-6) and then he talks about the common view of magic (which he does not deny) that a person can do what he wills through incantation of the gods. Then he says, "but if I have the(power) why are you not afraid of me?" (26). He then says he has done no malpractice even if he has been a magician (28, cf. 66). After some chapters, Apuleius returns again to the question of harm, but the harm has become deified. Apuleius tells of a Mercury statue to which he prays (and which the accusation has related to magic). Then, of a sudden, a curse comes out, "May this divinity bring upon you the enmity of the God.... but we are disciples of Plato." (64) Does this story show his belief in the god and yet his separation of his own power from that of the deity; any harm that comes comes from the deity! This, of course, would be the reverse side of the Apollonius-Hercules defense -- that Apollonius acted with the aid of Hercules. Is the story one of irony or of power?

The question about the Apuleian curse leads one back to post-apology story of Apollonius' "participation" in the death of Domitian. These stories confront one with what is a general problem for such apology-affirmations -- what is the actual role of the hero-speaker in these apologies. Thorndike says Apuleius composed his apology very fast and is incriminating himself (233) when he tells about Mercury's relation to incantations and forecasts of the future (Apol 31, 42). Thus, Apuleius is a magician. R. MacMullen, although he admits that Apollonius is both a charlatan and a philosopher, says that when Apollonius faces Domitian, Apollonius is acting as a philosopher rather than a charlatan (112-113). (MacMullen draws us to his cause by first describing philosophers as enemies of state; Apollonius is a death and emperor defying philosopher.) J. Z. Smith suggests apologies are meant not only to defend but to guard against the "sincere misunderstanding of admirers." The apology wants to point beyond miracles to a Son of God of whom they are the sign (25).[15]

Each of these suggestions illuminates the problem. Thorndike points toward the ambiguity of the Apuleian story about the statue. R. MacMullen points to the confrontation with authority as an important element in how we judge Apollonius. J. Z. Smith argues the double address of the apologies.[16] However, the points of each critic usefully abet those of the others. There is indeed an incriminating aspect to Apuleius' defense as Thorndike argues. But, in fact, the apology would seem like an affirmation of both good and evil power. Apuleius defends what the Magi do (using Plato), contrasts himself with those who do evil, but affirms apparently his power to arouse his statue.[17]

One may also agree with MacMullen when he pinpoints the "confrontation with authority" as important -- but disagree that "confrontation with authority" proves one a philosopher. As he admits, death is a possibility for magicians (124). When one looks at the confrontation in the story of Apollonius, the confrontation shows exactly where Apollonius differs from the ordinary philosopher. He is able to disappear at will and appear again in another place. He stands before the emperor knowing he (A.) will not die now (7:38; 8:5, 8). Such knowledge is claimed by and for certain philosophers, prophets and magi, as Pythagoras: (Iamblichus Life of Pythagoras 217), Proclos (Cassius Dio 67:16:2), Jesus (John 7:6, 30; Mark 8:31 par), Thrasyllus (Tacitus Ann 6:21) as well as Apollonius. One reason that the figure either fears or does not fear to act is that he knows what the future holds. The knowledge thus gives a death as well as a life option and power.

Knowledge of the time of one's own death also serves as a proof of knowledge of apocalyptic events (cf. forecast of one's own death in seven days as a proof of revelation: Phlegon, Mirabilia;[18] John 2:18; Ascletarius - Domitian's death and his own by dogs: Suetonius Domitian 15[19]). This may be the actual point of the forecasts in Mark 8:31 par; their coming to pass is proof that Jesus' other forecasts will also. A variant is that a person knows that his death will bring destruction upon those who kill him (Aesop - Delphi: Life 133; Jesus- Jerusalem: Mark 12, cf. Onias' death in Josephus Ant 14:25, R. Eliezer ben Hyrcanus: BM 59b, Teacher of Righteousness: IQH 2:8, 24, 7:12; Socrates: Plato Apol 39c). If destruction is the righteous recompense of the gods, the onus is taken off the prophet who might otherwise be accused of acting so that his enemies are hurt.

J. Z. Smith's presentation should be enlarged exactly at the points noted by MacMullen and Thorndike. Smith is quite right that Philostratus' Apollonius seeks to distinguish magic from what Apollonius does (7:39).[20] However, one may argue that the syndrome which Philostratus describes is not riddle-transcendence-emptiness but riddle-threat-promise. Good news is not no news; good news is bad news for some. The "vanishing" which Smith also notices does not connote "transparency" as Smith argues (28); the vanishing connotes power and produces portentous reaction. Apollonius has been said to fortell the death of those who acted ill toward him (1:12). Here his departure overly discomposes Domitian and shortly thereafter Apollonius is portrayed as participating (at a distance) in the death of Domitian (8:26). If one looks at Iamblichus' Life of Pythagoras, as Smith does,[21] one also sees that Abaris (follower-associate) does recognize that Pythagoras is not a charlatan but is "as a God". However, the author of the Life needs a contrast -- here, the tyrant Phalaris who not only blasphemes the gods but opposes Pythagoras (216-22). Although Pythagoras does say that all things are done as the heavens show and speaks of the oracles of Apollo, Pythagoras' true power is said to be shown when the insolent action of the tyrant "occasioned" the death of the tyrant (222). Thus again an event is forecast by heaven but brought about by Pythagoras and by those who act wrongly toward him. The magi-vates do have negative power and the negative power is available against those who oppose them. Thus, Pythagoras is said to be the one who helps man and yet who occasioned the death of one who acted insolently toward others (222). The gospel-aretology-apology shows an adversative situation where the powerful figure defeats the enemy (carrying out contested action, showing himself legitimate or confusing the enemy) and also proclaims his true role both as healer and destroyer. As Apollonius says, men need one who is regarded as a god -- to fear "to do what a god disapproved of," a "god sent down by wisdom"...."to wean them from lusts and passions." (8:7:7).[22]

Thus miracle doing and prophecy were important for Hellenistic society, but were damped by possible accusations of maleficia. However, although the accusations of maleficia were what the society used to catch the man of power, the reply to the accusation was what the man of power used to proclaim both the good he could do and the divine maleficia he could set in motion.

S 93 A CRITIQUE OF KELBER'S "THE HOUR OF THE SON OF MAN AND THE TEMPTATION OF THE DISCIPLES: MARK 14:32-42"

Gene Szarek
Mundelein College

Werner H. Kelber has recently edited a volume of essays, *The Passion Narrative in Mark* (Fortress Press, 1976). These remarks are intended as a starting point for discussion on the third essay of that book, his own, titled "The Hour of the Son of Man and the Temptation of the Disciples: Mark 14:32-42" [pp. 41-60]. In it Kelber proposes to advance scholarly consideration of the Markan Gethsemane pericope beyond the usual form-critical, source-critical, and history-of-traditions analyses. He chooses to accomplish this by employing redaction-critical methodology under the conscious presupposition that a fundamental intelligibility and coherence exist within the Markan corpus. He seeks to uncover the theological meaning of the pericope as given in the text and disclaims any further need to differentiate redaction from tradition. He accomplishes well what he sets out to do.

I will divide my criticism into three parts: first, a brief recapitulation of the successful results of his effort; next, some point for further consideration; and last, a few areas of disagreement.

I

A particularly valuable contribution of Kelber to the study of the Markan passion narrative lies in his recognition of the association of kingdom theology and passion christology. He develops this concept by relating the *coming* [ἤγγικεν] of the kingdom of God in 1:15 with the *coming* of the betrayer in 14:42. These are the only two loci in the gospel where this verb is used in this form, and both times the coming is an announcement of Jesus. Because of this association, Kelber can point to the eschatological dimension of the "deliverance" of Jesus. He strengthens his argument by demonstrating the manner in which the title "king" is attributed to Jesus only in the passion narrative [pp. 45-46].

Although I would not agree with every detail of his work on the three sleeping disciples, attention should be called to Kelber's very helpful correlation of the cluster *watching-coming-finding-sleeping* in both the parable of the doorkeeper [13:33-37] and the Gethsemane scene [14:32-42]. Because of the appearance of this cluster of words at the end of the Apocalyptic Discourse, he is able to suggest convincingly an eschatological character to the conduct of the disciples at Gethsemane [pp. 48-49].

Kelber's application of Bird's insights into some Markan *gar*-clauses[1] is commendable. In general, critical scholarship seems reluctant to acknowledge multiple layers of meaning within the Markan text except as a sort of cop-out when greater precision is out of reach. Kelber is quite correct, at 14:40, in supposing that the physical "heaviness of eyes" for Mark is a way of

[1]C.H. Bird, "Some *gar*-clauses in St. Mark's Gospel," *Journal of Theological Studies* n.s. 4 (1953), 171-187.

dramatizing a spiritual blindness of the disciples in the face of the events transpiring before their "eyes" [p. 49].

The triple visits of Jesus to the disciples [14:37-42] is matched structurally by Kelber with the three passion predictions [8:31; 9:31; 10:33-34], the three denials of Peter [14:68, 70, 71], and the three"hours" on the cross [15:25, 33, 34-37]. He is thus able to show not only the internal function of the three visits [the inexcusable blindness of the disciples] but to suggest an external relation of Gethsemane to other parts of the Gospel. Because of the affinity of these four scenes structurally, he is able to say: "The correlation of these four threefold scenes, which variously emphasize the divine necessity and human rejection of passion, underscores the tragically irreconcilable conflict between passion Christology and discipleship failure" [p. 53].

Finally, a word of appreciation ought to be registered for Kelber's method. He carefully works out the issues of the text itself and moves programmatically, first to the adjacent context, then to the larger context of the whole Gospel, finally to the Markan milieu. It is easy to follow his argument and to offer judgment on the various phases of his work. The earlier stages are tightly controlled and though the results may be modest, they are firm; the last stage, in which he moves towards ecclesial considerations, leaves me less confident. Overall, Kelber operates with considerable restraint, allowing--even inviting--further research. It is precisely this perceived invitation to collaboration by others that prompts my next remarks.

II

Kelber's association of a Markan kingdom theology with a passion christology [pp. 43-46] is an excellent result of the application of his method. However, he remains unconvincing in his judgment that at 14:35-36 Jesus "is not the suffering Righteous One, but one who seeks to escape his appointed fate of righteous suffering" [p. 44] and that "the request for the passing of the hour and the removal of the cup has every indication of a desire to bypass the cross" [p. 43] and that there must be a Markan reason "for forcing Jesus to the brink of refuting his mission" [p. 46].

A. SORROW UNTO DEATH

It would seem that other possibilities are more likely. The question needs to be raised: could the anguish and horror of Jesus be due to something other than his simple and unsurprising fear of death?

One of the possibilities emerging from the text is that Mark wishes to present Jesus as experiencing a deathly dread of soul, presumably equal to physical dying, if we are not to render περίλυπός ἐστιν ἡ ψυχή μου ἕως θανάτου [14:34] merely metaphorical. If the Markan intent is to suggest that Jesus is undergoing a kind of death in Gethsemane (and I will show below that this is very likely) then this "death" might be due logically to the following possibilities:

1. fear of physical death
2. fear of violating the Father's will: either
   a. by resisting death, or
   b. by accepting death
3. a crisis of meaning: the Markan Jesus is not just "dying" in Gethsemane because he will shortly be dying on Golgotha, but because he is genuinely doubting [failing to understand?] the utility of his physical death.

The first possibility, fear of physical death, is the common explanation of the attitude of Jesus in Gethsemane and is clearly the interpretation embraced by Kelber. This possibility cannot be discounted, but its adequacy may be questioned. I remarked above that a kind of death is occurring in the Gethsemane scene. Already at 14:34, death is mentioned. A purely figurative interpretation of this word does not do justice to the language of the text

...καὶ ἤρξατο ἐκθαμβεῖσθαι
   καὶ ἀδημονεῖν [14:33b]
καὶ λέγει αὐτοῖς·
περίλυπός ἐστιν ἡ ψυχή μου
ἕως θανάτου· [14:34a]

and renders the passage merely pious. Kelber admits the urgency and direct seriousness of the verbs in 14:33b [p. 43] for the understanding of ἕως θανάτου. I would further suggest an examination of the verb in the following verse:

καὶ προελθὼν μικρὸν <u>ἔπιπτεν</u> ἐπὶ τῆς γῆς [14:35a].

Πίπτω is used eight times in the gospel. Jairus fell at the feet of Jesus [5:22] and, in the cure of the child with the speaking malady [9:20], the child fell on the ground. In the Apocalyptic Discourse, the stars of heaven shall fall [13:25]. Apart from the solitary instance in which Jesus is given as falling on the ground [14:35], the only remaining instances of the use of this verb all occur in the Parabolic Discourse, where the falling of the seed is described in four ways:

4:4 ...some fell by the way [παρὰ τὴν ὁδόν]
4:5 ...other fell on rocky ground [ἐπὶ τὸ πετρῶδες]
4:7 ...other fell among the thorns [εἰς τὰς ἀκάνθας]
4:8 ...others fell into the good earth [εἰς τὴν γῆν τὴν καλὴν].

Only the latter seed fell "on the earth" and only this seed bears fruit. This association of seed falling to bear fruit and Jesus falling in the garden is not predicated simply upon the use of the verb "fall," but also upon the phrase "on the ground." Mt 26:39 modifies this and has Jesus falling "on his face." Lk 22:41 changes it altogether and has Jesus "kneeling down."

Consider further that there are two "deaths" in the image of the seed bearing fruit. Mk 4:8 has the seed which falls on the good ground bearing fruit, and Mk 4:29 has the delivery of the fruit which signals harvest time and the sending forth of the sickle. Both moments signify death. Clearly, the harvest is death, but a death that reaps bountiful nourishment. However, there is also an earlier death, the one without which the second is not possible; that is the death of the seed, when it is sown on the ground.

It is not stretching the image at all to suggest that the falling of Jesus in the garden is the first death, the death of the seed which in the parable is unfathomable, and that the crucifixion is the second death, the reaping of the harvest.

Thus, if Jesus endures "death" in the garden, it would seem appropriate to consider a deeper interpretation than fear of physical death.

The second possibility, that the anguish of Jesus is due to his concern for the Father's will, needs also to be considered because of the final line of his prayer:

...ἀλλ᾽ οὐ τί ἐγὼ θέλω ἀλλὰ τί σύ [14:36c].

With the indirect prayer for the passing of the hour [14:35b] and the direct prayer for the removal of the cup [14:36b], Jesus is depicted as having concern for his suffering. But the conclusion about the Father's will depicts Jesus as preoccupied also with the motivation of his prayer. Whatever happens, it should be according to the will of God. When this last line is taken seriously, two possible interpretations emerge: first, that the will of the Father might be violated by Jesus if he should resist death; second, that the will of the Father might be violated by Jesus if he should embrace death.

The common interpretation of 14:36c assumes that Jesus had earlier hoped for escaping death but here "allows for the possibility of ultimate consent to the divine plan of passion" [p. 43]. This interpretation need not be rejected, but its obverse should at least be examined, namely, that Jesus could logically be portrayed here as one who truly wishes to do the will of the Father but who has suddenly been overtaken by the terror of suspecting that the Father's will, after all, is *not* wrapped up in his physical death.

The awareness that the process of deliverance is already beyond recall coupled with the fear that he may be violating the Father's will precisely by accepting death could, logically, produce an agony unto death. Thus, the sense of the prayer would have to be something like the following:

"Do not let me spoil your plan, whatever it may be."

However, this "possible" interpretation breaks down with the use of the initial ἀλλ', which strongly suggests that the Markan Jesus' concern about the Father's will stands *in contrast to* his earlier prayer that "this cup might be removed from me." Thus, a logically possible explanation is, finally, textually impossible. Kelber's position on this correctly stands unchallenged. The agony of doing the Father's will remains related to the notion of resisting death rather than accepting it; and so we continue our search for the content of that agony. We move to a third consideration, which remains both logically and textually plausible.

The third possibility, that the anguish of Jesus is predicated on his uncertainty about the value or meaning of his death, finally makes the most sense. In this view it is necessary to understand both "hour" and "cup" as his present anguish, not as the future crucifixion. Jesus would, accordingly, be praying for freedom from the moral pain of this very moment, namely the doubt that his dying can possibly be victorious. Jesus is not asking to be rescued from death but from the possibility that his death will be useless. He could hardly be praying for the passing of the hour and the removal of the cup on the face of his inevitable death, but he could be praying to be spared the agony of his doubt. In this case, his "nevertheless not what I will, but what you do" should be connected, not with his acceptance of death [which is already beyond his control anyway], but his submission to death *without* meaning, a decidedly added burden.

Of course, an argument cannot be spun out of mere logical possibilities. And so, we turn to textual and structural considerations that support the contention that Jesus dreaded the possible uselessness of his death. These can partially be found in the Baptist stories: John is "delivered up" [1:14] to a totally futile death, caused by the intersection of an ill-conceived Herodian promise, a jealous woman's malice, and a capricious dancer's whimsy [6:22-25]. Since παραδίδωμι is used principally of Jesus as the one delivered up or of Judas Iscariot as the one who will deliver Jesus up [3:19; 14:10, 11, 18, 21, 41, 42, 44; 15:1, 10, 15], it is useful to notice its use in the single reference to the Baptist.[2]

There is nothing especially telling about the *meaning* of the Baptist's deliverance; rather, the quality of trivial and nearly accidental fatality is underlined. This is further brought out by Mark in the comment that Herod "feared John, knowing that he was a just and holy man, and kept him safe. When he heard him, he was much perplexed; and yet he heard him gladly" [6:20]. Further, Mark tells us that "the king was deeply grieved because of the oath he had made" [6:26]. Thus, the only one who permitted and ordered the death of the Baptist would himself have preferred another course. Mark has Pilate in pretty much the same situation vis à vis Jesus: Pilate marvelled at the conduct of Jesus' defense [15:5], wanted to release Jesus because he knew that the chief priests had delivered him up out of envy [15:10], and even asked the people why they wanted to crucify Jesus--"Why, what evil has he done?" [15:14]. Just as Herod wanted to please his reclining guests [6:26] and so ordered the execution of John, so also Pilate resolved to satisfy the crowd [15:15] and delivered up Jesus for crucifixion.

There is no doubt that Mark presents a tragedy of the first order; and to carry through on the total anguish of Jesus, he must even suffer in Gethsemane the ordeal of suspecting that his own will be another useless death. Only the reader of the gospel knows otherwise from the proclamation of the centurion at the foot of the cross: "Truly, this man was the Son of God" [15:39].[3]

This third possibility, then, in addition to being logically plausible and textually sensible, in fact also helps greatly to elucidate the cry on Jesus' lips as he died: "My God, my God, why did you forsake me?" [15:34]. It can be said that what Jesus had concluded at 15:34 in his death cry is very much related to his agonizing prayer in 14:35-36. Thus, the hour that was not spared him and the cup that was not removed both embrace dual considerations: the death itself and the feeling of abandonment or, put another way, the loss of meaning in the death.

---

[2]When this verb appears once at 9:31 and twice at 10:33 in the predictions of the passion-resurrection, the subject is the "Son of Man." In the Apocalyptic Discourse, when this verb occurs at 13: 9, 11, 12, there is registered the same sort of futility and unfairness as is found in the flashback to the Baptist's death [6:14-29]. But here, the instruction of Jesus includes the notions of purpose ["for my sake, as a witness to them," 13:10], consolation ["whatsoever shall be given you in that hour...the Holy Spirit shall speak," [13:11], and a final guarantee of salvation for those who perservere in spite of the oppression [13:13], something the disciples in Gethsemane fail to do.

[3]The Markan story-line does not, however, pursue a totally relentless drama in which Jesus feels only doubt. Much of the discipleship teaching of Jesus and the ὑπὲρ πολλῶν clause of 14:24 indicate that Jesus did grasp the significance of his death. The texts cited above simply provide the context for the suffering of Jesus, who could not know with certainty that his death would be other than the Baptist's. If Jesus had never anticipated the significance of his death, then there would have been no reason for him to accept death; if he had never doubted the significance of his death, then there would have been no tragedy.

A corollary of this hypothesis follows in the readjustment of the relationship between Jesus and the disciples. Both they and Jesus fail to understand. But only the disciples fail in faith; Jesus perseveres in executing the Father's will in spite of the severest doubt. Thus, it cannot be properly said that the non-understanding of the disciples here serves as a foil for the understanding of Jesus; rather, Mark spells out the primacy of faith in the face of non-understanding. The passion narrative given by Mark becomes a treatise on the relationship of faith and understanding.

B. TIME OF DELIVERANCE

The important phrase in 14:41c, d -- ἦλθεν ἡ ὥρα, ἰδοὺ παραδίδοται ὁ υἱὸς τοῦ ἀνθρώπου εἰς τὰς χεῖρας τῶν ἁμαρτωλῶν -- finds illumination not only in the immediate context of anguish and subsequent arrest, but in the wider context of the whole gospel as well.

The first gospel reference to time [ὅτι πεπλήρωται ὁ καιρὸς] occurs in the first statement of the preaching content of Jesus [1:15]. He has earlier been baptized in the Jordan by John [1:9] and driven into the wilderness by the spirit [1:2], where he was tempted by Satan [1:13]. The immediate temporal frame for this preaching of the fulfillment of time is given as the moment of John's "deliverance" [καὶ μετὰ τὸ παραδοθῆναι τὸν Ἰωάννην]. Although "hour" does not specifically occur here, this is already the "fulness of time"; and it is associated with deliverance, in this case John's. The elements that are salient for our study of collocations of time references and deliverance occur here:

1:14-15 "And after John was *delivered*,
Jesus came into Galilee,
preaching the gospel of God:
the *time* has been fulfilled
and the kingdom of God has drawn near;
repent and believe in the gospel."

The next collocation of "time arriving" and deliverance occurs in the context of Jesus' teaching about the kingdom of God in the parable of the harvest [4:26-29]. Thus, when the fruit is delivered up [ὅταν δὲ παραδοῖ ὁ καρπός], immediately the man who planted the seed sends forth the sickle, because the harvest-time has come [4:29]. This is the way the kingdom of God is [4:26]. The man who plants the seed sleeps and rises without ever knowing how the seed matures from blade to ear to full corn [4:27-28]. Still, harvest comes just as certainly as does the hour for the Son of Man [14:41], while the three sleep and do not know how to respond [14:40]. The sickle is sent forth precisely because it is time for harvest; so the crowd accompanying Judas brings swords and clubs [14:43]. Even more, the cross [15:25] figures as the sickle which has been brought out because it is now the time for the harvest. Although the salient elements of deliverance and time-reference appear here in parabolic form, there is no mistaking their similarity to the earlier text at 1:14, especially since both texts bear a relationship to the kingdom of God.

4:26, 29 "So is the kingdom of God,
as if a man should cast seed into the ground...
But when the fruit is *delivered up*,
immediately he sends forth the sickle,
because the *harvest* is come.

There is an additional association of time and deliverance in the Apocalyptic Discourse, at 13:9-13, which begins with the imperative Βλέπετε and continues παραδώσουσιν ὑμᾶς εἰς συνέδρια καὶ...[13:9]. This discourse continues: "Whatever is given to you in that hour [ὃ ἐὰν δοθῇ ὑμῖν ἐν ἐκείνῃ τῇ ὥρᾳ...], speak this, for you are not the ones speaking but the Holy Spirit" [13:11]. A description of that "hour" is given as brother betraying brother to death, and so father and son, children and parents: the disciples shall be hated by all men on account of his name [13:11-12a]. However, before that hour arrives, it is necessary that the gospel be preached to all the nations [13:10]. Mark has already established at 1:14 that the gospel is precisely the news of the fulfillment of time and the drawing near of the kingdom of God. The solitary respite from this prediction of eschatological doom resides in the promise that the one who endures to the end shall be saved [13:13b]. From the narratives of Gethsemane, it becomes obvious who endures to the end, and at what cost. The elements of deliverance and time-reference, thus, are extended here to the disciples for an eschatological significance.

13:9, 11 "But take heed to yourselves;
for they will *deliver* you up to councils...
And when they bring you to trial and *deliver* you up,
do not be anxious beforehand what you are to say;
but say whatever is given you in that *hour*,
for it is not you who speak, but the Holy Spirit."

After 14:41, ὥρα is used as an explicit temporal marker for the crucifixion [15:25, 33 (2x), 34]. Παραδίδωμι is used again at 14:42, 44; 15:1, 10, 15, but not in collocation with ὥρα or καιρός. The time has indeed been fulfilled and the kingdom of God has drawn near. The time of harvest has arrived and the work of the sickle has now to be performed.

III

My largest disagreements with Kelber lie in assessing his conclusions about the cultural and ecclesial milieu of the Markan community [pp. 58-60].

A. He judges that the discipular objection to passion christology "might find a historical explanation in the specific Mkan setting and in the general environment of early Christianity" [p. 58]. He feels that the situation in the Markan church might have been an exaggerated attention to the exalted, risen Lord. The Markan church, he suspects, would prefer bypassing the suffering Jesus in favor of the risen Christ.

Clearly, it is possible to present a story-line, as Mark in fact has done, in which the disciples resist, misunderstand, and fail to accept the passion of Jesus. But it also seems impossible, both logically and theologically, to have a community which, after the fact, gives credence to resurrection without yielding intellectually to a prior dying. One may push the argument farther by saying that the disciples themselves came to the truth of the resurrection only through their eventual insight into the meaning of the death. Put another way, the whole point in Mark about "not understanding" is related to the need for the Son of Man to suffer and die. This is what the disciples, for Mk, could not perceive; this is what kept them blinded. Accordingly, for the Markan community, who also may not be able to understand, only their faith insight into the meaning of the death of Jesus could render resurrection faith possible. Indeed, to the extent that a religious milieu is discernible through analysis of the Gethsemane pericope, it would seem to me that the weight ought not to be given to the polarity of discipular non-understanding vs. Jesus' understanding of the meaning of his death. (My earlier comments would suggest that Jesus too did not clearly understand.) Rather, the foil can be placed between the decisive movement forward of Jesus towards death on the cross (resulting from his "agony unto death" in the garden, the seed falling on the ground and dying, an unfathomable faith response) vs. the discipular scattering and running away from his death. In this way, the church is taught that the crisis resides not in its capacity for understanding, but in its unwillingness to follow Jesus to the cross. The problem faced by the Markan church, I would propose, is not intellectual but existential.

B. Kelber also concludes that "by setting standards over and against the three leading disciples the Mkan Jesus discredits the notions of apostolic leadership and succession" [pp. 59-60]. In fact, episcopal succession as an ecclesiastical issue flowed from a development in the understanding of the tradition of doctrine [the handing down of truth], and is therefore a problem that appeared in church literature only many decades after the composition of the gospel of Mark.[4] Although possible, it is extremely unlikely that so careful and sophisticated an understanding of succession and its attendant problems could have existed so early in the history of the church.

In conclusion, Kelber demonstrates very well the methodic process that flows from the application of redaction criticism and composition criticism to the Gethsemane pericope. Systematically he provides illumination on the text itself, then interprets the text in relation to the entire gospel, finally proposes some possibilities for explaining the purpose for which the gospel was written. The clarity with which he applies his method warmly invites further collaboration from students of Mark.

---

[4]Such succession is first written about ambiguously in 1 Clement and with fuller specificity only in Irenaeus, *Contra Haereses*, Book III. Details are given by E. Szarek, in an unpublished study, "Apostolic Succession in Didache, Clement of Rome, Ignatius of Antioch, Irenaeus, Tertullian, Hippolytus, Origen, and Cyprian," University of San Francisco, July 1970, 26 pp.

CHRISTIAN PROPHECY AND THE Q TRADITION

Richard A. Edwards

There is very little agreement about the extent of Q--even by those who accept the "Quelle" hypothesis. Because the 'second source' theory depends upon the acceptance of the priority of Mark, I see no alternative to a minimal definition of Q, i.e., Q is the material which Matthew and Luke share but which is not found in Mark. Although Matthew and/or Luke may be responsible for changing or modifying the "original" Q, there is no secure way to demonstrate such activity. Thus in each Q pericope there will usually be 1) precise agreement between Matthew and Luke, 2) words which are very close but because of context may be in a different case, person or tense and 3) words, phrases or sentences which are unique. It is only those words which fall into categories 1 and 2 which can be accepted as Q. All attempts to argue that Matthew or Luke has retained the original and that the other evangelist decided not to use it, I consider too speculative for our present task. When I refer to Q, it will be to this restricted body of material and there will be some segments too fragmentary to be of much use in a redactional study.

NUMBER	TITLE	MATTHEW	MARK	LUKE
1	The Preaching of John	3:7-10	1:7-8	3:7-9
		3:11-12		3:15-18
2	Temptations	4:1-11		4:1-13
3	Beatitudes	5:3-12		6:20b-23
4	Love of Enemies	5:38-48		6:27-36
		7:12		
5	Judging	7:1-5	4:24-25	6:37-42
		12:36-37		
		15:14		
		10:24-25		
6	Fruits	7:15-20		6:43-45
		12:33-35		
7	House on Rock	7:21-27		6:46-49
8	Centurion of Capernaum	8:5-13		7:1-10
				13:28-29
9	John's Question and Jesus' Answer	11:2-6		7:18-23
10	Jesus' Witness to John	11:7-19		7:24-35
		21:31-32		16:16
11	Commissioning the Twelve	10:1	6:6b-13	9:1-6
		10:7-11		
		10:14		
12	On Following Jesus	8:18-22		9:57-62
13	Commissioning of 70	9:37-38		10:1-12
		10:7-16		
14	Woes on Galilee	11:20-24		10:13-15
				10:12
15	Whoever Hears You Hears Me	10:40		10:16
16	Thanksgiving and Blessedness of Disciples	11:25-27		10:21-24
		13:16-17		
17	Lord's Prayer	6:9-13		11:1-4
18	Encouragement to Pray	7:7-11		11:9-13
19	Beelzebul Controversy	12:22-30	3:22-27	11:14-23
		9:32-34		
20	Return of the Evil Spirit	12:43-45		11:24-26
21	Sign of Jonah	12:38-42	8:11-12	11:16
		16:1-4		11:29-32
22	Sound Eye	6:22-23		11:34-36
23	Against the Pharisees	23:4-36	7:1-9	11:37-54

24	Fearless Confession	10:26-33		12:2-9
25	Sin against the Holy Spirit	12:31-32	3:29-30	12:10
26	Assistance of the Holy Spirit	10:19-20	13:11	12:11-12 21:14-15
27	Anxiety	1:25-34		12:22-32
28	Treasures in Heaven	6:19-21		12:33-34
29	Watchfulness and Faithfulness	24:42-51		12:35-48
30	Divisions in Households	10:34-36		12:49-53
31	Signs of the Times	16:2-3		12:54-56
32	Agreement with Accuser	5:25-26		12:57-59
33	Mustard Seed	13:31-32	4:30-32	13:18-19
34	Leaven	13:33		13:20-21
35	Exclusions from the Kingdom	7:13-14 7:22-23 8:11-12 19:30		13:22-30
36	Lament over Jerusalem	23:37-39		13:34-35
37	Great Supper	22:1-14		14:15-24
38	Conditions of Discipleship	10:37-38		14:25-33
39	Parable of Salt	5:13	9:49-50	14:34-35
40	Lost Sheep	18:12-14		15:1-7
41	Two Masters	6:24		16:13
42	Concerning the Law	11:12-13 5:18		16:16-17
43	Warning against Offenses	18:6-7	9:42	17:1-3a
44	On Forgiveness	18:15 18:21-22		17:3b-4
45	On Faith	17:19-20	9:28-29	17:5-6
46	Day of the Son of Man	24:23 24:26-27 24:37-39 24:17-18 10:39 24:40-41 24:28	13:19-23 13:14-16	17:22-37
47	Parable of Pounds	25:14-30		19:11-27
48	Precedence	19:28	10:41-45	22:28-30

A further presupposition of this paper is the use of the phrase 'community of Q.' I am assuming that the Q material was collected, used and preserved by a group of like-minded people whose interests and theology will be reflected in the traditions they find useful. This is a basic corollary of form criticism and does not necessarily imply any 'creativity' on the part of the community.

The matter of a definition of prophecy is much more difficult. It is the nature of the redactional approach that one begin with the present form of the text and work toward some statement of the self-understanding of the author or authors. This is especially important in a matter as broad and complex as an understanding of prophecy. There is a general assumption that any spirit-initiated activity can be labeled prophecy--that 'inspired' equals 'prophetic.' On the other hand, some others would suggest a definition which points to a specific content or theme as the determining factor, e.g., judgment saying, _Satz heiligen Rechtes_ , etc. This latter approach assumes that the definitions of prophecy which have been developed by Old Testament scholars, as e.g. Westermann, should be used for the New Testament.

Since there is specific mention of prophetic activity in the New Testament and because of the continuity between Old Testament and New Testament, the question about prophecy in Q is certainly legitimate. But my redaction critical approach leads me to argue that the first task is to seek some indication that the redactors or final editors had some interest in, or concern for, the whole matter.

It seems best at this point to summarize my overall understanding of the theology of the community of Q. The starting point is the recognition of the absence of any specific reference to the redemptive significance of Jesus' death. Rather than concentrate on the passion, the Q material is composed almost entirely of sayings of Jesus. When one tries to co-ordinate the content of these sayings and the themes which they contain, the following characteristics emerge:

1. an anticipation of the imminent return of Jesus as Son of Man.
2. a need to continue to proclaim Jesus' sayings (rather than proclaim his death and resurrection.)
3. a recognition that Jesus is still active within the community by inspiring prophets to speak in his name.
4. a need to prepare for his coming by fulfilling the demands placed upon them by the coming judge.
5. a consciousness of the negative reaction (persecution) toward those who speak and act as Jesus directs.

The emphasis throughout is upon the practical necessities of the end-time--one must prepare for the coming of the kingdom and its attendant judgment. The one who was here among men is soon to come again. But, in place of speculation about the final event, the Q community seems to stress the words spoken by the judge so that those who listen will be able to prepare for his arrival. There are a large number of wisdom forms in Q, in conjunction with both the eschatological and prophetic themes. I see this as an indication of the community's view of Jesus as a combination of teacher, prophet and wise man. His fate was similar to that of most of the prophets--they have all been persecuted or killed by the "fathers" of Jesus' (and the community's) opponents. Nonetheless, even though Jesus died, he will soon return as the judge. And because the judgement is near at hand, his followers are to prepare by following his teachings.

The immediate problem of this seminar is to determine whether any of the Q sayings originated as sayings of prophets, or of the historical Jesus, or from some other source. Gene Boring's article is an example and there have been enough references to his work in this seminar to assume that we all are aware of this approach.[1] D. Hill has argued, on the other hand, that it is impossible to establish that a specific statement was created by a Christian prophet.[2] As I understand it, Hill's point is that the evidence for the creative role of Christian prophets is indeed weak. In his analysis of Bultmann and others, the frequent reference to the book of Revelation, which he feels represents a separate and unique tradition, carries little weight. Moreover, neither John nor Paul offer any direct evidence that prophets spoke in the name of the risen Christ. Against Käsemann[3] he advises caution in moving from a literary feature (Satz heiligen Rechts) "to a judgment concerning the identity of those who may have employed the form: form-criticism cannot demonstrate the prophetic origins of the 'sentences' investigated." Käsemann goes too far, he feels, in assuming that only those "endowed with charisma" can recognize the criterion for divine judgment and proclaim it.

I tend to agree. There is some correlation between seeking to authenticate the sayings of Jesus and those of Christian prophets--in fact, one must argue that a saying is not from Jesus in order to argue that it comes from a Christian prophet. The limits of that task are well known.

The alternative is to seek an understanding of the Q community: the contours of its thought and self-understanding.

Some recent attempts to write a theology of Q have tackled the problem of prophecy. S. Schulz has argued that the "oldest layer" of Q material comes from a community which exhibits Post-Easter enthusiasm or eschatological-spirit-possession within an apocalyptic context.[4] Although he uses the word prophecy from time to time, his emphasis is on a prophetic-apocalyptic enthusiasm.

His argument, in brief, is that the lego humin formula demonstrates that the exalted Lord speaks directly through the mouth of his prophets. This formula is the key item. In addition, beatitudes and woes in an eschatological context, Satz heilgen Rechts, and other sayings are used to substantiate the main point.

The difficulty that Schulz has in demonstrating that these are prophetic statements is partly dependent upon his division of the material into older and newer (supposedly Hellenistic) layers as well as the fact that this combination of prophecy and apocalypse is also influenced by wisdom traditions. That is, we are dealing with a phenomenon for which we have no specific label other than the awkward combination--"eschatology-prophecy-wisdom." Thus our normal definitions and criteria for prophetic sayings do not fit precisely. This problem, on top of the basic problem of determining the authenticity of non-original tradition, has led to the general description of prophecy as 'inspired' speech.

It seems more profitable to seek to comprehend the outlook and self-understanding of the community. What can be said about prophecy or prophets in the Q community--even though specific evidence is lacking which would assign a particular saying to the creative activity of a Post-Easter prophet? The material we have to work with is not easy to deal with redactionally because we do not have any comparative sources (as we do with Matthew and Luke, viz. Mark). Nor do we know the order of the material, which eliminates any kind of composition analysis as in the study of Mark and Acts. Because Q is composed almost entirely of sayings of Jesus, we must use the structure and style of the argument of those sayings to uncover the intention of the community which preserved and used them.

I see three emphases in Q: eschatology, prophecy and wisdom. It is not merely a matter of three different, isolated or consecutive elements, but an interaction of the three which results in a combination that has its own distinctive character. That prophecy is tempered with elements of the other two needs to be demonstrated.

First, let me briefly indicate how I differentiate between wisdom and prophecy. A wisdom approach is characterized by its use of comparison, either explicitly with terms "like," "as," etc., or simply by juxtaposing two elements, a technique which leads to metaphor and parable. To make a point using this approach, one relies on a basic cultural atmosphere in which certain ideas and concepts are already present. Then by the juxtaposition and comparison of images or ideas, the hearer is encouraged to recognize the point one wishes to make. Thus wisdom depends upon a specific cultural basis as the background for the audience's experience.

Prophecy, on the other hand, I understand to be a means whereby new, revelatory information or data is presented in a declarative manner. Certainly the prophet makes use of the experience of his hearer, but he uses that experience as a way of illustrating the relation between current attitudes and/or practices and the demands or announcements of the Deity. Although one might easily acknowledge the validity of the prophetic announcement, its truthfulness is not based upon an argument from experience. One's agreement with the prophet rests on an acceptance of the source of authority from which he speaks--which usually leads to a similar assessment of the problem.

Although we might expect an eschatological emphasis in a prophetic statement, its presence within a wisdom context is unusual.

Evidence for prophecy in Q.

1. Prophets are mentioned in 6 places in Q:
   Lk. 6:22-23 (Mt. 5:11-12) In this final, lengthy beatitude the prophets are described as those who are persecuted. The point of the saying is that "you" will be reviled, as the prophets were reviled; so your reward will also be great.

   Lk. 7:26 (Mt. 11:9 and 11) John the Baptist is declared to be more than a prophet. The quotation from Mal. 3:1 implies that John is the messenger who is more than a prophet.

   Lk. 10:23-24 (Mt. 13:16-17) Luke places this saying about the blessedness of those who see and hear at the conclusion of the so-called synoptic Johannine pericope; Mt. places it at the conclusion of his explanation for speaking in parables. Many prophets desired to see and hear what 'you' see and hear, but did not.

   Lk. 11:47-51 (Mt. 23:29-32, 34-36) Among the woes against the Pharisees, they are accused of building tombs to the prophets who were killed by their fathers. More prophets will be sent, who will also be killed and persecuted. 'This generation' will repeat the misdeeds of their fathers.

   Lk. 13:34-35 (Mt. 23:37-39) Lesus laments over Jerusalem because they stone and killed prophets and 'those who are sent to you.'

   Lk. 16:16 (Mt. 11:12-13) A difficult saying in which the prophets are associated with the law; these are until John. Violence is mentioned, but not specifically associated with the prophets; it is a feature of the present.

2. The <u>lego humin</u> introductory formula, has often been considered as indication of prophetic activity and is quite prominent in Q.

Matthew: 14 in Q (7 more in a Q context)
11 from Mark (6 more in Markan context)
19 in "special M"

Luke: 14 in Q (9 more in a Q context)
9 from Mark (1 more in Markan context)
15 in "special Luke"

3. A traditional characteristic of prophetic speech is its style of announcement rather than argument. The prophet, it is argued, speaks as a messenger of YHWH who announces his (YHWH's) will and the results of present action. Sayings with this proclamatory force are found in Q primarily in a variety of judgment and warning sayings.

   Lk. 10:12 (Mt. 10:15) More tolerable for Sodom.

   Lk. 10:13-15 (Mt. 11:20-24) Woe to Chorazin and Bethsaida. More tolerable in the judgment for Tyre and Sidon.

   Lk. 12:8-9 (Mt. 10:32-33) He who acknowledges or denies, will be acknowledged or denied.

   Lk. 3:17 (Mt. 3:12) . . . but the chaff he will burn with unquenchable fire.

4. Two other factors which would help to support some of the earlier material are 1) the interest in John the Baptist and his preaching of judgment and 2) the use of quotations from the Old Testament prophetic books.

Although the material cited is of varying strength and usefulness, I find it significant enough to suggest that the Q community has given enough clues to one aspect of its self-understanding. However, it is far from certain that any or all of these sayings originated with the community. That is an issue which current methods cannot solve. The point to be stressed is their use of these sayings in conjunction with the emphasis on eschatology and a style that we usually designate 'wisdom.'

Thus the prophetic dimension in Q is tempered by its context--by wisdom and eschatology. There is a new outlook on life because of the imminence of the Son of Man. Wisdom forms and styles are often employed to express this concern.

In the material about John the Baptist (pericopes number 1,9,10), John is described as a prophet, and more than a prophet--he is the one sent before the messenger and the one who marks the beginning of the new age, an age of violence. As with other prophets, he is rejected. His preaching is full of criticism of those who come to hear him and he uses proverbial styles of speaking to emphasize the need to act as though the end were imminent for this generation. The Q material adds to the Markan account of his preaching (about the coming one who baptizes with the Holy Spirit) a note about fire and the parable about the threshing floor; the chaff and the wheat will be separated, and the chaff burned. Also, John's doubt about the authority of Jesus is answered with a quotation from the prophet Isaiah.

In pericope #12 'On Following Jesus' we have the declarative style of a prophetic statement in which a judgment or conclusion is proclaimed and not argued. These are the radical demands of the end-time which are expressed in parabolic language in one case, and with a command in the other.

Number 13 ends with the judgment upon the town which does not respond to those who come in Jesus' name. The basic purpose of the mission is to announce the approach of the kingdom of God. But the situation is described with the use of the harvest imagery and a comparison about wolves and lambs.

The same comparative approach is found in the 'Woes on Galilee' (#14). Judgment is specifically announced as a future event. It will come upon these towns of Galilee for their lack of response to the teaching; even the Gentiles to the north would have repented.

Number 15 is unusual in that the form of the saying (the Satz with present tense verb) is obvious even though the specific vocabulary differs. Käsemann has argued that the Satz is obviously a saying of a prophet because of its judgmental features. Here we lack the future verb in the apodosis and perhaps are moving closer to a wisdom 'sentence.' The phrase 'him who sent me' is close to the prophetic mission consciousness.

In #16 Luke has attached the beatitude about the disciples to Jesus' thanksgiving. The disciples are better off than "many prophets and kings (Lk), righteous men (Mt)" because of what they have seen and heard. If these two units belong together in Q, the content of the disciple's perception is the knowledge of the identity of the son and the father and those "things which have been delivered" to the Son. There is no mention of the further consequences of the possession of such knowledge, but the emphasis on proclamation found at other points in Q can be inferred. Although there is a reference to the wise, it is a typical prophetic dig about the ignorance of God among those who are wise to the ways of the world. The prophetic emphasis on revealed information is present throughout.

Number 18 contains specific wisdom comparative arguments but there is an assurance about the will and goodness of God.

In the Sign of Jonah complex (#21) the specific reference to the preaching of Jonah is the most noteworthy detail. The men of Nineveh "repented," yet "something greater than Jonah is here," viz, the preaching of the Q community, the presentation of the words of Jesus. The wisdom dimension is also present in explicit form with the same comparison between the wisdom of Solomon and the wisdom of the Q community.

The eschatological correlative which explains the enigmatic phrase, 'except the sign of Jonah,' may originally have been similar to Luke's version, with its emphasis on the effect of Jonah's preaching rather than his miraculous deliverance.

In the long collection of Woes against the Pharisees (#23), we find the theme of the persecution of the prophets mentioned above. Aside from the judgmental character of the 'Woe' form of statement, there is the curious problem of Mattnew's use of 'I,' over against Luke's 'the Wisdom of God,' in the statement about the sending of 'prophets' and 'apostles' (Luke),'wisemen and scribes (Matthew).'

The lament over Jerusalem (#36) states that the city is doomed because of the killing and stoning of the prophets and 'those who are sent to you.' The declarative announcement of the judgment is combined with the wisdom-like image of the hen and chicks. The closing beatitude underlies the image of coming or being sent.

Although the evidence is not precise, we have enough information to suggest that some, if not all, of the members of the Q community saw their role in the end-time in a way similar to that of the prophets of Israel. They announce the will of YHWH by repeating the words of Jesus, the Son of Man. So Jesus was presecuted, and as the prophets were persecuted, so they also have been and expect to be mistreated in the last days. However, along with the prophetic elements, there are wisdom sayings and forms, implying that the end-time has also given them a new insight into the meaning of man's relationship to the creation. There are lessons to be learned and communicated from the world of nature and social affairs which are not pronouncements but lead to similar conclusions. Prophecy is one element in a larger complex.

NOTES

1. M. Eugene Boring. "How May We Identify Oracles of Christian Prophets in the Synoptic Tradition? Mark 3:28-29 as a Test Case," JBL, 91 (1972), 501-21.

2. David Hill. "On the Evidence for the Creative Role of Christian Prophets," NT Studies, 20 (1974), 262-274.

3. Ernst Käsemann. "Sentences of Holy Law in the New Testament," New Testatament Questions of Today (Philadelphia: Fortress, 1969), 66-81.

4. Siegfried Schulz, Q: Die Spruchquelle Der Evangelisten (Zürich: Theologischer Verlag, 1972).

S 103 CHRISTIAN PROPHECY AND MATT 10:23: A TEST EXEGESIS

M. Eugene Boring
The Graduate Seminary, Phillips University

This paper has a limited purpose: to marshall the evidence that Matt 10:23 is an oracle of a Christian prophet, and to explore some of the implications of this for interpreting the text. Considerations of space therefore dictate that decisions on related critical issues can only be stated, rather than argued for. These are, with more or less assurance from case to case, as follows: (1) Matt 10 is Matthew's construction from Mark, Q, and M material, though some of it may have existed as tradition-clusters before its incorporation into the various sources. Traditionsgeschichte, and not just source analysis, must play a role in the consideration of our text. (2) Matt 10:23 is an original unit, independent of its context but not itself a composite from two independent sayings. (3) The saying originated neither from the historical Jesus nor the evangelist Matthew.

Although this verse has often been designated the product of Christian prophecy[1], this declaration has rarely been supported with evidence. Our method will be to indicate the points of contact between this logion and Christian prophecy as we otherwise know it, and inquire whether these are sufficient in number and power of persuasion to indicate that this logion originated as Christian prophecy. Our hypothesis is that this is in fact the case. The evidence is as follows:

1. Form Criticism

The five synoptic sayings Mark 9:1, 13:30, Matt 5:18, 10:23 and 23:39 possess a strikingly similar form: a solemn introduction with ἀμὴν λέγω ὑμῖν (Matt 23:39 may also have originally had ἀμήν preceding λέγω ὑμῖν), an emphatic (οὐ μή) declaration that something will not happen (4x ἕως ἄν , once μέχρις οὗ) before the eschaton, which at least four of the five cases is assumed to be near.[2] This form is appropriate to Christian prophets, but not to others. Not only is ἀμὴν λέγω ὑμῖν itself an indication of prophetic speech,[3] but a declaration that the eschaton will occur before some present state of affairs ceases to be is the kind of statement that can only be made ab ovo by one who knows himself authorized by charismatic power. Later scribes may repeat it, but not invent it.

The remarkably close similarity in form between the five sayings suggests the same Sitz im Leben. All four of the other sayings have been the subjects of arguments of varying strength to the effect that they are from Christian prophecy.[4] The cumulative effect of this argument is to suggest that this would also be the origin of Matt 10:23.

2. Relation to Tradition

Although Christian prophets originated characteristic forms for their oracles, they did not create the content of their message ex nihilo, but derived much of it from previous tradition. Revelation is a clear example. The line has been drawn too hastily and too firmly between prophecy and tradition. Christian prophets sometimes drew elements of their message from authentic words of Jesus handed on in the tradition. There may be a core of pre-Easter material in Matt 10:23, but if so, it is no longer possible to identify it, and it must in the nature of the case be minimal, if there at all[5]. A more likely possibility, which remains only a possibility, is that the early Palestinian church had taken over a Jewish tradition (Sota 9:15) that in the days just preceding the advent of the Messiah "the people of the frontier (or Gebul) should go about from city to city with none to show mercy on them"[6]. This tradition may have been adopted by the church and then re-formed and re-presented by a prophet as the word of the exalted Lord. But there is no evidence in whatever traditional material this logion may contain to link it to Christian prophets.

3. The "Wandering" Motif

The logion presupposes a setting in which bands of Christian missionaries go from city to city. If Christian prophets had been non-settled, wandering "free lance" figures, this would seem to be a solid point of contact between the saying and Christian prophecy. Harnack, still full of enthusiasm from the then-recent discovery of the Didache, pictured Christian prophets as being such independent extra-congregational figures, and his view has been widely influential. But this picture is overdrawn and too narrowly based. The NT in fact mostly describes prophets as congregational figures who function within the local church rather than as individuals. Such prophets may from time to time go from one church to another, or be sent by a church on preaching missions, but this is not of the esse of the prophets' role.

In any case, we must observe that it is the speaker of the oracle who is being suggested as a prophet, not necessarily those to whom the oracle is addressed. I would picture the oracle as originally having been delivered in a "commissionning" service in which a church was sending out missionaries, as in Acts 13:1ff. The saying is a word of consolation not for persecuted Christians in general (although Matthew later understands it this way), but for persecuted missionaries. Some of the "wandering" missionaries being charged by this saying may themselves be prophets--again as in Acts 13--, but the wandering motif per se cannot be used for or against the origin of the saying in Christian prophecy.

4. The Persecution Motif

The saying reflects not only mission, but persecution. It is not necessary to choose between these two[7], nor to divide the verse into 23a (persecution) and 23b (mission) as originally separate units[8], for both were fused in the experience of early Palestinian Christianity. Explicit references to persecution are not only an indication of post-Easter origin[9], but sometimes an indication of prophetic speech. Suffering and even martyrdom were already firmly a part of the picture of the true prophet in first century Judaism [10]. This aspect of prophecy was taken over by the church, and confirmed by its experience. The expectation that the missionaries would be persecuted is especially appropriate to Christian prophets who would tend to see the church's mission in prophetic terms, and may be taken as one evidence of the prophetic origin of the saying.

5. Response to A Concrete Issue

"In my opinion prophecy is the gift of understanding and expressing what the will of God is for a given present situation."[11] This is certainly one aspect of prophecy in the NT. When a community which wished to live by the word of its Lord faced situations for which there was no dominical saying in the tradition, a Christian prophet sometimes arose to deliver the word to that situation. The content of prophecy was not reflective, hypothetical, abstract, or speculative, but directed to a specific situation. Practical problems of church life received revealed answers, as is shown, e.g., in Hermas, Mandates iv, 1:4ff, 3:1ff, and the Apocalypse of John. The prophetic oracle contained in the earliest writing in the NT (I Thess 4:15f) is a response to a pressing practical problem. Although in dialogue with the tradition (both receiving materials from it and contributing materials to it), "belief in the Spirit could legitimize breaks with the tradition."[12] There was firm tradition that the Christian should stand firm in the face of opposition. Some of this tradition was from Jesus, but some was the creation of Christian prophets, as Revelation for example shows. But what if standing fast in the face of persecution endangers the mission with which the missionaries have been charged by the risen Lord himself? Should the missionaries stand fast, even at the risk of their lives (and of the mission), or flee? The latter course seemed not only to accept defeat, but to concede that the mission was illigitimate, since the true prophet does not retreat at the prospect of suffering. I think it was to such a situation that the oracle Matt 10:23 was directed. Flight in the face of persecution was not cowardice or strategy, but obedience to the exalted Lord, authorized by a word from his prophet. This authorization came not only by virtue of the form of the saying as a direct word from the heavenly Lord, but is supported by the content derived from the thought-world within which early Christian prophecy lived: eschatological-apocalyptic paraclesis.

6. Eschatological Paraclesis

In attempting to determine the meaning of the saying, it is very important to distinguish between the sense in which Matthew might have understood it as already a given part of his tradition, and the meaning which the logion was intended to express at its original promulgation. Thus the various ways of understanding the coming of the Son of Man in this text as referring to something other than the parousia at the end of history are at least possible for Matthew, however unlikely they may be: a meeting of Jesus and the twelve during the course of the mission,[13] Jesus' death and/or resurrection,[14] or the crisis of the Jewish war 66-73.[15] Such explanations may help a later generation--Matthew's or ours--to make acceptable sense of a saying which in its obvious meaning has become an embarrassment. But no one who wanted to speak of a rendezvous between Jesus and the twelve, or the resurrection, or the Jewish war, would choose to express any one of these meanings in the form in which Matt 10:23 now stands. The original meaning of this oracle must refer to the parousia at the end of history. The inner logic of the saying is this: "When you are persecuted, the heavenly Lord authorizes you to flee to another town. This is not cowardice, but is made necessary by the shortness of time before the eschaton and by the missionary imperative. Do not remain in an inhospitable town, because you will not have completed the assigned task of preaching in every city in Israel before the End. Matt 10:23b is the ground for the command in 10:23a, and it is such only if understood in its natural sense, eschatologically. It is on the basis of their claimed insight into the eschatological Heilsplan Gottes that the Christian prophets offer their word of command for the present situation. The command is not arbitrary, nor based on its authority as an inspired oracle alone, nor is the eschatological content speculative. Eschatological insight functions pastorally; pastoral "advice" is more than that, it is command grounded in a revealed eschatological mystery.[16] The Apocalypse is similar in form and function, though the resulting command is different. There, eschatological insight results in the charge to be faithful to the point of martyrdom; here, to flee persecution. Though the situation and content are different, the form and function are the same, and as we are clearly dealing with Christian prophecy in Revelation, we might well suppose that this is also the case in Matt 10:23.

7. Son of Man

I think a good case can be made that in the early post-Easter enthusiasm it was Christian prophets who first identified Jesus as the Son of Man, and that the whole tradition of Son of Man sayings depends on this early prophetic speech event. The transition from the proclaimer to the proclaimed was facilitated by Christian prophets who spoke in Jesus' name as the Son of Man. There was thus a middle term between proclaimer and proclaimed: Jesus the self-proclaimed Son of Man through his spokesmen the prophets.[17] The formative power of this original event impressed itself on the tradition, so that throughout the NT trajectory including the final redaction of each of the four gospels, Son of Man remains exclusively a self-description of Jesus in the first person.

This is not to say, however, that any particular extant Son of Man saying originated in Christian prophecy, for once the identification of Jesus and Son of Man was made, non-charismatics could also place Son of Man sayings in Jesus' mouth. This in fact was done, but, so far as the Synoptic Gospels indicate, rather sparingly. Matthew creates one Son of Man saying at the most, 13:36-43, and inserts Son of Man into only two contexts where it does not appear in his tradition, 16:28/Mark 9:1 and 26:2/Mark 14:1. Luke creates no Son of Man sayings, and inserts Son of Man redactionally only in 21:36, 22:48, and perhaps 6:22. These three factors, namely that most Son of Man sayings are secondary, that all are in the first person, and that there was a reluctance by non-prophets to formulate Son of Man sayings, would indicate that the presence of Son of Man in a secondary saying would increase its probability of having originated in Christian prophecy, and is one more reason to consider Matt 10:23 to be from a Christian prophet.

8. Authority

One of the most frequent arguments for the authenticity of this saying is that it would not have been preserved after its erroneous prediction became obvious unless, as Carsten Colpe states, "it really was a saying of the Lord."[18] Granted that some considerable authority must have been behind the statement for it to have continued in circulation after its lack of fulfillment was clear, we must not fall into the same trap as Colpe and assume that the authoritative sayings which the early church considered "really" from the Lord were all from the pre-Easter Jesus. It is of the nature of prophetic materials that their authority remains and the materials themselves are preserved even when their predictions fail of fulfillment.[19] Again, Revelation is "Exhibit A" in this regard. It too predicts the near advent of the Son of Man, was mistaken in this, but continued to be circulated as authoritative "Word of the Lord."

Matt 10:23 is here as in other respects a miniature Apocalypse, and has the same authority behind it: the risen Lord and his prophetic spokesman.

9. *Traditionsgeschichtlich* Context

I refer here not to traditional elements which may be contained in the logion (see #2 above), but to a saying's setting(s) in the process of transmission as an aid in determining whether it is of prophetic origin or not. This is a slippery approach in which the door is opened to an even greater degree of subjectivity than is usual in our enterprise, but it has not yet been sufficiently probed to determine whether or not it might be a helpful method. A few efforts have been made, thus far inconclusively.[20] The elements of this approach involve the following hypotheses: (1) Christian prophets functioned in proximity to the tradition and in dialogue with it. (2) Materials originating in or influenced by Christian prophets would tend to be clustered together in the transmission process. (3) Tradition clusters handed on in a setting where Christian prophets were active would tend to manifest characteristics associated with Christian prophecy. (4) Material located in a tradition-complex which has contacts with Christian prophets is itself suspect of prophetic origin or development.

If *traditionsgeschichtlich* context should turn out to be a helpful methodological approach in identifying the sayings of Christian prophets in the synoptic tradition, how would this method apply to Matt 10:23? There are at least four possibilities, whose potential in this regard remains unexplored: (1) The possible original connection of the sayings Mark 9:1, 13:30, Matt 5:18, 10:23, 23:39 in the *same Sitz im Leben*, temporally and geographically, would need to be investigated. Establishing *traditionsgeschichtlich* connections among the sayings, or showing that none exist (and not just observations on *formal* similarities) would clarify all of them, and help to decide whether all (or none) of them are from Christian prophets. (2) If 10:17-23 were originally or at some time in the tradition process a unit, as suggested by Lloyd Gaston,[21] the incorporation of this into the Markan little apocalypse, which is of Christian prophetic origin, would bring 10:23 into conjunction with Christian prophecy. (3) If 10:23 were originally or at some point in its transmission history the conclusion to the Q unit in Luke 12:2-12, as Schürmann argues,[22] the number of prophetic features in this passage suggest a connection of Matt 10:23 with Christian prophecy. (4) If the speech complex in Matt 10 as a whole had already taken some shape in the Matthean community before Matthew's final redaction, a community in which Christian prophets had been active, as argued by Käsemann, the features of Christian prophecy found elsewhere in the speech would suggest that the whole complex, 10:23 included, was shaped by Christian prophets.

Admittedly, such *traditionsgeschichtlich* considerations are very tenuous. They are offered as suggestions already made by responsible scholars which, if developed, might prove helpful. If any of the four possibilities became demonstrably probable, it would strengthen the case that Matt 10:23 is the oracle of a Christian prophet.

NOTES

[1]In addition to those listed by David Aune's index in SBL 1975 Seminar Papers, (Missoula: Scholars Press, 1975), p. 132 (Käsemann, Tödt, Perrin, Hasler, Vielhauer, Luck), some others are Eta Linnemann, Die Gleichnisse Jesu (Göttingen, 1961) 138ff; Walter Grundmann, Das Evangelium nach Matthäus (HKNT 1; Berlin, 1968) 294, and Lloyd Gaston, No Stone on Another (SNT 23; Leiden, 1970) 455; Douglas Hare, The Theme of Jewish Persecution of Christians in the Gospel according to St. Matthew (NTSMS 6; Cambridge, 1967) 111.

[2]See Gaston, Stone, 451ff, who does not include Matt 5:18 in his discussion. Gaston considers them four versions of a single saying; I would see them as five sayings with a single form.

[3]See e.g. Victor Hasler, Amen: Redaktionsgeschichtliche Untersuchung zur Einführungsformel der Herrenworte 'Wahrlich ich sage euch' (Zürich, 1969).

[4]See Aune's index cited above.

[5]Cf. Heinz Tödt, The Son of Man in the Synoptic Tradition (NTL; Philadelphia: Westminster, 1965) 62.

[6]E. Bammel, "Matthäus 10:23", Studia Theologica 15 (1961) 79-92.

[7]Contra Bammel, "Matthäus 10:23", p. 92, and Heinz Schürmann, "Zur Traditions and Redaktionsgeschichte von Matt 10:23", Biblische Zeitschrift NF 3 (1959) 82-88.

[8]Contra Erich Grässer, Das Problem der Parusieverzögerung in den synoptischen Evangelien und in der Apostelgeschichte (Beih. z. ZNW 22; Berlin, 1957) 137.

[9]Ferdinand Hahn, Mission in the New Testament (SBT; Naperville, 1965) 56.

[10]See J. Jeremias, New Testament Theology, Vol. I, The Proclamation of Jesus (New York, 1971) 280 and the literature given there.

[11]Hendrikus Berkhof, The Doctrine of the Holy Spirit (Richmond, 1964) 91.

[12]A. D. Nock, St. Paul (New York, 1938) 61.

[13]J. Dupont, "Vous n'aurez pas achevé les villes d'Israel avant que le Fils de l'homme ne vienne", Novum Testamentum 2 (1958) 228-44.

[14]Karl Barth, Church Dogmatics III/2, The Doctrine of Creation (Edinburgh, 1960) 499f, and W. F. Albright, Matthew (Anchor Bible; New York, 1971) 125.

[15]Peter Ellis, Matthew: His Mind and His Message (Collegeville, 1974) 51.

[16]Gaston, Stone, 55f.

17 M. Eugene Boring, Christian Prophets and the Gospel of Mark, unpublished Ph. D. dissertation (Vanderbilt, 1969) 200-13.

18 Carsten Colpe, "ὁ υἱὸς τοῦ ἀνθρώπου " TDNT 8:437; cf. also A. L. Moore, The Parousia in the New Testament (Supp. to Nov. Test. 13; Leiden, 1966) 99; V. Taylor, The Life and Ministry of Jesus (Nashville, 1955) 115.

19 Cf. Johannes Lindblom, Prophecy in Ancient Israel (Philadelphia, 1962) 199f.

20 See e.g. Ernst Käsemann, "Sentences of Holy Law in the NT", NT Questions of Today (Philadelphia, 1969), 77; Tödt, Son of Man 207-11; Gerd Theissen, "Wanderradikalismus. Literatursozialogische Aspekte der Überlieferung von Worten Jesu im Urchristentum", Zeitschrift für Theologie und Kirche 70 (1973) 25]; Sherman Johnson, The Gospel according to St. Mark (New York, 1960) 84.

21 Gaston, Stone, 454ff.

22 Schürmann, "Traditions und Redaktionsgeschichte", 82-88

23 Ernst Käsemann, in an unpublished Göttingen lecture series, 1964; cf. "Sentences", 77.

S 121
A 184

MIGRATION THEORIES VS. CULTURE CHANGE AS AN EXPLANATION FOR EARLY ISRAEL

George E. Mendenhall
University of Michigan

For at least three thousand years folk traditions and scholars alike have attempted to explain the sudden emergence of cultures new to a particular region on the basis of migration from some "mythical land of Oz that could never be located." Whether the early Hebrews, Philistines, Dorians, Hittites, Arabs, Etruscans, and so forth *ad infinitum*, folk- or scholarly-lore always traced them to some vague locality that has only to a slightest degree been vindicated by archaeological evidence.

Recently, Ernest Pulgram has vigorously attacked this migration theory in a work that should be required for anyone dealing with ancient history ("Linear B, Greek, and the Greeks," in *Glotta*, 1960). In effect, he is arguing for a position that should be self-evident, if not axiomatic: that all through recorded history, "race" (whatever that means), culture, and language have no necessary relationship to each other. The idea that they *do* is merely the result of attempts on the part of ancient or modern society to forge ideological bonding in a diverse, and always precarious, unity constantly on the verge of falling apart because of internal conflicts and competition. In other words, such legends of common origin and common "race, culture, and language" are a part of the ideological history of a particular culture, not an explanation of its origin; and usually that ideological history cannot be traced with any certitude until centuries *after* the origin.

The Problem of Migrations

Presumably even Ernst Pulgram would not argue that migration did not take place in ancient worlds. In the ancient Near East, as elsewhere, this is a highly controversial subject. My position is, as it has been for decades, that migration is a constant throughout the recorded history of mankind. However, migrations that became ideologically important to a much later society are very rare in comparison to migrations that carried no such ideological value. Those that became *immediately and lastingly* of importance to a new, emergent, culture number only two (I invite challenges to this position): the Exodus and the Pilgrim Fathers. The latter was without doubt modelled ideologically after the former, and therefore cannot really be cited as an independent historical example. If so, there is really only one example of a migration that furnished the ideological foundations of a "new society": ancient Israel. That a migration *did* take place at that time must be accepted, unless the scholar is willing to discard all the old poetry and prose traditions that attest to this fact. The traditional problem is one of reconciling those biblical traditions (many of which date to centuries after the event they purport to record) with the linguistic and archaeological evidence now available to interpret the events of the late 12th and early 11th centuries B.C.

Unfortunately for the proponents of the migration theory as an explanation for early Israel, the biblical traditions are insistent that only Joshua and Caleb succeeded in arriving in the "promised land," of those who emigrated from Egypt under the leadership of Moses, "the mixed multitude." Neither can really be plausibly associated with any identifiable large subsection of what later became "Israel," and neither became the "eponymous ancestor" of a tribe or even a sub-tribe. In other words, historical traditions that are difficult to explain and therefore to deny, are not readily compatible with the evidence we have from quite early sources concerning the early Israelite Twelve-Tribe Federation. Real history and social organization that claims validity from historical traditions rarely have anything to do with each other, except in ideology, usually enforced by social organization.

It seems to me that the real history that resulted in the formation of a large social unity is much more interesting than the official ideology that usually is used to justify the power structure that parasitizes the "official ideology," for its own purposes--usually for political purposes.

Migration, in other words, may or may not become ideologically functional in a community much larger than those (or the descendants of those) who were originally involved. If, as I maintain, migration has been a constant during historically recorded society, then migration *as such* explains little in human history, but it can have far-reaching effects in the areas of technology, social organization, and even ideology: the three elements that are inevitable to any culture.

Admittedly, migration is difficult to prove if we have nothing but archaeological evidence of similarities between two cultural areas, such as architectural, ceramic, or artistic *forms*. Such similarities have often been used to prove migration theories, but can often just as well be explained by trade, cultural diffusion ("borrowing"), or what some anthropologists term "stimulus diffusion." There is no need to elaborate further upon this very old debate between the "diffusionists" and the proponents of "independent origin" in the matter of formal similarity. To large extent, the debate is an accident of 19th-century organization of academia, and the consequent attempt of the proponents of one ancient culture or another to establish claims of "priority" or "originality" for their favorite culture over against others. (I shall refrain from comments upon modern political analogues, except to comment that neither academicians nor politicians have been able to understand the interdependence of humanity all through history.)

I had hoped originally to have a neat organization of this paper into the two separate topics of "migration" and "cultural change." It is impossible because the evidence we have strongly suggests, if it does not prove, what I think should be axiomatic: they are interrelated and inseparable.

We may start with the thesis of at least one anthropologist: "It is not continuity that needs to be explained; it is cultural change." The same is true to the nth degree when we are dealing with language. What accounts for the great changes that took place in the West Semitic languages from the Early Bronze Age to the Early Iron Age? (The same question can now be profitably answered with regard to the evolution of the

West Semitic writing systems, especially in the Bronze Age, in which all Semitic language writing systems have their origin *so far as we now know.*)

Though it is granted that cultural change is unquestionably caused by diffusion and the other factors mentioned above, it can hardly cause the kinds of radical discontinuity attested repeatedly in Near Eastern archaeological discontinuities with linguistic discontinuities; since language is the most distinctive and persistent trait of any culture, the conclusion seems inescapable that those periods of destruction and rapid change can be explained only by migration. The only question is the extent statistically to the pre-existent population, and the relationship of the immigrant populations and their cultural traits to those of the prior population.

The Correlation of Archaeological and Linguistic Discontinuities

1) As a preface, it seems very probable that already in the EB period, the West Semitic language area should be divided into three major regions: (*a*) the East Mediterranean Coastal area, designated here "Canaanite" and probably extending at least from the Gaza region (if not the Eastern Delta of Egypt) to the Gulf of Alexandretta; (*b*) the area East of the Lebanon-Amanus mountain complex, termed Proto-Aramean, extending from the rich agricultural and pastoral regions of Syria to the South of Transjordan where it becomes a rather narrow desert fringe; (*c*) the Jezireh of Syria (i.e. East of the Euphrates) and the Euphrates closely approach each other. This is termed "Amorite." Within each of the three regions I posit a high degree of mutual comprehensibility of local dialects, but less so between any two of the regions. It goes without saying that *within* any of the three regions, the further apart the local dialects, the less comprehensible they will be mutually.

This is doubtless an over-simplification, but it is at least an attempt to furnish a theoretical foundation for the existing linguistic evidence (and that forthcoming) for West Semitic languages in the Early Bronze Age. This tripartite division is based upon what I believe to be contrasts not only in linguistic/grammatical phenomena, but also in proven or probable geographical and cultural relationships. The relationships between the Mediterranean coast and Egypt can be traced to a time before the First Dynasty, and the Semitic linguistic elements in the Egyptian language have never, to my knowledge, been questioned. They must have derived from cultural or migrational influences dating long before 3000 B.C.

On the other side, Old Akkadian likewise exhibits many phenomena that can only be explained from much later West Semitic, as Gelb has ably demonstrated. The same is true of the entire so-called "East-Semitic" wing of the Semitic languages, i.e. Assyro-Babylonian. In this respect, what has long been termed "East-Semitic" parallels very well the West Semitic elements in the earliest Egyptian language. It follows that the entire region from the Egyptian delta to Mesopotamia proper was probably a West Semitic speaking region already in pre-historic times. Both in Egypt and in Mesopotamia an earlier Semitic language had been broken down in contact with a non-Semitic language, probably long before the beginning of the Early Bronze Age.

2) All the foregoing discussion deals with the prehistoric aspects of linguistic history, and is relevant here only to point out that what will be suggested below is nothing new in ancient Near Eastern linguistic history. At the same time, it should serve to warn against neat academic theories about continuous ethno-linguistic identities existing in isolation since the beginnings of time, which seems to be assumed in much 19th-century and even recent scholarship.

3) It must be strongly emphasized that our written documents stem from a political, merchant, or priestly elite, particularly before the popularization of the alphabet. Consequently, the language of the written documents may have minimal or even no relationship to the actual spoken language of the time and place from which they derive. Specialized groups, whether sociologists or truck drivers, always develop a dialect of their own, within the structure of an existing colloquial, but often enough such elite groups have used an entirely foreign language, such as Sumerian in Mesopotamia or Latin in Medieval Europe, or Aramaic in the Arab kingdom of Nabatea.

Cultural and Linguistic Discontinuities

1. From EB to MB

It is neither possible nor necessary here to discuss the details of this period, from the archaeological evidence. It is clear, however, from what we know *now* that the latest urban phase of the EB period in Syria was one that was characterized by a high degree of specialized literacy (the Tell Mardikh-Ebla archives). It is necessary to point out that proto-literate tablets of the Chalcolithic period have been found in at least three sites in the upper Euphrates valley in both Syria and Turkey, dating to the Warkan age. Potentially, an indigenous writing system could easily have been devised in this region even before the beginnings of the Early Bronze age, and I have no hesitation in predicting that ultimately evidence will emerge that inscriptions were actually produced in this area at least by the beginnings of the Middle Bronze Age, in an indigenous writing system, not necessarily related to the later Egypto-Canaanite system that ultimately became a more or less standard Phoenician alphabet by the 10th century B.C.

The transition from the Early Bronze age to the Middle Bronze age is highly controversial in detail, but no one doubts that there was a radical cultural and perhaps social change during this turbulent period. At the same time the Egyptian language made a transition from the Old Pyramid Texts to the "Middle Egyptian" language of the Coffin texts. In Mesopotamia at the same time, more or less, Old Akkadian died out and Sumerian as well (surviving as a specialized priestly linguistic competence for many centuries). Instead we have texts now termed "Old Babylonian." In the West Semitic area I posit that an old Canaanite written language represented in the Byblos Syllabic texts similarly gave way to a truly alphabetic writing system, at least by the beginning of the Middle Bronze Age, if not earlier *so far as we now know*.

The archaeological evidence for a radical change from the last phase of the Early Bronze age correlates with very far-reaching changes in language from Egypt to Mesopotamia. Those changes, however, are linguistically connected with what we may term the "Amoriticization" of earlier local dialects. It has been reported that the Tell Mardikh archives show no or little connection with the Amorite known, for example, from the personal names of the Mari archives (a half millennium or so later).

The Syllabic texts from Byblos similarly show almost no linguistic connections with Amorite, according to my decipherment of the meager corpus available. These documents must date (from internal evidence) either to the last phase of the Early Bronze age or the very early phase of the Middle Bronze Age, and are probably contemporary with the first intermediate period in Egypt and the Ur III dynasty of Mesopotamia.

The linguistic changes involved in the period under discussion are entirely internal (i.e. having to do especially with the linguistic areas described above as *b*, and *c*). In other words, we have no evidence that language change in that period was caused by radically different, non-Semitic languages introduced by an important non-Semitic speaking political superstructure, in the Syro-Palestinian area.

2. From MB to LB

Similarly, the considerable cultural change involved in the transition from the MB to LB correlates with the linguistic changes from Old Babylonian and Old Assyrian to Middle Assyrian and Babylonian. Unfortunately, we have no usable evidence from West Semitic dating to this transition period, though the contrast between the old myth and epic texts of Ugarit and the LB administrative texts does point toward a linguistic evolution that has not been sufficiently examined.

Though much of the foregoing discussion is not directly relevant to the topic of the explanation of early Israel, it is extremely important to recognize the fact that cultural change as revealed by archaeology does correlate to linguistic change. Further, the linguistic changes of the EB and MB periods cannot be explained merely by theories of diffusion; they must be the result of migration, and from the evidence now available, particularly from the Amorite sector of early West Semitic. It is generally conceded that Mesopotamia was largely dominated politically by Amorites by the 19th century B.C. but it has not been sufficiently realized that the same process must have taken place in the Mediterranean coastal region and perhaps Egypt at the same time, though Egypt during the Middle Kingdom was strong enough to ward off the process until the Hyksos period. This historical process is certainly reflected in biblical traditions concerning Abraham.

The Iron Age Discontinuity and Early Israel

As Weippert has pointed out, there have been only three major theories proposed by scholars to account for the sudden emergence of the ancient Israelite Twelve-Tribe system.

1) The classical theory of Alt and Noth is basically a migration hypothesis involving the idea that desert nomads gradually infiltrated Palestine and Transjordan, gradually became sedentary, and ultimately civilized. For this there is no support whatever in the biblical traditions. Other than the migration of Moses' little group, the biblical record knows only of a migration from N. Syria, attested not only by the Jacob-Laban story, but also in the ritual confession of Deut 26. The Aramean origin of Machir is also attested.

Migration *to* the South during the LB and EI age resulted evidently in an increase of population in Palestine and Transjordan that contrasts sharply to the situation as we know it in the Euphrates Valley. Our 1971 survey yielded evidence of a couple dozen LB sites, but only two clear EI ones. The catastrophe that struck the Hittite Empire evidently affected North Syria as well.

The thesis of Alt and Noth is thus completely contrary not only to the biblical traditions, but also the increasing evidence for migration patterns that we have from extrabiblical sources. Ironically enough, an Early Iron age site in the northern Hejaz (the traditional "land of Midian") yielded locally made imitations of Mycenean wares, and thus a northern cultural tradition of the Midianites themselves, completely parallel to, but not directly connected with, the Philistine culture.

Finally, an Israeli archaeologist gave a paper at the Biblical Colloquium last November in which he argued that the Alt-Noth hypothesis is simply incompatible with the archaeological evidence. Detailed information is not at present available.

To sum up, this classical theory has no foundations in biblical tradition, archaeological evidence, or in our greatly improved knowledge of ancient social organizations. It is an early 20th-century monument to 19th-century misconceptions and ignorance of ancient history.

2) The typically American theory got off the ground with Albright's work correlating biblical traditions with the results of excavations in Palestine. Key to his thesis was the identification of LB destruction levels with the Israelite Conquest, and for several decades it appeared that the process and chronology of early Israel was finally settled. The survey of Transjordan by Nelson Glueck, especially his "discovery" of a series of "border fortresses" in Edom that he correlated with the biblical traditions about negotiations with the king of Edom, and the subsequent route by-passing that territory, seemed to clinch the case. G. E. Wright did much to systematize the correlation of biblical with archaeological evidence, and for most of three decades the only serious debate was between the European source- and form-criticism school and the American archaeological school. The result was and is a standoff, with the Germans especially asking what evidence is there that those destruction levels were caused by the early Israelites?

Meanwhile, things had been happening in archaeological and historical research. Paul Lapp told me in 1965 that Nelson Glueck had dated those "Edomite border fortresses" at least two centuries too early, and they therefore had nothing to do with events during the lifetime of Moses. In fact, the three most competent specialists in Transjordan have assured me that at present we have not a single Early Iron age sherd between Wadi Mojib (=the River Arnon) and Qurayya in the land of Midian, now in Saudi Arabia.

In 1968 Albert Glock demonstrated that there exists no biblical or archaeological evidence that the early Israelites had any kind of military technology that would have enabled them to besiege and storm a LB city, and much evidence to the contrary, namely what I would term a "peasant guerilla warfare."

Elsewhere in the Eastern Mediterranean world also, evidence accumulated that few urban or town sites escaped destruction at this transition from the Late Bronze to the Early Iron ages. Consequently, the attribution of destruction levels in LB Palestine to the Israelite Conquest seemed more and more arbitrary. Perhaps the problem facing biblical scholarship was well put by G. E. Wright himself in a lecture that I vividly recall, but cannot remember when or where it was given. He asked, "How can we reconcile the high ethical sensitivity of the early biblical sources with the savagery illustrated in those LB destruction levels?" The answer is simple--there is no connection.

The problem of chronology must also be re-opened. The excavations at Ai and Heshbon (and perhaps Dibon as well) make it very difficult to correlate early biblical traditions with Late Bronze age occupations. It seems now most probable that the formation of the Israelite Twelve Tribe Federation took place during an early phase of the Iron age, and therefore had little or nothing to do with the archaeologically attested events of the end of the Late Bronze age. The Exodus would thus have taken place between 1225 and 1200 B.C., and the formation of the federation took place during the following quarter-century, from 1200-1175 B.C. I would not be at all surprised if these suggested dates will in the future have to be reduced by at least another quarter-century.

The American "biblical archaeological" school thus has no more foundation in ancient historical and archaeological reality than does the German school. Albright himself, so far as I can now recall, insisted that the Exodus involved only a very small "mixed multitude," but he never really faced the problem of how to account for a quarter of a million population in the Twelve Tribe system a mere generation later, according to his own estimate.

3) An alternative hypothesis was necessary. Both the German and the American theories could not really cope with the evidence for the religious/ideological aspects of early Israel, as Wright's plaintive remarks attest to. I argue now that there is no alternative to a theory that ancient Israel represented a popular movement against LB age political organizations, and particularly against their ideologies. No theory of the origins of ancient Israel is viable if it does not take seriously, and account for, this theological/ideological discontinuity. In spite of Wright's deep interest in biblical theology, I can see little evidence that he ever combined that with his equally deep interest in Palestinian archaeology, in any successful manner. It is curious that neither the European nor the American schools of thought really took seriously that which is most characteristic and unique to the biblical tradition, namely its religious ideology. It is understandable, however, since archaeologists and historians alike are ill-prepared to cope with the role of ideology in the larger framework of history, and particularly if that ideology is religious in nature (as I would maintain *all* ideological systems are).

It seems clear that the LB age involved much migration from the North. The archives of city states from Alalakh and Ugarit to Taanakh, and the Amarna texts all give evidence of non-Semitic population elements all over the Eastern Mediterranean region. The Deir'alla texts, the Philistine and Qurayya cultures all bear witness to a similar process, continuing into the early phase of the Iron Age.

Nevertheless, the migrations for which we have abundant evidence from both archaeological and linguistic sources cannot account for the existence of early Israel, even though the biblical traditions themselves attest such migrations from the North. Most emphatically those migrations cannot account for the unique features of early Israelite ideology. Therefore we are involved with the question of cultural and social change.

Early Israelite Cultural Change

1) The linguistic evidence is both crucial and overwhelming. Virtually all linguistic changes that took place between the LB and EI ages are common to both Phoenician and biblical Hebrew, even though I believe those changes have not been adequately examined linguistically. It follows that there cannot have been any important ethno-linguistic contrast between the early Israelites and the more-or-less "Canaanite" population of the pre-Israelite period. It follows also that there cannot have been any ethnic contrast of any discernable sort between the early Israelites and the non-Israelite population of LB-EI Canaan. This observation is strongly reinforced by the narrative of the *šibboleth* incident in Judges; whatever the linguistic analysis of that episode may become, it illustrates the *fact* that the Twelve Tribes of ancient Israel did not even speak a common dialect of West Semitic, and at present there is absolutely no reason to believe that early Israel was either linguistically or "ethnically" unified. Further, it seems to be demonstrable that the same linguistic changes took place in both the Israelite and the Canaanite regions, and therefore it is not possible to posit any significant ethnic contrast between the two groups. This conclusion is powerfully reinforced by the evidence from the archaic poetry of early Israel pointed out by Albright, Cross, and Freedman. Both the stylistic forms and the mythological motifs of that archaic poetry demonstrate that early Israel was actually an Early Iron age continuation of the LB Palestinian culture, but radically transformed, as everywhere in the Eastern Mediterranean region.

2) The cultural change characteristic of early Israel was certainly not technological. The early Israelites, from all the evidence we have, continued to be largely village peasants and shepherds, as they probably had been for at least a half-millennium. The change was primarily ideological, and it brought about a radical change in social organization, resulting in the Twelve Tribe Federation. The only migration that became ideologically significant was that of the Exodus, and we have no evidence that the persons involved, other than Joshua and Caleb, had anything to do with the Twelve Tribe Federation. The only plausible and acceptable conclusion is that early Israel was the result of a complex of cultural and ideological change in what must have been an extremely chaotic and traumatic period in the entire Mediterranean world.

The breakdown of the LB West Semitic phonetic and grammatical structure all over the coastal and inland areas can be best accounted for by the inundation of those regions by populations who spoke a non-Semitic language, Hurrians, Luwians, Hittites, and doubtless others not yet identified. Only in the remote areas of the desert fringe was this linguistic breakdown escaped, and the continuity of that Bronze age Semitic is what we know now as Arabic. Though the evidence is meager at present, all that we do know (especially from the Byblos Syllabic texts) indicates that Arabic is a continuity of the Early Bronze age language of the *coastal* region.

S 122, A 185

EARLY ISRAEL AND "THE ASIATIC MODE OF PRODUCTION" IN CANAAN

Norman K. Gottwald
Graduate Theological Union
Berkeley, Ca.

This paper starts off from the hypothesis that early Israel represented a revolutionary breach in the prevailing political economy of ancient Canaan, a notion first advanced (1962) and subsequently elaborated (1973) by George Mendenhall, independently proposed by the Czech scholar Jan Dus (1971), and extended and qualified synchronically and diachronically by this writer in articles (1974-1975) and in a major study now in press.

To sustain this hypothesis it is necessary to determine not only the political economy of pre-monarchic Israel but also the political economy of ancient Canaan. It is the latter task which this paper tries to define with more precision than has been customary to date.

I. Canaanite "Feudalism"?

Although with misgivings, scholars have generally treated Canaanite society as "feudal" in type, or, hedging their bets, have called it "quasi-feudal", i.e., somewhat like or resembling feudalism. I have gone along with this convention until now because Canaanite society seems politically "feudal" in its small balkanized units engaged in military competition fostered by a chariot warrior class, and it seems economically "feudal" in that a majority of the populace was locked into agricultural production whose surplus was appropriated by a ruling class and whose labor service could be demanded by the authorities at will. It is a serious question, however, whether such loose characterizations are sufficiently refined to be specific to feudalism.

Certain elements in the Canaanite setting are sensed to be either resistant or antipathetic to a specifically feudal analysis. The precisely formulated tenurial and personal relations between nobility and serfs so abundantly documented in medieval Europe are not clearly evident in Canaan. This omission seems not merely due to the fluke of a gap in legal documents, since diplomatic and administrative texts that touch upon the relations between the rulers and the ruled do not describe ties that are closely analogous to those in European feudalism. Still more problematic for a feudal reading of Canaanite political economy is the heightening of state authority in Syro-Palestine and the burgeoning of trade evident in the Amarna Age -- precisely opposite developments to the rise of feudalism in Europe which followed on the breakdown of the Roman, Merovingian and Carolingian Empires and the quiescence of trade.

Indicative of the analytic vacuum in which the discussion has gone on is the difference between William F. Albright (1926,1936) and Isaac Mendelsohn (1941,1955) over the appropriate characterization of the *ḫupšu*, whom both understood as peasants. Albright chose to call them "serfs", but Mendelsohn preferred to see them as "free proletarians", analogous to the *coloni*, the "tied tenant farmers" of the Roman Empire. More recently, M. Heltzer (1969) and H. Klengel (1965-1970, 1969) have argued that *ḫupšu* were a group largely in collective clientage to kings, "royal men", who owed various "service duties", mainly military but also in crafts and professions. They tend not to think that feudalism offers the suitable model for understanding Syro-Palestinian social organization, but they do not propose an alternative model. None of these analyses proceeds on a broad enough gauge to address fundamentally the question of the political economy of ancient Canaan.

II *Marx's "Asiatic Mode of Production"*

I am now disposed to argue that it is as erroneous to regard Canaanite society as a feudal society as it is to think that the first Israelites were largely pastoral nomadic. I have been delayed in reaching this judgment by long unfamiliarity with the details of Marx's analysis of "the Asiatic mode of production". Following its eclipse and distortion at the hands of Stalinists and anti-communists, the Asiatic socio-economic formation is once again coming in for lively discussion, for empirical testing and for theoretical refinement.

Notions of "oriental" or "asiatic" society have circulated since the seventeenth century and were particularly stressed by Montesquieu and Hegel. Marx and Engels worked out their theory of the Asiatic mode of production in the 1850s under three primary influences: 1) the economists John Stuart Mill and Richard Jones; 2) accounts of travels, memoirs and monographs on Eastern countries; and 3) studies Marx made of village communities in Scotland and Spain. Working backward from the impact of British capitalist penetration of China and India, they concluded that those lands -- together with ancient Egypt, Mesopotamia and Islamic societies -- had followed an essentially different route of political economy than had Europe in its procession from primitive communism through slavery and feudalism to capitalism. For Marx and Engels the Asiatic mode of production was a distinct variant type of class society, set off both from slavery and from feudalism by distinctive environmental and sociohistorical factors.

The essential features of the Asiatic mode of production were articulated by Marx in articles published in the *New York Daily Tribune* (1853-1860), in *A Contribution to the Critique of Political Economy* (1859) and most fully developed in his *Grundrisse* (1857-58). The most elaborately argued study of the Asiatic mode of production remains Karl Wittfogel's *Wirtschaft und Gesellschaft Chinas* (1931), a contribution little known in the West because in his subsequent *Oriental Despotism* (1959) the author was more interested in brandishing his later anti-communist sentiments than in building analytically on his earlier work. D. D. Kosambi has explored this mode of production in India (1956) and Maxime Rodinson in Islam (1966). Although highly compressed, the best treatment I have seen is by Ernest Mandel in chapter 8 of *The Formation of the Economic Thought of Karl Marx*, pp. 116-139 (1967, Eng. trans. 1971).

The following articulation of the distinguishing criteria of the Asiatic mode of production -- in contradistinction to slave or feudal socio-economic formations -- draws mainly on Marx, with elaboration by the early Wittfogel and by Mandel:

1) The absence of private ownership of land in favor of communal ownership of land.

2) The cohesion and persistence of the village community in spite of repeated conquests and changes of political regime.

3) The close union of agriculture and crafts within the village community.

4) The geographic and climatic necessity of large-scale hydraulic works for irrigation which in turn requires a central authority to build, repair and operate them.

5) The success of the central authority in concentrating a majority of the social surplus product in its own hands, through which it spawns social strata that exercise political hegemony over the politically weakened village communities.

6) The decisive economic subordination of towns to agriculture and the equally decisive political subordination of towns to the central authority.

7) Production of goods largely for use value rather than for exchange value.

8) Precisely because of the economic and political subordination of the towns, there is a persisting lag or retardation in the development of productive forces.

9) There are well defined social classes in addition to the political rulers and the peasants, namely, large landholders, merchants and bankers -- often enormously wealthy but limited in the full exercise of socio-economic and political power by their dependence on the state.

10) Although merchants strive to convert use values into exchange values, they are unable to dissolve the village community as the basic productive unit nor can they break free from central authority or seize it for their own unrestricted purposes.

11) Trade functions chiefly on the international frontier, as carrier or intermediary between peoples who continue for the most part to produce use values, while the supervisory state diverts much of the social surplus that would otherwise be available for consumption by the mass of peasant producers.

12) Trade and crafts, caught between state control and the persistence of communally owned land, are unable to foster either a free bourgeoisie or their necessary counterpart in "free labor". Without a large pool of labor severed from petty landownership or from communally landed property, the way is blocked to the unrestricted development of private capital.

13) The central authority functions for the whole of society, economically, politically and theocratically, but this does not in the least prevent the state from taking disproportionately large shares of the social surplus to benefit the social classes which it creates and supports.

14) While it may be said that there are "feudal" elements in the Asiatic mode of production (such as large-scale monopolized landed property existing _de facto_ if not _de jure_, cultivated by means of labor services or by the imposition of rent payments upon peasants), the essential point is that "this feudal class never became the ruling class. Its advances were always regarded as encroachments on the power of the state and the rights of the peasants" (Mandel, 135).

III _Entrepreneurial State and Village Community in Canaan_

What possible light does the hypothesis of an Asiatic mode of production throw upon ancient Canaanite political economy and upon the origins of Israel? What elements of the Syro-Palestinian socio-economic and political matrix are compatible with the hypothesis? What elements are neutral or ambiguous? What elements are resistant or contrary? What data are we lacking to be able to form a judgment? What data may be available but previously overlooked?

Without making any pretense of completeness, I shall now indicate some lines of analysis and reflection:

1) <u>On Centralized Hydraulic Works As The Basis Of Political Economy</u>. <u>Wittfogel's study of the Chinese version of Asiatic hydraulic society</u> has been taken up by several students of ancient Near Eastern society with varying degrees of interest and approval (Harris, 671-87). Many concede that the enormous task of taking full advantage of the waters of the Nile and of the Tigris-Euphrates had a great deal to do with an early development of strong states in those regions. Other scholars call attention, however, to additional functions of the state -- such as supervision of crop rotation, cultivation and security of the fields, military protection of villages, development of state craft sectors such as mining and metallurgy -- which they believe undercut or diffuse the priority and singularity of hydraulic works as the chief occasion for the rise of the hypertrophied state.

It is to be noted, however, that these non-hydraulic functions are handled in other societies by groupings of villages, by urban corporations or by local lords without development of an entrepreneurial state. The question persists: why was the entrepreneurial state specific to large-scale irrigation societies? Of comparative pertinence is the role of hydraulic projects in Meso-America, not only in the Aztec state but also in the much earlier statist society at Teotihuacán (c. 500 A.D.) where a shift from rainfall agriculture to an irrigation system, drawing on eighty springs in a small area, was associated with "rapid population growth, nucleation, monument construction, intense social stratification and expansionist warfare" (Harris, 1968: 686, reporting on the unpublished work of Sanders). Clearly, to test further the hypothesis of the hydraulic origin of a distinctive mode of production characterized by hypertrophied state-cum-village communities will require more sophisticated ways of coordinating measurements of irrigation works with measurements of the size and form of polities. Robert McC. Adams' demurrer (1966: 66-68) on the pertinence of the hydraulic hypothesis for explaining the striking socio-political evolutionary parallels between Mesopotamia and Meso-America preceded Sanders' findings on Teotihuacán.

More specifically, what is the relevance of hydraulic polity for Canaan, a land without the massive irrigation works of the Nile or of the Tigris-Euphrates? First, it needs to be recognized that there was a good deal more small-scale irrigation in ancient Canaan than often conceded. Recent archaeological work devoted to exploring the irrigation and terrace systems in the Israelite highlands has suggested that locally developed water systems (such as the apparently ancient installations at Jerusalem and in the vicinity of Bethlehem) probably had a lot to do with the successful Israelite agricultural settlements (de Geus; Wilkinson). Also to be considered are marsh drainage, dikes and canals as significant projects for communities along the upper reaches of the Jordan River and in the vicinity of coastal streams such as the Yarkon and the Kishon. Research on these water systems as functional totalities, going far beyond the earlier attention to isolated urban water tunnels and pools, is just beginning in a disciplined way.

Nonetheless, it is plausible that had the entire Near Eastern water supply consisted of such small rivers and streams and such localized highland springs, it is doubtful that the entrepreneur state would have been needed to take over irrigation from the village communities. Thus, the phenomenon of the hypertrophied entrepreneurial state in Syro-Palestine is probably to be explained by the region's strategic importance as a corridor between the major river valleys which created pressure on strong states at both poles to replicate their governmental formations throughout the corridor. From at least Hyksos times, the impact of imperial politics from the Nile, the Tigris-Euphrates and Anatolia led to diffusion of the entrepreneur state within the Syro-Palestinian corridor. Given the topography and modest irrigation possibilities, the central authorities in Syro-Palestine were generally small in scale, so that we conventionally speak of them as "city-states", but perhaps we do so largely on a measure of scale rather then on the basis of an accurate assessment of their internal organization. For example, ancient Near Eastern "primitive democracy", of which Jacobsen has spoken (1943), may be far less analogous to Greek city-states than to vestiges of village community organization not wholly stamped out within towns that served as administrative centers of the hypertrophied states.

2) *On The Social Structure Of Syro-Palestinian Entrepreneurial States And The Social Structure Of Early Israel*. The hypothesis of an Asiatic mode of production offers intriguing vistas for further theorizing and research. On the assumption that ancient Canaan was a feudal society, it is somewhat difficult to explain the village and tribal base of the Israelite social movement. As long as the Israelites were assumed to have been pastoral nomads, this was of course hardly a matter calling for explanation. With the dawning realization that pastoral nomadism was no more than a minor component in Israel and in any event was well integrated symbiotically into settled life (Gottwald, 1974), the village tribalism of early Israel cries out for analysis and clarification. For example, it is difficult to trace much social organizational continuity from the tribes of Gaul and Germany to the life of European feudal estates; the old communal forms of property holdings were long dissolved in the lord's unchallenged status as owner of the manor and in the serf's dependence on the lord. If the Israelites did not bring tribalism and notions of communal land holding with them from the desert, where did they get this form of social organization? Did they construct it out of whole cloth? The hypothesis of the Asiatic mode of production proposes that the cohesive village community had *not* been stamped out. The village community had been *imposed upon* by central authorities that did not alter the land ownership arrangements *de jure*, although *de facto* they seriously impinged upon and threatened the independent life of the peasants by a credit and loan system that threw them into practical bondage to absentee creditors and by the periodic levies which were demanded of the peasants as the price of economic and military security.

Viewed in this way, the Israelite tribes may be conceived of as a "revitalization" or "retribalization" movement (Gottwald, 1975), not so much unique in their basic form of segmented organization by extended families, protective associations and tribes, but decisively different in constituting a very broad alliance of such units that managed to throw off the central authority and take over its entrepreneurial socio-economic, military and religious functions at the village and tribal levels (Gottwald, in press, Parts VI and VII). On this model, everything depended on the Israelite revolutionary movement attaining *a sufficient scale and sophistication of coordination* to be able to provide the basic services that central authority had claimed as its prerogative. In particular, the Israelite movement had to be able to defend itself against the counter-revolutionary thrusts of the deposed authorities.

If other asiatic societies are any index, it is likely that more peasant uprisings occurred in the ancient Near East than the records of the central authorities were interested in reporting. What seems to have characterized most of these peasant uprisings under the Asiatic mode of production was a rapid reversion to central authority as new dynasties were installed by or took over from the rebels. It appears to have been a peculiarity of Israel that it sustained its non-authoritarian organizational thrust for some two centuries, persistently leveling all attempts to constitute a new central authority until it faced the Philistine threat. The Philistines posed a level of hostile statism and militarism which Israel could not cope with short of resorting to a strong military chiefdom which soon escalated into an Israelite entrepreneurial dynastic authority. In this way the old conflict between village community and state was imported into the Israelite community itself, but with a difference. The difference was that the Israelite state faced extraordinary infrastructural restraints and blockages to its enlargement based precisely in the fact that its villages communities were not insular units but had developed networks of self-rule and self-service. The village-tribal ethos and religion had been so well cultivated during Israel's first two centuries that it was this "lower" level of social organization that tended to shape the national culture and to stamp the religion as a persistent latent revolutionary force. One project clearly demanded is a careful inquiry into the contested and shifting division of socio-economic and political labor between state and village tribal networks throughout the course of the Israelite monarchy in its unified form and in its northern and southern branches.

IV On Testing And Applying The "Asiatic" Model In Canaan

The hypothesis of the Asiatic mode of production invites new investigation of the role of various social groupings reported in the Syro-Palestinian texts. Two examples may be cited. The *maryannu* "military aristocracy" has been reevaluated of late in ways that appear to question their feudatory standing as propertied lords. H. Reviv (1972), for example, finds that dynasts, growing fearful of a concentration of power in the hands of a charioteer military caste, began to appoint *maryannu* aristocrats to civilian posts and to draw lower class elements into the charioteer ranks, a move that tended to sever military performance from the independent wealth otherwise requisite to provide and maintain costly military equipment. M. Heltzer (1969) goes farther in denying that the *maryannu* ever were privileged aristocrats. In his view they were, like the *ḫupšu*, royal servants who owed service-duties, lived on royal land held conditionally and received all their arms and equipment from royal stores.

As for the notorious *ʿapiru*, they may perhaps be viewed, as Jankowska proposed (1969a) -- although her evidence is based mainly on Nuzi -- not so much as individual free-floating rebels or refugees but as groups of people pushed out of the security system of the family communes or village communities as a consequence of increasingly specialized production, e.g., fruits and vegetables in agriculture and handcrafts for trade. The *ʿapiru* may be viewed as a supplementary labor force which showed a tendency toward improvisation in socio-economic organization by adapting aspects of village community structure to occupational band or guild formations. Assuming that *ʿapiru* formed a sizable element in early Israel, it is probable that their organizational and military experience counted heavily in teaching other Israelites (derived from *ḫupšu*, *shosu* and pastoral nomads) how to cope with central authorities across previously constricting geographical, socio-economic and political boundaries.

Obviously our lack of law codes from Egypt and Syro-Palestine seriously handicaps efforts at more exact probes and testings of the hypothesis of an Asiatic mode of production in those regions. We can, however, go back to a fresh appraisal of the Mesopotamian and Hittite codes and of the administrative and diplomatic documents from Syro-Palestine. Hopefully, the recent archival finds at ancient Ebla in Syria may have something significant, even decisive, to tell us on these matters. Not least will be renewed attention to the biblical materials themselves and to the long neglected potentialities of historical cultural material strategies in archaeology which have proven so productive in Amer-Indian studies -- in fact productive almost everywhere else except in "biblical archaeology" with its dominant orientation toward literary and directly historical interests.

V The Tenacity Of The Village Community

Finally, one is tempted to ask whether it is at all reasonable to imagine that communal property holdings in villages -- and the accompanying socio-economic organization -- could have survived close to two millennia of relentless pressure by hypertrophied state power. Would not the heavy hand of state taxation in kind and impressment of the peasantry into army and labor service, of onerous loans at interest, of merchant profiteering, of famines, wars and migrations have completely destroyed the village commune in the course of a few centuries?

This question is all the more in our minds when we read Marx in the Grundrisse (Mandel's trans., 1967: 136-137):

> "Trade will obviously react to a greater or lesser extent on the communities between which it is carried on. It will subject production more or less to exchange value; it will push immediate use value further and further into the background, in proportion as it makes subsistence depend more upon selling than upon immediate utilization of the product. It disintegrates old established relationships. It thereby increases the circulation of money. It first of all seizes hold of the surplus of production, then increasingly takes over production itself".

Marx here describes a long-range tendency, "all other things being equal", and what his next remarks assert is that precisely in the Asiatic mode of production all other things are not equal:

> "But [trade's] disintegrating action depends to a great extent on the nature of the productive communities between which it is carried on. Thus, it hardly disturbed the ancient communities of India, or Asiatic conditions in general".

What had riveted Marx's attention in the first place, encouraging him to postulate the Asiatic socio-economic formation, was the remarkable fact that this juxtaposition and stalemate of hypertrophied state, on the one hand, and village commune, on the other, had persisted in the Far East into the nineteenth century.

How is the tenacity of the village community to be accounted for? In Canaan, was not the central authority so clearly superior in power that it should have snuffed out the village commune centuries before Israel appeared?

One answer is certainly that the tendency of state-sponsored trade to convert the village community's use values into exchange values did not go unchallenged. We hear enough about social justice, periodic reforms and overthrown dynasties to know that the village community possessed great socio-economic productive power, political resistance and over-all resiliency to "spring back" from the repeated incursions of landowning, merchant and banking classes legitimated by the entrepreneurial state. Israel's very emergence was one striking instance of a vigorous and sustained counterattack from coalitions of village communities against the predatory social strata instituted by the state.

This astonishing vitality of the village community is not after all unaccountable. Since private ownership of the means of production did not exist -- or at best can be said to have existed as a sort of temporary "franchise right" by entrepreneurial classes "licensed" by the state -- there existed no basis for the accumulation of private capital which could systematically break up the village communities and turn their peoples into urban hordes of "free labor". In the hands of central authority, a lucrative surplus in kind and in labor could be extracted from the village communities both for immediate use and for exchange for luxury goods by the privileged classes, for state sectors of the economy, for monumental construction and for military goods and services. However, the total of productive forces was not maximized rationally. Heavy-handed political power and crude deprivation of the peasantry were not matched by sufficient economic rationality for these Asiatic societies to reach a "take-off point" where the entrepreneurial clients of the state -- landowners, merchants and bankers -- had the power to seize control of the state or to infiltrate it and subject it to their ends. On the contrary, the state kept the entrepreneurial classes in tight rein, thereby assuring the constant reproduction of stalemate between grossly inflated political power and grassroots economic production. The dominant state and the defensive village communities were very imperfectly mediated by forms of new wealth that were not strong enough to break through the whole system, to bring about a radical increase in productive forces and thereby to achieve an overthrow of the general use-value infrastructure of the village communities. Because of this relatively low level of the productive forces, cities and towns never developed the aggressive economic energy of European centers, slavery never reached the proportions of the Roman Empire, nor was a "free" urban proletariat amassed by ejection from the land and by urban attraction, as occurred to some extent in the Roman Empire and more spectacularly in Europe by the heavy hand of enclosure and "rack-renting" which threw a majority of the populace on the mercy of burgeoning capitalism.

BIBLIOGRAPHY

ADAMS, ROBERT McC.
1966 The Evolution of Urban Society: Early Mesopotamia and Prehispanic Mexico, Chicago: Aldine.

ALBRIGHT, WILLIAM F.
1926 "Canaanite ḥapši and Hebrew ḥofši," JPOS, 6:107.
1936 "New Canaanite Historical and Mythological Data," BASOR, 63:29.

De GEUS, C. H. J.
1975 "The Importance of Archaeological Research into the Palestinian Agricultural Terraces...," PEQ, 107: 65-74.

DUS, JAN
1975 "Moses or Joshua? On the Problem of the Founder of the Israelite Religion," Radical Religion, 2, nos. 2/3: 26-41 (orig. pub. 1971 in German in ArOr, 39: 16-45).

GODELIER, MAURICE
1964 "Bibliographie sommaire des écrits de Marx et d'Engels sur le mode de production asiatique," La Pensée, April 1964.

GOTTWALD, NORMAN K.
1974 "Were the Early Israelites Pastoral Nomads?," Rhetorical Criticism. Essays in Honor of James Muilenburg, ed. J. Jackson and M. Kessler, Pittsburgh: Pickwick Press, 223-255.
1975 "Domain Assumptions and Societal Models in the Study of Pre-monarchic Israel," VTSup, Edinburgh Congress Volume, 89-100.
In Press A Sociology of the Religion of Liberated Israel, 1250-1000 B.C., 2 vols., Maryknoll: Orbis Books.

HARRIS, MARVIN
1968 The Rise of Anthropological Theory: A History of Theories of Culture, New York: Thomas Y. Crowell.

HELTZER, MICHAEL
1969 "Problems of the Social History of Syria in the Late Bronze Age," La Siria nel Tardo Bronzo, ed. M. Liverani, Rome: Orientis Antiqui Collectio, IX, 31-46.

HOBSBAWM, ERIC J.
1965 "Introduction" to Karl Marx, Pre-capitalist Economic Formations, New York: International Publishers.

JACOBSEN, THORKILD
1943 "Primitive Democracy in Ancient Mesopotamia," JNES, 2: 159-172.
1957 "Early Political Developments in Mesopotamia," ZA, 52: 91-140.

JANKOWSKA, NINEL B.
1969a "Extended Family Commune and Civil Self-government in Arrapha in the Fifteenth--Fourteenth Centuries B.C.," Ancient Mesopotamia: Socio-economic History, ed. I.M. Diakonoff, Moscow: Nauka Publishing House, 1969, 235-252.
1969b "Communal Self-government and the King of the state of Arrapḫa," Journal of the Economic and Social History of the Orient, 12: 233-282.

KLENGEL, HORST
1965-1970 Geschichte Syriens im 2. Jahrtausend, Teil I, 1965; II, 1969; III, 1970.
1969 "Probleme einer politischen Geschichte des spaetbronzezeitlichen Syrien," La Siria nel Tardo Bronzo, ed. M. Liverani, Rome: Orientis Antiqui Collectio, IX, 15-30.

KOSAMBI, DAMODAR
1956 An Introduction to the Study of Indian History, Bombay: Popular Book Depot.

LEACH, EDMUND R.
1959 "Hydraulic Society in Ceylon," Past and Present, 15 (April 1959), 2-26.

MANDEL, ERNEST
1967 "The Asiatic Mode of Production and the Historical Pre-conditions for the Rise of Capital," in The Formation of the Economic Thought of Karl Marx, New York and London: Monthly Review Press, Eng. trans. 1971, 116-139.

MARX, KARL
1853-1860 Marx on China 1853-1860; Articles from the New York Daily Tribune, intro. and notes by D. Torr, London: 1951.
1857-1858 Foundations of the Critique of Political Economy (Rough Draft), trans. with foreword by M. Nicolaus, Baltimore: Penguin, 1973 (first published in German as Grundrisse... 2 vols., Moscow: Foreign Language Publishers, 1939/1941.)
1859 A Contribution to the Critique of Political Economy, trans. by S.W. Ryazanskaya, edited with intro. by M. Dobb, New York: International Publishers, 1970.

MILLON, RENÉ
1967 "Teotihuacán," Scientific American, 216: 38-48.
1973 ed., Urbanization at Teotihuacán, Mexico, Austin: Univ. of Texas Press.

MENDELSOHN, ISAAC
1941 "The Canaanite Term for 'Free Proletarian' ", BASOR, 83: 36-39.
1955 "New Light on the Ḫupšu," BASOR, 139: 9-11.

MENDENHALL, GEORGE E.
1962 "The Hebrew Conquest of Palestine," BA, 25: 66-87 = BAR 3 (1970), 100-120.
1973 The Tenth Generation: The Origins of the Biblical Tradition, Baltimore: John Hopkins Press, 1973.

PRAWAR, J. AND S. N. EISENSTADT
1969 "Feudalism," International Encyclopedia of the Social Sciences, 3: 393-403.

REVIV, H.
1972 "Some Comments on the Maryannu," IEJ, 22: 218-228.

RODINSON, MAXIME
1966 Islam et capitalisme, Paris: Éditions du Seuil.

SANDERS, WILLIAM
1965 "The Cultural Ecology of the Teotihuacán Valley," University Park: Penn. State Univ., Preliminary Report of the Results of the Teotihuacán Valley Project, Dept. of Sociology and Anthropology, Penn. State Univ.

SANDERS, WILLIAM AND BARBARA PRICE
1968 Mesoamerica: The Evolution of a Civilization, New York: Random House.

VIDAL-NAQUET, PIERRE
1964 "Avant-Propos" to K. Wittfogel, Le despotisme oriental, Paris: Les Éditions de Minuit, 7-44.

WILKINSON, JOHN
1974 "Ancient Jerusalem: Its Water Supply and Population," PEQ, 106: 33-51.

WITTFOGEL, KARL
1931 Wirtschaft und Gesellschaft Chinas. I: Produktivkraefte, Produktions- und Zirkulationsprozess, Leipzig: C. L. Hirschfeld.

1957 Oriental Despotism: A Comparative Study in Total Power, New Haven: Yale University Press.

S 123, A 186

THE ROLE OF THE PEASANT IN THE AMARNA PERIOD

John M. Halligan
St. John Fisher College

It must be remarked at the outset that any description of Canaanite society in pre-Israelite epigraphy reflects the mind and interests "of the royal court, its administrative personnel," and the viewpoint of "the powerful upper strata of the society."[1] What may be known of the lower classes comes either when "they serve the court or rebel against it."[2] In Rib-Addi's complaint that his own *ḫupšu* have left him he also tells us of the extreme situation they are in.[3] Thus in politically chaotic times of revolt, such as that depicted in the Amarna period, "one learns more of the people, their exploitation and the defenders of the status quo" than in court records of the royal family.[4]

A. THE ELITE

The societal structure as found in the 18th-century Ugaritic texts is that of a city-state kingdom. The king is the keystone of the social order; he enjoys the communion of the gods and men, participates in the cult as high priest and mediator of divine revelation.[5] He was the dispenser of justice to all alike through *ad hoc* divine aid and his own natural wisdom guided by communal custom but not a codex of law. His men follow him with enthusiasm into war as a personal service for he is their leader.

By the 14th century he wages war by means of his military aristocracy whose names appear increasingly non-Semitic; following the Hyksos period Hurrian names as military chiefs may be found at Ugarit and in the Amarna letters.[6] In return for military service the king would grant a parcel of land *in perpetuum* to the *maryannu*-warrior, thus creating a feudal relationship of king and baron. But many others were granted land as payment for service as Gray reads:

> ...*šrm* (rev. 9-11), "singers," and *ngdm* (rev. 12-15), "shepherds," of whom we know that the chief priest *Atnprln* was the head. To these we should add *tgrm* (rev. 7-8), "doorkeepers," *mhsm* (rev. 25-26), "butchers," *šrm* (30-32-rev. 4), "butlers," and *trrm* (rev. 16-21), which we take as "inspectors" of either entrails or stars. If we are right in taking *mdm* (1-6), "measures," as custodians of weights and measures, they may reasonably be regarded as cultic officials, since weights and measures were anciently protected by divine sanction.[7]

All of these came from the class of cultic personnel. Among the military one finds besides the chariot experts (*maryannu*), two others that hold land grants: the *bdl mrynm*, substitutes for the *maryannu* who could not render service because of age or injury, and the *mr'u ebrn*, *mr'u skn*, groups of retainers, *mšrglm*, groups of armorers. Thus one might get land through service to the king either in the cultic capacities or the military; no provision is made in the texts for anyone else nor any other means save revolt.

The peasant might be conscripted for *corvée* labor on royal projects, or armed service as a *ḫubšu* (*ḫupšu*), possibly a yeoman in the infantry, or archer, or reserves in general. The terms *hpt* and *tun* occur in the Keret Epic ii. 90-91: "...*Peasant levies* without number, *trained regulars* beyond reckoning" [italics added]. The precise meaning of *hpt* and its relation to *ḫubšu* is still a matter of discussion.[8] The status of the *hpt* seems to be analogous to that of the *maryannu*: his freedom from working the lands to render capital for the king was his fief *in perpetuum* as much as land was that of the aristocratic *maryannu*; the *hpt* was bound to render military service instead of agricultural quotas. Yet it is not incompatible that in times of peace he did work the land for his own subsistence as the Alalakh texts suggest.[9] The plight of the peasant in the Amarna period was indeed desperate.

Whatever tribal organization may have preceded the rise of the feudal order, traces of it do not remain in the documents. By the time of the Late Bronze period legal documents, perhaps contemporary with El-Amarna, reflect a system of civil law parallel with the principles of the urban system of Mesopotamia.[10] The fact that *corvées* were reckoned according to district and not by tribe is a further indication of the administrative reach of the central power over population movement. It requires a fairly sedentary populace to enable the executive control to compute the numbers and exact action when ordered. Districts are constructs of the political regime and are significant only if they can be enforced; Alt's thesis that ancient territorial divisions outlive individual political powers has considerable merit if one understands the *Lebensform* of the peasantry.[11]

B. THE PEASANTRY

The picture of society that emerges from a study of the documents of the second millenium in Canaan is anything but primitive. In a "primitive society, producers control the means of production, including their own labor, and they exchange their own labor and its products" for goods deemed culturally necessary or for the service others may provide in return.[12] This is certainly not the case in a society based on feudal power as seen in Ugarit and Byblos. What has taken place is a transition from a tribal form to an urban form of living: the control of the means of production, viz., human labor, has passed from the individual to an executive group supported by force. The king surrounded by his military aristocracy was the executive group exercising total control over the fund of power, the productivity of the people and their land.

Every empire of the Ancient Near East was agriculturally based. It is equally true that a peasant society such as that of Egypt may exist without need of the city but the city cannot exist without the peasant. In Mesopotamia, Egypt and Canaan "the peasant group provided surpluses that are transferred to the dominant group of rulers" that "underwrite their own standard of living," then "distribute the remainder" to other nonagricultural groups, military and cultic personnel, for specific goods and services.[13] Goods are no longer exchanged between groups but are first furnished to a center and only later redirected.

Rib-Addi of Byblos informs the Pharaoh that his *ḫupšu* have pledged as *corvée* their own sons and daughters, and wooden tools for cultivating in the fields of Iarimuta for deliverance of their lives;[14] if he is not given grain to feed his peasants they will desert him for his enemy Abdi-Asirta;[15] and that his own peasants have been advised to kill him because he has not provided for their safety and subsistence;[16] and finally, that his own palace guard fail to protect him when attempted assassinations occur.[17] The social balance has completely deteriorated from the serene description in the Keret Epic. In the Amarna period the subsistence level of the *ḫupšu* was not being met; this in turn signified several other developments: (*a*) if he had not enough to eat, the peasant would not have enough surplus grain to provide seed for next year, or feed his livestock; (*b*) he has no way of replacing annual equipment loss for production and consumption;[18] in fact he has given them away to save his life; (*c*) he has no fund from which to carry on simple social relations such as a dowry or ceremonial offerings; (*d*) he is so destitute that in the asymmetrically based feudal order he cannot pay his taxes, rent for land use (since the king or a member of the upper class owned it).[19] The stark reality is vividly stated by Rib-Addi as he reports that his peasants are joining the SA.GAZ men, allies and confederates of his enemy Abdi-Asirta.[20] He is well aware that deprived of his peasants fund of rent he is deprived of his fund of power. This is essentially an urban system.

The peasant is a cultivator whose relationship to the city should be viewed as village-to-city. The cities in Canaan are not all alike: some are administrative centers such as those in the Execration Texts and the Amarna Tablets, some are equally religious centers such as Ugarit, Harran, Megiddo, Hazor and Hebron. Many were brisk trading centers such as Ugarit, Byblos, Tyre, Sidon, Hamath, Damascus, Jericho. Thus the relationship to the city will be determined by the type of demand the city places on the peasant or by what opportunities it provides for his welfare. In Egypt the political, religious and intellectual functions remained dispersed so there was no need for a center other than marketing.

The critical situation prevailing in Syria-Palestine during the 15th and 14th centuries according to the texts from Ugarit and Amarna indicate that the *ḫupšu* had two possible strategies to follow to meet both the demands of the royal tax collectors and his households' sustenance: (1) he might increase production, but this would depend on how he could manage the ingredients of production: land, labor and surplus (capital of some type); the data indicate that he had little possibility of going beyond or perhaps of meeting the minimal needs; (2) in politically chaotic times the "traditional liens on his fund for rent have weakened" because the central power structure has become ineffective;[21] therefore he can escape the demands to underwrite payments, can break traditional social ties for religious support by: (*a*) claiming the land for himself in the face of no opposition[22] or (*b*) withdraw from the old regime in favor of a stronger and more congenial one or withdraw from the land if he cannot succeed in any other manner.[23] The recurrent phrase that so-and-so has joined the SA.GAZ in all probability signifies that they have defected their political allegiance by joining the "out-party." Another alternative to the peasant, less dramatic but no less severe, would be to "curtail consumption."[24] Normally this is the first line of action taken in which only basic items are eaten, purchases minimized, and home grown produce relied on as much as possible. In this precarious situation any novelty may undermine the balance and therefore greater cleavage to tradition is enjoined. By nature the peasant is not a "joiner"; his necessity to meet the needs of staying alive without undue commitments to a larger system explains his grass-roots conservatism. In wartime the urbanite may easily be separated from his livelihood, but the peasant has the land and his ability to make it produce.[25] Thus it must be assumed that the *ḫupšu* of the Amarna period selected a path most convenient to their interests: for some it would mean remaining faithful to the regent, for others it was an opportunity to seize the land they worked, for yet others it was time to revolt by joining those who stood over and against their oppressors.

Canaanites were reknowned as merchants; Amorites were known to have carried on vast caravan trade with Sumer; and Hittite merchants from the city of Ura probably plied their goods into southern Palestine as well as Ugarit.[26] The urban system of network marketing was that practiced in Ugarit as the Administrative texts relate; it is also presumed to have been themodel for other centers throughout Canaan. In network markets there is a middleman, a professional, who stands between the primary producer and the consumer.[27] Thus one man may raise and sell his cattle to the merchant; the merchant may market the milk or slaughter the cattle and sell hides to the tanner, meat, fat to the consumer. The peasant finds himself in a market in which prices are not governed by custom or kinship as in the rural village, but by a stranger, by impersonal laws of supply and demand he may not entirely understand and which he certainly does not control. In this form of competition the peasant must be prepared to sell grain, milk, leather goods, pots and pans, whatever brings the best market, the price current. Between seeding and harvest the peasant may develop craft skills and products so as to be more flexible. It is not inconceivable that a cultivator also keep a herd of sheep, a few cows and goats, have a basic skill in leather and weaving just to meet needs. Because he has limited withholding power in times of depression, the peasant has few alternatives in short cycles of declining prices as obtained during periods of political chaos.[29] Times of political uncertainty are dangerous for the merchant as well, but they also afford chances for profiteering.[30] But the peasant may decide to do otherwise: he may tend the crops himself and send his wife to sell and buy, or keep some male members at home for the fields and send sons and daughters out for hire as cited by Rib-Addi.[31]

Caught in these economic binds, the peasant may confront the proliferation of middlemen by social exclusion, grouping all specialists of a kind different from himself and his locale as strangers and potential enemies. Thus he finds a social outlet and expression for economic domination within which he is powerless. He may very well find that he is not alone in his plight and so a *cosa nostra* may form of peasants like himself; a positive social relationship may develop but need not be enduring because its basis is not fundamental.[32] Local merchants such as smithys, leather workers, scribes who practice discounts and "little extras" for favored consumers may be included. The peasant's enemy is anyone who has a lien on his fund of rent. This can be the merchant, the tax collector, the royal production supervisor who sets quotas and market prices, the labor contractor, and ultimately, the king. They all have one interest in the peasant: grain. Thus, in the network market system, the merchant--even when he resides in the village--continues to be regarded as a stranger and an outsider.[33]

C. *LAND TENURE*

The land of the peasant belonged to the regent by right of domain, i.e., the lord held ownership by heredity or royal grant, for a definite period of time or in perpetuity.[34] The regent may parcel land to his peasants, grant hunting rights, rights to pasture, woodland and fuel. In return the peasant must pay in produce or labor. The peasant on his own level may "furnish housing to landless laborers in return for their labor" or sublease the land to tenant farmers. The lot of the slave or serf must have been that of the landless possibly in the service of the *ḫupšu*. Although a case may be made that the *ḫupšu* were "free proletarians" it would not take much stress on the system to have the *ḫupšu* become willingly or by force part of the serfdom.[35]

Gray concludes from Ugarit that the upper classes held land in perpetuity; thus, land held through inheritance is based on kinship and carries with it the right to receive tribute from its peasants.[36] Yet the Amarna texts reveal that the Pharaoh had appointed chiefs of his Canaanite provinces to administer his realm in his stead. Weber spoke of such domain as prebendal, i.e., the king granted officials land as income.[37] From the income derived from the peasants the regents had the right to keep some of the taxes collected and receive a salary from the central bureau. It afforded the king greater centralized control because the regents depended on his good will for their position. The feudal domain was more stable but also provided a permanent power source of opposition to the king from his landed aristocracy. Therefore it was necessary to "surround domain with ceremony" to lessen the edge of the single interest relationship: gain.[38] In addition it provided a much needed basis for a constant concern of rulers everywhere: it underwrites their claim to legitimacy. Through ritual the ruler may assume the power and glory of the god or king for his district in acting out myths of fertility for men and fields.[39] Festivals give occasion for the normal state of the society to be put aside to ease the peasants' tension, the Canaanites regulated every crisis of life from birth to the grave by customs designed to separate the participants from historical time and place them for a period in mythical time.

An in-depth study of the peasant's control of his land, water, seed, draft animals, tools and labor is needed to enable one to comprehend how his factors of production may and do become his debt titles. In the nature of their business, merchants could become creditors, money lenders, and bankers.[40] A peasant may have to pay to enjoy water rights; if he has no money he must borrow it and pay interest; the same may be true of his purchasing tools and yet again a rent for draft animals. Thus the creditor may keep the peasant permanently dependent at a subsistence level. If he deals in land and population density is heavy, he may land speculate and still create a competitive market for loans. However, if he keeps the peasant at a minimum capacity for repayment, he "freezes capital"; if he cannot always and easily recover his loan, and a bulk of laws indicate how real the possibility was, he will charge exorbitant interest rates of 50 to 75 percent.[43]

At a time of political unrest there will be a "steady turnover" of those who hold claim to lands and debt titles.[44] These short term relations make for quick money situations and increased tension between the impoverished peasant and the merchant group. The existence of a class of landlords and money-lenders whose real interests lie in living in urban areas removed from the countryside, who are aspiring for political office or favor, who exploit the rural opportunity as a means of accumulating wealth to further their own political and social ascendancy, creates a socially volatile moment. The city "benefits from the surplus" milked from the countryside by the "urban rent collectors without generating an expanded rural productivity."[45] The system is self-limiting because it reduces incentives by reducing the peasant's consumption to the bare minimum.

Caution regarding the shift in semantic range must be used as to the precise meaning of *ḫupšu* in texts that span the period from early to late second millenium, and are found in Babylon, Nuzi, Alalakh, Ugarit, Amarna and the Old Testament. From the Amarna usage it would be difficult to press the case that the *ḫupšu* were landless peasants or "free proletarians," tenant farmers. It is apparent that they were economically and legally bound to their regent (*hazanu*), the city-ruler appointed by Egypt. What is of immediate interest here is their relationship to the group termed the SA.GAZ-people.

D. THE SA.GAZ

It has been convincingly argued by Greenberg that the SA.GAZ of the second millenium were an ethnically heterogeneous class of people found in Mesopotamia, Syria and Palestine.[46] He states:

> "The core of the SA.GAZ/H. would seem to have been composed of uprooted, propertyless persons who found a means of subsistence for themselves and their families by entering a state of dependence in various forms."[47]

Within the successive ethnic movements of various peoples during the period there continued to be a social class of indigent, migrant peoples mixed with the settled populations. Once the social and political chaos diminished at the end of the millenium they seem to disappear as well. Yet even during the centuries of intense tribal migrations the SA.GAZ can be seen to be an element of the settled rather than the nomadic population. Nearly without exception cities and countries are given as their place of origin; they form special quarters in the city of Aleppo; they are given a city by Amanhatbi of Tusulti (EA, 185, 186); even when they are accused of plundering and burning the cities their base of operations is not the desert but the city.

The use of the term seems to indicate that one would not wish to be called a SA.GAZ by one's friend. Rival city-heads (*hazanu*) Shuwardata (Keilah is one of his cities), Milkilu of Gezer, Abdi-Hiba of Jerusalem are at various times allied with one another against a third member. Throughout the shifting alliances, they consistently regard their opponent as a SA.GAZ.[48] To be hostile to Rib-Addi of Gubla is "to become like the SA.GAZ." A difficulty with the Amarna usage is that while in the main the term SA.GAZ is used in a pejorative sense it is not true in every instance. However in the mind of Rib-Addi, who can bring no specific charge against Abdi-Asirta or Aziru, the term is charged with political sedition.

Rib-Addi is unable to convince the Pharaoh that his empire was virtualy lost because of the hostility of the SA.GAZ people. There were no invading hordes from the desert seizing the cities but a change in political control of the city-states, a change which the Pharaoh felt not worth the bother as long as he continued to receive tribute. It was through political intrigue, intimidation, bribery that the SA.GAZ gained control of a city and its territory.[49] Rib-Addi pleads that law and order could no longer be maintained, that his enemies derived their power from the lawless, rebellious element; even the Pharaoh's regents (*hazanu*) were joining them.

It is immediately apparent that the SA.GAZ were considered socially inferior. They were dependent and landless. They were displaced from their original social group either voluntarily or not, and they enjoyed no legal status within the extant feudal system. They took what they could get. In this context Rib-Addi's constant reference to Abdi-Asirta as a stray dog is a rather apt social sobriquet. But to live totally unattached would invite extinction, so some adherence to another political authority must be expected. This out-group not based on ethnic, folk or kinship ties would not be different from the in-group because of their legal status and political orientation. The mistaken notion that all SA.GAZ were impoverished may be avoided if one recalls that the regents, chiefs and military aristocracy became SA.GAZ in Syria-Palestine. Any dissident who no longer wished to be under the control of a given ruler could be a SA.GAZ -man. And although Abdi-Asirta and his Aziru were strong rulers in the eyes of Egypt, they could very well be SA.GAZ in the subjective view of Rib-Addi, for they stood outside the accepted political procedures of one regency respecting another.

Mendenhall reasons that there are three basic and constituitive factors in the term SA.GAZ: (1) loss of status; one must be ejected, fled or withdrawn from the previous group to qualify; (2) twofold loss of status in a legal/political community; (*a*) the SA.GAZ no longer feel bound by the customary legal obligations; "they do as they please," and (*b*) they are no longer enjoying the protection and privileges of the society; only force can deal with them; (3) they are said to use illegitimate force against the demands of the existing political structure.[50]

E. THE PERIOD BETWEEN AMARNA AND JOSHUA

Despite the major political disturbances in Syria-Palestine during MB, the cultural tradition remains fundamentally continuous.[51] However, a general deterioration in physical culture occurs between 1500 and 1100 B.C. The upheaval between 1250 and 1150 B.C. reaches from Alalakh to Lachish in which many cities were destroyed, most rebuilt but not immediately nor along the same lines. Glock sees three reasons promoting the political disturbances:

> a. New populations were moving in, for example, Philistines, Sea-Peoples, and Hebrews; b. *Habiru* and peasants generally were revolting against oppressive social and economic conditions in Canaanite life; c. also, Egypt was unable to police city-state intrigue.[52]

This is the proximate historical setting for the appearance of the new people in Palestine, the Israelites.

The political turmoil witnessed in the Amarna letters did not conclude with the last datable tablet, but continued piecemeal until the unification of the land by David. Defection from the political rule in Canaan during the 14th century in the form of cities and lands joining the SA.GAZ included members from every class of society. Likewise, in these times it is likely that new patrons will vie with established (legal) ones for peasant support and produce; a patron whose star is on the decline will lose his clients to one whose star is in ascendancy. For revolt, a common cause and coalition is needed. In times of political stress the opportunity is present--and as Amarna portrays was activated--for peasants to form coalitions. A major difference in the Amarna documents and those of early Israel is the lack of a tribal consciousness in the early 14th century and the marked awareness of it during the period of the Judges. A social and political transformation had occurred during the hiatus.

Seti I, Ramses II and Merneptah attempted to reassert effective political domination in Canaan following the Amarna period. Their limited successes at Beth-shan, Kadesh and Shechem and withdrawal subsequent to the arrival of the Sea-Peoples leaves considerable room for local developments. It is Mendanhall's contention that the Israelite settlement and the SA.GAZ movement of Amarna materials are one and the same political process, not necessarily a violent one but potentially so in certain cases.[54] Account must be taken of two factors in a peasant-based revolt: the peasant's tendency toward autonomy, and an equally strong tendency to form coalitions on a more or less unstable basis for short-range ends.[55] It may not be difficult to arouse a peasant group to common action, but it is equally arduous to maintain organization while in action and after the short term goal is achieved. Thus local periodic irruptions might continue over a long period of time without uniting into a major force for lack of a catalyst.

Racial distinction is a relatively modern notion that has come about since the rise of nationalism. The basic unit was the family associated with other families in a village. A cluster of families may constitute a clan with its specific village center. Several clans would comprise a tribe with a territorial center in some major city within its boundaries.[56] Clearly, a tribe would not be a racially pure group but simply an administrative unit within a federation of tribes. Noth is probably correct in assuming a prehistory for a tribe prior to incorporation, but this prehistory need not demand either ethnic purity or nomadic origin. Again, Alt may be quite accurate in his concept of the territorial division as a constant, for what had transpired was a change in political and social structure from the city-state to tribal, but not one of racially diverse population associated with cosmopolitan urban centers to racially new and pure groups haunting the uninhabited.

If one accepts the tribe as a social and administrative unit within a given territory which in turn is populated with cities and their villages, one may also conceive that a network of kinship ties between the urban group and those of the villages, through marriage or migration, might be maintained. However, the symbiosis between town and village would be disrupted if an external superior power group assumed control as the Sea-Peoples did in the 13th and 12th centuries. Gen 34 relates the blunder of a city prince violating a village maiden with the resultant havoc on the townsmen. Tribal formation may have come about as a result of sufficient numbers defecting from the cities with their military aristocracies; cities form their own coalitions as Josh 10 would indicate; they needed a similar alliance to cope with the Gibeonite treaty.[57] The military aristocracies met with their technologically inferior foe but lost to their wiliness. The Israelites possessed little military and technological power, but the traditions stress that they had an unparalleled unity of ethical cohesion.

It must be emphasized that the kingship ideal of divine origin was shared by Canaan with its neighbors.[58] The success of political and military power introduced into the city-state of Canaan a twofold disruption which was operative both in the ideology of the conqueror and that of the conquered. The most important deity is that which underwrites the legitimacy of those in power, and receives sufficient popular allegiance. A deity without a social following is at best effete. As it has been pointed out with regard to Mesopotamia, the pantheon reflects the political structure of the state and supports the *status quo*. The reciprocity involved subjects the gods to state manipulation. Aspects of the deities which were unpredictable become regulated through incarnation in the king and institutionalization in the priesthood. The Israelite movement was a radical rejection of this ideology; it proclaimed Yahweh as one, as king, as lord of the land, as judge, and as warrior; all were functions of the Canaanite aristocracy. The Israelites believed that political realities were a function of the religious ethic and not the exercise of the monopoly of force.[59] It is Mendenhall's thesis that:

> the biblical covenant was a systematic proclamation that no one was in control, and any social organization was a secular business that depended entirely upon its demonstrated value to human beings--and its willingness to remain within the ethical bonds to which all members of the community were obligated.[60]

The catalyst for mobilizing the large social units disaffected with Canaanite society was a band of immigrants, surely smaller in number than those native to the land but great enough to exert pressure. Thus the new forces were made up of a cross section of Canaanites (within this term must be grouped all smaller political and religious groups) predominantly of the lower classes (but not exclusively), some from the cities, the others from the villages, joined with a mixed group that migrated north along the eastern side of the Dead Sea bearing a fierce devotion to their god Yahweh and a vivid memory of what he had done for them in Sinai and in Egypt. The new faith was not something worked out over the next two centuries following entry but appeared compact and fully developed from the start.[61]

It is a fact that urban culture during the third and second milleniums suffered an ebb and flow pattern corresponding to the power of the current political regime. The periods of decline saw the influx of new peoples, the times of rise a strengthening of power. Urban-centered feudalism was the dominant social and political form that gave shape to the society throughout the second millenium. The Israelite movement is better characterized as a repudiation of the feudal system than a land appropriation by land-hungry nomads. The emnity between the Israelites and the Canaanites did not originate in the "age old hostility between the nomad and the sedentary farmer," but was a grass-roots polarization between groups within the society. The coalition that was successful in establishing a new order in Palestine was based on religious and ethical unity, i.e., a value system that transcended the old.[62]

This extended analysis of the social relations prevailing in Canaan during the Amarna age may shed some light on the dark decades that enshroud the period of Joshua. The peoples of Canaan were of many ethnic origins; many were landless for a myriad of reasons. The conditions were ripe for a major upheaval in which the traditional political system of city-states would be tested. It is the conclusion of this author that the Israelite movement was a throughgoing repudiation of the political and religious ideology which disallowed a disenfranchised peasantry reasonable participation in society.

NOTES

1. A. Glock, "Early Israel as the Kingdom of Yahweh," *Concordia Theological Monthly* 41 (1970) 578. Cf. Mendelsohn, "Society and Economic Conditions," *World History of the Jewish People*, Vol. 3, 39-51.
2. *Ibid.*, 578.
3. *EA* 85:12 ff., 114:21 ff.
4. Glock, *ibid.*, 578.
5. J. Gray, *The Legacy of Canaan. The Ras Shamra Texts and Their Relevance for the Old Testament*, SVT Vol. 5, 160; also, *idem*, *Archaeology and the Old Testament World* (New York, 1965) 138-139. In the latter work Gray compares the Davidic kingship with Canaanite, Mesopotamian and Egyptian models and concludes that the local feudal order long in existence in Canaan best illustrates the setting of the Davidic.
6. Names such as Biridiya (*EA* 242, 3), Widia (320, 5), Tadua (286, 2); at Ugarit King Nigmad (Nigmed), also S.F.N. Schaeffer, *The Cuneiform Texts of Ras-Shamra-Ugarit* (London, 1939) 16. Note also in the Keret Epic that the king marries a non-Semitic princess possibly suggesting the political symbiosis, J. Gray, *The KRT Text in the Literature of Ras Shamra: A Social Myth of Ancient Canaan* (Leiden, 1964) 2nd ed., 4-5. The Sardanu (Serdan) of *EA* 123, 15 are considered Aegean mercenaries by Gray; cf. *Legacy*, 162, esp. n. 3.

7. Gray, "Feudalism in Ugarit and Early Israel," *ZAW* 64 (1952) 50-51.

8. Gray, *Keret Epic*, 40-41; "Feudalism," 53-54; *Legacy*, 169-171. J. Pedersen, *Israel: Its Life and Culture* I-II, (Copenhagen, 1964[5]) 498-499; *idem*, "Note on the Hebrew Hopsī," *JPOS* 6 (1926) 103-105. R. DeVaux, *Ancient Israel* (New York, 1961) 88. W.F. Albright, "Canaanite *Hopšî*, 'free,' in the Amarna Tablets," *JPOS* 4 (1924) 169-170; *idem*, "Canaanite *hapši* and Hebrew *hopšî* again," *JPOS* 6 (1926) 106-108; *idem*, "New Canaanite Historical and Mythological Data," *BASOR* 63 (1936) 23-32; in this article he translates a portion of the *Keret Epic* ii. 90-91 as "three thousand myriads--serfs without number, peasants without count," 29.

9. D. J. Wiseman, *The Alalakh Tablets*, Occasional Publications of the British Institute of Archaeology in Ankara, No. 2, (London, 1953) 10-11.

10. F. Thureau-Dangin, "Trois Contrats de Ras-Shamra," *Syria* 18 (1937) 246-255; I. Mendelsohn, "On Corvée Labor in Ancient Canaan and Israel," *BASOR* 167 (1962) 31-35.

11. A. Alt, *Essays on Old Testament History and Religion*, trans. R.A. Wilson (Garden City, N.Y.: Doubleday, 1966) 175-221.

12. E. Wolf, *Peasants* (Englewood Cliffs, N.J.: Prentice-Hall, 1966) 3. Cf. G. Sjoberg, "'Folk' and 'Feudal' Societies," *AJS* 58 (1952) 231-239; note in particular his typology of the feudal system, 232-233.

13. Wolf, *ibid.*, 4.

14. *EA* 81, 33-41.

15. *EA* 118, 21-23; 125, 14-30; 85, 8-15.

16. *EA* 81, 6-14.

17. *EA* 81, 15-17; 74, 25-26. Cf. also, E.F. Campbell, *The Chronology of the Amarna Letters* (Baltimore, 1964); W.F. Albright, *The Amarna Letters from Palestine, Syria, the Philistines and Phoenicia, CAH*, Vol. 2, ch. 20, 23, 1966.

18. Wolf, *Peasants*, 5-6.

19. *Ibid*, Wolf, 7-9. Notice the elaborate description of the bridal-price in the Keret Text. C.H. Gordon, *Ugaritic Handbook, KRT*, iii.205 ff.

20. *EA* 73, 26; 74, 19; 88, 31-32; 84; 138, 93.

21. Wolf, *Peasants*, 15-16. Rib-Addi complains that he is virtually a prisoner in his own city (*EA* 81, 19-22); "Behold, thus I remain shut up in the midst of my city. I cannot go out of the gate ...."

22. A study of the Nuzi feudal system indicates that upon the death of the tenant farmer the land reverts back to the crown to be redistributed afresh by the *ḫalṣuḫlu*, the royal supervisor of the land. Rights of inheritance was a prerogative of the aristocracy and in times of political turmoil supervision of the land may slip back to the peasant. Cf. H. Lewy, "The Nuzi Feudal System," *Orientalia* 11 (1942) 22.

23. The SA.GAZ people do as they please to the point that Rib-Addi asks, who do they think they are. *EA* 76, 14-14; 104, 17-24. Perhaps the Deuternomic historian means as much in Jdg 21:25.

24. Wolf, *Peasants*, 16.

25. Wolf, *ibid.*, 17.

26. Gordon, "Abraham and the Merchants of Ura," *JNES* 17 (1958) 28-29. It is Gordon's conviction that Abraham was "a merchant prince; a *tamkârum* from the Hittite realm," 31; W. F. Albright, "The Excavations of Tell Beit Mirsim II," *AASOR* 17 (1936-37), p. 5 argues that there was sufficient pasturage for a wool industry here.

27. Wolf, *Peasants*. 42.

28. The Hebrew patriarchs are portrayed as wise in the ways of making one dollar earn two. Jacob outwits a nimble Laban, Isaac becomes a subject of envy to Abimelech's countrymen, Joseph requires that his brothers be honest before allowing them to trade.

29. Wolf, *Peasants*, 45.

30. Take for example the case of a peasant who must borrow grain from the merchant because he has had to sell his grain early to meet urgent demands. The merchant lends at interest due in harvest time. Then the peasant sells his grain at 2 minas of silver (the market price) to the merchant, plus interest. The merchant buys at 2 minas and resells it to the peasant at the next short period at 4 minas. Thus the peasant is economically controlled and oppressed by the merchant. Cf. Wolf, *Peasants*, 45.

31. Wolf, *Peasants*, 46.

32. Wolf, *Ibid.*, 47.

33. J. Nougayrol, *Le Palais Royal D'Ugarit*, IV, Mission de Ras Shamra, IX. dir. Claude F. A. Schaeffer (Paris, 1956), Texte 17.130, 103-105. An important letter of Hattusilis III to Niqmepa, king of Ugarit (1324-1274), answers the latter's complaint that the merchants of Ura were a burden to the city, instructed that they were to operate only during the summer, clear out by winter, and were not to own any land there. The term used for them signified "foreign traders," *tamkâru*. The inferior status of the merchant is further illustrated from the Hittite laws regarding the murder of a merchant. If anyone slays a free person or a slave in anger, or smites them causing their death he must surrender 2-4 persons in restitution, but if he slays a merchant a payment of coin will suffice. Cf. E. Neufeld, *Hittite Laws* (London, 1951), pp. 1-2, 134.

34. Wolf, *Peasants*, 49.

35. I. Mendelsohn, "The Canaanite Term for 'Free Proletarian,'" *BASOR* 83 (1941) 36-39; *idem*, "State Slavery in Ancient Palestine," *BASOR* 85 (1942) 14-17; *idem*, "New Light on the *Ḫupšu*," *BASOR* 139 (1955) 9-11. Note also Joseph's agrarian plan in Gen 47:13-26.

36. Cf. Gray, *ZAW* 64, 51-55. Cf. also H. Reviv, "On Urban Representative Institutions and Self-Government in

Syria-Palestine in the Second Half of the Second Millenium," *JESHO* 12 (1969) 283-297.

37. M. Weber, *Ancient Judaism* (New York, 1952), trans. and ed. H. H. Gerth and D. Martindale, p. 169. Here Weber is speaking of the Jerusalemite priests prebendal provisions placed under tighter state control by Joash. Cf. Wolf, *Peasants*, 51.

38. Wolf, *Peasants*, 52.

39. Neufeld, *Hittite Laws*, 45-46, deals with a consecration ritual for dividing a field, probably performed by a priest for a family. The inference is that he who owns the land has the power; would that the god act favorably in consort with the owner.

40. C. H. Gordon, "Abraham of Ur," *Hebrew and Semitic Studies*, presented to Godfrey Rolles Driver, ed. D. Winton Thomas and W. D. McHardy (Oxford, 1963) 78. In speaking of Abraham, Gordon states: "He had every opportunity to lend precious metal on interest in Canaan in accordance with the methods of *tamkârûtu* 'business enterprise'." The laws of Hammurabi provide that if a person given in surety dies in the house of the creditor because of ill-treatment, the owner of the pledged person shall convict the *merchant*, i.e., creditor. Cf. G. R. Driver and J. C. Miles, *The Babylonian Laws*, Vol. II (Oxford, 1955) 47, n. "j". Bourraburiash II, king of Babylon, complains to Amenaphis IV in the Amarna Tablets (*EA* 8) that his merchants were slain in Canaan, Egyptian land, and nothing has been done about it.

41. Wolf, *Peasants*, 55.

42. Wolf, *ibid.*, 56.

43. That such an elaborate system existed in the Ancient Near East seems beyond doubt as one reads the laws of Hammurabi dealing with equitable interest rates merchants who lend grain or money may charge. Cf. Driver and Miles, *The Babylonian Laws*, II, 39-41. Interest was fixed by CH: L and this might fluctuate with the relative value of the basic unit, the GUR. But other rates were recognized as well: (1) "interest of the city" fixed by the town officials, (2) "interest of the market" fixed by the seller-group, (3) "interest of the temple" regulated by local temple priests, and (4) the "interest of Shamash" fixed by royal temple at 20 percent. For as money lender to exceed these rates would not be unheard of depending on the instability of the government and desperation of the debtor. Cf. *Ibid.*, Vol. I, 174. Cf. also J. L. McKenzie, "Loans," *Dictionary of the Bible* (Milwaukee, 1965) 515; DeVaux, *Ancient Israel*, 170-177.

44. Wolf, *Peasants*, 56.

45. Wolf, *ibid.*

46. M. Greenberg, *The Hab/piru*, American Oriental Series, V. 39, eds. H. M. Hoenigswald, J. DeFrancis, G. Mendenhall (New Haven, 1955) 85-88. The full question of the identification of Apiru (Hab/piru) with the Hebrews will not be treated here. Cf. H. Cazelles, "Hebrew, Ubru et Hapiru," *Syria* 35 (1958) 198-217; J. Bottéro, *Le problème*

des Habiru à la quatrième rencontre assyriologique internationale, Cahiers de la Société Asiatique, XII (Paris, 1954). A wide range of opinion on the subject has been expressed over the years; cf. P. E. Dhorme, "Les Habiru et les Hébreux," *JPOS* 4 (1924) 162-168; G. A. Barton, "The Habiri of the El Amarna Tablets and the Hebrew Conquest of Palestine," *JBL* 48 (1929) 144-147; E. Chiera, "Habiru and Hebrews," *AJSL* 49 (1932-33) 115-124; E. Dhorme, "La Question des Habiri," *Revue de l'histoire des religions* 118 (1938) 170-87; H. H. Rowley, "Ras Shamra and the Habiru Question," *PEQ* 72 (1940) 90-94; J. W. Jack, "New Light on the Habiru-Hebrew Question," *PEQ* 72 (1940) 95-115; A. Guillaume, "The Habiru, the Hebrews, and the Arabs," *PEQ* 78 (1946) 64-85; E. G. Kraeling, "The Origin of the Name 'Hebrew'," *AJSL* 58 (1941) 237-253; H. H. Rowley, "Habiru and Hebrew," *PEQ* 74 (1942) 41-53; esp. *idem, From Joseph to Joshua* (London, 1952) 165-188. M. Gray, "The Habiru-Hebrew Problem," *HUCA* 29 (1958) 135-202; H. Klengel, "Halbnomaden am mittleren Euphrat," *Das Altertum* 5 (1959) 195-205; M. Rowton, "The Topological Factor in the Hapiru Problem," *Studies in Honor of Benno Landsberger*, Assyriological Studies 16 (Chicago, 1965) 375-387; R. DeVaux, "Le Problème des Hapiru après quinze années," *JNES* 27 (1968) 221-228; M. Greenberg, "Hab/piru and Hebrews," *WHJP* V. 2, 188-200.

47. *Ibid.*, 88.

48. *EA* 280, 290a, 289, 271.

49. Harrassment of the peasants prevented the harvesting of crops and the fields were abandoned. The technique is common practice for Abdi-Asirta, Azira, Labaya. Campbell notes that Biridiza's scribe often implies by "harvest" the meaning: "We were not able to pluck the wool." Thus all forms of peasant economy, even simple sheep herding, were shut down. The peasants would not survive if they remained loyal to the regent; their alternative was to join the SA.GAZ people. Cf. E. F. Campbell, "Shechem in the Amarna Archives," *Apud* G. E. Wright, *Shechem* (New York, 1965) 193, n. 4.

50. G. Mendenhall, *The Tenth Generation* (Baltimore, 1973) 131-135.

51. P. Lapp, "The Conquest of Palestine in the Light of Archaeology," *Concordia Theological Monthly* 38 (1967) 295. Also, Kenyon, *Amorites*, 5, states: "This continuity, from the Middle to the Late Bronze Age and into the Iron Age, is of particular importance, for this is the material culture that the Israelites found in the land. It is, moreover, the culture that they to a large degree adopted. One of the major difficulties in establishing the chronology of the entry of the Israelites is that at no point in a single site can one say that the material evidence shows that a new people had arrived."

52. A. Glock, "Early Israel as the Kingdom of Yahweh," *Concordia Theological Monthly* 41 (1970) 583; also B. Mazar, "Development," *WHJP*, Vol. 3, 3-22.

53. This would satisfy the Alt-Noth belief that it was peaceful and Lapp's need to explain the destruction of specific sites.

54. Autonomy should not be taken in terms of the American Declaration of Independence, but rather freedom from oppressive demands on his funds of rent and subsistence. Karl Marx, for all his love of the proletarian, was a realist when it came to ensuring peasant support; they must be led and represented by someone outside their class. The revolt Mendenhall speaks of is not a Marxist revolt but many elements are similar. Cf. E. R. Wolf, *Peasants*, 91-92.

55. Cf. C. U. Wolf, "Terminology of Israel's Tribal Organization," *JBL* 65 (1946) 45-49; *idem*, "Some Remarks on the Tribes and Clans of Israel," *JQR* 36 (1946) 287-298; J. H. Chamberlayne, "Kinship Relations Among the Early Hebrews," *Numen* 10 (1963) 153-164. A. Causse views the Hebrew invasion clashing with urban culture of Canaan producing a crisis for kinship relations among the Israelites; cf. "La crise de la solidarité de famille et de clan dans l'ancien Israel," *Revue d'Histoire de la Philosophie Religieuse* 10 (1930) 24-60. Cf. also B. S. J. Isserlin, "Israelite and Pre-Israelite Place-Names in Palestine," *PEQ* 89 (1957) 133-144. See also M. O. Sahlins, *Tribesmen* (Englewood Cliffs, N.J., 1968) 4-13 concerning their social and political roles.

56. B. D. Rahtjen, "Philistine and Hebrew Amphictyonies," *JNES* 24 (1965) 100-104.

57. Cf. J. Gray, "Canaanite Kingship in Theory and Practice," *VT* 2 (1952) 193-220. The author demonstrates the distinctiveness of Canaanite kingship in the midst of her most powerful rivals; however he is also wedded to a naive anthropology that conceives of primitive tribal societies supplying fresh blood to Canaanite culture through continuous incursions from the desert.

58. Mendenhall, *Generation*, 193.

59. *Ibid.*, 195.

60. McKenzie, *Judges*, 98; also, R. T. Anderson, "The Role of the Desert in Israelite Thought," *JBR* 27 (1959) 41-44.

61. It cannot be emphasized too strongly that "religion and politics are reciprocals" and operative in the formation of the new social order. It might be argued that the Israel of the Merenptah stele was a social class, a group as yet unleavened. Following the disruption of the Sea Peoples and the subsequent invasion of Yahwism Israel became a people. Cf. E. A. Speiser, "'People' and 'Nation' of Israel," *JBL* 79 (1960) 157-163.

S 137 JOSEPH AND ASENATH AND THE GREEK NOVEL

Richard I. Pervo

Seabury-Western Theological Seminary

The task set for this paper is the comparison of Jos. and As. to that body of literature commonly called the "Greek Novel" or "Romance."[1] One does not, hopefully, pursue questions of relationship for their own technical sake, but rather as part of a broader quest. "Greek" raises the question of cultural and religious influence and background as well as matters relating to date and provenance, while "novel" raises the question of literary form: what works should we read against Jos. and As. in order to clarify our understanding of its purpose and function?

The thesis I will set forth is that Jos. and As. belongs to the history of the Sapiential Novel in its Jewish manifestation at a stage when influence from contemporary Greek novels was quite appropriate and that, theologically as well as literarily, this work appears to be a parallel to the dualistic religious novels evidenced also in pagan and Christian circles. Jos. and As. is a "Sapiential Novel" of a branch of the Jewish Wisdom tradition which was evolving a gnosticizing theological position.

A convincing analysis of the ancient novel as a genre was long limited by several factors, including a highly erroneous chronology, intense concentration upon a small body of "erotic romances," and a prevailing atmosphere of literary disdain and/or condescension.[2]

Although the chronological arrangement proposed by E. Rohde in his classic study of the Greek novel could not withstand the refutation provided by papyrological recoveries, the effects of his chronological analysis continue to impact study of the ancient novel.[3] Rohde saw the novels all of a piece and considered them degenerate products of the Second Sophistic and the even more degenerate early Byzantine era. Both the tendency to treat the genre as a whole and the allegation of decadence have endured.

Focus upon the *Scriptores Erotici* has encouraged the relegation of similar works to the subsidiary level of forerunners or illegitimate spin-offs, and this attitude, in turn, has fostered an overly narrow view of the scope of the ancient novel and its potential for development.[4] Perhaps more importantly, insistence upon a narrow canon of about five works (which, in fact, imitate one another) created and reinforced the dogma of the ancient novel as a quite restricted and stereotyped genre, built around the two motifs of love and travel, each of which took literary form in recurring clusters of sub-motifs.[5] A full appreciation of the ancient novel requires, and is beginning to receive, a broader approach embracing a substantial body of narrative prose fiction and historical fiction.

Learned writers nurtured on the Classics have tended either to view most ancient novels with revulsion, as not worth reading,[6] or to point with condescension to their utterly banal quality.[7] This general context of cultural disappointment has, by and large, meant that most studies of the ancient novel incline toward examining them as an (unpleasant) phenomenon which must be explained in terms of literary-historical predecessors and causation. The unsurprising and not infrequent conclusion of inquiries so oriented has been that the ancient novel was a degeneration of one or more Classical genres, a typical product, in other words, of later Antiquity.[8] Preoccupation with the relationship of the novel to other genres has inhibited a fair appraisal of this form and its representatives in their own right. Stylistic and literary comparison of popular[9] novels to the great literature of Greco-Roman antiquity is neither reasonable nor appropriate. Whatever their esthetic deficiencies, ancient novels are extremely valuable for historians of popular culture, including historians of religion. These works provide us with important data about the hopes, aspirations and beliefs of relatively ordinary people in the Mediterranean world of the late Hellenistic and Roman periods. The dullest and most deservedly ephemeral of ancient novels give profile, both in style and content, to Jewish and Christian narrative writings of the same era.

When taken up in the broader sense, the novel is probably the most formless of all ancient genres. Because this form came into prominence in response to everyday needs and was most often written in a popular speech and style that failed to conform to the established criteria for "good" literature, the novel did not gain recognition in ancient times as a legitimate activity for educated persons. Critics did not even feel obliged to establish a name for this disreputable genre.[10]

As the most formless of genres, the novel was free from restriction and open to borrow whence it pleased and develop freely in response to changing times and tastes. To draw a phenomenological analogy, one might say that novels represented a sort of literary syncretism, quite parallel to the religious syncretism of the early centuries C.E. Jos. and As. is an excellent example of both literary and religious syncretism. In order to understand the rise of the novel in the Greco-Roman world we must look to cultural developments no less than to available and deteriorating genres of literature.

The novel as an undefined, open, syncretistic and somewhat unrestrained genre was very nicely suited to express the moods of a new age, a cosmopolitan era, a time in which old social, economic, religious, political and ethical barriers were liable to regular collapse and subsequent reconstruction along new lines. The most sympathetic and persuasive surveys of the ancient novel have interpreted the genre as a response to and expression of *Zeitgeist* rather than as the gradual distillation of a mechanical type of literary evolution.[11]

One final critical hobgoblin which vexes the study of ancient novels is the expectation that any sound member of the genre ought be "pure entertainment." Surviving novels nearly always have a message, a goal or a view of life recommended to their readers. These themes or ideals greatly vary and may be personal, social, intellectual or religious. The last of these examples is rather more important than present day readers might presume, or recognize. Religion, one could even argue, is a more consistent interest in ancient novels than either love or travel![12] Jos. and As. is by no means peculiar because it is a novel that propagates certain religious ideas and proclaims a particular god.

Limitation of the genre proper to the *Scriptores Erotici* has left the problem of the sub-classification of ancient novels at a primitive level.[13] In the following section I will attempt to illustrate the position of Jos. and As. among ancient novels by comparison with various species of the genre. The sub-types set forth here are not intended as a solution for the problem in general. They are rather *ad hoc* critical tools for the assessment of this particular book.

The historical novel was an important type of ancient literature in both literary (Xenophon's *Cyropaideia*) and more popular (The *Alexander-Romance*) spheres. Jewish and Christian literature includes a rich and continuous production of historical fiction. Among Jewish historical novels one may point to Judith, Esther, *Artapanus* and *Third Maccabees*. The apparently favorite type of historical fiction among Christians during the first few centuries was the Acts-literature. The majority of extant ancient historical novels are biographical in nature. Their most common organizational principle is the life and activity of a famous national, religious or intellectual figure or figures.

The mere presence of a known or presumed historical person as a principal character does not provide adequate basis for classifying an ancient novel as "historical." Even the surviving collection of *Scriptores Erotici* are historical in that sense. The writers of erotic novels normally used genuine or legendary local heroes to staff their novels and local legends as the nuclei of their plots.[14] If the term is to have any specific value for the classification and analysis of ancient literature, "historical novel" should be reserved for works which expound events of major significance in the life of a people, community, sect &c. The historical setting must be more than an envelope to hold the story. This criterion would seem to distinguish Jos. and As. from historical novels, proper. The major goal of the work is not the glorification of Joseph and his career. The leading character is Asenath, and her private experiences dominate the story. Jos. and As. is "historical" to about the same degree as the novel of Chariton, the earliest fully extant Greek erotic novel: a minor and colorless historical (or legendary) figure can be fleshed out as an example of an ideal type precisely because real or putative history has so little to say about her.[15] Jos. and As. does not retail a story for its historical interest. The two charaters and their experiences are the basis of this novel because they were perfectly suited to present a certain view of Diaspora Jewish life and belief.[16] Jos. and As. is not a historical novel in the strict sense.

One literary response of the proud old peoples of the East to the Hellenistic conquest was a continuing assertion, in the Greek tongue, of their own accomplishments and historical achievements. What Berosus, Manetho and Josephus, for example, attempted for educated readers was done in a more popular way through the dissemination of "National" or "National-Hero" Romances. These books, most of which constitute a specific group of historical novels, have survived, in the main, only in fragments or later editions.[17] As reconstructed, the National Romances appear to have been worked up from legendary or mythical material cast into a biographical pattern. In a manner reminiscent of apocalyptic, their references to past events often served as a vehicle for anti-Greek or Roman sentiments, as anachronistic allusions to contemporary events frequently indicate.[18]

Not a few Jewish writings, particularly those of the so-called "apologetic" variety, were composed or transmitted as pieces of national-religious fiction. One may point again to *Artapanus*, Judith and, also, Esther (Cf. *Third Maccabees* and *Aristeas*). Is Jos. and As. to be closely aligned with this type of literature? Although the book certainly glorifies the Jewish religion and presents a Jewish hero, comparison with the above works suggests that the objectives of the National Romances and Jos. and As. do not coincide. The political independence or position of the nation or people is not at issue, and the adulation of the hero Joseph is not the major theme. Jos. and As. is more concerned with private than with public affairs. It is not a "National Romance."

The tradition of ancient Jewish novels is related to the Persian as well as the Hellenistic and Roman periods. *Achikar*, Tobit and the first six chapters of Daniel represent a type of novel which appears to have had its origins in the era of Persian domination and to have flourished independently of Greek literary influence, however much their content and continued transmission was due to the later popularity of edifying novels. "Sapiential Novel" is a good designation for this type of literature because of its obvious affiliation to other Wisdom writings. The typical Sapiential Novel seems to have taken as a base one or more traditional popular stories, which may already have possessed cautionary or positive exemplary value, and enriched this core with rather substantial doses of contemporary wisdom material. The net result was (or was felt to be) an excellent medium for the widespread dissemination of wisdom views and values.[19]

Several characteristics of the surviving Sapiential Novels are important for the evaluation of Jos. and As. In its relatively short length, the work under discussion is rather much more comparable to the average sapiential work than to most novels of Greco-Roman provenance. The standard for size in the case of Jos. and As. seems to have been a bit old fashioned. In both structure and content, the Sapiential Novels tended to allow the edifying wisdom to overwhelm what might be regarded as the more interesting story. There was no deft balance between instructional and entertaining material, and the latter was often subordinate in the highest degree. In this regard, also, Jos. and As. as a literary work seems to stand in a close relationship to the older sapiential novel tradition. Comparison with the pagan religious novels of Apuleius and Longus makes the point especially clear.

These relatively primitive sapiential novels frequently inserted their wisdom material into and thus alongside of the story, usually by means of speeches.[20] The narrative elements can therefore easily be separated and distinguished from the conjoined sapiential passages. Greek and Latin novels were rarely so transparent in structure and technique.[21] Here, again, Jos. and As. is not unlike the Sapiential Novels of the earlier Jewish tradition. The long central section in chs. 9-19 which relates Asenath's conversion dominates both the structure and content of the book. The first two thirds of the work are occupied with symbolic and allegorical narrative. The story serves as a thin framework for a lengthy theological presentation.[22]

The character of Levi offers another similarity to the Sapiential Novel. He seems to be the kind of ideal sage frequently featured in these works. His role helps associate both sections of Jos. and As. to the Sapiential type of novel.[23]

The Book of Daniel provides most interesting comparisons with Jos. and As. In both, the traditional genre of sapiential novel is employed for the communication of a non-traditional kind of "wisdom."[24] For Daniel the new message is Apocalyptic, while Jos. and As. reflects a development of speculative wisdom that is verging upon Gnosticism. Both continue the "secular" orientation of the Sapiential Novels by illustrating the potential for success in the gentile world of impeccably religious Jews.[25] Both diverge strongly from the traditional Sapiential novel in that their "wisdom" is esoteric theological information deriving from supernatural revelation. With Jos. and As. in place we may trace the history of the Sapiential Novel in its ideological development: from secular to religious wisdom to Apocalyptic to Gnosis.[26] Jos. and As. belongs, to a large degree, within the context and history of the Sapiential Novel as a Jewish literary genre.

Because the book concerns the private and personal experiences of the two heroes, their meeting, marriage and later life, Jos. and As. invites comparison to another type of ancient novel, the so-called "erotic romances" which flourished in Roman Imperial times. Such action as the book contains is triggered by their love and the jealousy aroused by their marriage. Dynamics of this sort are very common to the plots of the standard "erotic" novels.[27] Jos. and As. thus shares with many Greco-Roman erotic novels their fundamental structural features. It is most likely that this similarity results from imitation. Just as the older Sapiential novels reflected contemporary taste, so Jos. and As. used the most up-to-date sort of plot. In this imitation our novel was by no means alone. The constant reutilization of successful formulae has been an enduring aspect of popular entertainment media.[28] Much more significant than the fact of imitation is its significance: the writer of Jos. and As. intended to appeal to popular taste by clothing the story in an entertaining form, however unsuccessful the attempt might have been.

The use and re-use of effective formulae and devices largely accounts for the frequent recurrence of certain motifs in ancient novels. Creativity was neither demanded by the public nor expected from the writers of these books. The repertory of stock items was employed with such regularity that attempts have been made to define the genre by means of the presence or absence of certain motifs.[29] Philonenko recognized the presence of many of these motifs in Jos. and As. and has pointed many of them out.[30] While the employment of numerous motifs found, among other places, in erotic novels does not establish Jos. and As. as a representative of the genre "Greek Novel," *per se*, it does offer further evidence that the writer wished to present his or her audience with a book that appealed to popular taste. There can be no doubt that Jos. and As. took up the structure of its plot and many individual features from the erotic novel of the contemporary Greco-Roman world.

Jos. and As. ought not be studied solely as an imitation or example of the ancient erotic novel. I have argued above that the book also belongs to the tradition of Jewish novel-writing that emerges in the Sapiential Novels of the Persian period. Similarity to contemporary entertaining and edifying fiction helps us to understand the intention of the book and enables us to place it within a general cultural context: the Greek-speaking Eastern Mediterranean world of the first two centuries of the Common Era.

Despite its similarity to contemporary novels, Jos. and As. may scarcely be described as nothing more than a pleasant and uplifting love story with an ethnic orientation. The centrality of its religious message, the frequently symbolic character of its narrative and certain religio-historical parallels place it within the rank of religious novels and require consideration of its possible bearing upon the hypothesis that the primary purpose of the erotic novels as a whole was aretalogical, the proclamation in cryptic fashion of various Mystery Religions.

The different forms of this hypothesis can be presented here only in outline. Although the names of Merkelbach and Kerenyi are often linked in discussions of the theory, their ideas and procedures are quite distinct. Kerenyi, observing that the erotic novels made use of mythical and legendary persons and patterns, argued that they represented a secularized exposition of religious texts and beliefs. To a certain degree Kerenyi was undoubtedly correct, and the phenomenon he describes is by no means unique in the history of ancient literature.[31] But Kerenyi pushed his argument further and maintained that the erotic type of novel was written to propagate Mystery (especially the Isis) Religions. His proposal has not met with general approval.[32] If Professor Merkelbach's method seems less sophisticated than Kerenyi's, he has avoided many of the obscurities and inexactitudes that have plagued appreciation of the latter's work. Merkelbach followed through on the ground laid by his predecessor by maintaining that the erotic novels were *Romans à clef*, veiled presentations of the actual cultic practice of various Mystery Religions. He interprets the details of the novels as references to specific actions and beliefs. Numerous objections have been raised against

Merkelbach's analysis of the erotic novels, and he has found little support.[33] Perhaps the major shortcoming of both Kerenyi and Merkelbach is that each wished to find a comprehensive theory explaining the origin of the ancient erotic novel.[34] The widespread rejection of their work has inhibited recognition of the importance of religion in at least some of the erotic novels.

At first sight Jos. and As. seems to suggest an overlooked piece of confirmatory evidence for the theories noted above. It is a love story, clearly religious in intention, which uses Mystery language and contains demonstrably symbolic narrative. Philonenko does briefly suggest that Jos. and As. lends support to the theories of Kerenyi and Merkelbach.[35] In fact, however, the opposite would be more nearly correct. This novel is so clearly a derivative product, in which the love story obviously serves as a scant frame for a religious message, that it provides no support whatsoever for the contention that the original motive force behind the composition of Greek erotic novels was religious propaganda. The Greek and Latin novels with a religious theme as a major purpose appear to be secondary.[36] Jos. and As. conforms to this general situation.

The major literary tradition underlying Jos. and As., then, seems to have been the Jewish Sapiential Novel, a tradition which antedated the widespread production of popular Greek fiction. The writer of Jos. and As. did not remain indifferent to current developments, however, but produced a work significantly influenced by the Greek novels of his or her own time. Jos. and As. is not a strange by-product of Greek literature. It is rather a representative of the natural development of a vital and responsive Jewish literary tradition. Within the context of Jewish and Christian literature, the book stands somewhere in the middle of a developmental history in which Daniel might represent one pole and the *Acts of Thomas* another.[37] To what extent the Jewish and Christian developments proceeded along independent lines probably cannot be ascertained with any degree of precision.

Despite its location within an active literary tradition, Jos. and As. suffers when compared to other religious novels, pagan, Jewish and Christian, as a work of literature. If the writer intended to write an exciting book, he or she did not succeed. The structure is jejune. The book falls readily into two parts: chs. 1-21, dealing with meeting, conversion, courtship and marriage; and chs. 22-29, which narrate married life and adventure. The second section is so attenuated that it can only be regarded as a brief *exemplum* of the divine blessings poured upon Asenath's earthly life after her conversion. When the structure of Jos. and As. is placed next to parallel works (such as canonical Acts 9, Xenophon of Ephesus' novel, 1, especially 1,1-4 and Apuleius, especially book 11), it gains the appearance of the opening section of a religious novel, with a "happily ever after" slapped onto the conclusion of the first book. Although there is no indication that this observation describes the literary *history* of Jos. and As.--that it is an abbreviation of a longer work[38]--it does accurately describe the structure of the book. Formally speaking, Jos. and As. is composed of two *novelle*, the Conversion Story and the Foiled Plot of the Jealous Rival. There are no other real "episodes" in the book.[39] The first of these *novelle* is a frequent component of religious novels and has widespread attestation in aretalogical texts, as Burchard has shown.[40] Nor is (miraculous or natural) delivery from a plot concocted by jealous rivals unusual in novels and aretalogies.[41]

The two *novelle* which make up the bulk of Jos. and As. are quite distinct in style. The adventure story is written in straightforward religious narrative prose. The first section, on the other hand, is permeated with symbolic passages and contains no small amount of allegory. Theologically the two sections of this work are also rather dissimilar. The second part does not continue the dualizing, esoteric religious thought and language of the opening chapters. Chs. 22-29 are perhaps derived from a source, while the author is mainly responsible for the first two-thirds of the book.[42]

There are other ancient novels written to communicate a dualistic world view based upon religio-philosophical speculation. Burchard has quite correctly called attention to the tale of Cupid and Psyche in Apuleius, an allegorical story which is important for the interpretation of the *Metamorphoses*.[43] An additional phenomenological parallel is the famous "Hymn of the Pearl" in the *Acts of Thomas*, 108-113, the function of which is very like that of Cupid and Psyche. Each of these three novels uses narrative myth and the language of religious mystery rites as the media for expressing their respective esoteric religious views.[44] Along with the similarities is a significant quantitative difference. Jos. and As. does not employ allegory or myth as the interpretive key to a long entertaining narrative. In this sense it may be strongly contrasted with the pagan and Christian counterparts. Jos. and As. is not a "Jewish equivalent" to the *Metamorphoses* or the *Acts of Thomas*. Direct competition with works of this sort would at least require a book of more substantial scope. As a novel within the Jewish literary tradition, it remains an important testimony to the continued vitality of the genre and its evolution along lines which are similarly attested in pagan and Christian writing and thought.

NOTES

[1]For ancient literature the terms "novel" and "romance" may be used interchangably. There is a basic bibliography of general works on ancient novels in my paper for last year's meeting of this Seminar, "The Testament of Joseph and Greek Romance," in *Studies on the Testament of Joseph*, ed. G. Nickelsburg (SCS 5; Missoula: 1975) 24 n.5.

[2]All of which derive from the classic study of E. Rohde which, at age 100, remains the major treatment of the field. *Der Griechische Roman und seine Vorlaeufer* (Hildesheim, 1960; reprint of 1914, 3d ed.). The classic corpus (*Scriptores Erotici*) are Chariton, Xenophon of Ephesus, Longus, Achilles Tatius and Heliodorus.

[3]In that the novels of the Second Century C.E. are regarded as normative for the entire genre. The late B.E. Perry proved that the "Sophistic Romances" are actually secondary, in the most comprehensive recent study of the ancient novel, *The Ancient Romances* (Berkeley, 1967), which is based upon his 1951 Sather Lectures.

[4]In addition to the types discussed below, antiquity saw examples of Utopian (Euhemerus, Iambulus), Comic or Satiric (Lucian's *Onos* and *Vera Historia*) and Picaresque (The *Satyricon*, ascribed to Petronius) novels. Neither the types nor the examples are exhaustive.

[5]The argument is fallacious because it is circular. Novels are based upon love and travel; ergo, works without one or both cannot be novels. No one really believes this.

[6]So Rohde.

[7]Parallels are often drawn with Hollywood movies of the 1920's-50's. So, to cite one example, O. Weinreich in his brief but excellent *Der Griechische Liebesroman* (Zurich, 1962).

[8]Thus Perry sub-titled his study "A Literary-Historical Account of their Origins," despite his rejection of the premises of earlier investigations and vigorous polemic against Rohde.

[9]"Popular" is here used in opposition to "literary." Not all ancient novels were popular. Literary works were much more liable to survive. Papyrus fragments, as well as Christian works, show that large numbers of novels were written for what might be called the semi-educated public.

[10]Often quoted in this regard is the Emperor Julian's "Letter to a Priest," 301c (=Loeb 2:326). See also Philostratus' Letter 66 (=Loeb p.534), which may refer to the writer Chariton.

[11]This is the line pursued by Perry. See also CJ 50:295-298, 1955. In different ways similar analyses are made by F. Altheim, *Literatur und Gesellschaft im Ausgehenden Altertum*, vol. I (Halle, 1948); K. Kerenyi, *Die Griechisch-Orientalische Romanliteratur* (Tuebingen, 1927) and *Der Antike Roman* (Darmstadt, 1971); R. Merkelbach, *Roman und Mysterium* (Berlin, 1962); F. Wehrli, *Mus. Helv.* 22 (1965) 133-154 and B. Reardon, *Phoenix* 23 (1969) 291-310.

[12]Of the classic corpus, only Achilles Tatius, which is something of a parody, appears to have no genuine religious element. See below.

[13]See n.4 above.

[14]Chariton uses known historical persons as his main characters. On the use of local legends in ancient novels see B. Lavagnini, *Studi sul Romanzo Greco* (Messina, 1950) 1-105.

[15]Regarding Chariton and the date of his work see Perry, pp. 96-148 and his references to other literature.

[16]Comparison with other Joseph literature (Philo, Josephus &c.) clearly reveals that the purpose of Jos. and As. is not to give historical or pseudo-historical information about this famous Jewish figure.

[17]On the "National Romance" see the paper referred to in n.1 above.

[18]For Apocalyptic outside of Jewish circles see S.K. Eddy, *The King is Dead* (N.Y., 1961) and R. MacMullen, *Enemies of the Roman Order* (Cambridge, Mass., 1966). The debate over the allegedly Roman date of *Third Maccabees* is relevant here.

[19]The cultural conditions under which the Sapiential Novel flourished seem parallel to the circumstances in which the later Greek novels thrived: peace, prosperity, an ecumenical empire and a universal language.

[20]For example, Tobit 4:3-21. 12:6-10. Achikar 8:1-41.

[21]There are, of course, exceptions. The *Cyropaideia* contains long speeches which amount to a treatise on ideal kingship. Some of the Apocryphal Acts are inundated with discourse.

[22]As is discussed below, the parallels adduced by C. Burchard (*Der Dreizehnte Zeuge* [FRLNT 105; Goettingen, 1970]) from Acts and Apuleius do not comprise anything near the relative length of their respective works as does the material in Jos. and As. 1-21.

[23]Daniel is An Ideal Sage of the first half of the Second Century, B.C.E. See Sirach 39:1-11.

[24]This statement should not be taken as a claim that Apocalyptic is essentially an offspring of the Wisdom movement.

[25]Note the emphasis on correct practice in Daniel 1:5-16 and Jos. and As. 8 and *passim*.

[26]See the study of sayings-collections by J.M. Robinson, "*Logoi Sophon*," in J. Robinson and H. Koester, *Trajectories through Early Christianity* (Philadelphia, 1971) 71-113.

[27]Love at first contact, marriage and subsequent problems raised by jealous rival suitors also constitute the opening book of Chariton's novel. The notion that the invariable pattern of an erotic novel should be love at first sight, long separation in travel and, at long last, marriage, has no basis in the ancient texts.

[28]So modern television and "genre" literature such as mystery, gothic and science fiction.

[29]Rohde, followed by many. See R. Soeder's study of the Apocryphal Acts, *Die Apokryphen Apostelgeschichten* (Stuttgart, 1932). Soeder took the motif approach to definition for granted.

[30]M. Philonenko, *Joseph et Aséneth* (SP-B 13; Leiden, 1968) 43f. and his commentary, *passim*.

[31]Classical Tragedy is only one example of this process. The treatment of myth by Ovid in his *Metamorphoses*, based on Hellenistic works, shows humanization and sentimentalization of older mythical literature.

[32]See Nock's review in *Gnomon* 4 (1928) 485-492 (=*Essays* 1:169-176).

[33]Probably least of all by Morton Smith, CW 57 (1964) 378. One adherent is H.H. Chalk, CR n.s. 13 (1963) 161-163.

[34]They may thus be said to have continued pursuit of the goal first set by Rohde: explanation of the "why" of the genre. Some studies of religious themes in individual novels are Altheim (n.11 above), H.H. Chalk, JHS 80 (1960) 32-51, and P.G. Walsh, (*The Roman Novel* [Cambridge, 1970]) on Heliodorus, Longus and Apuleius, respectively. For Xenophon of Ephesus, see below. Merkelbach's work ought not be rejected *in toto*. His chapter on Cupid and Psyche, for example, is excellent (*Roman*, 1-90). Kerenyi likewise developed many profound insights into the nature of ancient novels.

[35]*Joseph*, p.47.

[36]Xenophon of Ephesus, who wrote what is at least in part an Isaic novel, was clearly dependent upon Chariton. The Greek source of Apuleius is not extant, but the *Onos* ascribed to Lucian permits the conclusion that his ending was original and quite different. Longus' *Daphnis and Chloe*, a Dionysiac novel, was also dependent upon earlier romances.

[37]The later history of the Christian Acts-genre merges into hagiography. Philonenko shows the specific influence of Jos. and As. (pp.110-117, with references) on this type. The similarities of these Christian novels to their pagan counterparts are well known. See the study of R. Soeder, n.29 above.

[38]As is most likely in the case of Xenophon of Ephesus. See G. Dalmeyda in the introduction to his Budé edition (Paris, 1926) xxvi and the references there given.

[39]Ch. 22 introduces the beginnings of the conspiracy. Chs. 1-3 are introduction to the Conversion Story.

[40]*Dreizehnte Zeuge*, 52-105. Xenophon of Ephesus 1:4 is perhaps a secularized form of this type.

[41]For example, the Delos Sarapis Aretalogy, Acts 16:16-40 and Xenophon of Ephesus 4:2.

[42]In this respect, also, comparison with the Book of Daniel is interesting.

[43]*Metamorphoses* 4:28-6:24; *Dreizehnte Zeuge* 66-82.

S 139 THE SOCIO-RELIGIOUS SETTING AND AIMS OF "JOSEPH AND ASENATH"

Howard C. Kee

Byrn Mawr College

In 1888 Pierre Henri Battifol wrote that "The Prayer of Asenath", as our pseudepigraph is still frequently titled, was the product of a catholic Christian center of upper Asia Minor in the sixth century. He assumed that its author had built on a Jewish haggadic legend that achieved fixed form in the fourth century of our era, and that the work in its Christian form spread throughout the oriental Christian churches.[1] Although scholars are still in Battifol's debt for publishing the text and thereby making it available for subsequent study, few if any analysts of *Joseph and Asenath* (JA) would agree with his conclusions about its origins. Louis Ginzberg declares that there are only a few parallels to this apocryphal story of Joseph and Asenath in the rabbinic literature,[2] so that the assumption of an origin for JA in rabbinic lore is called into question. And the absence of any distinctively Christian language or of any allusions to the New Testament[3] requires us to consider other possible settings--religiously, socially and culturally--than either rabbinic Judaism or post-Constantinian Christianity as the place of origin of this romantic tract.

I

The adjective, "romantic", is wholly appropriate for JA. Its author evidences familiarity with the overall form and specific features of that popular, loose genre known as the hellenistic romance.[4] Represented in JA are the *characteristica* of the romance: the vivid portrayals of striking persons, the aura of the supernatural and the occult, the interest in miracles, the attention to piety, and above all, the fascinating narrative in which these elements are embedded. Examples of the vivid portraiture are the description of Asenath in her penthouse quarters and of Joseph when he appears in the chariot of the sun (5:4ff). One of the conventions of the romance is the inclusion of hymns to the deity at impressive moments in the unfolding of the narrative (Joseph in 8:10ff; Asenath in 12:1 ff). The most compelling narrative in the work is the long concluding section (23-28), in which Pharaoh's first-born son and his collaborators get their comeuppance. Philonenko seeks to differentiate three types of romance in JA: missionary romance, romantic novel, and mystical novel--which assumes more precise categories of romance than is warranted. Further, he suggests that there is a close kinship between JA and a romantic Egyptian tale from the 19th dynasty (ca. 1300 B.C.) in which the roles are reversed: a prince of Egypt falls in love with a Syrian princess who has been enclosed by her father in a tower.[5] Closer in time and plot, however, is the hellenistic version of the story of Helen of Troy, especially when Helen is identified with *Sĕlēnē* in her tower, as is the case in the Clementine Recognitions (2.12.4). In any event, the two-level view of reality, according to which the earthly narrative is a thinly-veiled vehicle for tracing the destiny of the soul, is common to the hellenistic romances and to JA. There can be little doubt that the author of this work is thoroughly familiar with the romantic genre of his epoch, and is consciously telling his elaborated version of the biblical narrative with the hellenistic romance as his literary model, with the apologetic aim that is characteristic of the genre.[6]

Linguistically, JA is written in idiomatic Greek of the hellenistic period. Even when the fact is taken into account that later recensions of the text took the trouble to smooth out parataxis and other stylistic infelicities,[7] the earlier state of the text is free of semiticisms and represents literate, though not elegant Greek. At many points there is evidence of the impact of the LXX on JA, but there is no unambiguous case of translation from a Semitic original. The etymologies closely resemble those found in Philo of Alexandria, and accordingly evidence little if any knowledge of Hebrew or Aramaic. A possible exception is the name, Asenath (אסנת), which is interpreted as coming from חוסנא , and interpreted as "strong place," or more specifically as "City of Refuge."[8] The credibility of this linguistic-etymological accounting for the change in Asenath's name is diminished, however, when we note that "City of Refuge" is used in other contexts (e.g., 4 Ezra 10:27, 50-54) as a designation for the inclusive religious community where the name, Asenath, does not appear at all. More telling yet against the notion of a Semitic original is the frequent use of terms for which there is no real equivalent in Hebrew or Aramaic: ἀθανασία, ἀφθαρσία 8:5,7; 20:8; 23:9; 29:3, as indicated by Philonenko.[9] θεοσεβής occurs 13 times in JA, which is half again as frequent as its appearance in the whole of LXX.[10] Like the cognate nouns, θεοσέβεια and εὐσέβεια , this is a favorite term of hellenistic Judaism. Of 7 occurrences of θεοσέβεια, all but two are from documents that originated in the hellenistic period; and εὐσέβεια is used 53 times in material from hellenistic times, 46 of them in the thoroughly hellenized 4 Maccabees alone! Thus both the terminology and the characteristic concepts of human virtue and destiny are widely represented in JA, in distinction from the older, more strictly Semitic biblical literature.

It is not surprising, therefore, that other features of hellenistic religious aspiration and piety should also be found in JA as well. The solar and astral interests of the writer of JA are obvious to any reader. In 5:4 Joseph makes a triumphal entrance as Helios, clad in a white robe of radiance, mounted on a gold-plated chariot drawn by four snow-white horses, wearing a radiant crown, with 12 precious stones and 12 rays, and wielding the scepter of royalty. Not only is he identified as "Son of God" (6:2), but it is explicitly stated that "the sun comes to us from heaven in his chariot and came into our house today" (6:5). It is quite proper to note that there is precedent for linking the figure of Joseph with celestial power in the biblical tradition (Gen 37:9), but the details here derive from Greek mythology and astronomical speculation rather than from the Bible.[11]

We have already noted the links between Asenath and Selene, a role for her which is consummated in the sacred marriage described in JA 15. Further, her confession of sin (12:1ff) as an alien from Israel who approaches in penitence Israel's God, is confirmed by the Morning Star (14:1). The astral imagery is developed in another direction by the use of sacred numbers, of which the twelve (for the signs of the zodiac) is only the most obvious.[12] This detail in JA recalls the passage in 4 Macc 17: 4-5, where the destiny of the faithful and the power of the stars are linked.

Equally apparent is the allegorical dimension of the narrative in JA. Asenath represents Wisdom, the consort of Joseph, who perhaps represents the Logos. The tower in which the heroine is imprisoned is perhaps her body, with the seven rooms and seven virgins depicting the various parts of the soul.[13] The windows of her quarters, facing three of the cardinal points of the compass (JA 2), including the bed facing the east (2:15), are more than an ancient interior decorator's description of luxurious apartments. The interrelation of the halls and the gates, the links with the elements and the four corners of the earth are indigenous to Jewish mysticism,[14] as well, as we shall note below.

Magical elements appear throughout the work: the mysterious appearance of the honeycomb (JA 16); the presence of the man from heaven in Asenath's apartment in spite of locked doors (14:5); in response to Asenath's prayer, the swords are wrenched from the hands of her attackers, and they are reduced to dust (27:8).

Still more prominent are the revelatory features of the narrative in JA. Joseph is able to see everything that is hidden (6:3; 19:2). Levi appears, not as priest, but as prophet in JA, and is able to foresee the future events (26:7). The supreme moments of revelation occur when Asenath partakes of the heavenly honeycomb (16:7-8). This is followed by the appearance of a chariot of fire in which a man from heaven appears at the conclusion of the sacred meal (17:6). The revealer figure closely resembles Joseph, and is almost certainly to be understood as Joseph's heavenly counterpart. In association with him, Asenath becomes as radiant as he (18:7).

The ethical virtues that are exemplified by Joseph and Asenath are self-discipline, penitence, humility (at least in the case of Asenath). At several points in the narrative, it appears that the merits of androgynous existence are being extolled, as when Joseph promises to treat Asenath as a sister (7:11), or even more explicitly in Asenath's description of herself in 15:2, where she is called a virgin, a male, a youth. Ultimately, there is no asceticism enjoined, since Joseph and Asenath do marry, have intercourse, and produce offspring (21: 6-8).

The most remarkable aspect of JA, when viewed against the background of hellenistic piety, however, is its thorough-going mysticism. This is evident in the importance attached to the sacred meal shared with the heavenly beings (15:14), in the sacred marriage (21:1ff), but especially in the sacred food and sacral anointing following her initiation (14:4-15:5) which probably reflect a sectarian liturgy. She is given a new name, a new lustrous garment. She is transformed and renewed. She is granted to participate in the bread of life, the cup of immortality and the anointing of incorruption (15:4). Her name is written in the Book of Life (15:3). And finally, she is told that she will be the bride in the sacred marriage (15:5). These mystical features not only have important details in common with pagan mystical rites of the hellenistic period, but they also are clearly akin to Jewish mysticism. The prominence given to the chariot of Joseph, Son of God and savior (26:7); the advent of the man from heaven who initiates Asenath; the emphasis on the radiance and the supernatural knowledge of the heavenly agents, as well as of their chosen beneficiaries; the celestial food of which they partake, and its revelatory effects--all these recall the facets of *merkabah* mysticism.

Several of the distinctive features of JA are to be found in the literature of the *merkabah* mystics. First is the hymnic response of the *mystai* to the revelation that is received: the chief examples in JA are Joseph's prayer in behalf of Asenath (8:10-11) and Asenath's confession and penitence (12:2-11). Both embody the short rhythmic lines and the parallelism that Gershom Scholem has indicated to be characteristic of *merkabah* hymns.[15] The second major element shared by Jewish mysticism and JA is the nature and intent of the revelation--what Scholem has called the "halakhic character of Hekhaloth mysticism."[16] In addition to initiating Asenath, the man from heaven tells her that she is to have a special concern for those of whatever race who turn to God in repentance. *Metanoia* is personified as one who prays always to the Most High in behalf of the penitent. He has prepared a bridal chamber for those who love Repentance, chief among whom is Asenath herself (15:7). Surprisingly out of keeping with the private nature of mystical disclosure, the rule of God that is being expounded and exemplified here is that of an open attitude toward penitent non-Jews; they are welcomed by God into relationship with Him, and should be so welcomed by His faithful people.

II

Is this document with its open attitude toward Gentiles to be understood as a Jewish writing from a mystical group? Although there would be a strong inclination to assign JA to Jewish origins on the basis of the heavy dependence on LXX and of the absence of quotation from or allusion to the New Testament, the affirmative case can be made even more strongly. There is an obvious importance attached to the observance of the sabbath as well as of the food laws. Joseph refuses even to eat at the table of his Gentile hosts on arrival at the home of Pentephres (7:1). Likewise, he refuses to allow Asenath to kiss him so as she utters with those lips prayers to the Egyptian gods (8:5). (Cf. the "holy kiss" in Origen's *Cant. Cant.* 1).

The story points, therefore, to (1) the problem of exogamy and (2) to the related issue of the admission of proselytes to the community as central concerns for the author and the community for which he is writing. Among Gentiles and Christians, these issues would be of no consequence. But they were clearly of major significance among Jews of the dispersion, especially among those who were seeking to establish or to maintain some degree of social rapport with their pagan fellow-citizens.

The continuing potency of the Jewish tradition is also evident in detailed features of the narrative. For example, Benjamin's utter rout of Asenath's enemies with sling stones is an expanded version of the exploit of David in his contest with Goliath (JA 27:1-6). The inscribing of Asenath's name in the Book of Life recalls the persistent Jewish tradition on this subject that reaches from Ex 32:32f, through the Psalms (69:28) and the prophets (Isa 4:3) to the apocalyptic writings (Dan 12:1; 1 Enoch 47:3).[17] Thus the writing presupposes a Jewish community living out of and appropriating anew its Jewish heritage.

But Judaism of what variety? We have already noted the lack of kinship between JA and the rabbinic traditions.[18] Can a link be demonstrated with other known Jewish sects of the hellenistic period? Even before the discovery of the Dead Sea Scrolls, a common candidate for kinship was the Essenes. Apart from the claim to revelatory experiences--which is by no means a monopoly of the Essenes--there is little in common with JA. In our document there is no eschatology, and the revelations have nothing to do with the end of the age. There is in JA no real interest in the temple or its cultus, while the Essenes longed to be restored to what they considered their rightful place as those who presided over the Jerusalem sanctuary. Levi, who for the Essenes was the leading figure of their history, both historically and in their eschatological expectations, appears in JA as a prophet devoid of priestly function or of messianic role. Although Asenath temporarily renounces the affluent life by throwing her gourmet dinner out the window of her tower to the dogs in the street below (10:14; 13:8), her action is a sign of her humility and penitence, not a vow of poverty or of world-rejection. Her withdrawal into her tower is a negative factor in the narrative, not an indication of her dedication, as was the case with the retreat of the Essenes to "Damascus" at what we call Qumran.

There are more points of identity between JA and the Therapeutae whom Philo describes so sympathetically.[19] Both report prayers to the rising sun (JA 2:14;[20] *De Contemp.* 89); both praise self control (*De Cont.* 34); both are interested in sacred numbers (*De Cont.* 66). There is a possible further link between the generous act of healing the wound of Pharaoh's son and the healing activity of the Therapeutae. JA and the Therapeutae are united in their denunciation of the Egyptian gods (*De Cont.* 8).

But the points of difference are great. In JA--unlike Philo's representation of the Therapeutae--there is no abandonment of property, no communal existence encouraged, no real rejection of luxury. The common meal of the Therapeutae seems to have had nothing of the mystical significance described in

JA in connection with the bread and wine. Even though both documents manifest an interest in allegory (*De Cont.* 28; 78), JA's treatment of scripture is more in the nature of narrative and symbolic elaboration than of real allegorization.

The closest similarities are probably with *merkabah* mysticism, details of which we have noted above. Since we know nothing about the organization, if any, that characterized this mystical movement in the hellenistic period, it is impossible to trace similarities or differences between the community behind JA and a community of the mystics. But if we can learn nothing of the structure of the JA community, we can make some safe inferences about its social stance.

III

The community behind JA was clearly open toward many aspects of hellenistic culture, as we have seen. Yet it regarded itself as able to maintain its own integrity and its own distinct Jewish identity, even while incorporating into its group religious life certain fundamentally hellenistic values. Stated negatively, there is no hint of a sociologically sectarian outlook reflected in JA, nothing of the "now-we-are-nothing; then-we-shall-be-in-control" stance of Qumran or other eschatological sects.[21] Since the highest religious value of the group seems to have been personal, revelatory experience, there is no evidence of concern for the destiny of the group. While there is no bar to use of astrological notions or to the incorporation of Stoic virtues into the system, there is a fixed line drawn at one point: the gods of Egypt are to be scornfully rejected. Thus there is no hint of compromise with a monotheistic position in JA. The presence of angelic or superhuman figures, such as the man from heaven (Joseph's *alter ego*), does not confound for the author the belief in the Lord as the sole ultimate sovereign.

But more is at work in JA than merely an open attitude conceptually toward certain aspects of pagan religion and culture. There is evident throughout the document a vigorous championing of the cause of conversion of the Gentiles. This is not a syncretistic movement, at least not consciously, since the goal is to bring "aliens" into the household of Israel's faith rather than to create an amalgam of religions. The main story line concerning the conversion of Asenath is meant to show that the most aloof, haughty, high-placed, affluent, self-possessed person can--when confronted by the powerful appeal of the true religion--be converted. The contrast between Asenath, the proud penthouse-dwelling princess, and Asenath, the abject maid seizing the opportunity to wash Joseph's feet (13:12; 20:3), dramatizes how great the change can be. The transforming effect of conversion is set forth in Joseph's hymnic prayer in behalf of Asenath:

> Lord, God of my Father, Israel,
> Most High, Powerful One
> Who makes all things to live,
> Who calls out of darkness into light
> and from error to truth,
> from death to life,

You indeed are the Lord
who made alive and blessed this virgin.
Renew her by your Spirit,
Reform her by your hidden hand,
Restore her to your Life,
and let her eat the Bread of Life
and drink the Cup of Blessing,
she whom I chose before her birth,
and let her enter into your rest (κατάπαυσις)
which you prepared for your Elect Ones.

What is envisioned for the proselyte is not only complete renewal, but the entering into a relationship which was preordained by God Himself. There is nothing concessive about proselytization; rather, it is the outworking of the divine plan.

Furthermore, God protects the proselytes as He protects those who are His own by birthright. Asenath is delivered from her foes by miraculous intervention in response to her prayer for help to her newly-found God (27:8). The reward for piety and the judgment of the impious is the major story line of JA, culminating in Joseph's enthronement as king (29:11). The reverse of that exaltation is that the enemies of God's people, both Jews and proselytes, go down in defeat. The heavenly Joseph depicts himself as "the leader of the troops of the Lord's house and commander-in-chief of all the heavenly army" (14:7).[22] Following the praise of God's sovereignty and the depths of her confession (12:1-7a), Asenath in her prayer petitions God to rescue her "from those that harass me", to snatch her from the hand of the enemy (12:8). The Devil is the father of the gods that she has repudiated (12:9), and she prays for deliverance from him. But then her final, impassioned words present her as one cut off from her family, "an orphan and alone" (12:11). Although this is not appropriate for Asenath in terms of the narrative, since there is no indication of rejection of her by her parents, it is fitting as a petition by or reassurance for proselytes who have been forced to sever family ties and who accordingly feel abandoned (13:1). The probability is that this strand in JA reflects the actual social situation in which the converts to this Jewish sect found themselves.

In contrast to Qumran, however, where hatred of enemies is enjoined, the moral attitude that JA urges is one of forgiveness and compassion. Building on the traditions of Deuteronomy (Deut 32:35) and the Holiness Code (Lev 14:17ff), JA insists on non-retaliation toward the perpetrators of acts of hatred and assumes that "neighbor" is a broad, inclusive term that encompasses even one's antagonists. The other half of the picture, of course, is provided by the accounts of God's miraculous punishment of those who oppose His elect (25:7; 26:3; 27:8; 28:1). Indeed the entire final section of JA, following the sacred marriage, is taken up with the issues of compassion toward enemies and divine retribution. It is plausible to suppose that this pair of themes reflects the social situation in which Jews and proselytes found themselves, when to align oneself with this wing of Judaism opened up the possibility of hostility from co-religionists (brothers) as well as from pagan civil powers (the son of Pharaoh). The author of JA counsels compassion toward the opposition and confidence in God to set things right.

When and where is such a work as JA likely to have been written? On grounds of its locale, of mention of place names in Egypt (especially Heliopolis), of the picture of Joseph's authority as continuing in Egypt, and of the clear kinship between aspects of hellenized Judaism in Egypt (both Philo and the Therapeutae of whom he reports), the most likely candidate for provenance is the Alexandrian Jewish community. Within wide limits, the time can be fixed with reasonable assurance: it cannot be earlier than the LXX, on which it builds;[23] it cannot be later than the time of Hadrian, who proscribed proselytizing.[24] There are no certain allusions to events in the Roman period, although the oppression by the pagan powers could be a veiled reference to the difficulties experienced in the Alexandrian Jewish community in the time of Caligula (cf. Philo's *Legatio ad Gaium*). Since the *merkabah* material is itself of uncertain date, its links with JA are of no chronological assistance. But since there is evidence of *merkabah* mystical influence on Paul's account in II Cor 12 of his heavenly transport,[25] a date after the turn of the eras would be reasonable.

The chief value of the work for the historian of this period is that it provides additional evidence of the mingling of factors in Judaism in the Graeco-Roman period in a manner that the traditional scholarly categories (Hellenistic Judaism, Palestinian Judaism, the four sects) are useless and misleading. Positively, we see in JA how deeply hellenistic culture had penetrated the thinking of a self-consciously Jewish community with its own brand of proselytizing exclusivism, its mingling of biblical and stoic piety, its blend of chastity and eroticism, its open attitude toward the surrounding culture tempered by its aspiration to mystical transport.

NOTES

1. H.P. Battifol, *Studia Patristica, études d'ancienne littérature chrétienne* (Paris, 1889) I 36-37.

2. Louis Ginzberg, *Legends of the Jews* (Philadelphia: Jewish Publication Society, 1947) V 374, n. 432.

3. Chr. Burchard, *Untersuchungen zur Joseph und Asenath* (WUNT 8; Göttingen, 1965) 99: "JA ist eine jüdische Schrift. Es gibt, negatif gesprochen, in ihr keiner Satz, der nicht jüdisch sein könnte" (99). Neither the teaching about redemption nor the ethical outlook is Christian (100). M. Philonenko (*Joseph et Aséneth: Introduction, Texte Critique, Traduction et Notes* [Studium Post Biblicum 13; Leiden: Brill, 1968]) asserts that the shorter recension of JA is purely Jewish, although the longer recensions may be Christian. He finds no allusions to the New Testament, however (100-101). K.G. Kuhn ("The Lord's Supper ...", in *The*

Scrolls and the NT [ed. K. Stendahl; New York: Harper, 1957] 74ff.) finds that--unlike Test XII--there was no Christian revision of JA.

4. Martin Braun's little book, *History and Romance in Graeco-Roman Literature* (Oxford: Blackwell, 1938), is more of an attempt to illustrate the range of subject matter and interest in the hellenistic romances than an essay in definition. Braun does point out, however, that the romances emerged as an instrument of national identity at a time when one-worldism was seeking to eradicate local and ethnic heritages.

5. Philonenko, *JA* 40-41.

6. Moses Hadas (*Three Greek Romances* [Garden City, L.I.: Doubleday, 1953] 8) declares that "Apologetics for a cult, or more properly for the cultural minority who are its votaries, is probably the earliest motivation for the ancient novel." The apologetic thrust of *JA* is patent.

7. Philonenko, *JA* 30.

8. Ginzberg, *Legends* V 374, n. 432.

9. Philonenko, *JA* 30; cf. K.G. Kuhn, "Supper" 261, n. 33.

10. In LXX, θεοσέβεια is a nominal conflation for fear of God (the Lord).

11. For details, see note in Philonenko, *in loc*.

12. Discussed by Philonenko, *JA* 71ff.

13. *Idem*.

14. G. G. Scholem, *Jewish Gnosticism, Merkabah Mysticism, and Talmudic Tradition* (New York: Jewish Theological Seminary, 1965) 32.

15. Scholem, *Jewish Gnosticism* 26-27. A semitic *Urtext* behind JA does not exist and probably never did, but there is a similarity of structure and function between the hymns/prayers of JA and what Scholem observes about the *merkabah* hymns.

16. Scholem, *Jewish Gnosticism* 9.

17. For bibliography, *JA* 182, in Note on JA 15:3.

18. Confirmed by E. Schürer, in the fourth edition of his *Geschichte des jüdischen Volkes*. In the second edition, on which the English translation was based (New York, Scribner, 1891), he considered the work to be a Christian product (II, iii, 151).

19. In *On the Contemplative Life* K.G. Kuhn ("Supper" 74ff.) thinks the sect behind *JA* was akin to the Therapeutae.

20. Although prayer is not mentioned in JA 2:14, the reason for orienting Asenath's bed toward the window facing east seems to be linked with meditations or prayers at the rising of the sun.

21. K.O.L. Burridge, *New Heaven, New Earth* (New York: Schocken, 1969).

22. There is a certain kinship between these celestial armies and those that are depicted in the Qumran material as doing battle with the enemies of the Lord on the upper stage of the universe. But in *JA* there is no hint of an apocalyptic struggle at the end of the age; rather the heavenly hosts assist in overcoming the earthly foes during the course of the life of the faithful, as is the case with Asenath and her royal enemy, Pharaoh's son.

23. The LXX Additions of Daniel and Esther likewise evidence the influence of the hellenistic romance. Martin Braun gives extended analytical treatment of the incident with Potiphar's wife in the romantic expension of that tale in Testament of Joseph, *History and Romance* 44-104.

24. So G.D. Kilpatrick, "The Last Supper", *ET* 64 (1952) 5. Followed by Philonenko, *JA* 108: Burchard, *Untersuchungen* 143; also K.G. Kuhn, "Supper" 74, n. 34.

25. G.G. Scholem, "The Four who Entered Paradise and Paul's Ascension to Paradise," in *Jewish Gnosticism* 14-19.

S 140 ILLUSTRATED MANUSCRIPTS OF THE ROMANCE OF JOSEPH AND ASENETH

Gary Vikan Dumbarton Oaks

The systemmatic investigation of illustrated medieval manuscripts can be organized according to several basically distinct methodologies. An art historian may, for example, concern himself with the isolation of groups of illuminated manuscripts which are interrelated through figure style, paleography, and codicological make-up. His ultimate aim in this case will be to identify individual miniaturists, scribes, and scriptoria, and thereby to help characterize the role of de luxe book production in the cultural life of a specific region and period. He may, on the other hand, organize his research on the basis of illustration to a single narrative unit, taking as his primary evidence all extant illustrated copies of a specific text, no matter how disparate their origins. In this case the art historian's goal will be to organize all relevant manuscripts into an iconographic lineage or stemma, to distill from them the purest and most original state of their lost pictorial archetype, and to circumscribe the temporal and geographic boundries within which that archetype was likely created. Not surprisingly, the methodology he employs will in many respects be similar to that developed by philologists for working out text recensions.[1]

Thanks to the research of Christoph Burchard, we know that there are eighteen surviving copies of the romance of Joseph and Aseneth in Greek.[2] Among this group are three late manuscripts wherein the text is accompanied by a series of simple illustration which, almost in comic strip fashion, visually translate successive stages of the drama. The present paper will be devoted to an examination of the iconographic recension which may be reconstructed from those three chance survivals.[3]

The Illustrated Manuscripts

1. Virginia Beach, Greeley Collection, cod. McKell (figs. 2,4,6,14-15):[4] Aesthetically the finest member of our pictorial tradition, this codex was produced in the Romanian principality of Wallachia around 1580, very likely for the reigning Voevod, Mihnea II.[5] An elegant witness to the revival of Byzantine culture beyond the Danube, it was transcribed and illuminated by Luke the Cypriot, a leading Romanian ecclesiastic and diplomat, and founder of one of the most sophisticated and influential Post-Byzantine scriptoria.[6] Its picture cycle, which is based on the subtle blending of traditional Byzantine figurative compositions into atmospheric, Italianate landscapes, includes seventeen illustrations to the Aseneth story. Beneath its sixteenth-century, westernizing veneer is a stylistic substratum whose figural proportions, gestures, vestments, architectural motifs, drapery mannerisms, and general "narrative idiom" strongly suggests a de luxe, fourteenth-century model.[7] Finally, the very

clear, archaizing minuscule in which it is transcribed reflects an ultimately Late Byzantine paleographic tradition perpetuated and cultivated by Luke the Cypriot and his school.[8]

2. Oxford, Bodleian Library, cod. Roe 5 (figs. 1,3,5,7-8, 10,13):[9] Artistically and paleographically much inferior to the McKell manuscript, this second member of our Aseneth iconographic recension betrays the more typically degenerate state of Post-Byzantine book painting. Produced in 1613 by a certain Georgios of Ainos, it includes an abridged vernacular translation of the Aseneth romance, accompanied by a cycle of twenty-one crude, heavily Turkish pen drawings. Although substantially abridged and thoroughly rewritten, the Roe narrative, along with that of McKell, has been assigned by Burchard to text family "b"--according to him the earliest and most original state of the narrative.[10]

That the McKell and Roe miniature cycles are indeed partial redactions ultimately dependent on a single, much larger pictorial archetype anterior to either, is demonstrable through the convergence of several types of evidence. There are, first of all, miniatures in both codices which include significant iconographic elements supported not by the text they accompany, but rather by some other variant reading of the passage. Consider, for example, the Roe depiction of Joseph's rebuke of Aseneth (fig. 1).[11] The passage above the illustration stipulates only that, when Aseneth wished to embrace him, Joseph "...δὲν την ἐδέχθην..."[12] Yet in the miniature, Joseph dramatically places a restraining hand against Aseneth's chest--a very specific action which is fully consonant with other, more explicit versions of the encounter, which relate that: "...ἐξέτεινεν Ἰωσὴφ τὴν χεῖρα αὐτοῦ τὴν δεξιὰν καὶ ἔθηκε πρὸς τὸ στῆθος αὐτῆς....[13] Similarly, the McKell portrayal of the celestial messenger as a winged angel (fig. 4),[14] conforms not to its accompanying text, which describes an "...ἄνθρωπος ἐκ τοῦ οὐρανοῦ...,"[15] but rather to a number of other romance variants which speak of an "...ἄγγελος Κυρίου...."[16]

Clearly, both miniature cycles iconographically transcend the textual limits of their own codices. Moreover, we may be quite certain that both illuminators drew on the same preexistent visual tradition, since in those instances where they illustrate the same episode, their respective iconographic interpretations are basically similar. Compare, for example, the McKell and Roe versions of Aseneth's repentance (figs. 2-3),[17] and of her subsequent encounter with the "angel" (figs. 4-5).[18] For the former episode both manuscripts show Aseneth standing in profile, facing toward the right; her arms are extended with palms up as she addresses the divine presence, symbolized by a radiating disk of light at the upper right of the composition. In the latter episode (figs. 4-5), both illuminators have portrayed Aseneth on her knees, her hands reaching toward an approaching angel. Notice especially the close correspondence in the placement of the angel's arms, and in the relative position of Aseneth before an arched doorway. Morphological parallels such as these could hardly be due to chance.

One very basic distinction between iconographic and textual studies lies in the fact that an illuminator may only partially and selectively copy his model, for no matter how few scenes he may ultimately choose to transmit, the continuity of his story line will still be maintained by the accompanying text. It is thus in no sense unusual that the seventeen McKell miniatures should thematically coincide with the twenty-one Roe miniatures on only four occasions.[19] Moreover, it follows by implication that the tradition upon which these illuminators drew once included much more extensively illustrated manuscripts.[20] Finally, it is clear that since both the McKell and the Roe picture cycles are substantially unique, each must play an equal and complementary role in reconstructing the maximal iconographic breadth of their shared recension--despite the fact that they are obviously unequal in their respective levels of execution, and in their relative positions of primacy within text family "b."

Yet, what may be said of the relative iconographic "quality" of these two cycles? Which, in the text critic's sense, gives a "better reading?" Consider again the two pairs of miniatures already cited (figs. 2-5). Although the arrangement of the essential figural core is fundamentally the same in both codices, their respective interpretations of the spatial ambience are distinct. In the McKell version of the repentance (fig. 2), Aseneth stands in an open landscape, her tower chamber only symbolically evoked by a toy-like replica behind her. In the Roe manuscript (fig. 3), on the other hand, she appears, as the text requires, in the interior of the first, or "great" chamber of her tower. Before her is a diagonally foreshortened wall with a small opening representing the "window toward the East"; behind and to the left is her "bed of gold," while at the far end of the room is a large door leading to her second chamber. Since all of these motifs are textually based,[21] and since the style of the McKell illuminator is otherwise marked by an idiosyncratic tendency to emphasize airy landscapes at the expense of interior space,[22] we may safely conclude that this Roe illustration, although later, cruder, and in the company of a paraphrased text, nevertheless gives a more accurate reflection of the original state of this scene than does McKell. A comparable relationship obtains between their respective versions of the embrace of Joseph and Aseneth (figs. 6-7).[23] In portraying Aseneth's retinue of virgins on a staircase descending from the tower, the Roe miniature is again more explicit in its visualization of the narrative context,[24] and thus has assumedly transmitted an element of original iconography deleted by the McKell illuminator (or by one of his predecessors).

From the accumulation of evidence such as this, it may generally be said that the Roe picture cycle, although aesthetically deficient, shows a consistent iconographic priority in its explicit portrayal of architectural setting, and in its retention of textually motivated auxiliary figures.[25] It includes, moreover, twelve scenes unattested in McKell. The latter manuscript, on the other hand, is unique witness to thirteen Aseneth episodes. Moreover, since it is free of Roe's thorough-going Ottoman transmutations, it undoubtedly gives a clearer image of the Byzantine style of their shared archetype.

3. Mount Athos, Koutloumousi cod. 100 (figs. 9, 11):[26] The third and final member of the Aseneth pictorial recension

was produced during the sixteenth century at the Koutloumousi monastery on Mount Athos. Although aesthetically and technically on a level with Roe, it represents a still more substantial abridgement, since it includes just three simple wash drawings in the company of a vernacular paraphrase only one fourth as long as that of Roe. Dr. Burchard has observed that its text is based on a model very close to, although not identical with that recorded in the Roe codex.[27] The same relationship holds true for its picture cycle.[28] All three of its miniatures overlap and closely match scenes in Roe, to which they are, moreover, generally "secondary" in terms of their compositional lucidity and narrative explicitness. Compare, for example, their respective visualizations of Joseph's first arrival at the court of Heliopolis (figs. 8-9).[29] That the two miniatures share a common parentage is clear from similarities in composition and detail: Joseph, at the back of a long, two-horse chariot, approaches from the right with a contingent of mounted lance bearers; Pentephres and his entourage await his arrival at the left beside the arched portal of the palace; and above, in a small window behind the palace parapet, is the face of Aseneth. Closer examination, however, shows that the Roe miniature gives a better, more original reflection of this episode since, unlike Koutloumousi, it clearly portrays the east portals of the courtyard through which Joseph is about to pass, and, in full conformity to the text, explicitly differentiates Pentephres and his wife at the head of the welcoming crowd.[30]

Yet, despite this unusually close, and seemingly derivative relationship, Koutloumousi could not possibly have been copied from Roe.[31] Burchard has shown that in several isolated cases its text appears to give a fuller, more original reading of a passage.[32] Basically the same relationship is indicated by a comparison of the Koutloumousi and Roe illustrations of the death of Pharaoh's son (figs. 10-11).[33] Both compositions show Aseneth in her chariot, and Pharaoh's son either fallen (Koutloumousi) or falling (Roe) from his horse. Only Koutloumousi, however, includes Aseneth's stone-hurling protector, Benjamin, beside her in the chariot. Moreover, that miniature is unique in clearly showing his victim's mortal head wound, and, at the upper background, the massacre of the soldiers of Pharaoh's son by the brothers of Joseph.[34] Clearly, the Koutloumousi miniaturist worked from a model even more densely illustrated than Roe. Quite possibly these two codices are independent descendents of a slightly earlier vernacular redaction of the romance. If so, Roe would likely provide an accurate reflection of at least the scope and style of that lost prototype, which certainly bore the heavy imprint of its surrounding Ottoman culture.[35]

The Pictorial Archetype

Like its accompanying textual tradition, the romance of Joseph and Aseneth iconographic tradition almost certainly developed from an original, individual creative effort. Accordingly an art historian, like a text critic, may legitimately concern himself with the probable appearance and origin of the lost archetype. From a critical examination of the forty-one miniatures in the three surviving cycles, a hypothetical original may be reconstructed with at least thirty-six distinct episodes.[36] Yet, when was this original likely produced?

The archetype's broadest temporal limits are, of course, dictated by the creation of the narrative itself, and by the date of the earliest extant illustrated witness: respectively, the first century A.D., and the sixteenth century.[37] This fifteen-hundred-year span may, however, be substantially reduced. The most important evidence for readjusting the terminus post quem lies in the fact that each of the three extant Aseneth cycles forms half of a coupled pictorial unit with a cycle of illustration to Pseudo-Ephraem's Life of Joseph.[38] Since neither cycle exists independently of the other, and since all three manuscript witnesses show a continuity of figure style, narrative idiom, and relative iconographic quality across both cycles, it is reasonable, if indeed not necessary to suppose that the Aseneth picture cycle was, from the first, conceived as part of a Life of Joseph/Joseph and Aseneth coupled unit. Even if the Life of Joseph were, as it purports to be, a Greek translation of a Syrian original by Saint Ephraem, a coupled picture cycle dependent on it could date no earlier than the late fourth century. Since, however, that attribution is suspect,[39] the terminus for both text and pictures should probably be shifted a century or two forward. It is certain that the romance of Joseph and Aseneth was known in Syria by the sixth century;[40] moreover, the history of the Armenian tradition of the narrative strongly implies that the LJ-JA coupled unit existed in that region soon thereafter.[41]

For art historians, the most important implication of this iconographic coupling, and of its associate change in terminus, lies in the necessary shift in pictorial archetype from a Jewish to a Christian milieu. The possibility that Jews invented extensive pictorial narratives in Late Antiquity has, for several decades, been enthusiastically debated.[42] Certainly the romance of Joseph and Aseneth would be a likely candidate for such visual expression, both because it was the product of a prospering hellenized Jewish community,[43] and because it presents an illuminator with a vivid story line, which, since it is non-canonical, would assumedly be less subject to the restrictions of the Second Commandment.[44] The apparent link between Aseneth illustration and Pseudo-Ephraem, however, necessarily removes the former as evidence of Jewish art.[45] Moreover, it provides graphic evidence of a purely literary channel whereby ultimately Jewish themes could enter Christian art.[46]

The evidence for fixing the terminus ante quem of the first Aseneth illustration is varied and indirect. That the pictorial archetype was created some time before the sixteenth century is, first of all, implicit in the surprisingly distant iconographic relationship between McKell and Roe. It has, moreover, already been suggested that the two vernacular cycles are probably descendents of an earlier modern Greek redaction, while the McKell codex was very likely copied from a fourteenth-century model. The terminus implicit in the McKell model may be carried back still further, since what is now known of the general development of Byzantine manuscript production favors the creation of such a full, inventive cycle of narrative illustration neither in the comparatively sterile Palaeologan period (1261-1453), nor in the tumultuous decades immediately before or after the fall of the Empire.[47] Rather, the Aseneth pictorial archetype would be much more at home in the unusually productive eleventh century, which saw the invention or major amplification of several comparable miniature cycles.[48] An examination of the iconographic substrata of the McKell, Roe, and Koutloumousi codices supports the same conclusion. For although the stylistic veneer of each is clearly distinct, and reflects a fusion of the model's style and the style of the period and region of production, the iconogrphic core over which that style is applied reflects a narrative idiom for which the closest parallels are forthcoming from manuscripts of the eleventh and twelfth centuries.[49] Compare, for example, the McKell and Roe illustrations of Aseneth in prayer (figs. 2-3) with the representation of Joasaph in prayer from a twelfth-century illustrated[50] copy of the popular romance of Barlaam and Joasaph (fig. 12). Although separated by more than four centuries, these images clearly draw on a common iconographic vocabulary, both for their evocation of prayer, and for their formalized rendition of interior architectural space.

To this point we have been able to circumscribe the archetype's temporal limits to somewhere between the sixth and twelfth centuries, with art historical evidence most supportive of the eleventh century. A final iconographic detail apparently corraborative of this later, Middle Byzantine <u>terminus</u> is the specific portrayal of the celestial messenger in the McKell and Roe codices (figs. 4-5). Both manuscripts show an angel (ἄγγελος Κυρίου) instead of a man (ἄνθρωπος ἐκ τοῦ οὐρανοῦ), and thus clearly align themselves with what Burchard appraises as the secondary state of their text family.[51] And while it has not been determined when "man" was raised to "angel," the retention of "man" in both the Syrian and Armenian translations, which are assigned respectively to the sixth and sixth-seventh centuries, suggests that in that early period the transformation had not yet taken place.[52]

<u>Relationship of Image to Text</u>

One need only compare the Western and Eastern traditions of Psalter illustration to realize that the Byzantine illuminator, when measured against his Latin counterpart, is typically literal, rational, and narrative in his approach to his craft.[53] It is thus in no way unusual to find that our hypothetical eleventh-century painter passed over the rich imagery and symbolism of the Aseneth romance in favor of a rather predictable, comic-strip like presentation of successive narrative events. Nearly every miniature is a purely literal visualization of the text passage to which it is bound. Consider, for example, the epidode of Aseneth receiving the mystical honeycomb (fig. 13).[54] Although this text passage must certainly have evoked for the illuminator images of the Last Supper and of the daily celebration of the Eucharist, there is nothing in his rendition of the scene to suggest the actual influence of contemporary images of either event. Instead, the iconography fully conforms to the text beneath it:

> Then the angel called Aseneth near, and coming forward she fell at the feet of the angel. And the angel, stretching out his right hand, placed it at the head of Aseneth... and the angel blessed her in [the name of] the Supreme God, and cut from that honeycomb and placed it in the

> mouth of Aseneth. And the angel said to Aseneth; Behold, you eat the bread of life....[55]

Of course no textual description can be so complete as to anticipate every aspect of a miniature. The role of artistic imagination is obvious, for example, in the detailed characterization of Pentephres' palace (figs. 8-9). Moreover, every illuminator tends to interpret his model according to contemporary fashions and formulae--even at the expense of narrative accuracy. In Chapter X Aseneth casts aside her golden crown and sumptuous garments for a simple black robe. Yet soon thereafter, as she bows before the celestial messenger, the McKell illuminator directly contradicts the text by dressing her again in the regal attire of a Byzantine queen--a standardized ensemble which she wears, almost without variation, throughout this entire cycle (fig. 4). In a similar manner the Roe miniaturist substantially disregards the detailed description of Joseph's entry into Heliopolis,[56] choosing instead to repeat a current and accepted iconographic <u>topos</u> for "imperial procession" (fig. 8).

Yet beyond such predictable, and relatively minor divergencies of text and image, there remain two miniatures wherein the Byzantine illuminator has creatively and independently used his craft to augment the Aseneth story line. The first is a royal portrait of Joseph, found at the head of the McKell text (fig. 14).[57] "Headpieces" much like this appear in many Byzantine manuscripts. Linked to no specific text passage, their role is primarily decorative, their intent simply to provide a visual introduction to the author,or, as in this case, to a leading player in the drama.

The second non-textual miniature is found in the same manuscript, at the end of the first section of the narrative (JAI) (fig. 15).[58] Here is portrayed the great feast in honor of the wedding (Chap. XXI.6): at the center is Pharaoh, to his right Aseneth, and to his left, Joseph. Yet flanking this group are Jacob (left) and Benjamin (right) who, according to the text, have not yet even made the journey to Egypt.[59] This unusual artistic liberty was probably taken in order that in image, if not in narrative fact, the five major personalities of Joseph's life could be united at the joyous feast celebrating the culmination of the romance.

The intent of the foregoing analysis has been threefold: to present the three illustrated copies of the Aseneth romance and organize them into an iconogrphic lineage; to establish the likely boundaries of the first Aseneth illustration; and to briefly characterize the relationship of Aseneth image to Aseneth text. I hope in the end to have given some idea of how the romance of Joseph and Aseneth is viewed through the eyes of an art historian.

NOTES

1. For the most systematic presentation of this methodology, see K. Weitzmann, Illustrations in Roll and Codex: A Study of the Origin and Method of Text Illustration (Studies in Manuscript Illumination: 2), Princeton, 1947 (2nd ed. 1970).

2. Two of the eighteen copies are in modern Greek. See C. Burchard, Untersuchungen zu Joseph und Aseneth (Wissenschaftliche Untersuchungen zum Neuen Testament: 8), Tübingen, 1965, pp. 4ff., 17; and more recently, C. Burchard, "Joseph and Aseneth Neugriechisch," (forthcoming), p. 1 (typescript). See also M. Philonenko, Joseph et Aséneth (Studia Post-Biblica: XIII), Leiden, 1968, pp. 3f., 16.

3. See G. Vikan, "Illustrated Manuscripts of Pseudo-Ephraem's Life of Joseph and the Romance of Joseph and Aseneth," unpubl. diss., Princeton, 1976.

Although images directly dependent upon the romance of Joseph and Aseneth account for a substantial majority of all Aseneth representations extant from the medieval period, she does appear occasionally in other narrative contexts. These other appearances are based either on the two passing references to her in the Bible (Genesis 41.45;50), or on one of the many Aseneth haggadoth (V. Aptowitzer, "Aseneth, the Wife of Joseph: A Haggadic Literary-Historical Study," Hebrew Union College Annual, I, 1924, pp. 239ff.). Although an examination of these scenes is outside the scope of the present investigation, the following studies may be consulted: Vikan, 1976, pp. 301ff.; W. Stechow, "Jacob Blessing the Sons of Joseph: From Early Christian Times to Rembrandt," Gazette des beaux-arts, XXIII, 1943, pp. 206ff.; J. Lebram, "Jakob segnet Josephs Söhne: Darstellungen von Genesis XLVIII in der Überlieferung und bei Rembrandt," The Priestly Code and Seven Other Studies, Leiden, 1969, pp. 145ff.; M. Levin, "Some Jewish Sources for the Vienna Genesis," Art Bulletin, LIV, 1972, p. 243; E. Revel, "Contribution des textes rabbiniques à l'étude de la Genèse de Vienne," Byzantion, XLII, 1972, pp. 126ff.; S. Dufrenne, "A Propos de deux études récentes sur la Genèse de Vienne," Byzantion, XLII, 1972, pp. 598ff.; S. Dufrenne, "Nouvelles remarques sur la Genèse de Vienne," Byzantion, XLIII, 1973, pp. 504f.; and J. Gutmann, "Joseph Legends in the Vienna Genesis," Proceedings of the Fifth World Congress of Jewish Studies, Jerusalem, 1969, Jerusalem, 1973; and note 52, below.

4. Formerly: Chillicothe, McKell Collection. See Vikan, 1976, pp. 607ff.; Burchard, 1965, p. 5; and J. and O. Pächt, "An Unknown Cycle of Illustrations of the Life of Joseph," Cahiers archéologiques, VII, 1954, pp. 35ff., pls. XII-XVI.

5. See Vikan, 1976, pp. 493ff.

6. See Vikan, 1976, pp. 405ff.; N. Şerbănescu, "Mitropoliţii Ungrovlahiei," Biserica Orthodoxă, LXXVII, 1959, pp. 768ff.; and L. Politis, "Eine Schreiberschule im Kloster τῶν Ὁδηγῶν," Byzantinische Zeitschrift, LI, 1958, pp. 282ff.

7. It was a major contention of O. Pächt's original publication of this codex (J. and O. Pächt, 1954, pp. 35ff.) that

it was copied from a sixth-century, east Mediterranean model close in style to the famous Vienna Genesis (Vienna, Nat. Lib. cod. theol. gr. 31; H. Gerstinger, Die Wiener Genesis, Vienna, 1931). The apparent stylistic similarity between the two manuscripts does not, however, bear up under detailed examination. It reflects instead the fortuitous convergence of two fully independent stylistic trends, one at the waning of Antiquity, and the other at the threshold of the Renaissance. For a thorough treatment of this difficult question, see Vikan, 1976, pp. 506ff.

8. See Politis, 1958, passim. Since Luke and his circle transcribed all types of liturgical texts in this same archaizing hand, it in no way bears on the antiquity of the model.

9. See Vikan, 1976, pp. 611ff.; Burchard, 1965, p. 17; H. Coxe, Catalogi codicum manuscriptorum Bibliothecae pars prima recensionem codicum Graecorum continens, Oxford, 1853, cols. 461f.; and Burchard, forthcoming, passim.

10. See Burchard, forthcoming, esp. pp. 2, 9f. (typescript). On the priority of family b, see C. Burchard, "Zum Text von 'Joseph und Aseneth'," Journal for the Study of Judaism, I, 1970, pp. 3ff.

11. Fol. 180v (Chap. VIII.5). See Vikan, 1976, pp. 320f.

12. Col. 2, line 2. For a transcription of Roe 5, see V. Istrin, "Apokrif ob Iosifě i Asenefě," Drevnosti (Trudy slavjanskoj kommissii Imperatorskago moskovskago archeologičeskago obščestva, II, 1898, p. 154, col. 2, line 1.

13. See Istrin, 1898, p. 154, col. 1, line 5, and note 4. See also, Philonenko, 1968, p. 154, and Burchard, forthcoming, p. 10, (typescript).

14. Fol. 75v (Chap. XIV.1ff.). See Vikan, 1976, pp. 327f.

15. Fol. 76r, lines 6-7.

16. See Burchard, 1965, p. 21.

17. Cod. McKell, fol. 69v; cod. Roe 5, fol. 181v (Chap. XI.1ff.). See Vikan, 1976, pp. 324ff.

18. Cod. McKell, fol. 75v; cod. Roe 5, fol. 181v (Chap. XIV.1ff.). See Vikan, 1976, pp. 327ff.

19. See Vikan, 1976, pp. 324ff., 327ff., 331ff., and 340f. The McKell codex lacks Chaps. II.3-X.1. In Roe, this text segment is allotted seven illustrations.

20. The evidence of surviving illuminated manuscripts has shown that the evolution of a pictorial tradition is generally marked by progressive condensation, and by a gradual deterioration in the accuracy of miniature to text. See K. Weitzmann, "Die Illustration der Septuaginta," Münchner Jahrbuch der bildenden Kunst, III-IV, 1952-1953, pp. 99, 114.

21. They conform to the description of Chap. II.1ff.

22. See Vikan, 1976, pp. 496ff.

23. Cod. McKell, fol. 88r; cod. Roe 5, fol. 184v (Chap. XIX.10). See Vikan, 1976, pp. 340f.

24. Chap. XIX.1.

25. See Vikan, 1976, pp. 564ff.

26. See Vikan, 1976, pp. 612f.; Burchard, 1965, p. 17; S. Pelekanidis, P. Christou, C. Tsimoumis, and S. Kadas, The Treasures of Mount Athos: I, Athens, 1974, p. 456, figs. 319-341; and Burchard, forthcoming, passim (pp. 2ff. with transcription).

27. See Burchard, forthcoming, p. 6 (typescript).

28. See Vikan, 1976, pp. 564f.

29. Cod. Roe 5, fol. 179v; Koutloumousi cod. 100, fol. 38v (Chap. V.2ff.). See Vikan, 1976, pp. 317ff.

30. For their respective texts, see Istrin, 1898, p. 151, col. 2, lines 9-13; and Burchard, forthcoming, p. 2 (typescript). It is significant that the simplification and apparent degeneration evident in the Koutloumousi miniature precisely parallels a corresponding simplification of its accompanying text. Roe stipulates that the east gate is opened and that Pentephres, his wife, and his household go forth to meet Joseph. Koutloumousi, on the other hand, does not mention the east gate, and speaks only of "Pentephres and all his family." This is one of several miniatures which suggest that our Aseneth illuminators did not always slavishly copy their models, but occasionally responded to changes in the text. For the methodological problems inherent in dealing with such iconographic "corrections," see Vikan, 1976, pp. 379ff.

31. If indeed the Koutloumousi codex may safely be assigned to the sixteenth century, the possibility of its having been copied from Roe is necessarily excluded. It lacks, however, a firm terminus ante quem.

32. See Burchard, forthcoming, p. 6 (typescript).

33. Cod. Roe 5, fol. 186r; Koutloumousi cod. 100, fol. 42r (Chap. XXVI.6ff.). See Vikan, 1976, pp. 351ff.

34. See Vikan, 1976, pp. 353f.

35. For evidence of specific Ottoman textual and iconographic influence on the Koutloumousi and Roe codices, see Vikan, 1976, pp. 445f.

36. However, the surprising density with which Chapter XXI is illustrated (five miniatures to just six verses of the Philonenko edition), suggests that the first Aseneth picture cycle may have been substantially more ambitious. For a critical presentation of the 36 episodes, see Vikan, 1976, pp. 312ff.

37. See Philonenko, 1968, p. 108. Burchard (1965, p. 143; 1970, p. 5) gives the time frame of 1st c. B.C. to early 2nd c. A.D.

38. For the Life of Joseph, whose typological prologue and legendary reworking of Genesis 37 to 46 together nearly equal in length the Aseneth romance, see J. Assemani, Sancti patris nostri Ephraem Syri: Opera omnia quae exstant; graece, syriace, latine, II, Rome, 1743, pp. 21ff. The LJ-JA textual unit is quite common, appearing in ten of the eighteen extant Greek copies of the Aseneth romance, and crossing all four text families. See Burchard, 1965, p. 29; and Vikan, 1976, pp. 20ff. The McKell, Roe, and Koutloumousi codices include 112 Life of Joseph miniatures, which may be critically distilled to seventy-five distinct episodes. The iconography of this cycle has, to a substantial degree, been adapted from a preexistent tradition of Septuagint illustration. See Vikan, 1976, pp. 46ff., 395ff.

39. See D. Hemmerdinger-Iliadou, "Éphrem grec," Dictionaire de spiritualité, Paris, 1960, cols. 800ff.

40. See Burchard, 1965, pp. 24f.

41. See C. Burchard, J. Jervell, and J. Thomas, Studien zu den Testamenten der Zwölf Patriarchen, Berlin, 1969, p. 18.

42. See J. Gutmann's "Prolegomenon" to No Graven Image: Studies in Art and the Hebrew Bible, New York, 1971, pp. xiff.

43. See Burchard, 1965, pp. 143f.

44. See K. Schubert, "Das Problem der Entstehung einer jüdischen Kunst im Licht der literarischen Quellen des Judentums," Kairos, XVI, 1974, pp. 10. 13.

45. Even if this link did not exist, a Jewish pictorial archetype would, on historical grounds, seem improbable. If the late first-century dating of the text advanced by Philonenko is approximately correct, there would remain only a few decades for its illustration before the repressive measures initiated by Emperors Trajan and Hadrian substantially mark the end of Jewish participation in the Greek cultural life of Egypt. See V. Tcherikover, "The Decline of the Jewish Diaspora in Egypt in the Roman Period," The Journal of Jewish Studies, XIV, 1963, pp. 20f.

46. See R. Stichel, "Ausserkanonische Elemente in byzantinischen Illustrationen des Alten Testaments," Römische Quartalschrift, LXIX, nos. 3-4, 1974, pp. 159ff.

47. See H. Belting, Das illuminierte Buch in der spätbyzantinischen Gesellschaft, Heidelberg, 1970, p. 7; and H. Buchthal, "Toward a History of Palaeologan Illumination," The Place of Book Illumination in Byzantine Art, Princeton, 1975, pp. 157f.

48. See K. Weitzmann, "Byzantine Miniature and Icon Painting in the Eleventh Century," The Proceedings of the XIIIth International Congress of Byzantine Studies: Oxford, 5-10 September, 1966, London, 1967, pp. 207ff.

49. See Vikan, 1976, pp. 515f.; 520ff.; 581ff.

50. Mount Athos, Iviron cod. 463; fol. 61v. See S. Der Nersessian, L'Illustration du roman de Barlaam et Joasaph, Paris, 1937, pl. IX, no. 32.

51. See Burchard, 1965, pp. 21f.

52. Another potentially significant source for dating the Aseneth archetype, and for plotting its influence, are illustrated copies of Vincent of Beauvais' Speculum Historiale, and of its fourteenth-century French translation, the Miroir Historial (see L. Delisle, "Exemplaires royaux et princiers du Miroir Historial," Gazette archéologiques, XI, 1886, pp. 87ff.; and G. Guzman, "A Growing Tabulation of Vincent of Beauvais' Speculum historiale manuscripts," Scriptorium, XXIX, 1975, pp. 122ff.). Since this encyclopedic text includes an abridged version of JA (Burchard, 1965, pp. 41f.), it is possible that the occasional Aseneth illustrations associated with it (Delisle, 1886, p. 92) may ultimatley depend on the Greek JA pictorial archetype. An appraisal of the significance of these scenes must, however, await an analysis of the relevant Latin and French codices.

Two scholars (Stichel, 1974, p. 176; and H. Voss, Studien zur illustrierten Millstätter Genesis, Munich, 1962, p. 74) have suggested the influence of JA iconography on specific cycles of Septuagint illustration (for Genesis 41.45;50). The examples they cite, however, show no compelling thematic or iconographic links to the JA recension under examination. Fully independent are the occasional Joseph and Aseneth double portraits appearing as headpieces to Armenian versions of the romance (see Encyclopaedia Judaica, Jerusalem, 1971, IV, p. 862).

53. See Weitzmann, 1952-1953, pp. 107ff.

54. Cod. Roe 5, fol. 183r. See Vikan, 1976, pp. 333f.

55. See Istrin, 1893, p. 163, col. 2, lines 20-32 (Chap. XVI.7ff.). (Line 22: ἀπτόχοντας should be ἀπλώνοντας).

56. Chap. V.5.

57. Fol. 60r. See Vikan, 1976, pp. 312f.

58. Fol. 91v. See Vikan, 1976, pp. 346ff.

59. They enter Egypt only during the seven years of famine (Chap. XXII).

Figure 1
Roe fol. 130v

Figure 2
McKell fol. 69v

Figure 3
Roe fol. 131v

Figure 4
McKell fol. 75v

Figure 5
Roe fol. 131v

Figure 6
McKell fol. 33r

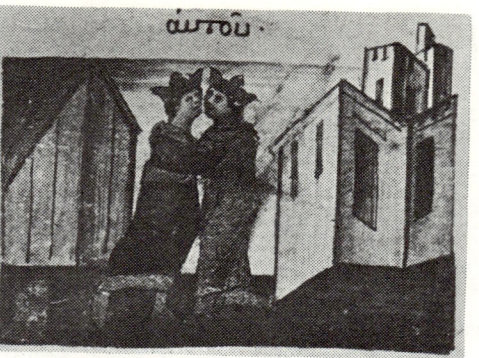

Figure 7
Roe fol. 134v

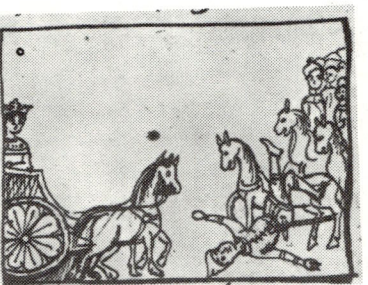

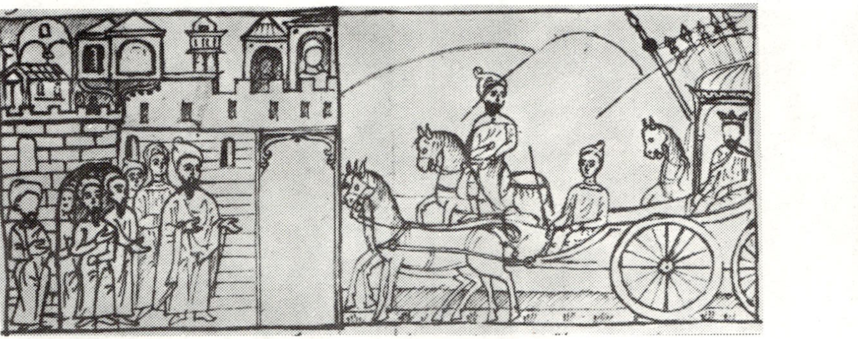

Figure 3
Roe fol. 179v

Figure 10
Roe fol. 136r

Figure 9
Kout. fol. 33v

Figure 11
Kout. fol. 42r

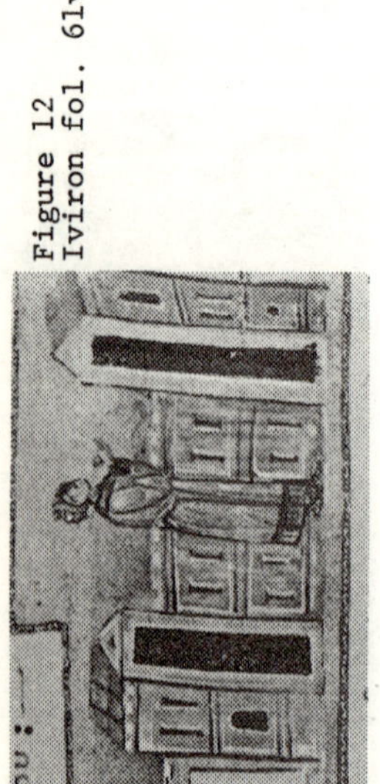

Figure 12
Iviron fol. 61v

Figure 13
Roe fol. 133r

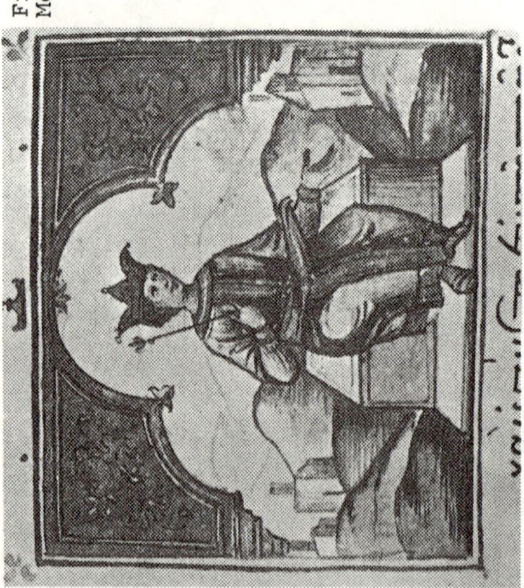

Figure 14
McKell fol. 60r

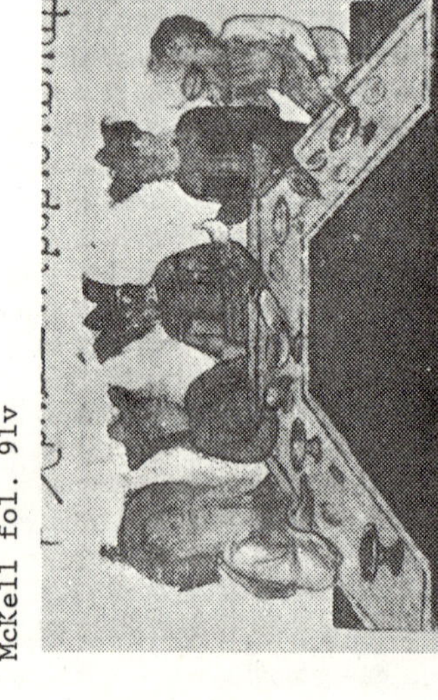

Figure 15
McKell fol. 91v

S 155 THE LUCAN BIRTH NARRATIVES IN TRADITION AND REDACTION

Lloyd Gaston
Vancouver School of Theology

At the 1975 meeting of the SBL Luke-Acts group K. Donfried presented a thesis for our further discussion together with a proposed procedure for testing it.[1] The thesis is that the broad strokes of Jervell's interpretation of Acts are correct and the procedure involves looking closely at texts which deal with the author's attitude to Judaism on the one hand and the Gentile mission on the other. I personally would agree with the thesis and find the proposed procedure potentially fruitful. The one section of Luke-Acts which strikes most readers as being closest to the atmosphere and aspirations of first century Judaism is Luke 1-2, which might provide a useful test case.[2] A completely adequate test would of course be a convincing commentary on the whole of the Luke-Acts. What follows is only in the nature of a plea to reconsider some neglected aspects in the discussion of redaction in Luke-Acts.

I

First, let us agree with the insistence of Jervell and others that Luke is addressing Christian readers in a specific situation, seeking to bring to bear the resources of the gospel to meet their specific concerns. But even if his analysis of Acts' specific concern is correct, and I think it is, he devotes very little time to recovering the situation addressed. I simply cannot agree with his offhand remark that "only in a milieu with a Jewish-Christian stamp would such a lengthy explanation of the justification of the circumcision-free Gentile mission be required,"[3] nor with his view of the actual historical relationship of the relative importance of Jewish-Christians in the period after 70 A.D.[4] It is surely Gentiles who were most in need of a theological justification of the legitimacy of the Gentile mission, for their own self-understanding as legitimate members of the people of God was at stake. This was presumably the greatest theological crisis to be faced by the early church, and Luke's solution of the problem according to Jervell is an impressive one.[5] In any case, Jervell's characterization of the Lucan situation does not seem vitally important to his overall thesis, and at one point he indicates a more satisfactory description. "The Jewish charges which Luke reports in his trial chapters reflect problems of his own milieu. Quite obviously there was some association with a Jewish environment, and it was necessary to offer some defense against charges aimed at the church."[6] That Luke was a Gentile Christian writing to the situation of Gentile Christians is according to Kümmel "das einzige, was mit Sicherheit aufgrund des Lk über seinen Verf. gesagt werden kann."[7]

Second, let us agree with the insistence of Jervell and others that the overall structure of a writing is an important clue in determining the theology of the final redaction. Let us further agree that architecture analysis is an important way of detecting literary patterns and that such patterns are a useful tool in distinguishing between tradition and redaction and thus in highlighting the specific theological concerns of the redaction.[8] But surely in order to be completely convincing there ought to be a constant interaction with the attempt to isolate and characterize sources, each enterprise acting as a check on the excesses of the other. The ultimate goal of synoptic research should be a convincing reconstruction of the whole process of the tradition from its beginnings to the significance of the whole work in its final context.

Third, let us agree with the insistence of Jervell and others that Luke is in control of his material, that he is not just a clumsy collector and transmitter of diverse earlier traditions nor a mere chronicler of past events for their own sake with no attempt to relate them to the present. This means that everything told in Luke-Acts must be compatible with the purpose of the author. U. Wilckens says for example, "Im jetzigen Zusammenhang der Apostelgeschichte sind die Reden gerade auch in ihrer Form, in dem zugrunde gelegten Schema, durchgehend von der theologischen Gesamtkonzeption des Lukas her verständlich."[9] Of course! But that does not mean that they were necessarily composed by Luke, only that they were useful for his purposes, and that does not mean that they could not also be equally verständlich in another Zusammenhang. In short, admiration for Luke's literary and theological accomplishments should not relieve us of the responsibility of also looking for sources.

Fourth, let us agree with the insistence of Jervell and others that justification of the legitimacy of the Gentile mission is a primary concern of Acts (p 41 and passim). This of course does not exclude other concerns, such as an anti-Gnostic emphasis,[10] and S. Brown[11] and especially S.G. Wilson[12] have given salutary warnings against seeking for a too rigid and a too narrow conception of Luke's theological purposes. Here again a sharper distinction between tradition and redaction may help us to see Luke's achievement in more modest perspectives. But in general, it has been demonstrated that this is at least one major concern of Luke and that in its present form it is to be ascribed to the final redactor.

Fifth, let us agree with Jervell and others that "Luke has excluded the possibility of a further mission to Jews for the church of his time because the judgment by and on the Jews has been irrevocably passed" (p 64, cf. pp 69, 174). Something similar has been said by J. Munck, E. Haenchen, J. Gnilka, H. Conzelmann, G. Bornkamm, A. George, J.C. O'Neill, W. Eltester, S.G. Wilson, and N. Dahl.[13] Of course, Jervell's very starting point has been his quite correct assertion that one cannot call the Jewish rejection of the gospel the decisive presupposition for the beginning of the Gentile mission. But it is not clear whether he realizes the full implications of his acknowledgment of the fact that for Luke the period of the fulfillment of the promises to Israel lies in the past.

Sixth, let us agree with Jervell's major contribution to the study of Luke-Acts, his extensive demonstration that for Luke the Gentile mission presupposes the fulfillment of God's promises to Israel, a repentent and faithful Israel which accepts the gospel. It is true that he has been taken to task for an overemphasis of this motif and for a tendency to suppress evidence to the contrary, by M. Moscato[14] and S.G. Wilson[15] among others. It may be that Jervell tends to see as alternatives what really are meant as complementary motifs. In any case the general thrust of Jervell's articles provides one of the most stimulating approaches to the study of Acts in recent time.

Finally, let us agree with Jervell on the importance of Luke 1-2 in understanding the total theology of Luke-Acts. At least I assume he would insist on their importance on the basis of two references and an article not available to me.[16]

If true, it is very distressing that "it is generally agreed that Luke added chapters 1 and 2 after he had already completed the body of his Gospel."[17] That the Proto-Luke of Streeter and Taylor failed to meet acceptance in spite of their valid observations surely has to do with their concept of the document as a "first draft" by Luke himself and thus with no distinctive outlook, a conclusion they might have avoided if they had not excluded Luke 1 and 2 from consideration. H. Conzelmann has been sufficiently reprimanded by P. Minear for ignoring the birth stories simply because they did not fit into his theory.[18] It is to be regretted that the most thorough recent commentary on Luke[19] and the most thorough recent NT introduction[20] both treat Luke 1-2 as a kind of afterthought, an appendix prefixed before the main work. Finally a paper presented to this group in 1975 also is inclined toward this assumption.[21] The main arguments seem to be as follows:

1. The synchronism of Luke 3:1f looks like a good beginning. But the possible parallel to the dating in 1:5 and especially 2:1f and Luke's own concern to set his work within the context of world history (e.g. Acts 26:26) surely undercut the force of what is only an impression.
2. The genealogy, Luke 3:23-38, should have been included in the earlier chapters if they were an original part of the whole. But there are alternative explanations for the position of the genealogy in Luke's outline.[22]
3. Both Mark and the kerygma (Acts 1:22, 10:37, 13:24) begin from the baptism of John. But it is not sure that the scope of a gospel must be determined by the scope of one form of the kerygma, a Lucan source may well have predated Mark, and it is clear that someone, presumably also Luke, *did* want to begin a gospel with the story of the annunciations and births of these two figures.
4. The birth stories "reflect a 'higher' and more developed Christology."[23] But Romans 1:3-4 is rather early than late, the title Son of God may be an addition to a source in 1:35, and it is possible that Luke 1-2 do not proclaim a virginal conception at all.[24]

Unless there are stronger arguments to the contrary, it seems best to understand Luke 1-2 to be an integral part of Luke-Acts (and I would add: of an important source). The consequences of rejecting them in any attempt to understand the whole are major.

II

It is difficult to avoid arguing in a circle when attempting to distinguish tradition and redaction. A redactor is one who by definition edits his material and makes it conform to a uniform style.[25] Nevertheless it is necessary to assume that he has not done so perfectly, so that some of the language, style, structure and conception of the source can still be discerned behind the redaction. This is particularly the case the further apart source and redactor are in general culture, outlook, and theological concerns. The isolation of specifically Lucan concerns can help in the reconstruction of sources; the distinction between source and redaction can help in identifying the concerns. In this way perhaps the circle can become a spiral.

If it is true that Luke was a Gentile Christian writing someplace outside the land of Israel and if it is true that some of his material is of Palestinian provenance, then intimate knowledge of Palestinian matters and the sharing of Palestinian concerns would be a sign of tradition, just as ignorance of these matters and concerns would be a sign of redaction. It is not necessary to rehearse here the impressive linguistic observations of Sahlin, Laurentin, Winter[26] and others, nor the intimate knowledge of a Palestinian milieu and the sharing of Palestinian aspirations which these chapters display.[27] On the other hand Conzelmann[28] and many others have pointed out Luke's basic ignorance of Palestinian matters. If redaction criticism can act as a check on some of the excesses of source and form criticism, nevertheless it still presupposes them. Form criticism began with the insight that stories tended to be originally told in self-contained units and that the joining of them together must be redactional. Let us go back to the beginning, to K.L. Schmidt's *Der Rahmen der Geschichte Jesu*.[29]

If there are any sources used in Luke 1-2 at all, Schmidt thought that it was possible fairly easily to distinguish them in broad strokes from the redactional composition. 1:1-4 is the obvious example of the hand of the final redactor. In addition, Schmidt argued that the Magnificat and Benedictus have been secondarily inserted into their present context and that a redactor has rewritten his sources in 2:1-5 and 2:22-24. He labels the following verses as redactional: 1:26a, 56, 67, 80; 2:19, 21, 39, 40, 41, 51, 52. Some of these seem to point very strongly in the direction of Luke. 2:21 is very awkward linguistically in its context, refers back to 1:31 and 1:59-63, and falsely assumes that Jewish children normally were not named until the day of circumcision. 2:1-5 betrays such Lucan language and concerns that we must assume a rather extensive rewriting of a source.[30] Something is wrong with 2:22-24; apart from certain linguistic difficulties it confuses the purification of the mother with the redemption of the first born.[31] 2:51b-52 round off the entire cycle by reference back to 2:19 and 2:40 and indicate a human interest in Mary. We shall return in a moment to Schmidt's other indications of redactional joinings and cross references.

K.L. Schmidt's isolated narratives can be analysed as follows:

A. Annunciation of the birth of John 1:5-23, 24-5.
B. Annunciation of the birth of Jesus 1:26b-38.
C. Meeting of Mary and Elizabeth 1:39-45, 56.
D. Birth of John 1:57-66.
E. Birth of Jesus 2:1-18, 20.
F. Simeon and Anna in the Temple 2:22-38.
G. Jesus in the Temple 2:42-50.

The independence of some of these stories has often been remarked. Thus the four stories concerning Jesus (B, E, F, G) do not refer to one another and have different concepts. On the other hand, while D does not refer back to B and C, it is the clear continuation of A. C presupposes A and B so clearly that it could never have existed independently of them. Finally, there are so many parallels between A and B that one must have been composed in view of the other. The usually assumed priority of A and D has been associated with the no longer tenable assumption of a Baptist source, and R. Brown's proposal that B is prior seems equally plausible to me.[32]

There is then evidence of a redactor, who certainly composed C and probably A and D (or alternatively B). Was that redactor Luke? If so it is strange that the one pericope which is most obviously redactional, C, betrays no obvious evidence of his hand, which seems to be most strongly represented in the narratives E, F and G. It may be that Luke 1-2 in its entirety is a Lucan composition and that Luke was a first century James Joyce who was able to adjust his style radically as appropriate to the subject matter. But if there were sources for the individual elements of tradition contained in these chapters, then there was also a pre-Lucan redactor, and the material must have come to Luke in something very like its present form. This means that it would be very difficult to determine whether some of the redactional elements Schmidt isolated stem from the source or from Luke.[33] It is also not possible to distinguish clearly, as older source critics sometimes naively thought, between all the details of the original and Lucan additions and rephrasings. But if it seems probable that there was a unified source behind Luke 1-2, then one could go on to ask about its extent and special theology.

The looseness of some of the hymns in their present context has long been noted. Quite apart from the disparity between content and situation, 1:56 is evidence of the secondary insertion of the Magnificat, and 1:67 after 1:64 argues for the secondary insertion of the Benedictus. D. Jones[34] would add the Canticles of Simeon 2:29-32, 34f, and F. Gryglewicz[35] also the hymn of the angels 2:10-11, 14. It is also conceivable that the annunciation to Zechariah existed before its present context was composed around it. I have argued elsewhere that all these are early Jewish-Christian hymns celebrating the salvation that had come to Israel in the Messiah Jesus, the eschatological prophet, the political savior of Israel; that the Benedictus must be understood as a unity having nothing to do with "Baptist circles"; and that the application of 1:68-79 and 14-17 to John the Baptist is due to the redactor of the source. I have also pointed out the correspondence in language and concept between the Benedictus and the speech in Acts 3:12-26.[36] This and other correspondences between the birth stories and some of the material in the early chapters of Acts raise the question whether or not it is possible to isolate a strand of tradition in Luke-Acts with a consistent Christology and a consistent attitude to Israel and the Gentiles. Insofar as it can be shown that this strand consistently reflects the concepts and aspirations of Palestinian Jewish Christians, it would be in that sense un-Lucan. I do not know if I have succeeded in demonstrating that a strand of Luke-Acts can be understood in this context.[37] But if it is a possibility, it would do two things relevant to our present concern. It would put to the test Donfried's proposed procedure. And it would underline the importance of the birth narratives for source criticism as well as redaction criticism.

III

It is to Jervell's credit to have pointed out that Luke can justify the Gentile mission of his own time only by insisting on the prior success of the mission of the church to Israel. It is only possible for salvation to come from Zion if it has previously come to Zion. There is a necessary relationship between Acts 28:28 "to the Gentiles has been sent this salvation (σωτήριον) of God" and Luke 2:30-32 "my eyes have seen thy salvation (σωτήριον) which thou hast prepared in the presence of all peoples; a light for revelation to the Gentiles and glory for thy people Israel."[38] It is very clear that Luke 1-2 are very important for Luke's purpose as understood by Jervell. It would after all be strange to find any traditions in Luke-Acts which were at sharp variance with Luke's own theology, for he has deliberately taken them up and absorbed them into his own wider scheme. There is nothing in Luke 1-2 which is incompatible with the Lucan intention, but there are concepts and hopes which could never have been composed in the service of that intention.

It must not be forgotten that the concept of salvation for Israel and thus as a consequence also for Gentiles is not peculiar to Luke but is also characteristic of Jewish eschatology at least since the time of Deutero-Isaiah.[39] It is not only Luke who would say that "only when Israel has accepted the gospel can the way to Gentiles be opened" nor even that "the unrepentant portion of the people cannot hinder the fulfillment of the promises to Israel."[40] But there might very well be substantial disagreement between Luke and, say, James about the relative size of the repentant portion as fulfilling the promises and how successful the Jewish mission would have to be in order to speak of Israel accepting the gospel. This is true even in terms of Luke's sanguine exaggerations, and the contrast is all the sharper if the mission of the church to Israel was in fact nearly a failure during the first generation and practically non-existent during Luke's lifetime. Insofar as the Gentile mission began before the complete eschatological fulfillment of the promises to Israel, then there is a sense in which Jewish rejection of the Gospel and a divine rejection of the Jews is a presupposition for Gentile mission, and Jervell should not minimize this motif.

If the motif of the rejection of Israel is a sign of Lucan redaction, the parallel motif of the fulfillment of the promises to Israel cannot in itself be taken as a sign of earlier tradition, as also Luke makes very important use of it. But this latter is not part of Luke's present experience or hope, and Luke 1-2 is one of the places where the hope for the salvation of all Israel is most enthusiastically and even naively expressed. "Here we are probably in touch with an early (and not defunct) Palestinian mentality in the church which, while not Zealot, was concerned with the national hope based on the promise to Abraham."[41] At Jesus' birth the angels proclaim "peace on earth to men of God's election" (2:14), and Jesus will "reign over the house of Jacob, on the throne of his father David"(1:32f), as the Messiah, the anointed of YHWH (2:11,26), the horn of salvation (1:69), the Branch (1:78), the Son of the most high (1:32), the prophet of the Most High (1:76). Thereby God "has visited and given redemption to his people" (1:68) and "knowledge of salvation to his people" (1:77) and "glory to (his) people Israel" (2:32), who were waiting for the "redemption of Jerusalem" (2:38) and the "consolation of Israel" (2:25). Now God "has helped his servant Israel" (1:54) giving them "salvation from our enemies and from the hand of all who hate us" (1:71). The Messiah has come "to make us without fear, rescued from the hand of our enemies"(1:74), and "to guide our feet in the way of peace" (1:79). All of this is the fulfillment of "the oath which he swore to Abraham our father, to remember his holy covenant" (1:72f), "as he spoke to our fathers, to Abraham and his seed forever" (1:55), and the promises are for the whole people of Israel (παντὶ τῷ λαῷ 2:10).[42] That these chapters could have been composed after the destruction of Jerusalem had made a mockery of the proclamation of the national peace of God to the people of the promise and after the results of the mission to Israel have been seen to be only partial and past seems utterly uncomprehensible to me. That these chapters fit very well into Luke's purpose is clear, but that they were first composed in the light of Luke's own situation is impossible. The question of the audience addressed is crucial in distinguishing tradition and redaction, and here if anywhere we are clearly dealing with a pre-Lucan source.

Probably few still agree with Conzelmann's threefold heilsgeschichtliches Schema for Luke. On the one hand he was wrong to separate Jesus from John the Baptist, and on the other hand his time of the church, at least if Jervell is right, must be seen to be differentiated between the time of the successful preaching to Israel as the fulfillment of the promises and the time of Luke's own church as the Gentile-Christian heirs to this period. In speaking of that earlier period Jervell writes "These Jewish Christians were the historically necessary transition to a predominantly Gentile Christian church" (p. 68). The parallel to Eckardt's concept of "the bridge generation"[43] is striking and has far-reaching implications for current relations between Christians and Jews.

Finally, let me conclude with the plea that redaction criticism take very seriously the question of Lucan sources for two reasons. First, the two approaches fructify each other, for the very achievements of redaction criticism provide more refined tools for identifying the sources, but then the recognition of sources acts as a check on some of the excesses of redaction criticism.[44] We can understand the emphases of the final redaction better if in terms of assigning importance to details we distinguish between a source which is modified to serve the purpose of the final author and what has been directly composed to this end. Rather than speak of Luke-Acts as a strictly Lucan creation, I would rather think in terms of a Lucan modification of and additions to a basically Jewish-Christian document in order to serve, and to serve quite well, the concerns of his own Gentile-Christian church. Second, we know very little about the Jewish-Christian church of the first century, and if Lucan source criticism can help us this is of potentially great importance. Let us not neglect the full richness of all that is contained in Luke-Acts.

NOTES

1. "Attempts at Understanding the Purpose of Luke-Acts," 5.

2. There is the added advantage of the possibility of discussion with another paper presented at that meeting, R. Brown's "Luke's Method in the Annunciation Narratives of Chapter One," later published in No Famine in the Land: Studies in Honor of John L. McKenzie (1975).

3. Luke and the People of God (1972) 175; cf. also 117, 176, 199. He has a similar view of the purpose of Romans: "Der Brief nach Jerusalem; Über Veranlassung und Adresse des Römerbriefs," ST 25 (1971) 61-73. Cf. also E. Trocmé, Le "Livre des Actes" et l'Histoire (1957) 67-75.

4. I am much more impressed by the arguments of W. Schmithals, Der Römerbrief als historisches Problem (1975).

5. The so-called problem of the delay of the parousia is really only an aspect of the crisis faced by the church in the unresponse of Israel and the premature beginning of the Gentile mission. Luke's eschatology should be reexamined in this light.

6. LPG, 174. Cf. the similar (and I think correct) characterization of the situation in S.G. Wilson, The Gentiles and the Gentile Mission in Luke-Acts (1973) 246-249.

7. Einleitung in das Neue Testament (1973^{17}) 118.

8. The reference is of course to C.H. Talbert, Literary Patterns, Theological Themes and the Genre of Luke-Acts (1974). But statements like "whatever one's judgment about the source" (p. 20 and often), while understandable in a work with a limited purpose, are ultimately unsatisfactory.

9. Die Missionsreden der Apostelgeschichte (1961) 99.

10. C.H. Talbert, Luke and the Gnostics (1966) and Literary Patterns.

11. "The Prologues of Luke-Acts in their Relation to the Purpose of the Author," SBL 1975 Seminar Papers, II, 1-14.

12. The Gentiles.

13. J. Munck, Paulus und die Heilsgeschichte (1954) 240f; E. Haenchen, Die Apostelgeschichte (1959^{12}) 90f, 653; "Judentum und Christentum in der Apostelgeschichte," ZNW 54 (1963) 155-187, 185; in Keck and Martyn, eds, Studies in Luke-Acts (1966) 278; J. Gnilka, Die Verstockung Israels (1961) 119-154; H. Conzelmann, Die Apostelgeschichte (1963) 149f; SLA 308; G. Bornkamm, SLA 201; A. George, "Israël dans l'oeuvre de Luc," RB 75 (1968) 481-525, 522; J.C. O'Neill, The Theology of Acts (1970^{2}) 75, 95; W. Eltester, "Israel im lukanischen Werk," Jesus in Nazareth (1972) 76-147, 111-120; S.G. Wilson, The Gentiles, 226. N. Dahl, SLA 151, has given a particularly clear summary: "1. Salvation of Gentiles was from the beginning envisaged by God and included as part of his promises to Israel.... 2. Luke wants to make it clear beyond doubt that in the course of events due respect has been paid to the priority of Israel.... 3. The priority of Israel is regarded as a matter of history; it is no longer a present reality for Luke and for churches like those of Corinth and Rome."

14. "A Critique of Jervell's Luke and the People of God," SBL 1975 Seminar Papers, II, 161-168. But surely one ought to speak of two interrelated motifs rather than two separate traditions.

15. The Gentiles, 222-224, 227-233.

16. LPG 91, 138, and "Den omskårne Messias," SEA 37-38 (1972-73) 145-155.

17. W. Wink, John the Baptist in the Gospel Tradition (1968) 58.

18. "Luke's Use of the Birth Stories," SLA 111-130. I find particularly ununderstandable Conzelmann's extraordinary statement: "die Authentizität der beiden ersten Kapitel sei fraglich (weshalb wir auch ihre besonderen Theologumena ausklammern)," Die Mitte der Zeit (1960[3]) 109.

19. H. Schürmann, Das Lukasevangelium I (1969) 18-21, 141.

20. W.G. Kümmel, Einleitung, 106-107.

21. R. Brown, "Luke's Method." Cf. also P. Benoit, "L'Enfance de Jean-Baptiste selon Luc I," NTS 3 (1957) 169-194.

22. E.g. Talbert, Literary Patterns, 46, 117. Rather than looking to Matthew 1 for a model, why not Exod 6:14-27?

23. R. Brown, "Luke's Method," 1.

24. Cf. J.A. Fitzmyer, "The Virginal Conception of Jesus in the New Testament," TS 34 (1973) 541-575.

25. There are sufficient "Lucanisms" in Luke 1-2 that if these chapters had by accident been transmitted in a different context, we would still be convinced by such arguments as R. Morgenthaler, Statistik des neutestamentlichen Wortschatzes (1958) 51f, to ascribe them to Luke. Cf. also P. Minear, "Luke's Use."

26. H. Sahlin, Der Messias und das Gottesvolk (1945); R. Laurentin, Structure et Théologie de Luc i-ii (1957); P. Winter's numerous contributions are listed in my No Stone on Another (1970) 258.

27. Cf. among others Schürmann, 145, and Wink, 61-62.

28. Die Mitte.

29. 1919, reprinted Wissenschaftliche Buchgesellschaft (1969) 310-316.

30. In addition to Schmidt, 312, also R. Bultmann, Die Geschichte der synoptischen Tradition (1958[4]) 323, and W. Bundy, Jesus and the First Three Gospels (1955) 17.

31. Various reconstructions of the original text have been proposed; cf. Bultmann, Geschichte, 326, and Sahlin, Messias, 243-246.

32. "Luke's Method." In addition to Brown's rejection of a Baptist (and Marian) source, see also W. Wink, John the Baptist, 60-72.

33. C. Talbert, Literary Patterns, 44f, finds two seven-part cycles of parallels in these chapters and argues that they are "the result of Lucan design." With respect to the first set, more probable is R. Brown's demonstration that they come from a common OT annunciation pattern. His second set is not so impressive (e.g. his 1,2 and 5), and where parallels are clear they are not to be ascribed to the overall structure but to Lucan (2:19, 21, 52) or possibly pre-Lucan (1:80; 2:40) redaction. Thus the very existence of these latter parallels is evidence of Lucan redaction of a source rather than free composition.

34. "The Background and Character of the Lukan Psalms," JTS ns 19 (1968) 19-50.

35. "Die Herkunft der Hymnen des Kindheitsevangeliums des Lucas," NTS 21 (1975) 265-273.

36. No Stone, 256-280.

37. No Stone, 244-369.

38. The unusual neuter σωτήριον comes of course from Isa 40:5 LXX, also cited Luke 3:5, the only places where the word occurs in Luke-Acts.

39. A pioneering study making this insight fruitful for NT study was B. Sundkler, Jésus et les païens (1937).

40. Jervell, LPG, 55.

41. W.D. Davies, The Gospel and the Land (1974) 263. How far this attitude to Israel is from the mind of Luke is shown not only by the ending of Acts but also by the fact that W. Marxsen, Introduction to the NT (1968) 159, feels called upon seriously to defend Luke of the charge of antisemitism in his redaction of the passion narrative.

42. The concept of a divided people of God is also present in the birth narratives (2:24f), but there is a great difference between a foreboding and a fait accompli. And Luke 2:29-32 is of course the expression of a Jewish Christian or Jewish attitude to the eschatological witness to the Gentiles.

43. A. Roy Eckardt, Elder and Younger Brothers (1967) 137-140.

44. E.g. if T. Schramm, Der Markus-Stoff bei Lukas (1971) is correct, and I have seen almost no discussion of his work, then much of what Conzelmann assigns to the Lucan redaction of Mark really comes from a source. His thesis should not be ignored but tested very seriously.

S 156 THE LUKAN SITZ IM LEBEN: METHODOLOGY AND PROSPECTS

Robert J. Karris
Catholic Theological Union

SETTING THE PROBLEM

What do we know about Luke's Sitz im Leben? That's a question I recently asked myself and was surprised by the answer "not much."[1] That answer becomes an embarrassment when I realize that some twenty years of redaction critical work have issued in the paltry result of "not much" and when I glance at what colleagues have been able to determine with considerable probability about the Sitz im Leben of John's Gospel and Matthew's Gospel. The goal of this paper is to challenge us to step up our pursuit of the Lukan Sitz im Leben.

In what follows I will suggest, in a very brief way, that our methods may have prevented us from getting a clearer fix on the Lukan Sitz im Leben. Led by the compass of these methodological suggestions, I will examine one prospect of getting at the concrete Lukan Sitz im Leben - the theme of poor and rich.[2]

METHODOLOGY

It seems that we Lukan scholars invest huge amounts of time in trying to pin down Luke's purposes, themes, and tendencies and then become niggardly with our time when it comes to pursuing the question of the Sitz im Leben which is determinative of that purpose or theme or tendency. It seems to me that for purposes, themes, or tendencies to have complete validity it must be demonstrated that they arise from a concrete situation within Luke's community. Otherwise, it is too easy for them to lose their grounding in reality and to float freely on some high level of abstraction where they can generate other ideas and combine with them to form clusters of ideas. These clusters of ideas may have captivating intrinsic beauty, but say little about the reality which they are supposedly designed to explain.

Examples will clarify my point. The "classical" Roman Catholic image of Jesus' human knowledge, equipped with beatific vision, shows how a theory can become divorced from the data and thrive on its own inner logic, e.g., Jesus would be the best general, king, nuclear physicist, etc. Conzelmann's hypothesis that Luke develops a theology of salvation history[3] in the face of the delay of the parousia is an example of a purpose and a Sitz im Leben which run the risk of being too abstract and divorced from reality. Thumb through Conzelmann's _The Theology of St. Luke_ and note how often he gives the nod to persecution, yet _does not_ use persecution as one of the Lukan Sitze im Leben. If he had, he would be more in contact with Lukan reality. The "delay of the parousia," besides being a faulty concept, is much too general, too abstract to be of much help in determining the Lukan Sitz im Leben.[4] To those who proclaim Luke as the universalist, the theologian of the Holy Spirit, the champion of the outcast or the first Christian apologist, I respectfully reply, "Show me the reasons _why_ Luke develops that theme."

If we steadfastly resolve to stalk the Lukan Sitz im Leben, then it behooves us to repeat the query made by Schuyler Brown during our last session: "The double tendency in Luke (evangelical and theological) does seem to presuppose two circles of readers, and perhaps some thought should be given to the question: what plausible Sitz im Leben in early Christianity might have given rise to a book with such diverse potentials?"[5] As we investigate the Sitze im Leben behind the various purposes, themes, and tendencies proposed for Luke-Acts, are we not forced to atomize Luke-Acts? That is, will we be proposing some twenty or thirty Sitze im Leben? What if Luke's situation was one in which there were persecutions, false teachers, greedy church leaders, insensitive rich folk, free lance miracle workers, etc., etc.? Would this view of Luke's community make that community so complex that it would defy historical probability? I doubt it. Life, even ecclesial life, is complex and pluralistic. Who's to say that it wasn't that way for Luke and his community?

In developing my prospect of the theme of poor and rich, I will doggedly raise the question of Sitz im Leben. Answers to that interrogation will hint at the complexity of the Lukan Sitz im Leben.

PROSPECT - THE THEME OF POOR AND RICH

I. DEFINITION OF TERMS

I follow Jacques Dupont in defining the poor as the indigent, those who lack the necessities, those who need alms.[6] The rich are those who have considerable possessions or money. I disassociate my definition of poor from that of Joachim Jeremias, who, while having many helpful comments on Lk 4:18, 6:20, and 7:22, gives a definition of poor which is so broad that it is not serviceable as a means of discriminating between the various materials on poor and rich: "Jesus used 'the poor' in this wide sense that the term had acquired in the prophets ... the hungry, those who weep, the sick, those who labour, those who bear burdens, the last, the simple, the lost, the sinners."[7]

II. PREVIOUS STUDIES ON THE THEME OF POOR AND RICH IN LUKE-ACTS

In this section I will whet our appetites for pursuit of the Lukan Sitz im Leben by summarizing and evaluating studies which make representative or major contributions to our thematic. I will underline what these authors have to say about the Lukan Sitz im Leben.

A. A MERE "CONCERN." It seems that many studies on Luke devote a number of pages to his "concern" for the poor. Quite often these discussions fall into the literary category of spiritual nosegay and betray not the slightest trace of an interest in relating this theme to the Sitz im Leben of Luke.[8]

B. HENRY JOEL CADBURY. As in so many other instances, Cadbury had a profound insight into the material on poor and rich. Some 50 years ago he wrote: "It is to possessors, not to the dispossessed, that Jesus speaks on alms and on the cares and pleasures of property." "But the rebuke of wealth ... betokens a concern for the oppressor rather than pity for the oppressed...."[9] Cadbury makes no statement about the Lukan Sitz im Leben.

C. HANS-JOACHIM DEGENHARDT.[10] I make two points. First, Luke separates the laos from the mathetai, the mathētai from the apostoloi. The admonitions to renounce wealth/possessions are given to the disciples who are the Amtsträgern of Luke's community - traveling apostles, missionaries, evangelists, wandering preachers, charismatic prophets, and resident community leaders. These are the ones who must follow the radical statement of Jesus about renunciation of possessions.[11] Further, there is also the danger and tendency among Luke's church leaders to become greedy, pleasure-seeking, and forgetful about almsgiving.[12]

My second point is that Degenhardt hedges on the primary Sitz im Leben, outlined above, and introduces another.[13] By means of his modifications of the inherited traditions behind Acts 2:41-47 and 4:31c-35 Luke confronts Gentile Christians who because of cultural conditioning have little or no concern for love of neighbor and almsgiving. Unless this cultural conditioning is confronted and transformed, the very existence of the Christian community as a fraternity will be in jeopardy. Moreover, Luke has to show these Gentile Christians that possessions can separate them from union with Christ (see Lk 12:21; 11:41; 12:15; 14:14; 18:18-27; cf. 12:16-20).[14]

Methodologically, Degenhardt's work is deficient because he does not deal with the Magnificat and the Zacchaeus story;[15] because it is not possible to separate out the "disciples" from the "people" and the twelve (apostles) with any type of consistency;[16] and especially because Degenhardt does not sufficiently discuss other material within Luke-Acts which deals with church leaders and thus does not provide a control for his methodology and conclusions.

While there are problems with some aspects of Degenhardt's monograph, he has made many valuable points. I single out two: 1) he takes very seriously the fact that Luke preserved radical material about possessions and asks the question why; 2) he surely is on to something very significant when he notes that Luke has to counter a cultural tendency within his Greco-Roman community, a tendency, which, if left unchallenged, would lead to the abandonment of the poor.

D. GERD THEISSEN.[17] While Degenhardt argues that Luke has preserved the "radical" Jesus material on possessions for church leaders, Theissen argues that Luke has preserved this radical material only to have Jesus rescind it in Lk 22:35f. This rescinding reveals Luke's Sitz im Leben: he is arguing against the descendents of the first itinerant charismatics who plague his church. For Luke there were only twelve legitimate apostles, the great itinerant missionaries of the earliest days.

It is highly questionable that Lk 22:35f. rescinds all the radical material in Luke's Gospel. I cannot deem Theissen's proposed Sitz im Leben plausible until more evidence is offered.

E. JACQUES DUPONT.[18] Dupont enters the discussion of our thematic via the beatitudes and woes. He argues that the beatitudes are addressed to the Christian community which is persecuted for its faith, poor, suffering deprivation. The woes are not addressed to Christians, but to people outside the Christian community. These people are incredulous Israel. The passages about the dangers of wealth show how wealth can lead to blindness, a blindness characteristic of incredulous Israel. Riches are also a very great danger about which Luke must warn his Christian community.

It is hard to understand why Luke has to warn his poor and persecuted community about the dangers of wealth. How could the message about the dangers of wealth really be relevant for these poor? Moreover, on p. 202 he explains the vitally important Lk 12:33, 14:33, 5:11,28, and 18:22 in one paragraph by subsuming them under the rubric of placing all one's security in God and not in mammon. Furthermore, he does not take into account Acts 2:41-47 and 4:31-35 about which he had written so perceptively in a previous article.[19] Lastly, Dupont seems to think of the Lukan community in monolithic terms, that is, the beatitudes and the woes cannot be addressed to the same community. This view must be challenged.[20]

In summary. With variations, Cadbury, Degenhardt, and Theissen agree that members of Luke's community had possessions. Cadbury and Degenhardt (at times) suggest that Luke's community was composed of a certain number of rich Christians. Dupont is the only author to champion the view that Luke's community was composed solely of poor Christians. Thus, these studies provide us with sound clues in our pursuit of the Lukan Sitz im Leben. The main clue is that Luke is more concerned with possessors than with the poor. In what ensues I will discuss the most important Lukan passages on poor and rich to see whether we can follow up on the clues of these previous studies, especially in the area of the Lukan Sitz im Leben.

III. LUKAN PASSAGES ON POOR AND RICH

A. Acts 2:41-47 and 4:31c-35. Degenhardt, Theissen, and Brown are quite accurate in granting major significance to these summary passages. I presuppose that these passages open the window onto the Sitz im Leben behind the Lukan theme of poor and rich.

Obviously, it is impossible to treat all the problems attendant on these verses. The following points must suffice. For some time now scholars have recognized the Greco-Roman philosophical utopian parallels to our passages.[21] Plümacher[22] and Charles H. Talbert[23] interpret these parallels as evidence of Luke's idealization of the primitive community as free from heresy and schism. It seems to me that they have read the summary passages of Acts 2 and 4 too narrowly. Luke uses the terminology of friendship to show that what was longed for, but rarely, if ever, realized has been realized in the Christian community. Luke's primary point is that Christians treat each other as friends. And because and when they do, they share what they have (give alms), and no one is in need. Put another way, Luke, by the use of Greco-Roman philosophical terminology of friendship, modifies his inherited tradition[24] in order to make it comprehensible to his Greco-Roman audience which does not share the Christian/Jewish concern for the neighbor in need and for the poor. Luke's point, then, is: the Christians aid the neighbor in need and the poor in the community because they view each other as friends.

In order for us to fathom the significance of Luke's modifications in Acts 2:41-47 and 4:31c-35, it is vital that we appreciate the general Greco-Roman cultural background on the poor and on almsgiving.[25] While it may not be possible to develop an absolutely pure typology, the evidence is considerable that almsgiving is not known among the Greco-Romans whereas it is a cultural expectation for those from an Egyptian/Jewish (oriental) background. The Greco-Romans would not come to the aid of a non-citizen; they would help a friend in need, but that only to collect IOU's against future contingencies.[26]

In sum, what emerges from the summary passages of Acts 2 and 4 is mission theology: how to make the Christian/Jewish teaching about the necessity of almsgiving and about fellowship intelligible to converts who come from a widely different cultural expectation. If the Christian community in Jerusalem, composed of so many different peoples, treated each other as friends, so too should the recent converts of Luke's own time. Luke's Sitz im Leben consists of propertied Christians who have been converted and cannot easily extricate themselves from their cultural mindsets. It also consists of Christians in need of alms. Luke takes great pains to show that Christians treat each other as friends and that almsgiving and care for one another is of the essence of the Way. If the converts do not learn this lesson and learn it well, there is danger that the Christian movement may splinter.[27]

In what follows I will examine passages in the Gospel where Lukan redaction is most manifest to see whether analyses of these passages may give greater specificity to the Sitz im Leben detected behind the Lukan redaction of Acts 2:41-47 and 4:31c-35.

B. Luke 3:1-9:50.[28]

1) Luke 4:18+7:22; 6:20-26. Almost all Lukan scholars would agree that 4:16-30 is programmatic: it describes Jesus' nature and mission. Also, it is clear that 4:18 is closely related to 7:22. But it is not clear who the poor are on the redactional level. I question whether it is totally legitimate to interpret the "poor" of 4:18 (7:22) on the basis of what that term might mean in Isaiah. I suggest that we turn to 6:20-26 in our quest to give content to the word "poor" on the redactional level.

I agree with Dupont's analysis that 6:20-23 refers to the Christian community of Luke's day. They are poor, suffering deprivation and persecution for their faith.[29] Thus, if we interpret the "poor" of 4:18 and 7:22 via 6:20-23, they are Christians of Luke's own time who suffer want and are persecuted for their faith. Jesus brings good news to them.

When it comes to an identification of who the rich are (6:24-26), the question is not as easy as Dupont thinks. I am not convinced that the rich are incredulous Israel.[30] Dupont's argument that Luke does not conceive of the recipients of the woes as present is not valid on the redactional level of analysis. If the woes are meant to be injunctions to repentance, is it intrinsically improbable that they be addressed to rich members of Luke's community? The rich members may be tempted to compromise their faith rather than suffer persecution and possible deprivation of property (see Hebr 10:34). They may be afraid to befriend their persecuted fellow Christians.[31]

Thus, it seems that one aspect of the Lukan Sitz im Leben is deprivation occasioned by persecution. This persecution may be seen as a real possibility for all times (see Acts 14:22) or something which the community has recently experienced or is experiencing. Within this Sitz im Leben Luke's purpose is to console the poor of his community. Luke <u>may</u> also be concerned with the rich members of his community whom persecution unmasks as too attached to their possessions. Luke edits the woes to warn them of the life-and-death decision which faces them. This proposed Sitz im Leben adds one factor to the Sitz im Leben suggested for Acts 2:41-47 and 4:31c-35, namely, persecution.

2) Luke 5:11,28. As mentioned above in note 20, I find no evidence in these texts that abandonment of possessions is the prerequisite for following Jesus. Peter and Levi are examples,

in much the same way as Barnabas in Acts 4:36f., and show what some people may do in response to the call to become disciples. At this point of the investigation this contention cannot be proven. We need the additional evidence of Luke 18:18-30, especially 18:28.

3) Luke 9:1-6; 10:1-12; 22:35f. It seems best to treat these three passages together, especially since 22:35f., although addressed to the apostles, refers not to 9:3, but to 10:4. As we have seen above, Theissen stakes a huge claim on his interpretation of 10:4 and 22:35f. Analysis will not allow his claim.

Luke 10:4 points to the total Christian hospitality shown to all traveling brothers and is not advocating an ascetic renunciation of worldly goods. "The disciples are to take nothing along <u>since they can have anything they need from those with whom they stay</u>."[32] Luke 22:35f. refers to a situation of persecution during which the Christian missionaries must finance themselves. Degenhardt is especially insightful on this passage: "Both injunctions, that of 10:4 and that of 22:36 have continued validity during the time of the church, each for a special situation. Luke 10:4 obtains during the peaceful development of the church and 22:36 for a time of persecution."[33]

Thus, these passages are concerned with the theme of poor and rich as it applies to Christian missionaries. The passages are not explicit on how the missionaries are to finance themselves during the times of persecution. Perhaps, the "missionary" Paul is their model.[34] These passages, especially 22:35f., supply additional evidence that the Lukan Sitz im Leben is one in which persecution is operative.

C. Luke 9:51-19-44 - TRAVEL NARRATIVE. After laboring industriously for decades on the Travel Narrative, scholars must admit that it has not given up its secrets.[35] We may be able to eavesdrop on this section as we study its materials on poor and rich. To use Kümmel's terminology, why does Luke have Jesus equip his disciples with so much teaching about poor and rich in this section?[36]

1) Luke 11:41. This passage is Lukan redaction. In it Luke surely underscores the importance of giving alms.[37] Yet such an observation does not do full justice to the verse. I believe that this passage will not yield its full meaning until Lukan scholarship clearly identifies the Lukan "Pharisees." It is obvious that Luke is not talking about the historical Pharisees in this passage which is set within the context of a meal (see 5:27-32; 7:36-50; 14:1-24; 15:1f.; Acts 11:2; 15:5; cf. Lk 16:14). Perhaps Jacob Jervell is on the right track when he observes: "Almsgiving is important for Luke, and only for him among the New Testament writers, as a sign of true adherence to the law (11:41; 12:33; Acts 9:36; 10:2,4,31; 24:17)."[38] <u>Maybe</u> the "Pharisees" represent those people within Luke's community who think they know what God's will is, those who know under what conditions a person should be invited to (full) table fellowship. Almsgiving may be raised to the level of a first principle by which other regulations of the law, like ritual cleanliness, must be judged. Proper participation at a meal is open to those who have given alms to the needy.

2) Luke 12:13-21,33f. Luke 12:13-34 should be interpreted as a unit. By means of the framework Luke gives to the parable of 12:16-20, he interprets it.

Luke is responsible for the barbarous Greek of 12:15; he adds ek tōn hyparchontōn autō to leave no doubt that abundance means abundance of possessions.[39] Dupont makes a viable case that 12:21 must be seen as a Lukan composition based on 12:33.[40] The rich fool is reproached because he did not transform his goods into heavenly capital, i.e., did not distribute them to the poor. Thus, by means of the framework he provides, Luke interprets the parable to mean: possessions are meant to be given in alms to those in need.

The Sitz im Leben behind 12:13-34 must be one where the members of Luke's community do have possessions, can be tempted to avarice, and can be admonished to store up treasure by giving alms. The conduct of the rich fool is to be eschewed like a cobra, for he neglected his obligations to the poor. This material is addressed to the rich within Luke's community who are tempted to believe that true life consists in the abundance of their possessions and who neglect the Christian poor.[41]

3) Luke 14:12-14; 14:25-33. Luke 14:1-24 is the Lukan symposium. At first blush, 14:12-24 seems to be concerned with the theme of God's call, which is addressed to and accepted by the poor and those excluded from cult. Those who were called are rejected.[42] This interpretation is compelling until one reflects seriously on the implications of 14:12-24, especially 14:12-14. For this latter passage to make sense it must mean that there are members in Luke's community who have the wherewithal to host festive meals. Luke 14:12-14 is addressed to them and goes against the common Greco-Roman reciprocity ethic: put your friends in your debt, so that at some future time you can cash in on their IOU's.[43] The affluent "Pharisees" are to invite in the poor and can expect no earthly return for their sharing. These same Pharisees are present for the teaching of the parable of 14:16-24, which does not highlight the divine maker of the guest list, but the excuses people proffer for not responding to the invitation to the banquet. These excuses betray overattachment to worldly concerns and are the typical excuses church people of Luke's time made to avoid conversion.[44] Thus, 14:12-24, especially 14:16-24 does not espouse a miniature theology of salvation history, but contains lessons for the rich and propertied in Luke's community: treat the poor as your friends; don't be seduced into supposing that care lavished on possessions is of greater value than deepened conversion.[45]

This analysis brings us to the doorstep of the awesome 14:33. Our entry into the meaning of 14:33, however, is barred unless we view it in its context. Dupont makes a sound case that 14:25-33 is related to 14:16-24 by means of the common theme of the detachment which is necessary for a lasting response to the call of the kingdom.[46] Luke 14:33 follows upon 14:28-32 and means in that context that Christians must show fidelity to what they have undertaken.[47] Now we are in a favorable position to enter into the interpretation of 14:33. This verse is clearly Lukan composition. Its verbs show that the proper translation should go: all disciples must be ready to renounce their possessions. The context (14:26f.) also suggests the situation behind Luke's redaction of 14:33. It is a persecution situation during which the Christians may have to suffer loss of possessions if they are to complete the walk with Jesus which they have undertaken.

In sum, 14:25-33, especially 14:33, is an important passage for any interpretation of the theme of poor and rich in Luke. As 14:16-24, especially 14:18-20, has already indicated, accepting the call to be a disciple and persevering in that call are not facile or petty matters for the Christian with possessions. Luke 14:25-33 points to the "cross" aspect of that discipleship, particularly in 14:26f. This persecution context is abetted by the two parables of 14:28-32 and issues in the final discipleship admonition of 14:33. The members of the Lukan community who have possessions must be ready to forego them if they stand in the way of their fidelity to Jesus Christ. Thus, Lk 14:12-33 provides further evidence that Luke's community had a somewhat high proportion of fairly prosperous members, who had to be exhorted to remember that the poor Christians were their friends. They also had to be advised that the cost of discipleship had been drastically increased because of persecution. This last point correlates well with the identification of the rich suggested above for 6:24-26.

4) Luke 16:1-31. It seems that the tendency in past scholarship has been to consider the two parables of this chapter in relative isolation from one another and from 16:14-18 or to single out 16:16 as if the rest of the chapter did not exist. I presuppose that ch. 16 forms a unity. My main question is: how is Lk 16:14-18 related to 16:1-13 and 16:19-31? I will fashion my answer by summarizing and criticizing the viewpoints of Dupont[48] and Degenhardt.[49]

(1) Dupont. He makes two major points. First, 16:14 is a Lukan redactional introduction to 16:19-31. Dupont virtually eliminates 16:15-18 from his discussion of the relationship of 16:1-13 to 16:19-31. Secondly, in relating 16:19-31 to 16:14, 9,13, Dupont makes these observations. Luke 16:14 shows the Pharisees' negative reaction to the teaching of 16:1-13 on the use of money. Luke 16:1-13 provides the positive statement on the conduct which evidences repentance/conversion (16:30,31). Luke 16:9 spotlights the conduct of a rich man who is attentive to the teachings of Moses and the prophets and gives alms to the poor. Contrast the rich man in 16:19-31, who should have made Lazarus his friend by giving him alms. Finally, 16:13 shows that the rich man of 16:19-31 needs a radical conversion because he worships mammon.

(2) Degenhardt. Relative to 16:14f., Degenhardt makes the valuable point that there are no Pharisees in Luke's Gentile community. Luke addresses himself to opponents in his church. He warns the greedy not to put their stock in their social position, for all depends on God's estimation of them. The opponents might view riches as evidence of God's favor. The sayings material of 16:14-18 might be continued in 17:1. If this is so, 16:19-31 may make a single point, analogous to that of 16:18, namely, the law (OT) of helping the poor still obtains.

These authors present a courageous, initial scouting report on the relatively unexplored question of how Lk 16:14-18 is related to 16:1-13 and 16:19-31. I would judge that Dupont has made a very plausible case for the connexion between the two parables. Unfortunately, he did not pause long enough to scout 16:15-18 adequately. I would take Degenhardt's sound interpretation of the Pharisees of 16:14 a step further. My scouting suggests that the rich (Pharisees) in Luke's community think that almsgiving is not important, perhaps because these folk maintained that Jesus abrogated the law and the prophets and their teaching about almsgiving. A corollary of their position, attacked in 16:15, is that riches are a sign of God's favor. In combatting them, Luke introduces the <u>pas</u> of 16:16: the kingdom of God is not just for some or the rich. Luke 16:19-31 provides him with additional armament for his combat: the poor who ostensibly are not blessed participate at the heavenly banquet while the favored rich suffer. Luke 16:19-31 also upholds the validity of the teaching about almsgiving contained in Moses and the prophets (see 16:16f.), a teaching which is continued in the preaching about Jesus (= kingdom of God in 16:16) who preached good news to the poor (4:18; 6:20; 7:22).

In summary. If my scouting report bears up under subsequent explorations, then 16:1-31 furnishes additional insights into the Lukan Sitz im Leben. The rich members of Luke's community strive to discern God's will and favor, and appeal to their wealth as a sign of that favor. Needless to say, this element of theological discernment complicates the Lukan Sitz im Leben considerably. It is not just a situation where the greedy rich fail to give alms to the Christian poor. The rich seem to have found theological justification for their self-centeredness. Thus, the Sitz im Leben, suggested by our analyses of Acts 2:41-47 and 4:31c-35 and augmented by subsequent analyses, might be modified further. Luke is not just arguing against rich Christians whose cultural conditioning blinds them to the needs of their brothers and sisters and who have too much to lose in the face of persecution. He may also be arguing against Christians whose cultural conditioning has been reinforced by theological speculations.

5) Luke 18:18-30. In this section it suffices to share and build upon the outstanding insights of S. Légasse.[50] Légasse's major contribution lies in his examinations of Luke's redaction. In 18:24-30 the rich ruler does not depart, but is present for what transpires: the rich ruler presents a moral case, a problem within the community. The attentuated response in 18:27 is rather severe; Luke omits "all things are...." The _ta idia_ of 18:28 is not just a stylistic variation for _panta_ of 18:22. Acts 4:32 must be taken most seriously as its interpretive parallel. "What Luke means here is not so much total dispossession as it is renunciation of that which is one's own for the sake of the ecclesial koinonia...." (104). "To the rich of the church Luke proposes the example of Peter and the apostles.... The apostolic group, which abandoned _ta idia_, along with the mother church of Jerusalem described in Acts, are for Luke types of his own ideal and the mediators of his message" (106).

In 18:18-30 Luke is addressing current problems about rich people in his community. Luke 18:28 refers back to 5:11 (5:28) and ahead to Acts 4:32 and shows one of Luke's major answers to the problems of possessions: voluntary sharing of _ta idia_ for the sake of the poor in the community. Thus, we note again the pivotal importance which Luke ascribes to Acts 2:41-47 and 4:31c-35. The possessors in Luke's community can escape from the chains of their cultural tunnel vision by imitating the examples of the apostles and the primitive Christian community of Acts 2 and 4.[51]

6) Luke 19:1-10. The key to the interpretation of this passage is found in 19:8, Luke's modification of the traditional story.[52] As Grundmann rightly notes, this modification makes the Zacchaeus story a contrast to 18:18-30. But Grundmann does not detail the content of this contrast. This redacted story contrasts to 18:18-30 as it shows that there may not be one dominant answer to the problems of possessions in the Lukan community. Zacchaeus is not required to sell all; nor does he voluntarily give all to the poor. It suffices that he donate half of his possessions to the poor.

The Sitz im Leben behind this passage is the problem of how a rich person should deal with his possessions. Luke answers that it is not necessary for a rich person to sell everything. Thus, the response which Peter and the apostles (18:28-30) gave to Jesus' invitation is not the only one possible. Zacchaeus' response is also a legitimate one. In sum, Luke's Sitz im Leben is one in which there are rich Christians. Their continued adherence to the Lord does not necessitate that they sell all. It does, however, necessitate that they give a genuine sign that they are not so attached to their possessions that they neglect the Christian poor.[53]

CONCLUSION

It is time to assemble the pieces of the puzzle of the theme of poor and rich in Luke to see whether they fit into a clear picture of the Lukan Sitz im Leben. Luke's community clearly had both rich and poor members. Luke is primarily taken up with the rich members, their concerns, and the problems which they pose for the community. Their concerns, as evidenced in 18:18-30 and 19:1-10, revolve around the question: do our possessions prevent us from being genuine Christians? The concerns of the rich are multiplied by the onslaught of sporadic, unofficial persecution (see 6:24-26 and 14:25-33). The rich Christians do not become conscious of their concerns in isolation from the rest of the Christian community. Luke confronts them with the problems which they raise for the Way and for the poor: your cultural conditioning inhibits you from easily helping the poor in the community and thus living up to Christian ideals (Acts 2:41-47 and 4:31c-35). Your view of who your fellow Christians are is unacceptably narrow (Lk 14:10-12). You are still too attached to your possessions (12:13-34 and 14:16-24) as our present persecution situation makes shamefully manifest (6:24-26 and 14:25-33). Riches are not an infallible sign of God's favor; Jesus did not abrogate the teachings of the law and the prophets on almsgiving (16:1-31). Repent before you lose your invitation to the heavenly banquet (14:16-24 and 16:1-31). This proposed Sitz im Leben has its greatest probability as it confirms Cadbury's insight that Luke's theme of poor and rich is principally addressed to possessors within his community. High probability must also be assigned to the element of persecution in Luke's Sitz im Leben. There is strong probability that all possessors in Luke's community had the same concerns. Likewise, it is probable that all possessors caused problems for Luke's community. It is less probable that all possessors were theologically facile in discerning that riches are a sign of God's favor (16:1-31).

In this paper I have suggested a method and have relentlessly pursued the Lukan Sitz im Leben behind the theme of poor and rich. You can well challenge me: Show us the city which is reflected in Luke-Acts! Show us that city's social structures! How did Christianity make inroads among the rich? What Jesus tradition was first preached to them? And I could challenge both you and myself by asking: could it be that the accounts of the non-Jewish converts in Acts are not mere apologetic stageprops, but contain genuine reflections of the fact that these first converts were rich, e.g., Simon Magus, the Ethiopian eunuch, Cornelius, Sergius Paulus? Could it be that Luke has scoured hill and dale to discover more material on poor and rich so that he can better address himself to the nobleman (= rich?) Theophilus' problems? Perhaps Theophilus is not so much concerned with peddlars of spurious Christological traditions as he is with the true meaning of possessions, especially in the teeth of persecution.

Admittedly, there are problems in pursuing the implications

of this paper's thesis. Yet I'm comfortable with these problems because they're the problems of growth in research and do not have veto power over the pursuit itself. Luke's sun does not rise and fall with his theme of poor and rich. Nevertheless, this theme does expose his community in broad daylight. If this paper has attained its goal of spurring us to discuss the Lukan Sitz im Leben with greater frequency and clarity, then it's been a success. Maybe through similar studies and discussions we can reverse the verdict on the Lukan Sitz im Leben from "not much" to "quite a bit."

NOTES

[1]That "not much" is reflected in the "official" scorecard of NT research. Werner G. Kümmel lists the following "purposes" for Luke's Gospel: 1) Luke answers the question of how the church of his time can remain in continuity with the period of Jesus which belongs to the past; 2) Luke is combatting Gnostic and especially Docetic false teaching. He lists eight "goals" for Acts without relating them to the Lukan Sitz im Leben. Introduction to the New Testament. Revised 17th ed. Nashville: Abingdon, 1975, 146f.; 163f. See also Kümmel's "Current Theological Accusations Against Luke," Andover Newton Quarterly 16 (1975) 131-145 (142f.).

[2]The sheer mass of material on poor and rich in Luke-Acts intimates that we can get at least a peek at the Lukan Sitz im Leben by studying this theme. The theme must have been of some importance within Luke's situation for him to have preserved so much material on it. - Space limitations prevent me from treating the other prospects I originally planned to consider: persecution, miracles, and church leaders.

[3]Because of Conzelmann's signal work and our debates with him, we seem to have been almost unconsciously seduced into viewing Luke as a systematic theologian, a first century Paul Tillich or Karl Rahner, who has one master theological matrix, the theology of salvation history. What would happen if we would view Luke as a pastoral theologian who preserves and edits traditions to meet his needs, does so in an orderly literary way, but is not catatonic over "contradictory" traditions and has no overarching theological idea which holds all the traditions together?

[4]E. Earle Ellis puts the matter neatly: "It was not delay qua delay but delay in the face of continuing death under persecution that caused hope to fade and apostasy to rise. 'Sunshine' delay poses no problems." The Gospel of Luke. Rev. ed. New Century Bible; London: Oliphants, 1974, 212.

[5]"The Prologues of Luke-Acts in Their Relation to the Purpose of the Author," Society of Biblical Literature 1975 Seminar Papers, Vol. II. Ed. George MacRae. Missoula: Scholars Press, 1975, 1-14 (6).

[6]Les béatitudes, Tome III: Les évangélistes. EBib; Paris: Gabalda, 1973, 42f.

[7]New Testament Theology: The Proclamation of Jesus. N.Y.: Scribner's, 1971, 109-113 (113). In Jeremias' definition the concept of the poor is swallowed up by the rubric of concern for the outcasts and sinners. Luke lays heavy stress on the Jesus who had table fellowship with toll collectors and sinners. This theme, however, should not be confused with the theme of poor and rich. Similarly, it is important to investigate Luke's picture of Jesus as a miracle worker as a theme in its own right and not neutralize the importance of that study by subsuming Jesus' miracles under the rubric of "care for the poor." Furthermore, the prophets are not the only OT voice on the meaning of "poor." The

various Jewish traditions about the poor are complex. In the OT one can note these four strains of tradition: 1) in pre-monarchic Israel there were clan egalitarianism, redistributional land tenure, and the ideal of a brotherhood where there was no poor person (see Deut 15:4; cf. Acts 4:34); 2) poverty as a scandalous condition. Clan egalitarianism is weakened by the power elite. See Amos 8:4-6. The King, as Yahweh's vicar, should care for the widows, orphans, and other needy; 3) poor person as a symbol for one's attitude towards God; poverty as spiritual childhood or religious ideal of humility. See Isa 66:2; Zeph 3:12; 4) the wisdom literature stresses the dangers of wealth (Sir 31:5), but also states that self-incurred poverty and beggary are hateful to God; riches can be a sign of God's blessing (see Prov 10:4,15; 14:20; Sir 31:1-11). At Qumran the poor person is the humble one who acknowledges his sinfulness and is saved by God's grace. Also at Qumran there was sharing of community goods and almsgiving. Martin Hengel summarizes the position of Rabbinic literature in this wise: "Jewish piety, which took its stamp from the message of the prophets and the social commandments of the Torah, did its utmost to eliminate or at least to alleviate the particularly abrupt contrast between the rich and poor in the Hellenistic Roman period" (Property and Riches in the Early Church. Philadelphia: Fortress, 1974, 19). Hengel also notes on p. 21 that the rabbis continued one facet of the wisdom tradition as they esteemed wealth highly and despised poverty. In apocalyptic literature, e.g., I Enoch 97, there is condemnation of the rich who think that their wealth is a sign of God's favor.

[8]Is Kümmel representative when he writes about the "human, moving features of Jesus"? Introduction, 139. Note also that Kümmel conflates "poor" with sinners and outcasts.

[9]The Making of Luke-Acts. London: SPCK, 1958 = 1927, 262f.

[10]Lukas, Evangelist der Armen: Besitz und Besitzverzicht in den lukanischen Schriften. Stuttgart: Verlag Kath. Bibelwerk, 1965. See also his "Die Liebestätigkeit in den Gemeinden der apostolischen Zeit," Volk Gottes. Festgabe für Josef Höfer. Eds. Remigius Bäumer; Heimo Dolch. Freiburg: Herder, 1967, 243-253.

[11]If one asks Degenhardt why Luke does this, he responds that Luke inherited these radical traditions and had to make contemporary use of them. See Lukas, 41, 214f.

[12]Lukas, 215f.

[13]For minor, additional examples of hedging: in Lk 16:14-31 Luke is arguing against libertine, Gnostic opponents (Lukas, 135 n. 20); in Lk 12:13-21 Luke has rich Christians in mind besides church leaders (Lukas, 80).

[14]Lukas, 221f.

[15]See Dupont, Béatitudes III, 152 n. 3.

[16]See I. Howard Marshall, Luke: Historian and Theologian. Grand Rapids: Zondervan, 1971, 207-209, esp. 207 n. 1.

[17]"Itinerant Radicalism: The Tradition of Jesus Sayings from the Perspective of the Sociology of Literature," Radical Religion 2, Nos. 2-3 (1975) 84-93 (91) = "Wanderradikalismus. Literatursoziologische Aspekte der Überlieferung von Worten Jesu im Urchristentum," ZTK 70 (1973) 245-271.

[18]Béatitudes III, 19-206, esp. 149-203.

[19]"La communauté des biens aux premiers jours de l'Eglise (Actes 2,42.44-45; 4,32.34-35)," Etudes sur les Actes des Apôtres. LD 45; Paris: Cerf, 1967, 503-519.

[20] I do not find persuasive the view of F. Hauck, Die Stellung des Urchristentums zu Arbeit und Geld. Gütersloh, 1921, 96 (as quoted in Degenhardt, Lukas, 210) that there were not many rich people in the community or else there would not be so many Jesus words about the difficulty of the rich entering the kingdom. - Space allows only the briefest comments on a provocative section in Schuyler Brown, Apostasy and Perseverance in the Theology of Luke. AnBib 36; Rome: Pontifical Biblical Institute, 1969, 98-107. Brown argues that in the Age of the Church "the readiness of all Christians to dispose of their property, however small it might be, for the benefit of the community corresponds to the totality of actual renunciation during the Age of Jesus" (101 n. 417). Even granting the validity of the theological significance which Brown places on the two Ages, I do not see how actual renunciation of possessions is a universal or even constant prerequisite for discipleship in the Age of Jesus. As I read Lk 5:11,28, I notice that Peter and Levi voluntarily left all; they were not commanded by Jesus to leave all. One cannot too quickly read 5:11,28 in the light of the troublesome 14:33.

[21] See Eckhard Plümacher, Lukas als hellenistischer Schriftsteller: Studien zur Apostelgeschichte. StUNT 9; Göttingen: Vandenhoeck & Ruprecht, 1972, 16-18 on 2:44f. and 4:32; the most complete parallels are found in Dupont, "Communauté."

[22] Schriftsteller, 18, esp. n. 61.

[23] Literary Patterns, Theological Themes and the Genre of Luke-Acts. SBLMS 20; Missoula: SBL/Scholars Press, 1974, 101f.

[24] In Acts 2:41-47 Luke uses this terminology in 2:44 to interpret his source's koinōnia (2:42); see Dupont, "Communauté," 505-509. In 4:31c-35 he uses the same type of terminology in 4:32bc to interpret his source material in 4:34; see Degenhardt, Lukas, 170-172 and "Liebestätigkeit," 247-249.

[25] This background is supplied by Hendrik Bolkestein, Wohltätigkeit und Armenpflege im vorchristlichen Altertum: Ein Beitrag zur Problem "Moral und Gesellschaft". Utrecht: A. Oosthoek Verlag, 1939 and A. R. Hands, Charity and Social Aid in Greece and Rome. Ithaca: Cornell University Press, 1968. Degenhardt, Lukas, 180f. has a most useful summary of Bolkestein's findings.

[26] In Acts 2 and 4 Luke does not argue against this reciprocity ethic. See below on Lk 14:12-14.

[27] You might grant that my suggested Sitz im Leben for Luke's redaction of Acts 2:41-47 and 4:31c-35 seems plausible enough and may even help to explain the materials in the Gospel. However, you muse, why does Luke spend so little time on this theme in the rest of Acts if it is so key for him? I would contend that Luke does devote space to this theme in Acts, but that it is not his only missionary concern. See the following passages, whose significance is little noticed in the literature, even by Haenchen: 1:18 (Judas); 3:2-10 (Peter and John do not have silver and gold to give as alms); 5:1-11 (an illustration of "the mortal danger present in the attachment to the world effected through possessions and riches" [S. Brown, Apostasy, 107]); 6:1-6 (care for widows); 8:18-25 (simony); 9:36 (the almsgiving of Tabitha); 10:2,4,31 (Cornelius is favored because of his almsgiving); 11:29 (relief sent to the famine-stricken brethren in Judea); 20:28-35, esp. 20:35 (Paul's farewell speech to the Ephesian elders [Degenhardt, Lukas, 174-176, rightly emphasizes this passage for it singles out Paul as a model for church leaders, not least because Paul worked with his hands (see also Acts 18:3) and because "to give" can be interpreted to mean "give alms"]); 24:17 (Paul

brings alms and offerings). The above passages indicate that poor and rich is a theme which is also present in Acts. Space limitations dictate that we can merely allude to these passages here.

[28]I omit 1:5-2:52; 3:10-14; 6:27-36; 8:3 because of space limitations. My surmise is that Lk 1:5-2:52, esp. 1:46-55, has much to say about our thematic. I make this most tentative suggestion: one way of looking at the Magnificat is to see it addressed to the rich Christians in Luke's community who feel that their riches are a sign of God's favor. To these individuals it is said that God's concern is for the lowly like Mary. I immediately concede that tapeinōsis (1:48) and tapeinoi (1:52) do not necessarily have to bear the full weight of my definition of "poor." The tapeinoi need not be materially poor at all.

[29]See also Heinz Schürmann, Das Lukasevangelium, Erster Teil: Kommentar zu Kap. 1,1-9,50. HTKNT III,1; Freiburg: Herder, 1969, 338f.

[30]Schürmann, Lukasevangelium, 338f. sees the woes in a different light: 6:24-26 mirrors opponents who are also attacked in Acts 20:29f.

[31]It is obvious that the identification of the rich suggested for this passage needs confirmation from other Lukan passages. These other passages will at least show that there are rich members in Luke's community.

[32]David L. Dungan, The Sayings of Jesus in the Churches of Paul. Philadelphia: Fortress, 1971, 45; emphasis his.

[33]Lukas, 67f. - We must beware of the temptation to imagine the Lukan community as some monolithic mass. In such a reconstruction of the data, the instructions for peaceful missionary work and beleagured missionary work must be handled by some such hypothesis as Conzelmann's Age of Jesus (peaceful) and Age of the Church (troubled). What happens if our reconstruction envisions a missionary community which experiences both peaceful and beleagured missionary endeavors - as described in Acts! - and has both rich and poor members? We must allow for seeming contradictions to exist side by side without trying to force them into a convenient reconstruction, whose convenience may only reveal our reluctance to cope with such apparent contradictions and our desire to put everything into pidgeonholes where there may be great order, but no life.

[34]See Acts 20:33-35 and Dungan, Sayings, 72-74.

[35]See Kümmel, Introduction, 141f.

[36]I cannot treat 11:13; see Wilhelm Ott, Gebet und Heil: Die Deutung der Gebetsparänese in der lukanischen Theologie. StANT 12; München: Kösel-Verlag, 1965, 108,111. I also omit 11:21f.; see S. Légasse, "L' 'Homme fort' de Lc 11,21-22," NovT 5 (1962) 5-9.

[37]See Degenhardt, Lukas, 59.

[38]Luke and the people of God: A New Look at Luke-Acts. Minneapolis: Augsburg, 1972, 140.

[39]Degenhardt, Lukas, 73f.

[40]Béatitudes III, 184f., based on the argumentation of 115-117.

[41]See Degenhardt, Lukas, 80.

[42]See J. A. Sanders, "The Ethic of Election in Luke's Great Banquet Parable," Essays in Old Testament Ethics (J. Philip Hyatt, In Memoriam). Eds. James L. Crenshaw; John T. Willis. N.Y.: Ktav, 1974, 245-271.

[43]See W. C. van Unnik, "Die Motivierung der Feindesliebe in Lukas VI 32-35," *NovT* 8 (1966) 284-300 (293f.); cf. above on Acts 2:41-47 and 4:31c-35.

[44]See Jacques Dupont, *Les béatitudes, Tome II: La bonne nouvelle*. EBib; Paris: Gabalda, 1969, 262-272.

[45]I do not have space to show how "wive" of 14:20 (see 14:26; 18:29) accords with the interpretation suggested here. See A. Stöger, "Armut und Ehelosigkeit - Besitz und Ehe der Jünger nach dem Lukasevangelium," *Geist und Leben* 40 (1967) 43-59, known to me only through *NTA* 12.197.

[46]Dupont, *Béatitudes* II, 262-272.

[47]In this and what follows I am dependent on Dupont, "Renoncer à tous ses biens (Luc 14,33)," *NRT* 93 (1971) 561-582.

[48]Dupont, *Béatitudes* III, 162-182.

[49]Degenhardt, *Lukas*, 113-135.

[50]*L'appel du riche (Marc 10,17-31 et paralleles): Contribution a l'étude des fondements scriptuaires de l'état religieux*. VS, collection annexe 1; Paris: Beauchesne, 1966, 97-110.

[51]It is not sufficiently clear to me that Luke is also attacking a view which regarded wealth as a sure sign of God's favor. He inherited "Who can be saved?" (18:26) from Mark. Of course, the new context which Luke provides for this eye-popping question clearly shows that he disagrees with its implications.

[52]See Walter Grundmann, *Das Evangelium nach Lukas*. THKNT III; 7. Auflage. Berlin: Evangelische Verlagsanstalt, 1974, 358-360.

[53]This analysis concludes our study of the Gospel passages on poor and rich. Space does not permit a study of 21:1-4.

S 179

THE DISCOURSE STRUCTURE OF THE FLOOD NARRATIVE

Robert E. Longacre
University of Texas at Arlington

The purpose of this paper is to approach the Biblical flood narrative from a standpoint of its discourse structure, as the latter is currently being studied in contemporary linguistics.[1] The author's credentials are those of a linguist rather than the Semitist--although he has a passing acquaintance with the Hebrew text.

The general goals and methodology of discourse analysis as here applied have been stated elsewhere (Longacre and Levinsohn, in press; Longacre, 1976; Grimes, 1976). To summarize here briefly, however: contemporary discourse analysis is interested in questions of genre classification, e.g., the matter of distinguishing a narrative discourse from other sorts of discourses such as procedural, behavioral, expository, and the further matter of distinguishing types within the same genre; the articulation of parts of a discourse such as formulaic beginnings and endings, episodes, and high points in the story (called peaks); the status of discourse constituents such as sentences, paragraphs, and embedded discourses; the cast of participants in a given discourse, and the thematic participant(s) of a given paragraph; author viewpoint and author sympathy as indicated in the text; the main line development of a discourse as opposed to subsidiary and supportive materials; the role of tense, aspect, particles, affixes, pronominalization chains, paraphrase, and conjunctions in providing cohesion and prominence in a discourse; ways of marking peak in a narrative; and the function of dialogue in discourse. In accordance with the charting technique described in Longacre and Levinsohn, and adapted to Hebrew, the Hebrew text of the flood story has been plotted out word for word in a multicolumnar arrangement. This charting facilitates separation of main line from subsidiary developments and tracking of participants through a discourse.

Discourse analysis of this sort may well revolutionize the contemporary scene in linguistics. It is being increasingly realized that the study of isolated sentences out of context is scarcely worth being called the study of language. Many facets of language from verb and noun morphology on up remain opaque to analysis when isolated sentences are analyzed. Discourse analysis of this sort is being applied extensively to the study of many aboriginal languages throughout the world. The author of this paper has recently been involved in such a discourse oriented research project[2] which embraced some thirty languages of Colombia, Ecuador, and Panama. The purpose of this paper is, as we have said, to bring these analytical tools to bear on the story as it occurs in the Bible.

1. A major problem in beginning the analysis of the flood narrative is the delineation of this narrative from the surrounding context. The flood story is part of the continuous ongoing narrative of Genesis, and as such, of course, has certain characteristics of embedded narrative--characteristics which betray that it belongs to something larger. As to the main peak of the flood story, there can be no doubt that in 7:17-24 we're in the very heart of the narrative itself. Somewhat more difficult to decide, however, is the precise place

that the flood story begins and ends. Take the problem of the beginning. The birth of Noah himself is given in Gen. 5:28-32, which seems very definitely not to be a part of the flood story proper. Gen. 6:1-4 recounts an incident (the sons of God going into the daughters of men) which likewise does not seem to be part of the flood story proper; but which may, on the other hand, pattern as the inciting incident which leads to God's decision to bring the flood. Gen. 6:1-4 is followed, however, by a section 6:5-8 (God's decision to destroy humanity) which apparently brings us up to the very onset of the flood story, with reintroduction of Noah as a main participant in verse 8.

We're confronted in 6:9 with the phrase 'These are the generations, toldot[3], of Noah'. Can this be taken to be the aperture of the flood story proper? First of all, the idea should be entertained that the phrase, 'These are the toldot of X' introduces a significant section in Genesis. Regarding a toldot section, it should be observed that (1) the participant for whom this section is named has been born and introduced prior to the beginning of the section itself; (2) much of the action may be by the descendant or descendants of the person for whom a section is named--so that the toldot of Isaac is actually concerned with the doings of Jacob and the toldot of Jacob is largely concerned with the story of Joseph; (3) the toldot section concludes with the death of the person for whom the section is named. By these standards then, the toldot section referring to Noah ends with verse 9:29, the death of Noah, and includes the post-flood incident of Noah's drunkenness and the cursing of Canaan, son of Ham. It is clear, therefore, the toldot of Noah includes more than the flood story itself. Nevertheless, the beginning of the toldot of Noah may well coincide with the beginning of the flood narrative proper. A difficulty here, however, is that Gen. 6:5-9 seems to belong to the flood story proper, but precedes the toldot title.

I propose for the present the following: Let Gen. 6:1-4 (the sons of God going into the daughters of men) be considered to be an incident preposed to the flood story proper. In the same way let Gen. 9:18-29 (the story of Noah's drunkenness and and cursing of Canaan, son of Ham) be considered to be a post-posed incident. Let Gen. 6:5-8 be considered to be a preview of the whole story--much like scenes flashed on the cinema screen (scenes which anticipate the substance of a story) while the names of the actors, directors, costume designers, composers, etc. are being presented. I will take the flood story proper as beginning with 6:9a: 'These are the toldot of Noah'. I will take verses 6:9b-12, which have to do with Noah and world conditions, as a stage of the entire story. The story will be considered to end with 9:1-17 which is God's discourse to Noah after the flood.

Having somewhat arbitrarily bounded the story from its surrounding context, I now proceed to distinguish the parts of the narrative according to their formal or surface features and their notional or deep structure characteristics.[4] The aperture, the toldot sentence of 6:9a is distinguished from the stage by the obvious title-like characteristics of the former and the rather striking juxtaposition of the proper name, Noah, in the Hebrew text: 'Now these are the generations of Noah. Noah was a righteous man,...'. In this section, as has been said, Noah and world conditions are described: Noah--righteous; world conditions--bad. Section 6:13-22 is an episode which deals with

God commanding Noah to build the ark, i.e., instructions as to the nature of the craft and Noah's acceptance of the command. I call this episode P-3--in which P stands for the peak of the story and -3 stands for the third episode preceding the peak. In 7:1-10 we have a section in which Noah is commanded to enter the ark and responds by entering. This I label episode P-2. In 7:11-16 we are given a description of the beginning of the flood. This reiterates the information that Noah, his family, and the animals go into the ark and is episode P-1. In 7:17-24 the flood grows in violence and prevails; we reach here a heighth of dramatic tension. There are very unusual surface structure features of paraphrase and repetition. Section 8:1-5, which has to do with the receding of the waters, I call P+1--i.e., the first episode following the peak. Section 8:6-12, which has to do with Noah sending out the birds, I call episode P+2. Section 8:13-19, which treats of Noah's leaving the ark, is episode P+3. Section 8:20-22 is episode P+4, i.e., Noah's offering sacrifice along with God's acceptance and response. Section 9:1-17 is P+5 i.e., God's blessing, the covenant, and the covenant sign. All this is summarized in Diagram I, which gives a general profile of the flood story, along with some further information as to how the sections are articulated (at top of page) and indications of thematic participants (at bottom of page).

While I propose in the balance of this paper to go through these sections in detail, it is useful to note here a few of the broad characteristics of the story. To begin with, we can expect different parts of the story to differ stylistically; they should. We should not expect the style at the peak of the narrative to resemble that of the more routine narration in other parts of the story. Nor should we expect the long quotes in which God is speaking to have the same style or syntax as the narrative portions. Nor should we expect background information of various sorts to sound like backbone narration. We can expect to find tenses and aspects used carefully and differently in the separate parts of the story.

As far as the slate of main participants for the discourse, apparently they are: God, Noah, the flood (variously referred to as the flood, the waters, etc.), and the ark. God is the central participant in that we are told His feelings and no one else's, not even Noah's. We are also told God's inner thoughts (but we are not told the thoughts and purposes of Noah although his actions are reported). In rank Noah is the next most important participant. Much of the story turns on Noah versus the flood waters. The flood, although inanimate, must be construed as a major participant. That the ark is a major participant is evident from its general importance throughout the story and its special prominence in Ep P-3 and in peak. Noah's wife, his sons, and his sons' wives are mentioned at several places, but nowhere assume an active role in the story. The animals, which are brought into the ark are minor participants. They, like Noah's family, are passively mentioned at most points in the story, except where the raven and the dove assume importance in Ep P+2. Various other entities are mentioned in the course of the story such as the parts of the ark, the fountains of the great deep, the windows of heaven, the rain, the earth, Noah's altar, the clouds, and the rainbow. Although these are minor participants (even props), on occasion certain of them (i.e., the animals and the earth) become thematic participants of a given paragraph or subparagraph. Some of the above are also associated with major participants,

Surface features	Profile	Content
ends with quote And God said to Noah " " " " " " " " " "	Ep(P+5) WRAP-UP	God's discourse to Noah: blessing, covenant & covenant sign 9:1-17
Noah → יהוה יהוה → Noah weak onset, but a distinct section	Ep(P+4)	יהוה receives sacrifice יהוה is thematic 8:20-22
ויהי and long setting (double dating)	Ep(P+3)	Leaving the ark 8:13-19
ויהי and date	Ep(P+2) DÉ. LOOSENING	Noah sends birds (assumes active role) 8:6-12
terminus (date) And God remembered Noah	Ep(P+1)	Receding waters 8:1-5
terminus	PEAK CLIMAX	The Flood prevails. Remorseless mechanism of judgment. God not mentioned Noah mentioned only at the end 7:17-24
יהוה shuts the door	Ep(P-1) RISING TENSION	Flood begins. Ends with a thematic יהוה verse 7:11-16
long date יהוה said Noah did	Ep(P-2)	Noah enters ark. יהוה thematic in first part 7:1-10
God said Noah did And God said to Noah	Ep(P-3)	The ark 6:13-22
toldot (may go with whole unit-- 9:20)	Aperture STAGE	Noah and world conditions 6:9-12
(character introduced before his toldot) dominance of יהוה as thematic participant	Preview	יהוה as thematic 6:5-8
run-down of previous paragraph		

DIAGRAM I: General Profile of the Flood Narrative (Gen. 6:5-9:17) e.g., the 'fountains of the great deep', the 'windows of heaven', and the 'rain' are associated closely with the 'flood' and the rising 'waters'--which indicate a major participant. The rainbow is closely associated with the covenant. The parts of the ark are, of course, closely associated with the ark itself.

The backbone of this narrative is carried here as in Hebrew prose narrative in general by waw plus prefixal verb--which is increasingly recognized as a special narrative tense for Hebrew. One of the special characteristics of this construction is that it does not tolerate any preposed element, not even the word lō 'not'. Any clause that has a preposed noun or the word 'not' must, perforce, be other than waw plus prefixal verb. The usual recourse in such circumstances is to the suffixal verb, but we may also have nominal clauses without any verb at all, or clauses with a medial verb hayah 'to be', or clauses with a participle serving as verb. All such clauses (including those with suffixal verbs) are CIRCUMSTANTIAL CLAUSES which add detail and background to the event line itself, but must be distinguished from the event line. Very commonly such clauses serve to introduce paragraphs, but they frequently occur paragraph medial as well.[5]

The status of negated verbs which sometimes appear to be on the event line (but which cannot employ waw plus prefixal verb) is somewhat problematical. Very often, as Grimes (1976) has observed for language in general, events which do not happen are not on the main line of discourses. It might, therefore, be argued that all such lō verbs are per se off the event line. However, this is simply a statistical generalization for language. There undoubtedly are discourses in almost all languages where negated events are a part of the very event line itself, i.e., it is important to the structure of a story that something did not happen. So we leave for a while this question unresolved. Maybe it will have to be resolved in each particular occurrence in the Hebrew narrative by resort to the structure of the narrative itself and semantic criteria.

The peculiar way in which Hebrew carries the main line of a story, viz. by clauses beginning with waw plus prefixal verbs, may possibly shed some light on a further feature of the present narrative (and Hebrew narrative prose in general), i.e., the frequent repetitive reference to the same event. Thus, e.g., the story contains several similar but differing lists of animals entering the ark, and tells us both in 7:6-9 and in 7:13-15 that Noah and the animals entered the ark. But that Hebrew uses such devices of recapitulation should not surprise us. Narrative structure in all languages demands some sort of recapitulation of old information while layering on new information--otherwise the pace at which the story proceeds will likely cause the listener/reader to loose the thread of the story. But --and this may prove important--the commonest and most standard method of recapitulation cannot be used in Hebrew along with the main line of the story. To illustrate: (1) in many languages a story proceeds by some such device as the following: "He did A. Having A'd, he B'd. Having B'd, he C'd. Finally, he D'd". Here A, B, C, and D represent main line activities in a story and the "having X'd" construction is a back-reference, initial in these sentences. This is a cohesive device of great importance and easy to document in European languages, Philippine languages, Mesoamerican, Papua-New Guinea, and South America--to name only areas where I have directly observed this device in action. But (2) Biblical Hebrew can not do this, since Biblical Hebrew uses a string of waw plus prefixal tenses to carry the main line of a story. The addition of any such sentence initial back-reference can not occur since it would make it impossible to use the very construction that carries the main line. Is it to be wondered, then, that the Hebrew style has features of recapitulation that are somewhat foreign to European literature?[6]

Of some importance is taking note of the Hebrew devices for establishing the thematic participant or participants of a given paragraph. Just as a story has a cast of participants, so a paragraph has its dominating participant(s). The difference between a paragraph and a discourse is that while the latter has a slate of major participants, a paragraph is usually dominated by one or at the most two participants, with other participants pushed off to the side. Hebrew does this in the text of the discourse under consideration by introducing the thematic participant(s) early in a paragraph (usually in the first or second sentence), repeating him a time or two, and (especially if he is not mentioned in intervening sentences of the paragraph) mentioning him afresh at the end of the paragraph. It is also the usual thing that the thematic participant becomes the subject of at least one clause on the main event line whether in the waw plus prefixal verbs of narrative, or the imperative or waw plus suffixal verbs of predictive/prescriptive discourse. The only exception in our present corpus to the rule that the thematic participant needs to be the subject of at least one main event line verb is in the set of instructions for making the ark (Ep P-3). Here, as we shall see in the examination of that section, the frequency of mention of the ark is such that it seems that we must consider the ark to be the thematic participant at this point. Also, there are other sections of the story where the ark is subject of main event line verbs. (For a set of rules for finding the thematic participant in Hebrew, see the appendix.)

In the detailed examination which follows, a number of features are considered: (1) establishment of thematic participants in paragraphs; (2) features that articulate paragraphs, especially those that open and close such units; (3) features of the internal structure of paragraphs (especially embedded paragraphs) and their component sentences; (4) main line development versus supportive, elaborative, and background material; and (5) special features which contrast the peak with more routine narration. The discussion will be largely inductive, i.e., I will first note features and then attempt to draw conclusions from them. As a whole, the discussion will proceed verse by verse much as in a commentary.

2. Preview of the story (Gen. 6:5-8).

This paragraph begins abruptly with a waw plus prefixal verb, 'And God saw...'. It is clear that this is a new paragraph largely because of the marked run down effect of the previous paragraph which ends in a quotation plus a few remarks that are almost parenthetical and are at least very clearly background in character. The thematic participant of this paragraph is Yhwh who is mentioned explicitly four times and is referred to in pronominal form once, plus three times as 'I' in the contained quotation of the paragraph. He is subject of all the main event line verbs: 'saw', 'was sorry', 'was pained in

His heart', 'said'. The final verb 'said' is quote formula for a quotation in which Yhwh speaks of His intention of wiping out man with other life from the earth. In the last sentence of this paragraph (6:8) Noah is abruptly introduced as one who found favor in the eyes of Yhwh. In that Noah is mentioned only once, he is clearly not the thematic participant of this paragraph. This is seen also by his late introduction in the ultimate sentence. Here the force of the waw is probably antithetical; Noah found favor in the eyes of Yhwh as contrasted with Yhwh's negative evaluation of everyone else.

3. Aperture and stage (Gen. 6:9-12).

Here, as we have observed, occurs a phrase, 'These are the generations of Noah' that probably serves to signal the onset of the flood story proper, but which also undoubtedly has reference to a larger stretch which ends at the end of chapter 9 with the death of Noah.

As we have also observed, the startling juxtaposition of the second occurrence of Noah, at the center of verse 9, signals the onset of the stage. Noah is described in three circumstantial clauses as 'a righteous man', 'perfect in his generation', and one who 'walked with God'. Noah occurs in the first and third of the circumstantial clauses and is referred to by pronoun in the center clause. Next follows a (waw plus prefixal verb on the event line with Noah as subject). 'And Noah begat three sons, Shem, Ham, and Japheth'. Noah, then is clearly established as thematic participant in this half of the paragraph. In the second half of the paragraph, there is a new thematic participant, 'the earth'. There are no special transition features between the former sentence and this one in 6:11. It, therefore, seems that we very probably have here but one surface structure, namely, a compound paragraph, the first half of which has a thematic participant, 'Noah', and the second half of which has a thematic participant, 'the earth': i.e., this paragraph treats of Noah and world conditions in his day.

In regard to establishing the thematic participant of verse verses 6:11, 12 note that the 'earth' is subject of two of the main event line verbs: 'And the earth was corrupted. And the earth was filled with violence.' While God is subject of the last main event line verb ('looked'), the 'earth' is mentioned twice in that sentence: 'And God looked out on the earth and behold it was corrupt, for all flesh had corrupted its way upon the earth'.

God apparently is not a thematic participant in either part of this paragraph. He comes in first in the third circumstantial clause of 6:9, 'Noah walked with God'. He is also mentioned in 6:11a, 'All the earth was corrupted before God'. While He becomes subject of a main event line verb in 6:12, God does not seem to be as prominent here as either Noah or the earth. If God is to be in any sense considered thematic, He would be secondarily thematic (in the paragraph as a whole).

4. Episode P-3 (Gen. 6:13-22).

The outer framework of this paragraph is what has been called for many languages in various parts of the world, an EXECUTION PARAGRAPH, i.e., a command (suggestion, etc.) is given and the command is followed out. Thus, we have in verse 6:13,

'And God said to Noah' while in 6:22 we find, 'And Noah did according to all that God had commanded him'. Verses 6:13-21 contain the substance of God's instructions to Noah.

The substance of the quote breaks apart into two paragraphs. The whole is probably a discourse with two points. Point one has to do with instructions for building the ark, and point two (from verse 17 on) has to do with what Noah is to do when the ark is built. The ark is thematic in the first of these paragraphs and Noah is thematic in the second.

The part of the quote found in 6:13 consists of two circumstantial clauses which serve as setting for the first constituent paragraph and probably constitute one sentence: 'The end of all flesh is coming before me, and lo, I am destroying them with the earth'. Notice the typical chiasmic structure here with 'before me' and the end of the first clause and 'lo I' at the onset of the next clause. Verse 6:14 contains a (main line) imperative: 'Make for yourself an ark of gopher wood'. No more imperatives are found in this paragraph. From here on the paragraph consists of elaborative material, i.e., prefixal verbs with preposed nouns. To be true, one waw plus suffixal verb occurs at 6:14b but it seems to be dependent on the previous verb with which it forms a unit. It appears, then, that the backbone command of the paragraph is in 14, which is in some sense the text of the entire paragraph; and that all of the remaining verbs of the paragraph express details as to carrying out of that main command.

The ark as thematic participant is first mentioned in 14a, 'Make you an ark of gopher wood', and is repeated in the next clause which is an elaboration of the first, 'Rooms shalt thou make in the ark', Reference to the ark is continued in the following waw plus suffixal tense which constitutes a continuation of the same sentence: 'and thou shalt pitch it within and without with pitch'. The details of making the ark continue with 6:15, 'And this is how you shall make it', with the ark referred to here (as in 6:14b) as a suffix on the sign of the accusative, i.e., 'otah. Verse 6:15 ends with three circumstantial clauses which evidently are conjoined into one sentence. In this unit, 'ark' occurs in the first clause and pronouns referring to the ark occur at the end of the next two clauses: 'Three hundred cubits (shall be) the length of the ark; fifty (shall be) its width; and thirty cubits (shall be) its height'.[7] The ark is referred to again in 6:16 where Noah is told to make a 'window' in the ark, and in 6:16b where he is told, 'The door of the ark thou shalt put in its side' (where the ark is referred to both by noun and by pronoun on the word 'side'). Finally, the ark is referred to still once more at the end of 6:16 as 'First, second, and third decks shalt thou make it'. It appears, therefore, that the ark here is very definitely the thematic participant by virtue of the continued running reference to it all through the passage--even though it becomes the subject of no verb at any point. As mentioned, however, we shall see below that it does become the subject of verbs in a subsequent part of the story and, in fact, at the very peak of the story itself.

The second paragraph of this quoted discourse begins with a circumstantial clause which is in some ways reminiscent of the setting of the previous paragraph (Gen. 6:13). Where verse 6:13 has, 'And behold I am destroying the earth', in 17 we find, 'And

I, lo I, am bringing a flood of waters upon the earth to destroy it...'. Here we find for the first time overt identification of the 'flood' (hammabbūl) by name. The verse continues with a purpose clause, 'To destroy all flesh which has in it the breath of life from under heaven' and adds on a second clause, 'all which is in the earth shall die'. (Here again we see chiastic arrangement within a sentence.)

Before going on to describe the body of the paragraph which is so introduced, it's important to note that in both the circumstantial clause of 6:13 and of 6:17, although God is mentioned very emphatically and although in 17 the flood is mentioned, neither are thematic participants of their paragraphs in that these participants are mentioned in only the setting of each paragraph and are not found further on in the same paragraph. There is, to be true, in 6:18 a waw plus suffixal verb which looks like the main line of the paragraph. It has as its subject 'I' which, of course, is God. This, however, is the last reference to God within the quoted discourse. There is no further such reference until 6:22 where we revert to the framework of the execution paragraph and are out of the quoted material within it. Furthermore, the force of the waw in 6:18 could conceivably be antithetical, i.e., 'but I will establish my covenant with you' as contrasted with God's purposes to destroy the rest of mankind. Thus, it may be that 6:18 links in some way more to the setting than to the body of the paragraph.

We have in 6:18b, however, another waw plus suffixal verb which certainly is on the main line of its paragraph, 'And you shall enter into the ark, you and your sons and your wife and the wives of your sons with you'. The use of the resumptive pronoun 'with you' at the end of the verb is extremely interesting. It is, of course, unnecessary. It probably serves here, however, to help establish the second person 'you' as thematic participant of this paragraph. In the balance of the paragraph a variety of devices serve to continue the second person orientation. (1) In 6:19 where Noah is told to take all the animals with him into the ark, the verb is prefixed for second person, 'You shall take' and the purpose clause also adds something very similar to a resumptive pronoun ('ittak 'with you') at the end, 'To preserve alive with you'. Again we may question whether there would be any real purpose for having 'ittak 'with you' at the end except to further help establish Noah as the thematic participant of the paragraph. (2) In 6:20 the animals are recapitulated in a similar but in some ways differing list as object (as they were in the previous verse) and again there is a second person reference 'They shall come to you to preserve life'. (3) In 6:21a, in place of a simple imperative 'take' we find that there are two devices used to continue the second person orientation. First of all, the verse begins with an emphatic pronoun w'attah 'and as for you'. This is followed by kaḥ lka... 'take for you...' where we find the indirect object pronoun lka 'for you' in the clause 'take for you from all food which is (to be) eaten' and so forth. (4) In 21b 'and you shall gather (it) to you' we find a second person suffix on a waw plus suffixal verb followed by 'eleka 'to you'. (5) And, finally, in 21c lka 'to you' occurs once more in 'and it shall be to you and to them for food'. It appears that the many references to the second person singular, the fact that it is the subject of waw plus suffixal verbs (main line in predictive discourse); the fact that in several cases resumptive pronouns are used which are otherwise unmotivated; and finally, the fact that the emphatic pronoun, 'as for you' occurs as sentence topic in 6:21 --all these features abundantly establish the second person singular 'you' (i.e., Noah) as thematic participant of this paragraph.

It is of some interest here that the ark is mentioned twice in the paragraph, 'Go thou into the ark' in 6:18 and, 'Cause to go various animals into the ark' in 6:19. The ark is not mentioned any further in this paragraph and does not establish itself as a thematic participant.

Finally, as noted above, in 6:22 we revert to the main framework of the paragraph, 'And Noah did according to all which God commanded him, thus he did'--which corresponds to 6:13a, 'And God said to Noah'. Note also here in 6:22 the fine chiastic structure of this sentence involving repetition of the verb 'do'.

5. Episode P-2 (Gen. 7:1-10).

The general framework of this paragraph is in 7:1 'Yhwh said to Noah "Enter the ark"', and 7:5 'And Noah did as Yhwh had commanded him'. This paragraph has an execution structure, i.e., 'A said something to B and B did it'. The balance of the paragraph (7:6-10) is an embedded subparagraph which further elaborates what Noah did as, 'And Noah went into the ark' (7:6), etc. This subparagraph has its own setting, its own conclusion, and its own thematic participants distinct from the paragraph in which it is found embedded. I first take up below the main paragraph and consider subsequently the embedded paragraph which elaborates the main one.

It is first of all necessary to establish the thematic participant(s) of the quote which is found within the first four verses. Here we find first person references (corresponding to Yhwh in the quote formula) to be somewhat prominent but there is also considerable use of the second person (corresponding to Noah in the quote formula) as well. The passage begins with an imperative, 'Go thou and thy house into the ark' (in which second person is prominent); continues with 'For you have I found to be righteous before me' (with first and second person referents) and continues with a second imperative, 'From all clean animals take for you (lka)...'. Verse 7:4 contains only first person referents. It begins, 'For in yet seven days I...' (with an emphatic topic pronoun, 'anokī) and continues 'am causing it to rain on the earth' (with participle as verb). This circumstantial clause is followed by a main line waw plus suffixed verb, 'I am going to wipe out every living thing from off the face of the earth which I have made'. In the latter there are two first person references.

What can we say as to the relevant dominance of first person versus second person in this verse, and whom can we pick out as thematic participant? A look at how the person references fit into the general framework of the paragraph is not too helpful. The second persons are found associated with the imperative and the first person forms are associated with the reasons for the imperative. Noah is told to enter the ark because God has found him righteous before Him in that generation and the command to enter the ark is further elaborated with the accompanying corollary command 'take with you various animals'. Then the whole first part of the paragraph has a further reason attached to it. It is introduced by a sentence containing a circumstantial clause and a main clause, 'For yet seven days I am causing it to rain on the earth...and I will wipe out...'. Looking at this complex picture, it seems to me probable that both God and second person you (Noah) are meant to be thematic participants in this paragraph. As thematic participant, God here is referred to as Yhwh, as He is back in the preview paragraph (6:5-8), where He is also thematic participant. This thematic prominence of deity carries over into the outer framework of the paragraph as well and correlates with the use of Yhwh in 7:1 and 7:5.

This situation forms a clear contrast to the subparagraph embedded at the end--which elaborates 'Noah did as Yhwh had commanded him' by explaining that this meant Noah's entering the ark. In the subparagraph, however, it appears that Noah and the flood are thematic participants. Two circumstantial clauses constitute 7:6, 'And Noah was a son of 600 years and the flood was upon the earth'. It appears that the first clause modifies the second clause, i.e., the first is circumstantial to the second and then that entire unit is circumstantial to verse 7: '(All this being so) and went in Noah and his sons into the ark and his wife and his sons' wives with him'. Notice again the resumptive pronoun at the end of verse 7. But verse 7 adds an additional phrase 'from the face of the flood'. Note, in both verse 6 and 7 the balanced emphasis on both Noah and the flood. The passage likewise ends with final references to both Noah and the flood. Thus, after verse 8, where there is an elaborate listing of all the forms of life which went into the ark, we are told in verse 9, 'They came to Noah to the ark, male and female, as God had commanded Noah'. Verse 10 ends with a final reference to the flood, 'And it came to pass in seven days that the waters of the flood were on the earth'. It appears then that not only Noah, but also the flood waters themselves are thematic. God, however, is not thematic in this subparagraph as He was thematic in the above paragraph. As non-thematic He is referred to in the only reference to Him as Elohīm (verse 10).

How does this episode move the story forward? To begin with, we must admit that the story moves forward slowly. Nevertheless, there is progress here. While God had previously expressed to Noah His desire that Noah, his family, and the animals take refuge in the ark which they were to build, now it is assumed that the ark is finished (presumably after some lapse of time). Noah and his family are now commanded to go into it. Again Noah is commanded to take animals into the ark but the instructions are amplified with the added detail that for clean animals and clean birds seven pairs were to be taken. To the original avowals of intent to destroy mankind and life in general (Gen. 6:7, 13, and 17, with first mention of a flood in the latter) is now added the more concrete and detailed prediction (7:4) that in seven days God is going to cause it to rain for forty days and nights. In the embedded subparagraph (7:6-10) Noah's entry into the ark is recorded, along with the entry of his family, and of the animals. As we have seen, this section is an elaboration of 'And Noah did as Yhwh had commanded him' (7:5).

6. Episode P-1 (Gen. 7:11-16).

This episode is just prior to the peak of the discourse and as such, contains some dramatic and some transitional features.

The new information which advances the story forward is mainly in 7:11-12 and 7:16, i.e., the causes of the flood (how the catastrophe was initiated) and God's shutting Noah in the ark. In between lies a recapitulative reference to entering the ark.

In general structure, the paragraph appears to have three main line verbs, 'And (there) was', 'And went in', 'And shut'. We can be initially suspicious of wayyhī 'And there was'/'it came to pass' as a main line verb. Very often it is in some sense introductory. It may, however, need to be construed as a main line verb here, because it seems to me to be the completion of the preceding suffixal verbs which occur in circumstantial clauses.[8] The first part of this paragraph (7:11-12) is simultaneous with what is reported in a suffixal verb in the second part of the paragraph, 'And that very day Noah went in' (7:13-14). There then follows in verse 14 a long reference (again) to the forms of life which went in to the ark, followed in 7:15 by waw with a prefixal verb (main line) which tells us that they all came to Noah to the ark two-by-two from all forms of life. This is, in turn, followed by further circumstantial elements, one of which is participial, 'And those going into the ark (were) male and female from all flesh'; and one of which has a suffixal verb, 'They went in as God had commanded him'. It is of some interest here that the coming of the animals to Noah is here for the first time featured on the main line of the narrative (7:15) while Noah's entry (already reported by means of a main line verb in 7:7) is here demoted to a circumstantial clause in 7:13.

So far the paragraph has simply reported two simultaneous actions: On the day that the natural events took place which resulted in the catastrophe, on that very day Noah and the animals went into the ark. Then very suddenly all this is followed by one short staccato verse, 'And Yhwh shut him in'. It appears that the entire structure of the paragraph is a sequence paragraph whose first event is an embedded simultaneous paragraph reporting the two events, the cosmic catastrophe and Noah's entering the ark, and whose final event is Yhwh's shutting them in.

In the embedded simultaneous paragraph undoubtedly Noah is indicated as thematic. The paragraph begins impressively with a long date, 'In the 600th year, the year of the life of Noah, in the second month, on the 17th day of the month, on that very day'. Note, moreover, the reference to Noah in this complex dating. In verse 13 Noah is referred to three times by name and once by pronoun, 'On that very day went in Noah and Shem, Ham, and Japheth, the sons of Noah, and the wife of Noah, and the three wives of his sons with them into the ark'. After the lengthy reference to the animals in 7:14, we are told in 7:15, 'And they came to Noah to the ark'. Noah is referred to by pronoun in 16, 'As God had commanded him'.

The first part of the paragraph, however, may indicate that a second thematic participant could be the events associated with initiating the flood; i.e., 'The fountains of the great deep were broken up' in 7:11a, and 'The windows of heaven were opened' in 7:11b, followed in 7:12 by, 'And there was rain on the earth for 40 days'. Nevertheless, while these look like indications of a thematic participant and may be so within the narrow confines of the verses indicated, they are not referred to again in the balance of the paragraph. Rather they constitute a complex of events which are pictured as contemporaneous with Noah's entering the ark. And, as we have seen, the long date at the start of 7:11 mentions Noah explicitly by name so that even the natural events are related to him chronologically.

As to the other participants, notice that the ark is referred to twice in 7:13 and in 7:15, but simply in the context that Noah went into the ark and the animals came to Noah to the ark. These two occurrences do not seem to be sufficient to qualify the ark as thematic participant. A somewhat better case can be made out that in the second paragraph possibly the animals are thematic. They assume a somewhat more active role than usual. Thus, while they are mentioned extensively in 7:14 (in a now familiar roster), they become subject of the waw plus prefixal verb in verse 15, then continue as subject of the participle and of the suffixal verb in verse 16. It may be then that in this half of the verse both Noah and the animals are thematic participants.

What do we do, however, with the striking clause, 'And Yhwh shut him in' at the end of verse 16? This clause seems to be something special. It represents an event which is subsequent to the simultaneous events which are reported in the embedded simultaneous paragraph which precedes it. Although cryptic and short, this sentence patterns as one of the main events of the story. In brief, God who has threatened to judge mankind and encouraged Noah to make extensive preparations to save himself from the catastrophe, now here deliberately shuts the gates of mercy on mankind while shutting Noah securely within. Further, it pictures God in an active role such as is not usual in other references to the catastrophe. Thus, in verses 7:11 and 12 the breaking up of the fountains of the great deep and the opening of the windows of heaven are reported as passives (suffixed niphal forms) and then rain ensues for 40 days and 40 nights. Neither here nor in the peak passage which follows is there any reference to deity. In the peak passage, God is not mentioned at all, but rather natural forces (initiated, of course, by God) are represented as taking over and destroying the earth. While the relevant conditions are not well understood at present, it appears that there may be special stylistic reasons for using Yhwh here rather than the name Elohim. It appears, at any rate, that the sequence of 7:1-16 presents the picture of a long chiasmus. Yhwh (along with Noah) is thematic in 7:1-5; Noah (along with the rain) is thematic in 7:6-10, and God is mentioned in passing simply as Elohīm. God is, as a whole, not mentioned in 7:11-14a, although He is referred to once at the end of this passage, 'As God had commanded Noah'. Rather, in this passage Noah and the animals are thematic. Then suddenly, at the end of 7:16b we find the deity referred to again as Yhwh where He appears to be thematic once more (in a one-sentence paragraph?). We have a chiasmus: Yhwh, Noah, Noah, Yhwh in terms of thematic participants.

7. Peak (climax) (Gen. 7:17-24).

The high point in a story is either its climax, i.e., the point of confrontation, or its dénoument, i.e., a decisive event which makes resolution possible. Either may be marked for peak.[9] If both are so marked, then a story has both a peak and a peak´. It is clear in the narrative here under discussion that there are some very special stylistic features which set apart 7:17-24 as a peak; that this story has but one such peak;

and that the peak coincides with the climax. The climax here is the prevalence of the flood and its possible threat even to Noah and his family in the ark.

I now trace in detail the progress of this paragraph with a look at its unique features. Verse 7:17 starts out with a wayyhi 'And there was a flood 40 days upon the earth'. This acts as setting for the entire paragraph which encodes climax. The events reported in the paragraph are not simple clauses, but are themselves embedded paragraphs. I will refer to these events as build-ups (abbreviated BU).[10] BU_1 is a slot filled by a sequence of three clauses found at the end of 7:17, 'And abounded the waters. And lifted up (they) the ark. And (it) raised up from off the earth'. The cycle begins again in verse 18 with another embedded unit of three clauses which fills the BU_2 slot. Again there is a beginning reference to the waters, 'And prevailed the waters. And they abounded exceedingly upon the earth. And drifted the ark on the face of the water'. Note also, as in the first cycle, the concluding reference to the ark.

From here on the paragraph develops a very striking structure. The third BU slot is filled by the material found in 7:19 and 7:20. While we could argue that in the above subunits, each waw plus prefixal verb forwards the event line of the paragraph, we come in 7:19 and 20 to a repetition of the waw plus prefixal form of the verb 'were covered'. Each of these in turn is itself a bundle of clauses not unlike the structures which fill BU_1 and BU_2 above. In brief, BU_3 is a paraphrase paragraph consisting of two sentences which are very similar in overall structure. While we could have found in the text that the second element of the paraphrase was not a waw plus prefixal form, but rather a circumstantial clause (as in the following verse), we do not find that construction employed here. Presumably such repetition in which the repeated verb is given the same structure as a verb on the main event line is a feature of the peak of a story--at least in epic style such as we have here. It is also interesting that in both halves of this construction, i.e., the half found in 19 and the half found in 20, the verse begins with a reference to 'the waters' even as BU_1 and BU_2 did above. This, however, by now is rather old information and the waters are demoted to a position of secondary importance (although they remain thematic). Thus, 19 begins with a circumstantial clause, 'The waters prevailed more and more upon the earth'. Likewise, 20 begins with a circumstantial clause, '15 cubits upward prevailed the waters'. Then these in turn are followed in 19 and 20 respectively by 'And were covered all the high mountains which are under the heavens' or, more simply, 'And were covered all the mountains'.

In verses 21, 22, and 23 a yet more elaborate paraphrase takes place which describes the destruction of life outside the ark. This whole unit fills BU_4. The first part of this paraphrase unit is itself a paraphrase unit in the form of a chiastic sentence. It begins with 'and died' wayyigwaʿ and ends with metū 'they died'. In between we find a long list of animals and forms of life, part of which goes with the first verb and part of which goes with the second. It is an extremely long and elaborate listing probably outdoing in complexity any previous list: 'all flesh which moves on the earth, with fowl, and with cattle, and with living things, and with every creeping thing which creepeth on the earth, and all men, all which stirs the breath of life in its nostrils, from all which is on the dry land'. This whole unit, itself containing a paraphrase, is then in turn paraphrased in 23, 'And was wiped out everything existing which is on the face of the earth from man to cattle to creeping things to birds of the heavens'. This construction which was introduced with a waw plus prefixal form is now in turn paraphrased by another waw plus prefixal form involving the same verb with a shift from singular to plural, 'And they were wiped out from the earth'.

The whole paragraph thus far then confronts us with a structure somewhat as follows: The flood is mentioned early in the first sentence, which is setting. Then for the two following BU's we find references to the flood and its interplay with the ark. Following this, there is a third BU in which there is an elaborate paraphrase in which the flood is now referred to in circumstantial clauses and the covering of the mountains is referred to by the same verb repeated twice in waw plus prefixal form. This in turn is followed by an even more elaborate paraphrase involving the death of life outside the ark. The first member of this paraphrase is a chiastic sentence with two synonyms for 'die', one occurring sentence initial and the other sentence final. The second member of this paraphrase is another paraphrastic unit in which the same verb occurs twice (with differing grammatical form) as waw plus prefixal form. There is an extremely extensive reference to varieties of animal life in the first main part of this overall paraphrase unit, and a more condensed reference to the forms of animal life that died in the last part of this unit.

The paragraph continues with the final BU (BU_n) where there is a reference again to Noah and those in the ark with him, 'And was left only Noah and those with him in the ark'. The paragraph terminates with another sentence which contains a final reference to flood waters, 'Prevailed the waters [Speiser: 'maintained their crest'] over the earth for 150 days'.[11]

For a graphic representation of the structure of this paragraph at peak, see Diagram IIA--which presents a transliteration of the Hebrew text--and Diagram IIB, which presents the same in a literal English translation (for ease in matching the two).

It is evident that the flood waters are thematic in this paragraph. They come in for repeated reference in the first three units, although they are eventually demoted to circumstantial clauses from their former position as subject of main line verbs. After an intervening involved reference to the death of animal life, the flood waters as thematic participant are again referred to in the last verse 7:24. The mountains are mentioned in 7:19 and 20 as thematic in the embedded paragraph which expounds BU_3. Animal life of various sorts is mentioned as thematic in the embedded unit which expounds BU_4. Noah is mentioned only briefly at the end in the next to the last sentence where he is referred to once by name, once by pronoun; he is not thematic. The ark is mentioned in 17 and 18 as raising up from the earth and drifting on the waters, and is mentioned again at the end of the entire passage, 'And only was left Noah and those with him in the ark'. It appears, therefore that the ark is a secondary thematic participant in the paragraph as a whole.

8. Episode P+1.

The onset of this new paragraph is signaled by a two-fold reference to God, Elohīm, who was not mentioned at all in the peak of the narrative. This same passage, 8:1 also contains a direct reference to the living things that were with Noah in the ark--none of which are mentioned specifically at the peak of the narrative although there is a summary reference in 7:24 to those with Noah in the ark. Thus, 8:1 begins, 'And God remembered Noah and all the living things and all the cattle which were with him in the ark' and continues with another reference to God, 'And God caused a wind to blow across the earth'. Thus, the first two main event line verbs of the paragraph (waw plus prefixal verbs) mention God as subject. God is not mentioned, however, in the balance of the paragraph and, therefore, does not prove to be a thematic participant. The next main line verb is, 'And the waters abated' in which 'waters' is the subject of the verb 'abate' and proves to be a thematic participant of the paragraph. The main line verbs, with reference to the waters or related phenomena, continue right through the remainder of a series of BU's in 8:2-3: 'And were shut up the fountains of the deep and the windows of heaven. And ceased the rain from heaven. And receded the waters from off the earth going and returning. And diminished the waters at the end of 150 days'. The BU_n at the end of this series is apparently climactic (witness the date) and has the ark as its subject, 'And came to rest the ark in the seventh month on the 17th day of the month on the mountains of Ararat'. The ark, which is mentioned in verse 1 and rementioned here as subject of a main line verb, probably qualifies, therefore, as a thematic participant. The paragraph ends with two circumstantial clauses, 'And the waters were going and returning and diminishing until the 10th month. In the 10th month on the first day of the month became visible the mountains'. Here the circumstantial clauses have preposed noun phrases and have suffixal verbs rather than the waw plus prefixal verb which characterizes the main line of the paragraph. In accordance with their structure as circumstantial clauses, these clauses are found in postclimactic position within the paragraph (after the BU_n, 'And rested the ark...') where they serve to terminate the paragraph.

The stylistic contrast between episode P+1 and the preceding peak is quite striking. Episode P+1 is a straight forward series of waw plus prefixal verbs which report successive events This series culminates with the ark coming to rest on Mt Ararat and then has some circumstantial clauses which terminate the paragraph. The clauses as a whole are short and almost no paraphrase is employed. In the peak, the successive stages in the growing vastness of the flood are reported not in clauses, but in embedded paragraphs with a large amount of paraphrase--often conveyed by main event line verbs rather than by main event line verb plus circumstantial clause. In both the climax and in the episode P+1 we find, however, that 'the waters' and 'the ark' are thematic participants.

In regard to the story as a whole, this episode represents a decisive turn of events which makes resolution of the story possible; it is, therefore (Longacre, 1976.213-17), the deep structure dénouement (DĒ in Diagram I). The peak ends with Noah, his family and the animals adrift on waters which, prevailing at crest for 150 days, show no sign of abating. Here, due to the intervention of God, the waters begin to subside, and the ark comes to rest.

9. Episode P+2 (Gen. 8:6-12).

This passage starts off with a wayyhi plus date clause (8:6a), 'And it came to pass at the end of 40 days'. This clause can be regarded as setting. It is followed (8:6b) by the first of a string of verbs which are main line (waw plus prefixal verb), 'And Noah opened the window [Speiser: 'hatch'] of the ark which he had made'. This first main event of the paragraph (structuring as BU_1) is of considerable interest in that it shows Noah (as he is throughout this paragraph) in an active role. His role has been passive during the flood and even before the flood in that the actions which he performed were in response to God's direct commands. Now in this episode Noah assumes a more active role. He is certainly thematic participant of this paragraph--but, the dove, prominent in the last three BU's is a secondary thematic participant.

There follow 13 more waw plus prefixal verbs. They do not apparently, however, form a simple string of successive events. Although they are all chronologically consecutive, they seem to group into subparagraphs which continue the series of BU's which was inaugurated by Noah's opening the windows of the ark (BU_1). BU_2 (8:7) is filled by a subparagraph which is concerned with the sending out of the raven. BU_3 (8:8-9) is filled by a subparagraph which includes five clauses all with initial waw plus prefixal verbs--as well as a purpose clause, a negative clause (lō plus suffixal verb), and a cause clause. This passage, which treats of the first sending out of the dove has some graphic detail--which is somewhat of a relief after the preoccupation with the vastness of the disaster. Thus, we are told that 'she [the dove] found no place to rest the sole of her foot', and that when she returned to the ark, 'Noah put forth his hand, took her, and drew her to him into the ark'. Verses 10 and 11 report (BU_4), the second sending out of the dove. This subparagraph is introduced by a temporal clause, 'And he waited yet seven days more'. Again, there is graphic--and highly relevant detail: 'And the dove returned to him at evening, and behold she had a freshly plucked olive leaf in her mouth'. This, in turn, leads to a sentence that is probably climactic in this subparagraph: 'And Noah knew that the waters had receded from the earth'. It appears that the climactic sentence (in its subparagraph) is chosen as the natural place to repeat 'Noah'--the name of the main thematic participant. Verse 12 constitutes another embedded unit (BU_n) which is also introduced by a temporal clause, 'And he waited yet seven days more'. This unit ends with the information that the dove came back to him no more--thus terminating the chain of events by removing one of the interacting participants from the story. In this episode, while the BU's are again complex (as in the peak), they do not involve paraphrase through main line verbs which so strikingly characterizes the peak of the narrative; rather, they are more like subepisodes within an episode.

This episode is, like the former, on the downslope of the story. The tension, built to a maximum at peak, is loosening here. The several graphic details concerning Noah's interaction with the dove provide relief from the overwhelming disaster which is so effectively described earlier in the story.

10. Episode P+3 (Gen. 8:13-19).

The most distinctive feature about this paragraph is its long setting expounded by an embedded paragraph. The embedded paragraph begins and ends with dates. Both dates are stages in the drying of the earth. The first date is given in a wayyhi clause: 'In the 601st year on the first day of the month'. The second date is found at the end of the embedded paragraph at the onset of verse 8:14: 'In the second month on the 22nd day of the month'. Verse 8:13, after the introductory dateline continues, 'dried out the waters from off the earth'. 'Dried out' here is a suffixal verb followed by a waw plus a prefixal verb, 'And removed Noah the covering from the ark'. This in turn is followed by another verb of the same construction 'And he saw that behold the face of the earth had dried'. Finally, the date at the beginning of verse 8:14 precedes another suffixed verb 'was dry the earth'.

It appears here that ha'areṣ 'the earth' is the thematic participant of this subparagraph. To be true, Noah is mentioned once as subject of a verb of the sort which customarily is main line in a narrative paragraph. There is a weak narrative line in this paragraph in the sequence 'And Noah took off the covering from the ark. And he looked'. Significantly though, Noah is not repeated. The Septuagint translation supplies the word Noah in the long date at the beginning of 8:13. Possibly, however, the Masoretic text is to be preferred here. The supplying of Noah, i.e., ' In the 601st year of the life of Noah' brings in a second reference to Noah which obscures the thematic structure of the paragraph as it stands in the Masoretic text--where Noah is mentioned only once and, therefore, cannot qualify as thematic participant, while ha'areṣ is mentioned three times and finally becomes subject of the last suffixal verb. Apparently, the long dates fore and aft in this embedded paragraph and the repeated reference to the earth result in some kind of thematic inversion of the structure of this paragraph whereby the weak narrative line, consisting of two waw plus prefixal verbs, proves not to be as important in the structure of the paragraph as the succession of perfects which refer to the earth. It can be argued that the line 'And Noah removed the covering of the ark' is simply a necessary prelude to his perceiving that the earth was dry.

The setting paragraph which establishes the drying out of the earth in two stages is followed by the body of a paragraph in the familiar execution form, i.e., 'God said to Noah, "Go out"' (verse 8:15) followed in verse 8:18 by, 'And Noah went out out'. In the reported speech of God in this paragraph, 'Go out' singular imperative, occurs in 8:15, 'Go out from the ark, you your wife, and your sons and the wives of your sons with you'. Verse 8:17 has a causative imperative, 'Cause to go out with you' with a long preposed conjoined noun phrase referring to the animals. The rest of verse 17 has three imperatives which anticipate the words of the blessing in chapter 9 and presumably are directed here to both men and animals, 'Increase in the earth. And be fruitful. And multiply on the earth'. In verses 18 and 19, which belong to the outer framework of the paragraph, the verb 'go out' is found again, 'And went out Noah and his sons and his wife and the wives of his sons with him'. Verse 19 continues with the other half of a chiastic construction, 'Every living thing, all that creeps, and all fowl, everything that stirs on the earth according to their families went out from the

	MAIN-LINE	CIRCUMSTANTIAL
SETTING: (7:17a)	wayyhī hammabbūl 'arba'īm yōm al ha'areṣ.	
BU_1: Narr Paragraph (7:17b,c,d)	wayyirbū hammayīm. wayyis'ū 'et-hattebah. wattaram me'al ha'areṣ.	
BU_2: Narr Paragraph (7:18)	wayyigbrū hammayim. wayyirbū m'od 'al ha'areṣ. wattelek hattebah 'al pnē hammayim.	
BU_3: Paraphrase Paragraph (7:19-20)	text { waykussū kɔl-heharīm haggbohīm 'ešer-taḥat kol haššamayīm. paraph. { waykussū heharīm.	whammayīm gabrū m'od m'od 'al ha'areṣ, ḥemeš 'esreh 'ammah milma'lah gabrū hammayîm
BU_4: Paraphrase Paragraph (7:21-23a)	text { text { wayyigwa' kol-basar haromeš 'al ha'areṣ...wkol ha'adam; paraph. { } paraph. { text { wayyimaḥ 'et-kal-haykūm 'ešer 'al pnē ha'damah.... paraph. { wayyimmaḥū min-ha'areṣ.	kol 'ešer nišmat-rūaḥ ḥayyîm b'appayw....metū.
BU_n: (7:23b) TERMINUS: (7:24)	wayyišša'er 'ak-Noaḥ wa'šer 'ittō battebah. wayyigbrū hammayīm 'al ha'areṣ ḥmiššîm ūm'at yōm.	

DIAGRAM IIA: Structure of Paragraph at PEAK (Gen. 7:17-24)

		MAIN-LINE	CIRCUMSTANTIAL
SETTING		And there was a flood forty days upon the earth	
BU_1:		And abounded the waters And they lifted up the ark And it raised up from the earth	
BU_2:		And prevailed the waters And they abounded exceedingly on the earth And drifted the ark on the face of the waters	
BU_3:	text	And were covered all the mountains the high ones which are under all the heavens	And the waters prevailed exceedingly, exceedingly on the earth
	paraph.	And were covered the mountains	Fifteen cubits upward prevailed the waters
BU_4:	text: text	And perished all flesh moving on the earth...and all men;	all which stirred the breath of life in its nostrils....died.
	text: paraph. / paraph.: text	And was wiped out everything existing which was on the face of the earth	
	paraph.: paraph.	And they were wiped out from the earth	
BU_n:		And was left only Noah and those with him in the ark.	
TERMINUS:		And prevailed the waters on the earth fifty and one hundred days.	

(Literal Translation into English)

DIAGRAM IIB: Structure of Paragraph at PEAK (Gen. 7:17-24)

ark'. Here 'according to their families' (lmišpotēhem) is found rather than 'after its kind' (lmīnah) which occurs in some of the former lists.

It seems that in the second half of this paragraph, it is the 'going out' that is thematic, i.e., there is a verbal theme. As for the participants, Noah, the animals, and the ark are all mentioned both early and late in the passage. It seems plausible to me that we do not have here three thematic participants as such, but that all these participants are subservient to the verbal theme of the paragraph, viz., the going out from the ark. The occurrence of the material at the end of verse 17 --the anticipation of the blessing in 9--is a bit puzzling, but it makes possible a two fold repetition of the word 'earth', thus, echoing the thematic participant of the first half of the paragraph, i.e., the paragraph which is embedded in the setting. Furthermore, anticipation of one section of a discourse in an earlier section is a cohesive device found in many discourses in many languages.

The place of this episode in the story is somewhat obvious. Loosening tension continues here; not only has the flood abated and the earth dried, but also the occupants of the ark are at last able to leave the craft in which they have been for so long confined.

11. Episode P+4 (Gen. 8:20-22).

This paragraph has a string of five main line, i.e., waw plus prefixal, verbs. 'And built Noah an altar to Yhwh. And he took...And he offered...And Yhwh smelled...And Yhwh said (in effect) "Never again!"' Noah is not the thematic participant of this paragraph. He occurs as subject of the first verb and is implied as subject of the next two verbs, but is not as such referred by name or pronoun again in the paragraph (although he is referred to by the prefix on the two prefixal verbs). The altar is a prop which is referred to twice in verse 20. It appears that the real thematic participant of the paragraph is Yhwh. Noah 'built an altar to Yhwh' in 20 and then we're told in 8:21 that, 'Yhwh smelled the soothing odor and Yhwh said in His heart...'. This gives a total already of four references to Yhwh, three by the proper noun and one by pronoun. In the quoted portion which follows in 8:21 and 8:22, we find further first person affixal references to Yhwh. Two are prefixal in negative verbs, 'I will never again curse' and, 'I will never again destroy' (both in verse 21) and one is suffixal in the clause 'which I have made'.

The adverb 'ōd 'yet, again' occurs twice in verse 21 and once more in verse 22. 'ōd-kol-ymē ha'areṣ 'yet all the days of the earth', i.e., 'as long as the earth continues'. This repetition of the adverb gives the whole passage a strong 'never again!' thrust. Taking off from the latter phrase, the verse ends with a quasi-poetic portion: 'As long as the earth continues, seed time and harvest, cold and heat, summer and winter, and day and night shall not cease'.

Although there are five main line verbs in this paragraph, they probably do not structure as a simple sequence of five sentences. Three of these verbs have to do with the actions of Noah and two have to do with Yhwh's response. Consequently, this paragraph probably forms some kind of an action-response unit with two embedded parts. The backbone of the embedded quote consists entirely of negated verbs, 'I will never again curse the earth', 'I will never again destroy every living thing that I have made', and 'Seasonal variations shall not cease'.

Again, it is instructive to note that deity is the thematic participant in this verse and as such He is referred to as Yhwh.

As to the place of this episode in the overall story, here the loosening tension procedes to the point where assurrance is given that such a judgement as the flood will never be repeated. This paragraph is, however, poorly delineated. It has no setting to signal the onset of a new unit; rather, the shift in thematic structure alone gives it its unity. It may well be, therefore, that this paragraph actually compounds with that found in Ep P+3. In effect, therefore, the offering of sacrifice and the divine response would be part of the complex of going out of the ark. I have not followed this alternative in that to me, the resulting complexity of paragraph structure is implausible. But if we were to take this passage 8:20-22 as part of a long unit 8:13-22, we would (1) still note that 8:20-22 is an embedded paragraph in the larger unity, and (2) probably represent 8:20-22 as climactic in the larger paragraph. As evidence of the latter, note the poetic or quasi-poetic nature of 8:22--where something special seems to be afoot.

12. Episode P+5.

This episode consists of a discourse of God to Noah, his sons, and all their wives. The form of quotation in 9:1 is two fold, 'And Elohim blessed Noah and his sons. And He said to them...'. The remaining verses from 9:1 to 9:7 give the words of God's blessing along with certain accompanying privileges and restrictions. The blessing proper occurs bracketing the passage i.e., in 9:1 we have, 'Be fertile. And multiply. And replenish the earth' and in 9:7 we have, 'And as for you, be fertile. And abound on the earth. And multiply in it'. In between there is some material in 9:2-6 which deals with privileges and restrictions. I will not go into it in detail here. While the blessing proper consists of imperative verbs and is main line, the intervening material consists of clauses which have preposed nouns and verbs in various tenses, i.e., prefixal tense in referring to future events and suffixal tense in referring to provisions which God had made. There is a niphal suffixal form at the end of verse 9:2, 'All have been given into your hands', and at the end of 9:3 an active suffixal form involving the same verb, 'I have given'. Finally, at the end of verse 6, following the prohibition against murder, we find another suffixal verb in the clause, 'For in the image of God made He man'.

In this embedded subparagraph which deals with the portion of God's discourse in which He blesses mankind, we find a number of second person plural references. The way for this is prepared in the quotation formula of the framework of the paragraph by the summary plural <u>lhem</u> 'to them'. This is cross-referenced immediately by the second person plural endings of the imperatives early in the paragraph. The second person plural suffix (-<u>kem</u> on nouns and on <u>l-</u>) continues the second person plural orientation through the following verses. About midway through 9:5 and in verse 6 the second person plural component fades out, only to be reiterated with force in 9:7

where the blessing is recapitulated, 'But as for you, be fruitful...'. I think it is clear that the addresses (second person plural) are thematic in this paragraph. I do not think that God is thematic in this portion. To be true, He refers to Himself several times in first person singular and there is a third person reference at the end of 9:6 to 'In the image of God made He man'. But the prominence of the second person plural suffixes, plus the imperatives that bracket the passage, and the strong second person plural reference in 9:7 (w'attem 'as for you') appear to be more prominent than the first person references. If God is a thematic participant, He is here a secondary thematic participant, not a primary one.[12]

In 9:8 the onset of the second portion of God's discourse to Noah and his family is signaled by the reintroduction of the quotation formula, 'And God said to Noah and to his sons with him saying'. The body of the paragraph starts off in 9:9 with the very solemn words, 'I, lo I, am establishing my covenant with you'. I suspect that in this section, i.e., 9:9-11, the covenant itself is thematic and that the partners to the covenant, God on the one hand and man on the other (expressed as 'I' and 'you'), are more incidental. 'Establishing the covenant' is mentioned in both 9:9 and 9:11. In 9:9 the word 'establish' is a participle in a circumstantial clause which continues through verse 10. In 9:11 the word 'establish' is a waw plus suffixal verb with the word 'covenant' following it again. The partners of the covenant are amplified in 9:10 in that it is made clear that the 'you' includes not just Noah and his family, but also all living creatures which are with them. Again a representative list of living creatures follows. This is summarized at the end of the verse as, 'from every thing coming out of the ark to every living creature on the earth'. The terms of the covenant are given in the balance of 9:11, i.e., the covenant is to the effect that God will not again destroy all flesh with the waters of a flood and that never again will there be a flood to destroy the earth. The two negative clauses contain lō plus prefixal verbs which probably here are main line in the quoted discourse. Again, the waw plus suffixal form cannot occur in the negative, and the two negative verbs appear to be a continuation of the waw plus suffixal verb in 9:11a.

The onset of the third point in God's discourse is likewise signaled by a quotation formula. This time the formula is much briefer. It does not emphasize that God said so-and-so to Noah and his family, but just states, 'And God said'. The full quotation formula is certainly appropriate in 9:1 where it sets the stage for the repeated 'you' plural which occurs as thematic in the quote itself. The full formula is likewise appropriate in 9:8 where it is followed by a quote in which God is one partner to the covenant and the addressees are the other part. This bilaterality is anticipated in the quotation formula 'And God said to Noah and to his sons with him, saying'. But in 9:12 apparently the full formula quotation is no longer necessary--partly because the speaker and addressees are already well identified and partly because the thematic participant of the quoted discourse is now different. In this portion 9:12-17 it is the covenant sign, i.e., the rainbow, which is thematic. It is first introduced in 9:12 in a non-verbal (nominal) clause. 'This (is) the sign of the covenant I am giving between myself and between you and between all living things which are with you'. Then, somewhat dramatically in 9:13 the rainbow is introduced in preposed position before a suffixal verb. 'My bow

I have given (placed) in the cloud'. This circumstantial clause is followed by a waw plus suffixal verb 'And it shall be for a sign of the covenant between Me and between the earth' where 'earth' here is used by metonomy for man and all other creatures on the earth. Verse 9:14 has two waw plus suffixal verbs. The first verb, however, is the verb hayah and is apparently somewhat introductory to the second verb, 'And it shall be in clouding over clouds over the earth, that shall be seen the bow in the cloud'. The string of waw plus suffixal verbs (normal for predictive discourse) continues in 9:15 and 9:16 broken only by a negative verb in the last clause of 9:15 where such a construction is impossible. Thus, we have in 9:15 'And I will remember the covenant which is between Me and you' followed by 'that not (to the effect that not) shall be again a flood to destroy all flesh'. In 9:16 there are two more waw plus suffixal verbs. Again, however, the first of these verbs is the verb hayah and may be somewhat introductory to the second, 'And (when) shall be the bow in the cloud and (then) I will see it to remember the covenant forever between man and between all living things with all flesh which is on the earth'. Clearly then, it appears that it is the sign of the covenant, the rainbow, which is thematic rather than the covenant itself. Also, as we have seen, the term 'rainbow' can occur without being associated directly with the word covenant--as in 9:13, 'My bow I have given in the cloud'; 9:14 'and the rainbow shall be seen in the cloud'; and in 9:16, 'And when the rainbow is in the cloud'.

Verse 9:17 concludes the entire discourse of God with special reference to the third point. Again there is a formula of quotation and again there is a reference to Noah: 'And said God to Noah, "This (is) the sign of the covenant which I have established between Myself and between all flesh which is on the earth"'. Notice that medial in God's discourse there is no indication of end of quote; rather, the quotation formulas of 9:8 and 9:12 introduce new points within a continuing (but quoted) discourse. The quotation sentence which occurs here closes the entire quoted discourse. It is also relevant to reiterate here that the variations in the form and extensiveness of the formulas of quotation are not random and unmotivated; rather, all contribute to unity and focus within the quoted discourse.

13. Conclusion and comment.

I have attempted to show in this application of contemporary discourse study to the flood account that the text of the flood story as it stands has a consistent and plausible discourse structure, that the variations in style found in certain parts of it are appropriate to the distinctions in the subject matter. Even small details of structure such as the presence or absence of resumptive pronouns and variations in the form of quotation formula will probably be eventually explicable here and elsewhere in the Hebrew Old Testament in terms of discourse structure.

I have also attempted to show that repetitive allusions to the same event--far from being evidence of more than one documentary source--are either (1) cohesive features which contribute to the unity of the discourse, or (2) features of parallelism and paraphrase which mark the prominence of the peak.

Especially, I have attempted to clarify the paragraph structure of this account, both in terms of the thematic participants which characterize the various paragraphs and sub-paragraphs and also in terms of the general progress and development within each paragraph. Thus, even the variation in divine names between Elohim and Yhwh seems not to be a matter of editorial patchwork, but seems to tie in to the matter of whether or not the deity is thematic in a given paragraph. I've attempted, also, to show that the various references to dates and chronology, far from being the hallmark of a special writer (P) are an integral part of the mechanism of introducing and closing paragraphs and maintaining discourse flow.

Apparent contradictions are actually minimal. Thus, when Noah is first told to build the ark, he is told to bring in the animals by pairs, but in a subsequent set of instructions he is told to take seven pairs of the clean animals and clean birds. Surely, if one allows the document to stand as it is, there is nothing implausible about a preliminary set of instructions being expanded and made more specific in a subsequent set of instructions--especially if a considerable time interval is implied (as seems plausible here). Likewise, I suspect that the chronology of the flood makes sense as it stands in the present text--although I have not had time to go into such problems in the present paper. It is mainly when one attempts to separate the text into earlier documents that one finds apparent discrepancies in the chronology.

It can, therefore, be rationally contended that the application of contemporary discourse study to this portion of Genesis makes the assumption of divergent documentary sources unnecessary and that such an assumption obscures much of the truly elegant structure of the story.

Appendix

Tentative set of rules for finding the thematic participant in Hebrew (based on limited corpus):

1. Is introduced early in the paragraph--usually the first one or two sentences (a secondary thematic participant is introduced as late as sentence 4 in Ep P+2, but this is still relatively early in what proves to be a long paragraph).

2. Is referred to several times successively by name (if third person) and/or pronoun (can be only pronoun if first or second person).

3. Whether or not mentioned in the middle of the paragraph, comes in for reiterated mention towards the end.

4. Is involved with the main event line of the paragraph--either by being subject of at least one event line verb or by repeated occurrence as other than subject in such clauses

5. Where two nouns vie with each other for thematic participant they may both be primary thematic participants (equal prominence), or one may be a secondary thematic participant (less prominent).

6. Occasionally, where there are apparently several thematic participants, all are probably subsidiary to a third entity, nominal or verbal, that is the real thematic entity.

NOTES

1. I acknowledge here the help of Sharon Bergstrom who not only typed up various drafts of this paper, but also offered many helpful criticisms.

2. NSF grant SOC 74-04763 and NEH grant RO-20280-75-5.

3. The transcription is somewhat of a makeshift in the absence of a Hebrew typewriter. Consonants are more or less traditionally represented. In the vowels, pathah and kameṣ are not distinguished, nor ṣere and seghol. Vowel letter h is retained but presence of yodh and waw as vowel letters is indicated with a long mark over the vowel. Shewa and hateph vowels are not symbolized. Daghesh forte is symbolized as a double consonant. Daghesh lene is considered to symbolize a subphonemic variation in the stops and is not, therefore, symbolized.

4. By surface structure is meant here the formal features which are usually called 'grammar' plus an extension of grammar to take account of formal features of larger units such as paragraph and discourse. By deep structure, I mean the notional or semantic features. Thus, while a discourse may formally mark beginning, end, and peak(s) (i.e., high point) of a story, it may indicate also some more elusive categories such as inciting incident, rising tension, climax, dénouement (an event which makes resolution possible), final suspense, and wrap-up (cf. Longacre, 1976.197-231). Such categories as the latter are the notional or deep structure of a discourse. The latter are intuitively recognized by the hearer/reader in that his own experience with the structure of stories leads him to expect them.

5. I am indebted here, as at many points, to Andersen, 1974. I acknowledge this debt without imputing to him any of the failings of the present paper.

6. As this article leaves my hands I have increasing doubts about the validity of the above argument--at least in the form stated. To be true, Biblical Hebrew can not prepose any element in the same clause as the waw plus prefixal verb. On the other hand circumstantial clauses are preposed to such main line clauses quite regularly. What does emerge, however, as extremely peculiar is that in no instance in the entire Flood narrative is a circumstantial clause clearly used for back-reference. The end result is the same as that argued in the body of the paper, viz. the devices of repetition and recapitulation that characterize Biblical Hebrew are quite distinct not only from European languages but also from every other language with which I have had experience in Mesoamerica, South America, the Philippines, and Papua-New Guinea (to name only areas that I have worked in for at least the better part of a year).

7. Hebrew here presents a usage similar to English, where with three clauses conjoined by 'and', the 'and' occurs only between the last two clauses rather than between each of the clauses.

8. For a quite differing partitioning of this passage and construing of relations among clauses, see Andersen, 1974.124-5.

9. For a summary of formal features found to mark peak (as so far observed in many languages) see Longacre 1976.217-228.

10. This analysis is not *ad hoc* to the present paragraph. It has become a convention in the analysis of narrative paragraphs by myself and those working with me to analyze narrative paragraphs as consisting essentially of the following slots: an optional Setting, two or more Build-up's, and an optional Terminus (Longacre, 1968.I.56-68). While I have not felt it worthwhile to refer to this apparatus everywhere in this presentation, the apparatus seems useful here in explaining somewhat in detail the paragraph structure at peak. It is also invoked in a few subsequent episodes.

11. For an alternative analysis of this passage--but one which points out the same features of parallelism and paraphrase which are noticed here--see again Andersen, 1974.124-5.

12. Presumably, as a secondary thematic participant, rather than as a primary one, deity is referred to as Elohim rather than Yhwh. In 7:1-5, where the first person (corresponds to Yhwh in the quote formula) is at least as important as the second person (Noah)--if not more important, deity is clearly a primary thematic participant. In the other passages (6:5-8 and 8:20-22) deity is clearly the participant which dominates each passage, and is referred to as Yhwh. The only possible problem concerning divine names in this passage is the occurrence of Yhwh in 7:16b. But, at all events, as explained above, there is something very special about that passage.

Bibliography

Andersen, Francis L. 1974. The sentence in Biblical Hebrew. The Hague: Mouton.

Buth, Randy. 1975. An introductory study of the paragraph structure of Biblical Hebrew narrative. Jerusalem. Ph.D. dissertation (unpublished).

Davidson, Robert. 1973. Genesis 1-11. Cambridge: University Press.

Fritsch, Charles T. n.d. In The Layman's Bible Commentary (Balmer H. Kelly, ed.) Vol 2., The book of Genesis.

Grimes, Joseph. 1976. The thread of discourse. The Hague: Mouton.

Longacre, Robert E. 1968. Discourse, paragraph and sentence structure in selected Philippine languages: Vol I, Discourse and paragraph structure. Santa Ana (California): The Summer Institute of Linguistics. Publication 21 of the SIL publications in linguistics and related fields .

_____. 1972. Hierarchy and universality of discourse constituents in New Guinea languages: Vol I, Discussion; Vol II, Texts. Washington: Georgetown University Press.

_____. 1976. An anatomy of speech notions. Lisse (Netherlands): Peter de Ridder Press.

_____. ed. (in press). Discourse grammar: studies in aboriginal languages of Colombia, Ecuador, and Panama. 3 volumes.

Longacre, Robert E. and Stephen Levinsohn. (in press). Field analysis of discourse.

Speiser, E.A. 1964. Genesis (In The Anchor Bible). Garden City (New York): Doubleday and Co., Inc.

Von Rad, Gerhard. 1961. Genesis, a commentary. Philadelphia: The Westminster Press. (translated by John H. Marks).

S 186 JOHN DOMINIC CROSSAN "EMPTY TOMB AND ABSENT LORD" A RESPONSE

John E. Alsup

Preliminary Note: For bibliographical references and a development of lines of questioning pertaining to the appearance tradition cf. the respondent's The Post-Resurrection Appearance Stories of the Gospel Tradition. A History-of-Tradition Analysis, Stuttgart, 1975.

Obviously conversant with a substantial portion of the history of research and arguing with a high degree of internal consistency and forthrightness, Crossan has offered an energetic and provocative solution to the thorny problem of the ending of Mark. This response is directed at the chief issues raised by his approach.

This reviewer shares Crossan's conviction that Mk intended to end his gospel at 16:8 and would therefore affirm the second half of the thesis sentence on p. 135. The question, of course, is what Mk intended to say by doing so. Crossan's reply is interesting not so much because of any uniqueness but because it combines a variety of positions advanced over the years. Wherever 16:8 has been taken to be the original ending the following views have been expressed:

1) The Empty Tomb (hereafter ET) has a direct relationship to the appearance tradition, i.e.,

a) Once upon a time ET itself was actually an appearance story of the resurrected Lord which was altered because of the inadequacy of women witnesses in a Jewish community.

b) ET replaced an appearance story - probably the "protophany" to Peter - which had to be suppressed because of ecclesiastical group conflicts.

c) ET does not directly replace an appearance story but points to appearances while declining to narrate them for theological reasons or because "stories" did not yet exist.

d) ET does not directly oppose the appearance tradition but a narration of such was not possible because of the concept of history behind the composition of Mk.

2) ET has only an indirect relationship to the appearance tradition or none at all, i.e.,

a) ET is a "translation" story, Mk's equivalent to the kerygma of I Cor. 15, an "anti-resurrection" translation aretalogy.

b) ET points not to appearance stories but to the Parousia in Galilee.

c) ET points not to appearance stories but to the presence of the Lord in his church's Galilaean ministry.

d) ET is motivated by polemic against anti-Christian accusations or heretical claims.

Against the backdrop of this varied NT discussion and in stated reliance upon a certain group of recent Markan studies C. constructs his understanding of the evangelist's theological intention: it is to be interpreted in the context of "intra-Christian polemic against theological opponents." They were interested in miracles and apparitions, had little sympathy with the Gentile mission, and appealed to the authority of the mother church in Jerusalem and its apostolic pillars. ET counters the appearance tradition, i.e. "...it was precisely to avoid and to oppose any such apparitions to Peter or the Apostles that he created most deliberately a totally new tradition...that of ET" (p. 146). The references in 14:28 and 16:7 are polemical and represent a judgment on the established mother church in Jerusalem; it had failed to heed the call "to inaugurate a mission to both Jews and Gentiles...the Jerusalem community led by the disciples and especially Peter, has never accepted the call of the exalted Lord communicated to it from the Markan community. The Gospel ends in a juxtaposition of Markan faith in 16:6-7 and of Jerusalem failure in 16:7-8" (p. 149). In brief, "both form and content of 16:1-8 coalesce as an anti-tradition to any concluding story of an apparition to the apostles or to any one of their leaders" (p. 150)... Mk "offers us an absent Jesus...the harsh negative of the ET and the Lord who 'is not here'" (p. 152).

Close examination of this picture sheds light on several problem areas. Most important is the question of the meaning of 14:28 and 16:7. While expressing agreement with some of the emphases behind C.'s position, E. Schweizer in a recent article resists any suggestion that Mk could be opposing the appearance tradition. He says, "If there was in fact a Christian community which had not yet learned of the appearances proclaimed by "all" they would certainly have become known through the very propaganda of their opponents. After reference has been made to the Resurrection in Mk 8:31; 9:9, 31: 10:34, and not once to the Parousia, the reader can only have connected 16:7 with the former coming immediately after the announcement of the Resurrection. If the evangelist had wanted to oppose such and discredit the disciples he would have described their lack of understanding and not excused them by not allowing the news of Jesus to reach them. As a matter of fact a Markan polemic against the disciples as representatives leading others astray by a miracle Christology is farfetched" (EvTh 33, 1973, p. 535 trans. mine). C.'s placement, moreover, of 16:7 in the particular context of rivalry and polemic between factions in Galilee and Jerusalem, while represented often enough in the history of research, has yet to be demonstrated.

Let us examine some of C.'s arguments in the light of alternative possibilities of interpretation! The methodological decision to suspend temporarily the historical question in analysing resurrection traditions is a good one; perusal of the literature shows the dominance of this question and the unfortunate neglect of form-critical and compositional considerations. Yet, without trying to follow a reconstruction (e.g. von Campenhausen) it must be asked if the question of historicity pertaining to ET is the same kind of question as the one pertaining to other resurrection traditions, especially the appearance traditions. The historical motif in general, moreover, as compositional element for Mk is a matter of debate. C. presupposes the "Jesus was buried by the same inimical forces that had crucified him" (p. 152) - a view advanced often enough by others (Lake, Baldensperger _et al_.; contra, Blinzler) - and refers thereby to Jn 19:31 (_not_ Acts 13:29?). This "reality" is then countered by Mk who introduces the tradition of ET; opposition to what "really happened" continues to manifest itself in the tradition's ongoing development. For C. there is no ET tradition in the strictest sense prior to Mk, only _presumption_ perhaps that the tomb is empty (p. 136). C. illustrates: Mk. undoubtedly "presumed Jesus had an infancy but there is no tradition of an infancy in Mark..." (_ibid_.) This manner of speaking about tradition is problematic _here_ because Mk's non-inclusion of an infancy is a matter of theological-compositional choice and does not preclude the existence of such a tradition. Mt and Lk are not its _creators_ as such any more than they are for their resurrection appearance stories (with one probable exception). C. presupposes as much in his allegiance to the "anti-tradition" hypothesis as a Markan polemical choice regarding the latter. "Occam's razor" granted, it is equally important not to jump too quickly to the conclusion that Mk has "created most deliberately a totally new tradition" (p. 146). Does this perspective do justice to the complexities of tradition processes in primitive Christianity? Are the issues of burial and discovery of the empty tomb in all cases identical? C. chooses to begin with Mk and the singular motif of the women as compositional element when speaking of ET tradition. Is it not possible to begin with the women themselves and some aspect of historicity on the question of traditional matrix? It is, after all, difficult to conceive of the tenacity of a tradition involving the witness of persons with as little "credibility value" in Palestine as women unless some kind of historical basis recommends it.

C. seeks additional support for the Markan creation hypothesis in Synoptic and Johannine comparison. A greater degree of differentiation is needed here. C. sees the accounts under comparison to be post-Markan and linear in development: "One discerns in all this a steady desire to replace the Women of Mk with Apostles, and the Messenger of Mk with Jesus himself" (p. 138). C. sees correctly that the tradition/redaction issue focuses on Jn. The guard motif in Mt is probably a redactional element, although not only Johnson but also more recently N. Walter and R. Kratz have made a case for a pre-Matthean tradition, a *Befreiungswunder*, shared by the Gospel of Peter. The matter of the apostles present at the tomb in Lk and Jn is also a subsequent development to the more original form. At this point, however, the question of Johannine sources becomes acute. Final redaction is clearly responsible for only some of the motifs (e.g. "beloved disciple"). Nevertheless, the need for apostolic substantiation (Jn 20:3-10) does succeed the original form of the story. But what of Jn 20:1-2 partem and 11-13? At this point, C. introduces the Gospel of Signs source, concludes that probability sides with the Gospel of Signs being dependent on Mk for ET, and says,"...WT in Mk is most likely the source for the residual WT in GS" (p. 141). Yet, the case for dependence is hardly self-evident. The argument based on catenae is difficult because the overall data is still too incomplete, and the suggested direction of dependence is complicated by the fact that form-critical indices point to the priority of Jn 6:16-21 over Mk 6:45-52. In general, moreover, the direct dependence of the Johannine tradition upon the Synoptics still appears to this reviewer to be extremely doubtful, the suggested alternative of "pure coincidental connection" nothwithstanding (p. 140). Admittedly the issues are complex, but a possible traditional matrix independent of Mk recommends itself on the basis of motif form and function.

Of key importance to C.'s argumentation is the ostensible attempt of the tradition after Mk to "replace" Mk's messenger with Jesus himself. C. points to Mt 28:9-10 and Jn 20:14-18 for support. Again greater differentiation is necessary. Strictly speaking, these two passages do not belong to ET at all. Their form is that of an appearance story and as such they constitute the seam between the ET and appearance tradition. The latter knows otherwise of no women participants nor localization at the tomb locale. Therefore, the question is: are these two accounts redactional constructs designed to "replace" something in ET as C. suggests or do they have an independent traditional base? In part C. is correct regarding Mt: form-critical comparison of 28:9-10 with the rest of the appearance stories leads to the conclusion that the account has been constructed by Mt to achieve a redactional seam between the two traditions. He has reproduced essentially the content of ET in the person of Jesus. This does not mean, however, "replacement" or "reduction" but rather reinforcement and heightening of the announcement in ET. The Mary Magdalene story, on the other hand, resists such explanation. The same form-critical comparison reveals that while the story has certainly been redactionally modified to accommodate it to its present location it does not simply reproduce the content of ET but functions as interpreter of that content and has all the critical earmarks of a traditional story comparable to the others. Hence, the direction of development for the question of ET, the women, and the resurrected One is to construct an account or to appropriate an already existing story as an extension and interpretive context for understanding ET, a tradition capable of a variety of interpretations (Jewish polemic or whatever!). This interpretive direction - from appearance tradition to ET - is also true for Lk. Is it true for Mk?

The question is raised in all due respect and seriousness for it represents the pivotal issue for interpreting Mk as theologian, a preserver and interpreter of the Jesus tradition. What kind of tradition does C. see Mk opposing in the appearance stories? The only concrete development of this question by C. comes in his reference to 6:45-51. Accompanying the reference is his acceptance of the Dibelius' hypothesis: "the historical sequence and development of the appearance tradition was from creedal <u>statement</u> (as in I Cor 15:5-7) to creedal <u>story</u>," and the identification of 6:45ff with the latter: "one example of such creedal stories is ...Mk 6:45-51. This is especially important because we are certain that Mk knew at least this one..." (p. 150). Measuring the form and statement-intention of the appearance tradition in this way is problematic at best. For one thing, a history-of-tradition analysis of the traditions involved in the Dibelius' hypothesis destroys it: the kerygma and story traditions do not stand in a linear/dependent but a complementary/independent relationship as two separate streams of tradition. For another, 6:45ff represents one of the so-called "displaced" appearance stories and their inclusion among the primary sources for evaluation of the tradition is beset with innumerable obstacles. To claim that, "Before Mk wrote his Gospel there was no 'before' and 'after' Easter," and that the story was "placed by Mk...safely in the earthly life of Jesus he had created" (<u>ibid</u>.) overtaxes the imagination. The claim, moreover, that "the form of Mk 16:1-8 is derived directly and deliberately from that of 6:45-51" (<u>ibid</u>.) and ostensibly is proven by the breakdown of formal elements in the chart comparing them (p. 151) is overdrawn. Besides the undifferentiated mixing of sources for comparison, the only significant points of overlap are characteristic of most Markan narratives where the identity of Jesus is intentionally shrouded in mystery and fear. When positing appearance story influences in pericopae of the earthly ministry, moreover, it is important to distinguish between appearance types; the Transfiguration in Mk 9, for instance, demonstrates far-reaching affinities with the "heavenly radiance" type (cf. Acts 9,22,26) but not the "anthropomorphic theophany" type characteristic of the gospel tradition.

When probing the relationship of Mk to the appearance tradition, therefore, it is imperative methodogically to make the comparison on the basis of that tradition as a whole. It is impossible here to rehearse an analysis of that tradition, but a summary of its findings might be offered as follows: the appearance stories in our gospels had a pre-redactional existence. As such their motifs and themes demonstrate extensive agreement, their statement-intention profound congruence, and their history-of-religion background probable similarity; they represent a NT

Gattung. Their probable background is the anthropomorphic theophany tradition of the OT. Their statement-intention is neither mere confirmation that he is alive again nor the legitimation of persons or places with the investiture of authority; rather they state that the crucified/resurrected Lord initiates and fulfills the restoration of fellowship with his own after its severance at the cross. The lack of recognition and the doubt of the participants in the appearances are overcome by faith and joy in that restoration and its promise of endurance, renewed commission, and service. To be sure, each of these motifs and themes is developed redactionally by the evangelists, but the source of each is embedded in the traditional matrix. This critical option for understanding the appearance stories offers itself as an alternative to C.: they "are the effects of Easter faith and not its cause or even its occasion" (p. 152).

Finally, then, is the notion of "absent Lord" the probable intention of ET for Mk? Strictly speaking, Lk's ending at 24:51 might come closer were it not for Acts. And yet, Mk does not in fact develop any notion of presence. Nevertheless, one must ask: if Mk is answering the question who Jesus is and calling for a life of discipleship "in suffering, in service, and in mission to the world" (*ibid*.) is it not more likely that as the community's common experience is the kerygma, baptism, and the Lord's Supper its members would interpret Mk and ET in the larger context of that Christian reality? Hence, absence as a category - while true enough for all those representing the Jesus tradition in one sense or another - is actually relative and conditioned by a broader understanding of divine presence and guidance which presumably did not leave Christian individuals or communities to their own devices.

[illegible] The [illegible] the entire [illegible] these [illegible] neither [illegible] the [illegible] as [illegible] life [illegible] and the [illegible] in the [illegible] and its purpose of [illegible] with the [illegible] the [illegible] of [illegible] the [illegible] that [illegible] of [illegible] (p. 155?) [illegible]

[illegible] the notion of [illegible] the [illegible] of [illegible] of [illegible] the question who Jesus is [illegible] in service, and in [illegible] it [illegible] that [illegible] the [illegible] baptism, and the [illegible] in the larger [illegible] those [illegible] the Jesus tradition [illegible] and [illegible] presence and [illegible] which [illegible] individually [illegible]

S 187

EMPTY TOMB AND ABSENT LORD: MARK'S INTERPRETATION OF TRADITION

Thomas R. W. Longstaff
Colby College
Waterville, Maine

In a new essay on Mk 16:1-8[1] John D. Crossan attempts to show that "Mk created the tradition of the Empty Tomb (ET) as the precise and complete redactional conclusion for his Gospel." Since my own recent work has concentrated on the synoptic problem and particularly on the redactional techniques of the author of the Gospel of Mark,[2] Prof. Kee was kind enough to suggest that I prepare a brief response to Crossan's article for consideration in the S.B.L. Seminar on Mark this year. He also suggested that I relate my comments to the importance of Crossan's work for the continuing discussion of the synoptic problem.

The first thing that needs to be said is that Crossan has made an important contribution to the understanding of Mark's Gospel. Although many of my remarks below will be critical ones, I must acknowledge at the outset that I found the essay exciting and interesting to read. The analysis has been carefully done and Crossan presents some very strong arguments for the thesis he proposes.

Nevertheless, from the point of view of one interested in the synoptic problem, it seems to me unfortunate that in the first section ("The Tradition Before Mark"), where Crossan discusses attempts to separate pre-Marcan tradition from Marcan redaction, no mention whatsoever is made of the possibility that Mark might have employed one or more of the other canonical Gospels as a source.[3] It may be true that the priority of

---

[1]John Dominic Crossan, "Empty Tomb and Absent Lord," *The Passion Narrative in Mark* (Philadelphia: Fortress Press, 1976). This essay was made available to me in galleys and thus citations below cannot include reference to specific page numbers.

[2]Thomas R. W. Longstaff, *Evidence of Conflation in Mark? A Study in the Synoptic Problem* (Unpublished dissertation, Columbia University, 1973; forthcoming from the Scholars Press in the S.B.L. Dissertation Series). In this study I have analyzed several known examples of conflation, attempted to define the literary characteristics which result from the use of this editorial method, and examined selected Marcan pericopae to determine whether the suggestion that Mark has conflated material taken from Matthew and Luke is a reasonable one. I concluded that it is and that the Griesbach hypothesis provides a viable alternative to the two-document hypothesis as a solution to the synoptic problem.

[3]Several theories suggesting such a possibility have been proposed, e.g., B. C. Butler, *The Originality of St. Matthew* (Cambridge: The University Press, 1951), W. R. Farmer, *The Synoptic Problem* (New York: The Macmillan Co., 1964), and R. L. Lindsey, *A Hebrew Translation of the Gospel of Mark* (Jerusalem: Duglith Publishers, no date).

Mark is an hypothesis sufficiently widely accepted as to require no further justification, and yet in an essay arguing that "there are no versions of ET *before* Mk" and "those *after* Mk all derive from him" this is a serious omission. To be fair to Crossan it must be noted that in the subsequent sections ("The Tradition After Mark" and "The Tradition In Mark") he does present a well reasoned account of the history of the development of the tradition of the Empty Tomb, discussing the ways in which the several versions of the tradition found in the other three Gospels may be understood as modifications of the Marcan narrative, and how the tradition in Mark itself may best be understood as the "complete creation of Mk himself." In this connection Crossan makes several points which seem to weigh in support of Marcan priority.

Among these points one of the more interesting and important is the suggestion that the Gospel of Signs (understood as a "narrative source underlying the Fourth Gospel") is dependent upon the Gospel of Mark for the basic tradition of the Empty Tomb.[4] Diagrammatically, Crossan's understanding of the literary relationships among the Gospels could be represented as follows:

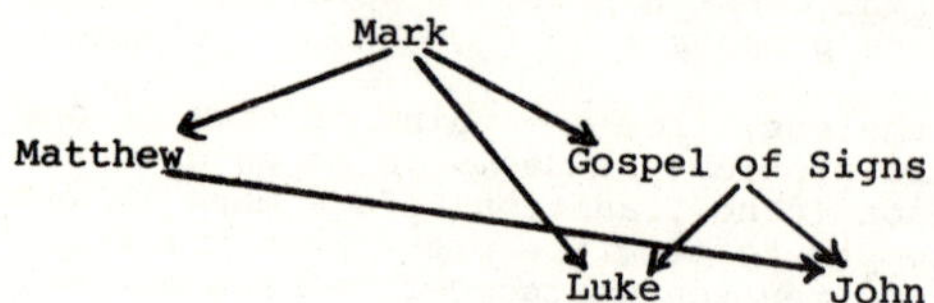

Although the implications of this suggestion cannot be explored in this paper (indeed, the whole range of material common to Mark and John would have to be examined with reference to the parallel passages in Luke) scholars familiar with the complexities of the synoptic problem will recognize that this diagram would be very difficult to reverse in order to place another Gospel in the position occupied by Mark.

Another point which might weigh in favor of Marcan priority emerges in Crossan's comments about the form of Mk 16:1-8. Calling attention to the formal similarity between Mk 16:1-8 and Mk 6:45-51 Crossan suggests that "the form of Mk 16:1-8 is derived directly and deliberately from 6:45-51" and further that the traditions describing appearances of the Risen Jesus (Mt 28:8-10 and Jn 20:14-18) are based upon this same narrative form. If a detailed form-critical study of these passages (which I have not yet undertaken) will indeed confirm these suggestions then the thesis that Mark has created the Empty Tomb tradition would be substantially strengthened. In this regard (although Crossan does not mention it) the form under consideration appears also in Matthew's account of the Women at the Tomb, however in Matthew the form seems to be somewhat disrupted since the Recognition (Mt 28:4) is by the guards although it is the women who receive the Greeting (Mt 28:5-6).

---

[4]While recognizing that a fuller understanding of the possible relationship between the Gospel of Signs and Mark is needed, Crossan does propose four arguments in support of the view that the author of the Gospel of Signs may have known Mark.

But while several such points in Crossan's essay may be understood to weigh in favor of Marcan priority, that hypothesis cannot be said to have been established in this work; it remains a presupposition with which the author begins. This needs to be pointed out for the acceptance of the theory has significantly affected the analysis and the conclusions.

For example, at the beginning of the second section ("The Tradition After Mark") Crossan, discussing the tradition about the Guards at the Tomb (Mt 28:4, 11-15; cf. 27:62-66), argues that this "element indicates that there was already a Jewish polemic *against the Mkan story* within the Matthean environment" and concludes that this tradition "is neither prior to nor independent *of Mk*" (emphases mine). But the case is stated far too strongly. Critical caution will require that one claim no more than that Matthew (or his source) knew a tradition about the Empty Tomb similar to that found in Mark (perhaps, but not necessarily, from that Gospel), either knew of or anticipated a Jewish polemic against the story, and either knew of or created a Christian response to the polemic. Although Crossan is correct (and helpfully so) when he reminds us that a presumption of fact is not the same thing as a tradition, it does not follow that there are no traditions prior to the time of the writing of the Gospels. It seems clear to me (and I suspect Crossan would agree) that the Evangelists have not only created traditions, they have also incorporated traditions (often with modifications) already present in oral and written form in their communities. Crossan's conclusion goes too far since it has not been shown that Matthew has taken this particular tradition from Mark. To be sure, Crossan indicates that he presupposes the validity of "Occam's razor,"[5] however that principle would support his statements in this instance only if it could be shown that Mark has created the tradition of the Empty Tomb and not himself taken it from a source (written or oral). But that is the general conclusion toward which Crossan is moving and the argument would become circular if the conclusion were used as an essential element in one of the steps by which it is reached.

It may be helpful at this point to note that there is no one Gospel which in every case preserves the earliest form of the tradition. Whatever solution to the synoptic problem one accepts as a working hypothesis there will be occasions when it will be necessary to acknowledge that the earlier form of a tradition is to be found in a Gospel considered secondary.[6] The fact that Mark preserves the earliest form of the tradition is not conclusive evidence that this Gospel is the source of the others. It is at least possible that Mark knew the tradition about the Guards at the Tomb (perhaps, but not necessarily, from Matthew) but wrote in a situation where and to people for whom the issue was unimportant or irrelevant.

---

[5]It may be noted, however, that among logicians and philosophers of science the validity of this principle is the subject of heated debate. Nevertheless, we can agree that the *unnecessary* postulation of multiple traditions is to be avoided.

[6]I am indebted to Reginald H. Fuller, who in recent years has devoted a good deal of attention and energy to the synoptic problem, for helping me to see this clearly.

Crossan's acceptance of Marcan priority has also influenced his discussion of the tradition in Mark. He understands Mark's Gospel to be

> an intra-Christian polemic against theological opponents characterized by (1) interest in miracles and apparitions rather than suffering and service; (2) very little sympathy with the Gentile mission especially insofar as this questioned the validity of the Law; (3) an appeal to the authority of the Jerusalem mother Church, based both on the family of Jesus and on the original disciples of Jesus: the twelve, the inner three, and Peter in particular.

Crossan does not recognize, however, that there is a strong similarity between his description of Mark's "theological opponents" and the perspectives of the other canonical Gospels. This similarity may be illustrated by the following details (which are not intended to be a complete or comprehensive list):

(1) An interest in miracles: In his study of the miracles Fuller has concluded that "Luke is more interested than the other evangelists in the miracles as facts of past history. They are part, and indeed the most important part, of Jesus' biography prior to his passion."[7] Fuller also points out that in Matthew the active role of the disciples in the miraculous feedings is more strongly emphasized than in Mark and that only in Matthew does Peter, like Jesus, walk on the water (Mt 14:28-31).[8] It is surely a safe conclusion that Matthew and Luke more strongly emphasize miracles than does Mark. Finally, the importance of miracles, understood as signs, for the Fourth Gospel may be noted.

(2) Little concern for the Gentile mission and concern for the validity of the Law: Here we need only point to two key passages in Matthew, passages which I would take to be important ones for understanding the theological perspectives of this author:[9] Mt 10:5-6, "These twelve Jesus sent out, charging them, 'Go nowhere among the Gentiles, and enter no town of the Samaritans, but go rather to the lost sheep of the house of Israel.'" (Cf. also Mt 15:24, "He answered, 'I was sent only to the lost sheep of the house of Israel.'"), and Mt 5:17-20:

> Think not that I have come to abolish the law and the prophets; I have come not to abolish them but to fulfill them. For truly, I say to you, till heaven and earth pass away, not an iota,

---

[7]Reginald H. Fuller, *Interpreting the Miracles* (London: SCM Press, Ltd., 1963), p. 87.

[8]*Ibid.*, pp. 79-80. See also Held's contribution in Günther Bornkamm, Gerhard Barth and Heinz Joachim Held, *Tradition and Interpretation in Matthew* (Philadelphia: The Westminster Press, 1963).

[9]See also Barth's contribution to the volume: *Tradition and Interpretation in Matthew, op. cit.*

> not a dot, will pass from the law until all is accomplished. Whoever then relaxes one of the least of these commandments and teaches men so, shall be called least in the kingdom of heaven; but he who does them and teaches them shall be called great in the kingdom of heaven. For I tell you, unless your righteousness exceeds that of the scribes and Pharisees, you will never enter the kingdom of heaven.

(3) The authority of the Jerusalem Church and the bases for that authority: Here three points will suffice by way of illustration. First, the author of Luke-Acts clearly understands Jerusalem to be the center (theologically and historically) from which the Gospel originates. This is evident (a) in the manner in which the narrative moves from its beginning with Zechariah in the temple at Jerusalem to its conclusion with Paul preaching quite openly and successfully in Rome, (b) in the manner in which Acts 1:8 likewise envisions the spread of the Gospel from Jerusalem to the whole world, and (c) in the manner in which the activity of Paul is understood to be based in Jerusalem (it is from Jerusalem that Paul embarks on his "missionary journeys" and to Jerusalem that Paul returns). Second, the importance of "The Twelve" in Luke-Acts (and especially as witnesses to the resurrection) is well known and particularly evident in Acts 1:15-26, the story of the selection of Matthias to replace Judas. This event is understood to take place in Jerusalem and the narrative clearly stresses not only the importance of the twelve but the primacy of Peter as well. Third, whatever one says about the much discussed passage in Mt 16:17-19 ("And Jesus answered him, 'Blessed are you, Simon Bar-Jona! For flesh and blood has not revealed this to you, but my Father who is in heaven. And I tell you, you are Peter, and on this rock I will build my church, and the powers of death shall not prevail against it. I will give you the keys of the kingdom of heaven, and whatever you bind on earth shall be bound in heaven, and whatever you loose on earth shall be loosed in heaven.'"), there can be no doubt but that this emphasizes most strongly the authority of Peter and the disciples in the Church.

Crossan's analysis, it seems to me, does not *require* the conclusion that Mark has created the tradition of the Empty Tomb. It could, in fact, present at least one problem for the theory of Marcan priority. If in theological perspective Matthew and Luke are frequently close to the views against which Mark directed his Gospel, how will one understand the ways in which these two might have used Mark as a source, re-introducing ideas which Mark might have found objectionable and yet apparently often with great respect for the Marcan text? Could Matthew and Luke instead be the "theological opponents" to whom Crossan refers? In view of the comments above and the vigor with which Farmer and others[10] have attempted to show that the Griesbach hypothesis is a viable alternative solution to the synoptic problem (indeed, one to be preferred) it is also unfortunate that this possibility was never considered.

---

[10]See Fuller's summary in Reginald H. Fuller, E. P. Sanders and Thomas R. W. Longstaff, "The Synoptic Problem: After Ten Years," *Perkins Journal*, XXVII (No. 2, Winter, 1975), pp. 63-68.

Thus far in this paper I have attempted to show that Crossan's assumption of Marcan priority is a serious methodological flaw in an essay which argues that there are no versions of the Empty Tomb tradition before Mark and that all those after Mark derive from him. I do not wish to argue here that the theory of Marcan priority is wrong, but I do want to suggest, as I have done in the dissertation referred to above, that the synoptic problem should be treated as an open question, especially in a study such as the one presently under review. Further, although I cannot present here a detailed analysis of the story of the Empty Tomb, I would like to suggest very briefly the direction which an alternative understanding of the history of the tradition, employing Griesbach's solution to the synoptic problem as a working hypothesis, might take.

The pericope in Matthew's Gospel begins with the simple comment that on the first day of the week the women (Mary Magdalene and the other Mary) came to see the grave. It is interesting to note that nothing is said about the reason for their coming and that therefore there is no suggestion in Matthew of an incomplete burial (Mt 27:59). It is possible (although support for this suggestion is not strong) that Matthew has in mind the custom (attested later, Sem. 8.1) of "watching" a grave for a period of three days to insure that the accidental interrment of a person still alive had not occurred.

Matthew next describes a scene in which, following an earthquake, an angel descends from heaven and (presumably in the presence of the women[11]) rolls away the stone from the entrance to the grave. It is important to note that the stone is not rolled away to allow the Risen Jesus to emerge from the tomb (as in the Gospel of Peter and *perhaps* in Mark and Luke). It seems very likely that for Matthew the stone represents a barrier to the discovery of the Empty Tomb (cf. Mt 27:60ff. and especially 27:66) which must be removed. It has already been suggested above that Matthew (or his source) has combined the tradition of the Empty Tomb with the Jewish polemic against it and the Christian response. The completeness with which this combination has been accomplished is evident in the fact that the guards appear not only in 27:62-66 and 28:11-15 but in 28:4 as well (but see my comment on this verse above). The angel next proclaims the resurrection[12] and instructs the women to tell the disciples that they will see Jesus in the Galilee.[13] The scene closes as the women depart from the tomb, with fear and great joy, to fulfill the angel's command.

---

[11]There seems to be no reason for the suggestion that the women found the tomb open, a suggestion made in W. F. Albright and C. S. Mann, *The Anchor Bible: Matthew* (Garden City: Doubleday & Co., Inc., 1971), p. 358.

[12]It should be noted that Crossan's observation that outside of Mk 16:6 the "almost titular" use of τὸν ἐσταυρωμένον is found only in Paul is not accurate. It is also in Mt 28:5.

[13]In this brief paper discussion of the meaning of προάγει ὑμᾶς εἰς τὴν Γαλιλαίαν is not possible (although the point is important). It seems to me that Matthew here anticipates the post-resurrection appearances of Jesus to the disciples whereas Mark anticipates the parousia.

Mt 28:9-10 describes the appearance of the Risen Jesus to the women. Crossan ignores the plain meaning of the words καὶ ἀπελθοῦσαι ταχὺ ἀπὸ τοῦ μνημείου (Mt 28:8) when he argues that Matthew and John are parallel in that both include an appearance of Jesus to the women at the tomb. In Matthew the appearance of Jesus serves to relieve the women's fears and to confirm the command given them by the angel. These verses can easily be removed from the narrative without disrupting the continuity (indeed, the narrative reads more smoothly without these verses) and the possibility should be explored that they constitute a later insertion into the Matthean account.

After the account of the bribing of the soldiers (Mt 28:11-15), a continuation of the Christian response to the Jewish polemic, Matthew reports the appearance of Jesus to the disciples in the Galilee, which is both the fulfillment of his promise and the Church's mandate to a more universal mission.

Mt 28:1-16, therefore, forms a complex but comprehensible unit, understandable as the Matthean interpretation of traditions known in his community.

Turning to Luke's account, one discovers several important differences in the narrative. In the first place, Luke does include a comment about the reason for the women's visit (they are bringing spices to anoint the body) and is, in fact, quite explicit about the incompleteness of the burial provisions (Lk 23:55-56). Luke, however, is not concerned about the barrier to inspection of the tomb (as Matthew might have been). He is concerned at once with the discovery of the Empty Tomb itself and therefore reports that upon arrival the women found the stone rolled away, entered the tomb, but did not find the body. Luke describes the women at the tomb, not as afraid, but as confused or uncertain until the angels (Luke mentions two) appear to remind them that Jesus had predicted his crucifixion and resurrection. It should be noted that the words προάγει ὑμᾶς εἰς τὴν Γαλιλαίαν, ἐκεῖ αὐτὸν ὄψεσθε have become in Luke μνήσθητε ὡς ἐλάλησεν ὑμῖν ἔτι ὢν ἐν τῇ Γαλιλαίᾳ. This change is, of course, explained by the fact that Luke places the post-resurrection appearances of Jesus in Jerusalem rather than in the Galilee. The change, however, may indicate that Luke knew the tradition in a form more like that now found in Matthew than that now found in Mark. Following the appearance of the angels the women return to tell the disciples what had happened but the disciples do not believe them.

If one accepts Lk 24:12 as authentic (as Crossan does), this verse will be understood both to provide apostolic confirmation of the emptiness of the tomb and to heighten the element of the disciples' failure to believe the report of the women.

Luke concludes his Gospel with accounts of several appearances of the Risen Jesus to his disciples, both in Jerusalem itself and in the surrounding area, and finally reports the ascension of Jesus from Bethany with the subsequent return of the disciples to Jerusalem (understood, as we have seen, to be the center from which the Gospel then spreads).

Examined in this linear way the accounts in Matthew and Luke emerge as strikingly different. Some of the more important differences may be indicated by a series of questions: (1) Why did the women come to visit the tomb on Sunday morning? Was the burial complete or incomplete? (2) Were guards placed at the tomb to insure that there be no fraud or not? (3) When was the stone rolled away and by whom? Were there any witnesses to this event? (4) What did the angel say to the women? Were there two angels? (5) What was the reaction of the disciples to the women's report? Did they believe or not? (6) Did Jesus appear to the women prior to appearing to the disciples? (7) Was Peter the first of the disciples to see the Risen Jesus? (8) Did Jesus appear to the disciples in the Galilee or in Jerusalem?

When considering the Marcan narrative from the alternate perspective of the Griesbach hypothesis reference must be made to the work of David Dungan. In two separate articles[14] he has convincingly demonstrated that it was often necessary for the philosophical and religious movements of the ancient world to defend themselves against the charges of rival movements that their beliefs were ridiculous because they were inconsistent or contradictory. Dungan is able to document a tendency in Christianity (as in the other movements he examines) to produce Gospel texts from which serious contradictions and inconsistencies have been removed (the most well known being, of course, the Diatessaron of Tatian). Although we cannot do justice to Dungan's detailed argument here, it can be noted that he concludes: "The suggestion of W. R. Farmer, that in its basic structure Mark seems to have been composed along a sort of neutral or middle-term principle, no longer seems as far-fetched as it did."[15]

And, indeed, Mk 16:1-8 can be understood as an attempt to find a middle ground between the views represented in Matthew and Luke and as an attempt to produce a Gospel useful to the Church in a situation where an expression of theological unity had become of great importance (perhaps at Rome toward the end of the first century). The Marcan narrative has similarities to each of the others. Among these are such details as the following: with Luke Mark mentions the reason why the women come to the tomb; with Matthew he comments on the size of the stone, but with Luke indicates that it had been removed before the women arrived; Mark agrees closely with Matthew in the report of the angel's words (and that there is only one messenger, perhaps not an angel in Mark) but with Luke in the suggestion that Jesus' earlier words are to be recalled; and with Luke Mark makes special mention of Peter (Mk 16:7/Lk 24:34, perhaps an anomaly in Mark if one accepts Crossan's analysis). With regard to the potentially divisive questions of to whom and where the Risen Jesus appeared Mark is silent and yet it must be noted that his account contains the essentials of Christian orthodoxy: the crucifixion (τὸν Ναζαρηνὸν τὸν ἐσταυρωμένον), the resurrection (ἠγέρθη, οὐκ ἔστιν ὧδε), and the expectation of the parousia (προάγει ὑμᾶς εἰς τὴν Γαλιλαίαν· ἐκεῖ αὐτὸν ὄψεσθε, καθὼς εἶπεν ὑμῖν). My own ex-

---

[14]David L. Dungan, "Mark--The Abridgement of Matthew and Luke," *Jesus and Man's Hope*, I (Pittsburgh: Pittsburgh Theological Seminary, 1970), pp. 51-97; and "Reactionary Trends in the Gospel Producing Activity of the Early Church? Marcion, Tatian, Mark," *L'evangile de Marc, Tradition et Redaction* (Louvain, 1975), pp. 188ff. These two articles will bear careful study.

[15]Dungan, "Reactionary Trends...," *op. cit.*, p. 202.

amination of this pericope has thus far given me no cause to abandon my earlier conclusion that the Griesbach hypothesis is a viable solution to the synoptic problem and one that in many ways is to be preferred over the two-document hypothesis.[16]

Within the context of the generally accepted solution to the synoptic problem, however, Crossan's essay provides some valuable and thought provoking suggestions about the way in which Mk 16:1-8 and the subsequent history of the tradition of the Empty Tomb might be understood.[17] But the discussion of this pericope should not be confined to such narrow parameters; other proposals about the literary interrelationships among the Gospels should at least be considered. In this regard it is interesting to note that one of the plenary sessions of the S.N.T.S. at its annual meeting this year was devoted to the synoptic problem (at the time this paper was written that meeting had not yet been held; by the time it is read the meeting will be past history). The procedure agreed upon called for the detailed examination of a single pericope with interpretations based upon several solutions to the synoptic problem being presented for discussion. The pericope selected as a particularly important (and neutral) test case (the selection was made by Prof. F. Neirynck, the Chairman of the S.N.T.S. Seminar on the Synoptic Problem who has himself written on the passage) was Mk 16:1-8.

I would hope that the S.B.L. Seminar on Mark would first give its careful attention to Crossan's essay and then widen the scope of the discussion to include other proposals which might reasonably explain the enigmatic ending of Mark's Gospel.

---

[16]Longstaff, *op. cit.*, pp. 251-255.

[17]There are, however, several factual errors to be corrected. I have attempted to point out some of these above.

S 188

THE SOURCES OF LUKE: A PROPOSAL FOR THE CONSULTATION ON THE RELATIONSHIPS OF THE GOSPELS

Joseph B. Tyson
Southern Methodist University

At the first sessions of the Consultation on the Relationships of the Gospels in 1975, the Synoptic problem was front and center. Some of us may have assumed that the title given to the Consultation was a euphemism for the Synoptic problem. As the sessions progressed, however, it became increasingly clear that, while many persons had substantial doubts about the prevailing hypothesis of Synoptic relationships, they nevertheless felt no urgency to solve the problem. There were several proposals that the Gospels should be studied as finished literary products rather than in their interrelatedness.

I should argue that the Consultation need not confine itself to the Synoptic problem but that the literary relationships of the Gospels need intensive study from a wide spectrum of scholarly perspectives. Since no such concentrated study is presently being pursued in the Society, it seems appropriate that it should become a matter of central concern for one seminar. As will become clear, I think that studies of the Gospels as finished products have an important place in the study of literary relationships. A Gospel writer is not simply a collector and arranger of received sayings and narratives; he is a redactor who has a certain aim in view and who controls his materials so that they may serve his aims. Studies which examine the Gospels as finished products should lead to an identification of those redactional aims which have guided the Evangelists. If these studies can proceed without dependence on a particular hypothesis of Synoptic relationships, they should be of significant help in the study of those relationships.

It is my suggestion that the Consultation seek to form a seminar, which will undertake to investigate various approaches to the literary relationships of the Gospels and which will, in particular, seek to formulate a convincing solution to the Synoptic problem. I suggest that this problem be kept central in the work of the seminar and that studies which promise to advance an understanding of the literary relationships of the Synoptic Gospels be encouraged.

In addition, I should like to suggest a project which would engage some, if not all, members of the proposed seminar. The project would be one which would focus attention on the Gospel of Luke and the probable sources used by the third Evangelist. Before I explain the proposal in detail, it will be necessary to explore the assumptions which undergird the proposal.

The first assumption is that the question of sources is vital in historical and literary studies. To speak of sources does not automatically mean the denigration of the integrity of literary documents.[1] For it is by no means certain that we can understand the purpose of an individual Evangelist unless we have some perception of the strictures under which he worked. Some of those strictures are to be found in the written documents that the Evangelist read, revered, and used. Moreover, the history of early Christianity includes the process by which those Gospels came to be written, and historical study which is not interested in the sequence in which they were written is simply uninterested in a part of that history. It is, of course, naive to think that the earliest Gospel, whichever it is, is *ipso facto* the most reliable in providing information about the historical Jesus. But surely our perception of the history of thought about Jesus is affected by our conception of the literary relationships of the Gospels.

The second assumption is based upon the recognition that there are currently two leading hypotheses that claim to explain the literary relationships of the Synoptic Gospels: the two-document hypothesis and the Griesbach hypothesis. To state the matter more correctly, the Griesbach hypothesis is the one which has emerged as the most serious competitor to the two-document hypothesis, which is affirmed by the majority of New Testament scholars. If this is an accurate statement of the current state of affairs, then it follows that prior attention should be given to these two theories. To be sure, a seminar on the relationships of the Gospels cannot ignore any hypothesis which is seriously advanced by a responsible scholar. Nevertheless, the seminar could agree that the prevailing theory and its leading rival, both of which have long histories and reputable scholarly sponsorship, should first have their day in court.

A third assumption is that the Gospel of Luke will provide a good place to test portions of the two leading hypotheses. This Gospel has a similar position in the two theories. In neither is it considered to be the earliest Gospel. Both theories recognize that its author made use of source material, some of which is no longer extant. Both maintain that Luke had access to one of our canonical Gospels, either Matthew or Mark. Of course a study of the sources of Luke will not constitute a full exploration of either theory, for it will not touch upon the relationship between Matthew and Mark. But it should be a fruitful study in that it should provide a means of falsifying one or both of the leading hypotheses. If it can be shown that Mark was a source for Luke, the Griesbach hypothesis has been falsified; if, contrariwise, we conclude that Luke used Matthew, the two-document hypothesis has been falsified. If neither or both were sources for Luke, both theories are falsified.[2]

A final assumption is that the Synoptic problem is probably not going to be solved by a blitzkrieg action or by the discovery of new evidence. Perhaps many of us wish that we could suddenly find the key that will automatically unlock the mysteries of the Synoptic problem, so that we could build important historical and theoretical studies upon this sure foundation. The failure of so many past attempts to solve the problem should and does make us cautious. Such caution was expressed by Joseph Fitzmyer in 1970, when he said that the Synoptic problem is "practically insoluble."[3] But Fitzmyer concluded his Pittsburgh paper without counseling that further work on the Synoptic problem should cease. He expressed some doubt that the re-opening of the question would yield good fruit, and he confessed his own attraction to the two-document hypothesis. But he also said that he intended to hold to this theory "until a more convincing way is found to present one or the other of [the alternatives]."[4] Fitzmyer represents a position which holds to the best available until a better comes along. That better will probably not come along through a sudden flash of inspiration. The Synoptic problem will be solved, if at all, through slow, perhaps plodding and apparently unexciting, but meticulously careful examinations of the important literary phenomena of the Gospels.

These four assumptions now lead to an explanation of my proposal. The proposal is that the seminar, or a task force thereof, examine the two leading source theories in their explanation of the relationship between Luke and the other two Synoptic Gospels. The seminar would take responsibility for the examination of two major questions: (*a*) Is there a direct literary relationship between Matthew and Luke? (*b*) What is the direction of the relationship between Mark and Luke? These two questions are carefully phrased in order to enable us to study both the two-document hypothesis and the Griesbach hypothesis and to do so evenhandedly. The first question, which focuses on the relationship between Matthew and Luke, asks about the nature of that relationship--whether direct, as maintained by the Griesbach hypothesis, or indirect, as maintained by the two-document hypothesis. The second question assumes a direct literary relationship between Mark and Luke and so focuses attention on the direction of the relationship--whether Mark is prior, as in the two-document hypothesis, or Luke as in the Griesbach. These two questions should guide the work of the seminar, as that work is carried on in the areas of research developed below.

There are certain preliminary tasks and certain areas of research which will need to be agreed upon.

Preliminary Tasks

1) The first preliminary task is that of preparing a bibliography, concentrating on recent studies in the Gospel of Luke, or in Luke-Acts. The bibliography will probably serve our needs best if it contains brief annotations, indicating the value of each entry for the work of the seminar. Prof. T.R.W. Longstaff has prepared a bibliography on the Synoptic problem and has recently updated it. This work could serve as a starting point for a bibliography to serve the needs of scholars working on the sources of Luke.

2) The preparation of a bibliography leads naturally to the second preliminary task: a history of recent source-critical research on the Gospel of Luke. Such a history would show how Luke has been perceived *inter alia* in the two-document hypothesis, the proto-Luke theory, the theory of Robert L. Lindsey, and in the work of W.R. Farmer.[5] It should also show how Luke is understood in the various debates about Markan priority (B.C. Butler, Pierson Parker) and in the debate about Q (Austin Farrer, T.R. Rosché, A.W. Argyle, Vincent Taylor). It should include analyses of the work of proponents and critics of current hypotheses. It should be of value in helping all of us to understand the current state of affairs. Its value will be increased if it is written as a critical history, in which the author is in serious conversation with his subjects.

3) The study of the Gospel of Luke in its finished state has an important part to play at this point. The third preliminary task is a study of the literary method and ideology of Luke conducted without dependence on any source theory. The studies of William G. Thompson and Jack D. Kingsbury on Matthew may serve as models for this study.[6] The work of H.J. Cadbury, Hans Conzelmann *et al.* provide valid insights into the literary method and ideology of Luke, but they will not substitute for what is needed now.[7] It is hoped that the study of the Gospel in its finished state will enable us to separate the redactional matter from the source material with greater precision.

Areas of Research

Upon the accomplishment of these preliminary tasks, the seminar could begin to work on the project itself by concentraing attention on certain areas as research.

Analysis of Individual Pericopes

A number of pericopes should be chosen for source analysis. In the case of material in the double tradition, the major question should be: Can we make sense out of the pericope on the assumption that Luke used Matthew as a source for this pericope? It should be possible for several scholars to work on several pericopes from the double tradition and to show what we should need to conclude about Luke on the assumption that he used Matthew. We could then look at these studies to see if they produce consistent results. For example, a comparison of Matt 8:5-13 with Luke 7:1-10, on the assumption that Luke used Matthew, would show that Luke has altered Matthew's story of the centurion of Capernaum by introducing some Jewish elders who act as intermediaries between Jesus and the Gentile petitioner. Luke has also removed the sayings about the exclusion of Jews and placed them in a passage where the condemnation does not so clearly fall upon Jews (Luke 13:28-29). We should probably conclude that Luke takes a softer line toward Jews than does Matthew. If so, we should then need to know if similar studies of other pericopes confirm or deny this conclusion. For material in the triple tradition, the task is a bit more complex. It will be necessary to compare Luke's version of the pericope with that in the other two and to make a preliminary judgment about the probable source. At this stage we ask: Is it more reasonable to conclude that Luke used Matthew or that he used Mark? If this preliminary judgment points to Mark, we must then examine the question of direction: Is it more likely that Luke used Mark or that Mark used Luke?

Organization and Sequence

A pericope-by-pericope analysis, even if complete, will not produce a convincing proof of Synoptic relationships. Serious attention must concurrently be given to larger matters such as agreements in organization and sequence. On the assumption that an editor is free to arrange his materials in line with his own intentions and so to structure his document, we should compare the organization of Luke with the other Synoptics and look for traces of influence. Are there, for example, suggestions in either Matthew or Mark that may have led Luke to compose his travel section in 9:51-19:27? We are, by now, familiar with the classical argument on order and with its refutation. It now appears that the argument, as a support for the two-document hypothesis, has been neutralized, and so it may seem that it is no longer fruitful to pursue studies of sequence. But not enough attention has been given to E.P. Sanders' contention that some agreements in the order of materials in Matthew and Luke have been overlooked because scholars have depended too heavily upon the pericope divisions of Tischendorf.[8] Moreover, Sanders' analysis and restatement of F.H. Woods's principles should be examined. Sanders restates Woods's principles as follows: "If Matthew and Luke generally agree with Mark...in the arrangement of the Marcan material, but disagree in the arrangement of the Q material, there is really only one explanation. Matthew and Luke have used two sources independently...But any agreements, even minor ones, between Matthew and Luke on a point of order which cannot be attributed to their independent use of Mark and Q will argue strongly that there must have been some other contact between the first and third gospels."[9] Sanders finds that Matthew and Luke do sometimes agree in the order of materials in such a way as to suggest that they were not independent of one another.

Verbal Agreements

A study of verbal agreements is a *sine qua non* in an examination of alleged literary sources. Considerable sophistication has been demonstrated in the past few years in studies by Solages, Honoré, and Morgenthaler.[10] The seminar should be able to capitalize on these works in the study of verbal agreements between Luke and the other Synoptics. Although it is simplistic to think that the Gospel which has the higher rate of verbal agreements with Luke is its source, a measure of verbal agreements is one in a concatenation of factors to be considered. While the rate of verbal agreements must be measured in each pericope to be analyzed, we should also have a perception of the rate in all comparable sections, in large expanses of material, and in different kinds of material. For example, in triple material does Luke have a higher rate of agreement with Mark or with Matthew? Does he have a higher rate of agreement with Matthew in double material than in triple material?[11]

Geographical Elements

Form critics usually attribute geographical elements to the redactional stage in the production of the Gospels. This is done on the assumption that the oral tradition was relatively free of location indicators and that the Gospel writers needed to include them to provide a sense of order and movement in their narratives. At the same time, critics such as Bultmann were prepared to admit that some geographical elements were retained within the oral tradition and transmitted by it.[12] Certain stories demanded certain locations. If a story makes no sense in a location other than the given one, or if it makes no sense with the given location removed, then that location indicator must have been a part of the story at the earliest date. Sometimes a location given in a story will conflict with the redactional principles of a Gospel writer, and it is in such places that we have signs of the use of a source. The redactor may even be led to provide a location for his material which is inconsistent with the one given in his source. Bultmann pointed to such a case in Mark 8:22-23. According to 8:23, the healing of the blind man occurred outside a village, while 8:22 has Jesus go into Bethsaida. Bultmann concluded that the reference to Bethsaida in Mark 8:22 was editorial.[13] An example in Luke is to be found in the feeding of the five thousand, which, by the very nature of the case, must occur in a deserted place (9:12) but is set by Luke in a city called Bethsaida (9:10b). Hans Conzelmann[14] called attention to the importance of geographical elements for understanding Luke's theology. Since he did not raise the question of sources, he did not examine geographical elements as signs of sources. Much of his work is, nevertheless, useful to those scholars who are interested in the source question.

Doublets

Doublets have classically been understood as signs of sources. J.C. Hawkins listed twelve doublets in Luke and concluded that most of them suggest the use of two sources, although one (Luke 12:11, 12; 21:14, 15) seems "to show that freedom of editors in using their own phraseology."[15] Surely the seminar can offer an occasion to examine the Lukan doublets afresh.

Adoption of Redactional Characteristics

Each gospel writer must have used words and phrases in such characteristic ways that they form a kind of hand-print.

If words or phrases which are judged to be characteristic of Mark or of Matthew show up in Luke, that should constitute a sign of the use of a source. W.R. Farmer stated the principle as follows: "That form of a tradition which exhibits words or phrases characteristic of a redactor whose hand is only traceable in another Gospel is to be adjudged secondary to the form of the parallel tradition in the Gospel where the redactor's hand can be clearly traced, provided the characteristic word or phrase occurs in the former Gospel only in passages closely paralleled in the latter, where the verbatim agreement indicates direct literary dependence."[16] Lists of words and phrases characteristic of Matthew and Mark are now being prepared and will be useful in studies in Luke.[17]

Other Evidence of Secondary Documents

The project should also include an application to the Gospel of Luke of E.D. Burton's six evidences of the secondary character of a document. Although these principles are well-known, it will be convenient to have them before us: "(1) manifest misunderstanding of what stands in one document on the part of the writer of the other; (2) insertion by one writer of material not in the other, and clearly interrupting the course of thought or symmetry of plan in the other; (3) clear omission from one document of matter which was in the other, the omission of which destroys the connection; (4) insertion of matter the motive for which can be clearly seen in the light of the author's general aim, while no motive can be discovered for its omission by the author if he had had it in his source; (5) vice versa omission of matter traceable to the motive natural to the writer when the insertion (of the same matter in the other Gospel) could not thus be accounted for; (6) alterations of other kinds which conform the matter to the general method or tendency of the author."[18] To these, Farmer's third canon of criticism should be added: "That form of a tradition which exhibits explanatory redactional glosses, and expansions aimed to make the tradition more applicable to the needs of the Church, is to be adjudged secondary to a form of the tradition which is free of such redactional glosses and expansions."[19] The application of these principles should be most helpful in identifying the probable source or sources of Luke. In this, as in all areas of research, methodological considerations must be kept constantly in mind.

These areas of research are suggestive of topics which might engage members of the projected seminar. They do not constitute an exhaustive list, and perhaps not all will be of interest. But the project as a whole is one which can marshal the energies and abilities of a number of scholars in an effort which has a chance of making progress toward the solution of a thorny problem.

NOTES

1. In his paper for the Pittsburgh Festival on the Gospels, Roland M. Frye warned against an excessive attention to sources which would result in "disintegrating criticism." See "A Literary Perspective for the Criticism of the Gospels," in *Jesus and Man's Hope*, ed. Donald G. Miller and D. Y. Hadidian (Pittsburgh: Pittsburgh Theological Seminary, 1971) II, 193-221. Frye said that disintegrating criticism "concentrates upon fragments at the expense of the literary work as a whole, and diverts attention from the literature as such" (p. 215). He maintained that this kind of criticism had been generally abandoned in humanistic studies. While I respond positively to much that Prof. Frye said in

this paper, I doubt that the proposal I have in mind can be considered to be a form of disintegrating criticism. The proposal calls for the examination of the possibility that Matthew or Mark may have been a source for Luke. Consequently, there will be a concentration upon these three gospels in their wholeness. There need be no suggestion that we substitute the sources for the Gospel of Luke itself. Rather the effort is to gain a clearer picture of the third Gospel. Although Frye says that modern critics of Shakespeare, Shaw, and Sherwood rarely turn to the sources which these dramatists used, he does not deny that a better understanding has resulted from a knowledge of them. His comparison of the Gospels with dramatic histories concentrates on the skill with which the dramatist has portrayed large events by representative characters and selected events. The aim of the dramatic historian is to point to an "essential truth," even though he may present an "inexact picture of some accidental facts" (quoted from G.B. Shaw; cf. Frye, p. 210). Frye has not made it clear how the literary critic identifies the dramatist's skill and measures his approach to "essential truth" without at some point comparing the finished product with the sources. Is it possible that the Shakespeare critic is able to concentrate upon the finished product *because* his work is undergirded by a source analysis in which all his colleagues have confidence?

2. The existence of the Book of Acts is an additional benefit. It can be used as a control document for the study of the Gospel of Luke.

3. Joseph A. Fitzmyer, "The Priority of Mark and the 'Q' Source in Luke," in *Jesus and Man's Hope* I, 131-170. It is not clear whether Fitzmyer meant that the Synoptic problem is almost insoluble or insoluble in practice.

4. *Ibid.*, p. 162.

5. Cf. Robert L. Lindsey, "A New Approach to the Synoptic Gospels" (Jerusalem: Dugwith, 1971); W.R. Farmer, *The Synoptic Problem* (New York: Macmillan, 1964).

6. W.G. Thompson, *Matthew's Advice to a Divided Community* (Rome: Biblical Institute Press, 1970); "An Historical Perspective in the Gospel of Matthew," *JBL* 93 (1974) 243-262; J.D. Kingsbury, *The Parables of Jesus in Matthew 13* (Richmond: John Knox Press, 1969); "The Structure of Matthew's Gospel and his Concept of Salvation-History," *CBQ* 35 (1973) 451-474; "The Composition and Christology of Matt. 28: 16-20," *JBL* 93 (1974) 573-584; "Form and Message of Matthew," *Int* 29 (1975) 13-23; "The Title, 'Son of God,' in Matthew's Gospel," *Biblical Theology Bulletin* 5 (1975) 3-31.

7. H.J. Cadbury, *The Style and Literary Method of Luke* (Cambrige: Harvard University Press, 1919); *The Making of Luke-Acts* (New York: Macmillan, 1927); Hans Conzelmann, *The Theology of St. Luke*, tr. Geoffrey Buswell (New York: Harper and Bros., 1960).

8. E.P. Sanders, "The Argument from Order and the Relationship between Matthew and Luke," *NTS* 15 (1969) 249-261. Cf. also my article "Sequential Parallelism in the Synoptic Gospels," *NTS* 22 (1976) 276-308. The article by F.H. Woods, referred to by Sanders, is "The Origin and Mutual Relations of the Synoptic Gospels," in *Studia Biblica et Ecclesiastica*, ed.

S.R. Driver, T.K. Cheyne, and W. Sanday (Oxford: Clarendon Press, 1890) II, 59-104.

9. Sanders, *op. cit.*, p. 252.

10. Cf. B. de Solages, *A Greek Synopsis of the Gospels* (Leyden: E.J. Brill, 1959); A.M. Honoré, "A Statistical Study of the Synoptic Problem," *NovT* 10 (1968) 95-147; Robert Morgenthaler, *Statistische Synopse* (Zürich/Stuttgart: Gotthelf-Verlag, 1971).

11. Prof. T.R.W. Longstaff and I are currently preparing a *Synoptic Abstract*, which should be of assistance in tracing patterns of verbal agreements. It is hoped that this book will soon be available.

12. Cf. R. Bultmann, *The History of the Synoptic Tradition*, tr. John Marsh (New York: Harper and Row, 1963), p. 338f.

13. *Ibid.*, pp. 64-65.

14. *Op. cit.*

15. J.C. Hawkins, *Horae Synopticae*, second edition, reprinted (Grand Rapids: Baker Book House, 1968), p. 81.

16. Farmer, *op. cit.*, p. 228.

17. Cf. e.g. W.O. Walker, "A Method for Identifying Redactional Materials in Matthew on Functional and Linguistic Grounds," an unpublished paper presented to the Southwest Seminar on Gospel Studies, 1975; David Peabody, "Linguistic Phenomena which are Characteristic of Mark's Gospel," a preliminary study presented to the same seminar, 1975.

18. E.D. Burton, *Some Principles of Literary Criticism and the Synoptic Problem* (Chicago: Univ. of Chicago Press, 1904), p. 198.

19. Farmer, *op. cit.*, p. 228. This is the third of four canons of criticism. The fourth was cited earlier. The first two have been questioned but should receive serious discussion from the seminar. For an application of these canons, with opposite results, cf. C.H. Talbert and E.V. McKnight, "Can the Griesbach Hypothesis be Falsified?" *JBL* 91 (1972) 338-368; and G.W. Buchanan, "Has the Griesbach Hypothesis been Falsified?" *JBL* 93 (1974) 550-572. Cf. also E.P. Sanders, *The Tendencies of the Synoptic Tradition* (Cambridge: Cambridge Univ. Press, 1969).

S 189 JOSEPH B. TYSON'S PROPOSAL FOR THE CONSULTATION ON THE RELATIONSHIPS OF THE GOSPELS

A RESPONSE

William O. Walker, Jr.
Trinity University

I find myself in substantial agreement with what I understand to be the basic intent of Tyson's proposal and with much of its content. In particular, I am attracted by the idea of attempting to *falsify* one or both of the two currently leading hypotheses that claim to explain the literary relationships among the Synoptic Gospels.[1]

Put most simply, Tyson wants us to examine two major questions: (1) Is there a *direct* literary relationship between Matthew and Luke? and (2) What is the *direction* of the relationship between Mark and Luke? If the literary relationship between Matthew and Luke is direct, then the Two-Source Hypothesis is falsified; if it is indirect, then the Griesbach Hypothesis is falsified. If Luke is dependent upon Mark, then the Griesbach Hypothesis is falsified; if Mark is dependent upon Luke, then the Two-Source Hypothesis is falsified.

As William R. Farmer has pointed out, however, it is not certain that these two questions can be answered in such a way as to solve the Synoptic Problem, at least not along the lines suggested by Tyson.[2] *The first question* probably cannot be answered, since no adequate criteria have been developed for determining whether a given literary relationship is direct or indirect. At best, criteria might conceivably be developed for showing that a direct relationship does not exist, in which case the Griesbach Hypothesis could thereby be falsified, but this is doubtful in my opinion. There is no way, however, in which it could be shown conclusively that a direct relationship does exist, since any similarity between Matthew and Luke, whether *verbatim* or not, is capable of explanation on the assumption of common use of one or more hypothetical sources, and, for this reason, Tyson's first question cannot be used as a basis for falsifying the Two-Source Hypothesis. Similarly, *Tyson's second question*, at least in the form proposed by him, cannot be used as a basis for falsifying the Griesbach Hypothesis. Most of the material shared by Mark and Luke is also found in Matthew, and wherever it is generally agreed that Mark has a more "primitive" version of this "triple tradition" material than Luke, Mark's version is very close to Matthew's; thus, it is quite possible that Mark, writing later than both Matthew and Luke and using both as sources, has in these instances reproduced Matthew's original version more faithfully than has Luke and that Mark's more "primitive" version is thus not evidence for Lukan dependency upon Mark, since both may have depended upon Matthew.[3]

I am by no means opposed to this Consultaton adopting Tyson's proposal, since the results of such a study of Luke would be extremely valuable for a variety of purposes. It is possible, however, that a much more modest project might accomplish the same purposes intended by Tyson, while at the same time avoiding the problems just mentioned. *This project would involve posing only Tyson's second question--What is the direction of the relationship between Mark and Luke?--and examining only the materials found in both Mark and Luke but not in Matthew*. This would bypass the problem of developing criteria for distinguishing between direct and indirect literary relationships posed by Tyson's first question, and it would also avoid the problems posed by the "triple tradition" material inherent in his second question. Admittedly, the material shared by Mark and Luke but not Matthew is limited in quantity, but it should be adequate for our purposes.[4] Since both the Two-Source Hypothesis and the Griesbach Hypothesis assume a *direct* literary relationship between Mark and Luke, if it can be shown that the *direction* of this relationship *ever* runs from Mark to Luke then the Griesbach Hypothesis is thereby falsified, if it can be shown that the direction *ever* runs from Luke to Mark then the Two-Source Hypothesis is thereby falsified, and if it can be shown that the direction sometimes runs from Mark to Luke and sometimes from Luke to Mark then both hypotheses are thereby falsified. If there is no *direct* relationship between Mark and Luke, then, of course, both hypotheses are false, but the investigation of this question would lie outside the scope of the present project.

It should be pointed out that a similar examination of the materials found in both Matthew and Mark but not in Luke would also be in order. Since both the Two-Source Hypothesis and the Griesbach Hypothesis assume a *direct* literary relationship between Matthew and Mark, if it could be shown that the *direction* of that relationship *ever* runs from Matthew to Mark then the Two-Source Hypothesis would thereby be falsified, if it could be shown that the direction *ever* runs from Mark to Matthew then the Griesbach Hypothesis would thereby be falsified, and if it could be shown that the direction sometimes runs from Matthew to Mark and sometimes from Mark to Matthew then both hypotheses would thereby be falsified. Again, if there is no *direct* relationship between Matthew and Mark, then both hypotheses are false, but the investigation of this question would again lie outside the scope of the present project.

To be sure, a great deal more work needs to be done on refining the criteria for identifying the direction of a direct literary relationship, but, as Tyson points out, both E.D. Burton and Farmer have already suggested certain criteria,[5] and their suggestions have been evaluated, sometimes modified, and utilized by E.P. Sanders,[6] Charles H. Talbert and Edgar V. McKnight,[7] and George Wesley Buchanan.[8]

A final word of caution is in order. The falsification of the Two-Source Hypothesis will not necessarily indicate the validity of the Griesbach Hypothesis, or *vice versa*, but the falsification of one or both of the currently leading hypotheses would represent significant progress, even if only of a negative sort, toward the ultimate solution of the Synoptic Problem.

The "more modest project" here suggested would not, of course, occupy the attention of the entire Consultation. Thus, it is not proposed as a substitute for Tyson's proposal or for other studies which the Consultation might undertake. The question of the relationships among the Gospels is a multifaceted question, and it can and should be approached from as many different perspectives and in as many different ways as possible.

NOTES

1. This is not to say that I am necessarily convinced that one or the other of these two hypotheses does, in fact, satisfactorily explain these relationships. With E.P. Sanders, "I rather suspect that when and if a new view of the Synoptic problem becomes accepted, it will be more flexible and complicated than the tidy two-document hypothesis" or, I might add, the Griesbach hypothesis; see E.P. Sanders, *The Tendencies of the Synoptic Tradition* (Cambridge: Cambridge University Press, 1969), p. 279. It should also be noted that the notion of falsifying one or more of the hypotheses is not new; see, e.g., Charles H. Talbert and Edgar V. McKnight, "Can the Griesbach Hypothesis Be Falsified?" *Journal of Biblical Literature*, XCI, 3 (September, 1972), 338-368; and George Wesley Buchanan, "Has the Griesbach Hypothesis Been Falsified?" *Journal of Biblical Literature*, XCIII, 4 (December, 1974), 550-572.

2. Much of this paragraph is based upon remarks made by William R. Farmer at a meeting of the Southwest Seminar on Gospel Studies on May 15, 1976.

3. This sentence is based upon a statement made by Farmer (see n. 2 above); I have not yet investigated the matter myself.

4. Elsewhere, Tyson says, "Less than two dozen verses are found in this class"; see Joseph B. Tyson, *A Study of Early Christianity* (New York: The Macmillan Company, 1973), p. 185. This represents an unnecessary restriction of the material, however. In addition to such *pericopae* as Mark 1:23-28= Luke 4:33-37; Mark 1:35-38=Luke 4:42-43; Mark 9:38-39=Luke 9:49-50a; and Mark 12:41-44=Luke 21:1-4, materials within the "triple tradition" *pericopae* which are found in both Mark and Luke but not in Matthew should also be included in the examination (e.g. Mark 2:4=Luke 5:19; Mark 3:3=Luke 6:8; Mark 5:18-20=Luke 8:37b-39; Mark 5:35-37=Luke 8:49-51).

5. E.D. Burton, *Some Principles of Literary Criticism and Their Applicatin to the Synoptic Problem* (Chicago: University of Chicago Press, 1904), p. 198; and William R. Farmer, *The Synoptic Problem: A Critical Analysis* (New York: The Macmillan Company, 1964), pp. 227-228. In private conversation, Farmer has indicated that he is removing his second "canon" from a forthcoming reprinting of his book, in light of further investigation by E.P. Sanders and others.

6. *Op. cit.*

7. *Op. cit.*

8. *Op. cit.*

S 190

JOSEPH B. TYSON'S PROPOSAL: "THE SOURCES OF LUKE..." - A RESPONSE AND COUNTER-PROPOSAL

Charles Thomas Davis, III
Appalachian State University

The language and literature of the NT is the product of an oral-aural culture.[1] The oral gospel, which forms the base of the written Gospels, was not subject to manuscript conventions much less to those of the post-Gutenberg world of print scholarship. Is not Tyson's proposal thus subject to serious question? The Gospels originate in a culture which did not know of "a redactor who has a certain aim in view and who controls his materials so that they may serve his aim." This has a clear ring of modernity; especially when Tyson proposes that: "On the assumption that an editor is free to arrange his materials in line with his own intentions and so to structure his document; we should compare the organization of Luke with the other Synoptics..." Is it valid to assume that such a concept of editorial freedom was known in the NT milieu? Luke 1:1-4 asserts quite firmly that there is precedent for writing the gospel and that such works stand in continuity with those who were eyewitnesses and ministers of the Word in the *Arche*. What was the precise nature of Luke's freedom? That is the key question.

Tyson's proposal rests firmly upon an assumption that something like modern individualism existed prior to Romanticism. In his book *A Study of Early Christianity*, Tyson reveals this limitation when he agrees with R. G. Collingwood that: "To know someone else's activity of thinking is possible only on the assumption that this same activity can be re-enacted in one's own mind" and then moves on to interpret this as an attempt to project ourselves backwards "to judge alternative responses which might be made to the situation."[2] It is in light of this assumption that we should interpret Tyson's stress on the "individual Evangelist" and his confidence in Burton's criteria. But is it valid to assume so easily that what is reasonable to us in a Cartesian, post-Gutenberg world of print scholarship was also reasonable in an oral-aural culture based on personal proclamation? Must we not first recognize the gulf between the modern, individualist mental set fostered by print culture and that of a pre-print culture and only then hazard claims to know someone else's mind well enough to "judge alternative responses which might be made to their situation"?

It is my opinion that Tyson's proposal, like so much of NT scholarship today, is bogged down in a dated, if not erroneous, construction of scientific method. Literary scholarship does not lend itself to the imagined, Newtonian precision of the controlled experiment.[3] The use of "scientific" sounding language like "hypotheses," "controls," "probably," "research," etc.; the call for the assembling of bibliography and history--which was done earlier in the original Taskforce on the Sequence of the Gospels--and the proposal to plod slowly but surely from certainty to certainty must not be allowed to prematurely comfort us with the thought that we are thereby scientists or that our task is a legitimately scientific one.

I would direct the Consultation's attention to some positive counter-proposals. Is it not time for us to abandon the atomizing 18th and 19th century procedures of analysis which are obsessed with dissecting phenomena and with individual genius? Michael Polanyi surely speaks to us when he says: "The falling apart of text and meaning, whether in the child or in the scientist, is the sign of a problematic state of mind. The seat of such confusion is always conceptual."[4]

Roland Frye has earlier directed our attention to our conceptual confusion and to our life in a theological ghetto.[5] His criticism provides a sound point of departure for our rethinking of our work. Let us direct our attention to language, to its nature and purpose in an oral-aural culture, to the intrinsic literary criticism which seeks to hear a writing in its own terms rather than to dissect it according to extrinsic historical and philosophical criteria.[6] Let us rethink our views of science, literature, theology and religion in light of the post-Newtonian science along the lines suggested by Polanyi in *Personal Knowledge*.

I propose that we establish a seminar which will take as its direct task that of clarifying concepts and of exploring the Gospels as distinct, discrete literary wholes directed towards the re-presentation of the "Christian experience"--the gospel. Until this task is undertaken the question of Gospel relationships is premature. Only in light of our respect for the integrity of a Gospel as a dramatic whole addressed to us as an audience, will a Gospel reveal the secrets of its deep underlying unity with other Gospels.

William Farmer has at least shown us the failures of the past two centuries of dissecting analyses such as this one proposed by Tyson. Let us go beyond the impasse. Is it not time to take up new options?

NOTES

1. Cf. W. J. Ong, *The Presence of the Word* (New Haven: Yale, 1967), esp. ch. 2.
2. (New York: Macmillan, 1973) 8-9.
3. Cf. Richard D. Altick, *Art of Literary Research* (New York: Norton, 1963).
4. Michael Polanyi, *Personal Knowledge* (New York: Harper and Row, 1962) 108.
5. "A Literary Perspective for the Criticism of the Gospels," *Jesus and Man's Hope*, ed. Donald G. Miller and D. Y. Hadidian (Pittsburgh: Pittsburgh Theological Seminary, 1971), 2, 193-221.
6. My "The Fulfillment of Creation: A Study of Matthew's Genealogy," *JAAR* 41 (4) 520-35, gives a small indication of how this can be done in NT interpretation.

CHRISTIAN PROPHECY IN LUKAN THOUGHT: LUKE 4:16-30 AS A POINT OF DEPARTURE

Waldemar Schmeichel
Kalamazoo College

There are two ways in which we can address the question at hand. We can isolate those pericopes in the Lukan narrative which display prophetic characteristics as these have been identified by acceptable criteria.[1] We then note their relative frequency, their consistency to each other, their distinctiveness over against non-prophetic material, their particular spacing in the Lukan narrative structure, and then make the redaction critical judgment as to their theological function and any possible sociological factors responsible for them. We then arrive at a likely source for Luke which may in part derive from his community. The value of such an approach is readily apparent, for it provides insight into the self-understanding of a community at some distance to its founder. It identifies a segment of leadership and how it excercised its power: By reference to the risen, contemporary Lord who comes to the community in the words of the historical Jesus mediated through a religious elite. Furthermore, the prophet is the institutionalized statement of the identity of the historical Jesus with the risen Lord.

The second way of responding to our question receives its initial legitimacy from the following observations. There appears to be a substratum of popular opinion which holds Jesus to be a prophet.[2] At the "opinion poll" requested by Jesus at Caesarea Philippi (Mark 8:28 par.) and given to Herod Antipas when the reputation of Jesus came to his attention (Mark 6:15 par.) the identification "prophet" figures prominently (Cf. also Matt. 21:11, 46). The interrogation before Pilate includes a popular request to prophesy (Mark 14:65 par.). In all of these, however, it is the <u>ochloi</u> and <u>alloi</u> who are making this allegation with an implicit distance to it both on the part of the reporting disciples and the gospel writers. Even when Jesus himself in the only exception quotes the popular proverb "A prophet is not without honor, except in his own country..." (Mark 6:4 par.), he is understood not to place any emphasis on the word "prophet" but on the phrase "not without honor."[3]

Against the background of such usage in Mark and Matthew where a distant and undifferentiated populace is permitted to have its uninformed say, the Lukan practice calls attention to itself. With unmistakable clarity Luke parallels the phrases "I must go on my way" and "for it cannot be that a prophet should perish away from Jerusalem" (13:33). The two Emmaus disciples matter-of-factly describe Jesus as one "who was a phrophet" (24:19). The resurrected Christ then uses this identification as a basis for clarification to the disciples that his suffering was a necessary consequence of such a prophetic role and should, therefore, be no cause for despondency. When the people of Nain exclaim spontaneously, "A great prophet has arisen among us" (7:17), we have once more a collective judgment. However, it is made in direct response to a specific act of Jesus, the resuscitation of a young man, and Luke lets it stand as a proper recognition of the role of Jesus as a visitation from God (7:16).

In 7:36-50 a woman "who was a sinner" anoints Jesus' feet with her tears and ointments. Jesus tolerates her ministrations in apparent ignorance of her religious unacceptability. To his host this raises the question of Jesus' identity as a prophet for whom such ignorance is compromising. By telling the story of the two debtors Jesus not only demonstrates that he has the expected knowledge and, therefore, a defensible claim to a prophetic identity, but then goes on to announce that the woman's sins are forgiven. This raises the question of whether the emotion and gesture of this woman signify gratitude for forgiveness previously received[4] or remorse and guilt in the absence of forgiveness. For the former to be correct the woman should have acted in consonance with Luke 15 - joy for the return of the Lost Son and the finding of the drachma and sheep - and "crashed" the Pharisee's meal with the request that everyone share her happiness. This is not the case, and we need to see her in a state of guilt until Jesus speaks, "Your sins are forgiven." The passive of aphiemi is a circumlocution for God's action[5] which Jesus announces to her in his role as a prophet. Luke, therefore, extends the idea of hidden prophetic knowledge from the interpersonal level to a knowledge of the will and action of God for man.[6]

The story begins with a questioning of Jesus' identity as a prophet because he appeared to lack prophetic knowledge. Jesus demonstrates that he has such knowledge by knowing the character of the woman and the thoughts of his host. He then transcends the popular conception of what a prophet ought to know and more substantially lays claim to a prophetic identity by the announcement of God's action toward that woman.

These observations first of all require our recognition that Luke has elevated an ascription of Jesus the tradition has handed down as a first, uninformed impression. He then placed it on the lips of Jesus and made it the judgment of close associates. We then need to examine how basic this ascription is for the Lukan christology. It has been an intermittant scholarly assessment that Luke understands Jesus as a prophet,[7] a conclusion prodded by the above observations and augmented by the Lukan use of the Spirit and the innocence of Jesus' suffering. However, such argument has not convinced because it failed to connect with an underlying Lukan thought structure. Finally, we need to make a judgment on the role of early Christian prophecy in this process. We are thus working with three components: 1.) A popular and fringe understanding of Jesus as a prophet; 2.) a Lukan and centrally Christian understanding of Jesus as prophet; 3.) the presence of Christian prophets who relate words of the risen Lord to the community. Is it possible that the mediators of the word have become mediators of identity and that the fusion of the words spoken by the historical Jesus with those spoken by the risen Lord prepared the fusion of identity along similar lines? Thus the Lord who comes to the community in the word of the prophet is in fact a "prophet Lord."

I shall opt for the second of the outlined approaches on the strength of these preliminary observations. What Luke understands by his association of the idea "prophet" with the figure of Jesus should be most accessible at the level he has extended it. In the inaugural introduction of Jesus in the Nazareth pericope (4:16-30) where the word "prophet" and imagery about it are central I postulate such extension.[8] I shall, therefore, examine this pericope under the stated question.

It has become axiomatic to regard this pericope as a statement of the Lukan "program." Cadbury has called it a "keynote speech."[9] Although there are studies which legitimately pursue the question of Jesus' program in this pericope,[10] my interest lies in the Lukan viewpoint which comes to expression here. The latter can be identified on two levels. First of all, linguistic usage is such that consonance can be obtained with the rest of the gospel.[11] While certain passages (vss. 18-19; 23, 24) clearly come from the tradition, [12] Lukan composition or at least editing of the whole is increasingly being granted.[13] Secondly, and in my judgment a more important indicator, the particular location of this pericope as the inaugural appearance and statement of Jesus identify it as editorial. In Mark (6:1-6) this scene occurs just before the Galilean ministry is drawing to a close; in Matthew (13:54-58) we find it at the climax of the Galilean ministry; in Luke, on the other hand, it prefaces Jesus' ministry as such. Furthermore, Luke alludes to activity in Capernaum (4:23), a city Jesus had not yet visited in the Lukan progression of events. Thirdly, without wanting to stress the "library" element of the way Luke produced his work, we cannot forget the fact that he had Mark in front of him.[14] The latter, of course, charts a different beginning and language for Jesus, and when he describes the Nazareth scene, does not, among other things, describe a sermon. Therefore, irrespective of whether or not one esteems Luke to be a composer or a conscientious editor of this scene, one touches on Lukan intentionality. The question is then only one of detail and degree.

But once the judgment is accepted that this is a programmatic scene, we need to specify with some care what it is Luke is emphasizing. Prompted by the Isaiah quote (the preaching of good news to the poor, release to the captives, etc.) and supported by the references to Elijah and Elisha in their rejection by Israel and concomitant turning to non-Israel, scholars have generally maintained that Luke is introducing the character and scope of Jesus' ministry and is pointing to that of the church in Acts.[15] Thus the story of Jesus begins in his <u>patris</u>, but because it is the kind of story it is and because his home town and home land are the kind of environment they are, this story cannot be completed there. Propelled by the dynamics of rejection the story of Jesus reaches into the Gentile community and legitimizes the Gentile mission.[16] But for this to be correct, would we not have to regard Luke 4:16-30 as a programmatic introduction not only to the gospel but more centrally to the Book of Acts as well? I do not know of any scholar who is prepared to do that. Furthermore, this focus on the ministry of Jesus loses sight of the fact that we are dealing with an author who has made no effort to extend Jesus and his work beyond Jewish territory. While the emphatic language of Matthew's gospel is absent ("I was sent only to the lost sheep of the house of Israel" 15:24; Cf. 10:5) Luke nevertheless did not reproduce the incident of the Syrophoenician woman with its location in the "region of Tyre and Sidon" (Mark 7:24; Matt. 15:21).[17]

To maintain, therefore, that the programmatic introduction of the story of Jesus has an internal logic which requires it to move beyond Israel stands at variance with the actual development of that story in the gospel. On the other hand, to recognize an anticipation of the experience of the church in that of Jesus is a reading of the Nazareth pericope from the perspective of Acts.[18] Perhaps what is necessary is a reevaluation of the Elijah-Elisha references as a paradigm of Israel's rejection of Jesus and his and his follower's necessary turning to the Gentiles. Is this what Luke wanted to indicate when he appropriated the experiences of these two prophets? I think not. That they are paradigms of rejection I do not intend to question, but that they are more than that, that in fact they represent a resolution to rejection, i.e. a welcome elsewhere beyond the rejecting community, I find difficult to recognize in the text.

In times of judgment over Israel Elijah is sent outside of the judged community not to another people but to one individual. He is further not sent to realize elsewhere what was impossible in Israel; he is sent to escape the consequences of Israel's judgment. Elisha also does not turn from Israel to another community, rather a non-Israelite seeks him out in Israel and becomes the beneficiary of the healing power of Israel's God. In both instances Israel is juxtaposed to <u>one member</u> of non-Israel, and that one member is not the object of religious or cultic attention. Rather, Luke wanted to make the statement of rejection so absolute that there was no single instance of acceptance to be found in all of Israel. To illustrate that total rejection and at the same time to demonstrate the continued availability of God's care and healing both prophets are related to one member, and one member only, of a non-Israelite community. Therefore, Zarephath and Naaman are not what Lydia was in Philippi, the first convert in a new missionary field, nor are they corporate personalities embodying in their individuality the larger nation. They are a minimal and necessary corollary to Israel's total rejection Luke wanted to depict. Zarephath and Naaman do not function on their own, they are a means to illustrate something about Israel. With them Luke has not left the sphere of Israel, but, rather, with the aid of a demographic model described total rejection. If this interpretation is correct, we cannot find any evidence of the Jewish-Gentile relationship in our text.[19] Two individuals from outside of Israel are simply acknowledged to exist and this not for their own sake but for the sake of Israel. Nor ought we to read this pericope from our knowledge of Acts 13:42-52; 18:6; 28:28. "Rejection by" does not immediately imply "movement to." It implies rather a qualified way of being in Israel. Our story is quite explicit at this point. The residents of Nazareth attempt to complete their rejection by an expulsion. Their inexplicable failure is only in part a Lukan corollary to John's "My hour has not yet come" (2:4). Fundamentally it separates the idea of rejection from that of expulsion, i.e. it qualifies the spacial dimension in the experience of rejection. To be sure, Jesus eventually "went away" (vs. 30), but he did that by "passing through the midst of them." If this scene prefigures the passion story, as is very likely,[20] Jesus passes through the midst of his people as one who is rejected. The movement from the home town to that fateful hill is a summary of the history of Jesus with his people. When Luke comes to the end of that history, he describes it in as neutral and dispassionate a manner as language will permit: "He went away." Therefore, rejection is the independent concern of our passage and of the gospel; the tension between it and expulsion is the theological issue in Acts.

This conclusion has ramifications for what we consider to be programmatic in our passage. It is not the ministry of Jesus in the process of changing constituencies. It is rather Jesus himself, i.e. Luke's particular understanding of who Jesus was! In an inaugural and carefully constructed scene Luke introduces the Jesus who will function in his gospel, i.e. at the commencement of his activity Jesus is presented in a summarizing overview that packs into one scene what will take the rest of the gospel to elaborate. Consequently, the first and central question we need to ask of this text is christological: What kind of understanding of Jesus seasoned by decades of church experience informs Luke? If the Nazareth scene still merits the adjective programmatic, as I think it does, and if the Lukan conception of Jesus makes up the center of the program, as I would advocate, then a careful study of this text will disclose a christology in its essential contours, as I hope to demonstrate.

One of the more puzzling aspects of this pericope is the abrupt and apparently unmotivated change in audience response to the words of Jesus. "All spoke well of him," is the conclusion of vs. 22; in vs. 23 Jesus refers to a (future) taunting challenge to make himself the beneficiary of his healing power. This contrasts markedly with an unambiguous story of rejection in the Markan _Vorlage_ (6:1-6) which is motivated by familiarity with Jesus' profession, mother, four named brothers and his sisters "with us."[21] Jesus in turn responds by quoting the proverb about a prophet's unacceptability in familiar surroundings, is unable to do any "mighty works there," and for his part marvels at the unbelief.

The incongruity in Luke has attracted sustained attention with a tacit assumption that it holds the key to a proper understanding of the pericope. In agreement let me review some of the more recent proposals which can be grouped in three methodological approaches.[22] The source critics operate with the view that there may have been two visits, one receptive, the other rejecting, or that Luke at least received contrasting traditions about such two visits.[23] More recently H. Schuermann[24] has proposed that vss. 17-21, (23a) and 25-27 derive from Mark and vss. 16, 22, 23b, 24 and 28-30 from the _Redequelle_. The discrepancy in Luke belongs to his sources, fidelity to which did not permit Luke to iron out the wrinkles. The fundamental reason for these discrepancies lies buried in the murky history of the tradition.

A variation of this approach combines traditional and editorial activities. Having received a story of rejection Luke superimposes an interpretation of success which relates itself to the rejection by requiring the movement of the gospel to the Gentiles.[25]

A second approach works with linguistic re-interpretation and has received its impetus from Jeremias' much discussed study.[26] Beginning with Semitic considerations behind martyrein, thaumazein and hoi logoi tēs charitos Jeremias argues that they without prejudice can be translated differently than has been the custom.[27] martyrein autō can mean "to bear witness against someone," thaumazein can express bewildered opposition, and hoi logoi tēs charitos does not have to mean "gracious words" (RSV) but "words of (God's) mercy." Jeremias then renders the passage: "They protested with one voice (pantes emartyroun autō) and were furious (kai ethaumazon), because he (only) spoke about (God's year of) mercy (and omitted the words about the Messianic vengeance)."[28] The omission took place when Jesus terminated his reading from the Isaiah scroll just prior to the reference of God's vengeance. From this perspective vs. 22 does not exhibit a break in the attitude of the audience to Jesus, rather "it records from the outset unanimous rage."

Attractive as Jeremias' suggestions are they need to be (and have been) criticized at their very strength. It seems highly implausible that within the compass of one crucial sentence Luke would employ three phrases of neutral meaning that he, however, intended to be understood in a very specific way. This is especially contradicted by vs. 28 where Luke has no difficulty finding adequate language to express anger.

A more recent but related study comes from J.A. Sanders[30] who approaches this passage from the centrality of the Isaiah quote and by the method of "comparative midrash" which is a form of extra-Biblical tradition-criticism. Jesus' midrash on Isa. 61 constitutes the offense, Sanders argues, and particularly the question of who the poor, the captives and the blind would be. For 11QMelch in which Isa. 61 is the central text these are representatives of the "in-group." The same expectation confronted Jesus in his home town synagogue. Jesus, however, by referring to Elijah-Elisha's reach beyond the "in-group" insists that these words apply "to those to whom God wishes them to apply." He thus plays the role of a true prophet in the classical tradition of the Elijah, Amos, Isaiah, Jeremiah type who cannot be "dektos by his own countrymen precisely because his message always must bear in it a divine challenge to Israel's covenantal self-understanding in any generation."

Thus Sanders denies the existence of any inconsistencies in Luke 4. What Luke presents is a growing acquaintance with the actual understanding Jesus has of Isa. 61 which then leads to unanimous rejection. However, Sanders' interpretation hinges on two debatable points. First of all, he structures his interpretation - to use his language - in an in-group, out-group tension. This ascribes the kind of significance to Elijah-Elisha's actions that I have argued they do not possess for Luke. Secondly, Sanders interprets all of Jesus' remarks as a commentary on Isa. 61 which in turn is seen too much from the perspective of 11QMelch. Sanders' comments about Jesus' prophetic function, on the other hand, are very useful.

A third approach toward an understanding of the Nazareth pericope is generally theological where Luke is construed to achieve a discernible purpose by the specific manner he tells the story. Thus H. Flender[34] recognizes two levels, historical narrative and preaching aimed at faith, on which this pericope moves. The tension between these levels can be illustrated by the intended ambiguity inherent in hoi logoi tēs charitos which on one level means "winsome words" and on the other "message of grace."[35] On the first level Jesus evokes curiosity and on the second he is vulnerable to rejection. The double entendre is the way Luke sees the relationship between revelation and concealment.

D. Hill[36] sees the tension within a time framework. Jesus announces that the year of God's favor has come. The people desire immediate evidence of its fulfilment. "This Jesus refuses by asserting that the prophetic ministry which will win acceptance (primarily with God) has to transcend the limits of his own land and people, as the scripture attests in the cases of Elijah and Elisha; irritated at being denied what they want, the people react violently and hustle Jesus out of town, with murderous intent."[37]

Bajard[38] argues analogously. Luke taken on his own terms has ordered his material so as to demonstrate that Jesus was rejected at Nazareth at the beginning of his ministry for the same reason that he was put to death at its end - his refusal to limit salvation to his own fatherland.

For R. Tannehill[39] the rejection of Jesus in Nazareth will benefit Capernaum and all the other cities of Israel. Vss. 25-27 complete the logic of this rejection and refer to the mission of the church which will move beyond Israel to the Gentiles. "Nazareth and the Gentile mission are the beginning and culmination of one movement.... The mission continues to encounter the rejection of Jesus' own people and the call of God to turn to others, a pattern which is first established at Nazareth."[40] Ch. Masson[41] puts the question this way: "If belonging to Israel does not entail a right to be healed by God, how much less does belonging to Jesus' own village."

This sampling of more recent attention to this pericope reveals a recurring theme: The actual experience of the Gentile church in Acts provides an overpowering magnetic force for the Elijah-Elisha remarks and transforms them into a Jewish-Gentile statement. It in turn is seen as a prefiguration of Acts, and interpretation in fact takes place _a majori ad minus_: The experience of the church is an imitation of the experience of her Lord. Since the experience of the former is more explicit and accessible, it forms the prism through which the less explicit function of Jesus is interpreted.

I would like to begin my own observations by focusing on the role of the Spirit in this pericope and in the preceding chapters. Luke has picked up the marginal idea in the tradition that Jesus is led or functions by the power of the Spirit[42] and then develops this association more fully. Although Luke shares with Matthew (1:20) the idea of Mary's conception by the Spirit, he explains that conception by the Spirit's "coming upon" Mary (1:35). Although he shares with Matthew (3:13:-17) and Mark (1:9-11) the descent of the Spirit at Jesus' baptism, for Luke this is not properly speaking a baptismal scene. It is a scene of the descent of the Spirit "upon him," the fact of the baptism having been reported in an introductory clause.[43] While once again Luke shares the synoptic leading (Mark:driving) of Jesus by the Spirit into the wilderness and temptation, Luke redundantly prefaces that statement that Jesus was "full of the Holy Spirit" (4:1). After the temptation Luke alone repeats that "Jesus returned in the power of the Spirit into Galilee" (4:14). Four verses later Jesus opens the Isaiah scroll and in his first public statement announces, "The Spirit of the Lord is upon me..." (4:18).

To the reader (and it is he/she who are Luke's primary audience!) who has accompanied Luke in his narrative so far, this is no great news. It is simply a statement of awareness and acknowledgment on the part of Jesus of something the reader had noted all along. The reference to Isa. 61, therefore, is first of all a summary of the experiential forms of the Spirit that impinged on Jesus' movement. Beyond this, however, the experience is now scripturally connected, i.e. it is confirmed and grounded in a divine purpose. The word "anointed," as M. de Jonge[44] has shown, emphasizes a divine calling, a special relationship to God in which "not the person as such, but his calling and his function are of importance."[45] When Jesus applies fulfilment of this scripture "today," this need not mean more than the commencement of Jesus' public activity when the Spirit which once called Trito-Isaiah[46] now anoints Jesus to his ministry.[47]

The Spirit's anointing of Jesus then receives functional content (_hou heineken!_): to preach good news (_euangelisasthai_)[48]...to proclaim...to set at liberty...to proclaim. This anointing sets Jesus apart for euangelizesthai by emphasizing God's claim upon him and his actions. What Jesus does is, therefore, an act of God, and the people glorifying God after Jesus has acted merely express their awareness of that fact (Cf. 7:16).

This is, however, only one observation we need to make about Luke's use of the Spirit. The other is yet more significant. After the Isaiah statement "The Spirit of God is upon me," we never again hear that Jesus is being led by the Spirit or performs any function under its guidance![49] This is particularly striking in contrast to the emphasis of such leading immediately preceding the quote. Jesus' movement throughout is controlled and motivated by the Spirit, i.e. until 4:18. At that point Jesus claims a Spirit anointment (not a Spirit experience!). From that point and based on the logic of the Isaiah quote we would expect an intimate association between Jesus and God's empowering Spirit. Just the opposite is the case. Jesus post-Nazareth is, as it were, on his own.

This observation rivets our attention on the Q saying, "But if it is by the finger of God (Matthew: Spirit of God) that I cast out demons, then the Kingdom of God has come upon you" (Luke 11:20// Matt. 12:28). The originality of the Lukan expression "finger of God" has been defended against Matthew's "Spirit" by the implausibility that Luke would have deleted a favored word.[50] Rather, ever since T.W. Manson Luke's wording is seen to be dependent on Ex. 8:15 and is generally granted dominical authenticity.[51] If my observation is correct that Luke's understanding of the Spirit pivots structurally on 4:18, we need to entertain the idea that Luke may have changed an original Q expression "Spirit of God" to conform to a specific understanding of the Spirit's function.

The popular response to Jesus' application of Isa. 61 is unequivocably favorable. "They all spoke well of him," is Luke's own summary to which he adds a heavily edited but equally favorable wonderment about Jesus' known origins.[52] It is at this point that Luke has Jesus forecast (ereite) the certainty of having the generally known proverb thrown into his face, "Physician, heal yourself!" (vs. 23). To this is added - no longer part of the proverb itself - a request to do something in "his own country" that he was reported to have done at Capernaum. Jesus responds to this postulated challenge by quoting a proverb of his own, "No phrophet is acceptable in his own country" (vs. 24).

This is an unmotivated extension of Jesus' remarks with a willful provocation toward hostility. What is being interpreted by vss. 23-24? Are they still part of the exegesis of Isa. 61? Commensurate with my earlier insistance that the Nazareth pericope develops a christology I would point out that a particular and serial understanding of Jesus is being unfolded. That understanding is of such a kind that a response of the people is inherent in it and completes it. A first element of that christology associated God's Spirit with Jesus and issued into Spirit directed activity that would benefit the poor, the captives, the blind and the oppressed. The people liked that.

The second element (vss. 23-24) disturbs this agreeable acceptance by raising, indeed, provoking the spectre of rejection and doing so under the suggested identity of a prophet. In Mark the reference to the proverb of the rejected prophet is a puzzled comment after a rejection has already taken place based on over-familiarity with Jesus' background and descent. It takes the form of three parallel phrases emphasizing the hostility of "his own country" to its native son. The fact that the word "prophet" is used to identify the native son, is not a matter of reflection for Mark. In Luke, on the other hand, Jesus' response pivots on the meaning of the word "prophet" and implies synonymity with rejection.

We now need to correlate these two elements in a coherent statement about one figure, i.e. Jesus understood as a prophet. As the bearer of

God's spirit this prophet will find acceptance, yet there is something about a true prophet that will quickly make him unacceptable.[53] How does Luke resolve this tension and, above all, how does he relate it to the Jesus he expects to function in his gospel?

I observed earlier that Luke abruptly terminates Jesus' guidance by the Spirit in his post-Nazareth narrative. I now need to make an attempt to explain why. In contrast to Paul[54] where the Spirit is more a psychological and inner-personal dimension, for Luke who under Hellenistic influence understands power in terms of substance,[55] it is an impersonal and objective power in history effecting the transcendent will in the Christian community. This power as a separate reality attendant upon the person of Jesus would first of all bring about his continued acceptance by the people and make a passion story incomprehensible. Furthermore, since for Luke the death of Jesus is innocently experienced, a miscarriage of justice, for which the resurrection serves as a divine restitution (Cf. Acts 5:15), a visible and continued association of the Spirit with Jesus could be expected to have averted such a death. Put differently, for Luke the death of Jesus is not a soteriological event.[56] To have the Spirit lead Jesus into a soteriologically unappropriated experience would place two inherently conflicting tendencies on a collision course. The Spirit upon Jesus expresses God's purpose, but the passion/death are antithetical to that purpose.

This returns us to the characterization of Jesus as a prophet both in the proverb and more intensely in the Elijah-Elisha references. That identity provides Luke with the corollary that helps him to explain the death of Jesus as both necessary and at the same time innocent suffering. "As early as the first century C.E. it had become a generally accepted teaching of Judaism that prophets had to suffer or even to undergo martyrdom."[57] Once Luke characterizes Jesus as a prophet, he is no longer under theological obligation to account for the death of Jesus. It inherently belongs to his having been a prophet as a confirmation of his role. The association between prophetic identity and the death of Jesus provides a mutually interpretive framework. But the prerequisite for this is that the motif of Spirit guidance be concluded when the motif of rejection is introduced. This happens in vss. 23-24. Thus Luke creates two sequential spheres of activity, one for the Spirit, the other for rejection. The inclusion of these two particular motifs is dictated by the prophetic christology. Their sequential order derives from the need to explain the death of Jesus without recurrence to soteriological categories. Suggestions for both motifs were provided by the tradition.

Finally, let me call attention to the phrase "in your own country" which occurs in conjunction with the Capernaum reference (vs. 23) and the prophet proverb. It is further implied by the identification of Nazareth as Jesus' home town (vs. 16) and the movements of Elijah and Elisha (vss.26-27). What is more natural than to interpret this phrase as a complaint that charity ought to begin at home, that Jesus is being charged with disloyalty to his native environment by turning either to Capernaum, or like Elijah to "the land of Sidon" or like Elisha to a Syrian? But, does Luke mean to say that the statement "No prophet is acceptable in his own country" actually implies that he would be acceptable somewhere else? Such interpretation would see the phrase in its obvious spatial and geographical sense, and I have questioned its legitimacy on other grounds above. Rather, a prophet is that kind of a person/role who will by definition achieve unacceptability because his message involves the radical questioning of his community's self-understanding before God.[58] He will repeat the Nazareth pericope as a biographical paradigm: It will begin with a word from God, include an application and lead to some high hill as a means of violent expulsion. Therefore, the phrase "in his own country" is a form of intensification of the idea of rejection by reference to "home" where one could at least postulate acceptability. Jesus could just as well have said, "No prophet is acceptable!" The role of the prophet and the status of acceptability are mutually exclusive entities, and a prophet's acceptability cannot be obtained by moving him about geographically. The point is that rejection is not a surprising experience for a prophet, it is rather a form of verification of the authenticity of his role.

Let me summarize my argument and the understanding of Jesus as prophet implicit in it. The tradition bequeathed to Luke a tangential and popular ascription of Jesus as a prophet which he brought into the center of his reflection about a Jesus whose death is not hyper hymōn/peri pollōn.[59] The tradition handed down to Luke an "undated" visit of Jesus to his home town which Luke "dates" as a beginning to Jesus' ministry, and with the aid of independent tradition transforms into a "keynote speech." In the total scene Luke develops his understanding of the Jesus who will function in his gospel and by that formal structure implies that interpretation cannot reach beyond the gospel.

A crucial element is the radical change of audience response between vss. 22 and 23 which has usually been interpreted by reference to the Isa. 61 quote and the Elijah-Elisha allusions as an implied movement of God from the Jews to the Gentiles. I have criticized the great dependence on Acts in such a conclusion, the predominance of spatial categories in the idea of rejection, the identification of Zarephath and Naaman with a movement to the Gentiles, and the lack of clarity of the programmatic focus of this scene. My alternative proposal begins with the Lukan understanding of the function of the Spirit in contextual and sequential forms. Contextually the Isa. 61 reference to the anointing Spirit provides a scriptural grounding and legitimizing of the experience of a leading Spirit with which the preceding chapters are replete. Sequentially the leading of God's Spirit is emphasized until 4:18 and not thereafter. The introduction of Jesus as a prophet who is rejected seems to account for this peculiar spacing of Spirit leading. Such leading makes the passion story as innocent suffering incomprehensible. It is, therefore, aborted precisely at the point where the rejection motif is introduced under the identity of Jesus as prophet. That identity under contemporary assumptions was synonymous with rejection, suffering and death and accounts for the programmatic and necessary response by the Nazareth audience as well as for Luke's ability to see Jesus' death as innocent suffering and a miscarriage of justice. The rejection of Jesus is, therefore, not a geographical category, but a way of functioning in Israel under the identity of a prophet.

NOTES

1. Cf. D.E. Aune, "Christian Prophecy and the Sayings of Jesus: An Index to Synoptic Pericopae Ostensibly Influenced by Early Christian Prophets," 131-42 and G.F. Hawthorne, "Christian Prophecy and the Sayings of Jesus: Evidence of and Criteria for," 105-29, both in 1975 Seminar Papers, Vol. 2.

2. R.H. Fuller, The Foundations of New Testament Christology (New York: Ch. Scribner's Sons, 1965), 125-29.

3. A. Plummer, A Critical and Exegetical Commentary on the Gospel According to St. Luke (New York: Ch. Scribner's Sons, 1907), 127.

4. J. Jeremias, The Parables of Jesus, trans. by S.H. Hooke (New York: Ch. Scribner's Sons, 1963), 127. W. Grundmann, Das Evangelium nach Lukas (Berlin: Evangelische Verlagsanstalt, 1961), 172 entertains the possibility that there must have been a prior association of Jesus with this woman at which time forgiveness was granted her. She now seeks this occasion to express her gratitude.

5. Jeremias, Parables, 127 note 59.

6. G. von Rad, Old Testament Theology, trans. by D.M.G. Stalker (London: Oliver and Boyd, 1965), Vol. 2, 80-98.

7. H. Flender, St. Luke. Theologian of Redemptive History, trans. by I. and R.H. Fuller (Philadelphia: Fortress Press, 1967), 88. G. Voss, Die Christologie der Lukanischen Schriften in Grundzuegen (Bruges: Desclee de Brouwer, 1965), 157-70. L. Gaston, No Stone on Another. Studies in the Significance of the Fall of Jerusalem in the Synoptic Gospels (Leiden: E.J. Brill, 1970), 276, 293. G. Schneider, Verleugnung, Verspottung und Verhoer Jesu nach Lk 22:54-71. Studien zur Lukanischen Darstellung der Passion (Munich: Koesel Verlag, 1969), 174. G.W.H. Lampe, "The Lucan Portrait of Christ," NTS 2 (1955-56), 168-69. B. Reicke, The Gospel of Luke, trans. by R. MacKenzie (Richmond: John Knox Press, 1964), 65.

8. My interest in this paper is not to interpret the Nazareth pericope in its various nuances nor to take up the issues raised by the secondary literature with any effort toward completeness. I would like to propose a thesis and develop it in a programmatic way. - The older periodical literature can be found in B.M. Metzger, Index to the Periodical Literature on Christ and the Gospels (Leiden: E.J. Brill, 1966), Nrs. 4368-71; 5522-31. Further bibliographical references can be found in F. van Segbroeck, "Jesus rejeté par sa patrie (Mt 13:54-58)," Bib 49 (1968), 167 note 1; C. Perrot, "Luc 4:16-30 et la lecture biblique de l'ancienne synagogue," RevSR 47 (1973), 338-40; H. Schuermann, "Zur Traditionsgeschichte der Nazareth-Perikope Lk 4:16-30," ed. by A. Descamps and A. de Halleux, Mélanges Béda Rigaux (1970), 187 note 1. To this should be added J.A. Sanders, "From Isaiah 61 to Luke 4," in Christianity, Judaism and Other Greco-Roman Cults. Studies for Morton Smith at Sixty, ed. by J. Neusner. Part one - New Testament (Leiden: E.J. Brill, 1975), 75-106 and the annotations on 104-06.

9. H.J. Cadbury, The Making of Luke-Acts (London: S.P.C.K., 1968), 189.

10. But compare Flender's (St. Luke, 153) judgment that an inquiry into the possible events at Nazareth blocks one's understanding of the Lukan pericope.

11. Cf. R. Tannehill, "The Mission of Jesus According to Luke 4:16-30," in W. Eltester, ed. Jesus in Nazareth (Berlin: Walter de Gruyter, 1972), 51-75.

12. H. Schuermann, "Traditionsgeschichte," 187-205. A.R.C. Leaney, A Commentary on the Gospel According to St. Luke (New York: Harper and Row, 1958), 50-54 identifies a separate tradition in vss. 16-22a; 23a; 25-30.

13. On Luke's dependence on Mark cf. M. Dibelius, From Tradition to Gospel, trans. by B.L. Woolf (New York: Ch. Scribner's Sons, n.d.), 110-11. R. Bultmann, History of the Synoptic Tradition, trans. by J. Marsh (New York: Harper and Row, 1963), 32. H. Conzelmann, The Theology of St. Luke, trans. by G. Buswell (New York: Harper and Ros, 1960), 31-36. Leany, St. Luke, 50-51.

14. Conzelmann, Theology, 32.

15. Tannehill, "Mission," 51. D. Hill, "The Rejection of Jesus at Nazareth (Lk 4: 16-30)," NT 13 (1971), 161. J.M. Creed, The Gospel According to St. Luke (London: Macmillan and Co., 1930), 66.

16. So Hill, "Rejection," 178.

17. Cf. Conzelmann, Theology, 189.

18. So H. Anderson, "Broadening Horizons: The Rejection at Nazareth Pericope of Lk 4:16-30 in Light of Recent Critical Trends," Int 18 (1964), 269.

19. Contra L.C. Crockett, "Lk 4:25-27 and Jewish-Gentile Relations in Luke-Acts," JBL 88 (1969), 177-83.

20. E.M. Prevallet, "The Rejection at Nazareth (Lk 4:14-30)," Scripture 20 (1968), 5-9. J. Bajard, "La Structure de la pericope de Nazareth en Lc 4:16-30," ETL 45 (1969), 165-71.

21. Cf. E. Graesser, "Jesus in Nazareth (Mc 6:1-6a)," in Jesus in Nazareth, 1-37.

22. With some help here from Anderson, "Horizons."

23. Cf. M.-J. Lagrange, Évangile selon Saint Luc (Paris: Gabalda et Cie, 1948), 146-47. The Jerusalem Bible even argues for three visits. The first one (vss. 16-22) in which Jesus is honored; a second one (vss. 23-24) reported also in Mark and Matthew at which he causes 'skandalon,' and the final threatening one (vss. 25-30) to be imagined at the conclusion of the Galilean ministry. A. Jones, ed. The New Testament of the Jerusalem Bible (Garden City, N.Y.: Doubleday, 1966), 99 note g. Cf. Conzelmann, Theology, 32-36.

24. Schuermann, "Traditionsgeschichte," 187-205.

25. Anderson, "Horizons," 266, 272. F.W. Beare, The Earliest Records of Jesus (New York: Abingdon Press, 1962), 124. Leaney, Luke, 51-52.

26. J. Jeremias, Jesus' Promise to the Nations, trans. by S.H. Hooke (Naperville, Ill.: Alec R. Allenson, 1958), 44-45.

27. Cf. Bajard, "La Structure," 165-71.

28. Jeremias, Promise, 45.

29. Anderson, "Horizons," 266-70. Hill, "Rejection," 163-65.

30. Sanders, "From Isaiah," 75-106.

31. Ibid., 79.

32. Ibid., 99.

33. Citing Bajard, "La Structure," for support.

34. Flender, St. Luke, 144-59.

35. Ibid., 153.

36. Hill, "Rejection," 161-80.

37. Ibid., 178.

38. Bajard, "La Structure," 165-71. This summary was assisted by Sanders.

39. Tannehill, "Mission," 62.

40. Ibid., 62-63.

41. C. Masson, "Jésus à Nazareth," Vers les sources d'eau vive (Lausanne: Librairie de L"université, 1961), 59.

42. G.R. Beasley-Murray, "Jesus and the Spirit," Mélanges Béda Rigaux, 463-64.

43. N. Perrin, The New Testament: An Introduction (New York: Harcourt Brace Jovanovich, 1974), 202.

44. M. de Jonge, "The Use of the Word 'Anointed' in the Time of Jesus," NT 8 (1966), 132-48.

45. Ibid., 147.

46. Cf. Sanders, "From Isaiah," 80 and the literature cited in footnote 11. The Targum on Isa. 61 actually reads, "The prophet says: 'The spirit of prophecy (come) from the Lord God is upon me...'" Cf. J. Schmid, Das Evangelium nach Lukas (Regensburg: F. Pustet, 1960), 112.

47. Technically the quote "The Spirit of the Lord is upon me" and the interpretation, "Today this scripture is fulfilled in your hearing" do not establish the connection between Jesus and the Spirit. Only reference to the preceding context does that.

48. As is often noted the verb euangelizasthai occurs only once in Matthew (11:5), not at all in Mark, 10 times in Luke and 15 times in Acts.

49. A vague exception is 10:21 where Jesus "rejoices in the Holy Spirit" and is moved to pray. Jesus' dying exclamation from the cross, "Father, into thy hands I commit my spirit" (23:46) is not Jesus' return of God's Spirit that descended upon him at his "baptism." Contra Perrin, Introduction, 201. "My spirit" and "myself" are interchangeable expressions.

50. N. Perrin, Rediscovering the Teaching of Jesus (New York: Harper and Row, 1967), 63.

51. T.W. Manson, The Teaching of Jesus (Cambridge: University Press, 1963), 82-83.

52. It is generally agreed that the Lukan tracing of Jesus' descent through Joseph rather than through (so Mark) does not convey criticism but is a genuine question of wonder.

53. Cf. Sanders, "From Isaiah," 99, 103.

54. Paul has frequent usage of the adjective pneumatikos, particularly in I Corinthians. Luke-Acts and the other gospels as well do not have the adjective.

55. E. Schweizer, Spirit of God, trans. by A.E. Harvey (London: Adam and Black, 1960), 40. Cf. G.W.H. Lampe, "The Holy Spirit in the Writings of St. Luke," D.E. Nineham, ed. Studies in the Gospels (Oxford: B. Blackwell, 1955), 193.

56. Cf. Cadbury, Making, 280. C.H. Dodd, The Apostolic Preaching in Its Development (New York: Harper and Bros., 1949), 25. Conzelmann, Theology, 201.

57. H.A. Fischel, "Prophet and Martyr," JQR 37 (1946-47), 279. Cf. J. Jeremias, "Mouses," TDNT, Vol. 4, 713.

58. Sanders, "From Isaiah," 99.

59. J. Jeremias, Eucharistic Words of Jesus, trans. by N. Perrin (London: SCM Press, 1966), 155.

S 196 CHRISTIAN PROPHECY AND MATTHEW 23:8-12
A TEST EXEGESIS

J. Ramsey Michaels
Gordon-Conwell Theological Seminary

Before attempting to trace the redaction of Mt. 23:8-12, it is worth asking whether there is any basis in the context for assigning all or part of that redaction to Christian prophets.[1] Is the Matthean community in any sense a prophetic community? The series of woes in Mt. 23 on the "scribes and Pharisee hypocrites" ends in vv. 29-32 with the charge that they "build the tombs of the prophets and adorn the sepulchres of the righteous" (v. 29). They are "sons of those who killed the prophets" and are said to "fill up the measure of your fathers" (vv. 31f.). Thus Jesus sees the conflict which went on in OT times between good and evil continued in his own day. The "fathers" of the Pharisees are those who killed the prophets in ancient times. The disciples of Jesus, however, are not called "sons" of the prophets; instead they are themselves "prophets and wise and scribes," and can expect a fate parallel to that of the OT prophets before them (v. 3, 4). The placing of Jesus' disciples in the succession of the prophets is not peculiar to this passage, but appears also in Mt. 5:11f., 10:40-42 and 13:16f., so that it can be provisionally regarded as a distinctive Matthean interest.

The one other place in ch. 23 where Jesus focuses on his disciples in particular is vv. 8-12. This section brings to a close that portion of the discourse addressed "to the crowds and to his disciples" (v. 1), an inclusive designation which allows Mt to bracket the material in vv. 1-7 with that in vv. 8-12. He probably takes his cue from Mk (as against Lk) in regarding the former as spoken primarily to the crowds, filling out the scanty Markan account with additional material (vv. 2-5) oriented in that direction. Then he appends vv. 8-12 specifically for the disciples. Within vv. 1-7 can be seen echoes of the Matthean sermon on the mount, particularly in v. 3b ("they say but do not do," cf. 7:21) and in vv. 5-7 ("to be seen by men," cf. 6:1, and "they love...the first seats in the synagogues and to be greeted in the markets," cf. 6:5).[2] Both here and in ch. 6, the description of the Pharisees' love of public recognition prepares for a contrasting statement about Jesus' disciples (<u>humeis de</u>; cf. <u>su de</u> in 6:3, 6, 17), which centers here as in ch. 6 on their relation to God as Father (23:9; cf. 6:4, 6, 8, 15f., 18 and especially vv. 9-13). We are thus dealing with some distinctive Matthean traditions fashioned here in a distinctively Matthean way.

As they stand, vv. 8-10 look like a series of three prohibitions:

(a) "Don't be called Rabbi, for one is your teacher and you are all brothers" (v. 8).

(b) "Don't call anyone on earth your father, for one is your heavenly Father" (v. 9).

(c) "And don't be called leaders, for one is your leader, the Christ" (v. 10).

The difficulty with this supposition is that the form of the second prohibition is active rather than passive. It has to do not with a title which the disciples might be given but with one which they might be tempted to give to someone else. Therefore if (a) and (c) refer to titles applied to leaders in the Christian community, (b) looks as if it should be interpreted differently. In Jewish literature, 'father' is less characteristically a title for contemporary Rabbis or religious leaders than for great men of earlier generations.[3] If this is the meaning here, Jesus is urging his disciples not to rely on their Jewish ancestry but on their new and unique relationship to their Father in heaven. The point is much the same as in the words of John the Baptist ("Don't presume to say to yourselves, 'We have Abraham as father'...," Mt. 3:9, Lk 3:8), and corresponds in a way also to the debate over Abrahamic and divine sonship in Jn. 8:33-47.[4]

When 23:9 is understood in this way, it can be read simply as an explanation of the term 'brothers' at the end of v. 8. The disciples are brothers not by virtue of a common human ancestry but because they are children of God. Therefore they must call no one but God their 'father.' Such an understanding suggests a twofold rather than threefold structure, one which has the advantage of incorporating vv. 11-12 naturally into its pattern:

(a) "*Don't be called Rabbi, for one is your teacher*; you are all brothers and must call no one on earth your father, for one is your heavenly Father" (vv. 8-9).

(b) "*And don't be called leaders, for one is your leader, the Christ*; he who is greatest among you will be your servant; whoever exalts himself will be humbled and whoever humbles himself will be exalted" (vv. 10-12).

There is a certain appropriateness to this structure. The underlined prohibitions of titles for oneself are parallel in form, and each is followed by some explanatory material stressing equality and mutual servanthood within the community. The titles, "teacher" and "leader," are reminiscent of the twin designations, "teacher" and "lord," applied to Jesus in Jn. 13:13 and implicitly in Mt. 10:24f.[5]

But two questions remain:

1. Why have two such similar injunctions been allowed to stand almost side by side? It is not easy to distinguish "teacher" (*didaskalos*) from "leader" (*kathēgētēs*) in this context, especially since 'Rabbi' in vv. 7-8 focuses less on the specific function of teaching than on the prestige and authority of the teaching office. The similarity in meaning between *didaskalos* and *kathēgētēs* makes v. 10 a virtual doublet of v. 8. This is even more obviously the case if *kathēgētēs* is accepted as the original reading in v. 8 as well (with ℵ*, D, Θ, and the Byzantine tradition), a possibility which should not be dismissed too quickly. Although assimilation of v. 8 to v. 10 cannot be ruled out, full account must be taken of the tendency of scribes to substitute a more familiar word for a less familiar one (especially if *didaskalos* was known to be the standard equivalent of *rabbi*, Jn. 1:38), and to favor what seemed to be a neat threefold series (teacher, father, leader) over a strangely redundant one (leader, father, leader). In this sense, *kathēgētēs* is the more difficult reading in v. 8 and can lay serious, though not conclusive, claim to originality.

2. Why are vv. 8 and 10, which are almost synonymous in meaning, separated by the statement on fatherhood in v. 9 with its strange partial resemblance to the warnings that precede and follow it? The repetition of the words heis gar estin humōn in vv. 8 and 9 (with only a slight difference in v. 10) surely creates the illusion of a threefold series even if, as we have seen, the real parallelism is between vv. 8 and 10.

The answers to the two questions just posed are the key to the redaction history of this passage:

1. The most likely reason why v. 10 appears to be a doublet of v. 8 is that it is intended to clarify or interpret v. 8. But why would v. 8 need clarification? Its meaning would have been perfectly clear in Jewish Christian congregations: Jewish honorific titles have no place among Jesus' disciples. In Gentile Christian communities the command would have been equally clear. If 'Rabbi' was not understood (and indeed Jn. 1:38 does take the trouble to translate it), its meaning could easily have been inferred from the last part of the verse: "for one is your teacher" (or "leader"). What was lacking in a Gentile setting was not clarity but applicability or relevance. What Gentile Christian would want to claim the title 'Rabbi' anyway? As it stood, Mt. 23:8 was an archaic word of Jesus as far as Gentile Christians were concerned. A Gospel intended for them had the choice of ignoring such a saying, preserving it intact in all its Jewishness to lend atmosphere and a sense of 'pastness' to its account, or re-interpreting the saying in language appropriate to a new situation.

Mt has adopted both the second and third of these alternatives. As C. H. Dodd perceptively notes,[6] he has made a 'translation'--in a way which we have come to think of as rather modern and sophisticated. He records the same thing twice: first as he received it, and then in an adapted form designed to achieve an equivalent effect in another culture. It is analogous to what Jn has done in 1:38, 41, 42, 20:16 (i.e. transcribing both the Hebrew word and its Greek equivalent), but at a much more significant level. Mt has translated the whole of v. 8 not into another language but into another cultural setting, thus attempting to preserve the principle he sees expressed in the prohibition of the title 'Rabbi.' In v. 10 he not only supplies a Greek equivalent for 'Rabbi' but puts it in the nominative plural rather than the vocative singular. This changes the statement from direct to indirect discourse: "Don't be called 'Rabbi'..." is rendered not as "Don't be called 'Leader'..." but as "Don't be called leaders..." (i.e. "Don't be known as leaders..."). It is no longer a matter of particular titles, but of a general attitude toward honor and authority, an attitude equally important among Jewish and Gentile Christians. The point is much the same as that of Mk. 10:42-44, preserved by Mt in 20:25-27. Appropriately enough, Mt immediately draws on a kindred tradition in 23:11 (cf. 20:26f.) which he reinforces with a generalization based on Q (v. 12; cf. 18:4, Lk. 14:11, 18:14).

The only real difference between 20:25-27 and 23:8-12 is that in the latter case Jewish rather than Gentile practice is used to undergird the warning. This is typical of Mt's procedure elsewhere; he shows an awareness of both a Jewish and Gentile constituency in his treatment of several topics.

Christian prayer, for example, is contrasted not only with Jewish (6:5f.) but with Gentile (6:7f.) prayer abuse. Both the mission to the Gentiles (28:20) and to the Jews (10:23) will last until the close of the age. Gentiles (25:31f.) and Jews alike (19:28) will be judged by the Son of Man before "the throne of his glory." Similarly, Christian patterns of authority are contrasted with prevalent attitudes among Gentiles (20:25f.) as well as Jews (23:7f), but the positive teaching about equality and servanthood is the same in both instances.

The closest parallel to Mt's translation technique in 23:10 is found in 5:22. There the Greek word mōre ("fool") serves to explain the Aramaic raka, while "the gehenna of fire" corresponds to "the Sanhedrin." Here too the purpose of the changes seems to be not only translation in a narrow sense, but the adaptation of sayings which originated with Jesus, or Palestinian Jewish Christianity, to a Gentile Christian audience. Thus if "Sanhedrin" had no contemporary meaning for Gentile Christians as a source of punishment, "gehenna of fire" (despite its Jewish origins) quite possibly did (cf. Mk. 9:43, 45, 47). If there was no "council" to punish sins within the community, there was in any case the threat of eternal retribution. The effect of the duplication in Mt. 5:22, as in 23:10, is to make an archaic word of Jesus relevant to Mt's readers by the use of words aimed at producing an equivalent effect in a different culture. In each case the old form is allowed to stand, but a new form is put beside it.

2. The second question was why 23:9 (and with it v. 8b, "you are all brothers") is sandwiched between the old and new forms of the same saying. The natural answer is that vv. 8 and 9 were so closely joined in the pre-Matthean tradition that the redactor was unwilling to separate them. The pantes de humeis of v. 8b picks up the humeis de of v. 8a, and serves to introduce v. 9. The twofold structure suggested above, in effect, takes the pantes de humeis as the beginning of v. 9. These words, together with the heis gar estin humōn of v. 9b, link v. 9 very closely to v. 8 with a 'catch-word' effect. Two slightly different, though related, thoughts are bound together by making the form as parallel as the content will allow.

As we have seen, the Matthean redaction appends v. 10 as the 'translation' of v. 8, and concludes the admonitions to the disciples with some appropriate traditional words on servanthood as the necessary style for Christian leadership. In the redactional process, vv. 8b-9 have not been simply ignored. The whole thrust of the 'translation' is to show what 'brotherhood' in the Christian community entails: not merely the avoidance of one honorific title, but the rejection of the self-seeking authoritarianism which causes people to think of themselves as "leaders" or "bosses." The positive alternative (i.e. servanthood) is then developed in vv. 11-12. The redactor has perceived that the heart of vv. 8-9 is really the statement, "you are all brothers," in v. 8b, and that v. 9 merely defines this brother- and sisterhood theologically. In his redaction he is concerned to make sure that its practical implications (to Gentiles in particular) are made equally clear. Instead of the heis gar estin humōn of vv. 8 and 9, the redactor varies the formula slightly: hoti kathēgētēs humōn estin heis ho Christos (v. 10b). The one leader is thus identified with "the Christ," which replaces kathēgētēs in the emphatic position at the end of the sentence.

The reason for the addition of "the Christ" at the end of v. 10 is not altogether clear. Perhaps *ho didaskalos* (v. 8) was sufficiently familiar as a designation for Jesus to require no further identification,[7] while *kathēgētēs*, not being a christological term, was thought to need such identification. But if *didaskalos* was original in v. 8, why the change in v. 10 to *kathēgētēs* at all? The redactor could easily have used *didaskaloi* and *didaskalos* there as well, yielding a formulation not unlike the *mē polloi didaskaloi ginesthe* of Jm.3:1. But instead he used *kathēgētai* and *kathēgētēs*, quite possibly because *kathēgētēs* was original in v. 8 as well. If so, the addition of *ho Christos* in v. 10 (or its absence in v. 8!) remains unexplained.

It should not be overlooked, however, that *ho Christos* has the additional function of linking 23:10 with its more remote context, specifically 22:41-45. Here the point is made that "the Christ" is *kurios*, and that it is therefore not adequate to call him David's son. What is to be true of his disciples is true of him first: he calls no one on earth his father (not even David). Although the question, "Whose son is he?" is never explicitly answered, the implication is that, as David's Lord, he is God's son. In 23:10, "the Christ" appears again, now as a kind of *primus inter pares*. He is the "one leader" of the disciples, but they are also (derivatively) his "brothers" (cf. 25:40, 28:10) because like him they acknowledge neither Abraham, nor David,[8] nor the prophets as father, but only God in heaven. Possibly the emphasis on sonship in 23:9 prompted Mt to re-introduce *ho Christos* in v. 10.

At any rate, the twofold structure outlined above is substantiated by our sketch of the redaction of this passage. Mt. 23:8-12 can be divided into two parts, each consisting of a warning or prohibition (vv. 8a and 10), followed by a positive statement about the nature of the Christian community (vv. 8b-9 and 11-12). The first (vv. 8-9) belongs to the pre-Matthean tradition, while the second (vv. 10-12) is the work of the Matthean redactor. The illusion of a threefold structure was created in part by the seeming refrain, "for one is..." in vv. 8, 9, and 10. Another factor, as we have seen, may have been the change of an original *kathēgētēs* to *didaskalos* in v. 8, resulting in three different predicates (teacher, father, and leader), and heightening the impression that v. 10 was a new and distinct prohibition rather than simply a gloss on v. 8. At any rate, the threefold structuring of the passage seems to have influenced our commonly-accepted verse divisions between vv. 8 and 9, and is at least as old as the *Epistle of the Apostles*.[9]

The task remains of determining whether the redaction of Mt. 23:8-12 can be attributed to Christian prophecy. Beyond our initial observation that the Matthean community saw itself as standing in the line of the OT prophets and as including "prophets, wise men, and scribes" (23:34), there is little direct evidence. In ch. 24, one of the characteristics of *false* prophets is that they either claim to be *ho Christos* (24:5) or to know where he is (24:23-26). But warnings against false prophecy do not exclude recognition of the true. It is *possible* that in 23:10 those who consider themselves as representing true prophecy may also be aligning themselves with "the Christ," specifically in repudiating earthly heritages and traditions, and in claiming to be the sons of God (cf. 5:9, 16,

45, 11:25-27, 13:16f., 16:17). The strongly egalitarian thrust of the whole passage may suggest a charismatic community at work.[10]

Opposition to a developing 'Christian rabbinate,' however, or to any potentially authoritarian teaching office, is not in itself sufficient grounds for ascribing the material in question to prophets in a specific sense. Certainly there is no discernible 'order' of prophets in the Matthean community. The Spirit (or the Christ) belongs to "all who do the will of my Father in heaven" (7:21, cf. vv. 22f.). Authority in the community is not visible, as if one could point to structures and say 'Lo, here' or 'There.' "The Christ" is absent in one sense, yet present wherever the mission goes on and where brother- and sisterhood is realized (18:15-20, 28:20). It does not take 'prophets' (by any customary definition) to accomplish the kind of editing that is going on in Mt. 23:8-12.

NOTES

[1]See, e.g. E. Käsemann, _New Testament Questions of Today_ (1969), pp. 84f.; E. Haenchen, "Matthäus 23," _ZTK_ 48 (1951), p. 43; R. Bultmann, _History of the Synoptic Tradition_ (1963), p. 146.

[2]Cf. Haenchen, _op. cit._, p. 42.

[3]H. L. Strack and P. Billerbeck, _Kommentar zum Neuen Testament aus Talmud und Midrasch_ I (1956), pp. 918f.

[4]Cf. C. H. Dodd, "A l'arrière-plan d'un dialogue johannique," _RHPR_ 37 (1957), pp. 16f. (see also his _Historical Tradition in the Fourth Gospel_ [1963], pp. 331f.); J. T. Townsend, "Matthew XXIII 9," _JTS_, n.s. 12 (1961), pp. 56-59.

[5]Even though _didaskalos_ in Mt is characteristically applied to Jesus by seekers (8:19, 19:16) or by opponents (9:11, 12:38, 17:24, 22:16, 24, 36) and only Judas calls him 'Rabbi' (26:25, 49), his activity undeniably centers around teaching, and in 26:18 at least he speaks of himself as _ho didaskalos_ (cf. _ho kurios_ in 21:3). This makes it likely that _didaskalos_ in 23:8 does refer to Jesus rather than to God.

[6]_Art. cit._, p. 16, n. 26.

[7]See above, n. 5.

[8]This in spite of 1:1. In Mt, as in Rom. 1:3f., the human descent of Jesus is acknowledged at one level, but ultimately transcended by his divine sonship (cf. 1:23, 2:15, 3:17, 4:1-11, 14:33, 16:16f., 28:18-20).

[9]Chs. 41-42, in both Coptic and Ethiopic. E. Hennecke and W. Schneemelcher, _New Testament Apocrypha_ I (1963), pp. 220f.

[10]So Käsemann (cf. n. 1), but why does he then assign the passage to Mt's _opponents_? Only because of his persistent assumption that Mt himself represents an "incipient Christian rabbinate," an assumption which explains neither the editing of this passage nor its final inclusion in the Gospel.

S 213, A 362 REVOLUTIONS IN NORTHERN ISRAEL

Simon B. Parker
Reed College

I. The Specific Biblical Data

According to the Books of Kings eight Israelite monarchs gained the throne by killing their predecessors. (In one case, that of Omri, the occupant of the throne committed suicide before Omri could get to him.) This mode of succession is usually referred to in the text by the formula: *wyqšr ʻlyw* PN (the usurper) *wykhw wymthw wymlk tḥtyw*, "PN rebelled against him and struck him down and killed him and reigned in his place" (1 Kgs 15:27-28; 16:9-10; 2 Kgs 15:10; 15:25; and, with minor divergences, 15:30). In the one case where an extensive narrative account appears, we have only *wytqšr* PN_1 ʻ(!) *l* PN_2 (2 Kgs 9:14). The verb *qšr* is not used of the moves against Zimri or Shallum (said to have reigned only a week and a month respectively). The formula may be punctuated with details of person, place, time or circumstances, and the immediate context may also give relevant information. For example, in three cases the coup takes place during a war, and in four cases the usurper is a military officer. Other information, though not directly expressed as relevant to the violent change of ruler, is provided by the larger context. Thus, in four cases the usurper strikes shortly after a regular accession to the throne, and in three of those cases the late king was himself a usurper.

In general, this information can be accepted as historically reliable, as far as it goes. It is the colorless, neutral stuff of an annalist. At the same time, it is largely formulaic and personal. It tells us practically nothing about the condition of, or developments within, the society at large. The account of Jehu's revolution presents us with material of a different sort. Here is lively, engaging, narrative literature, and it will have to be critically assessed as literature, before it can be used for purposes of historical reconstruction. Whatever the outcome of such an assessment, we are left with a very small amount of evidence about Israel's revolutions. Whatever the annalist's--or the narrator's, or the Deuteronomist's--criteria in selecting material, the final product seems pitifully inadequate as a basis for understanding the significance of these violent changes of monarch. Did the usurper act on his own initiative? If not, how widespread was his support, and in what segments of the society did it appear? And how articulate and organized was such support, if indeed it existed? What were the causes, and what were the events, that led to the killing of the king? What were the forces working against such an outcome? And what were the results of the usurpation? How far-reaching were the changes effected by the founding of a new dynasty? Did all the transitions we are concerned with fall into a similar pattern, or did they vary widely in character?

At this point it is appropriate to consider their distribution. The first three violent changes take place in the fifty years following the North's declaration of independence from Judah, and its foundation as a separate nation. The last four take place in the last twenty-five years of its existence under the threat of loss of independence and incorporation into the Assyrian empire. Between these two groupings there is a period of some one and a third centuries, which saw only one such disturbance--that which brought Jehu to the throne some thirty-five years after the establishment of the Omride dynasty. This distribution suggests that it may be appropriate to consider the first three usurpations together in the context of the early development of the new nation, and the last four together as having to do with the national emergency precipitated by the Assyrian advance. Whether Jehu's revolution was a last adjustment to new nationhood, or an early anticipation, in response to encounters with Assyria, or reactions a century later, it would seem to demand more independent treatment.

The distribution of the transitions *within* these groupings also deserves comment. In the first grouping, Baasha kills Nadab shortly after he has succeeded Jeroboam--some twenty-odd years after secession from the union under Judah. A quarter-century later, Zimri kills Elah just after the latter has succeeded Baasha. But this immediately precipitates Omri's move against Zimri. Within seven days, Omri is on the throne. But then there arises a third aspirant to the throne--Tibni, who is said to have had half the people behind him, but who is eventually overcome by Omri. Here the takeovers by Zimri and Omri have to be seen as part of the same disturbance, and, further, the unsuccessful bid by Tibni has to be included in any consideration of that disturbance.

In the second grouping there is a similar complex of events. Shortly after Zechariah has succeeded Jeroboam II, he is killed by Shallum, who in turn is killed a month later by Menahem. There is even evidence of subsequent opposition to Menahem in the reference to one city's holding out against him, and his exemplary treatment of it. These events, too, will have to be studied as part of a single disturbance. A decade later, Menahem is succeeded by his son, who is soon dispatched by Pekah. Pekah's reign, which must have been considerably shorter than that allowed in any of the textual traditions, was then cut short by Hoshea.

Turning our attention to the reverse side of the coin, from violent to peaceful succession, we find only two true dynasties in the two hundred years of Israel's existence as an independent nation: that of Omri, which lasted some thirty-five years (three reigns and a bit), and that of Jehu, which lasted almost a century (four reigns and a bit). Together these two cover sixty-five percent of Israel's history. Any explanation of Israel's usurpations should also explain the persistence of these two dynasties, and vice versa.

As a prolegomenon to such an explanation, there follows a selective and summary account of some social scientific contributions to the explanation of revolutions.

II. A Theory of Revolutions

"Revolution is not a discrete, relatively isolable, purely political phenomenon; the factors that contribute to it are as manifold as the elements comprising society itself, and abstract generalizations about revolution must reflect this extreme complexity. The analyst must therefore make use of sociological, psychological, military, and economic, as well as political, concepts and data."[1] It is difficult to write briefly and simply about so complex a phenomenon. Since most social scientific study of revolutions is based on modern revolutions--either the "Great Revolutions" or the innumerable smaller revolutions especially of the third world--it will be more profitable for us to turn to general, theoretical works, rather than specific, comparative works. A handy survey of "Theories of Revolution" is to be found in the article by L. Stone published under that title in *World Politics* 18 (1966) 159-76, and reappearing in updated form in the same author's stimulating study of the English revolution; *The Causes of the English Revolution* (New York: Harper, 1972), pp. 3-25. The following is based chiefly on C. Johnson, *Revolutionary Change* (Boston: Little, Brown and Co., 1966),[2] and subsequent page references in the text are to that work.

Johnson studies revolution as a species of social change, and his conclusions therefore presuppose an analysis of social change in general. But social change is meaningful only in relation to social stability. Drawing on the work of Parsons, Johnson says of stability and instability: "...the analysis of why one condition does or does not prevail is simultaneously the analysis of why its antithesis does or does not prevail" (p. 11). The model of society which Johnson expounds as susceptible of such an analysis is a synthesis of coercion theory and value theory. "Values and the division of labor are both independent variables...values and the circumstances of environmental adaptation must both be studied with regard to the way in which each does, or does not, complement the other" (pp. 38-39). Thus, whatever their origin, values either contribute to, or detract from the integration of society. In a stable society, the value structure authorizes, or legitimates, the use of force. Just as, in a market economy, trust in the system is as important as supplies of gold, so in a political system trust in the system is as important as supplies of force.

A society's division of labor is the product of its adaptation to its environment. The distribution of roles according to the division of labor is legitimated by its value system, which orders the different roles in a hierarchy of statuses. The interests of persons and groups occupying subordinate positions are thus normally neutralized by the value system. Such interests will remain latent, and the legitimacy of the distribution of roles will continue to be acknowledged, as long as the value system and the division of labor remain synchronized.

But this does not exclude the possibility of change--even of substantial structural change. Johnson takes over from Emmet the term "homeostasis," or homeostatic equilibrium, to denote the normal functioning of a (social) system, which includes correctives to disruptive tendencies. Homeostatic equilibrium is not static, but allows slight, individual variations in, e.g., role interpretation, or socialization. Even though the cumulative effect of such variations and adjustments may be changes in the structure of the society, the system will continue to operate through such changes. Homeostatic equilibrium is maintained as long as the value structure and the division of labor change synchronically. Social change of this kind, taking place within a functioning system, may be called evolutionary change.

Evolutionary change is to be distinguished from purposeful change, which takes place in a disequilibrated system, when the demand for change is beyond the resources of the normally functioning system. The social system is "disequilibrated" when the value structure and the division of labor are dissynchronized, that is, when one is changing without the other, or when both are changing "out of step" with each other. "The single, most generalized characteristic of a disequilibrated system is that values no longer provide an acceptable symbolic definition and explanation of existence" (pp. 72-73). Before considering purposeful change in a disequilibrated system, we should briefly review the possible sources of such a condition.

Johnson's analytic typology distinguishes four sources, according to whether they arise from within or without the society, and whether they have an initial effect on the structure of values or on the division of labor. Exogenous innovations in the value structure are easily recognizable and definable. Endogenous innovations in the value structure may come from "marginal persons" or "cultural hybrids" occupying new, poorly defined, or ambiguous statuses, or from "prestige-laden" persons of high status. Such innovations are rare, and more rarely accepted, though the number of marginal persons, or the influence of the prestigious person, will affect the diffusion of the innovation. Exogenous environmental change is again fairly obvious. It may take the form of economic stimulation as a result of foreign trade, importation of technology or skills, diplomatic relations, or, especially, military conquest, which will put new actors with new allegiances in positions of authority. Endogenous environmental innovation is again rare, and most obvious in the case of technological innovation. It usually takes some time for new values to develop, which will synchronize with such changes in environmental adaptation. Whatever the sources of pressures on a social system, their effects on the value structure and the division of labor, as the two determinants of equilibrium, are crucial for understanding the course of change.

If homeostatic processes cannot cope with such pressures, can policies be developed that will restore equilibrium? If the authorities recognize the need for change, and if they are willing and able to effect appropriate changes, homeostatic equilibrium may be restored. Appropriate changes in this context will be adjustments in the division of labor or in the value structure, or in the introduction of some overriding and unifying goal for the society, such as overcoming a foreign threat--which, however, may only temporarily alleviate the situation. Policies like these, directed at avoiding internal violence, even at the cost of, or by means of, structural changes, may be termed conservative. If the authorities do not undertake, or even recognize the need for changes, but adopt a reactionary policy, resorting to sheer force, if necessary, they are in effect admitting a loss of authority, or at least of legitimacy. Any sign of weakening may then precipitate sudden, violent change. If the authorities are unsuccessful in instituting changes, or refuse to innovate, and disequilibrated conditions persist, there is an increasing likelihood of conflicting policies developing. And since conflict is then no longer within the framework of the system, it is more likely to lead to violence. Indeed, in such circumstances, policies are likely to be formulated which are directed at changing the structure of the society even at the cost of, or by means of, violence. Such policies emerge as follows.

As the value system and the division of labor become increasingly dissynchronized, the status hierarchy loses its legitimacy, and the latent interests of persons occupying subordinate positions with inferior statuses become manifest, and are articulated in the form of ideologies. Johnson reserves the term "ideology" for an alternative value structure, which may emerge at any time among marginal persons, but only receives wide assent during a period of disequilibrium, as manifest interest groups form. "Ideologies are most typically crude rationalizations of a partially understood social situation,..." (p. 83), but over time they may develop a "goal culture"--that is, a model for a resynchronization of values and division of labor--and a "transfer culture"--a program for realizing the goal culture. Ideologies are generally exclusivist--both of the old synthesis and of rival ideologies--and are therefore not easily routinized, and tend to encourage violence. A significant factor affecting the legitimacy of political violence is the traditional attitude toward such in the society. "People...may be taught about the gains their ancestors won or liberties they protected through violence, teachings that often provide enduring justifications for violence in new circumstances."[3]

It follows from Johnson's theoretical presuppositions that a typology of revolutions would depend on a typology of social systems, which, in turn, would be based on the different sets of relations between particular value structures and the various modes of adaptation to particular environments. In 1966 he considered such a typology lacking. In general, he accepted provisionally a distinction between "traditional" and "modern" societies, the former being characterized by ascribed roles and lack of specialization, hence by a high degree of equilibrium, and a low degree of interdependence among the components of the society. Traditional societies may experience rebellions, but not revolutions--a distinction of respectable antiquity. Rebellions operate *within* a functioning system, or in a system with a relatively trivial dysfunction, such as the personal weakness of a monarch. Thus rebellions seek to change only the person(s) in authority, leaving the political and social systems intact. In fact, such rebellions are rare: "...societies with ascriptive values do not generate conflict when the eldest son of a ruler succeeds his father; and they normally tolerate, or systematically compensate for, the inefficiency that results if the son does not possess the temperament of a good ruler" (p. 26). When rebellions do take place, they are usually carried out in the name of king or church against a ruler regarded as a usurper or tyrant--or as the agent of a foreign king or church. Such rebellions generally lack a distinct ideology, although Johnson also allows a second category of "ideological rebellions," which revive a social ideal alleged to have existed in the society's past, and are justified, therefore, by claims of traditional legitimacy. Students of traditional societies, however, emphasize that in such societies, where the value system incorporates religious sanctions, movements of opposition generally appeal to the sanction of an alternative deity, mythology, or religion. Johnson, in fact, admits that ideological rebellions may aim to make substantial changes in governmental institutions. This is getting close to a "simple revolution," which involves changes in some values and institutions, that is, in the regime, or type of government. Johnson's final category is "total revolution" involving a change of the entire social system. Since 1966, G. Lenski has developed a typology of societies roughly consistent with Johnson's requirements.[4] In "advanced agrarian societies" he sees political violence as falling into two classes: assassination of the monarch by a rival member of the governing elite, and peasant rebellion.[5]

Johnson has some illuminating things to say about the coup d'état as a particular tactic of revolution (in the broader sense). A coup d'état generally presupposes certain characteristics of the antecedent disequilibrium, namely, a widely-felt need for change, and a relatively isolated and undefended governing elite. But it also faces more difficulty than other tactics in establishing legitimacy. In order to become acceptable to the people as a whole, the new government must respond to the real needs, on the basis of which it presumed to overthrow the preceding government. A military coup may have a better chance of success, in that the force of the army can support the new government as it seeks to establish its legitimacy. "An analysis of the political position of a system's armed forces always lies at the heart of any concrete study of a revolution" (p. 99). The sympathies of the army are a crucial factor in the success of an insurrection. If the officers are members of the governing elite, and their men well-disciplined, the army will generally support the establishment. However, if the army is close to the general populace in its origins and in its social contacts, that support may be lacking, and, indeed, the army may be the base of an insurrection.

In sum, the preconditions of revolution, the conditions under which revolution becomes possible, are twofold. The fundamental one is a disequilibrated social system, one in which there is a lack of harmony between the division of labor and the value structure. This has been connected with the psychological theory of relative deprivation, the core of Gurr's theory of revolution.[6] "Relative deprivation" is defined as a discrepancy between expectations and capabilities.[7] Gurr equates "expectations" with Johnson's "value structure," and "capabilities" with Johnson's "pattern of environmental adaptation" (division of labor).[8] The second essential precondition for revolution is an intransigent governing elite.

But to make a revolution probable, there has to be a specific "precipitator" or "accelerator." An accelerator exposes or suggests the inability of an already discredited elite to maintain its monopoly of force. Thus it might be particularly a military defeat, but also some sign of disunity among the elite, or the emergence of an inspired leader or prophet with a convincing ideology. The accelerator affects the timing and success of an insurrection.

III. An Approach to Israel's Revolutions

There seems to be general agreement that any adequate treatment of revolutions must be multi-disciplinary. In Stone's words, it "must necessarily range backwards over a long period of time and be multi-causal in its approach, laying as much stress on institutional defects and ideological passions as on social movements and economic changes."[9] One scholar has gone so far as to say that the determinants of revolution may be so various as to deny theoretical treatment, and may, of necessity, have to be left to the historian!

In the case of Israel, our evidence is so scanty that, as historians, we have to depend rather heavily on the theorist. That being so, any treatment of revolutions in Israel will have to be of the nature of interpretative case studies. Such interpretations will involve much historical reconstruction. The only control over a purely theoretical reconstruction will be the interpreter's attention to every scrap of evidence, and his nicety in interpreting it. In the brief space remaining, the first group of revolutions spoken of above will be discussed in light of the preceding theoretical analysis.

North Israel was founded by a revolution. According to the narrative in 1 Kgs 12, the point at issue was the exploitation--by compulsory service and contributions--of the population of the North by the monarchy of the South. The division of labor, serving the interests of Judah, clashed with the values and manifest interests of the northern tribes. For the Northerners, the authority of the king was conditional upon the maintenance of an equilibrium between his power and their traditional values. The precarious balance of the Union had deteriorated under Solomon, as the monarch's power and exploitation of it had increased, while the value structure of the North had remained more or less constant. Rehoboam's succession provided the Northerners with an opportunity to voice their discontent. They were met with intransigence, and so announced their secession from the political Union. Rehoboam relied blindly on the assertion of his authority: he sent his secretary of compulsory service into Israel to put his new demands into effect. The man was killed. This first act of violence was the final demonstration that the legitimacy of Rehoboam's sovereignty had been rejected. Rehoboam, resorting to simple coercion, planned an invasion of the North. But outright war was averted through Shemaiah (1 Kgs 12:22-24), speaking as a representative of the religious establishment in Jerusalem, which, while maintaining an ideology of all Israel as a single people under Yahweh's sovereignty (and presumably, therefore, itself as the ultimate legitimating institution), recognized a real shift in the distribution of power. In other words, it conservatively adjusted the value structure of the South to accord with the new political situation, and thus facilitated the restoration of "homeostatic equilibrium" in the South. Meanwhile, the North had made Jeroboam king of the seceding tribes, thus realizing in a new authority their divergent view of the source of legitimation and of the locus of power. Their values had apparently prevailed, though it would soon become apparent that a synchronized division of labor could not so easily be achieved. The institution of monarchy, an "exogenous environmental innovation, was not so adaptable to traditional values as the people perhaps supposed.

Jeroboam's previous career is of some relevance. Jeroboam ben Nebat was from Zeredah in Ephraim, we are told--a man, presumably of some traditional status, who had entered Solomon's service, been noticed for his hard work, and appointed supervisor of all Josephite labor. While in this office, he had attracted the attention of a figure of importance in a different context, a fellow-tribesman of his, Ahijah, from Shiloh, a "prophet" who told him that Yahweh would give him the North as his kingdom. Ahijah, representing a divergent--but traditional--source of legitimation for the North, had articulated the manifest interests of some of his people and given them a political focus in Jeroboam. Jeroboam's response is referred to as simply "raising his hand" against Solomon, who tried to have him killed. We can only surmise that this was a revolt that failed, perhaps because Solomon's authority was too great, his legitimacy too widely recognized. The value structure of the Union had, at least temporarily, gained general assent, and the traditional interests of the North were largely latent. This would explain how Jeroboam could have entered Solomon's service in the first place. Further developments, including Solomon's death, were necessary to bring those interests to the surface. At any rate, Jeroboam fled to Egypt, where he enjoyed the hospitality of the Egyptian king, returning to his homeland on the death of his persecutor. He thus enjoyed considerable status, both ascribed, in his original context, and acquired, through his experience in two courts. There is, therefore, no ground for introducing charismatic authority to explain the roles of Jeroboam, or Ahijah, or Shemaiah.

Jeroboam promptly set about establishing distinctive institutions for his new kingdom: a royal capital, border sanctuaries, religious institutions. These would not be absolutely new, any more than they would be perversions of Judahite institutions, as the sources suggest, but rather would have been based on indigenous traditions, at the same time expressing the national consciousness of the new, independent state. Presumably they were designed to be acceptable to the value structure of the people, but also to bolster the authority of the new king.

The new state was unable to hold onto the possessions of the Solomonic empire, and suffered the ravages of an invasion by Egypt. These developments meant military, political, economic, and prestige losses for the new king. At the same time, the border war with Judah, and the building up of the new royal centers at Shechem and Penuel necessitated the maintenance of a standing army (or frequent levies), and compulsory labor and contributions from the local populations. While Jeroboam's court must have been a very pale reflection of Solomon's, the burden of supporting it had to be borne by his own people (while Solomon had been able to exempt Judah, and lay the burden elsewhere). That would explain why the crisis after Solomon's death issued in secession, that following Jeroboam's death in internal revolution. The general conditions preparing the ground for revolution were much the same: a disequilibrium between the values of the general population and Jeroboam's manipulation of power, which perforce had begun to resemble that of Solomon. The situation was doubtless exacerbated by the sufferings consequent upon Shishak's invasion. Revolution was precipitated by the death of Jeroboam. The memory of the success of the popular insurrection after the death of Solomon was still fresh. The final trigger may have been some particular development in a war against the Philistines (1 Kgs 15:27). The blow was finally struck by Baasha, who is identified by patronymic and tribe; perhaps, therefore, a man with some traditional authority, apt to play the role of popular leader, not unlike Jeroboam himself. If he represented the discontents of the populace, and made some show of adjusting the monarchic division of labor to traditional values, he would have had no difficulty in quickly establishing the legitimacy of his takeover. Evidently the army--perhaps made up largely of traditionalists, and possibly dissatisfied with the political conduct of the war--accepted the changeover.

The border wars with Judah and Philistia continued, at least intermittently. Israel now suffered the ravaging of Naphtali by Damascus and the loss of much of Benjamin to Judah. Baasha moved to a new capital in Tirzah. The preconditions of the next insurrection thus seem to have been similar to those of the last: a continuing disequilibrium between the value structure, which was presumably fairly stable, and environmental adaptation, which involved the population in ongoing compulsory labor, contributions, and military service. Again the death of the king was a precipitant, and the fact that revolt broke out during a battle on the Philistine border (1 Kgs 16:15) again suggests some event in the course of that war as the final straw. Whether the reference to Baasha's heir drinking himself drunk with some of his cronies among the elite (16:9) can be taken as reliable evidence of Elah's incompetence is uncertain. In any case, the first to strike against him is Zimri, a man identified solely by his office: commander of half the chariotry. Presumably he was a man of negligible traditional status, who had risen to his present position through the army's more open opportunities for advancement, i.e. he is of achieved status. Thus he lacked popular support--but also the support of the army, as immediately becomes evident. He is an example of the unpredictable personal element that can enter into such situations, acting on his own initiative, and, from the point of view of theory, irrationally. Whatever triggered Zimri's action, it in turn triggered more momentous developments. Hearing of Zimri's assassination of the king, the army promptly proclaimed Omri king (16:16). He is introduced, as Zimri was, without patronymic, and is therefore also presumed to be of achieved status. But, unlike Zimri, who was his subordinate (Omri being commander of the army), he had the support of the entire army. With Omri at its head, the latter marched on the capital, of which Zimri had taken possession. When Zimri saw that he could not hold out against them, he burned the palace down on himself, and Omri occupied the city. However, Omri's support evidently did not extend far outside the army, for the sources report that now the country was split in two, half the people acknowledging Omri, and the other half supporting a Tibni ben Ginath. Again the patronymic suggests ascribed status. I suggest that Tibni is the representative of traditional values, heading a resistance movement to the encroachments of the relatively new monarchy. The disequilibrium of this value system and the division of labor developing under the monarchy must have been fairly constant through these decades, the latent interests of the general population occasionally becoming more manifest and organized, given sufficient provocation by, and sufficient signs of weakness in, the government. Perhaps both Zimri and Omri had hoped to capitalize on the discontent, focussing on the person of the previous monarch as scapegoat. But their moves had been seen as signs of disunity within the governing class, their acquired status was not acknowledged by those holding to traditional values, and a representative of those values with appropriate status had been found as a third claimant to the throne. Thus, a civil war broke out between the governing class and the army, with vested interests in the developing monarchy, on the one hand; and the traditional society of small town and country, with vested interests in a traditional (pre-monarchic) division of labor on the other. (Clearly, this will be an over-simplification.) Omri headed the superior force, and consequently prevailed. As 1 Kgs 16:22 delicately puts it: "The people behind Omri proved stronger than the people behind Tibni ben Ginath: Tibni died, and Omri ruled."

It is worth noting that Zimri is included among the kings of Israel, though he only occupied the throne for a week, while Tibni does not merit inclusion. Presumably, occupation of the capital meant de facto rule. But further, neither Omri nor Tibni (nor Menahem later) is spoken of as "rebelling" or "conspiring" (*qšr*) against the king whom he sought to replace--presumably because the legitimacy of that king was still in question a week (Zimri) or a month (Shallum) after his accession. (Tibni's insurrection is not dated, but seems to have taken place very soon after Omri's accession.)

In the first fifty years of its existence, then, the new state of Israel had suffered a continuing disequilibrium, arising from the inconsistency between the traditional values of the society and the division of labor evolving with the institution of monarchy. There is no question of the abolition of monarchy. Jeroboam, Baasha, and Tibni--if all three to some extent represent traditional values--are all accepted as (potential) monarchs. There is no suggestion that the dynastic principle is rejected. Rather for different social groups with different values, the best *timing* for an insurrection is immediately after a king's accession, whether by natural succession (Nadab, Elah), or by violence (Zimri, Omri). Nor are the various assassinations all simply palace coups, involving no more than intra-elite rivalry and a change of person at the top. Rather, as the debacle following Elah's accession makes clear, Zimri's coup, which looks most like a palace coup, precipitated the greatest turmoil in Israel's brief history: the army was first pitted against the new government, and then, more significantly, after Omri's initial success against Zimri, there was a relatively protracted conflict between government and army on one side, and the conservative majority of the population on the other. I am inclined to see continuity between the values expressed in the North's declaration of independence from the Union, and those represented by the movement behind Tibni, with Baasha possibly raising the same banner in his move for the throne. At the same time, I see the development of the new nation, i.e. of its central institution, monarchy, as entailing a division of labor decreasingly consistent with those values. The memory of the success of the move against Rehoboam would have reinforced hopes of success against native monarchs perceived as betraying their trust and abrogating their legitimacy. Thus, early Israel knew two different interpretations of the role of monarch: the traditional one, which severely restricted his responsibilities and privileges; and that of the incumbents and their retainers, which tended to exploit to the maximum the power of the office.

With Omri's successful quelling of the Tibni insurrection, a new force had established itself in Israelite society. Zimri and Omri suggest through their roles that a professional soldiery had been built up in Israel's army by this time. Omri's success meant the establishment of a unified military-political elite at the same time as the discrediting of the traditionalist movement under Tibni. The latter development must have contributed to acknowledgement of Omri's legitimacy. At least, we know of no challenge to his rule henceforth, or to that of his two immediate successors. In fact, Omri is able to found the first real dynasty in Israel. He laid the foundations for a strong, stable government that would last twice as long as that of either Jeroboam or Baasha, and that would survive three changes of person on the throne. The next question is twofold. How were the Omrides able to achieve that stability, and how was it lost by the time of Jehu? That question, and the further history of Israel's revolutions, awaits prior critical response to the present essay.

NOTES

1. C. Johnson, *Revolutionary Change* (Boston: Little, Brown and Co., 1966), p. xi.
2. Cf. his earlier monograph, *Revolution and the Social System*, Hoover Institution Studies, 3 (Stanford: Hoover Institute, 1964).
3. T. R. Gurr, *Why Men Rebel* (Princeton: Princeton University, 1970), p. 192.
4. G. Lenski, *Human Societies* (New York: McGraw, 1970).
5. *Ibid.*, pp. 250 ff.
6. T. R. Gurr, *Why Men Rebel* (Princeton: Princeton University, 1970).
7. *Ibid.*, p. 24.
8. *Ibid.*, p. 38.
9. L. Stone, *The Causes of the English Revolution*, p. 57.

PANEL DISCUSSION ON DIVINATION TECHNIQUES

S 228 Techniques in Early Dream Interpretation

Robert J. White, Hunter College

To one examining the history of dream interpretation, it becomes obvious that ancient dream writers seem to have had at least one common goal: to devise a uniform set of laws governing men's dreams and a workable system for categorizing dream material. This frequently took the form of distinguishing those elements in a dream which could be considered general or universal from those which were more personal and original. The dream interpreter tried to separate those dream images which exist in all persons simply because they are human beings from those that are peculiar to certain individuals or to members of certain classes.

The 2nd century dream writer Artemidorus is undoubtedly following what was traditional procedure in onirology when he instructs the apprentice dream interpreter to become familiar with the customs of the land in which the dreamer lives (1.8) and learn the dreamer's identity, age, personal habits, financial status, state of health, and occupation (1.9). This was based on the belief that the significance and prophetic value of a dream would vary in accordance with the dreamer's personal circumstances -- sex, nationality, economic position, profession. Such an approach to dream interpretation bears an obvious resemblance to the modern analyst's practice of ascertaining the general psychic situation of the dreamer, his mental associations, and the immediate precipitating cause of the dream before attempting any interpretation.

What separates Artemidorus and probably other 2nd century dream interpreters from their predecessors is a greater emphasis on the personal status of their subjects and an awareness that this method could be used to remove superstition from their profession and achieve a more scientific approach. For the 2nd century saw the development of two simultaneous but opposed movements in life and thought: on the one hand, a tendency toward the superstitious and the irrational, evidenced by such phenomena as the revival of the mystery cults of Isis, Cybele, and Mithra and the proliferation of exotic forms of prophecy, such as divining from cheese, crockery, spindles, sieves, and so on, while on the other hand, an opposite tendency toward the rational systematic structuring of knowledge, what we would call the scientific approach, evidenced by the work of Galen and Ptolemy, and by dramatic developments in the fields of medicine, astronomy, optics, geography, and others.

Artemidorus considers a knowledge of the dreamer's occupation essential to the interpretation of his dream. One can divide the trades and professions mentioned by Artemidorus into two classes -- (1) those that are imagined in dreams, and (2) those that are actually held by the dreamers and that must, consequently, be taken into account before a valid interpretation is possible.

Some idea of the extent and variety of 2nd century business and trade can be gained simply by reading Artemidorus' catalogue of occupations seen in dreams -- among them, farming, carpentry, tanning hides, metallurgy, secretarial work, moneylending, medicine, professional athletics. Artemidorus records more than forty occupations that recur frequently in dreams. He indicates whether a certain occupation is propitious or unpropitious for a subject to dream about, and then explains why this is so by interpreting the meaning of the occupation.

For example, if any man, regardless of his actual occupation, dreams that he is steering a ship in a dream, it is auspicious. Dreaming that one is employed as a cobbler, a jockey, or a carpenter is also universally auspicious. Dreaming that one is a goldsmith, a secretary, a tanner of hides, or a police and public works commissioner is, on the other hand, universally inauspicious. Many other occupations, such as sculpting, chasing metal, boxing, or commanding an army can be either, depending on the dreamer's actual occupation.

Dreaming that one is sculpting, drawing, casting a statue, or chasing metal (1.51) is inauspicious for all men except orators and forgers. The obvious implication of such an interpretation is that deception is an element common both to the occupations in the dream and the dreamers' actual occupations. Artemidorus himself draws this connection for us by stating that sculpting, drawing, and chasing metal "represent what does not exist as though it actually does." Dreaming that one is a professional boxer is inauspicious for all men except doctors, sacrificers, and cooks (1.61). Here blood, Artemidorus asserts, is the element which is common to all four occupations. Dreaming that one is an aedile, moreover, is inauspicious for all but medical students. This interpretation is also based on a similarity, forced and somewhat arbitrary, between the aedileship and medicine: a concern for food. For among the duties of the aediles was the *cura annonae*, the maintenance and distribution of the corn supply. And in Greek and Roman medicine, dietetics was the central factor in treatment, and thus an essential part of the curriculum of a medical student was the study of the general principles of dietetics, especially as they were related to fevers.

Artemidorus also treats the symbolism of various professions. For example, a moneylender or rent collector seen in a dream symbolizes, among other things, the dreamer's life or his daughter. If the dreamer is a household slave, the moneylender signifies a master who demands his hire pay. Public executioners and jailors are symbols of delay and pain. Innkeepers portend death for the sick but journeys for other men. Interestingly enough, Artemidorus devotes more space to dreams that involve cooks (3.56) and toll collectors (3.58) than to those involving any other profession.

Among the numerous occupations actually held by the dreamers, Artemidorus mentions some that are familiar to us because of the prominent role they play in Roman comedies and novels -- soldiers, slave-dealers, brothel-keepers, poets, painters, and mendicant priests. He also includes several professions that seem somewhat more specialized: thymelic musicians, beekeepers, water carriers, inspectors of weights and measures, and subscription collectors. Professional athletes, farmers, actors, and doctors are among the professions most frequently mentioned by Artemidorus.

Artemidorus' method of interpreting dreams is relatively straightforward. For each dream, Artemidorus provides a basic interpretation which is then followed by any additions to or deviations from the original interpretation. Dreaming that one has a large head, for example, is auspicious for an athlete, a moneylender, a banker, or a collector of subscriptions. For the athlete, it signifies victory. For the moneylender, banker, and collector of subscriptions, it foretells a great accumulation of wealth. It is, however, inauspicious for orators and soldiers.

The lore of the professional dream interpreter was based partly on experience and partly, as Aristotle states (*Div. Somn.* 2, 464 b 7), on supposed resemblances, on a system of analogies. It is not surprising, then, that Artemidorus concludes that dreaming that one has a shaved head is auspicious for a priest belonging to an Egyptian cult, that one has had sexual intercourse with the moon or has eaten some stars is auspicious for an astronomer, or that one has seen the god Apollo is auspicious for a musician, prophet, doctor, or philosopher. Nor is it surprising, conversely, that dreaming that one has a shaved head is inauspicious (and symbolizes a shipwreck) for a sailor -- Juvenal (*Satires* 12,81), Petronius (*Satyricon* 103-104) and Lucian (*Hermotimus* 86) all allude to the common practice of shipwrecked sailors to shave their heads when their disabled ship reaches still water -- or that dreaming that one's breasts have fallen off is inauspicious for a wet-nurse, that one's arms have disappeared is inauspicious for a juggler, or that one has seen the goddess Athena is inauspicious for a courtesan.

Artemidorus records more than one hundred dreams whose interpretation depends upon the dreamer's occupation. Although his prognostics are sometimes the result of arcane analogies, elaborate puns, forced anagrammatical transpositions, and obscure numerological procedures, he usually attempts to interpret dreams in a rational, practical way. Artemidorus seems determined to root out of his work much of the superstition and mysticism that flourished during the Antonine age. He dismisses as charlatans the astragalomantises -- prophets who divine the future from dice --, the Pythagoreans, practitioners of palmistry, the physiognomists -- even though his own interpretations of dreams involving birds (e.g. a nightingale's symbolizing a musician or singer, a vulture's signifying a pallbearer, undertaker, or tanner) seem derived from techniques similar to those employed by the physiognomists -- necromancers, and casters of horoscopes, the *mathematici*. His timid evasion in Book One of the *Oneirocritica* of the question of whether dreams are sent by the gods or whether they are motivated by something within the dreamer has, by Book Four (4.59), which was written sometime later, changed to a confident assertion that "dreams are products of the mind and are not caused by any outside influence."

Claes Blum, in his *Studies in the Dream-Book of Artemidorus* (Uppsala, 1936) has demonstrated convincingly the influence of the Empirical school of medicine on Artemidorus. Indeed, the three methods of the Empirical medical writers -- personal experience, transmitted experience, and analogy -- can be found throughout the *Oneirocritica*. For, in addition to Artemidorus' insistence that he is guided primarily by his own personal experience, he uses the word *historia* (transmitted experience) in Book Five of the *Oneirocritica* in a sense that seems closely related to the notion of the Empirics. Furthermore, the analogical approach of Galen and the Empirics, which they employed to diagnose unknown diseases from the symptoms of known diseases and to invent new medications from old ones, is also operative in many sections of the Oneirocritica.

Artemidorus' reliance upon the methods of the Empirics, then, and his abandonment of a simplistic system of prophetic dream interpretation that depended solely upon mechanical correspondences drawn between symbol and thing symbolized (e.g. a deep well invariably symbolizes imprisonment, irrespective of the context of the dream) for one in which subtler distinctions, based on the dreamer's occupation, can be made seem to suggest a shift in onirological emphasis from the spiritual to the scientific. Artemidorus' statement in Book Four that "dreams are products of the mind and are not caused by any outside influence" and his conviction that a man's personal status, his occupation especially, determines his dreams and consequently their interpretation may indicate that he was attempting to transform the art of dream interpretation into a logically arranged, systematized body of knowledge, that he was attempting to pay less attention to the role of the gods in dreaming and more to that of man, that he was attempting, in short, to move the profession of dream interpreter out of the realm of religion into the domain of science.

S 229 Fate and Freedom : Astrology vs. Mystery Religions

Jean Rhys Bram, Hunter College

In abbreviated accounts of the religious situation toward the end of the Roman Empire, it is fairly common to find a number of alien influences listed together, as, for instance, "addiction to astrology, belief in the efficacy of magic, divination and other occult arts", (Laistner, M.L.W., Christianity and Pagan Culture in the Later Roman Empire, Cornell, 1951). It is of course true that this series of beliefs effected changes in the world picture of the Empire, but closer examination discovers that they are based on very different attitudes toward the universe and man's place in it, and that a good deal of competition and hostility arose between the different practices. The writings of a fourth century practitioner of astrology, Firmicus Maternus, give us some insights into tensions.

Astrology for the most part had no place for a concept of afterlife and no divinities except the fixed stars and planets which are nothing but visible reminders of the inflexible law of nature. "Let the human race regard the stars with constant veneration", says Firmicus, 1,6,2.

On the other hand, magic, theurgy, the various mystery cults are all based on some variety of supernatural powers, or offer a hope of afterlife. The mysteries, in different ways, offered initiates a method of achieving ecstatic communion with divinity and often promised individual immortality after death. The practice of magic sought control over supernatural beings through ritual or verbal formulae. Astrology could provide only the cold comfort of knowledge of future events in this life. "We might well be astonished that a religion so arid and abstruse should have been able to conquer the ancient world", (Cumont, Franz, Astrology and Religion among the Greeks and Romans, Dover, 1960). Vettius Valens, a practising astrologer of the second century A.D. claimed that his art provided tranquillity of mind in the sure knowledge of Fate, in place of fear of the unknown. That would have been quite a different experience from mystic communion with the divine.

There were, of course, different degrees of committment to astrology. We hear of "circus astrologers", together with village haruspices and dream-interpreters (Cicero, De Divinatione, I, 58, quoting Ennius) who tried to pick up a few coins in public places by giving forecasts for a short period of time or a single project, as newspaper columnists do today. This was known as catarchic astrology and it was sometimes believed that its predictions could be circumvented if known in time.

Those who could afford it could procure from trained specialists a birthchart showing geometrical relationships between heavenly bodies at the time of birth (or conception). The lengthy manuals of Vettius Valens and Firmicus Maternus indicate the minute detail in which the client's life story could be mapped. The belief was that these charts, if correctly computed, outlined the entire life from birth to death, and its predictions were inescapable. "Let us", says Firmicus, "concede that nothing is placed in our power, but the whole is in the control of Fate. Whatever we do or suffer, the whole thing happens to us by this same judgment of Fortune." (I,9,3). In Manilius, who wrote a long poem about astrology in the time of Tiberius, we read:

> fata regunt orbem, certa stant omnia lege
> longaque per certos signantur tempora casus
> nascentes morimur, finisque ab origine pendet.

But he agrees with Valens that astrological predictions are helpful, since they release men from uncertainty about the future.

Naturally there was an attempt to protect the reputation of fatalistic astrology and to separate it from the practise of those who gave facile responses to the crowd. This was the type of astrology made respectable by Claudius Ptolemy in his Tetrabiblos in the second century A.D., an old-world type of Deism which regarded with awe the evidence of natural law in the mechanisms of the heavens. The concept of fatal determinism had penetrated the Mediterranean area from its Babylonian homeland where it seems to have been founded on the idea that the stars were autocratic rulers like terrestrial Mesopotamian monarchs, (David, M. Des dieux et le destin en Babylonie, Paris, 1949). In the Hellenistic world Stoic logos, sympatheia and providentia blended with and supported astral fatalism. "The Stoics", as Cicero remarked (De Div. I,6) "defended almost all kinds of divination," but astral divination became by far the most accepted. Tiberius, for instance, had no deep regard for the gods or religious feeling, we are told (Suetonius, Tib. 69), but was persuaded by his belief in astrology that the world was entirely ruled by fate.

The earliest signs of resistance to the inescapable rule of Fate were philosophic. There was a famous set of arguments which apparently stemmed from the Academician Carneades. They make two general points: astrological predictions are impossible and they are against morality. Cicero in De Divinatione quotes his teacher Panaetius (a deviant Stoic) along the same lines, and they are echoed through the years by Philo of Alexandria, Favorinus of Arles, Alexander of Aphrodisias, Sextus Empiricus, and, of course, St. Augustine. The Neo-Platonist Plotinus completely rejected determinism, (Enn. III, 1,10), but his followers tended to hedge. According to Jamblichus (De Mysteriis VIII,6) there are two souls, one from the First Intelligence, and one from the movement of the celestial bodies. The first soul is superior to the cycle of birth and delivers us from Fate.

Firmicus takes up these arguments one by one in his first book of Mathesis (mathematical astrology) and attempts to answer them. On the impossibility of determining the exact moment of birth he says it was much more difficult to chart than celestial phenomena. "Once the course of the stars has been found by mathematical observation, it is easy to see their powers and their spheres of influence " (I,4,11). On why Germans are all blond and Ethipians black if complexions are allotted by the planets: the nature of the five zones determines complexions in general, while the planets determine individual differences. The wisdom of the stars sees to it that everyone has a slightly different appearance, otherwise "what crimes would be committed if everyone had the same face!" (I,10,10). As for the characters of the various nations, they are not completely homogeneous either. For "the frivolity of the Greeks often takes on a serious dignity; the unbridled fury of the Scythians is sometimes tempered by clemency; many Spaniards lay aside the fault of boasting; the Gauls are growing in wisdom (I,10,12)."

But as to the moral problem, Firmicus has no compromise. "A just man maintains his life as a wretched beggar while another, stained by well-known crimes, accumulates the highest honors. See how a pirate after the murder of untold innocents gathers his happy children into his bloody embrace while another, innocent of all crime, is separated from his family (I,7,3)." All this is evidence of the power of Fate, which we should venerate because it is divine Mind at work. "We make men fear and worship the gods (the stars); we point out the will and majesty of the gods, since we are ruled by their divine motion (I,6,1)." Manilius (IV, 23 ff.) is just as rigid in his fatalism, but has a more cheerful view. "Without the influence of Fate, how would Aeneas have been able to reach Italy, how would Rome have been built, or its victories achieved?"

Firmicus' strict adherence to fatalism has a somewhat old-fashioned sound in the fourth century when mysticism was coloring most beliefs. He is most bitter against those who "try to creep in, as it were, through an underground passage to undermine our science." By this he refers to those who accept partial control of Fate, like Jamblichus, "that all things that pertain to our daily lives are in our power; only our death belongs to Fate (I,8,3)." Plotinus, he admits, was a pious man but met a grisly end -- "every day small parts of his inner organs were dissolved...he had thought virtue would protect him against the threats of Fortune...but in the end he realized the power of Fate and accepted the fiery judgment of the stars." (Served him right for rejecting astrology, Firmicus hints!) The exaggerated gruesome details of the death of Plotinus are probably Firmicus' own invention, according to Paul Henry ("Plotin et l'Occident", Specilegium Sacrum Lovaniense, 1934). In the same way he dwells on the tortures he attributes to Sulla -- "first Marius' legs were amputated, then his arms cut off, third, his tongue was torn out...then his eyes...." All of this is to show that the most wicked of men die happy and prosperous.

There is no hint of supernaturalism or concept of after-life in the Mathesis. Firmicus had not made up his mind whether or not he believed in the existence of gods, he says (I,1,6). But astrologers must "remember the sanctity of their oaths; guard their books with a pure mind and soul...and not reveal these secrets to the sacrilegious, (VII,23,2)." The astrologer should be "careful to keep honesty uncorrupted, avoid plots, shun disturbances...show the right road of life to erring men... and above all never be present at nocturnal sacrifices, whether they are held publicly or privately." That meant, never participate in mystery religions.

Firmicus is more rigid and fanatic in his adherence to determinism than any Stoic writer of earlier times. It may be that in the early Empire, when society was prospering under an autocratic ruler, a sense of stability in a universal law of Fate was more acceptable. But there is evidence that determinism was widely felt to be irksome and tyrannical in the third and forth centuries. There was a search for magic practices to give release from Fate. Chaeremon, Nero's tutor, was said to have taught him magical means to avoid his fate (Euseb. V,10,5). Vettius Valens maintains that Fate cannot be avoided "by sacrifices or prayers." According to Lydus (De Mensibus, II,10), the theurgoi (magicians) are not subject to Fate.

But the most effective way to escape destiny in this life was in a flight from this world, from the terrestrial body to a life after death. Most of the mystery religions operated on the principle of initiation which was the equivalent of rebirth, i.e. an escape from the original birthchart. Though the symbols of the starry heavens, and the flight of the soul past the Moon to the area of the Sun become part of the new beliefs, the soul is no longer dissolved into the Great Soul, as in Stoicism, but retains its individuality or is reborn. One meets again the old Orphic idea that the pious may fly off from the wheel of fate and escape the birth cycles, but the wheel is now the circle of the zodiac.

"I overcome Fate; Fate hearkens to me" is a declaration of Isis in the Isis hymn found at Cyme. She keeps the celestial bodies embroidered on her robe, since, as Egyptian Sothis, the dog-star, she was leader of the stars. The complex rituals of Mithra are permeated with astral symbols, but they offer release from Fate in afterlife. According to their doctrine, the soul as it descends picks up from each planet it passes the appropriate characteristics: sexual attractiveness from Venus, eloquence from Hermes, etc. In ascending after death it sheds these mortal traits again at the proper stations.

Even Christ is claimed as a "Releaser from Fate," at

least by the Christian Gnostics. According to the Valentinian Theodotos (Clement of Alexandria, Excepta ex Theodoto 69, i ff.) "the Lord delivers us from the astral powers. He has risen as a strange star and breaks the ancient power of the constellations....He decended on Earth to release those who believe in him from the reign of Fate...Fate is for non-Christians....The birth of the Savior put to flight the genesis of Fate."

It is not surprising that Firmicus warns his followers against the mystery religions. A few years after the publication of the Mathesis he was apparently converted to Christianity and wrote a new work, De Errore Profanarum Religionum, (Clifford H. Moore demonstrated that the two works are by the same author in Julius Firmicus Maternus der Heide und der Christ Munich, 1897). The second book, however, has nothing to do with the tenets of Christian doctrine. It does not mention afterlife -- or astrology. It is from beginning to end a fierce attack on the mystery religions, showing them as scandalous, wicked and depraved. He calls upon the emperor to punish severely the followers of the mysteries, and he quotes only the most vindictive passages from the Bible, mostly the Old Testament. "if your brother... entices you in secret saying, 'Let us go and serve alien gods,' you must not show him any mercy...but you must be sure to kill him." (Deut. 12,4). "Whoever worships the animal and its statue and lets its mark be put on his forehead or on his hand shall drink the wine of God's wrath, poured unmixed into the cup of his anger, and be tortured with fire and brimstone before the eyes of the holy angels." (Apoc. 14,9).

One feels that conversion has not altered Firmicus' personality or his basic beliefs. He has merely found a new way to attack his old targets.

S 230 The Two-Bean Method at Delphi

J.O. and C. Grandjouan (read by C. Grandjouan, Hunter)

Manteia is meant to get an answer to a human question from the non-human, whether that non-human is seen as Fate, the Universe, the Gods or God, or simply the mantic tool itself.

One of the intriguing aspects of this persistent component of human curiosity is the limited range of means, both intellectual and technical, by which answers are obtained in various civilizations.

Underlying these limited means is the idea that the answer exists, that the universe knows, and that all humans need to develop is the proper method of information retrieval. We might note that this basic assumption is the same one made by science, with some measure of success, and by social sciences, and political ideologies, with more uneven results.

The three basic techniques of mantic information retrieval can be summarized as Revelation, Decipherment and Inducement;

a brief glance at all three is needed before we can proceed further.

Revelation implies retrieving information through direct communication between the non-human, usually personalized as a spirit or god, and a human being. Included in this category would be the shamanistic vision, whether brought about by drugs or otherwise, the Delphic Pythia's "delirium", Joan of Arc's "voices" and all other trance states allowing humans to communicate with the non-human, not excluding dreams, aspects of which have already been discussed at this meeting. This direct communication can be fleeting, obscure or deceptive; it can also be prolonged, clear and elaborate, as with Mohammed taking dictation for the Koran or the Etruscan *Iucumones* listening to Tages. In the case of revelations clear and prolonged enough to produce a considerable body of information (e.g. Sibylline Books, Torah) that information once stored, usually in writing, becomes a stand-in for the answering power, spirit or god, and can also become a separate mantic tool (e.g. *sortes vergilanae*).

Decipherment implies retrieving information from preexistent patterns in the universe, patterns senseless to the common man but significant to the initiate or the learned. The pre-existent pattern, or message can be permanent, as in the stars which give us one of the important aspects of mantic decipherment, *astrology*, aspects of which have already been discussed at this meeting and where observers received encouragement when star patterns yielded useful seasonal information: or in landscape features which gave us the *fong shwei*, or Chinese "geomancy." Patterns can also be impermanent (bird flight, ground hogs, wind, thunder) or rarely occurring (comets, monstrous births, other *portents*). Finally, there is the important branch of decipherment of invited phenomena, as in *augury* from chickens fed by the augur, or *haruspicy* in its largest sense, that is observation of not only the internal organs but also the manner of death of a living being dedicated to the answering power (e.g. among the Celts).

Inducement implies retrieving information from a pattern which the human induces or compels from the answering power. The basic form of inducement is *cleromancy* again in its largest sense.

Cleromancy induces the answering power's answer through the arrangement or aspect of inanimate objects, usually tossed, cast or flung by the human consultant to minimize conscious arranging. Minor mantic forms -- such as reading tea-leaves or coffee-grounds -- may be considered offshoots of cleromancy.

Within cleromancy itself three methods appear to be used with remarkable consistency; they are in reality three aspects of the same method, and their technical means can be used interchangeably. They can best be defined through these three technical means: *specific lot*, *multiple-answer* and *Yes-No*.

Specific lot: this the most cumbersome and least flexible: objects, each representing a name (those who would be given to the Minotaur) or a course of action (war, flight, peace) or a future condition (drought, flood, prosperity) are placed in a container, one is blindly picked or tossed out and represents the information yielded by the answering power.

Multiple-answer: this is one familiar to us since we use one of the commonest multiple-answer mantic tools, dice, for many purposes in our own civilization, most of them connected with games, but occasionally truly mantic ("who will pay for the drinks?"). Before the invention of dice, and later alongside them, knucklebones, natural objects that are easy to handle and offer four different faces or answers, were commonly used.

Yes-No also continues to be used in our culture as heads-or-tails, and usually more for mantic ("which team will carry the ball?") than game(e.g. the Australian Two-Up) purposes. Yes-No is one of the most widespread (e.g. Hittite oracular responses, or Biblical Urim and Tummin) of cleromantic methods. It has also been argued that the entire development of computer technology is a simple refinement of this basic mantic tool.

In order to finally arrive at Delphi, we must consider briefly the most common ways of getting Yes-No answers. They are essentially two: the first, using two objects, or multiples of two, a simplification of the already rather simple-minded specific lot: one object for yes, one for no (e.g. black-balling a candidate: a black ball stands for no). The second, using both sides of a single object, or of several, the most common survival being heads-or-tails using coins, as mentioned above.

Most ancient -- and modern -- cultures use, separately or in combination -- yes-no and multiple answer. An intriguing development, that of using several yes-no objects to obtain multiple answers is the basis of the entire I Ching of China as well as the ancient Egyptian Tab or the Islamic and African "geomancy" (khatt-ar-raml). Two halves of a short stick, shell or nut provide four answers (◖◗, ◗◖, ◖◖, ◗◗). This repetition of the basic heads-or-tails seems to meet an equally basic need in humans to seek confirmation of the decree of fate, not to take no -- or even yes -- for an answer, to make sure, or, alternately, to compromise, hedge, and provides leeway.

Now that both the three basic categories of manteia and the three basic means of cleromancy are present in our minds, let us turn to the oracle at Delphi.

Revelation is the most conspicuous category of manteia used at Delphi. The Pythia, her trance and the ways to induce it, the interpretation given to her utterances are too well known to need repeating here.

Decipherment seems to be used mostly as haruspicy, in turn used to find out if conditions are favorable for Revelation, although there are obscure texts which may imply decipherment of some aspect of laurel boughs or leaves.

Inducement exists as the alternative form of oracular consultation, cleromancy. Tradition has this to be the gift of the mysterious, bee-like Thriai to Apollo through Hermes, and we are told that lots were kept in the Tripod, given instances of consultation by lots (e.g. the choice of the Eponymous Heroes at Athens) and even informed of the rate at which this consultation should be paid (the Skiathos inscription).

What remains obscure -- at Delphi and elsewhere -- is exactly which form the lots took. The Greek terms remind us what homely objects were commonly used:

kuamos	:	fava bean, lot
phruktos	:	roasted fava bean, lot (ballot)
ostrakon	:	potsherd, oyster shell, lot
psēphos	:	pebble, ballot
klēros	:	small stone, wood chip, lot

We already know something of Athenian methods (black and white balls in the allotment machine; inscribed potsherds for ostracism; elaborate metal ballots for courtroom use) and we know that knucklebones were used for some oracles. But there are few textual precisions for Delphi.

Let us nevertheless try to restrict possibilities by looking once more at the texts: late ones (Nonnos, Eudocia, Suidas or the Souda) tell us of lots (plural) kept in the Tripod and jumping about in it. Earlier texts refer more simply to consultation by the bean or beans, singular, plural, and in one instance apparently dual (*phrukto*).

As we have seen, widespread methods of lot-casting can exist simultaneously and it is clear that *specific answer* was used in Delphic cleromancy. *Multiple-answer*, at least with knucklebones, does not seem to have been common. That leaves us with the *Yes-No*, *Urim* and *Tummim* method (or a variant upon it through multiplication). It has been suggested that the *yes-no* at Delphi was based on two objects, one white and one black; that is certainly possible, but we should consider, given the emphasis on *phruktos* and *kuamos*, that the fairly flexible and responsive two-halves method may have been used instead of, or in addition to, the more simple-minded *specific lot*, or its black and white further simplification. One of the difficulties in accepting a bare black-and-white answer is that it leaves so little room for interpretation, something formal cleromancy is always careful to preserve. As Philochorus remarks (LXXXIV) "Many are the lot-casters: but few the prophets".

Texts and their interpretation are conveniently gathered in Pierre Amandry's *La Mantique Apollinienne à Delphes, Essai sur le fonctionnement de l'oracle*, Paris, E. de Boccard, 1950; the priciples governing cleromancy and their psychological implications are discussed in J.O. Grandjouan's *L'Astragale et le Pari*, Paris, G.P. Maisonneuve et Larose, 1969.

S 231 Omens and Oracles in the Classical Historians

Tamara M. Green, Hunter College

The meaning and use of oracles and omens in ancient historiography is part of the larger question of the classical understanding of the processes of historical causation. Every historian must deal with the question of causation, and he must deal with it on two levels: causation which determines the time, place and outcome of events, and causation which produces historical movement in time. In the debate over this problem, the classical historians have most often been faulted for attributing events in particular and the movement of history in general to the action of divine agency, either a god or fate or fortune. However, a careful examination of classical historiography reveals that this is not at all the case: rather, as we shall see, causation is considered by the ancient historians totally from the perspective of human action and behavior. If and when the forces of a divine agent are present, they will merely provide corroborating support or evidence for actions committed by men and initiated by men; for despite the seeming constant injection of the divine in certain of the classical authors (some historians, such as Thucydides, almost completely ignore it), historical determination turns out to be a product of human action, not divine. The divine may or may not respond to men, but it does not, in and of itself, cause events to occur.

The source of this view of causation is found in the belief expressed by the classical historians that, by and large, there is no divine plan for mankind. In the classical understanding of history, man can never know what, if anything, the gods expect of him; and this lack of knowledge forces man then to take an active role in determining history. Because this role is thrust upon man by the historians, they can never place ultimate determination of the historical process on an extra-human level.

Paradoxically, the use of oracles and omens serves only to point out more clearly the lack of the importance of the divine in history. Although frequently cited by the historians, stories of prophecy and divine intervention merely serve to underline the fact that it is men, and not gods, who cause events to happen. The historians are not interested in the omens and oracles in and of themselves, but rather, in the human interpretation of these events, and what this interpretation reveals about the nature of man.

The use of oracles by Herodotus illustrates this point. Oracles never determine the outcome of events, and when Herodotus writes

> Now I cannot deny that there is truth in prophecies and I have no wish to discredit them when they are expressed in unambiguous language (viii.77)

he is, in fact denying their validity, because oracles are always expressed in an ambiguous way. The oracle to Croesus is, of course, purposefully not clear, and Croesus is of course meant to misinterpret its meaning; for to Herodotus, it is Croesus's reaction to the oracle that is important, for the oracle is used to reveal human nature and behavior rather than a practical joke of Apollo. When the Lydian king attempted to blame the god for his defeat, he was reminded that it was he who had misinterpreted the words of the priestess, and therefore it was he who had to take responsibility for his loss. Indeed, the probability of misinterpretation of oracles and omens is what makes their use possible by the historians, for it is only then that man can be free to determine the course of history. Freedom of action, and thereby choice and responsibility, is what causes historical process. In order for there to be history as described by the ancient authors, man must act, he must seize the opportunity: he must respond. In Herodotus' account of the Spartan encounter with Mardonius, the historian writes that Pausanias, because his troops were in serious danger, called upon the goddess for help

> praying to her not to allow the Greeks to be robbed of their hope and their victory. Then, while the words were still on his lips, the Tegaeans sprung forward to lead the attack, and a moment later, the sacrifical victims were promising success. (ix.62)

The omens did not become favorable until the Tegaeans charged: human action was necessary first.

History, because it is about human action, must be rational to the extent that man is rational. In Thucydides, various characters speak on the unpredictability of war, declaring that it tends to produce such conditions so that rationality can no longer exist, but he makes it clear that anyone who places his hope in the divine, as did Nicias (vii.77), is sadly mistaken. The historian's account of the plague further illustrates his understanding. For when the Athenians saw how "quick and abrupt" were the changes of fortune, it had a devastating effect upon their behavior. To the Athenians, it was fear of divine punishment that had previously restrained them and that was now lacking, to Thucydides, it was merely one of the unpredictable things that happened during the war.

In the funeral oration of Pericles, the Athenian leader makes the distinction between what he could have foreseen (_gnome_) and what he could have not (_tyche_). Obviously, then, the Periclean definition of _tyche_ eliminates its divine quality; it becomes, instead, a deficiency in human understanding. It is what is unexpected that can be attributed to _tyche_, but even then, it is not seen by Thucydides as having divine cause. It is merely chance. In war the opportunity for accident may seem to increase, but it is man's actions which cause it. Thucydides will only operate on the human level: despite his statement in ch. 23 of the _Archaeology_, his use of oracles and omens in the rest of the history is merely to illustrate the effect of the war on the minds and behavior of the Greeks.

This same approach is also found in the later Greek and Roman historians. Although, for example, much has been written on Polybius's reliance on _tyche_ as the determining force in history, a consideration of his work reveals that although the historian makes frequent reference to _tyche_, it is really not an important factor. Rather, like Thucydides, he often uses it as a metaphor for events that are _para logon_: and in war, he sees, as does Thucydides, the proliferation of accidents. Even Livy, whose work at times seems overloaded with the expresions of belief in divine agency, uses the non-human only as a last resort. He is not a naive believer; rather, he, like his predecessors, recognizes that there are some events which are not totally explicable in terms of rational human behavior. Despite his insistence that the greatness of Rome had been foreordained, his constant attention to virtue and character negates the concept of Roman history as the fulfillment of some divine plan. Although Livy makes constant reference to the religious character of the Romans, it is certainly not necessary to conclude that the historian sees any divine consequences of Roman piety. It may further be pointed out that Livy's use of oracles and omens occurs primarily in the first books, which deal with the foundation of Rome. He himself remarks:

> there is no reason, I feel, to object when antiquity

> draws no hard line between the human and the supernatural; it adds dignity to the past, and if any nation deserves the privilege of claiming a divine ancestry, that nation is ours. (i.1)

Thus, his use of omens and oracles may be merely an expression of the historian's idealization of Roman origins.

The writings of Tacitus are filled with various asides on the nature of divine causes and divine manifestations. But again, as with the other authors we have considered, we must examine the context and the import of these stories. By focusing on the behavior and actions of men in both the *Historiae* and the *Annales*, Tacitus, in the tradition of the earlier historians, refuted his own statements about the divine. Like his predecessors, Tacitus attempts to look for the rational, i.e. human, understanding wherever possible; whenever there is a detectable cause, Tacitus will choose it over any divine agency. Human events are caused by the actions of men; perhaps it is this fact that accounts for the gloominess of mood. When human behavior becomes so extraordinary so that it can no longer be judged by normal standards of right and wrong, Tacitus then resorts to the divine, which once again becomes a metaphor for the lack of reason among men. And it would seem that to Tacitus, it was the unpredictability of events in time of political chaos that had produced this confusion of mind:

> Ignorant minds found something very sinister in the very shortage of water, feeling that even the rivers on which the Empire had for so long depended for defense were now deserting us. In time of peace, this might have been attributed to chance or natural causes; now it was called fate or the anger of Heaven. (*Hist.*, iv.26)

How seriously, then, can we take the omens and oracles that appear in his history?

Saint-Beuve once remarked that "history seen from a distance undergoes a strange metamorphosis; it produces the illusion -- most dangerous of all -- that it is rational." By the writing of history, the ancient historians attempted to understand the process of history, for the very act of writing implies that history can be comprehended. History was to be useful; if there were lessons to be learned from history, then *tyche* or *fortuna* or any manifestation of the divine, could not be a factor in the historical process, for otherwise, it would be impossible to use that knowledge which one had gained from the process of *historia*, or inquiry. For the classical historians, the study of history affirmed their belief in rational man in a rational world: their writings attempted to give substance to that "illusion."

S 238 THE STUDY OF RABBINIC PARABLES: SOME PRELIMINARY OBSERVATIONS

Robert M. Johnston
Andrews University

0. This paper consists of some observations possibly of interest to students of the parabolic genre, drawn from a yet unfinished doctoral dissertation dealing with interpretations of parables *(meshalim)* ascribed to Tannaim (scribes and rabbis who flourished before ca. C.E. 220). Though neither the dissertation nor this paper attempts to apply sophisticated Structuralist tools to these materials, it may be that the extensive corpus of specimens collected, the problems encountered, and some of the things learned will have relevance as a test for some of the new methodologies and categories.

In preparation for this research, a rather large selection of classical rabbinic sources was combed through, including the Mishnah, the Babylonian and Palestinian Talmuds, the Tosefta, Mekilta, Sifra, Sifre (on Numbers and Deuteronomy), Aboth de Rabbi Nathan (version A) and other Minor Tractates of the Talmud, the Midrash Rabbah, Midrash on Psalms, Midrash Samuel, Pesikta de Rab Kahana, Pesikta Rabbati, and the Pirke de R. Eliezer. Over 1400 items were collected, being found in every one of the forementioned sources, of which somewhat over three hundred were adjudged as attributed to Tannaim and as qualifying as parables according to the criteria set up for the purposes of the research/1/.

1. Deciding what items to collect was no small part of the problem. At first the net was cast wide, but such inclusiveness only postponed the time of reckoning, when principles of selection had to be defined and applied.

1.1 There are two opposite ways to approach the definition of parable in a literary corpus such as the New Testament or the rabbinic literature. One way is the normative, or deductive approach, which sets up an a priori definition based on form, content, function, or all three, and dismisses anything which does not fit into the a priori definition. The other way is the descriptive, or inductive approach, which seeks to base a definition on generalizations derived from the analysis of concrete specimens. In practice both approaches are forced to make compromises. The normative approach is likely to find few if any specimens in real life which perfectly fit into categories too strictly defined, and so it begins to speak of modified or "mixed" forms in relating the specimens to the rather artificial categories. The inductive approach finds itself in a vicious circle, for before it can manufacture a description of the specimens it has selected it must first select the specimens on the basis of some preliminary criterion. It is easy to define a bird as a vertebrate which flies if we base that generalization only on a collection of specimens, however large, which was chosen by looking only for specimens which are vertebrates and which fly. Granted that we should base our concept of the nature of parables on an examination of the things themselves, our selection of what things we shall examine already implies some preconception.

1.11 The normative-deductive approach has advantages. It supplies a clear starting-point for selection. It makes generic distinctions clear. It is convenient. It has universality: its categories can be applied to (or imposed upon) any corpus, thus making comparisons between corpora easy. But this approach also has serious disadvantages. It suffers from artificiality and overprecision so that there is difficulty in applying it to real data--the category is narrower than the species being categorized. Its irrelevance to historical questions is too easily overlooked, so that there is a temptation to draw conclusions about what is primary, what is secondary, etc., on the basis of an artificial definition. This happened, for example, in the work of Jülicher (1910), who imposed Aristotelian categories upon a literature to which they were alien. And this approach also falls into a pitfall of circularity: a parable is thus; everything that is not thus cannot be a parable--which begs the question.

1.12 The descriptive-inductive approach has advantages. Since it is inductive, there is no problem in squaring its categories with live specimens. It puts historical and form-critical conclusions upon a more legitimate basis. It avoids, at least in theory, a priori judgments. But it has disadvantages. It must compromise itself in order to make a beginning: there must be a principle of selection. Categorical arbitrariness can never be perfectly eliminated without making the universal coterminous with the individual item, which is to deny the validity of all meaningful classification. And since the descriptive approach seeks to let its categories grow out of the corpus at hand, not imposing an alien system, it makes comparison between corpora (e.g., rabbinic literature and New Testament) more difficult, or possible only to the extent that the corpora can be considered genetically or generically related.

1.2 There are two complementary approaches to the classification of literary items: (1) One may set up a class by content, and subdivide according to external forms; or (2) one may set up a class by external forms, and subdivide according to content (Smith: 79). The classical Jülicherian approach involved the counting of points of comparison between *Sache* and *Bild*. More recent efforts to refine the Jülicherian model and preserve the distinction between parable and other genres (e.g. allegory) have been less objective, more "mentalistic." Thus one of the earlier writers to take this tack (Findlay: 8, 10) suggests: "The essence of a parable is that it contains what I may call a 'bolt from the blue,' whether the parable is in narrative form or consists of one or more paradoxical sayings . . . . The essence of the parable . . . is the element of surprise." This abandonment of formal or objective criteria in defining parable is typical. The essence of parable, it is maintained, is that it stands conventional values upside down. Such a function, of course, cannot be divorced from content, and in this connection there have been attempts to objectivize deep structures, but the methods and categories evolved so far for determining the latter have yet to produce uniform results or command universal acceptance among their practitioners. One of the most interesting efforts (to an outsider) along these lines is Crossan's (1974:82-112; note especially the definition on p. 98)

1.21 Since Jülicher it has hardened into an orthodoxy to be defended that parable must at all costs be distinguished from allegory. Thus Funk (1974:68) refuses to think the unthinkable: "If Jesus choses [*sic*] an authority figure each time to model God, we are driven in spite of ourselves back in the direction of allegory." This struggle to distinguish parable from allegory appeals now to literary theory, but aesthetic approaches would seem to provide a slippery foundation upon which to base any scientific conclusions. Even though one confesses that the use of any models in hermeneutics is heuristic, not explanatory, such criteria as have now become fashionable seem too subjective to yield consistent results. While some mentalism is perhaps inevitable in the definition and delimitation of "parable," the departure from objectivism should be as conscious and explicit as possible/2/.

1.3 Our problem is breaking out of the circularity: One must decide what a parable is before he can collect them; he must analyze a collection before he can decide what one is. Since our study is of rabbinic parables, or *meshalim*, perhaps no better or more objective starting point can be found than the one stated with brutal directness by Pautrel (1936:8-9): "Nous appellerons empiriquement mashal (rabbinique) ce que les rabbins ont appelé tel." But Pautrel's list of marks which identify the items labelled as *meshalim* by the rabbis can be amplified and refined. And there is a more serious practical difficulty in the fact that the word *mashal* covers a very wide range of meanings and genres which by modern analysis appear distinct. Furthermore, when we compare the rabbinic corpus with the New Testament, we find that the rabbinic *mashal* and the gospel *parabolē* largely cover the same semantic area but are not perfectly identical; for *parabolē* seems to cover a somewhat more restricted range of genres, but in one case may extend over a domain not covered by *mashal*: the example story. There is thus a tension between two worthwhile aims: How can we obtain results from the study of rabbinic *meshalim* which will illuminate the gospel parables without prematurely imposing New Testament categories on the rabbinic literature, which would be to assume something which can be legitimate only as a conclusion of our study? Still another technical problem is presented as an obstacle to the literal-minded: There are many items in the rabbinic literature which are morphologically and functionally identical to items called *mashal*, but which are not themselves explicitly so labelled.

1.31 Our policy will therefore be to select as *meshalim* those items which are designated as such by introductory formulae, and also items which, though not explicitly designated *meshalim* in their contexts, have structural characteristics identical to the others. That is our principle of inclusion.

But in order to make our project manageable we must add to this a principle of exclusion: We shall concentrate only on *meshalim* which describe a past or typical event. These criteria must not be applied woodenly, but all deviations must be made only with due deliberation and for due cause. But it is necessary to define the territory still more clearly.

1.32 The morphological marks of the typical narrative *mashal*, whether it describes a specific event *(Parabel)* or general situation *(Gleichnis)* may be here laid out in advance, on the basis of the examination of hundreds of items. It will be noted that we have limited ourselves to narrative items, for the word *mashal* can be found applied to anything from a *bon mot* to an extended story (but not to exempla or example stories, as hereafter noted); a rough equivalent is the homiletician's term "illustration" (but not the German *Bildwort*, which has taken on a much more restricted meaning).

The marks of the narrative *mashal*, which with few exceptions effectively distinguish it morphologically from other varieties of *mashal*, can be summarized as four: explicit labels, abbreviated labels, special formulae, and peculiar structural characteristics. The first two marks are alternatives to each other, and the third renders the first two optional.

1.321 Explicit labels. Often the introductory formulae to the items explicitly label them as *meshalim: mašal l . . . ; 'emšōl lak mašal . . . ; maš*^{e}*lû mašal l*^{e}*mah hadabar dōmeh l . . . ;* etc.

1.322 Abbreviated labels. Frequently the introductory formulae are abbreviated in such a way that the word *mashal* itself is omitted: *l . . . ; l*^{e}*mah hadabar dōmeh l . . . ; k . . . ;* etc. No student of the matter has questioned the functional equivalence of these abbreviations with the fuller forms. Lists of these introductory formulae can be found in Feldman (1924:15, n. 1), who lists twenty-five, and in Guttmann (1929:3-6), who lists seventy-five, though he considers for study only those items introduced by the first twenty-three, the rest not belonging to the "Mašal-Gattung" (6). In rabbinic sources the fuller and abbreviated forms are virtually interchangeable, the difference belonging mainly to the province of manuscript criticism.

1.323 Special formulae. Certain special types of narrative

meshalim are sometimes designated *meshalim* by explicit or abbreviated label, but often not. Since however, they bear their own peculiar marks, they can always be identified. Those most common of this type begin, "It is the custom of the world that . . . ," or "A (king) of flesh and blood . . ." They are most often descriptions of general situations *(Gleichnisse)*.

1.324 Structural characteristics. The immediate environment and internal structure of the typical narrative *mashal* in its fullest form can be set forth as follows:

(1) Illustrand (the point to be illustrated);

(2) Introductory formula, whether full or abbreviated;

(3) The parable proper *(Bildhälfte)*;

(4) Application, usually introduced by *kak* or equivalent link-word or phrase;

(5) Scriptural quotation, often introduced by "as it is said" or "as it is written." This is sometimes followed by a second application, which itself can become an illustrand, thus producing a chain.

The last two parts are often omitted; the first two are but rarely lacking. We would not ordinarily count an item as a parable for our purposes if it lacked (2) unless all the other components were used. This last mark, then, embraces also the first three, relating them to the rest of the *mashal* structure.

1.4 It will be seen that we have made morphology the criterion for defining the rabbinic parable, rather than function. But having gathered a corpus on the basis of morphology we can then study function. In a general way, all narrative *meshalim* function in their contexts to illustrate or to prove, and the great majority serve as handmaidens to exegesis. But the same functions are performed by items which are morphologically and structurally quite different, such as the proverb, the example story, and the anecdote. It will help to define our territory by noting some of the forms left outside the fence.

1.41 By-words. In Baba Bathra 15a the personage Job is called a *mashal* (= "type" ?) by Resh Lakish.

1.42 Proverbs. These are also called *meshalim*, such as R. Levi's citation of the saying, "One who has been bitten by a snake is afraid of a rope" (Songs R. 1:2:3).

1.43 Parabolic acts, such as the object lessons used by R. Meir in the disputation recorded in Gen. R. 4:4.

1.44 Object lessons from nature, such as the series of lessons drawn from the behavior of the ant (Deut. R. 5:2), no doubt inspired by Prov. 6:6 ff.

1.45 Simile. The dividing line between simple simile and parable can be quite thin, the difference sometimes being only a matter of length (cf. Dodd 1961:7). But such an item as the comparison in Songs R. 1:2:3 of the Torah to water, wine, oil, honey, and milk seems clear enough: "Just as water has not taste unless one is thirsty, so the Torah has no taste unless one labors at it."

1.46 Metaphor. Expanded and introduced properly, a metaphor can become a parable, for from the rabbinic point of view there was no substantive difference between simile and metaphor. But a clear case of simple metaphor is in Gen. R. 34:10, "How wretched must be the dough when the baker himself testifies it to be poor!"

1.47 Fables. Partly analogous but not homologous to the object lessons drawn from the ant are the "fox-fables and fables of Kybisses" (Suk. 28a, Soferim 16:8, etc.; cf. Jacobs: 221). These can all be traced ultimately to Indian or Hellenistic sources, but they became popular also among the rabbis, perhaps as early as Johanan b. Zakkai. Only if a fable is dressed up fully in the garb of the autochthonous *mashal*, as is sometimes done, can we count it in our number; such "mashalized" fables were designated by Samuel Back (1875-84) as "uneigentlich." It is perhaps unfortunate that Ben-Amos (1976:140 ff.) subsumed the rabbinic *mashal* under the rubric of fable.

1.48 Imaginary dialogues. Somewhat akin to the fable are the imaginary dialogues between men and animals or even inanimate creatures, and between Scriptural or historic personages. An example is the fanciful interrogation of the serpent in Deut. R. 5:10.

1.49 Anecdotes. The typical rabbinic anecdote involves named historic personages, and it usually implies a value judgment upon the persons who provide the subject--the eloquence of this rabbi, the purity of that one, the wickedness of Hadrian, etc. But there is no explicit "Go and do thou likewise," and it is this which distinguished it from the example stories, to which they are otherwise very similar.

1.410 Example stories differ from other anecdotes in that they illustrate a positive or negative duty, concluding with an admonition, which may be moral or prudential. Unlike most anecdotes, example stories often do not name the persons involved. The following story lacks any introductory formula, commencing abruptly after the point it illustrates or proves:

> A woman went to her neighbor's house to kneed some dough, having in her purse two denarii. These fell into the dough and were baked into the bread. She discovered that the money was missing and went home to search, but she did not find it. She returned to her neighbor's and said to her: Give me my two denarii which fell out in your house. The neighbor said: I swear I know nothing about it. If I know, may my son be buried! And her son was buried. Returning from the cemetery she heard people saying: If the matter had been as she said she would not have had to bury her son. Whereupon she repeated her oath, and another son died. When people came to console her and they broke the bread for the funeral meal, the two denarii fell out of one loaf. The affair teaches: Whether you are innocent or guilty, do not lightly make an oath. (J. Shebuoth 6:5; cf. Lev. R. 6:3.)

The explicit moral which concludes the story is formally quite different from the applications usually attached to *meshalim*. Besides the differing linking formula, it is to be noted that the lesson derived is expressed as an imperative, rather than a statement in the indicative. Applications attached to rabbinic *meshalim* are almost always in the indicative.

1.4101 It is impossible to lay out here all the variant forms of rabbinic anecdotes and example stories, but we must make note of one striking fact which includes both anecdotes and example stories. In the rabbinic corpus both of these two types of narrative are sharply distinguished from parable. This distinction is seen first of all in terminology. The parable is called *mashal*; anecdotes and example-stories are never called *meshalim*, but the term uniformly used for them is *maᶜăśeh*. There is also a complete difference of formulary. As illustration or proof the *meᶜăśîm* are often introduced also by the Aramaic contraction *dîlᵉmah*, "here is a confirmation" (Jastrow: 300). In Hebrew the story may be introduced *maᶜăśeh* š . . . followed by a verb (as in Rosh HaSh. 2:8) or *maᶜăśeh b* . . . followed by a noun followed by š and a verb (as in Eccl. R. 1:8:4).

1.4102 In real life, some specimens flirt dangerously with

the borderline of their territory, and some even lounge casually astride it. Thus while there is a clear terminological and morphological distinction between the *maʿaśeh* and the *mashal*, there can sometimes be cases in which the former shades into something approaching the latter. We shall offer here one example, giving also the illustrand to which it is attached:

> What is the difference between the death of the young and the death of the old? R. Judah and R. Nehemiah give answers. R. Judah says: When a lamp is extinguished of its own accord, it is good for the lamp and for the wick; but when it is not extinguished of its own accord, it is bad for the lamp and for the wick. R. Nehemiah says: When the fig is gathered in its due season it is good for the fig and for the tree; but when it is not gathered in its due season, it is bad for the fig and for the tree.
>
> Here is an illustration *(dîlᵉmah)*. R. Hiya the Elder and his disciples--others say: R. Simeon b. Halafta and his disciples or R. Akiba and his disciples--were sitting and studying beneath a fig-tree. The owner of the tree arose early to gather its fruit. They said: Let us change our place lest he suspect us [of stealing his figs]. So they sat in another place. On the morrow the owner of the tree arose early to gather his figs but did not find the Sages there. He went after them and, on finding them, said: You performed a pious act for me [by studying beneath his tree], and now you withhold it from me. They exclaimed: Heaven forfend! He asked them: Why then did you leave your place and sit elsewhere? They answered: We said, Lest he suspect us. He said to them: Heaven forfend! But I tell you why I arose early to gather the fruit; it is because it becomes wormy when the sun shines upon it. That day he left the fruit without gathering it, and they found that when the sun shone upon it the figs became wormy. They remarked: The owner of the fig-tree knows well which is the proper time for the figs to be gathered and gathers them accordingly. Similarly the Holy One, blessed be He, knows when is the proper time for a righteous man [to die] and then removes him. (Eccl. R. 5:11:2; J. Ber. 2:8 [7].)

The morphological parallels to the structure of a typical *mashal* are striking in this story, but the formal parallels serve to point up the differences. First there is an illustrand; but it is not an exegetical point, as is usually the case with *meshalim*; it is itself a metaphoric illustration. The story is introduced by an introductory formula, which is, however, not a *mashal*-formula but a *maʿaśeh*-formula. The story is presented as a factual account involving historical persons who are named (although there seems to be some uncertainty about their precise identity, even this is expressed in such a way as to indicate a concern for historicity). The object lesson concludes with an explicit application introduced by *kak*, but there is no clinching scripture.

The number of miscellaneous formal types could be much added to, including many items which are almost *sui generis*, but the foregoing list will assist the delimitation of the *mashal*-genre. We now turn our attention exclusively to the latter.

2. My research being not yet complete, I cannot now present a mature synthesis of its results in a systematic way, and indeed many important observations will lie outside its scope. What will be presented in the rest of this paper will therefore be a series of representative specimens which I adduce to illustrate typical features and facets of the rabbinic *mashal*.

In the examples which follow, as far as possible the full pericopes will be given, including illustrand and application, as well as the parable proper. These three parts will be set off from each other by the use of indentation. Scriptural quotations will be capitalized.

2.1 While it might be legitimately said that the parables of Jesus are intended to reverse conventional values, it is clearly the case that rabbinic parables are intended to reinforce them. This is strikingly illustrated in an item frequently quoted because of its similarity to the parable of the Laborers in the Vineyard (Mat. 20:1-16):

> When Abun b. Hiya died, R. Zeira went to eulogize him: SWEET IS THE SLEEP OF A LABORER, WHETHER HE EATS LITTLE OR MUCH (Eccl. 5:12). It is not written, WHETHER HE SLEEPS LITTLE OR MUCH, but WHETHER HE EATS LITTLE OR MUCH.
>
> Unto what was Rabbi bar Hiya like? He was like unto a king who hired many laborers of whom one was more industrious than the others. What did the king do? He called him out and walked up and down with him. In the evening the workmen came to be paid. He gave also a full day's pay to the man he had walked with. When the other workers saw this, they complained and said: We have been working hard all day, and this one who only labored two hours receives as much wages as we do? The king answered: It is because this one has done more in two hours than you in a whole day.
>
> Likewise R. Abun, although he had studied the Torah only until the age of twenty-eight, he knew it better than a scholar or pious man who would have studied until a hundred. (J. Ber. 2:8 [7]; Songs R. 6:2:6.)

The similarities underline the contrast. But it may well be excessive to claim that all Jesus' parables provide such a reversal or such a contrast. The point of the parable of the Two Sons (Mat. 21:28-32) is not greatly distant from that of the rabbinic parable of the Overambitious Sharecropper (Ex. R. 27:9).

2.2 Though it has become a form-critical commonplace that it is a poor parabler who has to explain his parables, it is nonetheless true that the great majority of rabbinic parables have an explicit explanation, or "application," attached. The following item is one of the most frequently reoccuring parables in the whole rabbinic corpus:

> R. Simeon b. Yohai says: They parable a parable. Unto what is the matter like? It is like unto one who was walking along the road, and he encountered a wolf and was saved from him. And he was going along recounting the story of the wolf. Then he encountered a lion and was saved from him. He forgot the story of the wolf and went along recounting the story of the lion. Then he encountered a serpent and was saved from him. He forgot the story of both of them and went along recounting the story of the serpent.
>
> Even so is Israel. Later troubles cause the former ones to be forgotten. (Mekilta, Pischa 16:67 ff.; cf. Tos. Ber. 1:11; Ber. 13a; J. Ber. 1:9 [5]; etc.)

The various contexts in which this parable of The Escape From Three Perils occurs, and the illustrands for which it is used, all differ somewhat, though they are related--all different historic troubles, or sometimes different deliverances, as in Mekilta. Furthermore, this is the only place where it is explicitly ascribed to Simeon b. Yohai. But the parable circulated as a unit with its application, almost verbatim, and it never occurs without this exact application. With other parables the application can be found to vary--they are recycled, as it were, and reapplied to new lessons. But the presence of an application is usual, and the one here is unaverage only in its brevity.

2.21 It is quite common for the application to conclude with one or more scriptural quotations, following a pattern which became stereotyped, as in the parable of the Stupid Depositaries (Sifre on Deut., 357):

> When God takes away the souls of men, He has the wicked taken away by the grim and terrifying angels; but when God takes the souls of the righteous, He takes them away with the spirit of peace.
>
> They parable a parable. Unto what is the matter like? It is like unto a trusted man in a city to whom all came to leave deposits [for safe-keeping]. Then when one came to collect [his own] he brought it out and returned it to him, for he knew exactly where it was to be found. But when he left the responsibility to his son or his slave or his delegate, then everything was turned upside down because they did not know where each was.
>
> Even so when God takes away the souls of the righteous He does so with the spirit of peace. But when He takes away the souls of the wicked He turns them over to

> the grim and terrifying angels that they may wrench away their souls. Thus is says: A CRUEL MESSENGER WILL BE SENT OUT AGAINST HIM (Prov. 17:11) and it says: THEY DIE THROUGH THE SHAKING OUT OF THEIR SOULS (variant on Prov. 36:14).

The application virtually repeats the illustrand and then adds proof texts. It is to be especially noted that it involves a rather detailed explanation of the parable.

2.3 Since Jülicher it has become orthodoxy to distinguish sharply between parable and allegory. In allegory, it is said, every feature must be decoded, while a true parable can have only one *tertium comparationis* between the parable *(Bild)* and the reality to which it points *(Sache)*. Dodd (1961:4) even went so far as to assert that allegory, so defined, was a purely Hellenistic and un-Jewish phenomenon: "The probability is that the parables could have been taken for allegorical mystifications only in a non-Jewish environment. Among Jewish teachers the parable was a common and well-understood method of illustration, and the parables of Jesus are similar in form to rabbinic parables . . . . In the Hellenistic world . . . the use of myths, allegorically interpreted, as vehicles of esoteric doctrine, was widespread . . ." It is difficult to understand how such a mistatement could be made, or how it could become so widely accepted. Rabbinic literature, even in its earliest available sources, is replete with *meshalim* which hinge upon multiple *tertia comparationis*, such as The Slave and the Rotten Fish (Mek. Beshallach 2:107 ff.):

> They [the Egyptians] said: If we had been plagued without letting them go, it would have been enough. But we were plagued and let them go. Or, if we had been plagued and let them go without our money being taken, it would have been enough. But we were plagued, let them go, and our money was taken.
>
> A parable. Unto what is the matter like? It is like unto one who said to his slave: Go get me a fish from the market. The slave went and brought him an ill-smelling fish. He said to the slave: I decree that you eat the fish or receive a hundred lashes or you pay a hundred *manah*. The slave said: I will eat it. He began to eat but could not finish. He therefore said: I will take the lashes. After receiving sixty lashes he could stand no more. He therefore said: I will pay the hundred *manah*. The result was that he ate the fish, received the lashes and paid a hundred *manah*.
>
> So it was done to the Egyptians. They were plagued, they let Israel go, and their money was taken.

There can, of course, be no question here of the "allegorizing" application being secondary; the parable was clearly manufactured to explain precisely these three points, and the whole pericope is of one piece.

2.31 Fiebig (1904, 1912), who was one of the first to make a systematic investigation of the rabbinic parables, quickly saw the inapplicability of Jülicher's Aristotelian categories to the parables of rabbinic literature and the parables of the Synoptics, which he recognized to be of the same genre. Yet he tacitly used those categories, speaking of "pure parable," "allegorical parable," and "mixed-form parable." It was in the positing of this last category that he chiefly challenged Jülicher, for the latter had declared in a famous dictum, "Halb Allegorie und halb Fabel [pure parable] sind nur mythologische Wesen" (1910:107). Others have continued to use such categories, even when opposing the Jülicherian orthodoxy by pointing out that the so-called "mixed form" is by far the most common type of rabbinic parable. But in fact, it is doubtful whether such alien categories are useful at all. The rabbis were quite unconcerned about whether only one, or all, or nearly all, or merely some features in their parables were *tertia comparationis*. The parable of the Beneficent King (Mek. Bachodesh 5:2 ff.) is typical:

> I AM THE LORD THY GOD (Ex. 20:2). Why were the Ten Commandments not said at the beginning of the Torah?
>
> They parable a parable. Unto what is the matter like? It is like unto a king who entered a province and said to the people: May I be your king? But the people said to him: Have you done anything good for us that you should rule over us? He built the city wall for them, he brought in the water supply for them, and he fought their battles. Then he said to them: May I be your king? And they said to him: Yes, yes.
>
> Likewise, God. He brought the Israelites out of Egypt, divided the sea for them, sent down the manna for them, brought up the well for them, brought the quails for them. He fought for them the battle with Amalek. Then He said to them: I am to be your king. And they said to Him: Yes, yes.

Aside from the implicit metaphors of king/God and provincials/Israel, one may ask whether there are strong "allegorical" features here. Against the counting of multiple *tertia comparationis* stands the lack of numerical correspondence: the king does three benefactions, God does six. On the other hand, the water supply answers to the well, and in both *Bild* and *Sache* the benefactor does battle on behalf of the people. In Fiebigian terms, it is a mixed specimen--if such terms are useful.

2.32 The parable of the Beneficent King may also serve to illustrate a common function of rabbinic parables: to answer a question, solve a problem, or resolve a perplexity.

2.4 The last specimen introduced us to the phenomenon of standard metaphors in the parables--what Fiebig called "geläufigen Metaphern" (1904:99-100). Such figures as king/God, son/Israel, and robbers/enemies of Israel were apparently so well understood that "decoding" was automatic. The meaning of the following parable of Johanan b. Zakkai is clear not only from the illustrand to which it is attached, but because of its transparent metaphors, even though it lacks an explicit application:

> Why did Israel go into exile into Babylon rather than into all other lands? Because of the fact that the home of Abraham was from there.
>
> They parable a parable. Unto what is the matter like? It is like unto a woman who disgraces her husband so that he sends her away. He sends her away to the home of her father. (Tos. B. K. 7:3.)

In this particular case, however, the message conveyed by the standard metaphors is somewhat confused by the fact that not only the figure of the husband, but also the figure of a father usually represent God. Apart from knowledge of the illustrand, the hearer's understanding of the parable would have been contaminated by this inept selection of tropes, so standard had the father/God figure become. The metaphor of father/Abraham is logical enough in the immediate context, but in the context of the hearer's thesaurus of parabolic imagery it was a mistake. We therefore find a somewhat later transformation of the parable which seeks to eliminate this problem:

> A parable. It is like unto a man who becomes angry with his wife. Whither does he send her? To her mother's house. (Pesahim 87b.)

The Talmudic editors felt the incongruity of representing Babylonia by the father, a figure more appropriate for God, and they therefore changed father to mother, even though "her mother's house" would have been an unusual expression for the parental home, unless the mother be a widow! That such a transformation of the parable was deemed necessary is testimony to how powerfully entrenched many of these stereotyped metaphors were, many of them deriving in fact from biblical imagery.

Does the presence of such standardized metaphors in a parable make it an allegory? Fiebig said it does, Bultmann

(1972:187) says it does not. The Rabbis would not have understood the question. To them, allegory was a way of interpreting the scriptures, especially the Song of Songs; the term was irrelevant to the enterprise of constructing and interpreting *meshalim*.

2.5 Another common phenomenon met with in the rabbinic parables is the transference of the point of comparison, which can also be seen in many of the gospel parables (e.g. The Growing Seed, Mark 4:26-29, where the attention is immediately shifted from the man to the seed). All morphologically determined rabbinic narrative parables have a comparison word, which is the word that fills in the blank in the formula, "It is like unto a ________ which . . ." One might logically expect that the person or thing introduced thus at the beginning of the parable would continue to occupy our attention as the principle *Bild* to which the *Sache* is compared; but such is not the case in a large number of items. This can be illustrated by the parable of The Stubborn Caretaker (Mek. Beshallach 5:60 ff.):

> AND MOSES STRETCHED OUT HIS HAND OVER THE SEA (Ex. 14:21). Immediately the sea began to withstand him. Moses ordered it in the name of the Holy One, blessed be He, to divide itself but it would not submit. Moses then showed it the staff, but still it refused to yield.
>
> A parable. Unto what is the matter like? It is like unto a king who had two gardens, one inside the other. He sold the inner one, but when the buyer came wishing to enter the inner garden, the keeper would not let him. The buyer spoke to the keeper in the name of the king, but the keeper would not yield. He then showed him the king's ring, and he still refused to yield. So the buyer had to go and bring the king himself with him. As soon as the buyer came, conducting the king, the keeper started to run away. The buyer then called out to him: The whole day I have been speaking to you in the name of the king, but you would not accept it; and now why are you running away? The keeper answered him: It is not on account of you that I am fleeing, it is on account of the king.
>
> Even so, Moses came and stood by the sea. He told it in the name of the Holy One, blessed be He, to divide itself, but it would not consent. He showed it the staff, but it would not consent, until the Holy One, blessed be He, revealed Himself over it in His glory. And as soon as the Holy One, blessed be He, revealed Himself in His might and His glory, the sea began to flee, as it is said: THE SEA SAW IT AND FLED (Ps. 114:3). Moses then said to it: All day long I have been talking to you in the name of the Holy One, blessed be He, and you would not listen, and now wherefore are you fleeing? WHAT AILETH THEE, O THOU SEA, THAT THOU FLEEST? (Ps. 114:5). The sea answered him: It is not because of you, Moses, it is not because of you, son of Amram. It is only because: TREMBLE THOU EARTH AT THE PRE-

> SENCE OF THE LORD, AT THE PRESENCE OF THE GOD OF JACOB, WHO TURNED THE ROCK INTO A POOL OF WATER, THE FLINT INTO A FOUNTAIN OF WATERS (Ps. 114:7-8).

The center of the action is the buyer/Moses, or possibly the keeper/sea; but the parable begins: "It is like unto a <u>king</u> who . . . ," even though the king plays a secondary, though determinative, role.

2.51 Thus the <u>comparison</u> <u>word</u> does not always signify what is really being compared. There can be a disjunction between the main <u>point</u> of comparison and the comparison <u>word</u>. By far the most common comparison word is "a king," or "a king of flesh and blood." Out of the 324 Tannaitic parables we have collected, 180 employ the figure of a king as the comparison word, and Ziegler (1903), who collected all manner of items in which a king or kingdom figures, listed no less than 937. With few exceptions, whenever a parable involves a king figure he is used as the comparison word, even when he almost immediately walks off the stage and leaves the central action to others. It may also be said that the king almost always represents God, with but one or two dubious exceptions.

The next most frequent comparison words are "one" (49 times) and "a man" (40 times). "Two men" and "a woman" serve as comparison words each four times. A few others occur two or three times, and some threescore others only once each. In the case of the less common comparison words, the comparison word is much more likely to be also the figure which the parable is really about.

2.6 It was noted above (2.2) that parables could be reapplied, or the applications modified. An interesting example of this emerges from a comparison of the two versions of The Wise and Foolish Servants (Shabbath 153a and Eccl. R. 9:8:1). The first version reads:

> We learnt elsewhere, R. Eliezer said: Repent one day before your death [cf. Sirach 5:7]. His disciples asked him: Does one know on what day he will die? He said: Then all the more reason that he repent today, lest he die tomorrow, and thus his whole life is spent in repentance. And Solomon too said in his wisdom: LET THY GARMENTS BE ALWAYS WHITE; AND LET NOT THY HEAD LACK OINTMENT (Eccl. 9:8).
>
> R. Johanan b. Zakkai said: A parable. It is like a king who summoned his servants to a banquet without appointing a time. The wise ones adorned themselves and sat at the door of the palace. They said: Is there anything lacking in a royal palace? The fools went about their work.

> They said: Can there be a banquet without preparations? Suddenly the king desired the presence of his servants. The wise entered adorned, while the fools entered soiled. The king rejoiced at the wise but was wroth with the fools. He said: Those who adorned themselves for the banquet, let them sit, eat, and drink. But those who did not adorn themselves for the banquet, let them stand and watch.
>
> R. Meir's son-in-law said in R. Meir's name: Then they too would merely look on, being in attendance. But both sit, the former eating and the latter hungering, the former drinking and the latter thirsting, for it is said: THEREFORE THUS SAITH THE LORD GOD: BEHOLD, MY SERVANTS SHALL EAT, BUT YE SHALL BE HUNGRY; BEHOLD, MY SERVANTS SHALL DRINK, BUT YE SHALL BE THIRSTY; BEHOLD, MY SERVANTS SHALL REJOICE, BUT YE SHALL BE ASHAMED; BEHOLD, MY SERVANTS SHALL SING FOR JOY OF HEART, BUT YE SHALL CRY FOR SORROW OF HEART (Isa. 65:13 ff.).

The juxtaposition of illustrand and illustration is the work of editors, for Eliezer's dictum must be later than the parable of Johanan, his teacher. Eliezer himself may have applied or reapplied Johanan's parable to the lesson: Always be ready for death. That was probably not quite Johanan's original point, which was probably: Always be ready for the coming of the Messiah. Our suspicions in this regard are already aroused by the banquet in the parable, which is an obvious reference to the Messianic Age. Our suspicions are confirmed when we compare the parallel version, which has an explicit application attached: "Even so in the Hereafter *(le*ᶜ*atid labo')*, as Isaiah declares, BEHOLD, MY SERVANTS SHALL EAT, BUT YE SHALL BE HUNGRY." The Hebrew expression refers to the Messianic Age (see references in Jastrow: 1129). Thus Johanan's parable (like those of Jesus in Mat. 22:11-14 and 25:1-13) originally had reference to the coming of the Messiah, but Eliezer (or the Talmudic editor) reapplied it to the coming of death to the individual. The two meanings are, to be sure, congruent to each other.

2.7 To attempt here to lay out a classification of the rabbinic parables according to content (cf. Ziegler, 1903; Rabbinowitz, 1972; Feldman, 1924) or structure (see especially the interesting work of Pautrel, 1936-38) would take us far beyond the scope allowable in this paper. We must therefore be content to conclude with an example of a type of parable which is especially characteristic of the earlier sources, and which may be called the "geminate" type. A geminate *mashal* is one which places in symmetrical parallelism two contrasting examples, or two contrasting situations or modes of behavior for the same example. Positive and negative are neatly opposed. Usually one example is completely dealt with before its opposite is taken up; each is in complementary contrast with the other. In the true geminate parable, first one subject is paraded onto the stage, dressed in white or black; and then the second subject, identical to the first in all things except for being dressed in the opposite color, is brought on after the exit of the first. The audience is asked to vote its approval for one or the other in a choice thus rendered as easy as possible to make. In the parable of the Well-Rooted Tree (Aboth 3:18) the parabler, as if the audience might yet be left in some doubt, further instructs them with apposite scriptural comments (which indeed appear to be the original inspiration for the parable) after each subject has occupied the spotlight:

> He whose wisdom is more abundant than his works, unto what is he like? He is like unto a tree whose branches are abundant but whose roots are few. And the wind comes and uproots it and overturns it.
>
> As it is written: HE SHALL BE LIKE A TAMARISK IN THE DESERT AND SHALL NOT SEE WHEN GOOD COMETH, BUT SHALL INHABIT THE PARCHED PLACES IN THE WILDERNESS (Jer. 17:6).
>
> But he whose works are more abundant than his wisdom, unto what is he like? He is like unto a tree whose branches are few but whose roots are many; so that even if all the winds in the world come and blow against it, it cannot be stirred from its place.
>
> As it is written: HE SHALL BE AS A TREE PLANTED BY THE WATERS, AND THAT SPREADETH OUT HIS ROOTS BY THE RIVER, AND SHALL NOT FEAR WHEN HEAT COMETH, AND HIS LEAF SHALL BE GREEN: AND SHALL NOT BE CAREFUL IN THE YEAR OF DROUGHT, NEITHER SHALL CEASE FROM YIELDING FRUIT (Jer. 17:8).

A simpler example is The Married Woman (Tos. Kid. 1:11):

> R. Jose says in the name of Rabban Gamaliel: Everyone who has a handicraft, unto what is he like? He is like unto a woman who has a husband. Whether she adorns herself or not, no one gets fresh with her. If she does adorn herself she will have no fear. Everyone who has no handicraft, unto what is he like? He is like unto a woman who has no husband. Whether she adorns herself or not, everyone is fresh with her. And even when she does not adorn herself, she has fear.

For the most part, such parables describe general situations *(Gleichnisse)* rather than specific past events. Sometimes the verdict is explicitly requested, as in Mat. 21:28-32; other times the verdict is not explicitly requested, but wrung quite involuntarily from the jury-audience, as in Mat. 7:24-27 and these two specimens.

3. Classified on the basis of morphology, there can be no reasonable doubt that the rabbinic and Synoptic parables partake of the same genre. When the relatively small sampling of parables which come down to us from the sayings of Jesus are merged with the much larger collection we have from the Tannaim--not to mention the parables of the Amoraim, which are not basically different, but perhaps more elaborate and more stereotyped--classifications and characteristics emerge which would otherwise escape us. In this paper we could only hint at them. But viewed in the light of intent and function, the contrast between the parables of the two corpora is equally apparent, though it should not be exaggerated. The gospel parables seek to turn conventional values and expectations upside down; the rabbinic parables seek to reinforce them. The former surprise; the latter confirm. The parables of Jesus create perplexities; the parables of the Rabbis seek to resolve perplexities. The rabbinic parables mostly exegete the Torah; the gospel parables mostly expound the Kingdom.

NOTES

/1/ The process of collection was well begun by Harvey K. McArthur, my dissertation adviser, who also suggested this area of study to me. We project the publication of a jointly authored study guide to rabbinic parables, which will hopefully appear not long after the completion of my dissertation.

/2/ I here follow the example of modern descriptive linguistics as practiced by H. A. Gleason and his circle, which would not define a noun, for example, as "the name of a person, place or thing," which is rather circular and inexact, but in terms of its morphological and syntactic behavior. In an analogous manner, I propose to define a parable in terms of morphology and contextual function, with the emphasis on morphology. See H. A. Gleason, *An Introduction to Descriptive Linguistics*, revised ed. (New York: Holt, Rinehart and Winston, 1961), pp. 92 ff.

SECONDARY WORKS CITED

Back, Samuel
1875-84 "Die Fabel in Talmud un Midrasch," *Monatsschrift für Geschichte und Wissenschaft des Judentums* 24: 540-55; 25: 126-38, 195-204, 267-75, 493-504; 29:24-34, 68-78, 102-14, 144, 225-30, 267-74, 374-78, 417-21; 30: 124-30, 260-67, 406-12, 453-58; 33: 23-33, 34-35, 114-25, 255-67.

Ben-Amos, Dan
1967 "Narrative Forms in the Haggadah: Structural Analysis." Unpublished doctoral dissertation, Indiana University.

Bultmann, Rudolf
1972 *The History of the Synoptic Tradition.* Translated by John Marsh. Revised ed. New York/ Evanston: Harper and Row.

Crossan, John Dominic
1974 "The Good Samaritan: Towards a Generic Definition of Parable." *Semeia* 2: 82-112.

Dodd, C. H.
1961 *The Parables of the Kingdom.* Revised ed. New York: Charles Scribner's Sons.

Feldman, Asher
1924 *The Parables and Similes of the Rabbis: Agricultural and Pastoral.* London: Cambridge University Press.

Fiebig, Paul
1904 *Altjüdische Gleichnisse und die Gleichnisse Jesu.* Tübingen/Leipzig: J. C. B. Mohr (Paul Siebeck).

1912 *Die Gleichnisreden Jesu im Lichte des neutestamentlichen Zeitalters: Ein Beitrag zum Streit um die "Christusmythe" und eine Widerlegung der Gleichnistheorie Jülichers.* Tübingen: J. C. B. Mohr (Paul Siebeck).

Findlay, J. Alexander
1951 *Jesus and His Parables.* London: The Epworth Press.

Funk, Robert W.
1976 "Structure in the Narrative Parrables of Jesus." *Semeia* 2:51-73.

Guttmann, Theodor
1929 *Das Mašal-Gleichnis in tannaitischer Zeit.* Inaugural-Dissertation zur Erlangung der Doktorwürde der Philosophischen Fakultät der Universität zu Frankfort a. M. Frankfort a. M.: Hermon Druckerei und Verlag.

Jacobs, Joseph
1901 "Aesop's Fables Among the Jews." *The Jewish Encyclopedia* 1: 221-22.

Jastrow, Marcus
1967 *A Dictionary of the Targumim, the Talmud Babli and Yerushalmi, and the Midrashic Literature.* 2 vols. Reprint ed., Brooklyn, N. Y.: P. Shalom Pub. Inc.

Jülicher, Adolf
1910 *Die Gleichnisreden Jesu.* Zwei Teile in einem Band. Tübingen: J. C. B. Mohr (Paul Siebeck). Reprint ed., Darmstadt: Wissenschaftliche Buchgesellschaft, 1969.

Pautrel, Raymond
1936-38 "Les canons du Mashal rabbinique." *Recherches de science rêligieuse* 26: 6-45; 28: 264-81.

Rabinowitz, Louis Isaac
1972 "Parable." *Encyclopaedia Judaica* 13: 73-76.

Smith, Morton
1968 *Tannaitic Parallels to the Gospels.* Journal of Biblical Literature Monograph Series, Vol. VI. Philadelphia: Society of Biblical Literature.

Ziegler, Ignaz
1903 *Die Königsgleichnisse des Midrasch beleuchtet durch die römische Kaiserzeit.* Breslau: Schlesische Verlags-Anstalt v. S. Schottlaender.

S 239 HIDDEN TREASURE PARABLES IN LATE ANTIQUITY

John Dominic Crossan
DePaul University

"The story must be told and its telling is a record of the *choices*, inadvertent or deliberate, the *author* has made from all the possibilities of language."

W. H. Gass: 7 (italics added)

"At each crossroads of the action sequence, the *narrative* ... *chooses* between several possibilities, and this choice involves at any given moment the very future of the story; obviously the story will change according to whether the door on which one has knocked will open or remain closed, etc. ... It goes without saying that, where an action is faced with an alternative - having this or that consequence - the *narrative* invariably *chooses* that from which it profits, i.e, that which assures its survival as narrative."

R. Barthes: 7 (italics added)

1 Alternative Stemmas

My purpose in this paper is to compare eight parables on *finding hidden treasure* in the literature of late antiquity. Behind this is a general intention of raising certain methodological questions within the SBL Parables Seminar which may be of assistance to the SBL Genres Project in the area of parables.

I am going to consider as parables *very short stories with overtly didactic purpose*. My only qualification to this is a reminder that didactic can become "metadidactic" (Politzer) so that there are also parables which, as paradoxes, probe and question the limits of the didactic itself. The even more pressing problem is the little use to which such standard historical disciplines as source and redaction criticism can be put for the comparative analysis of these parables. Questions of chronology are answered in centuries rather than in decades in some cases and problems of genetic causality become impossible under such circumstances. And that ignores the fact that creativity within the narrative possibilities of the same theme may very well result in quite similar stories in very different times and places.

Two examples will suffice for the moment. First, we know that Book II of Horace's *Satires* was published in 30 B.C.E. (Fairclough: xii, xix). In it he refers to a presumably well-known folktale concerning the finding of hidden treasure. In writing his commentary on Horace, Porphyrio of Tyre (232-304 C.E.) gives a fuller and clearer version of this folktale. But how sure are we that what Porphyrio gives us is actually what Horace referred to in synopsis? If we had to base genetic arguments on the existence of Porphyrio's version before 30 B.C.E., how secure would such conclusions be. Second, what are biblical critics doing when they compare Jesus' parables with those of the Rabbis? Are they forging chronological and/or genealogical relationships? And if this is what they are doing, what happens when all the Rabbinical parables known to us date from after 70 C.E.? (Neusner, 1971, 1972:360, 368). Unless we postulate highly selective (Neusner, 1972:390) literary destruction during the period of the Roman revenge, we might conclude that parables were not much in use among the Rabbis of that earlier period, and what would that do to any genetic-historical criticism of Jesus's parables?

My intention, then, is to take whatever historical or genetic information we have on these stories and their interrelations but not to make such data, or its absence, the major interest of the study. Instead, I plan to consider these eight parables as discrete actualizations of narrative possibilities latent in the theme of finding hidden treasure. This means that I can make almost no use of chronological or genealogical stemmas and must look instead for some alternative critical system in which and through which to consider these parables comparatively.

The eight parables are spread across Jewish (P1,P2, P4,P6; Strack-Billerbeck: 1.674), Gnostic (P5), Christian (Jesus, P8), and other Graeco-Roman (P3,P7) literature. Since a *chronological* and *genealogical* stemma is of little help with these materials, I intend to organize and study them through a *narralogical* tree. This narrative stemma involves looking at the actual narratives available *but also and afterwards* looking at the logic of narrative possibilities. This latter concern taken by itself is almost infinite even within a set theme and its arboreal presentation can easily become a logical and theoretical forest primeval (Bremond; Güttgemanns). I intend, therefore, to stay as close as possible to my eight stories and to construct the *minimum narralogical stemma* necessary to explain the narrative choices (see epigraphs) which created their present format.

I hope for four main results from this method. First, it should be possible for others to discuss and criticize such a narralogical stemma, just as they might do with chronological or genealogical ones, since they can propose alternative versions and indicate why such might be more useful or fruitful than my own suggestion. This will hopefully render the analysis less solipsistic or impressionistic. Second, rather than negative or doubtful conclusions on genetic relationships, I should conclude with positive conclusions on narralogical relationship. Third, such narralogical comparison should assist in making more precise determinations of meaning, especially in cases where a narrative choice represents a radical new direction within a given tradition. Fourth, if other stories are to be considered within this same theme, either newly discovered or newly created ones, such can be fitted into the stemma with this latter bifurcated wherever it is necessary in order to make narrative space for the newcomer. For example, my entire stemma of eight parables is within the rubric of *finding* hidden treasure. But it has been claimed that "American treasure tales usually end with treasure not being found" (Hurley: 197), that is, "The treasure has been located. There is all manner of expert help in the search. Is it recovered? In American buried treasure tales the answer is, with very few exceptions, *no*" (204). Hence, American treasure stories reduce my entire stemma to one major narralogical choice: finding (late antiquity) or not-finding (American).

All of which raises very important questions, two of which may be noted in passing. Methodologically, are narralogical, chronological, and genealogical stemmas three consecutive steps in a total analytical process which must always proceed *in that order* even if it cannot proceed through all three stages in certain cases? Philosophically, are narralogical base-choices what we sometimes term historical destiny?

2 Narralogical Choices

The decision tree for these eight parables is given here as Table 1:

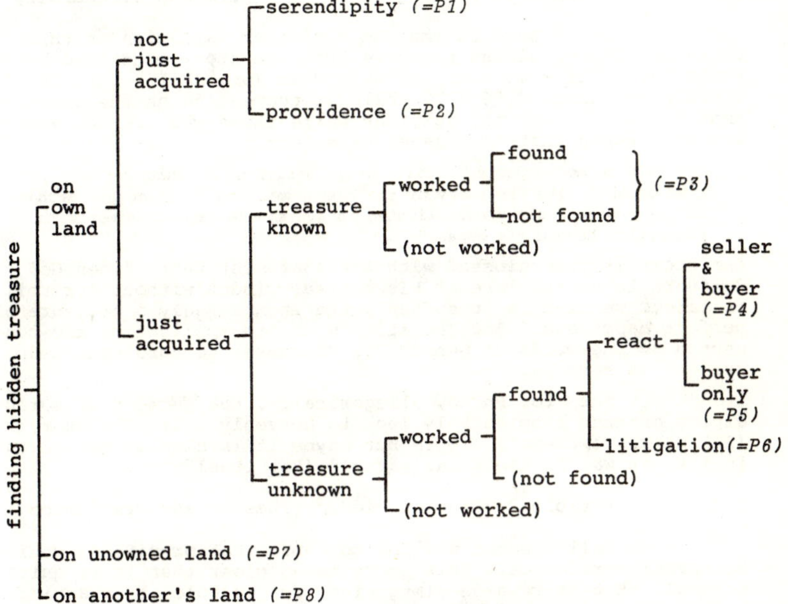

Although it was established after investigation of the individual narratives, it can be presented here initially since it dictates the order of their presentation.

The first choice is whether the treasure is found on one's own property or on that of another, and this binary opposition presents an immediate medial possibility of the treasure's being found on nobody's property, on free or open land. On one's own property is the only choice which is developed within the present miniature corpus of eight parables (P1-P6), with only one example for nobody's property (P7), and one for another's (P8). When the treasure is found on one's own land, it may be taken as sheer luck, pure serendipity (P1), or else as evidence of providential rewarding of one deserving of such gifts (P2). In neither case is there any complicating element to distract from these points. But what if one's property had recently been acquired from another? New possibilities open up immediately. If one had been informed that the acquired (inherited) land contained a treasure, one would probably search for it, and then what would happen? (P3). But if one knew nothing about the treasure's existence, but set out industriously to work one's newly acquired land, one could thereby find the treasure, thus a triumph of industry over indolence (P4) or of knowledge over ignorance (P5). Unless, of course, the entire affair ended up in court (P6).

3 Thematic Variations

The eight parables can now be studied in detail within this general narralogical schema.

3.1 Parable 1: Finding Hidden Treasure and Serendipity

It is hard to imagine a simpler variation on this topic of finding hidden treasure than the story mentioned by Philo (30 B.C.E - 45 C.E.) in *Quod Deus Immutabilis Sit*, 20.91 (Colson-Whitaker: 3.56-57). Philo is commenting on the paradox that those who seek may not find while those who are not searching may obtain what they never expected:

> "It is a common experience that things befall us of which we have not even dreamt, like the story of the husbandman who, digging his orchard to plant some fruit-trees, lighted on a treasure, and thus met with prosperity beyond his hopes."

The story is then glossed with the statement that, "when God delivers to us the lore of His eternal wisdom without our toil or labour we find in it suddenly and unexpectedly a treasure of perfect happiness." And the story with its application are connected to the words of Gen 27:20, "Because the Lord your God granted me success."

Thus for Philo, allegorically, the paradox of serendipity extends from earthly luck to heavenly gift. The story (P1) seemes extremely simple but maybe it is also as mysterious in its own way as the final parable (P8) itself.

3.2 Parable 2: Finding Hidden Treasure and Providence

Philo seemed willing to admit that providence could be rather paradoxical. This story makes clear that it is quite ethical, that it rewards almsgiving, for example, by granting hidden treasure as divine alms.

There are three almost identical versions of this parable, in the *Palestinian Talmud*: Horayoth, 3.4(7) (Schwab: 6.276) and in *Midrash Rabbah*: Leviticus, 4.4, and Deuteronomy, 4.8 (Freedman-Simon: 4:66-67; 6.97-98). All three versions are given as amplifications of a saying in Prov 18:16. But the *LevR* and *pHor* versions are much closer to each other than to the *DeutR* account. There are three small but interesting differences. This latter text (1) does not mention R. Akiba among the visitors, (2) has nothing about any cow or any broken leg while ploughing, and (3) specifies the amount given to the visiting Rabbis as "five gold pieces" before the treasure was found, and also adds that the finder gave them "one hundred gold pieces" on their return visit.

For my present purpose, however, it will suffice to consider the account in *LevR* 4.4. A pious and generous man named Abba Judan had become impoverished but when "R. Eliezer and R. Joshua and R. Akiba" came seeking alms for poor scholars, his wife "who was even more saintly than he" advised him to sell half of their last field and give the proceeds to the visitors.

> "They prayed for him, saying: 'May the All-present make good your deficiency!' After some days he went to plough the half field he had retained; and as he was ploughing, his cow fell and its leg was broken. When he went down to lift it up, the Holy One, blessed be He, gave light to his eyes, and he found a treasure there. Said he: 'My cow's

> leg was broken, but it turned out to be for my benefit.'"

Later when the Rabbis came back, they found Abba Judan fabulously wealthy and he acknowledged that their prayer for him had been answered. They assured him that on their list his name led all the rest and they gave him a seat with themselves.

Once again, the point is quite clear. The general proverbial wisdom that it's an ill wind that blows nobody some good is repeated in the story of the cow who breaks her leg against a hidden treasure. But the story has carefully framed this proverbial wisdom with moral and theological lessons. The alms of Abba Judan and the prayer of the Rabbis are detailed most fully before the finding and are also recalled after it. And what crowns his life is not just his newly-found wealth but his being seated among the Rabbis. It is also underlined that he found the treasure because "the Holy One, blessed be He, gave light to his eyes." Finally, the story exemplifies the saying in Prov 18:16 that "A man's gift makes room for him and brings him before great men."

3.3 Parable 3: Finding Hidden Treasure and Industry

In Table 1 I coded this parable as "finding" *and* "not finding" hidden treasure. The story is "The Farmer and His Sons," Aesop's Fable 42 (Hausrath: 57-59; Perry: 338) and it has been translated as follows (Daly: 111, 271):

> "A farmer, who was about to die and wanted to familiarize his sons with his farm, called them to him and said, 'Boys, a treasure is buried in one of my vineyards.' After he died, they took plows and mattocks and dug up their whole farm. They didn't find the treasure but the vineyard repaid them with a much increased crop.
> The story shows that work is a treasure for men."

When this P3 is compared with P4,P5,P6 the crucial difference is that in P3 those who acquire the land are told there is a "treasure" hidden in it. This known/unknown choice is more important than whether the field is bought or inherited since, no doubt, a buyer would act in the same way if a seller informed him the field contained a treasure.

3.4 Parable 4: Finding Hidden Treasure and Industry/ Indolence

To compare P3 and P4 is very interesting. In P3 the treasure *is* the increased crop so that work, not luck, produced this "treasure." But P4 has it both ways because indolence fails to find the actual treasure which industry then obtains. It is the Horatio Alger moral that, if one works very hard (*and* is very lucky), one will do well. But as we shall see later there are certain transformations of P4 which omit both the unreal treasure of P3 and the real one of P4 and detail instead how work produces increment directly without any mention of treasure at all (see 4.11).

Two different versions of this parable are attributed to Rabbi Simeon ben Yoḥai, a third generation Tannaite from the period around 130-160 C.E. (Strack: 115). Both are connected allegorically with the relations between the Israelites and Egyptians at the time of the Exodus.

3.41 The Dunghill.

The one version locates the hidden treasure in a dunghill (P4a) newly inherited, in *Midrash Rabbah*: Song of Songs, 4.12.1 (Freedman-Simon: 9.219-20):

> "R. Simeon b. Yoḥai taught: [The Egyptians were] like a man who inherited a piece of ground used as a dunghill. Being an indolent man, he went and sold it for a trifling sum. The purchaser began working and digging it up, and he found a treasure there, out of which he built himself a fine palace, and he began going about in public followed by a retinue of servants - all out of the treasure he found in it. When the seller saw it he was ready to choke, and he exclaimed, 'Alas, what have I thrown away.'"

This story is then applied allegorically to the feelings of the Egyptians after they had allowed Israel to depart, in Exod 13:17.

3.42 The Distant Residence

The other version (P4b) locates the treasure in an inherited but distant residence, in *Mekilta de-Rabbi Ishmael*: Exodus 14:5 (Lauterbach: 1.198):

> "R. Simon the son of Yoḥai, giving a parable, says: To what can this be compared? To a man to whom there had fallen as an inheritance a residence in a far off country which he sold for a trifle. The buyer, however, went and discovered in it hidden treasures and stores of silver and gold, of precious stones and pearls. The seller, seeing this, began to choke with grief."

Once again, the story is applied allegorically to the dismay of the Egyptians at the Exodus, but to Exod 14:5 rather than 13:17.

3.43 Comparison of P4a and P4b

The similarities and dissimilarities of these two accounts are equally obvious. Both are attributed to the same Rabbi, as already noted. Both are allegorically connected with the moment in the Exodus when Pharaoh repents of having let Israel depart from Egypt: Exod 13:17 or 14:5. And both mention that the seller had inherited the possession which he then sold for a trifle.

The differences may be summarized as in Table 2:

P4a: The Dunghill (*SongR*)	P4b: The Distant Residence (*Mek*)
	formal parabolic opening
"a piece of ground used as a dunghill"	"a residence in a far off country"
"working and digging ... and ... found"	"went and discovered"
"he built ... a fine palace, and ... a retinue of servants"	"hidden treasures and stores of silver and of gold, of precious stones and pearls"

Two points may be indicated in these differences. First, the same basic version from the same named Rabbi can be given with or without the formal parabolic opening: משל למה הדבר דומה ל... Second, P4a, with its treasure in a field, was able to underline the *morality* of work. The seller is qualified as "being an indolent man" and the new owner "began working" before finding the treasure. P4b, on the other hand, by locating its treasure in a residence, lost something of this moral application unless, of course, it is implicitly present in "went," i.e., to "a far off country." But P4b has gained a tighter connection with biblical history in that its "stores of silver and of gold" correlate very precisely with the "jewelry of silver and of gold" which the departing Israelites were to obtain from the Egyptians in Exod 3:22.

3.5 Parable 5: Finding Hidden Treasure and Ignorance/Knowledge

There is a variation in the *Gospel of Thomas* 109 (=98:31-99:2) which is very close to the preceding P5. It reads as follows (Guillaumont: 55):

> "Jesus said: The Kingdom is like a man who had a treasure [hidden] in his field, without knowing it. And [after] he died, he left it to his [son. The] son did not know (about it), he accepted that field, he sold [it]. And he who bought it, he went, while he was plowing [he found] the treasure. He began to lend money to whomever he wished."

When P5 is compared with its close parallel in P4, two important differences are immediately apparent. First, there is the mention of inheritance. P4a had "a man who inherited a piece of ground ... sold it" and P4b had "a man to whom there had fallen as an inheritance ... sold it." But here the one who bequeaths the inheritance is left quite implicit and only the inheritor-seller is explicitly mentioned. Gos Thom 109 has expanded and emphasized this point so that both inheritor and owner explicitly appear and each is specified as *not knowing* about the treasure. One presumes that the purpose is to stress this reiterated ignorance. Second, there is the more difficult question of the closing comment on interest. On the one hand, this seems no more than another way of mentioning the finder's enjoyment of the treasure, as also at the end of P2 ("servants ... goats ... camels ... oxen") or of P4a ("fine palace ... retinue of servants"). But, on the other hand, the attitude of Gos Thom towards such a materialistic activity is elsewhere quite negative. For example, in Gos Thom 95 (=96:35-97:2): "[Jesus said]: If you have money, do not lend at interest, but give [them] to him from whom you will not receive them (back)." One could say that a gnostic author was primarily interested in changing the opening of the folktale of the Hidden Treasure and Indolence/Industry into that of Ignorance/Knowledge and allowed the ending to stay as it originally was in his source, thus, with Turner (Montefiore-Turner: 100), "the discrepancy here may be due to the faulty redaction of original sources." Or, more positively, that he was willing to make his allegorical point even through usury just as Jesus (P8) was through dishonesty, thus, with Montefiore (Montefiore-Turner: 56), "True knowledge is as precious as treasure found in a field; and in the heart of a true believer it multiplies itself and increases its influence."

This comparison of P5 with P4, against the possible common background of P3 (Cerfaux-Garitte: 315), shows how well Gos Thom has gnosticized the story. He has (1) doubly stressed the theme of ignorance (not indolence) at the start of the parable (Schrage: 197) and he has (2) omitted any reference to the seller's fury at the end since the non-gnostic does not even know that something has been missed (Haenchen: 47). It is probably not necessary to push the gnostic allegorization much further, for example, by invoking reincarnation in connection with the initial father-son-buyer trilogy (Gärtner: 238) or by connecting the terminal lending at interest with the parable of the talents in Matt 25:24-27 (Grant-Freedman: 194). And, if one wishes a genealogical rather than a narralogical stemma, it is much more likely that P5 is a gnostic version of P4 (with or without P3) than it is of P8 (Dehandschutter: 214) since this latter parable represents very different narralogical choices and it would be impossible to get from P8 to P5 except through P4.

3.6 Parable 6: Finding Hidden Treasure and Litigation

This sixth variation is deeply involved in the difficult problem of "the relations between the Talmudic Alexander traditions and the Alexander Romance" (Wallach: 80). Whether one decides negatively (Lévi, 1883:84-85; Klausner: 380 [note 21]) or positively (Wallach: 63-80) on its Greek existence prior to any Jewish adaptation, it is certain that this "narrative about the treasure is a variation of an Alexander legend, which has [had] a great vogue in Jewish literature" (Ginzberg: 6.351 [note 35]), and that its subsequent wanderings into both Arabic and Western literature are almost as widespread (Lévi, 1881b, 1883: 91-93). This single variation opens up three different areas of historical research into the genetic relations between (1) the Greek and Jewish Alexander legends, (2) the various Jewish versions themselves, and (3) the subsequent eastern and western versions of the legend.

For my present purpose I am limiting consideration to four texts and leaving aside any later versions judged to be genetically dependent on one or more of these. The four units in question are the *Babylonian Talmud*: Tamid, 32ab (Simon: 26-29); the *Palestinian Talmud*: Baba Metzia, 2.5 (Schwab: 6.94); *Midrash Rabbah*: Genesis, 33.1 (Freedman-Simon: 1.258-59); and *Pesiḳta de-Rab Kahana*, 9.1 (Braude-Kapstein: 171-72). Later derivative versions such as those in *Midrash Rabbah*: Leviticus, 27.1 (Freedman-Simon: 4.342-43); *Midrash Tanḥuma*: Emor, 9 (Buber: 2.88-89); etc. (Lévi, 1883:90-91), will not be considered.

The four basic texts to be studied here contain three separate stories concerning Alexander's legendary travels in Africa: (1) Female War; (2) Gold Meal; (3) Treasure Judgment. These are combined in the four Jewish texts as indicated in Table 3:

Alexander	Female War[1]	*PsCall*	*bTamid*[1+2]	*Pesiḳta*[1& 2+3]
	Gold Meal[2]			
	Treasure Judgment[3]		*pBMetzia*[3+2] *GenR*[2+3]	

It is only with the third unit that I am directly concerned and the others are discussed only to isolate this one more precisely.

(1) The Female War. The Amazons confront Alexander with this dilemma in *bTamid*, 32a: "If you slay us, people will say that he killed women, and if we slay you they will call you the king who was killed by women." The story is also found in "the Romance composed probably in Alexandria sometime before the fourth century A.D. by an unknown author whom certain manuscripts falsely name Callisthenes, kin of Aristotle and companion and historian of Alexander the Great" (Wolohojian: 1). Exactly the same dilemma is presented but by letter from the Amazons to Alexander in the

various versions of the hellenistic Alexander Romance, *Pseudo-Callisthenes*, for example, in the Greek (3.25; Bergson: 170), the Syriac (3.15; Budge: 129, 229), or the Armenian (252; Wolohojian: 142) transcriptions. The Female War, then, derives originally from the Greek Alexander Romance (Lévi, 1883:82; Wallach: 54).

(2) The Gold Meal. This is presumably a satirical comment on Alexander's greed for gold. He is offered bread (and/or other food) of gold and must, of course, decline the meal. In *bTamid*, 32ab the Gold Meal is presented to Alexander by the Amazons immediately after the Female War unit. There is no equivalent to it in *PsCall* (by letter!).

The other three texts with which I am concerned (see Table 3) all connect the Gold Meal with the Treasure Judgment (King Kazia) rather than with the Female War (Amazons). Either (1) the Female War is completely omitted and the sequence is (a) Gold Meal and Treasure Judgment, as in *GenR*, or (b) Treasure Judgment and Gold Meal, as in *pBMetzia*. Or (2) the Female War is present but there is a clear separation so that the Female War is connected with the Amazons but the Gold Meal and the Treasure Judgment are both connected with King Kazia, as in *Pesiḳta*. Which *may* mean that "l'histoire des pains d'or était une création de l'imagination juive" (Lévi, 1883:83). In any case, the Gold Meal is not an integral part of the Treasure Judgment itself.

(3) The Treasure Judgment. This unit, then, is found in three main texts: *pBMetzia*, *GenR*, and *Pesiḳta*. I am not presently interested directly in the historical or genetic relations between these texts and I shall simply indicate three points of debate. First, the combinatory activity of *Pesiḳta* in bringing together all three stories concerning Alexander is somewhat crude. Although they have been given an external unity by the preliminary statement that "the continued existence of the world depends on humbler creatures ... than men," their internal unity is not so happily accomplished. King Kazia is mentioned; the Female War story follows; Alexander goes to "another principality" where "the people" offer him the Gold Meal; then the Treasure Judgment begins "before the king" and this is the point where the name of King Kazia might be expected to appear rather than in isolation at the very start of the complex. *Pesiḳta* seems to have combined the Alexander stories from *bTamid* and from *pBMetzia* and/or *GenR* (Lévi, 1883:89). Second, it is debated whether *pBMetzia* derived from *GenR* (Lévi, 1883:87-88) or *GenR* from *pBMetzia* (Wallach: 63-65). Third, it is also debated whether the story of the Treasure Judgment is originally from Greek or Jewish sources. Thus, "il paraît d'origine juive .... comme aucun écrit antérieur ne rapporte cette légende, on est en droit de supposer, jusqu'à preuve du contraire, qu'elle est le produit de l'imagination juive" (Lévi, 1883:84, 85); as against, "our investigation has clearly established the Greek origin of the legend" (Wallach: 75). The arguments for the former position seem much stronger since "this story of a Greek character is repeated throughout the Jewish *Midrashic* literature but is not found at all in Greek literature; it is not in accordance with the Greek spirit" (Klausner: 380 [note 21]). The main argument offered by Wallach for a Greek origin is the two Greek loan-words indicated in his translation given below. Lévi and Klausner would seem to have the best of the argument.

Apart from these debates over origin (Greek or Jewish), genetic sequence (*pBMetzia* to *GenR* or vice versa), and context (with or without the Gold Meal unit), the story itself is extremely similar in all three texts even in rather minor details. And in all three texts the conclusion has King Kazia reprimand Alexander by asserting that only God's concern for the animals obtains rain in the country of one so evil as Alexander, thereby "fulfilling" Ps 36:7(6), "Man and beast thou savest, O Lord" (i.e., here, man *for* beast thou savest!). Because of this similarity any of the three texts might have been used here but I shall take the translation of *pBMetzia* given by Wallach (63-64) in order to show the Greek loan-words he has noted in it:

> "Alexander of Macedon visited King Kazia. The latter showed him much gold and silver. Alexander said to him: 'I do not need your gold and silver. I came only because I wished to see your method [פרוכסין . πρᾶξις], how you act and how you dispense justice. While he was arguing with him, a man came with a complaint against his neighbor who had sold him an unploughed field, and in digging it the buyer happened to find a treasure of denars [in a dunghill]. The buyer agreed: I bought [the field and] the dunghill [in it], but I did not buy the treasure. The seller maintained: I sold [the field and] the dunghill and all it contained. While both were discussing the problem, the king said to one of them, 'Have you a son?' 'Yes', he replied. Then he asked the other, 'Have you a daughter?' 'Yes', he said. Said the king to both: 'Then marry them and let the treasure belong to both.' Alexander laughed [at the king's decision] and the king asked him, 'Why are you laughing? Have I not judged well? Had this happened among you [in your empire], how would you have judged?' Alexander replied, 'We should have killed both, and the treasure would have gone to the king'. Said the king to Alexander, 'How very fond must you be of gold and silver!' He offered Alexander a meal [אריסטון.ἄριστον] ...."

In *pBMetzia*, as noted above, the Gold Meal follows here and then the incident terminates with the application of Ps 36:7(6).

In this parable (P6), as distinct from P4, both buyer and seller are so virtuous that neither wishes to incur possible guilt by claiming the treasure. The seller even wants to extend the mishnaic laws of *Baba Bathra*, 4 (Danby: 370-72) on selling "it and all that is in it" to include treasure as well! Hence a situation calling for Solomonic judgment. In P6 the focus of interest has shifted from the buyer-seller conflict (P4) to the king-emperor conflict but it is clear that the parable actualizes an obvious possibility of litigation and judgment as a next step in the seller-buyer relationship.

3.7 Parable 7: Finding Hidden Treasure and Stupidity

The six preceding parables were all developed from the initial narralogical choice of having the treasure discovered in one's own property. P7 is a parable which cannot be told with its intended point unless the treasure be found neither in one's own field nor in the property of another. The treasure is found in free, open, or ownerless property. In fact, one would not even make this comment except when P7 is placed in comparative analysis with P1-P6 on the one hand and with P8 on the other.

Two versions of this parable are found in Graeco-Roman literature, one in Horace and another in Porphyrio. There is no substantive difference between them except that Horace's lean and economic lines do in thirteen words what Porphyrio does in sixty-one.

3.71 Horace

Satires, 2.6.1-15 opens with Horace ensconced in bucolic beatitude on his Sabine farm. He assures Mercury, god of gain, that he desires nothing more "save that thou make these blessings last my life long" (4-5). He guarantees Mercury that he at least will never utter two such foolish prayers as these. First, he will never ask to have his lands expanded just to make their shape more pleasing to the eye (8-9). Second, he will never pray,

> "O that some lucky strike would disclose to me a pot of money, like the man who, having found a treasure-trove, bought and ploughed the self-same ground he used to work on hire, enriched by favor of Hercules!"

Why exactly does Horace consider this second prayer to be "stultus" (8)? It was not that the wishful dreaming of the prayer was itself stupid since in the story it was granted. What renders the initial prayer useless is the stupidity of the servant whose imagination cannot absorb the implications of his new and god-given wealth. What Horace ironically contemplates and satirically castigates is the stupidity of one who continues to plough as owner what once he worked as servant. He never considers hiring and paying another to plough in his stead as *his* servant. His imagination is too weak for the actual transition from *mercennarius* to *mercatus*. Put proverbially, you can take the plougher out of the field but you can't take the field out of the plougher.

It must be noted, therefore, that Horace's story does not envisage a case where the servant (1) found a treasure while ploughing (2) in the field (3) of his master and (4) bought the field to obtain the treasure. This would be a most unwarranted intrusion from P8 into P7. Horace's text reads as follows:

> "O si urnam argenti fors quae mihi monstret, ut illi,
> thesauro invento qui mercennarius agrum
> illum ipsum mercatus aravit, dives amico
> Hercule!"

The correct Loeb translation cited above may be compared with this Modern Library one (Kraemer: 71; my italics):

> "If only I could accidentally find a pot of gold, like the hireling who discovered the treasure and bought and ploughed in his own right the field *where he found it*. Hercules was a good friend to him!"

This is not Horace's Latin (P7) but Matthew's Greek (P8). Such a mistranslation loses quite totally the ironic point of Horace's story and would have proved the servant's wily sagacity rather than his unchanged stupidity (Derrett: 2-3). It is clear, however, that since Horace is assuring Mercury of his own contentment and wisdom, what impresses him about the story is the foolishness of the one who cannot relax and enjoy the riches Hercules, god of treasure-trove, has bestowed upon him. He, Horace, knows when and how to say, "bene est" (4).

The story's supercilious and ironic moral claims that a peasant enriched is just an enriched peasant. This point is clear even in the summary form in which Horace records the folktale. Its heart is the lack of change from the peasant as servant to the peasant as owner.

3.72 Porphyrio

A longer version of this folktale is given much later by Porphyrio of Tyre (232-304 C.E.), a Neoplatonic philosopher, student and editor of Plotinus. This longer but still Latin version (Havthal: 321-22; Holder: 313; Morris: 222) reiterates the satirical moral even more clearly than had Horace:

> "The story is told about a certain laborer who continually implored Hercules to grant him some favor. Hercules obtained the assistance of Mercury and had him discover a hidden treasure-trove. The man dug it up, bought the field he usually labored in for pay, and proceeded to work there just like before. Thus Mercury was proved correct in what he had already told Hercules, that nothing could make such a man live at ease ("beatum vivere") since he continued to work then as always."

Horace, it can be noted, kept Mercury in the context but outside the story (5) while retaining Hercules inside it (13), and he gave no hint that the story's moral had been foretold by Mercury to Hercules, as in the longer version of Porphyrio. But, in any case, the point of both versions is exactly the same and Horace must have known some account very similar to Porphyrio's in order to explain the Mercury/Hercules combination in his text. The presence of the two gods does not change the story's moral but serves, more clearly and fully in Porphyrio than in Horace, to reiterate and reinforce the ironic point.

3.8 Parable 8: Finding Hidden Treasure and Paradox

This parable is found in Matt 13:44 and I have argued elsewhere that the story goes back to Jesus himself (Crossan, 1973:34-36).

> "The kingdom of heaven is like treasure hidden in a field, which a man found and covered up; then in his joy he goes and sells all that he has and buys that field."

Derrett (1) has noted that the "moral quality of the tale seems to be unnecessarily questionable" and that the "parable perplexes because the finder, in buying the field without revealing the presence of the treasure, has apparently taken a mean, or even dishonest, advantage of the owner of the field." Derrett's (13) own conclusion is that the finder's actions are perfectly legal: "Since the owner of the field had no rights in the treasure there was no reason whatever why he should be told of it." He interprets the situation as that of a day-laborer or servant who (1) cannot *lift* the treasure while in the landowner's employment or he would be acquiring it for his employer but (2) can leave the master's employment and then return and take the treasure for himself. Indeed, he would not even need to buy the field to do so. He is presuming, not implausibly, that later Talmudic codification gives us at least some idea of the legal principles operative at the time of Jesus.

But it is not at all clear that the Talmudic places he cites could be applied to a case of *treasure hidden on an employer's land*. The point at issue in *bBMetzia*, 10a or 12b or 118a (Daiches-Freedman) is whether "an ownerless object" [see note b(1) for *bBMetzia*, 10a] found by a laborer in the course of assigned work belongs to the laborer or to his employer. The same principles would not seem to apply at all to a case of hidden treasure found by a laborer on an employer's property. What the Rabbis were considering was whether a laborer under contract to another could legitimately take time to pick up ownerless objects for himself or whether any such serendipity accrued always to the employer.

Imagine three situations. First, an owner hides his own valuables in some emergency situation such as war or invasion. This is the case to which Solon's maxim, "Take not up what you laid not down" is applied by Plato in *Laws*, 11.913 (Bury: 2.389-90): "treasure: that which a man has laid by in store for himself and his family (he not being one of my parents), I must never pray to the gods to find, nor, if I do find it, may I move it." Since an owner will hardly sell land with such a treasure buried in it, this case is not of present interest. Second, if such a man dies and the heirs do not know of the treasure's existence, the situation is much more complicated. The legal logic ("a man has laid by in store for himself *and his family*") and moral ideal of Plato's interpretation of Solon would argue against retaining a treasure discovered in property bought from its unwitting heirs. And Jewish law would also be on their side if one can extrapolate from the discussions concerning one to three coins (!) in *bBMetzia*, 25b (Daiches-Freedman). The principle there is that the finder must announce or proclaim the find if there is any chance of its true owner correctly identifying it and legally claiming it back. This might certainly entail a complicated legal suit but the moral ideal is rendered quite clear by a version of the Treasure Judgment (P6) given as an example of the repentance of Nineveh in *Midrash Jonah* as summarized by Ginzberg (4.251):

> "A man found a treasure in the building lot he had acquired from his neighbor. Both buyer and seller refused to assume possession of the treasure. The seller insisted that the sale of the lot carried with it the sale of all it contained. The buyer held that he had bought the ground, not the treasure hidden therein. Neither rested satisfied until the judge succeeded in finding out who had hidden the treasure and who were his heirs, and the joy of the two was great when they could deliver the treasure up to its legitimate owners."

Third, the situation where either the position or the content of the treasure renders it quite impossible that anyone legitimately "owns" it any longer. In such a case one would not even have to proclaim it but could take it immediately as one's own. Note once again, one would not even have to buy the field in this last case. I presume that the cases involved in the Jewish stories (P4,P6) studied earlier all fall into this situation. Hence there can be no litigation to spoil the fuming/consuming climax to P4, and, unlike the Nineveh situation just cited where "heirs ... legitimate owners" were discoverable, it can be presumed that the dilemma of P6 arises both from this being impossible as well as from the superlative virtue of the litigants.

All of which comes down to the fact that, *pace* Derrett, the finder's action in P8 is of doubtful legality and questionable morality - if one wishes to raise such questions. Certainly, the landowner had not buried the treasure himself or he would not sell the field. But unless one gives the finder the benefit of a careful moral decision that the treasure need not be proclaimed because it could not possibly be owned by anyone, it must be admitted that his action is of doubtful legal and moral standing. And that, of course, is precisely why he *must hide* it and *buy* the field rather than simply claiming the treasure as his own discovery. Which means that the real question is why did Jesus choose this precise variation with its less than ideal morality to give as his parable? If he was not promoting doubtful morality, what necessitated this rendition as distinct from any other possible variation?

P8 is distinct from P1-P6 in that the treasure is found on another's land, and from P7 which has it discovered on open land. But only when P8 has it on another's land can it introduce a new functional element: "sold all." It is to obtain this element, I would argue, that the preliminary narralogical choice of "on another's land" was made. Thus the point of P8 "would lie in the sphere of sacrifice, or total investment, which we prefer to designate as 'total commitment'" (Kingsbury: 115). I would like, however, to qualify this conclusion and not just because "total commitment" is one of those expressions so radically trivialized by the sixties that it will have to be warmed in God's hands for a thousand years before it is again fit for human meaning.

The point of P8 pushes beyond sacrifice into mystery: "what is depicted here is not a simple, open transaction; there is something mysterious in the sale for it is only afterwards that it can be seen that the man has made a good bargain .... We are confronted not with a paranetic exhortation, 'You must sell all that you own for the sake of the kingdom', but with a hint of mystery: the strange activity of one who has found something which, in his eyes, is more valuable than all that he has. He sacrifices everything to possess what he has found" (Gerhardsson: 23).

This mystery *in* the parable reflects the much greater mystery *of* the parable. I prefer the term paradox for this, and here we return to the initial paradox of Philo in P1. Philo had noted how often the seeker does not find and the finder has not sought. Jesus' paradox is much more devastating. The kingdom of God demands *all* we have. If we take this *all* seriously, and the mystics of all the great religions have assured us that we must, it means that the kingdom of God takes from us also our narrativity and our linguisticality, in fact, it takes from us even this parable itself (Crossan, 1976).

Possibly the best way to *hear* Jesus' parable is to counterpoint it with another Jewish one, the beautiful story with which Gershom Scholem concluded his magisterial *Major Trends in Jewish Mysticism* and with which Elie Wiesel began his novel *The Gates of the Forest*:

> "When the Baal Shem had a difficult task before him, he would go to a certain place in the woods, light a fire and meditate in prayer - and what he had set out to perform was done. When a generation later the 'Maggid' of Meseritz was faced with the same task he would go to the same place in the woods and say: We can no longer light the fire, but we can still speak the prayers - and what he wanted done became reality. Again a generation later Rabbi Moshe Leib of Sassov had to perform this task. And he too went into the woods and said: We can no longer light a fire, nor do we know the secret meditations belonging to the prayer, but we do know the place in the woods to which it all belongs - and that must be sufficient; and sufficient it was. But when another generation had passed and Rabbi Israel of Rishin was called upon to perform the task, he sat down on his golden chair in his castle and said: We cannot light the fire, we cannot speak the prayers, we do not know the place, but we can tell the story of how it was done. And, the story-teller adds, the story which he told had the same effect as the actions of the other three."

When the place is lost, the fire unlit, and the prayer forgotten, there is still the story, the parable itself. But the question of Jesus is, what happens when the story too must go? *All* consumes the very parable itself. Or, as Arnold Schoenberg reminded us almost half a century ago, Israel left behind at Sinai a statue of shattered gold *and* a tablet of shattered stone.

4 Methodological Considerations

Two general methodological problems arise from the preceding narralogical comparison of stories for which chronological and/or genealogical study is of doubtful value. One concerns theme and structure, the other concerns chart and stemma.

4.1 Theme and Structure

The common *theme* of these eight parables was finding hidden treasure. But within this theme there was a striking difference in *structure* between, for example, P4, on the one hand, and P8, on the other. Leaving aside the seller's role in P4 since it has no equivalent function in P8, the sequence was from Acquiring to Finding in P4 while it was from Finding to Acquiring in P8. In this instance the common theme makes the divergent structure very evident.

But this draws attention to a much more complicated case where there is no common theme between two stories and yet they evince the same clash of structures just noted within the common treasure theme. For example, compare the following *thematic transformations* on P4 and P8 respectively.

4.11 Transformations on P4

There are five (P4/T1-T5) Rabbinical parables with the same structure as P4 but *without* any mention of hidden treasure: in *Midrash Rabbah*: Exodus, 20.5,9; Song of Songs, 4.12.1 (Freedman-Simon: 3.246, 250; 9.220); and in *Mekilta de-Rabbi Ishmael*: Exodus 14:5 (Lauterbach: 1.197-98). It can be noted that three of these stories accompany hidden treasure versions: P4/T3 and P4/T4 are with P4a (*SongR*) and P4/T5 is with P4b (*Mekilta*). Also that P4/T4 and P4/T5 are extremely similar although P4/T4 (*SongR*) attributes the parable to R. Jonathan, a third generation Tannaite around 130-160 C.E. (Strack: 114) while P4/T5 (*Mekilta*) attributes it to R. Jose the Galilean, a second generation Tannaite around 90-130 C.E. (Strack: 113). These five parables can be summarized under the rubrics of Acquiring, Working, and Finding which are the three main functions of the buyer in P4, as in Table 4:

<table>
<tr><th></th><th>The Spring
P4/T1
ExR 20.5</th><th>The Necklaces
P4/T2
ExR 20.9</th><th>The Woodworks
P4/T3
SongR 4.12.1</th><th>The Garden
P4/T4
SongR 4.12.1</th><th>The Garden
=P4/T5
Mekilta:Ex</th></tr>
<tr><td>Acquiring</td><td>field with heap of stones</td><td>heap of precious stones</td><td>thicket of cedars</td><td colspan="2">a very small field</td></tr>
<tr><td>Working</td><td>removes heap of stones</td><td>strings them into matched necklaces</td><td>makes boxes, towers, and carriages</td><td colspan="2">digs wells and plants orchards and gardens</td></tr>
<tr><td>Finding</td><td>finds running water underneath</td><td>sells them for great profit</td><td>---</td><td colspan="2">---</td></tr>
</table>

Table 4 also makes clear that these several transformations steadily close the gap between P3 (work *is* treasure) and P4 (work *finds* treasure). In P4/T1 one still finds something but it is running water rather than treasure. In P4/T2 one sells the work and makes money. And in P4/T3-T5 the work is left as its own obvious reward. But in all cases the sequence of Acquiring, Working, Finding/"Finding" is retained.

4.12 Transformations on P8

Compare this with the two transformations on P8: P8/T1 as found in Matt 13:45 and Gos Thom 76 (=94:14-18) and P8/T2 in Matt 13:47-50 and Gos Thom 8 (=81:28-82:3). These two parables, the Pearl and the Great Fish (Crossan, 1973:34-35; Quispel: 273-76) can be summarized in tabular form using the same rubrics as for P8. But note that P8/T1-T2 have no equivalent functions to the *finding in another's property* and the consequent *hiding* of P8. This is presumably why the gnostic author of Gos Thom could accept these two transformations from Jesus but had to avoid P8 itself, opting instead for a gnostic version of P4, as seen earlier. Thus, in Table 5:

	The Pearl (P8/T1)	*The Great Fish* (P8/T2)
Finding	a very valuable pearl	a very large fish
Giving Up All	sells all other goods	abandons all small fish
Acquiring	very valuable pearl	very large fish

What is the point of all this? In making comparisons of stories or parables where genealogical relationship is either non-existent or non-verifiable, equal attention must be given to thematic and to structural groupings and it will be especially important to compare in careful detail *divergent structures within the same theme*. Structural differences which might otherwise be missed across different themes become very evident within the same one. I would presume that structural groupings are far more significant in the long run than thematic ones.

4.2 Chart and Stemma

One final point on this mini-corpus of eight parables. How exactly does the mind correctly construe the point of each parable or, conversely, what is happening when we debate the meaning or meanings of such stories?

What we are actually confronted with is a temporally sequential series of *functions*, in Propp's sense of the word, which, in the simple type of stories involved here, can be fairly adequately reduced to gerunds, as in Table 6 on the next page. When this chart is read vertically, it gives the sequence of functions for each parable. Read horizontally, it emphasizes these points. First, and quite expectedly, Finding (and note "Finding" in P3) is present in all of them. Second, Working-Finding is a sequential combination in P1 through P7 but not in P8. Third, the sequence is Buying-Finding in P4,P5,P6 but Finding-Buying in P7,P8.

My suggestion is that upon hearing and as we actually hear any one of these parables we are immediately and simultaneously mapping the sequential functions unto the narralogical stemma so that in recording, quite implicitly and quite intuitively, that *this* choice was made we also record which one was thereby eliminated. It is the sum total of all such narralogical choices that constitutes this parable as this rather than some other. Such comparative techniques as charts and stemmas do no more than formalize and render consciously explicit the far swifter processes of mental scanning and storage that constitute a message's reception (Culler: 127, 141).

Table 6: Comparative Sequence of Functions in the Eight Parables

Parable 1: Serendipity	Parable 2: Providence	Parable 3: Industry	Parable 4: Indolence/ Industry	Parable 5: Ignorance/ Knowledge	Parable 6: Litigation	Parable 7: Stupidity	Parable 8: Paradox
	alms-giving						
	praying					praying	
				not-knowing			
		inheriting	inheriting	inheriting			
			not-working				
		knowing		not-knowing			
			selling	selling	selling		
			buying	buying	buying		
working	working	working	working	working	working	working	
finding	finding	finding	finding	finding	finding	finding	finding
	using		using	using			
			fuming				
					litigating		
					judging		
							hiding
							selling-all
						buying	buying
						not-using	

WORKS CONSULTED

Barthes, R.
1971 "Action Sequences." Pp. 5-14 in *Patterns of Literary Style*. Ed. J. Strelka. Yearbook of Comparative Criticism, 3. University Park & London: The Pennsylvania State University Press.

Bergson, L.
1965 *Der Griechische Alexanderroman Rezension* β. Acta Universitatis Stockholmiensis: Studia Graeca Stockholmiensia, 3. Stockholm: Almqvist & Wiksell.

Braude, W. G. & I. J. Kapstein
1975 *Pesikta de-Rab Kahana*. Philadelphia: Jewish Publication Society of America.

Bremond, C.
1966 "La logique des possibles narratifs." *Communications* 8: 60-76.

Buber, S.
1946 *Midrash Tanḥuma*. 2 vols. New York: Sefer.

Budge, E. A. W.
1889 *The History of Alexander the Great. Being the Syriac Version of the Pseudo-Callisthenes*. London: Cambridge University Press.

Bury, R. G.
1961 *Plato: Laws*. 2 vols. Loeb Classical Library. London: Heinemann.

Cerfaux, L. & G. Garitte
1957 "Les Paraboles du Royaume dans L''Évangile de Thomas.'" *Le Muséon* 70: 307-27.

Colson, F. H. & G. H. Whitaker
1962 *Philo*. 10 vols. Loeb Classical Library. London: Heinemann.

Crossan, J. D.
1973 *In Parables*. New York: Harper & Row.

1976 *Raid on the Articulate*. New York: Harper & Row.

Culler, J.
1975 "Defining Narrative Units." Pp. 123-42 in *Style and Structure in Literature*. Ed. R. Fowler. Ithaca, N.Y.: Cornell University Press.

Daiches, S. & H. Freedman
1962 *Hebrew-English Edition of the Babylonian Talmud: Baba Meẓi'a*. London: Soncino.

Daly, L. W.
1961 *Aesop Without Morals*. New York: Yoseloff.

Danby, H.
1933 *The Mishnah*. London: Oxford University Press.

Dehandschutter, B.
1971 "Les paraboles de l'Évangile selon Thomas. La Parabole du Trésor caché (log. 109)." *ETL* 47: 199-219.

Derrett, J. D. M.
1970 *Law in the New Testament*. London: Darton, Longman & Todd. Pp. 1-16 = "Law in the New Testament: The Treasure in the Field (Mt. XIII,44)." *ZNW* 54 (1963) 31-42.

Fairclough, H. R.
1955 *Horace: Satires, Epistles and Ars Poetica*. Loeb Classical Library. London: Heinemann.

Freedman, H. & M. Simon
1961 *Midrash Rabbah*: 1.Genesis 1; 3.Exodus; 4.Leviticus; 6.Deuteronomy & Lamentations; 9.Song of Songs. 10 vols. London: Soncino.

Gärtner, B.
1961 *The Theology of the Gospel of Thomas*. Trans. E. J. Sharpe. London: Collins.

Gass, W. H.
1970 *Fiction and the Figures of Life*. New York: Knopf.

Gerhardsson, B.
1972-3 "The Seven Parables in Matthew XIII." *NTS* 19: 16-37.

Ginzberg, L.
1913-28 *The Legends of the Jews*. 6 vols. Philadelphia: Jewish Publication Society of America.

Grant, R. M. & D. N. Freedman
1960 *The Secret Sayings of Jesus*. Garden City, N.Y.: Doubleday.

Guillaumont, A. *et al.*
1959 *The Gospel according to Thomas*. Leiden: Brill/ New York: Harper & Row.

Güttgemanns, E.
1973 "Einleitende Bemerkungen zur strukturalen Erzählforschung" & "Narrative Analyse synoptischer Texte." *LingBib* 23/24: 2-47 & 25/26: 50-73. ET in *Semeia* 5 (1976).

Haenchen, E.
1961 *Die Botschaft des Thomas-Evangeliums*. Theologische Bibliothek Töpelmann, 6. Berlin: Töpelmann.

Hausrath, A.
1940 *Corpus Fabularum Aesopicarum: 1.Fabulae Aesopicae Soluta Oratione Conscriptae:1*. Leipzig: Teubner.

Havthal, F.
1866 *Acronis et Porphyrionis Commentarii in Q.*

Horatium Flaccum. Vol. 2. Berlin: Springer.

Holder, A.
1967 *Pomponi Porfyrionis Commentum in Horatium Flaccum*. Hildesheim: Olms.

Hurley, G. T.
1951 "Buried Treasure Tales in America." *Western Folklore* 10: 197-216.

Kingsbury, J. D.
1969 *The Parables of Jesus in Matthew 13*. Richmond, Va.: John Knox.

Klausner, J.
1926 *Jesus of Nazareth*. Trans. H. Danby. New York: Macmillan.

Kraemer, Jr., C. J.
1936 *The Complete Works of Horace*. New York: Modern Library.

Lauterbach, J. Z.
1933-35 *Mekilta de-Rabbi Ishmael*. 3 vols. Philadelphia: Jewish Publication Society of America.

Lévi, I.
1881a "La légende d'Alexandre dans le Talmud." *Revue des Études Juives* 2: 293-300.

1881b "Les traductions hébraiques de l'histoire légendaire d'Alexandre." *REJ* 3: 238-65.

1883 "La légende d'Alexandre dans le Talmud et la Midrasch." *REJ* 7:78-93.

Montefiore, H. & H. E. W. Turner
1962 *Thomas and the Evangelists*. SBT 1/25. Naperville, Ill.: Allenson.

Morris, E. P.
1909 *Horace: The Satires*. New York: American Book Company.

Neusner, J.
1971 *The Rabbinic Traditions about the Pharisees before 70*. 3 vols. Leiden: Brill.

1972 "Types and Forms in Ancient Jewish Literature: Some Comparisons." *History of Religions* 11: 354-90.

Perry, B. E.
1952 *Aesopica. 1.Greek and Latin Texts*. Urbana, Ill.: University of Illinois Press.

Politzer, H.
1960 "Franz Kafka and Albert Camus: Parables for Our Time." *Chicago Review* 14/1 (Spring): 47-67.

1966 *Franz Kafka: Parable and Paradox*. 2nd ed. Ithaca, N.Y.: Cornell University Press [[1]1962].

Quispel, G.
1969 "Gnosis and the New Sayings of Jesus." *Eranos Jahrbuch* 38: 261-96.

Schrage, W.
1964 *Das Verhältnis des Thomas-Evangeliums zur synoptischen Tradition und zu den koptischen Evagelienübersetzungen*. BZAW 29. Berlin: Töpelmann.

Schwab, M.
n.d. *Le Talmud de Jérusalem*. 6 vols. Paris: Maisonneuve et Larose.

Simon, M.
1948 *The Babylonian Talmud: Ḳodashim, Tamid*. London: Soncino.

Strack, H.
1969 *Introduction to the Talmud and Midrash*. New York: Atheneum.

Strack, H. L. & P. Billerbeck
1922-28 *Kommentar zum Neuen Testament aus Talmud und Midrasch*. 4 vols. Munich: Beck.

Wallach, L.
1941 "Alexander the Great and the Indian Gymnosophists in Hebrew Tradition." *Proceedings of the American Academy for Jewish Research* 11: 47-83.

Wolohojian, A. M.
1969 *The Romance of Alexander the Great by Pseudo-Callisthenes*. Translated from the Armenian Version. New York: Columbia University Press.

<u>S 240</u> BY LAND AND BY SEA: A STUDY IN ACTS 13-28

Vernon K. Robbins
University of Illinois at Urbana-Champaign

The accounts of Paul's travels throughout the Mediterranean world begin in Acts 13. Prior to this chapter Paul (Saul) was present at Stephen's death (8:1), temporarily blinded and permanently converted on the road to Damascus (9:1-9), blessed and baptized by Ananias (9:17-19), and transported by night out of Damascus so the Jewish residents could not kill him (9:20-30). After some time Barnabas took Paul to Antioch where they spent a year together with the Christian community (11:25-26). When Barnabas and Paul were selected to take relief offerings to Jerusalem (11:29-30), they brought John Mark with them on their return (12:25).

Throughout all of this, Paul travels on land. In fact, in all of Lk and Acts 1-12 no one travels on the sea. In contrast to Mk and Mt where Jesus frequently travels on the Sea of Galilee, in Lk Jesus never even goes alongside the sea (παρὰ τὴν θάλασσαν).[1] On two occasions Jesus gets into a boat and goes onto or across "the lake" (ἡ λίμνη: 5:1, 2; 8:22, 23, 33). This "lake" is called Gennesaret in 5:1; never in Lk does Jesus go to or across "the Sea of Galilee." The author's choice of vocabulary indicates that he distinguishes between "the lake" and "the sea." "The lake" is a body of inland water on the eastern edge of Galilee. A person can sail across this lake (or "down" it, καταπλεύω : 8:26) to the land of the Gergesenes (or Gerasenes or Gadarenes) which lies opposite Galilee (ἀντιπέρα τῆς Γαλιλαίας : 8:26). In contrast, "the sea" is that expanse of water which can take you to Cyprus, Macedonia, Achaia, Crete, or Italy. Jesus sets a precedent for sea travel on the lake, but Jesus himself never travels or voyages on the sea. Even Peter and John are never portrayed as travelling on the sea. Only Paul and his associates face the challenge, adventure, and destiny of voyaging across the sea.

Sea travel appears for the first time in Acts 13. Paul and his company sail from Seleucia to the island of Cyprus, then from Cyprus to Pamphylia (13:4, 13). This sea travel holds little adventure or danger. Only two short clauses relate the means of travel; all the narrated episodes occur on land. Two more short clauses recount sea transportation in this section of Acts. Paul and Barnabas are taken back to Syrian Antioch in a boat (14:26), and Barnabas and John Mark go to Cyprus in a boat after the disagreement with Paul (15:39). Still, however, no detailed sea voyage occurs. Only in chapter 16 do extended sea voyages begin, and when they occur, the narration moves into first person plural "we."

The coincidence of sea voyages and first person plural narration in Acts is striking. There are four we-sections in Acts: 16:10-17; 20:5-15; 21:1-18; 27:1-28:16. In each instance, a sea voyage begins as the first person plural narration emerges. A survey of literature in Mediterranean antiquity indicates a strong propensity toward first person plural narration in sea voyage accounts.[2] The <u>Odyssey</u> of Homer was a major influence. As the author stages Odysseus recounting his voyage from Troy to Phaeacia in <u>Odyssey</u> 9-12, first person plural narration firmly establishes itself within the speech pattern. Because this technique was used in the primary epic literature of the Classical world, it pervaded much Hellenistic and Roman literature.[3] In the tradition of the sea manuals (οἱ περίπλοι), the most poignant example of first person plural narration is in the _Voyage of Hanno the Carthaginian_. This Punic document, which was translated into Greek between 350-125 B.C., shifts from third person to first person plural narration at the beginning of the sea voyage just like the accounts in Acts.[4] The most famous Semitic voyages do not use first person plural narrative style. Neither the biblical accounts of Noah nor Jonah use this technique. The influence appears to lie firmly in the Classical, Hellenistic, and Roman literary milieu.[5]

The author of Luke-Acts employs the sea voyage genre with great skill. His narrative builds toward a conclusion which is reached through a dramatic sea voyage. First plural narrative style is a feature of the sea voyage genre. This style emerges in the sections which present "mission by sea." There is evidence to suggest that Paul's voyages across the sea were in view during the composition of the first volume of the work. To explain the role of the sea voyages which contain first plural narration, we will approach them from three angles. First, the primary features of the sea voyage genre will be explored, and the we-passages will be examined for the presence of these features. Second, the position of the we-passages in the structure of Acts will be investigated. Third, we will posit a conclusion regarding the function of the we-passages in the purpose of Luke-Acts.

The We-Passages as Sea Voyage Literature

The sea voyage literature in Mediterranean antiquity contains basic features which make it possible to speak of a sea voyage genre.[6] These features arise out of the dynamics of sailing on the sea, landing in unfamiliar places, and hoping to establish an amiable relationship with the people in the area where the landing occurs.[7] During the short stay on land before resuming the voyage, two kinds of episodes are especially frequent. First, an event often occurs in which some people of the area are friendly toward the voyagers. This event usually leads to an invitation to stay at someone's home.[8] The voyagers seldom remain neutral visitors in a locale where they land. Thus, a second event will divide the people of the area over whether or not these voyagers are to be trusted. Usually the leader of the voyage will become involved in a major episode in which his extraordinary abilities are displayed. Often he will speak eloquently and perform some unusual feat.[9] If the voyagers are not driven forcibly from the place where they have landed, an emotional farewell scene occurs in which the people bring provisions and other gifts to the boat.[10]

A sea voyage account often opens with a statement regarding the purpose of the voyage, a comment about preparations for it, and a list of some of the participants in it.[11] When the voyage is under way, there is an account of the places by which the voyagers sail, and frequently short descriptive comments are given about the places. Also, the length of time it takes to sail from one place to another usually is indicated, and frequently the span of time is linked with the direction and force of the wind.[12] Gods are portrayed as determining the fate of the voyage. Visits of the gods, and signs and portents, frequently attend the voyage. In response, prayers are offered, altars are built, and sacred rituals are enacted.[13] At some point, almost every good sea voyage account portrays a storm which threatens or actually ends in a shipwreck.[14]

Virtually all of the features of ancient sea voyage literature are present in the we-passages in Acts. The first we-section, 16:10-17, begins in response to a vision which occurs during the night. In this vision a Macedonian says to Paul, "Come over to Macedonia and help us" (16:9). The narrator interprets this summons to mean that God is calling them to this area to preach the gospel (16:10). The success of this venture is assured by divine destiny no matter what obstacles threaten to undo it. Especially the sea voyages of Odysseus and Aeneas established visions, signs, and portents as a characteristic feature of this kind of literature. The first we-section emerges in the narrative of Acts with a dynamic which is well known in Mediterranean sea voyage literature.

As first person plural narration begins and the boat is launched for Macedonia, the narrator recounts the places by which they sail and the time it takes to sail the distance (16:11-12). This is the first instance of a detailed account of a voyage in Acts, and it includes a comment about the prestige and role of Philippi--a typical feature in a sea voyage account. The narration of the voyage ends with the statement: "We remained in this city some days." This is a customary clause at the end of a paragraph in a voyage manual.[15]

Once they land at Philippi, a series of events occur which lead to the imprisonment and spectacular release of Paul and Silas. Only the first two events are narrated in first person plural. In the first event (16:13-15) the voyagers meet some women and begin to talk to them. A woman named Lydia "opens her heart" so that she invites them to come to her house and stay. This scene is a typical component of voyage narratives, and it contains first plural narrative style.

The second event (16:16-18) begins with first person plural narration, but makes a transition to third person narration in 16:17. This event has a dynamic which is often present in sea voyage accounts. Paul performs an extraordinary act of power, and this act causes a disturbance among the local people. In this instance, Paul drives a spirit of divination out of a slave girl who brings money to her owners by soothsaying. As the episode develops into a detailed event in the city, first plural narration is left behind. With the re-emergence of third person narrative style, the events move from the sea to "the land." The next series of events does not conclude with a return to the boat; Paul and his company travel to Amphipolis, Apollonia, and Thessalonica on foot (17:1).

The transition from first plural to third person narration is achieved through the phrase "Paul and us" (16:10). This phrase is a signal to the reader that the events lead away from the boat to the land and its challenges. The same technique appears at the end of the third we-passage (21:18). At the end of the final we-passage, the transition is made by indicating that Paul was permitted to remain "by himself" with only the soldier guarding him (28:16). In all three instances the transition takes the events away from the sea; third person narration centers on Paul's influential activity on land.

The second we-section, 20:5-15, is the first half of a sea voyage to Jerusalem. First person plural narration emerges at the conclusion of a list of people who accompany Paul on the voyage (20:4). As in the first we-section, the voyage opens with a detailed account of the places to which they sailed and the duration of time. This introduction ends with the comment that they stayed in Troas for seven days (20:5-6). Again, first person plural narration begins as a boat is launched on the sea, and the opening verses are a typical beginning for a sea voyage account.

An event is recounted at Troas before the voyage continues, and it is narrated in first plural style (20:7-12). The episode begins as a farewell scene (20:7), but it ends as a spectacular event performed by Paul. When Paul's speech lasts far into the night, and a young man falls out of a third story window and is dead, Paul embraces him and revives him. This miraculous event is placed on the first day of the week, and Paul appears to "break bread" both before and after he brings the young man back to life. This setting for the event is not interpreted by the narrator, but it creates a context similar to the one created by the vision at the outset of the first voyage. This voyage is in the hands of God. Paul carefully follows the religious rites of the Christian community, and the power of God works through him. The reader knows (19:21) that Paul is headed for Jerusalem, and the reader also knows what happened to Jesus at Jerusalem. As the danger of taking this voyage to Jerusalem becomes prominent in the narrative, the will of God for Paul to go to Rome (19:21) becomes increasingly important. If Paul truly is an apostle through God's will, then he will fulfill the proper religious rites and receive the benefits of God's favor. For a person in the Hellenistic world, this feature is a natural part of a sea voyage account. It was the will of Zeus/Jupiter that both Odysseus and Aeneas complete their voyages without suffering death. All the delays, hardships, and apparent reversals of the decision are overcome by the rituals the voyagers perform and the destiny the supreme gods refuse to alter.

The final part of the second we-section (20:13-16) contains a typical detailed account of sailing from place to place and meeting people to take them on board. It ends by thematizing the purpose of the voyage: Paul "was hastening to be at Jerusalem, if possible, on the day of Pentecost" (20:16). At this point there is an interlude in the voyage. They have sailed as far as Miletus, and Paul summons the elders of the church at Ephesus to come to him there. This event features Paul giving a speech, and third person narration is used to recount Paul's meeting with these church leaders (20:17-38).

The third we-section begins as soon as the Ephesian elders bring Paul back to the ship. The parting scene depicts them kneeling in prayer and bidding Paul farewell with weeping, embracing, and kissing. As the first person plural narration resumes, again there is a detailed account of the voyage which ends with a remark about the length of their stay in the city where they landed (21:1-4). This opening part reiterates the purpose of the voyage as the disciples tell Paul not to go on to Jerusalem.

The next two verses contain another typical parting scene. All the disciples, with their wives and children, accompany the voyagers to the beach, pray with them, and bid them farewell (21:5-6). After this, typical voyage narration occurs until they reach Caesarea (21:7-8). At Caesarea a prophet enacts a scene which foretells Paul's arrest and delivery to the Gentiles when he reaches Jerusalem (21:8-14). In the sphere of literature in the Hellenistic world, this scene is like Odysseus' encounter with the prophet Teiresias in _Odyssey_ 11.90-137. Both the reader and the protagonist in the story know the dangers that lie ahead and the outcome. For the moment, however, Paul forgets that "he must go to Rome" (19:21). He is ready "not only to be imprisoned but even to die at Jerusalem" (21:13). The destination at Jerusalem is the sole concern of the voyage, and scenes which are typical components of sea voyage literature are used to emphasize the danger that lurks at the end of the voyage.[16]

The final verses of the third we-section describe the trek from Caesarea to Jerusalem (21:15-18). Since the destination of the sea voyage is Jerusalem, first person plural narration continues until Paul goes in to James and the elders (21:18). At this point the events are committed to land, and the narration moves back to third person style. As the first we-section stopped once Paul and his company began the activity which brought them before the leaders of the city (16:17), so the second and third we-sections stop once Paul and his company begin the consultation with James and the elders at Jerusalem. The trials which ensue are Paul's mission on land once he has voyaged to this area.

The fourth we-section, 27:1-28:16, presents the final, climactic sea voyage of Paul and his company. There is a dramatic progression in the length and drama of the we-sections in Acts. The first we-section is brief (16:10-17), and it takes Paul and his associates on a straight sailing course from Troas to Philippi (16:11). The drama of the voyage arises from the vision at the outset, the invitation to stay at Lydia's house, and the encounter with the slave girl who has a spirit of divination. The second and third we-sections are longer (20:5-15; 21:1-18), and they take Paul and his company on an episodic, tearful voyage which systematically moves to Jerusalem. The drama of the voyage emerges through the farewell speech which develops into a miraculous event when Paul revives a young man (20:7-12), the farewell speech and scene with the Ephesian elders at Miletus (20:17-38), the farewell scene at Tyre (21:5-6), and the prophetic enactment at Caesarea of Paul's imprisonment and delivery to the Gentiles (21:8-14). The fourth we-section is longer yet, and more dramatic.

As Paul is taken to the boat to sail for Rome, first plural narrative again emerges in Acts (27:1). The opening part contains the typical information about sailing from port to port, and passing islands and other places (27:1-8). Beginning with 27:4, the narrator introduces the dynamic which furnishes the drama for this voyage. The wind is against them, and the sailing becomes more and more difficult. The second part of the section thematizes the danger which is increasing and features Paul in conversation with the people in charge about their plight (27:9-12). Paul's advice that the voyage temporarily be aborted is overruled by a majority of the people on the boat. The narration of the increasing danger impels the action to the next part with skill. The wind grows into the fury of a storm, and the detailed portrayal of the inability to control the ship, the necessity of throwing the cargo overboard, and the absence of sun and stars for many days takes the reader to the heart of sea voyage narratives (21:13-20). Paul knows the divine destiny of the voyage which includes storm and shipwreck, just as Odysseus knows what will happen when the Sirens, Scylla and Charybdis threaten to kill every mortal on board including himself (*Odyssey* 12.35-126). Therefore, Paul tells them they should have listened to him, and he tells them what the outcome of this storm will be (27: 21-26). As Paul predicts, the ship runs aground as the crew attempts to beach it, and everyone is forced to abandon ship and escape to the island of Malta (27:27-44). The detailed description of the maneuvering of the ship by the sailors, the sounding for fathoms, the casting of anchors, and the manning of ropes and sails ranks this account among the most exciting depictions of storms and shipwrecks in the sphere of Greek and Roman literature. In the midst of it Paul takes bread, gives thanks to God, breaks it in the presence of all, and begins to eat (27:35). As all the members of the ship eat, the sacred ritual for receiving God's favor is performed. Everyone escapes safely to land, in spite of plans by the crew to abandon the ship (27:30) and intentions by the soldiers to kill the prisoners (27:42). Divine destiny holds the controlling hand when storm and shipwreck dash ships and mortals back and forth upon the sea.

The storm and shipwreck take the voyagers to the island of Malta. The opening scene portrays the islanders as unusually friendly (28:1-6), and the islanders become even more kindly disposed before the voyagers depart. When a viper bites Paul and he does not fall down dead, the islanders perceive Paul as every bit as godlike as Odysseus or Aeneas (28:6). The warm relationship between the islanders and Paul grows even more when Paul heals the father of the chief man of the island. Not only does the chief man receive them and entertain them for three days, but the scene develops into a general healing episode after which the islanders bid them farewell by bringing gifts and provisions to the boat (28:7-10). These events on the island are narrated in typical sea voyage style. All detail is suppressed except the information that highlights the welcome to the island, the spectacular abilities of the protagonist on the voyage, and the farewell scene.

The final part of the voyage contains the customary sailing information as the boat proceeds from Malta to Rome (28:11-16). Details about putting in at ports and staying for a few days are included; the favorable winds and the warm receptions at the harbors also receive attention. As the boat lands, Paul offers the proper prayer to God and takes courage that the voyage has concluded with God's favor still upon him (28:15). The voyage is ended, and third person narration emerges once again as Paul turns toward his new mission on land (28:18).

The final we-section in Acts represents the sea voyage genre _par excellence_. Each time a we-section begins the drama heightens; movement through space becomes a voyage across the sea. The final voyage takes the gospel to ports and islands far away, and the adventure, danger, and fear bring "Paul and us" to Rome with thanksgiving.

The We-Passages in the Structure of Luke-Acts

If the dynamic of sea voyaging is crucial for understanding the we-sections in Acts, the place of the passages in the arrangement of this two volume work is as important. There are two perspectives from which the arrangement is important for interpretation. First, the we-sections occur in the last half of Acts. Comparison of Lk with Acts indicates that both volumes contain a long travel narrative which leads into the concluding scenes. This feature suggests that the volumes contain some type of parallel structure. Second, the portion of Acts in which the we-sections occur represents the last fourth of this two volume narrative. In this final segment, Paul's travels spread the gospel "to the end of the earth" (1:8; 13:47). It will be important to discover the techniques by which the author has brought the entire narrative to its dramatic conclusion. The first aspect of the arrangement will be discussed here; the second aspect will be discussed in the next section.

The we-sections occur in a portion of Acts which shows significant points of relation with Lk. The journey narrative in Lk 9:51-19:28 is a distinctive feature of the Lukan narrative,[17] and the journeys of Paul in Acts 13:1-28:16 comprise the highpoint of the narrative of Acts. In general terms, Jesus' journey in Lk corresponds to Paul's journeys in Acts. The journeys reflect the movement through time and space which is a central feature of Luke-Acts.

Closer observation reveals that specific architectonic parallels exist between the journeys in Lk and Acts.[18] There are three sections in Acts which correspond to three sections in the Lukan travel narrative. Paul's mission to the churches in Asia Minor, Macedonia, and Greece (Acts 13:1-19:20) corresponds to the mission of the seventy (Lk 10:1-24).[19] Paul's journey to Jerusalem (Acts 19:21-21:26) corresponds to Jesus' journey to Jerusalem (Lk 13:22-19:46). Agrippa's handing over of Paul to a centurion to be escorted to Rome (Acts 27:1-28:16) corresponds to Pilate's handing over of Jesus to the chief priests, the rulers, and the people to be crucified (Lk 23:26-49). Because of these correspondences, this study could include detailed analysis of Lk as well as Acts. Our immediate goal, however, is to interpret the role of the we-sections in the overall setting of Paul's journeys. Therefore, having noticed this parallel architectonic structure, we will proceed with analysis in Acts only. In the next section, more features of Lk will come into the discussion.

All three sections of Paul's journeys contain we-passages, and the length of the we-sections increases as the end of the narrative draws near. The first journey section (13:1-19:20) only contains eight verses of first plural narration (16:10-17). The second journey section (19:21-21:26) contains twenty-nine verses of first plural narrative style, and the third journey section (27:1-28:16) is entirely a we-section (60 verses). Of course, the increasing amount of first plural narration is linked with the increasing amount of sea travel. The increasing length of sea voyage material affects the structure of Acts 13-28.

Perhaps the most striking aspect of the structure in the journey sections is the chiastic arrangement which unifies the first and second sections. The second half of the first section (15:1-19:20) and the second section (19:21-21:26) represent a generally balanced chiastic structure.[20] The perimeters of the chiasmus are the Jerusalem council in 15:1-33 and Paul's return visit to Jerusalem in 21:15-26. The inside of the chiasmus is filled out by three balancing units and a series of episodes at the center. The travel and imprisonment in 15:36-17:15 is balanced by the travel and prophecy of arrest and imprisonment in 21:1-14. The speech at Athens in 17:16-24 is balanced by the speech at Ephesus in 20:17-38. The assembly at Corinth and subsequent travel in 18:1-23 is balanced by the assembly at Ephesus and subsequent travel in 19:21-20:16. The center of the chiastic structure is found in 18:24-19:20. This, therefore, is the chiastic outline:

A	15:1-34 Jerusalem council	A'	21:15-26 Report to Jerusalem Leaders
B	15:36-17:15 Travel and Imprisonment	B'	21:1-14 Travel and Scene of Binding
C	17:16-24 Speech at Athens	C'	20:17-38 Speech at Ephesus
D	18:1-23 Assembly at Corinth and Travel	D'	19:21-20:16 Assembly at Ephesus and Travel

E 18:24-19:20 Spreading the Gospel Throughout Asia from Ephesus

The center of a chiastic structure, in relation to the outside portions, reveals the essential dynamic of the literary arrangement.[21] Events at Ephesus where Paul corrects inadequate or improper understanding of the gospel stand at the center. Paul's encounters with the authoritative leaders at Jerusalem stand on the perimeters of the structure. The literary arrangement presents an interplay between Jerusalem and Ephesus as centers for spreading the gospel. Ephesus is the center for preaching the gospel to all residents of Asia, both Jews and Greeks (19:10). This assertion stands at the heart of the Ephesus events. Jerusalem is the locale from which Paul's mission to Jews and Gentiles is authorized. Ironically, Paul's mission to Rome also issues from Jerusalem.

The relation of the we-passages to the chiastic arrangement introduces another dimension of this portion of Acts. There are no we-passages in the first half of the initial travel section (13:1-14:28), and this part of the first section is not a segment of the chiasmus. In other words, all of the we-sections except for the final dramatic voyage are included in the material which has been given a chiastic structure. This means that only with the chiasmus is mission "by land" and "by sea" emphasized.

With regard to structure, therefore, the initial travel section (13:1-19:20) has two halves. The Jerusalem council (Acts 15) stands between the first and second half. The first half portrays Paul establishing and nurturing churches in Galatia and Cyprus. This mission is inaugurated by the Holy Spirit who says, "Set apart for me Barnabas and Saul for the work to which I have called them."[22] After the prophets and teachers at Antioch fast and pray, they lay their hands on Barnabas and Saul and send them off (13:2-3). The Barnabas and Saul mission occurs in 13:1-14:28. This mission does not have the blessings of the Jerusalem leaders, and it does not take Paul "to the other side of the sea." Travel by boat is included in this first half (13:4, 13; 14:26), and "Saul" becomes "Paul" after he has "sailed" to Cyprus (13:9). Paul and Barnabas travel by boat, but their mission occurs prior to the Jerusalem council and is limited to the easternmost portion of the Mediterranean Sea.

With the Jerusalem council (15:1-35) a new phase enters into Paul's mission activity. He no longer travels with Barnabas, and his mission is not limited to the environs of the eastern portion of the Mediterranean. Beginning with the Jerusalem council, the material is balanced chiastically, and after this council there is an interplay of mission "by land" and "by sea."

Paul's authoritative mission "by land" begins in Acts 15:36. Severing his relation with Barnabas, Paul chooses Silas and establishes a valid mission to the churches in Syria and Cilicia by delivering to them "the decisions which had been reached by the apostles and elders who were at Jerusalem" (16:4). But Paul does not stop with this; his mission by land is on the move in a way it could not be before the Jerusalem council. Paul and Silas travel through Phrygia and Galatia and would appear to have "a clear road ahead." But then the mission by land is temporarily hindered. The Holy Spirit will not allow Paul and Silas to speak the word in Asia, so they are forced to go down to Troas (16:6-7).

The apparent hindrance to Paul's mission by land inaugurates a new phase: mission "by sea." The first we-section introduces this phase (16:10-17). In contrast to the previous sea travel by Paul (13:4, 13; 14:26), now the destination lies "on the other side" of the sea. In a night vision a man of Macedonia says to Paul, "Come over to Macedonia and help us" (16:9). In response the first true sea voyage is launched, first plural narration emerges, and a new mission area opens to Paul and Silas.

Once Paul and Silas have reached Macedonia, their mission spreads "by land" (16:19-17:13). When Paul goes to another new area, Achaia,[23] again he goes "by sea" (17:14-15). The effort of the author to assert this mode of opening the mission at Athens has created an unusual grammatical construction in 17:14. The verse states that the brethren at Beroea sent Paul out "to go as far as upon the sea" (πορεύεσθαι ἕως ἐπὶ τὴν θάλασσαν). The peculiarity of ἕως and ἐπί in sequence caused copyists either to omit ἕως or replace it with ὡς.[24] The problem evidently arises because Beroea is not a coastal city, and the author wanted to indicate that Paul went to Athens "by sea." The meaning is clear, because the verse is constructed in parallel with 17:15a: οἱ δὲ καθιστάντες τὸν Παῦλον ἤγαγον ἕως Ἀθηνῶν ("those who conducted Paul brought him as far as Athens"). In like manner, the brethren at Beroea sent Paul out to go (by land) as far as "upon the sea." The narrator distinguishes between spreading the gospel "by land" and "by sea." The gospel spreads to new areas, e.g. Macedonia and Achaia, "by sea." Once Paul and his company arrive at a new area, the gospel spreads "by land." Later in the narrative, Paul travels "by land" between Achaia and Macedonia (20:2), but the initial mission is "by sea."

The irony of the chiastic structure is that mission "by sea" to Macedonia is balanced with mission "by sea" to Jerusalem. It would be wrong to think this is accidental. The sea voyage which takes Paul and Silas to Philippi where they are imprisoned and miraculously released (16:10-40) is balanced by the sea voyage which takes Paul to Caesarea where the prophet Agabus symbolically enacts the binding of Paul and his delivery to the Gentiles (21:1-14). Both voyages are we-sections, and Paul's voyage to Jerusalem is mission "by sea." Prior to this Paul has not had an opportunity to spread the gospel in Jerusalem. This area was closed to him. Now he goes to Jerusalem "ready not only to be imprisoned but even to die at Jerusalem for the name of the Lord Jesus" (21:13). His voyage to Jerusalem opens up an extensive mission "by land" from Jerusalem to Caesarea. Paul spreads the gospel not only to the people in Jerusalem (22:1-21) but also to the Sanhedrin in Jerusalem (23:1-10), the governor Felix in Caesarea (24:10-21), and to King Agrippa (26:1-29). Mission by sea has taken Paul not only to Macedonia and Achaia; it has taken Paul to Jerusalem itself and the political leaders who rule the area. Counterbalanced we-sections open both areas of mission to Paul "by sea."

As Paul's mission by sea to Macedonia provides the base for mission by sea to Jerusalem, so Paul's mission by sea to Jerusalem provides the base for mission by sea to Rome. All three missions are by sea, and all three missions are inaugurated by we-sections. The long, dramatic voyage to Rome (27:1-28:16) stands in notable contrast with the circumscribed beginnings of Paul's mission in the easternmost part of the Mediterranean Sea (13:1-14:28). On the way to Rome Paul even has a mission "upon the sea." When the voyage becomes dangerous, Paul begins conversation with the people in charge (27:10), and when a storm begins to hurl them mercilessly about on the sea, Paul has the opportunity to tell the people on the ship about the God to whom he belongs and whom he worships (27:21-26). The foreknowledge of events which he receives from an angel of his God not only proves to be accurate, but it provides the opportunity for Paul to take bread, give thanks to God in the presence of all, and eat (27:35). And, says the narrator, "they all were encouraged and ate some food themselves" (27:36). This imagery will certainly not be missed by the reader; Paul has "broken bread" with the entire group on the ship. But this still is not enough. Paul's mission on the sea is made complete by miracles which attend his leadership.[25] When he sustains a viper bite, the natives on the island of Malta think he is a god (28:3-7); and when Paul heals the father of the chief man, Publius, all the diseased come to him and are cured (28:7-10). This mission "upon the sea" takes Paul to Rome. The remaining part of Acts presents Paul's mission by land in and around Rome.

The we-sections play a decisive role in the section in Acts which narrates the journeys of Paul. These sections add mission by sea to mission by land. By careful structuring throughout chapters 13-28, the author includes sections of sea voyage material which open new areas until the gospel spreads "to the end of the earth." By composing the journeys in three sections (13:1-19:20; 19:21-21:26; 27:1-28:16), the author develops a linear schemat which portrays the spreading of the gospel from the land east of the Mediterranean to Italy. By a chiastic arrangement of the episodes from the Jerusalem council to Paul's return to Jerusalem (15:1-21:26), the author counterbalances the mission "to Macedonia and Achaia" with the mission "to Jerusalem and its environs." The first person plural sea voyages furnish the dynamic for the movement through space, and the careful structuring of the episodes relates Paul's mission to Jerusalem and Rome.

The Function of the We-Passages in Luke-Acts

Analysis of the structure of Acts 13-28 indicates that the author uses the we-sections to create a special role for mission by sea. In this section of the paper the analysis moves a step further. Three aggregates of information suggest that the entire two volume work is designed to replace the Sea of Galilee, which dominates Mk, with the Mediterranean Sea. The we-passages systematically increase in length to focus all attention on the Great Sea which lies between Jerusalem and Rome. We recall that Paul's journeys in Acts 13:1-28:16 correspond to the long journey of Jesus in Lk 9:51-19:46. This suggests that the travel sections in Acts were designed to bring Lukan themes and actions to a dramatic conclusion. Our interest is to find any relationship between Lk and Acts which illumines the role of the we-passages.

The first items of importance are found in the vocabulary of Lk and Acts. The author never allows Jesus to go alongside or onto a "sea" (θάλασσα) in Lk. This stands in notable contrast to Mt and Mk where Jesus does both many times.[26] This difference arises, because the Sea of Galilee is never mentioned in Lk; it does not seem to exist in Lukan geography. Instead, there is a place on the eastern edge of Galilee which the author calls "the lake" (ἡ λίμνη: Lk 5:1, 2; 8:22, 23, 33). Once this lake is called the Lake of Gennesaret (5:1).

The existence of "the lake" but not "the sea" in Lk appears to relate to the overall purpose of the author. It is designed to limit Jesus' activity in a particular way. Jesus is allowed to go to the lake only twice in Lk. All other occasions when Jesus went to the Sea of Galilee in Mk are omitted. On the first occasion, Jesus goes out in a boat with Simon, and James and John, the sons of Zebedee (5:1-11). The entire episode moves toward the conclusion in which the three fishermen become disciples of Jesus and turn to "catching men" (5:10-11). On the second occasion, Jesus gets in a boat and sails to the other side of the lake (8:22). This setting allows for the inclusion of the accounts of the calming of the storm and the healing of the demoniac in the country of the Gerasenes (8:22-39).

Each of the occasions when Jesus is linked with the lake in Lk has a twofold dimension in Luke-Acts. On the one hand, the occasions set a precedent for later action in the narrative. When Jesus goes onto the lake in 5:1-11, circles around, and comes back, he evokes the image of the disciple as one who travels on water and fishes for men. It appears to be important that he does not go "across" the lake. This episode sets a precedent which corresponds to the situation in Acts 13:1-14:28. We recall that this section in Acts presents the first instance of sea travel. The Holy Spirit calls Barnabas and Saul to "the work" to which they have been called (13:2), and they sail out from Antioch in a circle to Cyprus, then to Pamphylia, and back to Antioch (13:4, 13; 14:26). When Paul and Barnabas return, they are sent to Jerusalem where they are sanctioned as apostles to the Gentiles (15:23-29). Paul and Barnabas have travelled on the sea; therefore they "have risked their lives for the sake of our Lord Jesus Christ" (15:26). Paul has been called to his work as the disciples are called to their work in Lk 5:1-11. But Paul does not go "across" the sea until after the Jerusalem council.

In Lk 8:22-39 Jesus sets the precedent for "crossing over" the sea which occurs for the first time in the initial we-section (Acts 16:10-17). In the Lukan episode, Jesus gets into the boat and announces, "Let us go across to the other side of the lake" (8:22). This corresponds to the Macedonian's call to Paul, "Come over to Macedonia and help us" (Acts 16:9). With the voyage across the body of water, God's work is spread to Gentile territory. The author of Lk revises Markan vocabulary in the account of the storm on the lake to orient the story toward the climactic voyage and storm in which Paul participates at the end of Acts. Jesus and the disciples "set out from shore" (ἀνήχθησαν: Lk 8:22), just as Paul and his company "set out" on a boat many times.[27] As they are "sailing along" (πλεόντων αὐτῶν: Lk 8:23), Jesus falls asleep. References to sailing are frequent in the voyages of Paul.[28] The revision of Markan vocabulary suggests that the author already has the sea voyages of Paul in view as he composes.

The other dimension of these two episodes in Lk has already been mentioned. But it must be recalled as we move to the next feature of Lukan composition. The author suppresses any reference to "the sea" in episodes with Jesus and the disciples. Only Paul and his company voyage on the sea. In the first episode not only Jesus but Simon Peter is in the boat. But Peter never voyages on the sea in Luke-Acts; he was called to his work by sailing in a boat on "the lake" (Lk 5:1, 2). Likewise, the author suppresses any reference to "the sea" in the storm episode. Instead of saying the wind and the sea obey Jesus (Mk 4:41), the disciples refer to the winds and "the water" (Lk 8:25).

The selection of vocabulary in the first volume suggests that the author is setting precedents during the time of Jesus which become the major challenge during the time of the church. In order to do this, the author presents corresponding episodes in Lk and Acts, and he suppresses certain features in the account in Lk so these features can be more dramatically carried out during the time of the church.[29]

This vocabulary usage grows in importance when other information is added to it. Although the author never depicts Jesus on or alongside a "sea," he betrays special interest in "the sea" in sayings of Jesus. He does not refrain from including the saying about being cast into the sea with a millstone around one's neck (Lk 17:2) and the saying about the sycamine tree that can be rooted up and planted in the sea by faith (Lk 17:6). Lk is the only gospel which refers to the "distress of nations in perplexity at the roaring of the sea and the waves" in the apocalyptic discourse (Lk 21:25). The sea has a special place in his theology even in the gospel of Lk, but the author will not link Jesus directly with it. The sea is linked with Paul's mission to the Gentiles. This conception is further indicated by the references to God "who made the heaven and earth <u>and the sea</u>" in Acts 4:24 and 14:25. Also it is probably not accidental that Simon Peter is associated with "Simon a tanner, whose house is by the sea" in the dramatic sequence of episodes in which the Gentile Cornelius is converted and blessed by Simon Peter (10:6, 32). The sea is linked with mission to the Gentiles, and the author systematically builds toward mission by sea in Lk and Acts 1-12.

Perhaps the most important piece of information which indicates that the author is composing toward a dramatic finish which is achieved through sea voyages is "the great omission" in Lk.[30] Lk shows dependence upon Mk as a source for most of the material in Mk 1-6:44. But beginning with Mk 6:45 through Mk 8:26, this Markan material is not recounted in Lk. The proposal in this paper is that the manuscript of Mk which the author of Luke-Acts used contained Mk 6:45-8:26. He omitted this section of Mk because it took the ministry of Jesus too far into the type of mission which he wanted to portray for Paul.

As Lk used the material in Mk 1-6:44 he systematically omitted references to the sea.[31] As we have just previously noticed, Lk places the call of the disciples (Mk 1:16-20) and the stilling of the storm and healing of the Gerasene demoniac (Mk 5:1-20) on "the lake." In this way, he avoids reference to the sea. But when he gets to Mk 6:45 the mission of Jesus develops into a mission all around the Sea of Galilee and deep into Gentile territory.[32] Precisely with the episode where Jesus walks on the sea (Mk 6:45-52) the author begins to omit all of the material. After this episode, Jesus and his disciples cross the sea again (Mk 6:53-56), a rationale for

Gentile mission is established (Mk 7:1-23), then Jesus travels through Tyre and Sidon (7:24-37). Since the boat and the sea continue to play an important role through 8:21, the author of Lk omits all the episodes in the section from the walking on the sea (Mk 6:45-52) until the confession of Peter in 8:27-33. By omitting this material, the author narrates an uninterrupted ministry of Jesus in Galilee without excursions into Tyre and Sidon and other Gentile territory. Also, the author keeps Jesus out of a boat and off of a body of water that may begin to play a major role in the ministry of Jesus.

In sum, the vocabulary of Lk, the two episodes where Jesus goes onto the lake, and the great omission indicate that the two volume work of Luke-Acts has been designed to replace the Sea of Galilee with the Mediterranean Sea. The role of the we-passages is to orient early Christianity toward the sea which lies between Jerusalem and Rome. The author disapproves of the emphasis upon the Sea of Galilee in Mk. No inland body of water in Palestine should be called "the sea." The sea which explains the history of early Christianity is the Great Sea which extends to the end of the earth.

Conclusion

Why, then, does the author use first plural "we" as he narrates those voyages which move the Christian church "across the sea"? First, it appears that the natural tendency to employ first person plural style within the sea voyage genre was a major factor. The second reason appears in the prologue. As the author, a member of the church, pens his narrative sitting in Rome, the question is how "we" got here when we started out in Jerusalem. This author feels a strong sense of union with the early Christian leaders about whom he writes. He says that all of the things about which he writes have been accomplished "among us" (Lk 1:1). This includes all of the events he recounts in the gospel of Lk as well as the narrative of Acts. For him, the conception and birth of John the Baptist (Lk 1:5-80) is an example of an event which happened "among us." The author participates in these events even when they are transmitted to him by others (Lk 1:2). Therefore he can say both that these things happened among us and that they were delivered to us. As he sits in Rome, he participates in the events of the Christian church, and explains to "Theophilus" how his community of believers got to be where they are (Lk 1:3-4). A Christian in Rome who knows the events well enough to pen them as this author does becomes a full participant in them. This is true even if he has experienced these events only through oral transmission and the written page. Thus he can say in his prologue that the activities of Jesus, the disciples, and the apostles happened "among us." As Paul voyaged across the sea, "we" got here.

If the author felt such a close relation to all of the events he wrote about, why didn't he use first person plural all the way through? Why did he use it only in the we-sections? He didn't use first person plural only in the we-sections. He used it in the two settings where it is eminently appropriate if the author construes his work in the genre of historiography or historical biography in the Hellenistic milieu toward the end of the first century A.D. These two settings are prologues and sea voyages.

NOTES

1. θάλασσα occurs 18 times in Mk, 17 times in Mt, and 3 times in Lk. Each of the occurrences in Lk is in a saying rather than narration: Lk 17:2, 6; 21:25.

2. Vernon K. Robbins, "The We-Passages in Acts and Ancient Sea Voyages," BR 20 (1975) 5-18.

3. Ibid., pp. 6-12. 4. Ibid., p. 15.

5. The voyage of Jonah raises the most interesting possibilities because of its widespread popularity. Beginning with the end of the third century A.D., Jonah's voyage appears frequently in sarcophagi. For this information, see Cornelia C. Coulter, "The 'Great Fish' in Ancient and Medieval Story," Transactions of the American Philological Association 57 (1926) 32-50; Joseph Engemann, Untersuchungen zur Sepulkralsymbolik der römischen Kaizerzeit (Jahrbuch für Antike und Christentum 2; Münster, 1973) 70-74. First person plural narration does appear in the Islamic account of Jonah's voyage: Koran Sure 37:139-141. See Richard Delbrueck, Probleme der Lipsanothek in Brescia (Theophaneia, Beiträge zur Religions- und Kirchengeschichte des Altertums, 7; Bonn, 1952) 22-23. I am grateful to Professor Emeritus John L. Heller for these citations.

For a study of the Jonah traditions in the NT see Richard A. Edwards, The Sign of Jonah SBT 2d Series 18 (London: SCM, 1971).

6. Cf. Eduard Norden, Agnostos Theos (Leipzig: Teubner, 1913) 313-327.

7. For all kinds of information about ships and sea travel on and around the Mediterranean, including information about Paul's voyages, see the four works by Lionel Casson: Travel in the Ancient World (London: Allen and Unwin, 1974); Ships and Seamanship in the Ancient World (Princeton, NJ: Princeton University Press, 1971); The Ancient Mariners (New York: Macmillan, 1959); Illustrated History of Ships and Boats (Garden City, NY: Doubleday, 1964). For an account of the search for the remains of ancient ships, and the estimates regarding the number of ships which travelled the Mediterranean and went down in the deep, see Willard Bascom, Deep Water, Ancient Ships (Garden City, NY: Doubleday, 1976).

8. Cf. Voyage of Hanno 6; Vergil, Aeneid 3.80-83, 306-355; Dio Chrysostom 7.3-5; Lucian, A True Story 1.33; 2.34; Achilles Tatius 2.33; Heliodorus, Ethiopian Story 5.18.

9. Cf. Odyssey 9.43-61, 195-470.

10. Cf. Vergil, Aeneid 3.463-505; Lucian, A True Story 2.27; Achilles Tatius 2.32.2.

11. Cf. Voyage of Hanno 1; Lucian, A True Story 1.5.

12. Cf. Voyage of Hanno 2-6, 8-17; Vergil Aeneid 3.124-127, 692-708.

13. Cf. Voyage of Hanno 4; Vergil, Aeneid 3.4-5, 19-21, 26-48, 84-120, 147-178, 358-460, 373-376, 528-529; Lucian, A True Story 2.47; Achilles Tatius 2.32.2; 3.5.1-4; 3.10.1-6.

14. Cf. *Odyssey* 9.67-73; Vergil, *Aeneid* 3.192-208; Dio Chrysostom 7.2; Lucian, *A True Story* 2.40; 2.47; Achilles Tatius 3.1.1-3.5.6; Heliodorus, *Ethiopian Story* 5.27.

15. Cf. Voyage of Hanno 6: παρ' οἷς ἐμείναμεν ἄχρι τινὸς, φίλοι γενόμενοι.

16. Cf. the danger which awaits Odysseus when he returns to Ithaca.

17. Cf. Hans Conzelmann, *The Theology of St. Luke*, trans. G. Buswell (New York: Harper, 1960) 60-73.

18. For an explanation of architectonic structure and the correspondences between Lk and Acts, see Charles H. Talbert, *Literary Patterns, Theological Themes and the Genre of Luke-Acts*, SBLMS 20 (Missoula: SBL and Scholars, 1974) esp. 1-65.

19. *Ibid*., p. 20.

20. *Ibid*., pp. 56-58. Our analysis varies some from Talbert's, though agreement with regard to the extent of the chiasmus exists.

21. For an excellent analysis of a chiastic structure see Joanna Dewey, "The Literary Structure of Controversy Stories in Mark 2:1-3:6," *JBL* 92 (1973) 394-401.

22. For the relation of statements by the Holy Spirit and prophets, see Ernst Haenchen, *The Acts of the Apostles* (Philadelphia: Westminster, 1971) 395.

23. During the first century, Achaia included the areas in which both Athens and Corinth were located, but it did not include the area in which Philippi and Thessalonica were located.

24. Evidently the reading with ὡς would mean that they sent Paul away pretending that he would go by sea but actually going by land: "as though to go upon the sea" or "to go as it were upon the sea." See Bruce M. Metzger, *A Textual Commentary on the Greek New Testament* (New York: United Bible Societies, 1971) 455.

25. Cf. Acts 19:11-20. **26. See note 1.**

27. Cf. Acts 13:13; 16:11; 18:21; 20:3, 13; 21:2, 2; 27:2, 4, 12, 21; 28:10, 11.

28. Cf. Acts 21:3; 27:2, 6, 24.

29. For a well known example of the technique in Luke-Acts, cf. Mk 14:62 with Lk 22:69 and Acts 7:56.

30. For a summary of discussions of the great omission, see Walter E. Bundy, *Jesus and the First Three Gospels* (Cambridge: Harvard University Press, 1955) 265-267. He concludes that "there is no satisfactory explanation" for this omission (p. 265).

31. Mk used θάλασσα 12 times in 1:1-6:44.

32. See Werner Kelber, *The Kingdom in Mark* (Philadelphia: Fortress, 1974) 57-62.

S 241 THE PORTRAIT OF PAUL IN ACTS AND THE PASTORALS

Stephen G. Wilson

Carleton University, Ottawa

This paper is part of a larger thesis in which it is argued that the author of Luke-Acts also wrote the Pastorals. Two scholars have defended this view in recent years - C.F.D. Moule,[1] who discusses only a few of the similarities; and A. Strobel,[2] who concerns himself mainly with linguistic and stylistic matters. Most recently N. Brox[3] has attacked this view. He correctly notes that one of the major difficulties of this thesis is the apparent divergence between the portrait of Paul in Acts and in the Pastorals. In this respect Brox represents the almost universal view that the author of the Pastorals (= the Pastor) did not know Acts, since his picture of Paul is so different. This view is based on two main observations: first, that whereas in the Pastorals Paul is the apostle, in Acts he is not considered to be an apostle at all; and second, that the setting of each epistle in general, and the movements of Paul and his companions in particular, cannot be harmonised with the narrative of Acts. This paper will deal only with the first of these issues, and will consider the image of Paul under three aspects: conversion, suffering and martyrdom, apostleship.

A. Paul's Conversion

The allusions to Paul's conversion in the Pastorals, especially I Tim. 1:12-17, do not concern themselves with psychological explanations of that event; rather, they are theocentrically orientated. They do contrast the pre-Christian and Christian periods of Paul's career, but they do so in order to emphasise the gracious activity of God and not to pry into the mental state of Paul. In this they are in accord with both Acts and the Pauline epistles.

The only reference to Paul's pre-Christian life in the Pastorals is found in I Tim. 1:13:

> I formerly blasphemed and persecuted and insulted (βλάσφημον καὶ διώκτην και ὑβριστήν) him; but I received mercy because I had acted ignorantly in unbelief.

Two observations are made here about Paul's pre-Christian career: first, that he was an enemy and persecutor of God and the Church; and second, that these actions were excused on the grounds of ignorance. That Paul persecuted the Church, and thus indirectly Christ himself (cf. Acts 9:4), is indisputable. It is confirmed both by Paul himself (I Cor. 15:9; Phil. 3:5f; Gal. 1:13f) and by Luke (Acts 8:3, 9:1-2,13-14,21, 22:4-5, 26:11). It has been suggested, however, that the other two terms (βλάσφημος ὑβριστής) convey a different picture from both Paul and Acts. Thus G. Klein argues that βλάσφημος is used in I Tim. 1:13 in a general, unqualified sense akin to I Tim. 6:4, Tit. 3:2, and is not parallel to Acts 26:11 where Paul tries to force Christians to blaspheme.[4] It may be true, as many have suggested, that the terms were suggested to the

Pastor by the catalogue of vices, but it is also clear that in I Tim. 1:13 the blasphemy is directed against Christ. In this respect the better parallels are I Tim. 1:20, 6:1, and Tit. 3:5 rather than the more general use in I Tim. 6:4, Tit. 3:2 - if, indeed, such a distinction is valid. G. Kittel, for example, notes that even in the conventional vice-catalogues 'a predominantly religious connotation is present even when it is not expressed'.[5] Acts 26:11, therefore, is a valid parallel to I Tim. 1:13. The second term (ὑβριστής) is found elsewhere in the New Testament only in Rom. 1:30, but it is not essentially different from the vivid descriptions of Paul's persecuting activity in Acts. The use of ignorance as a mitigating factor in the evaluation of Paul's pre-Christian activities finds close parallels in Acts. With respect to both Jews (Acts 3:17, cf. Lk. 23:34, Acts 13:27) and Gentiles (Acts 17:30), ignorance is also used as a relative excuse for the behaviour of non-believers.[6] There is no direct parallel to I Tim. 1:13 in Luke's description of Paul's pre-Christian career, but since he (alone in the rest of the New Testament) uses the concept elsewhere, a statement such as I Tim. 1:13 is consonant with Lukan authorship. In their description of Paul's pre-Christian activity and their use of ignorance as an excuse Luke and the Pastor can thus be seen to be in harmony.

Their agreement is the more marked when we contrast what they say with Paul's own statements. Thus it is often observed that of the three terms used in I Tim. 1:13 only 'persecutor' fits Paul's specific case and that, in view of Phil. 3:4f, 'it is conceivable that Paul would have used βλάσφημος or ὑβριστής of his own past'.[7] The use in I Tim. 1:13 of ignorance as a relative excuse does not preclude an emphasis on divine grace nor does it imply sinlessness, and it is not inconceivable that Paul could have written it; however, since it is open to such a misinterpretation, it is unlikely that it was written by Paul.[8] Finally, we may note that the statement in I Tim. 1:15 that Paul is the foremost (πρῶτος) of sinners, whether it is taken to mean 'first' or 'greatest', is unlikely to have been made by Paul, but is conceivable as a Lukan assertion. It is remarkable, therefore, that while the statements in I Tim. 1:13f do not recall Paul's own statements, they are essentially in accord with Acts.

The allusion to Paul's conversion in I Tim. 1:12-17 has two main features. First, since he has been portrayed as the foremost of sinners (v. 16) his conversion becomes an example, or perhaps even a prototype (v. 17 ὑποτύπωσις is ambiguous), of Christian conversion. Second, in making this point, the Pastor vividly contrasts the two periods of Paul's life. His pre-Christian past stands in dramatic contrast to his Christian present. Both of these features in I Tim. 1:12-17 contribute to the end product - a stylised, ideal portrait of Paul, a man whose conversion is both a model and a source of hope for all non-believers. The perspective is unmistakably post-Pauline, offering a retrospective assessment of Paul's dramatic turnabout and using it for paranetic purposes.

While this perspective on Paul's conversion is not found in his own writings, it is found in Acts. The description of Paul's conversion there clearly makes use of the 'contrast-effect'. The vivid descriptions of Paul's persecution activity in Acts 9,22,26, where it is described in progressively more violent terms, is designed to dramatise the subsequent conversion and emphasise its miraculous nature.[9] In one dramatic move, as a result of divine intervention, the chief persecutor becomes the chief missionary of the Church. Moreover, while there is no direct statement to the effect that Luke views Paul's conversion as exemplary or archetypal, it can scarcely be doubted that this is one of his motives in repeating the account three times and at some length. That this is not specifically stated in Acts, and that other themes such as the importance of this event in the history of the Early Church do not appear in the Pastorals, is to be expected given the difference in subject matter, purpose and genre. Similarly, while it is true that in Acts the accounts of Paul's pre-Christian activities and conversion are far more detailed, this is chiefly because of the narrative form. One would not expect such details in an epistolary setting.

It is reasonable to conclude, therefore, that Luke and the Pastor not only agree with each other but diverge from Paul. Both give fundamentally the same post-Pauline view of Paul's conversion and pre-Christian life. There is nothing which contradicts the theory of common authorship, and much to recommend it. It is perhaps worth adding that it has often been suggested that the faithful saying in I Tim. 1:16 - 'Christ Jesus came into the world to save Sinners' - is based on Lk. 19:10 - 'The Son of man came to seek and to save the lost'. And if there is no direct connection, it remains true that Lk. 19:10 is the closest parallel to I Tim. 1:16.

Paul's Suffering and Martyrdom

One of the most consistent features of the portrait of Paul in the Pastorals is the image of him as a deserted, persecuted apostle, suffering for his faith and, according to II Timothy, conscious that his martyrdom was both inevitable and imminent. The whole of II Timothy is suffused with this theme, but it is shown most clearly in 1:3-18, 2:9-10, 3:10-13, 4:6-22.

In II Timothy Paul is described as a deserted and lonely figure. Timothy, his close and beloved companion, had previously departed 'with many tears' (II Tim. 2:4) - an allusion which some would place historically at Acts 20:37.[10] Paul mentions that he longs to see Timothy again (II Tim. 1:4) and asks him to come soon (II Tim. 4:9). In addition, most of his other close companions are scattered far and wide (II Tim. 4:10f) and Luke alone is with him (II Tim. 4:11).[11] At an earlier stage Onesipherous had made a great effort to visit Paul (II Tim. 1:16-18), but many of the Asians, including Hermogenes and Phygelus, had deliberately denied him (II Tim. 1:15) and, during his 'first defence', he notes poignantly that everyone deserted him (II Tim. 4:16).

In addition to Paul's sense of loneliness and desertion, the Pastor repeatedly emphasises his sufferings as a Christian. His appointment by God to be an apostle, preacher and teacher necessarily involves suffering (II Tim. 1:11-12, 2:9, 3:11). This suffering accompanies his whole career (II Tim. 3:11), but is brought to a climax by his imprisonment (II Tim. 1:6, 2:9). That this suffering is neither fortuitous or associated solely with Paul is indicated in II Tim. 3:12 - 'Indeed all who desire to live a godly life in Christ Jesus will be persecuted' - and in II 1:8,23 where Timothy is exhorted to 'take your share of the suffering for the gospel....'

Finally, in II Tim. 4:6f, with remarkable equanimity, Paul views his imminent death. He has 'fought the good fight' and 'kept the faith', so he can be proud of his past as he looks back. His future lies with the Lord who will now, as before, 'rescue him from all evil' and ensure his salvation (II Tim. 1:18) and due reward (II Tim. 1:8). It appears that he had already undergone an earlier hearing or trial and had been able to turn the tables on his captors by preaching to the Gentiles. If the reference is to an earlier trial and subsequent period of freedom, then this preaching presumably refers to the continuing Gentile mission; if it refers to the first of two hearings then the preaching was presumably in court, in front of his accusers and judges. Either way, 'that the preaching of the chief apostle to the Gentiles should find its climax in a trial situation exemplifies the view of the whole epistle - i.e., that persecution and suffering are an integral part of the preaching of the word'.[12]

How does the Pastor understand this aspect of Paul's career? Primarily, Paul is being presented as a paradigm for Christian believers. In the same way that his conversion is seen as an example, so is his whole career. He is the archetypal faithful steward of the gospel - persecuted and finally martyred for his faith, but firm in his commitment to the end. As II Tim. 1:8, 3:12 (and 2:11?) make clear, what happens to Paul is an example of the fate of all believers. It has often been assumed on this basis, probably correctly, that the recipients of the Pastorals were themselves undergoing persecution. It is possible, too, that the Pastor goes beyond seeing Paul as a mere example:

> Therefore, I endure everything for the sake of the elect, that they also may obtain the salvation which in Christ Jesus goes with eternal glory.
> (II Tim. 2:10)

It might be argued that this recalls the notoriously obscure verse in Colossians 1:24, where Paul seems to claim that his suffering is in some sense vicarious, endured on behalf of his brethren and completing the suffering of Christ.[13] However, the notion of a fixed amount of suffering prior to the End, which probably lies behind Col. 1:24, is not even hinted at in II Tim. 2:10, nor is it clear that Paul's suffering is vicarious.[14]

With respect to Paul's suffering and persecutions, Acts, like the Pauline epistles, offers many parallels. He was persecuted by the Hellenists in Jerusalem (Acts 9:29), perpetually harrassed by the Jews (Acts 13:50, 14:2,5,19, 16:19-24, 17:5-9, 18:6,12f, 21-24), assaulted by Artemis worshippers (Acts 18:23f) and finally taken into custody by the Romans (Acts 24-28). Moreover, the suffering is seen by Luke to be an integral part of Paul's divinely designated role as chief missionary to the Gentiles, and is declared to be such at his conversion (Acts 9:16, 26:21). When speaking to the Ephesian elders Paul himself intimates that suffering is a concomitant of the Christian ministry (Acts 20:19,23-4). And Acts, like the Pastorals, recognises that Paul's suffering and imprisonment do not hinder the spread of the Gospel (II Tim. 2:9; Acts 28:30-31), for in both there is an overriding sense of divine control.

There is no direct parallel to II Tim. 4:6f in Acts, since Acts 28 tells us almost nothing about his imprisonment. There are hints earlier in the book, however, which suggest a similar outlook on Paul's death. The review of his past career in which he claims to have 'run the race' and 'fought the fight' recalls not only the specific use of the same metaphor in Acts 20:24, but also the general tenor of Acts 20:19-23. It is in this same speech that we get one of the few allusions in Acts to Paul's ultimate fate (Acts 20:24-5,38, cf. 21:10-14). However, apart from these few allusions, there is no description of Paul's ultimate fate even though presumably it was known to both author and readers. The ending of Acts is, of course, one of the book's greatest enigmas, for Luke concludes with a vague reference to Paul's two-year house arrest in Rome, which allowed him unhindered preaching of the gospel (Acts 28:30-31). The image of the lonely, deserted apostle facing imminent martyrdom would thus have to be considered as an addition to the information in Acts. Of course, II Timothy does not describe Paul's death any more than Acts does, but that is inevitable in an epistle ascribed to Paul!

However, it is important to note that this is not a substantial discrepancy. If the Pastor either knew or believed that Paul was released after his two year detention and that his death came at a later stage, there would be no contradiction with II Timothy. If, on the other hand, he located II Timothy during the imprisonment of Acts 28, the difference becomes explicable if one allows for the different purpose in each case. Acts 28 is the climax of a narrative which is concerned more to convey a sense of the triumphal progress of the gospel from Jerusalem to the ends of the earth (Acts 1:8) than it is with the fate of the individual Paul, and more with a general statement about his last two years than with a detailed description of his last few months. There is no difficulty in supposing that the author of II Timothy 4:9f understood it to be a description of Paul's circumstances at the end of his two year detention mentioned in Acts 28. Indeed, it may be that II Timothy confirms a recent explanation for the enigmatic ending of Acts. C.K. Barrett suggests that Acts ends where it does because "an account of the martyrdom itself, especially if at that time Paul was deserted by his friends and the victim of some kind of treachery, would not enhance the record of Paul's devotion and might detract from the sense of confidence, victory and unity that pervade the book".[15] It may be precisely such a situation which Luke, writing at a later date and for a different purpose, hints at in II Tim. 1:15, 4:9f. It is not clear exactly what II Tim 1:15 refers to, but it could be that 'all those in Asia' not only 'turned away' from Paul, but also conspired in his imprisonment and death. II Tim. 4:9f refers to the desertion of Paul by most of his travelling companions and v. 16 claims that 'at my first defence no one took my part; all deserted me'. Is it possible that this reflects what Luke knew when he wrote Acts, namely that there were Christians who had a hand in his death, either by positive action or passive compliance? Paul's death could not, of course, be narrated in II Timothy, but Luke took the opportunity to use the picture of Paul as the deserted, lonely, suffering apostle to good effect. It would have made a poignant but anticlimactic ending to the narrative of Acts, but in II Timothy it enhances the idealised portrait of Paul as the archetypal Christian believer who holds firmly to his faith whatever befalls him.

C.H. Talbert has suggested that the portraits of Jesus, Stephen and Paul in the Lukan writings are used as an anti-gnostic device. In particular, he argues that Luke rejects the connection between Jesus' death and the forgiveness of sins, and portrays it instead as the death of an innocent martyr. The purpose is to counter the view of those gnostics who rejected martyrdom in principle (Iren. Adv. Haer. XXXIV, 3-6; Tert. Adv. Haer. I).[16] It will be argued below that this is not the most probable setting for Acts, though it is for the Pastorals. One might argue, therefore, that the portrait of Paul in II Timothy is motivated by the gnostic refusal of martyrdom and, in turn, this is one reason why there are more specific allusions to Paul's martyrdom in II Timothy than in Acts.

It is scarcely in dispute, however, that Luke thought Paul's career was of central and exemplary significance. It is clear that whatever historical or antiquarian interests he may have had, he was also telling his story with an eye on his contemporaries and their needs. Thus while the account of Paul may serve several functions (historical, polemical, etc.) one of these is to present his life as a paradigm. There is a message for the readers of Acts not only in the teaching of the apostles but also in the way they lived. There is no hint that Paul's suffering was vicarious, but then such a notion cannot certainly be found in II Timothy either. In general, the information which Luke and the Pastor provide on Paul's suffering and death is consistent. There are many similarities, and where II Timothy gives additional information it is always consistent with the narrative of Acts.

Paul As Apostle

It has been asserted that when the Pastorals single Paul out as the apostle, the sole guardian of the truth and source of sound teaching, they contradict not only Acts, where the apostles are the Twelve and Paul is simply one link in the chain of tradition, but also those genuine epistles where Paul recognizes his dependence on his predecessors.[17] There are two issues at stake: first, the use of the word 'apostle'; and second, the exclusive concentration on the figure of Paul in the Pastorals.

It is significant that the Pastorals seldom use the word apostle. It occurs five times of which three are in the standard introductory formula of each epistle (I Tim. 1:1; II Tim. 1:1; Tit. 1:1). The use in II Tim. 1:11 is not particular emphatic: 'For this gospel I was appointed as preacher and apostle and teacher'. The title apostle is used as one of several ways in which Paul's role is described. A similar statement in I Tim. 2:7 connects 'apostle' and 'preacher', but here there is also a firm parenthetical affirmation - 'I am telling the truth, I am not lying'. The formulaic uses at the beginning of each epistle are predictable if, as seems likely, the author knew at least some of the genuine Pauline epistles (Rom. 1:1; Cor. 1:1; II Cor. 1:1; Gal. 1:1; Col. 1:1 etc.). The same can be said of I Tim 2:7, since in Rom 9:1, II Cor. 11:31, Gal. 1:20 Paul makes similar affirmations. On a formal level it is scarcely appropriate in a personal letter to Timothy, who would need no such reassurance, but it may be that some in Ephesus did. It is more likely, however, that this is one of the many instances where the genuine Pauline letters have influenced the wording of the Pastorals. It is noticeable, therefore, that apart from I Tim. 2:7 there is little emphasis on the title apostle as such. Certainly, when it does occur it is always with reference to Paul. But this is not because there is any desire to belittle the Twelve or any others who traditionally bore the title; it is part of the broader problem of the exclusive concentration on the figure of Paul in the Pastorals, and it is to this that we now turn.

The Pastorals unambiguously portray Paul as the sole source of genuine tradition and, by implication, assert that Timothy and Titus and any successors they appoint are those who preserve this tradition. This is clear in the format of the letters which are addressed by Paul to his companions Timothy and Titus and which contain instructions both for them and for the communities they oversee (I Tim. 1:18, 3:14, 4:6,11, 5:21, 6:2,11,14; II Tim. 1:6, 2:14, 3:14, 4:1; Tit. 1:5, 2:1,15, 3:8). More specifically, I Tim. 6:20, II Tim. 1:1-214 speak of the deposit (παραθήκη) which has been entrusted to Paul, which he entrusts to Timothy, and Timothy is to entrust to his successors (II Tim. 2:2). It is, therefore, Paul above all who is the source of sound teaching and truth for the communities to whom the Pastorals are addressed.

The information in Acts is more ambiguous. With respect to the title apostle, it is usually concluded that Acts differs not only from the Pastorals but from Paul. The key passages for our argument are Acts 14:4,14, since it is only here that Luke attributes the title to Paul (cf. Acts 1:21-22 which ostensibly give the qualifications for apostleship). I have argued elsewhere that the various attempts to show that Acts 14:4,14 do not represent, or perhaps even contradict, Luke's view of apostleship are not persuasive.[18] Whatever one makes of these verses it seems that at the very least they indicate that Luke did not have a rigid conception which confirmed the title to the Twelve and that he had no objection to its application to Paul (and Barnabas). Perhaps he believed it was originally confined to the Twelve and later used more widely. Or perhaps he believed that Paul and Barnabas were not apostles in the same sense as the Twelve, but for historical and not dogmatic reasons - the Twelve had a unique and unrepeatable function: 'Their (Paul and Barnabas) apostolic task was not to found and care for the infant Church in its initial stages of growth for they were later converts. Nevertheless, because they founded and cared for churches in the initial stages of the Gentile mission, they were equally apostles'.[19] However one explains them, if one thinks Luke wrote the Pastorals, Acts 14:4,14 undoubtedly give a precedent for the application of the title apostle to Paul in those letters.[20]

Acts provides a more complete picture of Paul's position within Christian tradition than the Pastorals, since there is a considerable amount of information about his relationship with his precedessors as well as his successors. This double aspect of Paul's work has been most thoroughly discussed by G. Klein. He argues that while Paul is wholly subordinated to his predecessors, he has absolute authority over his successors.[21] His conclusions are, I think, too rigid and they break down at several crucial points in the narrative of Acts. Thus he argues that Acts 13:1f narrates the legitimizing of Paul's transformation from subordinate to leader, the church at Antioch already having been legitimised by the Twelve. But since the agent of that legitimising was Barnabas (Acts 11:22f), it is curious that the Church at Antioch should be commissioning him as well as Paul! Klein notes, but does not successfully answer, this objection. Similarly his attempt to find significance in the changing order in which Paul and Barnabas are mentioned as a pair puts an unwarranted strain upon the text. It is surely no more than a literary variation, of which Luke is fond, and is without theological significance. Despite this, there is some substance to Klein's observations. It is clear that Luke attaches Paul closely to the original Christian community in Jerusalem. He meets the Twelve soon after his conversion (Acts 9:26-30), ends each journey in Jerusalem (Acts 15:2, 18:22, 21:17), is assigned by the Church at Antioch to represent them on the Gentile issue in Jerusalem (Acts 15:1f), and accepts the decisions of the apostles and elders (Acts 16:4). However, it is also clear that there is no attempt to subordinate Paul to the Twelve or the Jerusalem Church. His conversion is an independent event, since Ananias is not seen as the representative of the Twelve.[22] He is commissioned by the Church at Antioch (Acts 13:1f) and his dealings with the Church in Jerusalem are as much with the elders and James (Acts 15:22, 21:18) as with the Twelve. Thus while Paul clearly has a close and amicable relationship with the Jerusalem Church, he is not subordinated to them any more than he is to the Church at Antioch.

With respect to his successors, the information in Acts accords well with the Pastorals. Acts 14:23 reports that Paul and Barnabas appointed elders in the new churches they had founded. According to Acts 19:1-7, Paul has authority over those who know only the baptism of John and is the means whereby they receive the Spirit. It is, however, to Acts 20:17-33 that we must turn for the most complete picture. In a speech which in both form and content is unique in Acts, Paul bids farewell to the Ephesian elders. It is his only speech to Christian leaders and, like the speech to the Gentiles in Acts 17:22f, is clearly intended to be archetypal. It is an ideal scene, where Paul takes leave not only of the Ephesian elders but of all church officials and congregations. Moreover, this speech affords one of the most remarkable parallels to the Pastorals, in particular to II Timothy. The similarity goes far beyond the observation that they are both examples of a particular literary genre - the farewell speech.[23] Almost every detail of Acts 20:17-33 can be found in the Pastorals.[24]

1. Paul looks back on his past career with some confidence, believing that he has fulfilled the tasks designated to him (Acts 20:18-21,25-6; II Tim. 4:6f). Moreover, the striking metaphor of an athlete finishing his race is used in both Acts 20:24 (ὡς τελειώσω τὸν δρόμον μου) and II Tim. 4:7 (τὸν δρόμον τετέλεκα). At the same time he is deeply concerned with the fate of the Church in his absence. This is indicated by the whole of Acts 20:17-35 and each of the Pastorals letters.

2. The problem Paul foresees and warns of is heresy, which will assault the church from within and without (Acts 20:29-30; I Tim. 1:3f, 3:1f, 6:20f; II Tim. 2:14f, 3:1f). The heresy appears to be an early form of gnosticism and its centre is in Ephesus (Acts 20:17f; I Tim. 1:3). Paul urges constant alertness (Acts 20:31; II Tim. 4:2f).

3. The responsibility for resisting the false teaching is placed on the church leaders or on Paul's assistants. The

church leaders are, in both cases, elder-bishops (Acts 20:17-28; I Tim. 5:17; II Tim. 2:2; Tit. 1:5f), and it is Paul's example and instruction which will be their chief weapon (Acts 20:27, 30-5; I Tim. 3:14; 4:11f, 6:20; II Tim. 1:8f,13-14, 3:10f; Tit. 1:5).

4. Paul speaks of his own suffering for the sake of the gospel (Acts 20:19-24; II Tim. 1:11-12; 2:3, 3:11) and indicates that for him a martyr's death lies ahead (Acts 20:25,37; II Tim. 4:6f).

5. The ministers whom Paul appoints and exhorts are warned of the dangers of the love of money (Acts 20:33-5; I Tim. 6:9-10; Tit. 1:11).

6. Paul commits his successors to the Lord and his grace (Acts 20:32; II Tim. 4:22).

How is this speech to be assessed within the context of Acts? E. Haenchen suggests a variety of motives.[25] An obvious one is the desire to present Paul as the archetypal Christian minister, the prototype for later generations. This motive would, of course, be fully in line with the Pastorals. Haenchen also suggests that, since the churches in Asia Minor had succumbed to gnosticism soon after Paul's death (Rev. 1-2), Luke wishes to absolve Paul from any responsibility. Paul is blameless for he has not shrunk from declaring anything to his successors. G. Klein more plausibly suggests that a quite different motive was at work.[26] The problem was not that Christians were accusing Paul of failure, but that the gnostics were claiming Paul as the authority for their teaching. The speech asserts that, despite their claim that Paul is their authority, in reality they are excluded from the genuine Pauline tradition and do not have the Pauline 'deposit'. The repeated claim that Paul has witheld nothing from the elders (Acts 20:27,30,35) is not a claim of innocence, but an assertion that Paul's appointed successors alone have his true teaching, and they have all of it. There is only one Pauline tradition, so that any claim to possess a secret Pauline tradition is opposed by Paul himself!

On this note we can now turn to a consideration of some of the explanations of the similarities and differences between the portrait of Paul in Luke-Acts and the Pastorals. With particular reference to Acts 20:17-35 W. Schmithals says, 'I consider the speech to be a piece, reworked by Luke, of the so-called "itinerary", the author of which stood close to the author of the Pastorals or was even identical with him, though I cannot at this time more fully establish this assumption'.[27] It should be noted that Schmithals considers the Pastorals to be 'wholly non-Lukan' and ascribes them to a quite different stream of Christian tradition. The Pastorals he places in the stream of Gentile-Hellenistic-Christianity and Luke in the stream of Jewish-Hellenistic-Christianity. However, as I shall argue below, while Schmithals' observations confirms the similarity between this speech and the Pastorals he does not offer convincing evidence for the non-Lukan origin of Acts 20:17-35, nor does his observation account for the many similarities between Luke and the Pastor which lie outside the itinerary. N. Brox offers a broader explanation for this phenomenon.[28] He suggests that the Pastor drew on a variety of Pauline traditions that were preserved in both written and oral form by his successors and supporters. The Lukan traditions were one among many sources which the Pastor used. This is a possible explanation but, in my view, does not go far enough. C.H. Talbert suggests that the similarities between Acts and the Pastorals, especially those between Acts 20:17-35 and II Timothy, are because both Luke and the Pastor were combating gnosticism.[29] This is, of course, part of his overall thesis that Luke-Acts are primarily anti-gnostic documents. This does not seem to me, however, to be the most probable explanation of the purpose of Luke's writings, and especially of Acts.

In the course of arguing for Lukan influence on the Pastorals A. Strobel[30] offers a curious explanation for Acts 20:17-35. Commenting in particular on the use of the same athletic metaphor in Acts 20:24 and II Tim. 4:7, he argues that the latter is neither a literary fiction nor a secondary construction based on Acts 20:24. Rather, when Luke wrote Acts 20:24, at a later date, he drew on his memory of the authentic words of Paul. He then notes that when II Tim. 4:12 indicates that a short time beforehand Tychicus had been sent to Ephesus, this was probably to convey a similar message to Acts 20 and possibly also to deliver I Timothy. This is a puzzling series of statements,[31] not least because Strobel nowhere else discusses exactly what he means by Lukan 'authorship' of the Pastorals or how he views the chronological relationship between the Lukan writings and the Pastorals. All we have are a few obscure and confusing hints. If he is implying that II Timothy (and I Timothy?) are Pauline this contradicts his own attempt to show that they are 'Lukan'. The appeal to the sending of Tychicus in II Tim. 4:12 is presumably meant to suggest that II Timothy was, like I Timothy, written to Timothy while he was in Ephesus, thus forging a connection with Paul's farewell address to the Ephesian elders. He seems to be implying that Luke was Paul's companion, that he wrote Acts after the Pastorals, and that Acts was based in part on his first-hand knowledge of Paul's activities. One must assume then that he thinks Luke was Paul's scribe, and that the Pastorals are a mixture of Pauline dictation and Lukan influence. In other words, his explanation of the relationship would be the same as Moule's.[32] Valuable as Strobel's article is in drawing attention to the many similarities between Luke and the Pastor, his obscurity at the crucial stage of explanation does not enhance the defence of common authorship.

Both the similarities and differences in the portrait of Paul seem to require a different explanation from those considered above. The nub of the problem is this: if Luke wrote the Pastorals why, in those letters, is the title apostle confined to Paul and why is exclusive attention paid to him at the expense of his predecessors in the Christian tradition? If one accepts that Acts provides precedents for the application of the title apostle to Paul, then it should be remembered that we are dealing here not so much with a contradiction as with a difference of emphasis. The emphasis on Paul's relationship with his successors and the description of it are the same in Acts and the Pastorals..It is the omission of any reference to his predecessors and the resulting concentration on Paul in the Pastorals which is different from Acts. One level of explanation could be as follows: Luke reconstructed Paul's career as best he could, given the limitations of his sources and his own predispositions, but without any polemical purpose. Since he was intent on writing an account of the expansion of the church he had to write about Paul and about Paul's predecessors and his dealings with them, for they were an integral part of the story. Consideration of them is forced upon Luke by the historical realities of his chosen subject matter. On the other hand, if he wrote the Pastorals too, though in the name of Paul, the question of predecessors did not arise any more than it did in every genuine Pauline epistle. There the issue arises only for specific reasons related to the situation of the community to whom it is addressed. Moreover, concentration on the figure of Paul can be explained in large part precisely because the letters are written in Paul's name, as over against Acts where both the stage and the number of players are far larger. Such an explanation of the differences may be a partial answer to the problem; but there is another level of argument yet to be pursued.

The portrait in Acts of Paul in particular and the Gentile mission in general appears to be motivated in part by problems facing the communities for whom Luke wrote. In particular they suggest that these were Gentile communities founded by Paul, but were living in a predominantly Jewish environment.[33] It is probable that these communities were under attack by Jews or Jewish Christians who accused them of apostasy, directing the attack in particular at their founder, Paul. Although it is not possible to draw a direct line of connection between this situation and the violently anti-Pauline strand of Jewish Christianity which produced the _Kerygmata Petrou_, the latter do give an indication of the opposition Paul's teaching could meet even after his death.[34]

The Pastorals, on the other hand, were written in the face of a quite different threat both to Paul and to the Church. The threat came from gnostic enthusiasts who infiltrated the churches in a more subtle manner: they did not attack Paul; on the contrary, they used him. For it was to Paul and his writings that they appealed as the basis for their teaching. N. Brox has argued convincingly that the Pastorals are not an attempt to rehabilitate Paul for the church as a result of misuse of his views by gnostics, as if the letters are intended to authenticate the author; rather, it is the teaching of the Pastorals, the genuine Pauline tradition, that is being authenticated by Paul.[35] That gnostics were active in Ephesus is indicated not only by Acts 20:17-35 and the Pastorals but also by Revelation 1-2, which speaks of the infiltration of the Nicolaitans into the churches of Asia Minor. That there were gnostics who used Paul's writings to support their views is indicated most clearly by II Peter 3:15-16.

It is these two quite different situations, both intimately connected with the figure of Paul, which provide the most adequate explanation of the difference in emphasis between Acts and the Pastorals and which allow a defence of their common authorship. When he wrote Acts, Luke was faced primarily with an anti-Pauline opposition of a Jewish or Jewish-Christian character. This is why Paul's faithfulness to his Jewish heritage and his harmonious relationship with the Jerusalem church are emphasised. Luke is refuting those who argue that Paul is an apostate Jew, a renegade who had lead his wing of the church into heresy. Paul and the churches he founded remained true to their Jewish heritage and, ironically, if anything it was the obduracy of the Jews which precipitated the expansion into the Gentile world. On the other hand, when he wrote the Pastorals the problem was quite different. The opposition was now pro-Pauline. They claimed Paul as their chief authority and bolstered their case with reference to his own writings. In the face of this more subtle assault on Paul's teaching, there was no need to emphasise Paul's Jewishness or his relationship with his predecessors. The problem was with the tradition which came after, and in part emanated from, Paul. The crucial issue was, therefore, who had the true Pauline 'deposit' and how it was to be transmitted to subsequent generations. And thus the concentration is almost exclusively on the figure of Paul and his successors.

Perhaps a slightly modified version of this argument will serve my purpose as well. It could be argued that although the primary problem facing Luke when he wrote his account of Paul in Acts was anti-Paulinism, the inclusion of Acts 20:17-35 suggests that this was not the only problem. Likewise, while the Pastorals almost wholly concerned with guaranteeing the preservation of the genuine Pauline tradition, there is at least in I Tim 2:7 (cf. I Tim. 1:12-16; II Tim. 1:11) a modest but firm defence of Paul's rank as apostle. Perhaps the situation was as follows: when Luke wrote Acts anti-Paulinism was the major threat, but the gnostics had appeared on the horizon. They were not as yet a major influence but they clearly spelled trouble ahead, and Acts 20:17-35 is Luke's attempt to head them off before they became more influential. However, at a later date it was clear to Luke that the gnostics were becoming increasingly influential. They had not died a natural death nor had they been effectively countered. The number of their adherents was increasing and they had infiltrated many churches and, what was worse, they used Paul's writings as their authority. In the face of this Luke returns to the task he had begun in Acts 20:17-35, but with two important differences: first, he attacks them at much greater length and with more vehemence; and second, he counters their use of Pauline writings by producing anti-gnostic writings in the name of Paul. At the same time there may still have been a few Jews or Jewish-Christians who took an occasional shot at Paul and the communities he founded, reviving an earlier controversy. It is not the chief problem any longer, but it warrants a brief response (I Tim. 2:7 etc.).[36]

This scenario may also be used to explain the slight shift of perspective which can be found between Acts and the Pastorals. In Acts 20:29 Paul warns that the heretics will be active 'after my departure (μετὰ τὴν ἄφιξίν μου)'. This is often taken to mean that Paul is seen as the last of the great heroic figures in the heresy-free apostolic era. When he departs, heresy arrives.[37] Thus while he can foresee what will happen and warn his successors, he is not himself directly involved in the conflict. The Pastorals, on the other hand, place Paul in the thick of the battle.[38] This contrast is weakened if we take ἄφιξις to refer not to his death, but to his departure from Fphesus. This would be feasible even with the other allusions to Paul's death in the speech and even if one reads it as an ideal, paradigmatic scene. The Ephesian elders will not see Paul again, but as the narrative unfolds it is clear that his death is a few years off. If one imagines that Luke located the Pastorals chronologically in the period after the imprisonment of Acts 28 there would then be no problem. But if he located them within the narrative of Acts, in particular I Timothy and Titus to a period prior to Acts 20:17-35, then clearly he would have imagined Paul to be disputing with gnostics in Ephesus and Crete <u>before</u> his farewell speech to the Ephesian elders - and that would contradict either interpretation of Acts 20:29. We shall return to these chronological issues in the next chapter. A different, and perhaps more satisfactory argument, would be that Luke, writing a few years after he had completed Acts and faced with an urgent need to counter the gnostic threat, momentarily forgets the perspective of Acts 20. In his desire to introduce the voice of Paul into the dispute over who were the true interpreters of the Pauline tradition, he places Paul in the thick of the battle. Of course, even in the Pastorals Paul's involvement is indirect, in the form of epistles; he is not physically present in Ephesus or Crete. Also, in the Pastorals there is some oscillation between the prediction of future false-teaching and the recognition that it is present (II Tim. 3:1f). However one assesses this point I think the shift of perspective, when seen in content, is not a serious objection to common authorship. Certainly, it is no more of an anomaly than some of the discrepancies we can certainly ascribe to Luke, such as the differences between the dating and description of the Ascension in Lk. 24 and Acts 1.

All in all, an analysis of the image of Paul in Acts and the Pastorals lends support to the hypothesis of common authorship. There are differences of emphasis, but they are the result in part of purely literary factors and in part of the different contexts in which the works were written. There are many similarities, the most striking of which is between Acts 20 and II Timothy. It is not only feasible, but likely, that Luke was the author of both.

NOTES

1. C.F.D. Moule, 'The Problem of the Pastoral Epistles: A Reappraisal', BJRL 47 (1965), 430-52.

2. A. Strobel, 'Schreiben des Lukas? Zum sprachlichen Problem der Pastoralbriefe', NTS 15 (1969), 191-210.

3. N. Brox, 'Lukas als Verfasser der Pastoralbriefe?', Jahrbuch fur Antike und Christentum, 13 (1970), 62-77.

4. G. Klein, Die Zwölf Apostel (Gottingen 1961), pp. 133-8, esp. p. 134.

5. G. Kittel, art. βλασφημία, TDNT, Vol. I, pp. 621-5, here p. 621.

6. M. Dibelius and H. Conzelmann, The Pastoral Epistles (Philadelphia 1972), p. 24; E. Haenchen, The Acts of the Apostles (Oxford 1971), p. 410; S.G. Wilson, The Gentiles and the Gentile Mission in Luke-Acts (Cambridge 1973), pp. 209-10.

7. Dibelius-Conzelmann, Pastoral, p. 28. Also Klein, Apostel, p. 133.

8. C.K. Barrett, The Pastoral Epistles (Oxford 1963), p. 45.

9. Contra Klein, Apostel, pp. 114-44. See Wilson, Gentiles, pp. 157-9.

10. Although Acts does not mention that Timothy was left behind after Paul's farewell speech to the Ephesian elders, he is not mentioned subsequently. If Luke was the author of the Pastorals, it may be that he believed that Timothy was left behind at this stage and that II Timothy was composed during the Roman imprisonment of Acts 28.

11. It should be said, incidently, that II Tim. 4:11 is not necessarily contradicted by II Tim 4:21, since in the former passage he is speaking of his close companions who had regularly accompanied him on missionary tours and in the latter of local Christians who could give him some moral support but could not replace close friends.

12. N. Brox, Die Pastoralbriefe (Regensburg, 1969), p. 276.

13. J.N.D. Kelly, A Commentary on the Pastoral Epistles (London 1963), p. 178; J. Jeremias, Die Briefe an Timotheus und Titus (Gottingen 1963), p. 48.

14. Dibelius-Conzelmann, Pastoral, pp. 108-9; Brox, Pastoralbriefe, p. 243.

15. C.K. Barrett, 'Pauline Controversies in the Post-Pauline Period', NTS 20 (1973-4), 229-45, here p. 240.

16. C.H. Talbert, Luke and the Gnostics (New York 1966), pp. 71-82.

17. Brox, Pastoralbriefe, pp. 68-74.

18. Wilson, Gentiles, pp. 116f.

19. J. Andrew Kirk, 'Apostleship since Rengstorf: Towards a Synthesis', NTS, 21 (1974-75), 249-64, here p. 264.

20. Wilson, Gentiles, p. 117. One might even go beyond this and argue that as the title is of no great importance in the Pastorals neither is it in Luke-Acts, where it serves mainly as a convenient designation for all or some of the Twelve.

21. Klein, Apostel, pp. 162-84.

22. Wilson, Gentiles, pp. 173f.

23. See the formative article by J. Munck, 'Discours d'adieu dans le Nouveau Testament et dans la littérature biblique', Aux Sources de la Tradition Chrétienne (Neuchatel 1950), pp. 115f.

24. See Talbert, Luke, pp. 65-8, 114; Brox, Pastoralbriefe, pp. 72-3; H. von Campenhansen, Ecclesiastical Authority and Spiritual Power (London 1969), pp. 111-12; H. Windisch, 'Zur Christologie der Pastoralbriefe', ZNW 30 (1935), 213-38, here 232.

25. Haenchen, Acts, pp. 596-7.

26. Klein, Apostle, pp. 183-4.

27. W. Schmithals, The Office of Apostle in the Early Church (Nashville 1969), p. 249.

28. Brox, Pastoralbriefe, pp. 72-4.

29. Talbert, Luke, p. 114.

30. Strobel, Schreiben, 203-5.

31. Brox, Lukas, p. 71.

32. Moule, 'Pastoral', 434.

33. Wilson, Gentiles, p. 248, based on J. Jervell, Luke and the People of God (Minneapolis 1972), pp. 174-77.

34. For a general exploration of Pauline tradition see Barrett, 'Controversies', 229-45; H.M. Schenke, 'Das Weiterwirken des Paulus und die Pflege seines Erbes durch die Paulus-Schule', NTS 21 (1974-75), 505-18.

35. Brox, Pastoralbriefe, pp. 66-77. See also Dibelius-Conzelmann, Pastoral.

36. Barrett, Pastoral, pp. 14-17 also suggests that these two strands provide the most intelligible background to the Pastorals. The author attempts to rescue Paul from both his professed enemies and false friends. He does not, however, distinguish the level of importance of these two groups nor, of course, is he arguing for Lukan authorship.

37. E.g., Klein, Apostel, p. 181; Haenchen, Acts, p. 593; C.H. Talbert, Literary Patterns, Theological Themes and the Genre of Luke-Acts (Montana 1974), pp. 101-3.

38. So Barrett, 'Controversies', 241.

<u>S 246, A 409</u> METAPHOR AND REALITY IN HOSEA 11

J. Gerald Janzen
Christian Theololical Seminary

Among the various modes of divine address to Israel which are to be found in the Book of Hosea, is that mode of address which takes the grammatical form of a question. This mode of address occurs only sparingly, yet it punctuates the divine address as a whole in such a way as to imbue the whole with its own peculiar significance. This is especially the case in Chap. 11, where a divine question to the people inaugurates perhaps the boldest portrayal of "the living God" in the OT. It is the purpose of this paper to explore the theological implications of this mode of address in Hosea, especially in its climactic occurrence in Chap. 11. This exploration will involve a consideration of what it means to ask oneself a question, of what it means to ask that question of another, and of what it might mean for God to ask questions of himself and of others.

Since this paper is being offered for discussion in a hermeneutical seminar, perhaps I should say something at the outset about hermeneutical method. Or rather, perhaps I should make a confession. I do not customarily lay down hermeneutical ground rules for myself, and then follow them methodically to conclusions, the soundness of which I assess partly by the proper employment of such methods. Rather, I characteristically try to approach a text with no specific posture or strategy, but with a sort of general alert emptiness--what Alan Watts, I suppose, might call *Kendo*[1]--in which the sum total of what I know about things sleeps in readiness within me. The general intention is to allow the text to set the agenda by raising questions or posing issues or opening perspectives through the specific elements of the text which claim my special interest. When such interest has been awakened, I tend to pursue it in whatever fashion, or with whatever combination of resources of understanding, seems to offer promise of illuminating the text. The control on such a pursuit is, of course, the text itself. In my view, the pursuit may operate on as short or as long a leash as one's hermeneutical imagination is comfortable with, so long as, in the end, the results respect the integrity, and indeed illuminate the integrity, of the text. In the terms of the present paper, the question of hermeneutical method is an *existential* question, and as such can be answered only at the *end* of the hermeneutical process.

Since this paper is quite long, I should outline the course which my exploration of Hos 11 will take. *First*, I will place the topic before us, by a simple presentation of the relevant texts, together with a brief comment on their contexts, and with some quotations from the commentaries of James Luther Mays and Hans Walter Wolff which will provide a point of entry into my hermeneutical explorations. *Secondly*, I will engage in some general reflection on what it means to ask a question, for us, and possibly for God. *Thirdly*, I will consider briefly several aspects of the OT from the perspective gained through the general reflection. *Fourthly*, I will return to the Book of

Hosea and its divine questions, and explore their significance from the achieved perspective. But then, because of a specific issue raised by the text, in section *five* I will undertake another general reflection on the existential challenge posed by a genuine impasse, for us, and possibly for God. Then I will return to Hos 11 for a *final* exploration of its theological overtones. In the course of this multi-phase exploration, I will freely introduce a variety of resources not native to technical biblical scholarship. For this I make no apology; the justification, in my view, depends upon the integrity of the result, by which I mean the explication, and not the violation, of the text. One hermeneutical assumption should perhaps be disclosed here: I assume that the relation between text and interpreter is dialogical.

I

The first divine question occurs in the context of *Hos 6:1-6*, of which vv 4-6 read as follows:

(4) What shall I do with you, O Ephraim?
What shall I do with you, O Judah?
Your devotion is like morning mist,
like dew that soon disappears.
(5) Therefore I have fought (them) with the prophets,
slain them with the words of my mouth,
and so my justice goes forth like light.
(6) For I desire devotion, not sacrifice,
the knowledge of God, rather than burnt offerings.

Mays and Wolff both take this passage as a divine oracular response to the people's liturgical act of penitence portrayed in 6:1-3. Whereas such a liturgical act normally would be expected to evoke an affirmative and encouraging oracle from a cultic spokesman for Yahweh, in this instance the divine word through Hosea takes the form of a question. In this question, says Wolff, "God is pictured struggling with himself (cf. 11:8)."[2] Mays comments,

> The opening questions express a perplexed frustration at Israel's penitence....Without reserve God discloses the frustration caused by the inconstancy of his people. In the election of Israel Yahweh involved himself in the consequences of their acts. He is the true subject of Israel's history; but he is inextricably by his own free choice a part of the history of which Israel is subject. The history of Israel is the sphere of the struggle and dialogue between man and God--and here the dialogue is like that between husband and fickle wife, father and prodigal son.[3]

This divine question is followed, in v 5, by an indication of Yahweh's way of dealing with his people. Apparently the verse refers to palpable historical calamities visited upon the people in accordance with prophetic announcements of judgment. Given a "dynamic activistic conception of the word of Yahweh" (Mays, p. 97), the historical agency of judgment in this instance is left unmentioned, in favor of an emphasis upon that divine agency of prophetic speech which the people have failed to heed and which therefore, through its actualization, will destroy them.

The second question occurs in the context of *Hos 8:1-14* of which we need quote only vv 5-6:

(5) Your bull, O Samaria, is rejected;
my anger burns against them.
How long will they be incapable of innocence?
(6) For what has Israel to do with it?
An artisan made it!
A god it is not!
Yea, splinters shall become
Samaria's bull.

Wolff identifies this question as a lament, by its opening element, and comments that "the lament juxtaposed with the expression of divine wrath indicates how jealous judgment and grieving, expectant love for Israel struggle within Hosea's God" (Wolff, p. 141). Similarly, Mays comments,

> 'How long...' is an interrogatory exclamation used repeatedly in songs of lament....The question which it introduces is rhetorical; the line is really a cry of anguish and sorrow over Israel's inability to live in innocence, free of the deeds that disqualify for relation to God....In this juxtaposition of lament and burning wrath the God of Hosea discloses the suffering in which the election of Israel has involved him. His anger is not bitter hatred; it is the passion of purpose that will not surrender in spite of frustration and rejection. (Mays, pp. 118-19.)

This divine question is followed, in v 6 and in following verses, by an indication of Yahweh's way of dealing with his people--a variety of historical calamities construed as divine judgments.

The third question occurs in the context of *Hos 11:1-11*, and introduces the central and pivotal section of that long divine address, the section comprising vv 8-9:

(8) How can I make you, O Ephraim,
consign you, O Israel,
how can I make you like Admah,
dispose you like Zeboiim?
My heart transforms itself upon me,
my change of mind grows fervent altogether!
(9) I will not act out my burning anger,
I will not turn to destroy Ephraim--
for I am God and not man,
the Holy One in your midst--
And I will not come to consume.

In this instance the divine question to Israel reaches an extraordinary intensity of passion, in confronting a baffling impasse which calls forth a remarkable disclosure of the interior dynamics of the divine life. Mays characterizes the question in v 8 as a form of "intense...impassioned self-questioning by Yahweh," in which the divine father "pours out mingled sorrow and love in rhetorical questions which deny just punishment." He goes on to say, "as a literary expression of the suffering into which the covenant God has been drawn by Israel's faithlesness, the questions are similar to those in 6:4" (Mays, p. 156). The intensity of the self-questioning arises out of the divine envisagement of a judgment upon Israel so complete and so final as to be analogous to the terrible doom long ago visited upon Admah and Zeboiim, cities which along with Sodom and Gomorrah stand in the OT as eminent instances of total and irreversible annihilation. The questioning of such a prospect achieves such passionate intensity because of the long and intimate relationship which has grown up between Yahweh and Israel, a relationship which had its ground in the divine love (11:1) and which took the character of a relation between father and son. Because of this intimate relation, the divine question to Israel is, as Mays says, precisely a *self*-questioning. As I will argue, it is this *self*-questioning which reveals most deeply what it means to say, in Mays's words, that "[Yahweh] is the true subject of Israel's history" who in part by such questions "discloses the suffering in which the election of Israel has involved him" (see above, in Mays, comments on the first two occurrences of the divine question). That is to say, in view of the nature of the threatened relation between God and people, the question here raised is as much a question of the future of Yahweh as it is a question of the future of Israel. In this instance, now, the disclosed outcome of the divine question is decidedly different than in the two earlier instances. Though, in this third passage, divine wrath does in part come to expression in palpable judgment, nevertheless this judgment will not be on the order of Admah and Zeboiim, but is qualified by an emphatically reiterated negative resolve (v 9) which leaves both Israel's future and Yahweh's future open to the prospect of eventual reconciliation and restoration. Between the questions of v 8 and the negative resolves of v 9 lie the pivotal, all-important and fatefully significant two lines which Wolff translates

> My heart turns against me,
> my remorse burns intensely

and which Mays translates

> My heart has turned itself against me;
> my compassion grows completely warm.

Later, I shall want to examine the translation of these two lines more closely, and to explore their theological implications in some detail. But at this point it is sufficient to note the contrast which they pose to the contexts of the two earlier divine questions. In 6:4 and in 8:5 the questions are followed purely by references to divine judgment of Israel, that is, to a form of divine action which brings about a decided change in Israel's own experience. But in 11:8-9, while the question still leaves room for judgment, this time there also occurs a form of divine action which transpires completely *within* Yahweh himself and which has the character of "intramural" change or transformation. I would emphasize that this transformation occurs as the outcome of an intense *self*-questioning, to which Israel is made privy through the prophetic word. Again, whereas in 6:5 the divine question issues in a prophetic word which slays the people with a word of judgment witnessing against *them* and ushering in *their* punishment, in 11:8-9 the question is contained within a prophetic word which, as Wolff comments, witnesses not so much against Israel and Israel's history as to "the divine love which struggles with Israel *as within itself*" (Wolff, p. 203; italics added). One might say, in other words, that this prophetic word, in the form of this divine question, has to do first of all with the history of *Yahweh*, and only then, and within that *milieu*, with the history of Israel.

II

With this introductory look at the divine questions in Hosea, and at some recent commentary on them, I would like now to explore in a general way what it means to ask a question--for man, and possibly for God. I am not concerned here with the sort of question that poses a request for information about an already existing state of affairs which happens to be unknown to the questioner. Nor am I concerned with rhetorical questions [though of the three questions in Hosea, the last two are explicitly described as rhetorical by Mays], except to note that such questions involve that which is well known by the questioner, and so are not intended to elicit an answer, but are posed for rhetorical effect.

Rather, I am concerned with what I would call *existential questions*. As I mean this term, an existential question has to do with the fact of being alive. And being alive is a matter of exhibiting personal growth and becoming, understood as a temporal process through the power of decision exercised in active response to possibility which stands before one. Such presented possibilities pose themselves as the question of one's existence. What I mean is set out in a well-known passage of a letter by Rainer Maria Rilke, in which he responds to a young man's questions about life. Rilke writes,

> ...no human being anywhere can answer for you those questions and feelings that deep within them have a life of their own....You are so young, so before all beginning, and I want to beg you, as much as I can, dear sir, to be patient toward all that is unsolved in your heart and to try to love the *questions themselves* like locked rooms and like books that are written in a very foreign tongue. Do not now seek the answers, which cannot be given you because you would not be able to live them. And the point is, to live everything. *Live* the questions now. Perhaps you will then gradually, without noticing it, live along some distant day into the answer. Perhaps you do carry within yourself the possibility of shaping and forming as a particularly happy and pure way of living; train yourself to it--but take whatever comes with great trust, and if only it comes out of your own will, out of some need of your inmost being, take it upon yourself and hate nothing.[4]

In this passage, Rilke provides a sensitive description of what it is to experience, to entertain, to enter into the power of an existential question. Such a question is not to be answered, if by answer we mean some piece of information or some notion foreign to the questioner which is brought or drawn toward the questioner who remains stationary. Rather, such a question is to be *lived toward*, in such a way that, in time, the self which one has become is the "answer." The relation between this kind of question and its answer is the relation between inchoate and relatively indeterminate possibility, and determinate actuality.

Moreover, the *power* to live toward such a question arises from the question itself, and this power arises within the person as the question is taken in and entertained attentively. For the power lies in the tension between who and what one *is* at a given point, and who and what one vaguely but importantly senses one may *become*. (This connection between the future as question, or hope, and strength for becoming, is illustrated in some of the Hebrew words for hope, in their root meanings and in their usage. *Tiqwah* can mean either "hope" or "cord." Its root *qwh*, "to wait for," is cognate with Arabic *qawiya*, "to be strong" and *qawwatun*, "strength" or "a strand of rope." Job, in 6:11, asks "What is my strength, that I should wait?/ And what is my end, that I should be patient?" Second Isaiah answers (Isa 40:31), "They who wait for Yahweh shall renew their strength.") Potential for existence is potency for existence.

The *question*-character of this potency consists in the fact that one's most significant and encompassing possibilities for becoming never present themselves in clearly determinate form; rather, they are sensed, or felt, as a directional thrust or pull, which at best may be represented typically, through images and symbols. In this respect, existential questions resemble informational questions, in that the one who entertains an existential question cannot say precisely what it is that one is directed toward by means of the question. Indeed, one may suggest a correlation in which question is to answer as faith is to knowledge. But whereas faith sometimes is *criticized* as being a mere belief as to the character of what could right then be (but in fact is not) known, so that faith is a poor, and sometimes bad, substitute for knowledge, in the here-advocated sense faith is the one possible avenue *to* knowledge. For faith in this sense concerns that which not only is not yet known but is not yet knowable because it does not yet *exist*--it is "the essence of things hoped for." The point is that questions lead *to* existence by being believed *in*. This connection between faith and existential questions is the central point in William James' classic essay, "The Will To Believe." In this essay, James illustrates his central thesis with reference to questions concerning personal relations, as when one asks another "Do you like me, or not?" In many instances, he points out, the way in which the question is asked, the trust and expectation which is invested in the question, "the previous faith on my part in your liking's existence is in such cases what makes your liking come." So, more generally, he concludes, "there are, then, cases where a fact cannot come at all unless a preliminary faith exists in its coming."[5] Robert Frost was deeply indebted to James for this understanding of the role of belief, and recurred to it again and again in poems, essays and interviews. In one interview he said,

> The Founding Fathers didn't believe in the future,...they believed it *in*. You're always believing ahead of your evidence. I believe the future *in*. It's coming in by my believing it. You might as well call that a belief in God.[6]

And in the essay, "Education By Poetry," he wrote,

> There are two or three places where we know belief outside of religion. One of them is at the age of fifteen to twenty, in our self-belief. A young

> man knows more about himself than he is able to prove to anyone....In his foreknowledge he has something that is going to believe itself into fulfillment....
>
> There is another belief like that, the belief in someone else, a relationship of two that is going to be believed into fulfillment....
>
> Then there is a literary belief. Every time a poem is written, every time a short story is written, it is written not by cunning but by belief. The beauty, the something, the little charm of the thing to be, *is more felt than known* ....No one who has ever come close to the arts has failed to see the difference between things written...with cunning and device, and the kind that are believed into existence, that begin in *something more felt than known*....
>
> Now I think--I happen to think--that those three beliefs that I speak of, the self-belief, the love-belief, and the art-belief, are all closely related to the God-belief, that the belief in God is a relationship you enter into with Him to bring about the future.[7]

Understood in this way, existential questions need not present themselves in the form of a *grammatical* question, but simply in whatever form implies a not-completely-determinate, directional possibility. So far as grammar is concerned, they may take the form of invitation, or suggestion, or enticement, or even command. But all of these specific forms of presentation may be said to have the character of a question, insofar as they initiate a process of response which may (but need not) eventuate in the respondent's becoming that which is not fully determinate until the becoming is complete. To sum up this paragraph, I suggest that an existential question is a source of power for becoming, which power is exercised in the mode of active belief. I want now to come at this matter from a somewhat different angle, which I will illustrate with a brief "Heideggerian" word-play and then relate to biblical modes of thought.

Already in Latin, *ex(s)istere* appears to have functioned as an intransitive verb meaning "to emerge and stand out, to appear, to exist." But this verb was built from the components *ex* and *sistere* which means "to cause to stand" from *stare*, "to stand." This illustrates the notion that what exists, what emerges and stands forth with actuality, does so not out of its own aboriginal power for becoming, but by a power derived from a situation of being *caused* to stand forth. I suggest, then, that what exists stands forth in response to a *call*, in the form of a presented possibility for existence, a call in the form of an existential question. This brief suggestion as to what it means to exist may be taken to explicate two creation texts which are, I believe, not unrepresentative of the OT. Isa 48:13 reads

> My hand founded the earth
> and my right hand spread out the heavens;
> when I call to them,
> they stand forth together.

And Ps 33:6-9 reads, in part,

> By the word of Yahweh the heavens were made,
> and all their host by the breath of his mouth.
> ....
> For he spoke, and it came to be;
> he commanded, and it stood forth.

According to these passages, existents emerge and stand forth in response to a call. But they are not merely ushered passively and inertly into existence; they are called to appear, to present themselves. And their existence, consequently, is as much a function of their active response as it is of the initiating call. Moreover, I suggest, this active response does not merely confer actuality upon a potentiality whose details are in all respects pre-determinate. Rather, the call is always general enough to allow for some contribution of specific detail and originative character on the part of the existent. In other words, the existent partly shapes and determines what and who he will become. To give a well-known biblical example, Abraham comes to be who he is through his response to the possibility placed before him by God. This possibility, this awareness of something foreign to his early existence in Haran, something not yet clear to him (and by Gen 15:2 and 16:2 still not clear), something he can only live toward and thereby believe *in*, is Abraham's existential question.

Now I want to suggest that, as power for becoming, one's existential questions are to be husbanded through discreetly channelled living toward them, and not dissipated through indiscriminate disclosures. For the disclosure of one's own questions to others admits them into the sphere of one's inner counsel which is the sphere of one's power of becoming. Thus admitted, others share in that power, for good or ill, and so share in the determination of the final outcome. For example, at least as portrayed in the Gospels, the messianic secret may be shared at the right moment, within a close circle, but for the time being must be kept from the indiscriminate many, lest the outcome lose all resemblance to the initial possibility.

When, through a venture of trust, one's question, while yet a question, is fruitfully shared with another, then the outcome will be somewhat different from what it would have been if pursued in solitude. For the other, having been drawn into the sphere of power of one's question, now shares in that power, and so contributes his own determinations to the eventual "answer." Such situations at the outset constitute a coming together, a *covenant* in the root sense of that word, in the mode of promise and vow. At the outset, not only does each share in the *power* of the other's question, but each becomes a *part* of the other's question--that is, by the very act of admitting another to one's own question, one allows that question to become re-defined so as to include the other as an element in it. The eventual actualization, the *embodiment* of the question wherein the two become one flesh, has the character of a concrete unification, what one Jewish tradition might call a *yihud*, which is coming together or covenanting in the mode of fulfilment. In this unification, each has become a part of the other's answer. So understood, the dialogical character of true covenant relations consists in the sharing of personal power in risk and vulnerability through the mutual disclosure of existential questions. It may be noted, incidentally, that such comings together may arise for the sake of narrow or limited or brief purposes, or for the sake of the most comprehensive and unqualified possibilities in which the total destines of the parties are at stake.

There is, of course, another way of disclosing one's existential questions, which avoids the risks of indiscrimination, but which is devoid also of the rewards of mutuality. This sort of disclosure occurs after one's own given question has been lived (believed) into one's own answer. The power for becoming has been exercised and the person has become something at that stage determinate and complete, at least with reference to that question and that phase of the person's existence for which it was powerful. But the power of that question is now spent for that person as a power for *growth*. He must entertain fresh questions, or cease to grow, and instead just lapse into being, through that stationary dance in which he embraces the (now fully determinate) question and repeats the (already achieved) answer. Yet the question which for him is spent may still be offered to another, for whom, given the other's comparative stage of growth, it may be a source of genuine power. Of course, there is here no risk for the giver of the spent question. For he is already complete with reference to this question, and therefore nothing which the other does with the power of this question can any longer affect his own becoming. I suggest that this is one way to understand the nature of a rhetorical question: it may contribute to the becoming of the one who receives it; but it in no way contributes anything to the one who poses it. He expects no answer to his rhetorical question. For he already possesses, or rather already is, his answer. In this instance, the other does not enter into one's own sphere of power, to share in the determination of one's own destiny. Rather, the other receives one's no longer needed power. Here, no *covenant* arises.

The issue toward which this whole discussion has been moving, is this: Can God entertain existential questions? Or is God, by his very nature, restricted to the entertainment of rhetorical questions only? For classical western thought, including Christian thought generally the dominant answer is clear: God can ask himself no existential questions. Still less can he share such questions with others. Any questions he may pose to himself or to others are rhetorical. As posed, they may enter into the becoming of others, but not into his own. For he does not become; he just *is*.

For process thought generally, the perspective on this issue is quite different. In this perspective, static perfection is not a virtue but a fatal liability. For "even perfection will not bear the tedium of infinite repetition."[8] Rather, the divine perfection is understood to consist in the capacity to change with perfect adequacy in the direction of the divine aim and in league with a fluent world. Indeed, the fluent world itself is understood as receiving its dynamism for change from the God whose own becoming arises out of the divine appetition or "Eros which is the living urge towards all possibilities."[9] The divine Eros may be said to consist in the aboriginal power to pose existential questions as means to the advance of the divine life in its own self-enjoyment. This Eros is a *directional* urge, aimed at the enjoyment and the realization of *types* of possibility, rather than at envisagements which are totally specific and determinate.

But the self-creativity of God does not proceed in solitude. Rather, divine self-creativity goes hand in hand with the emergence of the world in its multifarious forms and occasions of existence. The multifarious existents (the "hosts of heaven and earth") emerge into existence as responses to the disclosed, presented, and so shared divine urge toward novel possibility. This shared divine urge is received locally in the form of what Whitehead calls propositions or "lures for feeling," that is, felt awarenesses of what might be. Such propositions function, in form of the sort of belief of which Frost speaks in the passages quoted above, an awareness of "something, the little charm of the thing to be," an awareness "more felt than known." This awareness often takes on focus in the form of images and metaphors and symbols, which retain the intense feeling of directional lure and indeterminateness with respect to actualization. Precisely how "what might be" is actualized, and the specific shape and character which the existent takes, depends in some degree upon how the existent exercises the power of becoming which it receives in the form of the presented lure or question.

With the completion of the occasion of local becoming, that which now exists as a fully determinate finite actuality is received into God, "unto whom are all things." But for process thought, the only way in which anything can meaningfully be said to be received by God is if that entity enters as an ingredient into the divine becoming, where it contributes its finite and local determinateness to the comprehensive determinateness which is the fulness of God in his perfection as at that moment. As Rilke puts it,

> If he is the most perfect, must not the lesser
> be *before* him, so that he can choose himself out
> of fullness and overflow?--Must he not be the last,
> in order to encompass everything within himself,
> and what meaning would we have if he, whom we long
> for, had already been?[9a]

To sum up this brief statement of process thought, in the terms of the primary question of this paper up to now, God whose own life proceeds toward existential questions posed out of the aboriginal fund of his own appetitive imagination, discloses his own existential questions to that which is not himself, thereby at once calling forth new creatures into existence, and also sharing with them his own sphere of power, and his own becoming. In this, there is complete mutuality of becoming between God and the hosts which make up the world. It is with God and the world (apart, perhaps, from the specific sexual roles) as depicted in these lines of Lawrence Ferlinghetti:

> then this dame
> comes up behind me see
> and says
> You and me could really exist

III

What, then, of the OT? Are its portrayals of God in his own existence and in his relations with the world patient of interpretation in this perspective? At first one begins to hunt for passages which might be adduced in support of a process versus a classical view of God. Suddenly one realizes that the shoe really belongs on the other foot, and that, in many respects, the OT reads much more naturally and suggestively for theology in a process perspective than otherwise. One massive piece of evidence for this is the hermeneutical difficulties which early synagogue and church faced in attempting to read the OT in the light of theological categories developed under the influence of Greek metaphysics, categories which assumed the impassibility and the immutability of the divine life. The hermeneutical solution was to cry "metaphor" and "anthropomorphism," and in effect to demythologize by converting the "oriental imagery" into philosophical categories. The problem with this practice was not *that* it was attempted, but *how* it was carried out. At certain key points, it seems to me, the conversion did not carry what the text itself implied. Rather, the text was inverted and made to say exactly the opposite of what the metaphors implied. For instance, those passages which portrayed a God who is internally related to the world, and so capable of feeling and change in response to change in the world, were explained *away*, as accommodations to our human understanding, rather than explored as they stood for their theological implications. By contrast, a process view of things may dispense with many traditional hermeneutical devices designed to "save the [biblical] appearances," since it provides a currency of thought and language into which we may most naturally convert those OT portrayals where God's passionality and mutability are either asserted or assumed. Let me adduce a few items in support of this general assertion.

1. *Gen 6:5-8*. Two points are noteworthy here. The divine decision for the flood is accounted for, not by appeal to the inscrutable caprice of God, but by appeal to the state of affairs in the world. This world, it may be said, arose as the means to the fulfillment of the divine urge to creation, and to enjoyment of its own creation (Gen 1:1-4). The enjoyment of the creation, and of the divine self as creator, assumed the "goodness" of that creation (Gen 1:4). But the state of affairs has become so incompatible with the divine creative aims and enjoyment, that the indignant pain which it gives him leads God to change his mind concerning the viability of such a world as a means to those aims. But, secondly, the fact of Noah's existence in righteousness effects a modification in the changing divine purpose. Both with respect to the world in general, and with respect to Noah in particular, the natural conclusion is to suppose that God is internally related to his creation.

2. *Gen 18:16-33*. Again the state of affairs, this time concerning a local region, comes to the point where God purposes to visit that region in his justice. In this instance, the way in which Abraham is admitted into the sphere of power of God's question concerning these cities, could not be more graphically portrayed. For God has visited Abraham in the persons of three men. Now as God, or these three men, set(s) out toward Sodom, God decides to make Abraham privy to his intention, and the reason for this soon becomes apparent. While *two* of the men go on toward Sodom, Yahweh remains standing before Abraham.[9b] Of course, the later scribes with philosophical clarity recognized the implications of such a divine action, and in one of their rare deliberate alterations of the text they revised it so as to have Abraham standing before Yahweh. The implications of the original text are clear and

momentous, in at least two ways: by standing before Abraham even while he proceeded toward Sodom, the text suggests that God himself was not finally decided, or resolved, concerning the future of Sodom. That is to say, the future remained open to at least two types of possibility, and so posed itself as a question for the divine purpose. Further, in remaining before Abraham to see what he would do or say, God drew Abraham into that sphere of decision-making power within which Sodom's fate would be decided. And Abraham's intercession was simply the form which his determining action took.

3. It is not too much to suggest that the prophets generally, whether as intercessors or as announcers of the divine word to which they have become privy, are to be understood as standing within the sphere of power of God's questions concerning the future. For the announcement of Yahweh's word, even where it has the grammatical force of a warning, or a seemingly inescapable sentence, at a deeper level has the character of an existential question. As Martin Buber puts it, in *The Prophetic Faith*,

> The true prophet does not announce an immutable decree. He speaks into the power of decision lying in the moment....The power and ability are given to every man at any definite moment really to take his choice, and by this he shares in deciding about the fate of the moment after this, and this sharing of his occurs in a *sphere of possibility* which cannot be figured either in manner or scale. It is to this personal decision of man with its part in the power of fate-deciding that the prophetic announcement of disaster calls.[10]

Of course, it can be objected that the fate which is decided by this power is the fate of the world only, and not the fate of God; so that what we have here is not the disclosure of a divine existential question, but of a question which is existential for man but only rhetorical for God. Buber himself, after probing the significance of prophetic activity so sensitively, ends up on a note which, in my view, robs what he has said of its full potential for theological reflection, and betrays his education in the classical philosophical and hermeneutical tradition. For, in turning to a discussion of the Book of Jonah, with its paradigmatic dramatization of the dialogue between man and God within the sphere of shared possibility, and its portrayal of human repentance followed by divine repentence, Buber writes,

> Human and divine turning correspond the one to the other; not as if it were in the power of the first to bring about the second, such ethical magic being far removed from Biblical thought, but--"Who knows."

This sentence is an astoundingly clear example of how classical modes of thought about God can bewitch the otherwise sound hermeneutical perceptions of a sensitive student of the Bible. For it is clear that the "ethical Magic" really is on the other foot! What else can we call it but magic, when we have two actions in temporal sequence, such that the second *appears* to follow from the first, and yet there is no *discoverable* causal relation and indeed there is said to *be* no causal relation;

and nevertheless the moral and existential climate of urgency indicates that we are to attend to both actions as though they had something to do with one another? In the absence of a causal relation, simply to introduce the phrase "correspond to one another" is to wave the wand of a magic incantation over a process which one cannot or will not venture to understand. In Jonah, as in Jer 18:5-11, the conclusion which we must draw, if we are not to destroy the force of the passages altogether, is that man is privy to the sphere of power by which the future is decided. And this future is not just the future of the world, but it is also the future of God. For when men's actions bring about a change in God's purposes for the world, they thereby bring about a change in God himself. For there is little if anything that is more definitive of one's own inner existence than one's own purposes, and it makes no sense to speak of God's (or anyone's) purposes as external to himself.

4. The capacity of man to share in the determination of the life of God is shown in a number of other ways, of which only a few may briefly be alluded to here. *Item*: In the OT, the act of blessing, whether undertaken by God to man, or by one man to another, is portrayed as an efficacious enrichment of the one blessed by the very power of being which quickens the one who blesses. Now, in worship Israel is said to bless God (e.g., Ps 103). On what biblical or other basis do we decide that the context of worship, and the nature of the recipient, gives blessing a meaning different than that which it otherwise has? Is it not at least worth considering that the significance of the general act of blessing indicates the true character and importance of the act of worship? *Item*: Ps 51 has God repudiate sacrificial offerings. On what basis? That he has no need of bulls and goats? Or is it that, as the text asserts, bulls and goats are already his, but that, as the whole psalm implies, there *is* a sacrifice which God looks for and which is *not* his unless it is *offered*--the offering of human thanksgiving together with a life of covenant integrity? It may be *ḥesed* which God desires, and not sacrifice (Hos 6:6). But this means that it is not the logic of sacrifice which is in question, but its content. The word "desires" indicates that which lies in man's power to offer for, or to withhold from, the enrichment of the divine life. *Item*: One is bidden to love God and to love one's neighbour as oneself. On what biblical or other basis does one understand the second action to contribute to the neighbour's well-being, while one demurs from understanding the first to contribute to God's? Surely the ultimate biblical motive for ethical existence is not man's well-being, but God's pleasure. But what does it mean for God to take pleasure in the lives of his creatures? Even if it be objected that God's concern for man's ethical existence arises out of a concern for *man's* welfare, and not out of a concern for the divine self-enjoyment, this only pushes the issue one step further back. The point remains that one or another kind of human behaviour toward another human being can and does bring joy or pain to the divine care for the world; but that care is not external to the divine life, it is part of its very intrinsic character. And the ethical history of the world is etched upon, or rather etches, the contours of the biography of the divine care, for which not even the welfare of the foreigner or the eunuch is ever forgotten (Isa 56:3-5). *Item*: God not only works and rests according to his own self-

determined schedule (Gen 1:1--2:3, Exod 31:17), but he can be made to labour and become weary under the burden of a people which misuse the power which he has shared with them (Isa 1:14; 43:24). *Item*: God can bind himself to man by an oath concerning the fulfillment of a promise, such that the violation of that oath will rend the divine life in two (Gen 15:7-21, especially v 17; note that it is not Abraham who passes between the divided parts, but a numinous presence). Insofar as the self-binding has to do with a future which is open but directed, that self-binding constitutes the entertainment and the appropriation and the husbanding of the power of the divine Eros in one of its forms; and insofar as that self-binding is undertaken in the presence of a man, that man is drawn into the sphere of power of the oath, and indeed becomes a part of the very question itself.

5. It is sometimes said that, in contrast to the Gods of the Ancient Near East, "Yahweh has no myth concerning his life." (The source of this sentence is lost to me.) The intention of such a saying is to take note of an obvious difference between the divine myths of the Ancient Near East, and the OT. But I suggest the difference is thereby misconstrued. Insofar as the myths concern the lives of the Gods, they do so by portraying the mutually internal relations between the Gods, and the vicissitudes of their several life stories arising out of those internal relations. What strikes me about these myths is that, while the Gods affect one another, by existing together within that "sphere of possibility" (to use Buber's term) and sphere of shared power which constitutes the Divine Council; and while their actions affect man and so constitute man's existential questions; yet the myths give little space to the actions of man as significant or determinative for the Gods. While it is true that human ritual action and prayer is assumed to be efficacious in winning the response of the Gods, it does seem significant that, in the myths themselves, taken as portrayals of the fundamental character of things, little or no place is made for human determination of the course of events. At most, man is a servant of the Gods, who provides for their personal needs while they shape the course of events by their interactions. There is a long but direct line from the ancient Gods and their monopoly on the power of fate-deciding, and contemporary determinisms arising from a consideration of the workings of natural laws. By contrast, in the OT the whole story has to do with the inter-relations between Yahweh and the *human* community, while so-called encounters between Yahweh and the other Gods appear around the edges of the drama. But it is not as though myth has been pushed to one side, and the life of God rendered invisible. I suggest that just the reverse has happened. Man has been drawn into the myth and now shares the stage with divinity. The sphere of power is no longer somewhere else, *in illo tempore*, across the plains or on the summit of the cosmic mountain or at the sources of the double deep; it is that public and present world which man inhabits. The whole OT is the myth concerning Yahweh's life.

6. Finally, the very notion of covenant, which by common consent is fundamental to the OT, involves the mutuality of shared power by the mutual disclosure of existential questions between God and man. There is an intrinsic resemblance, which spans the difference in magnitude and tone (and perhaps importance) between

You shall be my people
and I will be your God

and

You and me could really exist.

What it means for Israel to have Yahweh as her God, is an open question; and it is likewise an open question for Yahweh, as to what it means for him to have Israel as his people. It is within the sphere of this all-encompassing open question that all local and specific questions arise, including the three which are explicitly posed in Hosea and to which we may now finally return.

IV

In Buber's words, the prophetic word in Hosea, taken as a whole, may be said to have been spoken "into the power of decision lying in the moment," which in this instance was the historical situation in which Israel existed at that time. This word did not function to "announce an immutable decree." How *could* it, since long ago already Yahweh had admitted Israel (as, in one way or another, the whole creation) into the "sphere of possibility," the "power of fate-deciding"? The power of action arising out of Yahweh's own existential questions was no longer solely in Yahweh's hands such that he could issue unilateral immutable decrees. Rather, this word functioned to elicit a *turning*. But it became apparent that Israel's own defective behaviour with its consequences made such a turning to Yahweh increasingly difficult and unlikely, as Israel became "increasingly bound to that behaviour until eventually it [was] enslaved (5:4a; 9:10b, 16a; 13:1f)."[11] The prophet's announcement of disaster was delivered into such an extreme situation as a last possibility for touching "the innermost soul," in order "to evoke the extreme act: the turning to God" (Buber). But this means that, as such, Hosea's announcement of doom, for all its declarative mode of address, at a deeper level had the character of a *question*, as if to ask, What will you, now, make of this imminent probability, which threatens to be inescapable, and which *will* be inescapable if present tendencies are without alteration merely extended into the future?

This deeper character of the prophetic word of Hosea as a whole comes to the surface, like stone outcroppings in the foothills of Colorado, in the three explicit questions which punctuate the divine address to Israel. In these questions, the true force and purpose of the total address becomes evident. It is not that the announcements of disaster are a mere *bluff*. For disaster is an all-too-likely outcome. The specific trajectories of historical momentum which combine to define Israel's situation of crisis, drive toward the doom which is announced, a doom which, at one and the same time, Israel calls down upon herself, and Yahweh visits upon her. But the future is never completely foredoomed. There is always a margin for decision, a margin of negotiability within which both Israel and Yahweh must find the way forward. Granted, then, that these divine questions are "a cry of anguish and sorrow over Israel's inability to live in innocence...," and as such, a disclosure of "the suffering in which the election of Israel has involved [God]" (Mays, p. 119), one may ask, what is the purpose of such a passionate disclosure? Is it not to speak, in this most vulnerable and therefore perhaps most persuasive and finally efficacious mode, into Israel's power of fate-deciding, and thereby--who knows--evoke a turning? Is it not, perhaps, to punctuate the announcement of doom in such a way as to show that, precisely in their declarative force, these announcements have as their aim to jolt Israel out of the somnambulistic assurance of its wrongheaded ways, and to bring Israel back to the awareness that it stands within that sphere of becoming which it properly shares with Yahweh? But if this be the case, then the questions are not rhetorical but existential.

The questions show Yahweh placed before an impasse, which seemingly can be overcome only by choosing one of two ways forward, either of which is unthinkable: either to execute the righteous judgment of God in that overflowing of wrath which would break off the covenant relation; or to continue to overlook Israel's persistent subversion of God's aims, and thereby (as surely as by a judgmental severance of relations) to fail to bring Yahweh and Israel to that "answer" implied in that divine existential question which initiated the covenant relationship. How is this impasse to be negotiated, without loss to the divine aim?

According to Wolff and Mays, the impasse is overcome in the course of a *conflict* within God himself, which is resolved through the overthrow of the divine wrath by the divine compassion or love, intensified or spurred on by the divine remorse (Wolff). Mays translates the last two lines of v 8,

> My heart has turned itself against me;
> my compassion grows completely warm.

On these lines he comments, in part,

> To be like Admah and Zeboiim is to exist only as a memory of swift and final calamity. In face of such a fate for Israel Yahweh has become like a man in whose self-consciousness wrath and love battle with each other. His heart, the seat of consciousness and will, assumes a hostile position against the punishment which he has already announced (9:6, 11-13; 10:8, 14f). Compassion, the tender emotion which parents feel toward the helpless child, grows increasingly strong and displaces wrath....Yahweh speaks of himself in the human genre to disclose in emotional terms that his election of Israel is stronger than their sin. (Mays, p. 157.)

This is a bold interpretation indeed, one which envisions the divine life at odds within itself, such that

> Yahweh speaks as a man incapable of action because of his divided feelings, caught by the growing power of desire and emotion which oppose what he must do. (Mays, p. 157.)

This boldness, however, is then blunted by Mays' cautionary recollection of the metaphorical mode of this biblical portrayal of Yahweh, which should remind us that "Hosea's many anthropomorphisms are meant as interpretive analogies, not as essential definitions." But unless we are simply to *replace* such analogies with essential definitions derived from elsewhere,[12] how do we move from metaphor to essential definition? Now, for all their manifold richness of overtone and allusion, metaphors at their center do imply one thing and not another; and the most natural procedure is to take the metaphor as adumbrating an essential character which is analogous to the metaphoric vehicle, and not contrary to it. When Mays goes on to say, "He is wrathful and loving *like* man, but *as* God," I take him to be on firm ground. But I will propose that the difference which his assertion alludes to is to be identified otherwise than as he suggests. But first let us consider what Wolff has to say on these two lines. Wolff translates,

> Mein Herz kehrt sich gegen mich,
> meine Reue entbrennt mit Macht,

which is rendered in the English version of his commentary,

> My heart turns against me,
> my remorse burns intensely.

He comments on these lines,

> Yahweh's will is directed against himself, i.e. against his wrath (v 9a). In the phrase "my heart turns against me," ...*ᶜalay*...has a hostile sense. The rarely used word "remorse" (*niḥumim*) ...emphasizes *the turning point* in Yahweh's will attested in v. 8....His remorse (over his wrathful intention to judge) "grows hot," i.e., it provokes him and dominates him....Again and again we see the God of Hosea in conflict with himself over Israel. (Wolff, p. 201; italics added.)

Apropos the immediately following lines in v 9, Wolff goes on to say,

> It is important to note that the concept of Yahweh's holiness, appearing only once in Hosea, provides the foundation not for his judging will but for his saving will, to which he had committed himself from the very beginning of Israel's saving history. (Wolff, p. 202.)

And in this context he also says,

> God proves himself to be God and Holy One in Israel in that he, unlike men, is independent of his partner's actions. Remaining completely sovereign over his own actions, he is not compelled to react....The final period of the nation's history is not to be dominated by the consequences of Israel's deeds (vv. 5-7); rather, the future will be determined [sic] by Yahweh's decision to let his love rule. (Wolff, p. 202.)

This interpretation does take the figurative language with unflinching seriousness, and attempts to draw consequences for theology which preserve the implications of the figures. Wolff says later,

> Of great theological significance in this chapter is its disclosure that Israel's election and guidance is founded upon God's love (vv. 1,4); this love is not some inconstant characteristic but proves to be the incomparable, holy essence

> of God himself. Yahweh cannot set aside his love just as he cannot set aside his divinity. (Wolff, p. 203.)

The clear implication of this last passage, that unlike his love God's wrath is an "inconstant characteristic" and therefore not an element in his "holy essence," is explicitly stated in a comment upon another passage, where Wolff writes, "His wrath is to be distinguished from his essence, as a tool is distinguished from the master craftsman who uses it" (Wolff, p. 114; compare, less explicitly, Mays, p. 90). If this distinction is correct, then it is clear that God may set aside his wrath without setting aside his divinity. But then the internal conflict, after all, cannot be much of a struggle, for it is an uneven and fore-doomed match between God's holy essence and some inconstant characteristic or occasional instrument. Indeed, in this case the portrayal of God as "a man incapable of action because of his divided feelings" would have to be said to be overdrawn, or to be merely a rhetorical--a misleading rhetorical--device with no genuine impasse indicated. But it is doubtful that the wrath of God is to be given so slight a status in the divine life. It may be that he is *slow* to anger, and *abounding* in steadfast love (Ps 103:8); but this difference by itself does not place the two feelings upon a different basis within the divine nature.[13] To set aside his wrath is as essentially problematical for Yahweh in the OT as to set aside his love. Yet, in summing up the commentary of Wolff and Mays on this point, it may be said that this is how they see Yahweh overcoming the impasse. In so overcoming it, Wolff asserts, God in his sovereign freedom and power acts independent of his partner's actions, toward which he is not compelled to react. Now, such an interpretation is, in Wolff's words, "of great theological significance" indeed! The significance is one with which I would have such difficulty that I should have to resolve my own mind by a process such as they ascribe to God, by a denial of one part of me for the sake of another part--were I able in the first place to accept the translations of the text upon which their interpretations are based. But the translations, in my judgment, are forced, and do not follow the most natural meaning of the text. It will be necessary, then, to examine the linguistic elements of these two lines in some detail, before continuing with this hermeneutical exploration.

The Hebrew text reads as follows:

> *nehpak ᶜālay libbî*
> *yaḥad nikmᵉrû niḥûmay*

Now it is acknowledged freely that the opening verb can be used to refer to polemical actions of "overthrow." This is the case primarily with the simple, or qal, stem of the verb, and in all instances of the cognate noun *mahpekāh*, which always (6 times) refers to the overthrow of Sodom and Gomorrah. Also, the niphal stem (the stem in Hos 11:8) functions once, in the passive voice, to describe the (projected) overthrow of Nineveh, in Jon 3:4. Wolff's comments (p. 201) assume that because of the mention of Admah and Zeboiim in v 8, this aspect of the meaning of *nehpak* must be, or at any rate is, dominant in its occurrence in the line in question. Certainly, given the plurisignative way poetic language does its work, one can hardly fail to hear such overtones. In my judgment, such overtones function to create tensive contrast. But the attempt to elevate these overtones to the status of primary meaning breaks down. Let me try to show this by quoting again a comment by Wolff: "Yahweh's will is directed against himself, i.e., against his wrath." In this sentence, Wolff asserts, in a footnote, "Yahweh's will" is identified with "my heart"--presumably indicating his true and deepest and essential purpose. The pronoun "me" Wolff takes to refer to "himself, i.e. ....his wrath (v. 9a)." Now, in order for Wolff's interpretation to work, so as to have the verb *nehpak* somehow function with the overtones of the polemical uses of this root, we have to imagine that Yahweh's (saving) will overthrows his wrath. We could do this, if the subject of the verb, *libbî* = "my heart/will," governed a *transitive* form of the verb, so as to give a reading "my will overthrows me" or the like. Or we could do this if the *niphal* stem which is in fact used were to be taken in the passive voice (as in Jon 3:4), with "me" as subject, to give "I am overthrown by my heart" or the like. But the text allows neither of these possibilities. It does not allow us to understand the verb *nehpak* as indicating a polemical relationship between "my heart" on the one hand and "me" on the other, with the heart the victor. Among polemical options allowed by the syntax, the best we could manage would be a reading "my heart is overthrown upon me," in which case the actor, and victor, is a third party not identified. If we take *nehpak* as reflexive, we might try to imagine a civil war, "my heart overthrows itself..."--but there is no analogy for such a connotation of this verb in the reflexive voice.

But the verb *hāpak*, both in the qal and in the niphal stem, also has another very common meaning in the reflexive voice, which fits the present context much more naturally, and yet carries sufficient dramatic force to sustain and even to provide a climax for the emotional intensity to which Hos 11 has been building since the first verse. That meaning describes some kind of *change* having the character of a *transformation.* In such instances, the verb describes a qualitative change affecting the totality of the entity to which it refers. Thus, for instance, it may refer to a change in the colour of one's skin (Lev 13:55, Jer 13:23), a change in the quality of one's physiological awareness (1 Sam 4:19), a change in the quality of one's pervasive emotional state (Jer 31:13),[14] or a change in one's attitude toward another (Ps 105:25). The verb may also describe a change or transformation in the total character of a person. This is implied in the analogy of Jer 13:23, and it is made explicit in 1 Sam 10:6, "and you shall be turned into another man," a transformation described in 10:9 in these words: "and God gave him another heart." This last text collocates the verb *hāpak* and the noun *heart* in a portrayal of non-polemical transformation. All of these usages indicate the naturalness with which the verb *hāpak* may be taken to refer to a change or transformation of heart. This meaning for the line in question in Hos 11 is supported by the preposition which accompanies the verb there, as we shall now try to show.

Wolff analyzes the preposition as having "a hostile sense." Again, it is granted that this preposition often does occur in polemical contexts with the meaning "upon = against." Yet this is hardly the most natural meaning in the present context. For the word is also used frequently in descriptions of changes in the inner, emotional state of a person. In such instances, the force of the preposition "upon" is to portray the subject as in some manner experiencing or undergoing his own changing state, so that he is the recipient who "suffers" this change.[15] In some instances of this usage, the relation between the object of the preposition and the action in the verb is complex, so that somehow the subject is both *agent* and *recipient*. An instructive example, in which the niphal stem occurs with reflexive force, is Neh 5:7 *wayyimālēk libbî ᶜālay* (grammatically and semantically an almost exact parallel to *nehpak ᶜālay libbî*): "my heart took counsel upon me," or "I took counsel with myself." It need hardly be pointed out that here no polemical overtones are present in the preposition. Other examples in which the subject is both agent and recipient of action, are Ps 42:5 "I will pour out my soul upon me," and Job 10:1 "I will let loose my complaint upon me."[16] In short, then, the preposition in such instances gives vivid expression to that awareness which accompanies certain intensely felt actions in which the actor himself undergoes change. So then, I propose (in basic agreement with Wilhelm Rudolph[17]) that the most natural translation of this line is "my heart transforms itself upon me."

Parallel to this line, the Hebrew text proceeds to say,

yaḥad nikmᵉrû niḥûmay

The verb *kamar*, which occurs only in the niphal stem, means "to grow intensely warm, or hot." In three of its four occurrences in the OT, it describes a surge of fervent positive feeling (see Gen 43:30; 1 Kgs 3:26, where the feeling arises in relation to one's child or one's brothers). What is it that surges fervently, in Hos 11:8? It is *niḥûmay*, which may translate "my compassions" or the like. Wolff, however, understands the word to signify the *intransitive* rather than the *transitive* aspect of its root meaning.[18] This is clear both from his translation "remorse" (Reue), and from his comment that this "rarely used word...emphasizes the *turning point* in Yahweh's will attested in v. 8" (italics added). That is to say, I take the two locutions, *nehpak libbî* and *niḥûmay*, as synonymous, referring to a change or transformation which takes place within Yahweh. The second line, then, is to be read in part "my change of mind grows fervent...." But this process is characterized by the emphatically positioned adverb *yaḥad*, a word which is of great significance for our discussion.

The root *yḥd* occurs in verbal form only rarely in the OT. In the qal stem it occurs twice, in the negative (Gen 49:6; Isa 14:20), to indicate that someone is not to *join* a group of people in their particular mode of assembly; in the piel stem it expresses the prayer that Yahweh might *unite* the worshipper's *heart* to fear his name (Ps 86:11). These few occurrences show that the meaning has to do with togetherness, or existence in concert. By far the majority of the occurrences of this root take the form of an adverb, either *yaḥad* (as in the present instance) or *yaḥdāw*,[19] which carries the basic meaning "together." In a large number of instances, the adverb characterizes a situation in which a number of persons come together to take counsel for some specific purpose (e.g., Josh 9:2; 11:5; Ps 2:2; 71:10; Isa 45:21). The adverb functions to indicate, not just their physical togetherness, but their unanimity in counsel and purpose which constitutes them as an assembly (*qāhāl*), an intimate privy council (*sôd*) (Gen 49:6). The covenanting[20] character of such a coming together is shown in Ps 83.6 (5, EVV):

> they conspire *with one accord*,
> against thee they make a covenant.

One might say that in such contexts the adverb describes the process whereby "the many become one." The unity thereby achieved arises with reference to some *purpose* to which all are privy and with which all are in accord. The root also describes an analogous process as it may occur within an individual. (Indeed, it is highly suggestive that the form *yaḥîd*, which most often means "only, only one, solitary," can occur as a synonym for *nepeš* or self, in Ps 22:21 and 35:17). The prayer in Ps 86: 11, "*unite* (*yaḥēd*) my heart to fear thy name," clearly is to be connected to the injunction to love Yahweh with all one's heart, and to the quality of inner integrity or undividedness expressed in the phrases *tām lēb* (Gen 20:5,6) and *lēb šālēm* (1 Kgs 8:61 and often). One may consult also 32:39, and 1 Chron 12:17.[21]

We are in a position, now, to appreciate the significance of the plural form *niḥûmay* and the ingressive force of the verb *nikmᵉrû*, in Hos 11:8: the transformation which takes place in Yahweh is "wholehearted"; all the components of the divine life grow fervently together in the new purpose to which he resolves himself.

What the two lines together describe, then, is a process of transformation which takes place within Yahweh, a transformation in which the dilemma is dealt with in such a manner that the outcome is an undivided feeling and attitude and purpose, a transformation in which Yahweh is both initiator and outcome. It is by *this* means, and not by a divided purpose in which one element dominates and overrules the other, that the impasse is negotiated. Moreover, I suggest, it is this difference which provides the basis for the assertion of an emphatic contrast between God and man in v 9. How, then, may we interpret this transformation and understand this contrast? Since the contrast makes implicit appeal to the way man characteristically acts in such impasses, it is appropriate (indeed, one may say the text with assertorial lightness directs us) to reflect upon such human action in general.

V

The general phenomenon of human decision making shows that all too often such an impasse is resolved by choosing in favour of one or other of the components of deep feeling. The tragedy is that such a decision results in something less than existential wholeness; the decision cuts off a palpable and organic part of the actual situation, including an organic part of the deciding self. For what has happened is that one component feeling has been identified as relatively evil, and the other component feeling as relatively good, and the evil has been rejected and the good adopted. But since, in the case of a genuine impasse, each component arises as a momentum of personal energy, a concrete, determinate power of action which makes its own efficacious claims on the total situation, to choose one over against the other is to lose part of the total power and efficacy of the situation. And insofar as one is internally related to that situation, this means to lose part of one's own concrete self.[22] One may, after a fashion, negotiate the impasse and enter into the kingdom, but one does so minus an eye, or a hand, or a foot, or (vide Origen) something else. Such a diminishing choice may, in such situations, be the best that man, as man, can carry through, and as such it partly gives the human condition its character of tragedy.

But even for human finiteness in its tragic weakness, there is the *challenge*, as Buber argues in *Good and Evil*, not to reject the evil impluse (the *yeṣer hārāᶜ*) in favor of the good impulse (the *yeṣer haṭōb*), but to unify all the impulses, in an act which sustains one's relation to the total passional situation and at the same time to the fundamental direction of one's life. Buber's development of the Talmudic doctrine of the two urges is worth introducing here at some length, for the light it may shed on Hos 11:8-9, as well as for the possible extension which the general argument of this paper may indicate for that doctrine. Buber writes,

> In the creation of man, the two urges are set in opposition to each other. The Creator gives them to man as his two servants which, however, can only accomplish their service in genuine collaboration. The 'evil urge' is no less necessary than its companion....Man's task, therefore, is not to extirpate the evil urge, but to reunite it with the good.... Man is bidden...: 'Love the Lord with all thine heart,' and that means, with thy two united urges. The evil urge must also be included in the love of God [,] thus and thus only does it become perfect, and thus and thus only does man become once more as he was created: 'very good.'...But how is the evil urge to be prevailed upon to permit this to happen to it? Why, it is nothing but a crude ore, which must be placed in the fire in order to be moulded....

Buber goes on to characterize the two urges thus:

> ...the evil 'urge' as passion....which, left to itself, remains without direction and leads astray, and the 'good urge' as pure direction, in other words, as an unconditional direction, that towards God.

And he concludes,

> To unite the two urges implies: to equip the absolute potency of passion with the one direction that renders it capable of great love and of great service. Thus and not otherwise can man become whole.[23]

I will interrupt these extended quotations at this point, to suggest that, within the perspective of this paper, the "unconditional direction" of which Buber speaks may be interpreted in terms of the fundamental divine existential question, by admission to the sphere of power of which man receives his high calling and task. Of course, Buber confines this task of unification (what this Jewish tradition calls *yiḥud*) to man, and limits the scope of what is to be unified to man and his world; and he explicitly repudiates the notion of "this unification as taking place 'in' God."[24] As will shortly be seen, the notion which he repudiates is here adopted, and will be the very meaning claimed to be implicit in Hos 11:8-9. Meanwhile, one further quotation may be introduced:

> ...By decision we understand, not a partial, a pseudo decision, but that of the whole soul.... Good can only be done with the whole soul. It is done when the soul's rapture, proceeding from its highest forces, seizes upon all the forces and plunges them into the purging and transmuting fire, as into the mightiness of decision. Evil is lack of direction and that which is done in it and out of it as the grasping, seizing, devouring, compelling, seducing, exploiting, humiliating, torturing and destroying of what offers itself. Good is direction and what is done in it; that which is done in it is done with the whole soul, so that in fact all the vigour and passion with which evil might have been done is included in it.[25]

These quotations indicate the challenge which is posed whenever a genuine impasse arises in the path of existence, that is, in the path of becoming. The challenge is not merely to sustain or maintain oneself, nor merely to restore a unity as it previously existed, but rather to forge a wholeness which, since it must encompass new elements including impulses and efficacious passions which have arisen in the new situation, is a *new* wholeness. If, in this process, man becomes once more as he was created--"very good"--it becomes clear that in this process man participates in creation.

Now, in a process perspective, I suggest, the existential task of *yiḥud*--the task of holistic becoming through unification of one's world--characterizes not only, nor eminently, the life of man, but first of all and eminently the life of God. For the divine unity is not a static but a dynamic perfection. This dynamic perfection arises out of God's internal relatedness to the world. God (after Rilke's words quoted earlier) chooses himself out of fullness and overflow, "in order to encompass everything within himself." The unity of God is realized ever afresh through his sovereign freedom and power whereby, in each new occasion of the divine relation to the world, he draws the world in all its multifarious determinateness into himself, passionately conforms himself perfectly to these finite forms of determinateness, and yet does so in such a manner as to sustain the original *direction* (cf. Buber) indicated by his own Eros, his own aboriginal existential question. In this view, the sovereign freedom and power is not demonstrated in his independence of his partner's actions, to which he is not compelled to react (Wolff). Quite the opposite! His sovereign freedom and power emerge in the process by which, having conformed with perfect passional sympathy to the actions of his partner, and thereby, so to speak, having his own agenda set for him by his partner's actions (for what else could genuine dialogue between God and man mean?), he goes on to act in a manner which sustains both the total relationship with his partner, in all its concrete particularity, and the aboriginal divine purpose.

This process of "choosing" involves struggle, wherein the various mutually discordant components and vectors of purposive energy in the world are drawn into an ideal unification or harmonization. As discordant and incompatible among themselves in the world, the component energies in the world tend--with varying vectors of efficacious momentum--toward their own destruction. Since their discordancies arise out of their own several decisions, this destruction or doom may be said to be brought upon themselves. But this doom or wrath is not merely "the way the world works," as though wrath were to be understood solely as a kind of "natural law" of moral retribution originally ordained by God but now operating purely in the world and externally to God. Rather, this wrath is quite appropriately, and I would argue most properly, to be understood as the wrath of God.[26] For, in my understanding of process thought, God receives the world into himself initially without qualification, aberration, or remainder (unto him are *all* things). In the technical language of Whitehead, God makes no negative prehensions. He carefully, that is fully and with care, receives every quantum of energy and emotion and impulse and action that arises in the world, in and with its peculiar quality of feeling and direction of aim, into himself, by his own conformal or passional power. Therein he allows himself to be determined by the multifarious determinatenesses of the world. He makes these passions his own--he owns them. In this way, the wrath which arises in the world in the form of mutually discordant, eccentrically-misdirected efficacious actions tending to the destruction of some region or all of the world, *becomes* the wrath of God. At this point, the complete fact is the wrath of *God*; and it is only by a retrograde abstraction that we may think of it as wrath operating by some kind of natural law in the world. God's wrath, then, arises from the world through his perfect conformal feeling of the world. There is an analogy here with human experience, in which wrath arises within one, not as a deliberate intention, but as a passion which acts upon one. Were God merely to exclude or reject or deny any least such wrathful feeling, he would to that extent fail to know and relate to that part of the world with perfect adequacy. But on the other hand, merely to "know the world as it is," and to acquiesce in its settled determinateness and its vector energies, and so to allow its vectors to determine the divine future, would be to lose sight of the aboriginal divine aim within the sphere of which the relation with the world has been established and pursued. To lose *either one* of them--either the totality of the determinate vectors of the world inclusive of its wrathful components; *or* the aboriginal divine aim of which the world has been made a constituent member--would be, I suggest against Wolff, to "set aside his divinity," in favor of one or other of what would by themselves become demonic forces.[27] Therefore, an act of *transformation* is called for, by means of which the disparate ingredients in the divine wrath are incorporated into a wider, deeper vision which is consonant with the aboriginal vision and to which they may ultimately contribute.

It is important to note here that, as I view it, this transformation does not imply a material change in the elements of the world themselves. God does not tamper with the results of our decisions, so as to undo what we have done and thereby in effect rob our power of decision of its reality and importance. What God's transformation does imply may be adumbrated in two aspects. First, it implies a transformation in the specific forms of relevant possibility by which the aboriginal divine Eros may achieve its aims. That is to say, the transformation is something which occurs in the mode of imaginative vision within God himself. The transformation effects an imaginative reconciliation of the world within God, by means of which the unity of the divine life is a *new* unity. (This, I suggest, is a way of understanding the assertion that "Yahweh sits enthroned over the flood,//Yahweh sits enthroned as king for ever"--Ps 29:10.) But this unity is not something thereby actualized. It is a unity which is *imaginatively* achieved, but which remains to be rendered concrete. This imaginative unification constitutes the new form of the divine existential question. Were God to achieve such a unity, to actualize it, by his solitary action, we should have to take any questions arising for the world out of this new situation as being only *rhetorically* posed for the world by God. But, in the perspective here being argued, such is not the case.

A second implication of God's transformation now emerges: This new form of the question, this imaginative vision, is then offered to the world, so that the world is drawn into its sphere of power. It is offered to the world as a translucent garment of possibility which clothes[28] all the determinate elements and vector forces of the world, including the components tending toward wrath. The garment does not itself change the settled world. Rather, the garment, by a kind of refraction which may alter the world's vision for itself, opens the way for the world to understand itself in a new way.

That is to say, God's imaginative transformation of the world, including such a transformation of the wrath, is offered as a new way of understanding the world including its wrath. Where the margin of negotiability in the world permits it, the creatures in the wrathful situation have the opportunity to turn from their destructive course and, by bringing the concrete trajectories of their efficacious power into harmony with the new divine vision, avert the immenent wrath. In some critical situations it is highly uncertain, or even extremely doubtful, that such a margin exists, but as the King of Nineveh says, "who knows?" But where the margin of negotiability proves too narrow to avert actual disaster, because the momentum of historical efficacies for destruction cannot be reversed or sufficiently deflected, still there is room for the creatures within this doomed situation to assess the situation, not *just* within its own terms as doom, but from the perspective of the transcendent divine aim, which transcends the doom in virtue of its transformed character. In such situations, the doom is not the end, but has the character of a time of tribulation (biblical *ṣārāh*, or *thlipsis*) and of travail, on the way to an end which lies beyond these turbulent immediacies. This tribulation can only, then, be undergone and suffered in hope, by man and by God.

Two more points may be made, by way of a general understanding of the divine transforming action as displaying God's sovereign *freedom* and *power*. In a process view, the sovereign *power* of God is displayed not as an instance of unilateral and independent action (*pace* Wolff), but as an instance of relational action, displaying both passional and active aspects. It is as such that we may understand the divine life to be the eminent exemplification of "Power as the Capacity to Sustain a Relationship."[29] But what of the sovereign *freedom* so displayed? According to Wolff, and Mays, and other commentators,

God's freedom is displayed in the choice by which he denies or displaces his wrath in favor of his love. But action which *divides* the self by actualizing the potential of only some of the passionate impulses, is not a display of freedom but of compulsive behaviour. In Tillich's words,

> freedom is the possibility of a total and centered act of the personality, an act in which all the drives and influences which constitute the destiny of man are brought into the centered unity of a decision. None of these drives compels the decision in isolation.[30]

If this properly describes freedom, one should hesitate to take Hos 11:8-11 as demonstrating that Yahweh's actions arise out of some one element in him at the expense of another. But it may be questioned that the text *does* this. Indeed, at this point we may appreciate how the text in fact refuses to attribute the transformation to any one discrete aspect of Yahweh, but rather simply indicates that it takes place in the divine life. In this way, the text preserves the mystery of the divine freedom of action, even as it vividly asserts that the transformation takes place. Here, the significance of the idiom *nehpak ᶜālay libbî* perhaps comes fully into view. As suggested above, the peculiar force of the preposition here demonstrates that the action is something conceived as at the same time happening *to* the agent, so that the agent is in some sense the outcome of his own action. All this may be understood in a process perspective through the following remarks of Bernard Loomer:

> The self in its freedom, in its self-creation, is its uniqueness and its mystery. The self in its freedom cannot be reduced to its conditioning causes. Its decision is not simply a function of its motives, however vital they are in the constitution of the self. The choice of the self cannot be explained. The decision cannot be rationalized. The individual cannot tell another, finally, why he made the decision he did because he *is* that choice, that decision. In answer to the question as to why he made the choice that he did the individual can only reply that he is the person who made that choice. If he could "explain" his decision, he would be a function of his explanation or his motives. He would also have lost his selfhood and his own mysteriousness.[31]

VI

Within the perspective gained through the above general discussion, let us now attend once more to Hos 11:8-9 and its sequel in 11:10-11. Verse 8, lines 1-4, portrays Yahweh as confronted with a genuine impasse. The wrath which arises in and from Israel's situation and which becomes the wrath of Yahweh, in and of itself has as a projected result the final destruction of the people and thereby the final termination of the Yahweh-Israel relation. This is intolerable to Yahweh. But the wrath inherent in the situation cannot simply be rejected, if Yahweh is to continue to be God of heaven *and* earth, or, in Second Isaiah's terms, if Yahweh is to be the *first* as well as the last. The wrath must be drawn into the power of the divine decision, into what Buber calls the transmuting fire wherein the future is adequately forged. In a process which is veiled from our view within the mystery of the divine freedom, God's heart--his complete affective, cognitive, and purposive self--displays a transformation which pervades the totality of the divine life. The outcome is that, whereas the *initial* form of the divine feeling with its wrath would have been a departure, a turning, from Yahweh's aims for Israel, the *transformed* divine aim ensures that Yahweh "will not *turn* to destroy Ephraim."[32]

It is in this divine act which eminently and perfectly exemplifies the true character of *yiḥud*, of existential decision toward holistic becoming, that the emphatic contrast emerges which distinguishes God as the Holy One from man. Whereas man in his finitude and brokenness constantly falls short of, and misses the mark of, such decisions and such becoming, God achieves it ideally within himself. But by virtue of the fact that this Holy One is in man's midst, the divine imaginative *yiḥud* becomes also man's task. The imaginative unification takes place first of all within God himself, within that *sōd Yahweh* which is his own privy solitariness where no one is his counsellor. But the prophet, by virtue of his calling, becomes privy to the divine *sōd*; and by the announcement of the message received in this intimate context--in this instance, by the announcement of Hos 11:8-11 to the people--the whole people is drawn into the *sōd*, the inner council.

This last sentence leads us into a concluding heuristic speculation on the character and function of the sort of eschatological language which appears in Hosea. As 2:14-15 (EVV) already shows, the new future beyond judgment is portrayed largely in the terms which characterized the old relationship: new wilderness, new entry into the land, new covenant. (Note the terms in which the last feature is expressed: "and there she shall *answer* as in the days of her youth,//as at the time when she came out of the land of Egypt." The eschatological covenant, like the original covenant, will arise through the posing of an existential question to Israel, and will be concluded through a lived response which will be Israel's answer.) So also, 11:10-11 portrays a future which in part resembles the past: it will be a deliverance from Egypt (and, this time, Assyria); and it will be effected under the aegis of Yahweh the divine warrior, in the image of the roaring lion.[33] This tendency to depict a saving future by the use of images which have arisen as characterizations of the past comes to its most comprehensive biblical expression, of course, in Second Isaiah. The significance of this type of portrayal may be indicated, in the perspective of this paper, as follows.

First, the divine portrayal of the future is not merely an accommodation of the divine omniscience concerning a totally determinate future, to the limitations of human powers of envisagement. For the future is not envisaged in its precise details even by God, but is entertained, even in the divine life, in the form of the directional and inclusive Eros. It is this indeterminateness of eschatological vision which provides the arena of freedom within which both God and man may share in the "power of fate-deciding." But this means that the eschatological images and metaphors function as symbols for God as well as for man. But secondly, the resemblances between past and future give assurance of the fundamental faithfulness with which the new aims of Yahweh further the original purposes shared with Israel under the old covenant. In this way there is disclosed "the passion of purpose that will not surrender in spite of frustration and rejection" (Mays, p. 119). That is to say, the possibilities which had once become a live question for Israel, but which now threaten to become a dead issue, by the announcement of Hos 11:1-11 once again become an open question. In this question lies the fount of freedom and power by which Israel may, eventually, turn and "go after Yahweh" (Hos 11:10).

Thus it is seen that eschatological existence for Yahweh and Israel is existence within the sphere of power of the deepest and most comprehensive of existential questions. Perhaps the most painful and searching of specific questions to arise within the sphere of eschatological existence, is the cry which arises on *both sides* of the relationship--"how long?" That question is neither a request for information nor a rhetorical outpouring of futile feeling or useless passion. Rather, a life which is lived in the power even of such a specific question is a life which remains open to the envisaged future, and which keeps itself open to the "answer" which the other party may yet give through existential decision. Thereby, the eschaton may be said to be believed *in*, even where the belief takes the form of questions which also give voice to poignant doubt. If the eschaton proves to be more than its images were capable of showing, that is because each party was "saying as you go more than you even hoped you were going to be able to say, and coming with surprise to an end that you foreknew only with some sort of emotion."[34] Which is to say that, for Yahweh and for Israel, eschatological existence is existence in faith, a faith into the sphere of power of which, even as he is subjected to other wrathful forces, Ephraim is already being invited by the disclosure of the divine word in Hos 11.

NOTES

1. See Alan W. Watts, *Nature, Man and Woman* (New York: Vintage Books, 1970), p. 86: "No amount of drilled-in rules or reflexes can prepare the swordsman for the infinity of different attacks which he may have to face....He is taught, therefore, never to make any specific preparation for attack nor to expect it from any particular direction....He must be able to spring immediately from a relaxed center of rest to the direction required." James Dickey advocates a similar approach to poetry: "...our encounter with any poetry...requires that we rid ourselves of preconceptions and achieve, if we can, a way of reading an established poet as though we had never heard of him and were opening his book for the first time. It requires that we approach him with all our senses open, our intelligence in acute readiness, our critical sense in check but alert for the slightest nuance of falsity, our truth-sensitive needle--the device that measures what the poet says against what we know from having lived it--at its most delicate, and our sense of the poet's "place," as determined by commentary, textbook, and literary fashion, drugged, asleep, or temporarily dead. Like most ideal conditions, this one cannot be fully attained. But it is certainly true that an approximation of such a state is both an advantage and a

condition productive of unexpected discoveries in reading poets we thought we knew." (Introduction to Morton Dauwen Zabel, ed., *Selected Poems of Edwin Arlington Robinson* [New York: Collier Books, 1972], p. xi.) Is it naive to suggest that Dickey's approach to poetry is relevant to serious biblical hermeneutics?

2. Hans Walter Wolff, *Hosea*, trans. Gary Stansell (Philadelphia: Fortress Press, 1974), p. 119. (Hereafter, this book will be cited simply by author's name and page number, in the text.)

3. James Luther Mays, *Hosea* (Philadelphia: The Westminster Press, 1969), pp. 96-97. (Hereafter, this book will be cited simply by author's name and page number, in the text.)

4. Rainer Maria Rilke, *Letters to a Young Poet*, trans. M.D. Herter Norton (New York: W.W. Norton & Company, Inc., 1962), pp. 34-35.

5. William James, *The Will to Believe, and Other Essays in Popular Philosophy* (New York: Dover Publications, Inc., 1956), pp. 23-25.

6. Edward Connery Lathem, ed., *Interviews with Robert Frost* (New York: Holt, Rinehart & Winston, 1967), p. 271.

7. Hyde Cox and Edward Connery Lathem, eds., *Selected Prose of Robert Frost* (New York: Holt, Rinehart and Winston, 1966), pp. 44-46.

8. Alfred North Whitehead, *Adventures of Ideas* (New York: The Free Press, 1967), p. 258.

9. *Ibid.*, p. 295.

9a. Rainer Maria Rilke, *op. cit.*, pp. 49-50.

9b. The Massoretic text (and English translations) has Abraham standing before Yahweh. This is by deliberate scribal alteration from an earlier form in which the text had Yahweh standing before Abraham.

10. Martin Buber, *The Prophetic Faith* (New York: Harper & Brothers, 1960), pp. 103-104.

11. James M. Ward, "The Message of the Prophet Hosea," *Interpretation*, XXIII/4 (October 1969).

12. For example, with the essential definitions of a static divine perfection involving divine impassibility and immutability.

13. In the definitive divine self-disclosure in Exod 34:6-7, the divine wrath enjoys the same essential status as the divine steadfast love, even if the two characteristics of the divine relation to man may be qualified differently as "slow" and "abounding." Note also the expression in Ps 95:11, a verse that is sloppily translated as "Therefore I swore in my anger"--as though Yahweh swore in the heat of a momentary and transient state. An examination of all occurrences of the verb "to swear" followed by the preposition *bᵉ*, shows that what is sworn by is not something transient or inessential, but rather (as we might expect in an oath formula) by something enduring. When Yahweh swears, it is by his name, his *nepeš*, his glory, and his holiness. According to Ps 95:11, then, he swears *by* his

wrath, that is, by this constant and essential aspect of his own being. Wolff's reading of Hos 5:10 ("upon them I will pour out my wrath like water") will not wash. The imagery of "pouring out" no more indicates the instrumentality of the wrath than does the "pouring out" of the soul (Ps 42:5) indicate the instrumentality of the latter!

14. In Jer 31:13, the statement "I will turn their mourning into joy" is followed by the verb *niḥamtîm* (cognate to *niḥûmîm* in the last line in Hos 11:8), which is usually translated "and I will comfort them." This translation does not really bring out the force of this verb, which basically "describes a change of mind or heart, either in an intransitive sense [where it means to 'repent, change one's own mind concerning something']...or transitive 'to comfort' [i.e., to change someone else's mind]" (E. A. Speiser, *The Anchor Bible: Genesis* [Garden City, New York: Doubleday & Company, Inc., 1964], p. 51.) The true force of the verb is to be seen in the internal change effected in the attitudes of the people: mourning to joy; gladness for sorrow. The synonymity of the verbs *hapak* and *niḥam* in this verse in Jeremiah is parallelled, I will suggest, in the forms *nehpak//niḥûmîm* in Hos 11:8.

15. See Francis Brown, S.R. Driver, Charles A. Briggs, *A Hebrew and English Lexicon of the Old Testament* (Oxford: At the Clarendon Press, 1957), p. 753, classification II.1.d.

16. On Ps 42:5, see above, note 13.

17. Rudolph translates the line "verwandelt ist in mir mein Herz," in which the verb has reference to change by transformation or transmutation. On the preposition he writes, "*ᶜl* hier nicht 'gegen' (Wolff), sondern Ausdruck 'bei leidenschaftlich erregten Stimmungen' (GB sub *ᶜl* Nr. Iaç)." Wilhelm Rudolph, *Hosea*: *KAT* (Gütersloh: Gütersloher Verlagshaus Gerd Mohn, 1966), pp. 208, 212.

18. The word *niḥûm* occurs only three times in the Hebrew Bible. In its other two occurrences it is commonly translated "comfort," but the context suggests that "comfort" is not quite the force of the word (see note 14 above). A brief examination of the two occurrences will perhaps make this clear. *Isa 57:18* reads "...I will requite him with *comfort*, creating for his mourners the fruit of the lips." As the following clause indicates (and in parallel with Jer 31:13), *niḥûmîm* here indicates that Yahweh will bring about a *change* in the basic felt attitude of the one referred to. The same force inheres in the occurrence in Zech 1:13. The context makes this clear: (1) The angel of the LORD utters a lament: "O LORD of hosts, how long wilt thou have no mercy...?" (2) The LORD answers gracious and comforting (*niḥûmîm*) words to the angel. (3) The angel no longer laments to God, but now turns to the prophet and instructs him to "Cry out, Thus says the LORD of hosts: I am exceedingly jealous for Jerusalem and for Zion." The very change in the felt attitude of the angel, from lament to cry of hope, illustrates what is referred to in Jer 31:13 and Isa 57:18. To sum up, it appears that in two instances, *niḥûmîm* can indicate "change of mind" in a transitive sense. In Hos 11:8, I maintain, it indicates such a meaning intransitively.

19. Recent discussion of the root *yḥd* may be traced in S. Talmon, "The Sectarian *yḥd*--A Biblical Noun," *Vetus Testamentum* III (1953), pp. 133-140; J.C. de Moor, "Lexical Remarks Concerning *yaḥad* and *yaḥdaw*," *Vetus Testamentum* VII (1957), pp. 350-355; and J. Maier, "Zum Begriff *yḥd* in den Texten von Qumran," *Zeitschrift für die Alttestamentliche Wissenschaft* 72 (n.f. 31, 1960), pp. 148-166.

20. I am not persuaded by Talmon's attempt to establish a widespread occurrence of *yḥd* as a *noun* in the OT; nor by his attempt to establish for it a *technical* meaning "to enter into a covenant." Nevertheless, his discussion does show the natural affinity between the basic meaning of this root and the basic notion in covenanting as a binding together for future purposes.

21. In 1 Chron 12:17, it may be suggested that "if you have come to me *l*^{e}*šālôm*....I will be toward you *lebab l*^{e}*yaḥad*" describes a situation in which two parties to an agreement are to enter into it wholeheartedly, and without deceit or hidden intent to betray (see the second half of the verse). The genuine unity of such an agreement thus depends upon the genuine unity within each party for the agreement.

22. It is a commonplace of contemporary psychological understanding, that refusal to accept and "own" the negative aspects of one's own experience results in internal splits and dissociations which, among other effects, diminish the resulting width and intensity, and general richness and vitality, of one's sense of life.

23. Martin Buber, *Good and Evil* (New York: Charles Scribner's Sons, 1953), 94-97.

24. Martin Buber, *Hasidism and Modern Man*, ed. and trans. Maurice Friedman (New York: Harper & Row, 1966), p. 215. On man's task of *yiḥud*, see futher, e.g., *The Origin and Meaning of Hasidism*, 133-135.

25. *Good and Evil*, pp. 130-131.

26. For an attempt to develop a process understanding of, among other things, the wrath of God, see my paper, "Modes of Power and the Divine Relativity," *Encounter* 36/4 (Autumn, 1975), pp. 379-406. It may be noted that this issue is given entirely to papers written under the theme "Process Philosophy and Biblical Theology."

27. For a suggestive discussion of the "warm, passionate" power of the past, and the "cool" power of the future, which when disengaged from one another and from the power of transformation become demonic as *Lucifer* and *Ahriman*, see Owen Barfield, *Unancestral Voice* (Middletown, Connecticut: Wesleyan University Press, 1965), especially pages 56-61 and 96-103.

28. See "Modes of Power and the Divine Relativity," pp. 389-390, and especially these lines: "In this sense only is God 'subversive' of the world as settled: he 'clothes' it with the translucency of his novel aims....The past world is conveyed by God into the present finite occasion without physical 'refraction,' but clothed with the slightest and yet most enticing capacity to produce a refraction at the mental poles of inheriting finite occasions."

29. Bernard Loomer, "Two Conceptions of Power," *Process Studies* 6/1 (Spring, 1976), pp. 5-32.

30. Paul Tillich, *Systematic Theology, II: Existence and the Christ* (Chicago: The University of Chicago Press, 1957), pp. 42-43.

31. Bernard M. Loomer, "Dimensions of Freedom," in Harry James Cargas and Bernard Lee, *Religious Experience and Process Theology* (New York: Paulist Press, 1976), p. 326.

32. The verb *šûb* in this line is commonly translated adverbially, as the syntax certainly will allow. But the context of the whole passage (and indeed the whole book), with its preoccupation with defection from covenanted purpose, suggests that the verb here connotes a possible (but here denied) divine defection from covenanted purpose. Though Wolff and Mays both adopt "again" in their translations, in their commentary they implicitly follow the other interpretation: "Yahweh will not turn from his election of 'my son' and destroy the Ephraim creation by his saving acts" (Mays, p. 157); *šûb* denotes...not only the repetition of an action, but also the restoration of previous conditions, or the nullification of a deed" (Wolff, p. 202).

33. Verse 10 is often held to be secondary to the chapter (e. g., Wolff, and Mays). The main objections are succinctly stated by Mays: (1) the style of divine saying of vv 1-9 and v 11 (divine first person) is dropped for the style of a report with Yahweh in third person; (2) Hosea elsewhere uses a different word for Yahweh as lion; and (3) elsewhere Yahweh as lion depicts ravaging wrath. In my judgment, these considerations are too slight to disturb the other indications of the verse's place in the passage: (1) Since this verse begins the depiction of an event in the indeterminate future, and so away from the present, the shift to third person is not unnatural (moreover, elsewhere in the OT, third-person references in the midst of first-person address is not impossible; compare Jer 2: 2-3). (2) Since Hosea elsewhere uses a different word for Yahweh as lion only *twice* (5:4 and 13:7), it can hardly be insisted that he has a pronouncedly characteristic usage from which the present instance would be a peculiar departure. Are synonymous expressions not allowable? (3) It hardly will do to rule out this verse because elsewhere in Hosea the lion figure connotes wrath. The difference in connotation of the lion figure is a function of the difference in general *context*: the other two instances occur in contexts where judgment is being announced; the present instance occurs in a context where hope is being announced. When we consider that Hosea deliberately is capable of suggesting that the old name "Vale of Achor" is susceptible of new connotations in the future, "Door of Hope," (2:15 EVV), we should not be surprised if he similarly in 11:10 suggests that the sound of Yahweh as lion will in the future have a transformed significance for the exiles. It may further be suggested that, in addition to the affinities of v 10 with v 11, v 10 picks up a motif which runs through vv 1-7 and rings a nice change on it. Verse one says that they *went* from Yahweh (the verb is *hālak*) to sacrifice to the Baals. Thereafter, the familiar

Hoseanic theme, of Israel's refusal to turn back to Yahweh, is reiterated. Now, in v 10, that turning back in the future is described by means of the same verb as was used in v 2 to describe the defection: they shall *go* (*hālak*) after Yahweh. In this description, the occurrence of the divine name Yahweh (which momentarily throws the self-reference into the third person) simply emphasizes that there will be no ambiguity in their future allegiance: it will not be to a "lord" (*baᶜal*) whose identity is ambiguous (cp. 2:16-17 EVV), but to one who is unmistakably called Yahweh.

34. Edward Connery Lathem and Hyde Cox, eds., *Selected Prose of Robert Frost* (New York: Holt, Rinehart and Winston, 1966), p. 46.

S 259 THE PORTRAIT OF MOSES IN EZEKIEL THE TRAGEDIAN

Carl R. Holladay
Yale Divinity School

One of the more intriguing facets of religious propaganda is the manner in which revered figures of the past are interpreted by the adherents and proponents of the religious heritage in which those figures played a formative role. Critical analysis of these interpretations yields valuable historical information on at least two fronts. First, the mirror-image syndrome implicit in such interpretations makes it possible to achieve greater historical clarity about the personality types and ethical ideals dominant within a given era and sufficiently popular to elicit or repel admiration and imitation. This obviously yields valuable information about the proponents themselves. Second, our understanding of the inner dynamics of religious propaganda is broadened. Traditions about religious figures are notoriously susceptible to historical transgressions. The resulting portraits easily render the historical figures giving rise to them unrecognizable, but the same process that tends to detach the portrait from history produces the distinctive modifications within the traditions. These modifications become the raw data for reconstructing the distinctive features of the portrait as well as for recognizing the distinctive stages through which the propaganda has passed.

An unusual tradition about Moses preserved by Ezekiel the Tragedian, a Hellenistic-Jewish author who flourished in the mid-second century B.C.E. in Alexandria, poses some interesting questions when examined as one of the numerous cameos of Moses which emerged within Hellenistic-Jewish propaganda. The passage is as follows:

λέγει δὲ αὐτὸς ὁ Μωσῆς δι' ἀμοιβαίων πρὸς τὸν πενθερὸν οὕτως πως·

‘ Ἔδοξ' ὄρους κατ' ἄκρα Σιναίου θρόνον
μέγαν τιν' εἶναι μέχρις οὐρανοῦ πτυχός,
ἐν τῷ καθῆσθαι φῶτα γενναῖόν τινα
διάδημ' ἔχοντα καὶ μέγα σκῆπτρον χερὶ
εὐωνύμῳ μάλιστα. δεξιᾷ δέ μοι
ἔνευσε, κἀγὼ πρόσθεν ἐστάθην θρόνου,
σκῆπτρον δέ μοι παρέδωκε καὶ εἰς θρόνον μέγαν
εἶπεν καθῆσθαι· βασιλικὸν δ' ἔδωκέ μοι
διάδημα καὶ αὐτὸς ἐκ θρόνων χωρίζεται.
ἐγὼ δ' ἐσεῖδον γῆν ἅπασαν ἔγκυκλον
καὶ ἔνερθε γαίας καὶ ἐξύπερθεν οὐρανοῦ,
καί μοί τι πλῆθος ἀστέρων πρὸς γούνατα
ἔπιπτ', ἐγὼ δὲ πάντας ἠριθμησάμην,
κἀμοῦ παρῆγεν ὡς παρεμβολὴ βροτῶν.
εἶτ' ἐμφοβηθεὶς ἐξανίσταμ' ἐξ ὕπνου.’

ὁ δὲ πενθερὸς αὐτοῦ τὸν ὄνειρον ἐπικρίνει οὕτως·

‘Ὦ ξένε, καλόν σοι τοῦτ' ἐσήμηνεν θεός·
ζῴην δ', ὅταν σοι ταῦτα συμβαι<ν>ῃ ποτέ.
ἆρά γε μέγαν τιν' ἐξαναστήσεις θρόνον
καὶ αὐτὸς βραβεύσεις καὶ καθηγήσῃ βροτῶν;
τὸ δ' εἰσθεᾶσθαι γῆν ὅλην τ' οἰκουμένην
καὶ τὰ ὑπένερθε καὶ ὑπὲρ οὐρανὸν θεοῦ·
ὄψει τά τ' ὄντα τά τε προτοῦ τά θ' ὕστερον.’[1]

The passage occurs in the Ἐξαγωγή , notable among other things for being the longest extant fragment of a Hellenistic tragedy. One of several tragedies composed by Ezekiel, it is a five-act drama which probably spanned the events of Moses' life from his birth to the encampment at Elim. As one might expect, Moses is the Biblical figure who receives the most attention in the drama, although he is but one of the dramatis personae, along with Zipporah, Chum, Raguel (= Jethro), God, and a member of the pursuing Egyptian army; brief reference is made at the outset to Jacob. A perusal of the extant 269 lines of the drama reveals that Ezekiel's aim was more than simply to depict the life of Moses. The dream-scene apparently served to bridge the gap between the first and second act.

The portrait of Moses in the dream seems clearly intended for outsiders in spite of Tcherikover's insistence that Hellenistic-Jewish Alexandrian literature was written to bolster the faith of Jews who were coming to grips with Hellenization. If Jewish aversion to the theatre still obtained in Alexandria at this time as the less than complimentary reference to Theodektes in Epistle of Aristeas 316 suggests, this would hardly have been the ideal way of addressing Jews. Moreover, the lengthy description of the origin and manner of celebrating the Passover (Denis 212: 30ff.) would be an admirable attempt to explain this apparently strange custom to persons unfamiliar with it, or perhaps curious about it. Propagandic intentions are further suggested by the speech of the Egyptian soldier (ἄγγελος , Denis 214:3) into whose mouth Ezekiel places the description of the crossing of the Red Sea. Towards the end of the soldier's speech Ezekiel employs the common stylistic device of placing a confessional formula in the mouth of a pagan, a point that would not easily be missed by a pagan reader. But perhaps the most cogent argument suggesting Ezekiel's ulterior motives is his choice of Greek tragedy as a literary genre. Some idea of the extent of his literary pretensions is the mere inclusion of the dream-scene itself. For the most part Ezekiel adheres closely to the LXX. Even when he embroiders it, as when he fills in the gap between Exodus 2:10 and 2:11 by including a brief resumé of Moses' childhood, it is mild in comparison with the highly embellished birth-youth traditions in Josephus (Antiq. 2. 205-37). Neither the dream nor the interpretation is found in the Biblical account, and considering Ezekiel's usual scrupulous adherence to the Biblical narrative, this is all the more remarkable. The most plausible explanation is provided by those who have noticed his dependence upon classical Greek models, Euripides in particular. Since it was a stock stylistic device to incorporate a dream into the narrative of Greek tragedies, it is clear that Ezekiel includes the dream-scene to impress his readers with a knowledge of Greek literary conventions as well as his finesse in handling them.

One major interpretive problem is that of determining the fundamental portrait of Moses which Ezekiel intends to emerge from the dream scene. Those who see the image of Moses as king as the dominant element of the portrait point to the prominence of the heavenly throne (lines 4, 9, 10, 12) and the conferral of the regal trappings upon Moses. Yet this image is neither undiluted nor pervasive. If the dominant image of the dream is Moses the king, the dominant image of Raguel's interpretation (lines 20-26) is Moses the prophet. The throne motif of the dream is picked up in Raguel's interpretation (line 22), yet his subsequent role is not articulated with βασιλεύειν terminology, as one might expect, but in the somewhat surprising formulation καὶ αὐτὸς βραβεύσεις καὶ καθηγήσῃ βροτῶν (line 23). Even more remote from the kingship image is Raguel's final prediction in line 26. The net result is a double exposure of two distinct images.

The juxtaposition of two distinct images may be intentional as was Philo's quintuple portrait of Moses over a century later (V. Mos. 2. 2f.). Or, it is possible that the prophetic image, being the interpretation of the dream, is intended to override the monarchical image. Another possibility is that a common portrait lies beneath both images and that what appear to be separate images are but different aspects of this common image. This third possibility we shall pursue in this paper.

The question of sources and interpretation are, as always, difficult to separate, for if the sources upon which Ezekiel drew in composing the dream scene could be isolated and identified with any degree of certainty, one could perhaps interpret the overall portrait with greater assurance.

The depiction of the heavenly throne in the dream employs OT motifs but their final blend results in a peculiarly distinctive image. The OT records frequent exchanges between Moses and God (Ex. 3:1-4:17, 21-23; 5:22-7:19; passim.), but the throne of God motif does not figure in them. A throne in the heavens is common enough in the OT (Ps. 9:5, 8; 10:4; 44:7 (?); 46:9; 88:15; 92:2; 96:2; 102:19), but it is not identified with Sinai. Under the monarchy Israel's kings as God's appointees in a sense sat upon God's throne since He established the throne and since the throne as an institution extended beyond a single ruler and thus could be called θρόνος βασιλείας κυρίου ἐπὶ τὸν Ισραηλ (1 Chron. 28:5). It is most often associated with David and Solomon, who figure most prominently in Rabbinic speculations about the throne of God, although the Rabbis understood Moses' reception of the rod of God (Ex. 4:20) to mean that he was given the royal sceptre of God (Midr. Ps. 21.2)

Certain motifs Ezekiel may have derived from the dreams which he knows from the OT, especially the dreams of Jacob (Gen. 28), Isaiah (Isa. 6), Daniel (Dan. 7), and possibly Joseph (Gen. 37), although the differences are striking. The unadorned throne of the dream-scene (lines 4-5) sharply contrasts with the elaborate and sometimes grotesque imagery which characterizes the throne descriptions of Isa. 6:1ff., Ezek. 1:26 (cf. 10:1), Dan. 7:9ff. (cf. 1 Kg. 10:18; 2 Chron. 9:17). The anthropomorphic appearance of the figure seated upon the throne (line 6) is far closer to the figure in Ezek. 1:26 than to the enthroned Lord of Isa. 6:1, or even to the Ancient of Days of Dan. 7:22. Although it is never explicitly said that the figure seated upon the throne is God, the fact that the throne reaches to the vaults of heaven (line 5) makes this identification probable.

As for Moses' being seated on the heavenly throne on which he assumes the sceptre and crown, Ezekiel's rendition of the vision is singular when compared with other traditions depicting dreams involving the throne of God. In the Biblical visions connected with prophetic calls (Ezek. 1:4-2:11; Isa. 6:1-13) the throne of God appears but no mention is made of the prophets taking a seat upon the throne. The throne and the accompanying imagery bear no direct connection with the prophet nor his call except to underscore the majesty and sublimity of the God who issues the commission.

The *Targum of Jonathan* on *Gen.* 28:1, which mentions "Jacob the pious, whose likeness is inlaid in the throne of glory," although illuminating because it shows how the patriarchs were glorified in Rabbinic traditions, does not bear directly upon our passage since Jacob is not made to sit on the heavenly throne. There are also parallels in the Midrashic interpretation of *Exodus* 7:1, in which God's declaration to Moses, "I appoint you a god ..." is interpreted as a display of God's magnanimity. Unlike a mortal king who allows no one else to ride his horse, sit on his throne, wear his crown, God "assigns glory to those who fear him," i.e. He shares the signs of His dignity with His vicegerents: Solomon sits on his throne, Elijah rides on His horse (i.e. the whirlwind), Moses holds His sceptre, Messiah wears his crown, Israel wears His mantle, Moses is called by His own name (*Ex. R.* 8.1; also *Ps. R.* 21.2). Nevertheless, the distance between these Midrashic passages and the Moses-dream in Ezekiel is considerable.

Much closer, both in verbal and conceptual similarity, is the enthronement of the Messianic Elect One in *1 Enoch*. In almost identical language *1 Enoch* tells of the Lord who seats the Elect One upon His throne from which he executes judgment and righteousness upon the earth (62:1ff.; cf. 55:4; 61:8; 69:27). Moses' vision of the heights and depths of the universe along with his knowledge of heavenly things (lines 13-14, 24-25) closely resembles the description of Enoch's vision in *1 Enoch* 17-18. This raises the interesting possibility that certain features of Ezekiel's portrait are derived from apocalyptic traditions although it should be noticed that the strong eschatological note of *1 Enoch* is absent from Ezekiel. While it is true that the throne mentioned in Raguel's interpretation is to be erected in the future and that line 21 may be a cryptic reference to the distance of the event, there are no indications that Ezekiel has in mind a final judgment scene in which Moses will be God's vicegerent who judges all men as is the case in *1 Enoch* 61-62.

Another motif which may have OT antecedents is the submission of the "host of stars" to Moses (lines 15-16) which may recall *Gen.* 37:9, since the astral motif within a dream is common to both.

This admittedly sketchy review of the traditions which have been suggested as the sources upon which Ezekiel draws in formulating the dream-scene succeeds only in underscoring the multiplex nature of the portrait rather than providing a coherent interpretation of the portrait of Moses which emerges. Although a certain reluctance is thus required in proposing yet another tradition which may illuminate the Moses-portrait, there are justifiable reasons for doing so.

To state the thesis briefly, the portrait of Moses which emerges from the dream is heavily influenced by the image of the *mantis* as it had developed in the Greek classical tradition. This image not only provides the basis for a coherent interpretation of both the dream and interpretation, but suggests a plausible explanation for the emergence of this portrait within an Alexandrian *Sitz im Leben*.

Heinemann may very well be correct in asserting that Ezekiel borrows only the technique of including a dream, not the content of the dream itself, from the Greek dramatists, but there are features of the dream-scene which suggest otherwise. The prediction that Moses, from his vantage point of his newly erected throne, will see "the present, the past, and the future" (line 26) is a strikingly non-OT depiction of the prophetic role. Yet it bears a remarkable resemblance to Homer's description of the mantis Calchas: ὃς ᾔδη τά τ' ἐόντα τά τ' ἐσσόμενα πρό τ' ἐόντα (Iliad I.70). The identical formula is employed in Hesiod, Theogonia 36-39, of the Muses; also worth noticing in this same connection is Theog. 32 where the inspired poet's role as spokesman for the gods is indicated by his reception of the sceptre; compare lines 7 & 10 of the dream-scene. Of Proteus the seer (vates) Vergil, Georg. IV, 392-3 writes: ... novit namque omnia vates, quae sint, quae fuerint, quae mox ventura trahantur. Similarly, in Ovid, Metam. I, 517-18, it is said of Apollo: ... quod eritque, fuitque, estque patet ...

By employing what appears to have been an ancient Greek formula for describing prophecy Ezekiel clearly intends to locate Moses within the tradition of the Greek seer. His omission of the actual term mantis may be owing to its unfavorable connotations in the LXX (cf. Deut. 18:10, 14; 2 Kg. 17:17; et al.). In Euripides and the tragedians the mantis is a familiar and respectable figure, as seen in Euripides, Iphigenia Taurica 711-14, where it is implied that for a mantis to practice deception is exceptional behavior.

If our suggestion is correct that Ezekiel's portrait of Moses in line 26 was drawn from the Greek mantis tradition, it is possible to interpret the throne motif within the same conceptual framework, thus resolving the apparent conflict of two distinct images in the dream-scene.

The incorporation of classical Greek depictions of the throne of Zeus into Jewish depictions of the throne of God is seen as early as Aristobulus, Ezekiel's near-contemporary and fellow Alexandrian whose dependence upon Orphic traditions is indisputable.

In Euripides Iphigenia Taurica 1249-58, in which Apollo's oracle is being vindicated over against Iphigenia's dream, the mantis and the throne motif occur in a combination strikingly similar to what we find in Ezekiel. Phoebus establishes his right to the oracles and from this "throne of truth" (ἐν ἀψευδεῖ θρόνῳ, IT 1254) dispenses the divine oracles to mortals (IT 1255-56). Thus it is from this throne that he executes his mantic role over mortals. The same combination is seen in Aeschylus, Eumenides 616, where Apollo issues his judicial verdict μαντικοῖσιν ἐν θρόνοις. Cf. also v. 29, ἔπειτα μάντις ἐς θρόνους καθιζάνω.

A coherent interpretation is thus achieved if lines 20-26 are seen as portraying Moses in the role of the Greek mantis, most notably Apollo. The dream and Raguel's interpretation are also seen to be logically coherent when it is remembered that as a mantis Apollo issues his oracles under the promptings of Zeus. In fact, lines 4-17, especially 10-12, of the dream-scene may very well have been inspired by a passage such as Aeschylus, Eumenides 17-19, in which Zeus seats Apollo as mantis upon his throne with the result that Apollo becomes Διὸς προφήτης.

As the spokesman for Zeus, Apollo can function in a judicial role as when he is called upon to be the advocate for Orestes (Aeschylus, Eumenides 609-21). Not surprisingly, the mantic role of Apollo shades off into his legislative role. The widespread influence of the oracle of Apollo at Delphi was connected with his role as the one who issued divinely given laws, and he was indeed looked to as the source of divine law; he was also regarded as the "national expositor."

Against this background Ezekiel's portrait of Moses becomes more intelligible. The interchange between Moses and God may be seen as an intentional counterpart to the Zeus-Apollo relationship in which Apollo serves as the spokesman for Zeus. The divine investiture signals the authentication of Moses as God's spokesman. By incorporating the dream into the drama Ezekiel has no intentions of portraying Moses as a king per se. The throne he is to set up is the throne on which he is to act as arbiter and guide of mortals, on which he has access to the divine secrets of the universe, and to the knowledge of the present, past, and future; in short, the mantic throne--or, if properly understood, the prophetic throne. By formulating the dream in these terms he is consciously placing Moses in direct competition with Apollo, the spokesman of Zeus, the one who issues divinely given laws, the arbiter and guide of mortals. The ecumenical tendency, as reflected in the extensive use of universal language (lines 13, 16, 17, 23-24), cannot be unintentional and serves to underscore the universal extent of Moses' influence. The audience (readers) would hardly fail to see the point of the dream-scene: Sinai replaces Delphi as the place where the divine oracles are issued; Moses replaces Apollo as the spokesman for God; accordingly, the whole of mankind is to seek the divine will not from the oracle of Apollo at Delphi, but from the law of God given to Moses at Sinai.

NOTES

[1]Text and line numeration from A. M. Denis, Fragmenta Pseudepigraphorum Quae Supersunt Graeca Una Cum Historicorum et Auctorum Judaeorum Hellenistarum Fragmentis (Leiden, 1970) 210. References cited to the text in Denis are as follows: page number in Denis followed by line(s) number.

S 260 THE RULE OF TYCHE AND HELLENISTIC RELIGION

Luther H. Martin

Any investigation of the place of chance in the Hellenistic world would do well to begin with that great erotic novel of the mid-second century AD, The Golden Ass or Metamorphoses of Lucius Apuleius.[1] The opening story of Aristomenes whom Lucius, the hero of the novel, encounters on his way to Thessaly, not only foreshadows the plight of Lucius, but suggests the plight of man in the Hellenistic world as a whole. Aristomenes tells Lucius of his chance meeting with a long-lost friend, Socrates, who had fallen onto bad luck and had been reduced to a beggar. Socrates tells his friend that he was attacked by bandits while on a business trip to Macedonia. He finally escaped to an inn only to fall under the power of a sorceress, Meroë. Ultimately, however, Socrates blames neither the bandits nor Meroë, but Fortune, for his present condition and chides Aristomenes for his ignorance of the capriciousness of Fortune, thus establishing the theme of the novel.[2] Before long, Lucius, a sort of Hellenistic Everyman, too will experience the buffetings of Fortune.

A. The Rule of Tyche

1. Universality. Tyche/Fortuna was commonly worshipped by the third century BC and possessed temples in nearly all the great Greek cities.[3] Her influence extended into the Roman period as Apuleius' novel indicates. Likewise, Pliny, writing in the first century AD, attests her universality:

> Everywhere in the whole world at every hour by all men's voices Fortune alone is invoked and named....and we are so much at the mercy of chance that Chance herself, by whom God is proved uncertain, takes the place of God.[4]

The universality of this goddess has often been viewed as the last stage in the secularization of religion[5] in which, as Pliny notes, the personification of the unpredictable and the unexplained "takes the place of God." But she has also been referred to as the most important deity of the Hellenistic era because of her universal sovereignity over mortals and immortals alike.[6] Such a universal principle, encompassing even the gods, suggests that Tyche/Fortuna is a cosmological metaphor.[7]

Claudius Ptolemy, the second century contemporary of Apuleius, formulated finally and definitively a cosmological image which had its first inception in the pre-Socratic philosophers.[8] We can suggest the general acceptance of this Ptolemaic image of cosmology by the height of the Hellenistic period. In contrast to the integrated image of traditional cosmology, the Ptolemaic system greatly expanded and bifurcated the cosmos. Earth was depicted as a flat cylinder, or as a sphere, suspended in space and surrounded by seven planetary spheres, the whole contained within the spherical realm of the fixed stars. Within this contained whole the cosmos was divided into the superlunar celestial realm of the divine and the sublunar terrestrial realm of the profane. With this bifurcation of the traditional cosmological image, integration gave way to differentiation and the criterion of this differentiation was cosmologically grounded. That is to say, the primary cosmological criterion of differentiation within this new world view was lunar. The power of this lunar reality is exemplified by the great "Regina caeli" or prayer to the "Blessed Queen of Heaven" by Lucius, occassioned by the dazzling power and majesty of the full moon.

> About the first watch of the night, when as I had slept my first sleep, I awakened with sudden fear, and saw the moon shining bright as when she is at the full, and seemingly as though she leaped out of the sea. Then I thought with myself that this was the most secret time, when that goddess had most puissance and force, considering that all human things be governed by her providence; and that not only all beasts private and tame, wild and savage, be made strong by the governance of her light and godhead, but also things inanimate and without life; and I considered that all bodies in the heavens, the earth, and the seas be by her increasing motions increased, and by her diminishing motions diminished.[9]

The dominant Earth Mother mythology of traditional cosmology had become the governing luminous principle of the night sky, the lunar Queen of Heaven, of Ptolemaic cosmology. Tyche/Fortuna, inconstant as the moon itself, was the name of this Hellenistic feminine cosmic principle in its experienced ambiguity.

2. <u>Capriciousness</u>. Tyche/Fortuna means chance or luck, good and ill.[10] The ambiguity or capriciousness of Tyche/Fortuna, i.e., her double nature, positive and negative, embodied in a single image, is her most characteristic trait. Again to illustrate from Pliny:

> [Fortune is] alone accused, alone impeached, alone pondered, alone applauded, alone rebuked and visited with reproaches; deemed volatile and indeed by most men blind as well, wayward, inconstant, uncertain, fickle in her favours and favouring the unworthy. To her is debited all that is spent and credited all that is received, she alone fills both pages in the whole of mortals account...[11]

In terms of cosmologically determined symbolism, Tyche/Fortuna personified man's necessary experience of the world as the deities withdrew across the cosmic sublunar abyss to the celestial realm beyond. Her ambiguity personified disorder within the boundaries of the closed cosmos itself. Although an order of things was assumed to exist, it was veiled from the terrestrial vision of man. The protective cosmic circumference apparently had been breached by chaos.

B. <u>Response to the Rule of Tyche</u>

1. <u>Philosophy</u>. Hellenistic man responded to the rule of Tyche in several ways.[12] One response was rational or philosophical. This response can be illustrated by Plutarch, who argued that what separates man from lower forms of life is:

> Prometheus, or, in other words, the power to think and reason....In all of this, therefore, there is no element of chance at all but solely and wholly sagacity and forethought.[13]

For Plutarch, and the philosophical position generally, Tyche/Fortuna is a power which rules only animals and unthinking men. It is mind and reason which separates man from the animals, and it is precisely this Promethean power to think and to reason which gives man his freedom from the rule of Tyche/Fortuna.[14] But the philosophical path was the path of the elite and was incomprehensible or inapplicable to the day-to-day experiences of the populus.

2. Prognosis. More accessible to the populus was a second response to the rule of Tyche/Fortuna, the prognosis of divination. As a universal or cosmological alternative, nowhere was divination as prognosis more attractive to human imagination in the Hellenistic world than as astrology. In contemplating the order of the superlunar reality, it became possible astrologically to order the sublunar terrestrial effects of Tyche by bringing an external cosmic source of order to bear upon the conditions of human existence. In the words of Ptolemy:

> what could be more conducive to well being, pleasure, and in general satisfaction than this kind of forecast (prognostikos), by which we gain full view of things human and divine?[15]

Prognosis, for Ptolemy, was not so much prediction of the future as it was a matter of foreknowledge grounded in the perception of the order of things, not so much a matter of predicting the unknown, as of overcoming ignorance in order to know the knowable. Ptolemy contrasts the unchangeability of the observable and regular motions of the superlunar celestial realm with the unpredictable, seemingly chance, changes in the sublunar, terrestrial world.[16] Ptolemy's name for this sublunar transitoriness is symbebekos, chance event, i.e., deanthropomorphized Tyche.[17]

Thus astrology shares with philosophy the assumption that order in the face of rule by Tyche exists within the cosmic order of things, and that knowledge of this order is available directly to man, whether terrestrially by means of a Promethean exercise of reason, or celestially through the terrestrial application of astronomical observation. Divination, however, like philosophy increasingly became unavailable to the populus because of its very success and the specialization required to practice it.

3. Providence. The third response of Hellenistic man to the rule of Tyche/Fortuna was based on a recognition of the ambiguity of her nature: she was not simply the personification of a negative principle to be overcome, but she was equally positive and providential in her influence. As the Fortune of Cities, she was represented as wearing a turreted crown symbolizing the protective fortifications of the walled city, and bearing the nourishing cornucopia of abundance and the scepter of sovereignity.[18] Likewise, Apuleius refers not only to the

buffetings of ill fortune, but also to the benefits of good fortune. Isis herself is revealed to be true Fortune.[19] This beneficial aspect of the capricious feminine was known as Agathe Tyche, good fortune, or Tyche soteira, Tyche-saviouress. Tyche/Fortuna, the chaotic buffetings of fortune, is overcome by the saving goddess, who is true Fortune. Pindar already exemplified this character of the goddess when he prayed:

> Daughter of Zeus the Deliverer! thou saving goddess Fortune (soteira Tyche)! I pray thee.... But never yet hath any man on earth found a sure token sent from heaven to tell him how he shall fare in the future, but warnings of events to come are wrapped in gloom.[20]

Thus Pindar suggests what is made clear by Apuleius, that it is only Tyche-soteira who is able to intercede on behalf of man in the face of the capriciousness of Tyche/Fortuna. This relationship between the capriciousness of Tyche and Isis as true Fortuna is summarized in the speech of the priest of Isis to Lucius following his transformation. The priest tells Lucius that neither his nobility nor his education had been able to thwart the capricious torments of blind fortune. Now, Lucius is told, he is "under the protection of that fortune that is not blind," the providence of the goddess Isis.

> Behold, here is Lucius that is delivered from his former so great miseries by the providence of the goddess Isis and rejoiceth thenceforth and triumpheth of victory over his fortune.[21]

It was only Isis, the feminine as saviouress, who was able to overcome Tyche/Fortuna, the feminine as capricious; only Tyche remanifest as the soteriological "Queen of Heaven," is victorious over "cruel Fortune." Whereas philosophy and divination assumed an order within the cosmos available to man, whether manifest through reason, or through astrological observation, this third response was grounded in the providence of the goddess, symbolized in the fullness of the cornucopia, and revealed to man finally through cult epiphany.

> I am she that is the natural mother of all things, mistress and governess of all the elements, the initial progeny of worlds, chief of the powers divine, queen of all that are in hell, the principal of them that dwell in heaven, manifested alone and under one form of all the gods and goddesses....my true name, Queen Isis.[22]

4. Redemption. Philosophy, divination, and revelatory epiphany all shared an essentially positive view of the cosmos. In the face of Tyche/Fortuna, the experienced disorder of the cosmos, an innate order was assumed to exist which by one technique or another (philosophy or divination), or through cult epiphany, was available to human perception. Astrology, because of its success as a universal cosmic system, nevertheless ordered the closed universe at the price of an oppressive determinism.

This negative manifestation of the feminine was cosmically experienced by Hellenistic man as Heimarmene, the abstract feminine symbol of man's condition of alienation from the ruling Goddess of life, separated from the gods, and imprisoned by the enveloping spheres of the planetary powers.[23] The Poimandres from the Corpus Hermeticum explicitly sets forth this cosmic nature of Heimarmene:

> God...created seven Rulers (i.e., the planets), which encircle the world perceived through the senses. Their government is called Heimarmene.[24]

Heimarmene was the necessary conclusion to be drawn from the Ptolemaic astrological ordering of the cosmos, a cosmic order also shared by philosophy and the mysteries. When Tyche/Fortuna lost her capricious--and consequently her ambivalent--character, and showed primarily her unfavorable side, the dominance of Heimarmene moved into the foreground.[25]

In the Gnostic and Hermetic traditions, the symbolically feminine nature of the totality of the cosmos was itself now understood as defective. This view of the feminine cosmos as defective is mythologically illustrated, for example, by the cosmogonic fall of Sophia.[26] In the face of this anti-cosmism, there developed a fourth response by man to the heimarmenic rule of Tyche/Fortuna, a redemptive, otherworldly alternative. The masculine redeemer[27] of Mithraism, Gnosticism, and Christianity who, in the face of symbolically feminine anti-cosmism, charted in their revelatory ascent, the "Way" back through the celestial spheres for the faithful to follow in their own transcendence of Heimarmene:

> Therefore a strange and new star arose doing away with the old astral decree, shining with a new unearthly light, which revolved on a new path of salvation, as the Lord himself, men's guide, who came down to earth to transfer from Heimarmene to his providence those who believed in Christ.[28]

C. <u>Conclusions for an Understanding of Hellenistic Religion</u>

1. To the extent that Tyche is related to Moira,[29]

a. Tyche is a more ethical concept than older *moira*. Whereas Tyche is perceived as both positive and negative, such values are not generally attributed to the personified Moira, but only to her effects as one's "share" or "portion" in life.

b. Consequently, whereas one cannot escape the effects of *moira*,[30] one may overcome, or escape altogether the effects of Tyche.

2. Tyche/Fortuna is a personified cosmological feminine principle discernable by philosophy or divination, or mythologically manifest positively as providence, negatively as Heimarmene. The mythological manifestation of Tyche/Fortuna is central to the self-understanding of the mystery and Gnostic movements of the Hellenistic world.

3. As a cosmological principle, Tyche/Fortuna is a universal principle. Consequently the various responses to rule by Tyche/Fortuna constitute a cross-section of religiosity in the Hellenistic world and thus provide some understanding of the coherent pattern underlying the historical confusion named by syncretism.

NOTES

1. Apart from the general tone, Apuleius describes this as a Grecian story (Fabula Graecanica), Meta. I,1. The story, borrowed from a lost Greek work, Lucius or Ass, by Lucius of Patrae, is generally considered to be autobiographical, especially Book XI. In another work, his Apologia, Apuleius states "I have taken part in a number of initiation ceremonies in Greece." J. Gwyn Griffiths, who cites this passage, concludes "We may confidently infer that the Isiac rites were among these." The Isis-Book (Metamorphoses, Book XI). 1975, pp. 3f.

2. "O my friend Aristomenes, now perceive I well that you are ignorant of the whirling changes, the unstable forces, and slippery inconstancy of Fortune..." (Meta. I,6).

3. Percy Gardner. New Chapters in Greek Art, 1926, reprinted 1971, pp. 257-268; Martin Nilsson. Geschichte der Griechischen Religion, II, second edition, 1961, pp. 202f.; W. W. Tarn. Hellenistic Civilization, third edition, 1952, p. 316; Paul Wendland. Die Hellenistisch-Römische Kultur, third edition, 1912, p. 104; Franz Cumont. Oriental Religions in Roman Paganism, 1911, reprinted 1956, p. 179.

4. N.H.II,22.

5. Nilsson, p. 202.

6. As opposed to the negative evaluation of Tyche as the last stage of secularization, compare the evaluation of Cumont: "Thus belief in Fate not only (1) became a source of moral inspiration to noble minds, but also (2) provided a justification of the necessity of positive worship." Astrology and Religion Among the Greeks and Romans, 1912, reprinted 1960, p. 89.

7. H. R. Patch concludes that Fortuna under the Empire "is in control of the universe, but she is quite arbitrary about it." "The Tradition of the Goddess Fortuna in Roman Literature and in the Transitional Period." Smith College Studies in Modern Language, Vol. III. No. 3, 1922, p. 147.

8. Tetrabiblos I-III. For a survey of ancient cosmological theory, see Milton K. Munitz (ed.), Theories of the Universe. 1957, pp. 1-138.

9. Meta. XI,1. The lunar goddess is not yet known to Lucius as Isis. (Griffiths, p. 115). Isis as a lunar goddess is attributed to the interpretatio Graeca. (Griffiths, p. 125).

10. Nilsson (p.202f.) states that Fortuna and Tyche are not the same. G. Dumézil, on the other hand, states with respect to Fortuna that "The influence of the Greek representations of Tyche, improbable in the beginnings, is later positive, from the time of the first Hellenizing poets." Archaic Roman Religion II. 1970, p. 423; likewise Pauly-Wissowa: "tyche [ist] in späterer Zeit mit Fortuna gleichgesetzt." Certainly those

Latin authors like Apuleius or Pliny who explicitly draw from a Greek background for their material employ Fortuna in the tradition and meaning of Tyche. For an extended discussion of Tyche see Pauly-Wissowa, zweite Reihe, Bd. VII, 1643-1697; and Fortuna, Bd. VII, 12-42. The point for this paper is her well-known ambiguity or capriciousness, i.e., the double character of Tyche/Fortuna, positive and negative, embodied in the single image.

11. N.H.II,22

12. A. J. Festugière suggests that one's principle of organization in examining so vast a topic ought not to begin with the peculiarities of the contents, but with genetic conditions. "Cadre de la mystique hellenistique" in Aux Sources de la Tradition Chrétienne. Mélanges a Goguel, 1950, pp. 74-85. Jan Bergman. "I Overcome Fate," in Helmer Ringgren (ed.), Fatalistic Beliefs in Religion, Folklore, and Literature, 1967, pp. 48-50; and W. W. Tarn, pp. 351ff., offer typologies of the response of Hellenistic man to "Fate."

13. Moralia, Peri Tyche, 3

14. H. R. Patch, p. 149

15. Tetra. I,3. H. R. Patch notes that "Astrology and the predictions of soothsayers are ways of getting in touch with the great scheme of the universe, methods of discovering the plan [i.e., having to do with Fate]; lots, geomancy, fortune-telling in general, aim to fit haphazard media to a haphazard order [i.e., Fortune], p. 147, n. 59.

16. F. E. Robbins (ed.). Tetrabiblos, p. 4, n. 1.

17. Tetra. I,3

18. Gardner

19. Meta. XI,15

20. Olym. Odes, XII,1-9.

21. Meta. XI,15

22. Meta. XI,3f.

23. For an extended discussion of Heimarmene, see Pauly-Wissowa, Bd. VII, 2622-2645.

24. C.H. I,9

25. C. J. Bleeker. "Chance-Fate-Providence: Some religio-phenomenological reflections" in The Rainbow. 1975, p. 183.

26. E.g., Iren. ad Haer, II,IV. On the relationship between the lunar goddess and Sophia, see Hans Jonas, The Gnostic Religion, pp.107ff.

27. Whereas soter is attributed to both males and females, "redeemer" is consistently attributed to male figures.

28. Ex. Theod. 74f.; Wilhelm Anz suggested that escape from the effects of Heimarmene was the central teaching of Gnosticism, in Zur Frage nach dem Ursprung des Gnostizismus. 1897.

29. John Ferguson. The Religions of the Roman Empire. 1970. p. 77.

30. "Greek tragedy teaches that fate is inescapable." Bleeker, p. 189.

APPROACHING THE SYNOPTIC PROBLEM FROM THE SECOND CENTURY: A PROLEGOMENON

S 268

by

Arthur J. Bellinzoni, Jr.
Wells College

One of the most widely accepted conclusions of synoptic studies has been the hypothesis that Mark was the earliest written gospel and that Matthew and Luke used Mark, a second source Q, and one or more additional sources as the basis for the writing of their gospels. More than a century of scholarly research on the synoptics amassed such overwhelming evidence in support of the Two-Source Hypothesis (or the Four Document Hypothesis as it is called in B. H. Streeter's classic statement[1]) that alternative explanations have been virtually given up, even by the great majority of Roman Catholic scholars, who earlier had what might be regarded as a vested interest in the priority of Matthew.[2] In 1964 William Farmer reopened the synoptic problem in a way that has been particularly painful, especially to those of us whose published research is based on the priority of Mark.[3]

Specifically, Farmer has subscribed to what has been called the Griesbach paradigm; namely, he has called for the rejection of the priority of Mark and of the whole idea of a second source Q, employed independently by Matthew and Luke; and he has instead called for a return to the hypothesis of Johann Griesbach (long since ignored or even forgotten by the authors of our standard texts) that Matthew is the first of the synoptic gospels, that Luke copied his Markan and non-Markan parallels from Matthew, and that Mark put together his gospel as a conflation of Matthew and Luke.[4]

It is far too early to predict what new hypotheses or modifications to old hypotheses will establish themselves when the evidence has been re-examined in light of Farmer's thesis, but it is appropriate for us to begin to test the suggestions that have disturbed, if not shaken, the critical consensus that has developed in synoptic research over the last hundred years.

---

[1]Burnett Hillman Streeter, The Four Gospels: A Study of Origins (London: Macmillan and Co., 1953).

[2]On June 19, 1911 the Biblical Commission enacted a decree affirming the traditional authorship, date of composition, and historical character of St. Matthew's Gospel. "In deciding the priority of St. Matthew's Gospel in its original language and substance, the Biblical Commission has solemnly disapproved of any form of these theories which maintains that St. Matthew's original work was not a complete Gospel or the first in order of time." Francis E. Gigot, "Synoptics," The Catholic Encyclopedia, edited by Charles G. Herbermann and others (New York: Robert Appleton Company, 1912), Volume XIV, p. 394.

[3]William R. Farmer, The Synoptic Problem: A Critical Analysis (New York: Macmillan, 1964).

[4]"A Demonstration that Mark was written after Matthew and Luke" by J. J. Griesbach, University of Jena, 1790. Translated into English from the Latin text by Bernard Orchard o s b., Beda College, Rome 1975. (Circulated in typewritten form.)

D. Wenham in the Tyndale Bulletin of 1972[5] and more recently J. A. T. Robinson in the July 1975 volume of New Testament Studies[6] have begun to look at synoptic material afresh, although as Robinson admits his work is "but a small sample dip into the mass of material that needs to be looked at afresh."[7]

Rarely has the literature of the second century been consulted for clues that might help in solving the so-called synoptic problem. By general assent the relationship among the synoptic gospels has been established primarily, if not exclusively, by examining and comparing parallel material in the gospels themselves. This method is surely sound; yet I would maintain that a close study of certain second century materials may well cast considerable light on the synoptic problem. What I hope to accomplish here is to share my thoughts as to where we might begin to look in the literature of the second century for witnesses to the relationships among the synoptics. I frankly view this paper as a prolegomenon to a study that might, if properly pursued, yield results that could help in the solution of the synoptic problem.

A first challenge might be to seek clues to synoptic relationships in the Apostolic Fathers. The view of Vincent Taylor that "in the Gospels the 'tradition' has attained a relatively fixed form" and "is no longer subject to change, except as it is altered by copyists or by the writers of the later Apocryphal Gospels"[8] needs clearly to be rejected. Helmut Koester has examined the extent of the formative period of the synoptic tradition and has argued (some would say convincingly) that in the period of the Apostolic Fathers there is dependence upon both written and oral tradition.[9] Koester has argued that unaltered quotations of the words of Jesus from the synoptic tradition are quite rare among the Apostolic Fathers and are apparently limited to very short sentences (2 Clement 2:4; 6:1a; Didache 9:5).[10] A great number of alterations are dependent upon the application of the sayings of Jesus to a particular situation (2 Clement 3:2; 4:2; 9:11; 13:4; etc.);[11] and quite frequently Koester identified passages which clearly harmonize parallels from Matthew and Luke (2 Clement 4:2, 5; 5:4; 9:11; Didache 1:3; 1:4),[12] a tendency which, according to Koester's view, apparently developed quite early in the history of the

---

[5]D. Wenham, "The Synoptic Problem Revisited: Some New Suggestions about the Composition of Mark iv, 1-34," Tyndale Bulletin, XXIII (1972), pp. 3-38.

[6]J. A. T. Robinson, "The Parable of the Wicked Husbandman: A Test of Synoptic Relationships," New Testament Studies, XXI, 4 (1975), pp. 443-461.

[7]Ibid., p. 443.

[8]Vincent Taylor, The Formation of the Gospel Tradition (London: Macmillan & Co. Ltd., 1957), p. 1.

[9]Helmut Koester, Synoptische Überlieferung bei den apostolischen Vätern (Berlin: Akademie Verlag, 1957).

[10]Ibid., p. 264. [11]Ibid. [12]Ibid.

synoptic tradition and which only later developed into the full-blown harmonies of Theophilus of Antioch and Tatian. Koester's thesis is, of course, based on Streeter's solution to the synoptic problem.[13] Clearly a fresh look at certain key passages in the Apostolic Fathers in light of alternative solutions to the synoptic problem is in order (e.g., 1 Clement 46:8, which Koester believes belongs to a stage behind the synoptics, possibly Q;[14] and the passages in 2 Clement and the Didache which Koester believes harmonized parallel material in Matthew and Luke). Evidence from the Apostolic Fathers may prove to be indirect; but it is, I believe, worth asking if there is evidence in the Apostolic Fathers for the existence of Q (or M or L). Or perhaps more precisely, it is worth asking whether there are variations in synoptic type traditions in the Apostolic Fathers that might confirm the Streeter hypothesis with respect to pre-synoptic "sources."

A second challenge might be to seek clues to synoptic relationships in the Gospel of Thomas. In the year 1908 Emil Wendling[15] argued that the saying in Oxyrhynchus Papyrus 1 (saying 6 — "No prophet is acceptable in his fatherland, and no physician performs healings among those who know him") is more primitive than the parallel passage in Mark 6:1-6. This result was confirmed by form-critical analysis by Rudolf Bultmann long before the discovery of the Gospel of Thomas.[16] Since the discovery of the complete text of this gospel to which Oxyrhynchus Papyrus 1 belongs, a number of scholars have sought to strengthen their arguments for the secondary and heretical character of the Gospel of Thomas by the hypothesis of its dependence on the synoptic tradition. The list of scholars who have thrown their weight on this side of the controversy is impressive: Robert M. Grant and David N. Freedman,[17] Ernst Haenchen,[18] Bertil Gärtner,[19] and H. E. W. Turner[20] to name but a few. No less impressive is the list of those who have argued in one way or another that Thomas is dependent upon a source distinct from our synoptic gospels, perhaps an independent

---

[13] Ibid., p.3.

[14] Ibid., pp. 16-19.

[15] Emil Wendling, Entstehung des Markus-Evangeliums, p. 54.

[16] Rudolf Bultmann, History of the Synoptic Tradition (New York: Harper & Row, 1963), pp. 31f.

[17] Robert M. Grant and David Noel Freedman, The Secret Sayings of Jesus.

[18] Ernst Haenchen, "Literatur zum Thomas-Evangelium" and Die Botschaft des Thomas-Evangeliums.

[19] Bertil Gärtner, The Theology of the Gospel of Thomas.

[20] H. E. W. Turner, "The Theology of the Gospel of Thomas," in Thomas and the Evangelists, ed. Hugh Montefiore and H. E. W. Turner.

earlier stage of the sayings tradition: Hugh Montefiore,[21] Helmut Koester,[22] James M. Robinson,[23] R. McL. Wilson,[24] R. A. Spivey,[25] as representative. Clearly the relationship of the Gospel of Thomas to the synoptic tradition has not been resolved. Equally clearly the decisions reached with respect to the Gospel of Thomas bear directly on the question of the relationship among the synoptic gospels and any proposed solutions to the synoptic problem. As Koester indicates, "Further studies should involve a fresh analysis of the parallel sections in the synoptic gospels: the collections of parables and sayings underlying Mark 4 and Matthew 13; the basis for the Markan sayings used in Mark 2 and 3; [the so-called] Q sections underlying Matthew 5-7 and Luke 6 as well as other [so-called] Q material now occurring in Matthew 11:7ff.//Luke 7:42ff.; Matthew 21-22 par., etc.; and, finally, the sources for the special Lukan material in Luke 12 (Luke 11:27-12:56 is paralleled by no fewer than thirteen sayings in the Gospel of Thomas, seven of which have parallels only in Luke)."[26] Such study is bound to clarify certain aspects of the controversy that now centers on the solution to the synoptic problem, especially as it enables us to identify the primary and secondary material within the synoptic gospels as well as in the Gospel of Thomas.

A third challenge might be to seek clues to synoptic relationships in certain post-synoptic tradition. That harmonizing of the synoptic gospels was a well-developed practice in the early church can be seen from an examination of several second century sources. Some of the papyrus fragments are well-known for combining features from several gospels (cf. especially Papyrus Egerton 2). As has already been indicated, Koester

[21] Hugh Montefiore, "A Comparison of the Parables of the Gospel according to Thomas and of the Synoptic Gospels," in Thomas and the Evangelists.

[22] Helmut Koester, "Gnomai Diaphoroi: The Origin and Nature of Diversification in the History of Early Christianity," and "One Jesus and Four Primitive Gospels," reprinted in Trajectories Through Early Christianity by Helmut Koester and James M. Robinson.

[23] James M. Robinson, "Logoi Sophon: On the Gattung of Q," reprinted in Trajectories Through Early Christianity.

[24] R. McL. Wilson, "Thomas and the Growth of the Gospels," HTR 53 (1960), pp. 231-250; "Thomas and the Synoptic Gospels," ExpT 72 (1960/61), pp. 36-39; Studies in the Gospel of Thomas.

[25] R. A. Spivey, The Origin and Milieu of the Gospel According to Thomas. See also Ernest W. Saunders, "A Trio of Thomas Logia," Biblical Research 8 (1963), pp. 43-59; Robert North, "Chenoboskion and Q," CBQ 24 (1962), pp. 154-70. See as well G. Quispel, "Some Remarks on the Gospel of Thomas," NTS 5 (1959), pp. 276-290.

[26] "Gnomai Diaphoroi" in Trajectories, p. 132; see also "One Jesus and Four Primitive Gospels," in Trajectories, especially pp. 168ff. where Koester begins to analyze some of this material.

believes that 2 Clement and the Didache have certain harmonistic features. And in the case of Justin Martyr, as early as the nineteenth century such scholars as von Engelhardt,[27] Sanday,[28] and Lippelt[29] saw the use of a gospel harmony of some sort, a view that has now been confirmed by my own study of the sayings of Jesus in the writings of Justin Martyr.[30] And according to Jerome (Ep. 121. 6. 15 ad Algasiam), Theophilus of Antioch composed a gospel harmony in the late second century. The Diatessaron of Tatian, therefore, stands at the end of a long tradition, not at the beginning as is often thought. The question to consider is whether the evidence of the second century fathers supports the view that Matthew and Luke in their reworking of Mark and Q stand at, or at least near, the beginning of that long tradition of harmonizing, or can evidence be found among the second century witnesses to support the view that it was rather Mark who epitomized Matthew and Luke? It would be especially interesting to compare passages that are paralleled in all three of the synoptic gospels to related material in Justin and other fathers who are apparently dependent upon post-synoptic tradition. Specifically can the tendencies in the development of the synoptic tradition in the second century witnesses instruct us with respect to the development of synoptic tradition in the first century? And what conclusions, if any, can be drawn from the fact that the fathers of the second and third centuries seem to prefer one or another of the synoptic gospels?

In conclusion, I am persuaded that considerable light can be cast on a solution to the synoptic problem by examining relevant second century material in the Apostolic Fathers, the Gospel of Thomas, and the post-synoptic tradition found in the harmonized texts of Justin Martyr and others. But what is needed is not simply a reconfirmation of Streeter's two-source or four-document hypothesis or a Griesbach-Farmer variation. What is needed is a more comprehensive hypothesis which seeks to incorporate the Apostolic Fathers, the Gospel of Thomas, Justin Martyr, and others into the history of the synoptic tradition. As Walter Bauer clearly indicated in his epochal work Orthodoxy and Heresy in Earliest Christianity, the distinctions between orthodox and heretical, canonical and non-canonical are obsolete. Only when the larger history of the synoptic tradition is written will we be paying more than lip service to Bauer's acute observations, and in the process we may have cast more light on the relationships among the synoptic gospels.

---

[27] Moritz von Engelhardt, Das Christenthum Justins des Märtyrers (Erlangen, 1878), pp. 335ff., especially p. 345.

[28] William Sanday, The Gospels in the Second Century (London, 1876), pp. 136ff., note 1.

[29] Ernst Lippelt, Quae Fuerint Justini Martyris ΑΠΟΜΝΗΜΟΝΕΥΜΑΤΑ Quaeque Ratione Cum Forma Syro-Latina Cohaeserint (Halle, 1901), p. 35.

[30] A. J. Bellinzoni, The Sayings of Jesus in the Writings of Justin Martyr (Leiden, 1967).

S 274, A 458

BEYOND BRUXISM

Kent Harold Richards

Iliff School of Theology

> brux-ism 'brək,sizəm . . . the habit of unconsciously gritting or grinding the teeth esp. in situations of stress or during sleep.[1]

A kind of bruxomania pervades biblical scholarship. We gnash our teeth in article after article on subject after subject because the discipline is in "flux" or "things" are uncertain or critical issues are undecided. We even seem to revel in the mania. I have wondered what kind of students we hope to gain if we communicate this disease in lecture and seminar!

The field of biblical theology has not been free of bruxism. The word "crisis" seems to have evolved as the "right" descriptive word, while less picturesque than bruxism, it does present an image which evokes the same sense of apprehension, hesitancy, stress and failure of nerve. This bruxism cannot be healed with a single prescription, nor can a magic therapy be devised which will cure the problem. I do believe that there are some positive proposals appearing within biblical theology which will allow us to go beyond bruxism. One of these is the dialogue between biblical scholars and process theologians.[2]

In this age of rapid change and instant analysis we grasp the moment thinking that if we hang on tight enough we will be able to slow down the momentum. We have not found with much satisfaction a way to gain instant insight. This paper does not offer a total cure for bruxism nor a way to instant insight, but it does affirm some of the possibilities being generated out of one segment of the discussions surrounding biblical theology. The first part of this paper will be a survey and report. The second will be my reflections "beyond bruxism".

I

An official of the Rand Corporation has recently described how specialists in different fields can work together.

> In our population studies, for example, we draw on the perspectives of economists, geographers and sociologists. Economists know the price of everything but the value of nothing. An economist, it is said, would marry Elizabeth Taylor for her money. The geographer, of course, believes that everything is connected to everything else, only more so, the nearer things are to each other. And the sociologist is someone who can spend a hundred thousand dollars of somebody else's money to discover that a house of ill-repute is located just around the corner. He reports this finding in a language that no one can understand. The hallmarks of an interdisciplinary study then, are that it seems overpriced, it shows that everything depends on everything else, nobody really understands what it says, and the money (it costs) turns out to have been yours.[3]

Since those of us working in religion never have any money, part of the force of this quotation may be lost. Nevertheless it can serve as a word of caution.

In a working paper discussed last January at the Center For Process Studies[4] I discussed some of the functional and conceptual problems confronted in research involving two sets of languages, methodologies and conceptualizations. Anyone can come up with the problems and propose some solutions, but I wanted us to develop realistic expectations for the continuing dialogue between biblical scholars and process philosophers. To some extent it would be accurate to say that the discussions thus far undertaken have been unstructured and random. This has the positive effect of allowing and encouraging experimentation. Nevertheless it has seemed to me that some more comprehensive plan of research might be developed to determine if in fact the discussions between biblical scholars and process philosophers will eventuate in positive findings. I would hope that some discussion about how we might proceed could be undertaken.

For example, several areas might be fruitful for group research. First, a study of commentaries jointly undertaken by biblical scholars and process philosophers. The philosophical presuppositions (explicit or implicit) found in selected commentaries would present concrete examples of the interface between philosophical and the historical-literary categories. Second, some probes of major issues important to both fields could be productive. The issue of the nature of authority[5] in both philosophical and literary-historical areas might prove to be of infinite value at least to biblical theologians. Another area could center around the understanding of actual and observable events. Still another might focus upon the relationship between the network of propositional language found in philosophical discourse and efforts to recover the non-propositional power of narrative structures. These suggestions are not intended as a programatic statement, but as an indication of some topics which might be examined more systematically. Others will come to mind and then some decision about those of greatest interest could be pursued.

In order to bring outsiders up to date on the discussions and to begin to collect the bibliography for those involved over the past years, I will list the work undertaken and items I am familiar with that are in progress.

In late February of 1974 Christian Theological Seminary called together a group of scholars to discuss the relationships between biblical studies and process philosophy. Clark M. Williamson and J. Gerald Janzen convened the conference which was financially backed by the Oreon E. Scott Foundation. The majority of those papers and responses are published in <u>Encounter</u> 36 (Fall 1975).[6] The conference paper read by George Pixley and its response by Clark Williamson appeared in <u>Process Studies</u> 4 (Fall 1974).[7] These initial papers consist of ones read by both process philosophers and biblical scholars.

In the Fall of 1974 at the AAR-SBL National Meeting in Washington, three papers of a fairly broad scope were discussed.[8] Three more papers were read at the 1975 National Meeting in Chicago.[9] There have been a corps of approximately twenty-five participants with many additional parties sitting in on the sessions at the two national meetings. There are three papers, including this one, being discussed at the 1976 National Meeting.[10]

In addition to the AAR-SBL group there are a number of

other items which should be mentioned. William Beardslee and John Cobb have been two of the most active individuals in stimulating ideas and carrying on work of their own. Professor Beardslee listed five general characteristics of a process hermeneutic in the paper which he read at the 1974 National Meeting. It might be well to excerpt his major points for those new to the discussion.

> 1. It will be a realistic hermeneutic. That is, it will set the task of interpretation not only to take account of human consciousness in the world as directly perceived in consciousness, but it will assume, in however limited degree, we do have knowledge of reality in that interpretation had, among other things, to deal with the relation between the world of the text and reality. That is not to say, of course, that many interpretive acts may not justifiably bracket out the question of reality and concentrate on understanding the world of the text.
> 2. It will be a mediating and comprehensive hermeneutic. Whitehead says of philosophy that it may not neglect the 'multifariousness of the world--the fairies dance, and Christ is nailed to the cross.' In the context of interpretation, this will mean openness to a pluralism of methods, with the conviction that when carried far enough, they will illuminate each other. It will mean resistance to a stance which claims that only one center is an appropriate vantage point from which to seek for illumination of a text.
> 3. It will be attentive to actual occasions as the loci of reality, and to the relatedness of occasions.
> 4. It will also be attentive to the role of symbols in providing vehicles for the connection of occasions in historical existence.
> 5. It will be sensitive to the tension between interpretation as risk-taking and interpretation as achieving clarity, both of which can be helpfully explicated in a process framework.[11]

Professor Cobb's writings at a number of points generate discussion about the relationship of biblical studies and process philosophy.[12] He has been responsible for establishing the Center for Process Studies in Claremont. There have been several discussions and unpublished papers read over the last two years at the Center for Process Studies.[13]

Several dissertations are underway in this general area.[14] I think that in the future we could develop a system of communication whereby work underway both at the dissertation level, as well as research going on among established scholars, could be made public. It has been my hope that within the AAR-SBL group we could have a time slot for reporting on dissertations and research underway. I am sure that there are many others working in this area and that papers have been read in various places with which I am unfamiliar.[15] I would be happy to collect any new information and add it to that which I have. We could very easily in the publication of seminar papers for 1977 print a comprehensive bibliography of work thus far undertaken and a list of work in progress.

While a number of individuals are making efforts to self-consciously work with the disciplines of process philosophy and biblical studies, many others are raising questions and making observations which are related to the thrust of those directly involved in the discussions. One can see this in the work of James Robinson and Helmut Koester in the volume entitled, Trajectories Through Early Christianity. They speak of the necessity of developing new categories for the interpretation of the New Testament and say that what must take place in New Testament studies is "a dismantling and reassembling of perhaps the most embracing and foundational category of all: the traditional static, substantial, essence/accidence-oriented metaphysics which gave our inherited categories their most basic form. It suggests the need to replace that metaphysics with a dynamic, historic, existence/process-oriented new metaphysics, in terms of which a whole table of restructured categories may be envisaged."[16] Norman Perrin may have most precisely stated what lies before us when he says that "one of the characteristics of the contemporary situation in biblical scholarship is that it challenges us to do things that we have not done before."[17] The work thus far undertaken by the Process Hermeneutic and Biblical Exegesis Group is preliminary and tentative but has demonstrated an ability to go "beyond bruxism".[18]

II

My reflections can be divided into two major categories: first, some general remarks on the interchange between the two disciplines; and second, some specific observations of implications for a biblical theology developed in light of the interchange between these disciplines. These remarks and observations are not meant to be comprehensive but rather to indicate how one person from the biblical studies side has reacted. One could say that there have been at least three types of individuals from biblical studies involved in the discussions: those who are thoroughly acquainted with the categories and language of process philosophy; others could be described as onlookers who wish to be informed about what has been going on but not willing to participate directly; and a group of those interested in how process categories can affect their work and willing to experiment occasionally with it but who are not thoroughly versed in process philosophy. I understand myself to be in this last category.

This first set of reflections upon the general discussion between the disciplines can be focused on three areas: 1) the language and conceptualization provided by process philosophy; 2) the necessity to examine philosophical presuppositions; and 3) ways of developing criteria for the relationship between philosophy and the historical-literary-theological categories of biblical studies.

First, anyone acquainted with the language of process philosophy[19] is aware of its complexity. There have been times within our discussions when the point of debate between process philosophers has totally eluded me largely because of my ignorance of the technical terminology being employed. This does not mean that the point of debate which eluded me was unimportant. To be sure there are times when outsiders wonder what the purpose of a debate is, but this is not peculiar to process philosophy. It has surely been the experience of every biblical scholar to have a student or some individual come up and ask what difference does it make?!

I have personally discovered categories of process philosophy enabling me to articulate more precisely ideas and concepts originally stimulated from within the biblical corpus itself. For example, the proposals by John Cobb regarding historical routes of occasions.[20] He is able to use categories from process thought to explain both the common forms transmitted in a tradition as well as the transmission or canalization of novelty. Until I had seen his discussion I was experiencing an element within the biblical text, but unclear as to how I might be able to explain it. The dual phenomena within a single tradition of radical change and the perpetuation of the status quo was present, but more adequately brought to understanding through the category of a living historical route.

While I have experienced assistance in my own perceptions of biblical materials, I am concerned that the conceptual frames which are employed by all disciplines have some commonality. Another way to phrase this would be to ask if the conceptual framework of process philosophy can become the language of university discourse? Notice I have not asked if it can become the language of universal discourse! Process philosophy claims some of its origins in the sciences of the 20th century, yet if as a biblical scholar I come into acquaintance with these categories and then come upon a conversation with a physics or biology instructor, will I need first to explain the categories? I do not know the answer to this question. I think that one of the distinct advantages in the past of the employment of existentialist categories was that individuals in a wide variety of disciplines could engage in discussion. Existentialism infiltrated and influenced not only philosophy and biblical studies, but the entire panoply of disciplines within the humanities. Even the scientist, whether professionally or personally, frequently understands and appropriates some aspects of existentialism. It could be that our individual disciplines and subgroups within them have become so isolated and insulated that university discourse is an unattainable ideal, unfortunate as that may be. If process philosophy can aid the biblical scholar not only in more adequately perceiving and articulating his own subject matter, but also provide a language of university discourse then it would become most appealing.

Second, I have been totally convinced that as a biblical exegete-historian-theologian, it will become a help to me to be aware of my philosophical presuppositions. Biblical scholars need not become philosophers. They need not be in search of *a metaphysic* or philosophy. It is a misconception to think that one has *a metaphysic*, rather one has a set of metaphysical assumptions. Frequently these assumptions are in tension with each other or even contradictory. As one becomes aware of these assumptions and presuppositions, one is able to test the interplay between them. Having gained a sense of our own entangling assumptions, we might be able more adequately to discover some of them within the ancient texts and traditions with which we work. We may even find that some ancient tradition was aware of its own entangling assumptions and found a way of resolving them.

For example, have we biblical scholars really come to the creation traditions of Israel prepared to allow the text its own voice? Speaking quite frankly, my own 20th century assumptions are not completely clear regarding the "cut" of my conceptions of creation. I am not at all certain that I do not place upon a text such as Genesis 1 or 2 my problems demanding a solution.

Furthermore when these creation traditions get used in Deutero-Isaiah, I am totally unprepared since I have neither understood the originating impulses regarding creation in Israel nor the historical route which creation took. While much experimentation needs to be undertaken, the examination of the philosophical presuppositions and metaphysical assumptions of the biblical scholars could lead to a genuine hearing of the text. This is not "new talk" for those in biblical studies, but it frequently is just that, "talk". The conversations with process philosophy raise cosmological concerns among others which we have rarely examined in our own philosophical makeup, not to mention the underlying framework of the biblical traditions. Israel's initial and developing perceptions of creation need to be seen not in isolation but in the total set of entangling philosophical presuppositions of her time.

I think that it should also be mentioned that in becoming aware of our philosophical presuppositions, we may find that some of the American philosophical traditions can be of great assistance to us. To be sure, continental philosophy has played the greatest role in recent years. It would also be accurate to say that most of us American biblical scholars know more about the history of European biblical scholarship than we do about our own. It would be interesting to find in the renewed interest in American biblical scholarship an interest also in the American philosophical traditions, especially those employing empirical methods.

Third, is it necessary and possible to develop criteria for relating a philosophical position to biblical studies?[21] One could put it even more bluntly. Is there a "best" philosophy for biblical work? I am not at all certain that just because one needs to become conscious of one's philosophical presuppositions that one necessarily asks the question about the "best" philosophy. If one assumes that individuals operate with metaphysical assumptions and not with *a metaphysic* then one would need not find the single "best" philosophy or metaphysic. One should look toward developing criteria for the inter-relationship between philosophical assumptions and the various dimensions of biblical studies.

The adequacy of existentialism has been discussed by both those attracted to it as well as its distractors. Some have maintained that its philosophical perspectives corresponded very closely to the perspectives found in the Bible. The points at which correspondence was the greatest were those points at which the text was most meaningful. This correspondence criterion is not peculiar to existentialism for one can find it in the papers stemming from those engaged in the Process Hermeneutic and Biblical Exegesis Group. Biblical scholars almost unwittingly fall into the correspondence criterion principle. We want to find the text meaningful and relevant. We are always pleased when our contemporary notions correspond with those in the text. However, we have surely learned that a text which is at odds with our contemporary perceptions can also provoke and stimulate the imagination. We know that correspondence need not be the key.

It would seem to me that the most adequate philosophical presuppositions for the biblical scholar are ones which encourage and demand that actual occasions, the "stuff" of the biblical traditions, provide the context for constant scrutiny of any philosophical categories. Any set of philosophical presuppositions should in some way or another sensitize the biblical scholar to what is in the text. The crucial point is that texts must have the power and freedom to challenge constantly the adequacy of the philosophical presuppositions. Part of the task of philosophy is to articulate explicitly the shared notions of humanity, but it can only be developing those from the actual occasions and experiences of traditions. The biblical scholar needs to be aware of his role in the conversation between disciplines, but also should remember that there are some important implications for biblical studies itself. To understand a text or tradition one needs to realize that the mere description of the text or tradition is not enough. We need to discuss and critique the text or tradition within the horizon of the ancient philosophical assumptions. In that context we can more accurately come to understand how a text or tradition "cuts."

There has been a great deal of discussion in the papers of this group about characteristics of process philosophy which make it a good partner with biblical studies. The areas are numerous and need more critical study. There have been some discussions regarding a theory of text. Is there any way in which process philosophy can assist? What is the nature of understanding? This is an area which is under constant reflection in other groups as well.[22] There has begun to be a great deal of discussion about the place of imagination. It really does not take much insight to suggest that biblical studies must rediscover the magic and imagination which the Bible once had. Some have indicated that process philosophy can be a tool in this rediscovery process.

The participation in this discussion between process philosophers and biblical studies has a great deal of room. Diversity is healthy. An awareness of what led to the bruxism in biblical studies is important, but what is necessary is the vision beyond that toward constructive, innovative proposals across the entire spectrum. I believe this is not idle fancy but an imperative which has sounded forth here and in other quarters.

I would like to turn now to the second part of my reflections focusing upon some implications for biblical theology developed out of the interchange between biblical studies and process philosophy. Two preliminary asides should be made. First, this is not a systematic, thorough examination of biblical theology setting the stage for a new approach. That would demand another context. I selected the area of biblical theology for reflection since it seems so caught up in the "bruxism."[23] I am aware of the problems, but believe that some clearings are in sight.[24] Second, these remarks will consider three areas related to biblical theology discussions. Behind these remarks lies the affirmation that my acquaintance and study with people in process studies--from a seminary mentor, John Cobb, to colleagues on two faculties--has been instrumental in stimulating my interest and reflections on theological issues. I am, on the other hand, not persuaded that I need to become a biblical scholar totally influenced by the process conceptualities. The impact of my Doktorvater, Rolf Knierim, has taught me that the biblical scholar's work must be thought of in terms of a concert.[25] Many factors will contribute to the enterprise; it must not be a solo. Some may say that what is reflected in this discussion paper could have been instrumented from any number of disciplines besides process thought. That could be, but it is not the case in my experience.

The three areas I want to speak to are: 1) the search for a "center"; 2) the meant-means distinction; and 3) the place of the Bible in the theological enterprise. These issues are interrelated in such a way that it is difficult at this point in my thinking to keep them separate. Part of my concern, on the one hand, is that I may be blurring some essential distinctions in such categories as exegesis, hermeneutic and theology. On the other hand, I want to take that risk in an effort to expose the interrelationships.

First, it should come as no surprise to those involved in biblical studies that we seem intent on finding the "center" of the Old and/or New Testament. We want to know that single idea or concept or theme or event which holds it all together. Surely it is correct to say that in New Testament studies one of the great achievements of the post-World War II period was Bultmann's ability to identify the center and normative element in the New Testament despite its diversity and multiplicity. The kerygma of the early church provided the center. Developments beyond the primitive church sometimes strayed from the center or were thought to have lost the real meaning of Christian existence.

In Old Testament circles, the question of the center has been of "considerable importance."[26] Hasel, in his survey of Old Testament and Old Testament theology,[27] is able to describe the center as perceived by Eichrodt, Vriezen and others, but when he comes to von Rad problems exist as everyone knows. While Hasel is aware in example after example that the search is sometimes illusive and more frequently than not detrimental to a proper understanding of the text, he still goes on to say,

> The ultimate object of a theology is then to draw the hidden inner unity out of its concealment as much as possible and to make it transparent.[28]

This "hidden inner unity" for Hasel (as well as several other scholars) is God, ". . . the dynamic, unifying center of the OT."[29]

I am not at all certain that the drive to find the center (or as the image more frequently used to be the "unity")[30] will be productive. The vitality of the religious movements which brought forth the Old and New Testaments, and hence the books themselves, may well be found in the changing, reforming, novel dimensions. To identify the center may be to locate the patterns of conformity and even decay. The mere repetition of the past forms in contemporary theologies will miss the importance of the Bible both for contemporaries, as well as be misleading in regard to their significance in the past. If one were to stay with the center language and imagery, it must be far more dialectically stated. For example, the center of the Old Testament may be found in the dissolution of developing ideas, concepts, symbols, themes and in the emergence of novel, originative impulses. The center is a kind of infinite helix. Or stated still another way, the center is always the future.

The discussion of the center has developed primarily in terms of the "descriptive task" of a biblical theology. This leads to the second area of reflection, the meant-means distinction. Stendahl's classic article[31] has been formative to several generations of graduate students. It delineated carefully between what a text meant and what it can mean. It distinguished between the meaning which a text had in its original context and the meaning which it might have in the present. The description of what a text meant could not answer normative questions. "History does not answer such questions; it only poses them."[32] The descriptive task ". . . yields the original in its own terms, limiting interpretation to what it meant in its own setting."[33] The hermeneutical task was understood as something which took part after the descriptive task. The description of the "'original' beyond the presuppositions and the inherited frame of thought of our immediate predecessors"[34] was of extraordinary significance. The "original" had always run the danger of being submerged, except (of course!) in the Reformation. With a clearly worked out descriptive biblical theology then the systematic theologian has a "live option to attempt a direct translation of the biblical material, not a revision of a translation of a revision of a translation. . ."[35] Without the "original" the

> . . . history of theology would be an uninterrupted chain reaction of a philosophical nature, with Augustine correcting the early fathers, Thomas Aquinas correcting Augustine, Luther refuting Thomas, Schleiermacher touching up Luther and Barth, and Tillich carrying the traditional discussion up to our own time.[36]

The recovery of the "original" text provided by the descriptive biblical theologian was and is a major accomplishment. Biblical scholars must continue their work with linguistic, historical, sociological, anthropological and more than a dozen other disciplines. The experimentation with new methodologies and coalitions of disciplines has provided new insights. I do not in any way wish to denigrate these accomplishments. I want to make use of them, but some new directions need to evolve.

The methodologies attached to the descriptive side are not purely "objective" entities. They are in the matrix of history and do attempt answers to questions. They do have sets of entangling philosophical presuppositions. We biblical theologians must take the responsibility of dealing with the underlying meanings and ontological assumptions of our descriptive methodologies. Process thought might be able to present a new and more consistent ontology than was available with existentialism.[37] It might be able to resolve some of the problems associated with the subject-object issues which have plagued us since Descartes and Kant. I would have to agree that there is a "continuing anti-theological bias of biblical scholarship" in America,[38] and I would add an anti-philosophical bias as well. We ask the systematic theologian to use the "original", yet in the new alignment the theological-philosophical categories must not taint the descriptive biblical theologian.

The question of the meaning of the Bible has been left unattended by biblical scholars. When we describe what a text "meant" we cannot escape entirely what we think it "means." The dialogue with a philosophical partner who takes seriously our historical and literary tasks as biblical scholars, will assist us in focusing the questions of meaning. We should not forget that the biblical texts and traditions can assist us as well. The meant-means distinction has an appealing neatness which upon careful evaluation becomes illusive in the "doing" of biblical theology. For process thought "meant" and "means" are both separable and inseparable. They are both the product of the past and the anticipation of the future. The hermeneutical task can only with considerable risk be kept apart from the descriptive task. Hermeneutics encompasses the entire process and does not begin where description leaves off.

Finally, some brief comments about the place of the Bible in the total theological enterprise.[39] Theological method must encourage some differentiated tasks. Biblical, historical, systematic (just to mention three) theologians need to continue developing their own specialized methodologies. Each group has some distinctive tools and skills which must not be lost. Differentiation must be encouraged but it is necessary to set some common purposes.[40] The various types of theologians must determine what is worthy of support, and if they are Christians or Jews or whatever, they must determine what Christianity or Judaism is all about. These are surely minimal demands.

There must be some consistent use of the Bible in the theological enterprise. This does not mean that there will be unanimity. To seek a consistent methodology will mean that various systems will be in competition and debate, struggling to determine the most appropriate means of using the Bible. To search for a consistent method does not mean that a method would be insensitive to change. One of the major criteria might be the ability of the methodology to accommodate various contingencies.

Whatever consistent methods of relating the Bible to the entire theological enterprise are developed, none will dare blithely proceed from the *sola scriptura* principle. That principle has become all too frequently little more than a cliché. Kelsey's study, despite its basic, descriptive character, makes abundantly clear the inconsistencies arising out of the use of the principle among various theologians. Biblical scholars cannot expect theologian-philosophers and others to parade perfunctorily before us this principle. We must begin to delineate the power of the Bible for the theological enterprise. Surely it will not be found in some kind of super-naturalism. It must emerge out of the Bible's originative, contingently determined, novel historical routes. This will mean that the contemporary, pluralistic perceptions of the Bible--whether as "pagan classic"[41] or the canon of a community--will play a role in developing the place of the Bible in the theological enterprise. It will mean that the Bible's inner-textual commentary upon itself will assist in the endeavor. The panoply of present and past communities of understanding will need to be questioned in order to arrive at a consistent method. This will certainly provide a more catholic stance than we have normally sought.

III

In conclusion I want to express my hope that this discussion paper might function in several ways. First, to begin to collect the work which has been undertaken and is being developed in this dialogue between biblical and process studies. Bring items which you feel should be added. Second, to discuss some of the directions which might be pursued in the immediate future. What areas of individual and group research can be established? Third, to suggest that we critique some of our old conceptualities, not because they are old but in order to discover how they can function in our contemporary scene. Finally, I would like to experiment with some of my reflections by engaging in the actual "doing" of a biblical theology. This will necessitate a turn toward the text in our discussions.

NOTES

[1]Philip Babcock Gove (ed.), Webster's Third New International Dictionary (Springfield, Mass.: G. and C. Merriam Co., 1961), 287. The word is derived from the Greek βρύχω. The only New Testament occurrence is Acts 7:54. There are 5 LXX occurrences all meaning to gnash the teeth as an act of hatred by the "enemy."

[2]I have used the terms exegete, theologian, historian and/or scholar for those working in the biblical area. I refer to those from process studies as philosophers and/or theologians. There has never been a discussion about this so I use the terms primarily for variety. It would indeed be interesting to have some discussion of this from both disciplines since some of us prefer one term or another. For example, I tend to prefer exegete or theologian.

[3]Saturday Review of the Sciences 1 (1973) 15.

[4]"Collaboration and Conceptualization: Biblical Studies and Process Philosophy" (Unpublished paper).

[5]Lyman T. Lundeen, "The Authority of the Word in a Process Perspective," Encounter 36 (1975) 281-300. This was an initial effort to discuss the problem of authority for those involved in both biblical studies and process philosophy.

[6]The following were the initial papers published in Encounter:

Lundeen paper mentioned in note 5.

William A. Beardslee, "Narrative Form in the New Testament and Process Theology," 301-315.

Theodore J. Weeden, "The Potential and Promise of a Process Hermeneutic--A Response to William Beardslee's Paper," 316-330.

Bernard E. Meland, "Response to Paper by Professor Beardslee," 331-341.

David R. Griffin, "Relativism, Divine Causation, and Biblical Theology," 342-360.

Bernard M. Loomer, "Response to David R. Griffin," 361-369.

George W. Coats, "Response to David R. Griffin," 370-375.

David R. Griffin, "Response to George W. Coats and Bernard M. Loomer," 376-378.

J. Gerald Janzen, "Modes of Power and the Divine Relativity," 379-406.

Helga Reitz, "Biblical and Cosmological Theology: A Process View of Their Relatedness," 407-432.

[7]George V. Pixley, "Justice and Class Struggle: A Challenge for Process Theology," 159-175.

Clark M. Williamson, "Whitehead as Counterrevolutionary? Toward Christian-Marxist Dialogue," 176-186.

[8]William A. Beardslee, "Notes on a Whiteheadian Hermeneutic" (Unpublished paper). The two respondents were William A. Doty and Bernard M. Loomer.

Theodore J. Weeden, "A New Angle of Vision: The Synoptic Material" (Unpublished paper). The two respondents were William R. Baird, Jr. and Bernard Lee, S.M.

John B. Cobb and David Griffin, "Some Basic Principles of Whiteheadian Process Thought: Outlined with an Eye Towards Their Relevance for Biblical Historiography and Hermeneutic" (Unpublished paper). The respondent was Kent Harold Richards.

[9] John B. Cobb, "Trajectories and Historical Routes" (Unpublished paper). The respondent was James M. Robinson.

Russell Pregeant, "The Matthean Undercurrent: Process Hermeneutic and the 'Parable of the Last Judgment'," Society of Biblical Literature 1975 Seminar Papers, Vol. II, ed. George MacRae (Missoula: Scholars Press, 1975), 143-159. The two respondents were H. Edward Everding and Clark M. Williamson.

George W. Coats, "The King's Loyal Opposition: Obedience and Revolution in the Kingdom of God" (Unpublished paper). The two respondents were Lewis Ford and J. Gerald Janzen.

[10] J. Gerald Janzen, "Metaphor and Reality in Hosea 11" appearing in this volume. The two respondents are James Luther Mays and Edgar A. Towne.

Theodore J. Weeden, "Caesarea Philippi: Toward a Process Synthesis of the Pluralism in Markan Interpretation" (Unpublished paper). The two respondents are Delwin Brown and James Goss.

The respondent to this paper is David R. Griffin.

[11] "Notes on a Whiteheadian Hermeneutic" (Unpublished paper). Among Professor Beardslee's works one would want to examine the following: "Openness to the New in Apocalyptic and in Process Theology," Process Studies 3 (1973) 169-178; A House for Hope (Philadelphia: The Westminster Press, 1972).

[12] A number of his works have been helpful but I continue to return to an older paper I have in unpublished form, "Bible, Revelation and Christian Doctrine."

[13] William A. Beardslee, Loren Fisher, David Griffin, Rolf Knierim, Kent Richards, James Robinson are among those who have offered papers for discussion. Upon occasion others have spent portions of sabbaticals at the Center and discussed their research.

[14] There are several dissertations underway by students at the Claremont Graduate School and other institutions. Some dissertations have already been completed. Russell Pregeant did one in 1970 at Vanderbilt entitled The Meaning of Matthew's Christology: A Hermeneutical Investigation in Conversation with the Theology of Schubert M. Ogden. These need to be catalogued so that the work can be coordinated.

[15] Norman Pittenger, "'Personal Survival' in Biblical Thought and Process Thought," Encounter 36 (1975) 91-100. I read a major paper last year at the Catholic Biblical Association of America. It was entitled "New Frontiers: A Process Hermeneutic" (Unpublished paper).

[16] James M. Robinson and Helmut Koester, Trajectories Through Early Christianity (Philadelphia: Fortress Press, 1971), 9.

[17] Norman Perrin, "Eschatology and Hermeneutics: Reflections on Method in the Interpretation of the New Testament," Journal of Biblical Literature 93 (1974) 13.

[18] It would be impossible to mention all of the recent, important works by individuals and other groups looking for "restructured categories." Possibly most symbolic of the new vitality emerging in biblical studies itself is the establishment of Semeia which has as its purpose the "exploration of new and emergent areas and methods of biblical criticism."

[19]When I refer to process thought in this paper, I will be thinking of the work of Alfred North Whitehead and those most heavily influenced by him. Certainly there are many others who fit into a process perspective. The majority of individuals working in the Process Hermeneutic and Biblical Exegesis Group influenced by Whitehead.

[20]The Cobb paper referred to in Note 9.

[21]This was discussed preliminarily at the Center for Process Studies in a paper by David R. Griffin, "The Criterion for the Best Philosophy for Biblical Exegesis" (Unpublished paper).

[22]One example among many would be the work of the Task Group on Methodology and its History (cf. Martin J. Buss (ed.), "Theses for Biblical Hermeneutics," Society of Biblical Literature 1975 Seminar Papers, Vol. I, ed. George MacRae (Missoula: Scholars Press, 1975), 33-38.

[23]The opening line of Gerhard Hasel, Old Testament Theology: Basic Issues in the Current Debate (2d. ed. rev.; Grand Rapids: William B. Eerdmans Publishing Co., 1975) mirrors this: "Old Testament Theology today is undeniably in crisis" (9). The title of Brevard S. Childs, Biblical Theology in Crisis (Philadelphia: The Westminster Press, 1970) and other works develop this image of bruxism. It should be said that the two works mentioned above present new proposals, and in fact Childs actually experiments (also see his Exodus commentary). Nevertheless one senses that the context for the proposals is desperation, rather than a creative opportunity.

[24]I have not had time to examine thoroughly the recent issue of Interpretation 30 (July 1976) which has a number of interesting articles and reviews in this area of biblical theology.

[25]He referred in print once to the "concert of the exegetical disciplines" ("Old Testament Form Criticism Reconsidered," Interpretation 27 (1973) 468), but many times this image has come to mind as he has explained a text.

[26]Rudolph Smend, Die Mitte des Altes Testament (Zurich: Evz-Verlag, 1970).

[27]Hasel, 77-103.

[28]Hasel, 141.

[29]Hasel, 100.

[30]H. H. Rowley, The Unity of the Bible (Living Age Edition, New York: Meridan Books, 1957).

[31]Krister Stendahl, "Biblical Theology, Contemporary," Interpreter's Dictionary of the Bible, ed. George Arthur Buttrick, A-D (1962), 418-432.

[32]Ibid. 424.

[33]Ibid. 425.

[34]Ibid. 430.

[35]Ibid.

[36]Ibid.

[37]For example, it has been thought by some of us and referred to by Schubert Ogden as the "structural inconsistency" of Bultmann. Bultmann had developed an anthropological ontology but insisted that authentic existence depended on God's action in the historical Jesus.

[38]Robert W. Funk, "The Watershed of the American Biblical Tradition: The Chicago School, First Phase, 1892-1920," Journal of Biblical Literature 95 (1976), 21.
Funk speaks of the failure of the biblical scholar to examine the "Scripture question." He focuses the issue in slightly different ways than I see it, but I believe the point of American biblical scholarship trading on "sentiment" is certainly present. Look at the Holy Land tours we lead!! What the implications of his "suggestive" remarks are need some fleshing out. What it would mean to "afford full dignity to an ancient and honorable discipline without a scriptural crutch" (22) would be intriguing to pursue.

[39]David H. Kelsey, The Uses of Scripture in Recent Theology (Philadelphia: Fortress Press, 1975). There is an excellent review in Interpretation 30 (1976), 299-303. I have indicated earlier that this entire issue of Interpretation has articles on the much neglected issue of the place of the Bible in the theological enterprise. It arrived too late for any real comment.

[40]Hasel says the following, "For the systematic theologian it is indeed appropriate to operate with philosophical categories, because his foundations are on a base different from that of the Biblical theologian. The Biblical theologian draws his categories, themes, motifs, and concepts from the Biblical text itself. The Biblical theologian stands in danger of surreptitiously introducing contemporary philosophy into his discipline." (130). At other points Hasel indicates that the two theologians are not to compete. Nevertheless I think this quote indicates a kind of distance which is too great.

[41]John A. Miles, Jr., "The Debut of the Bible as a Pagan Classic," Bulletin of the Council on the Study of Religion 7 (June 1976), 1ff.